EMORY UNIVERSITY STUDIES IN LAW AND RELIGION

John Witte Jr., General Editor

BOOKS IN THE SERIES

Faith and Order: The Reconciliation of Law and Religion
Harold J. Berman

Rediscovering the Natural Law in Reformed Theological Ethics
Stephen J. Grabill

*Lex Charitatis: A Juristic Disquisition on Law
in the Theology of Martin Luther*
Johannes Heckel

*The Ten Commandments in History:
Mosaic Paradigms for a Well-Ordered Society*
Paul Grimley Kuntz

Religious Liberty, Volume 1: Overviews and History
Douglas Laycock

Building Cultures of Trust
Martin E. Marty

*Suing for America's Soul: John Whitehead, The Rutherford Institute, and
Conservative Christians in the Courts*
R. Jonathan Moore

Theology of Law and Authority in the English Reformation
Joan Lockwood O'Donovan

Power over the Body, Equality in the Family: Rights and Domestic Relations in Medieval Canon Law
Charles J. Reid Jr.

Religious Liberty in Western Thought
Noel B. Reynolds and W. Cole Durham Jr., eds.

Political Order and the Plural Structure of Society
James W. Skillen and Rockne M. McCarthy, eds.

*The Idea of Natural Rights:
Studies on Natural Rights, Natural Law, and Church Law, 1150-1625*
Brian Tierney

The Fabric of Hope: An Essay
Glenn Tinder

Liberty: Rethinking an Imperiled Ideal
Glenn Tinder

Religious Human Rights in Global Perspective: Legal Perspectives
Johan D. van der Vyver and John Witte Jr., eds.

*Natural Law and the Two Kingdoms:
A Study in the Development of Reformed Social Thought*
David VanDrunen

Early New England: A Covenanted Society
David A. Weir

God's Joust, God's Justice: Law and Religion in the Western Tradition
John Witte Jr.

Religious Human Rights in Global Perspective: Religious Perspectives
John Witte Jr. and Johan D. van der Vyver, eds.

LEX CHARITATIS

*A Juristic Disquisition on Law
in the Theology of Martin Luther*

Johannes Heckel

Translated and edited by
Gottfried G. Krodel
in collaboration with
Henning F. Falkenstein (†) and Jack A. Hiller (†)

from the second edition of
*Lex charitatis. Eine juristische Untersuchung
über das Recht in der Theologie Martin Luthers*

Preface by Martin Heckel

WILLIAM B. EERDMANS PUBLISHING COMPANY
GRAND RAPIDS, MICHIGAN / CAMBRIDGE, U.K.

First published in 1973 in German under the title
Lex charitatis. Eine juristische Untersuchung über das Recht in der Theologie Martin Luthers,
second edition, published by Böhlau Verlag GmbH & Cie Köln Weimar.

This English edition
© 2010 William B. Eerdmans Publishing Company
All rights reserved

Published 2010 by
Wm. B. Eerdmans Publishing Co.
2140 Oak Industrial Drive N.E., Grand Rapids, Michigan 49505 /
P.O. Box 163, Cambridge CB3 9PU U.K.
www.eerdmans.com

Library of Congress Cataloging-in-Publication Data

Heckel, Johannes, 1889-1963.
[Lex charitatis. English]
Lex charitatis: a juristic disquisition on law in the theology of Martin Luther /
Johannes Heckel; translated and edited by Gottfried G. Krodel;
in collaboration with Henning F. Falkenstein and Jack A. Hiller;
preface by Martin Heckel.
p.   cm.   — (Emory University studies in law and religion)
Includes bibliographical references and index.
ISBN 978-0-8028-6445-1 (pbk.: alk. paper)
1. Law (Theology) — History of doctrines.
2. Luther, Martin, 1483-1546 — Theology.
I. Krodel, Gottfried G.   II. Title.

BR333.5.L3H4213   2010
241'.2 — dc22
                                            2009043731

The translation of Johannes Heckel, *Lex charitatis. Eine juristische Untersuchung über das Recht in der Theologie Martin Luthers*, 2d ed. expanded, edited by Gottfried G. Krodel (Cologne: Verlag Böhlau, 1973), is by permission of Verlag Böhlau, Cologne

"What I write to you, I write to all."

Luther to Justus Jonas

Sept. 20, 1530

WA.B 5:630.56

Contents

Preface by Martin Heckel	xi
From Martin Heckel's Preface of the Second German Edition of Lex charitatis, *1973*	xiv
Introduction	xvi
Abbreviations	xxiii

WHICH CONCEPT 'LAW' DID MARTIN LUTHER AFFIRM?   1

Part One
The Present Interpretation of Luther's Idea of Law in the Context of Its Theological Origin and of the Main Stages of Its Development

1. The Problem	5
§1. *The Present Situation in Research*	5
§2. *The New Formulation of the Problem*	12
2. The Theological Origin of Luther's Doctrine of Law and the Development of Luther's Doctrine of Law	16
§1. *The Sovereignty of the Divine Law*	16
§2. *The Development of Luther's Doctrine of Law*	19

Contents

Part Two
The Basic Features of Luther's Doctrine of Law

SECTION ONE
THE BASIS OF LUTHER'S DOCTRINE OF LAW:
THE DOCTRINE OF THE TWO KINGDOMS

3. The Origin of Luther's Doctrine of the Two Kingdoms   25
4. The Kingdom of the World   27
5. The Kingdom of Christ   30
6. The Kingdom of God at the Right and at the Left of God   33

SECTION TWO
LUTHER'S DOCTRINE OF LAW

7. The Connection of the Doctrine of the Kingdoms with the Doctrine of Law   39
8. The Divine Law in the Status of the Incorrupt Nature   43
   - *§1. The Divine Natural Law*   43
   - *§2. The Divine Positive Law*   51
   - *§3. Summary*   52
9. Human Law in the Status of the Corrupt Nature during the Age of Unwritten Law   54
   - *§1. The Substantive Secular Natural Law*   54
   - *§2. The Institutional Secular Natural Law*   70
10. Written Law   81
11. The Law of Christ   84

Contents

**Part Three
The Existence of the Christian
in the Legal Structures of This World**

12.	The Christian as a Member of the Church in the World	97
13.	The Christian in the Estate of Marriage	102
14.	The Christian in the *Politia*	105
	§1. The Spiritual Basis of the Christian's Freedom in the Politia	105
	§2. The Christian as a Legal Associate in the Politia	106
	§3. The Christian as a Subject in the Politia	107
	§4. The Doctrine of the Tyrant	110
	§5. The Christian in the Office of Governmental Authority	114
	§6. Luther's Doctrine of the 'Christian Body' Especially in To the Christian Nobility of the German Nation	118
	§7. Retrospect	127

**WHAT HAPPENED TO
LUTHER'S DOCTRINE OF LAW?**   129

Appendixes

I.	Luther's Doctrine of the Right of Resistance to the Emperor	133
II.	The *Cura Religionis* of the Evangelical Prince	140
III.	In the Maze of Luther's Doctrine of the Two Kingdoms	145
IV.	Church and Ecclesiastical Law in the Frame of the Doctrine of the Two Kingdoms	176
V.	The Unfolding of the Doctrine of the Two Kingdoms as a Doctrine of Kingdoms and Governances	204
VI.	Announcement of *Initia Iuris Ecclesiastici Protestantium*	216
VII.	Announcement of *Lex Charitatis* and of "Widerstand gegen die Obrigkeit?"	223

Contents

Notes	233
Titles of Cited Luther Texts	506
Short Titles and Place of Full Citation	512
Index of Bible Passages	527
Index of Subjects	531

Preface

For the scholarship of our generation, Johannes Heckel in *Lex charitatis* was the first to develop Luther's ideas about church and law on the basis of the fundamental connection of their theological and juristic positions. In so doing, he also established directives for the proclamation of the church and for the present-day appropriate efforts to shape the legal form of the church in agreement with the gospel. The book, the result of decades of investigating the sources, was published in 1953; a second edition was published in 1973, and that edition is now presented in an English translation.

Lex charitatis was a groundbreaker in Luther research since it presented the whole of Luther's doctrine of law systematically. Further, the book may be considered to be of epochal significance for the history of ecclesiastical law. The results of the book overcame the self-sufficient legal positivism and the historicism which up to that point dominated ecclesiastical law and its history; they eliminated the sterile separation of the method of theology and of jurisprudence which had fatal consequences for the legal praxis of the church and for the church's relationship with the state; and they provided the theological foundation for evangelical ecclesiastical law on which it depends for its existence, especially in an increasingly secular society. The author developed a clear picture of the significance the central doctrine of Luther's Reformation — justification of the sinner by grace alone — had for the understanding of divine and of man-made law, and of ecclesiastical and of secular law; he demonstrated the connection between that understanding and

Preface

evangelical ecclesiology; and he worked out the consequences of that understanding for the way in which the Reformation viewed and shaped the office of pastor, the sacraments, marriage, secular governmental authority, and the right of resistance within the church and within the secular commonwealth. In this process he precisely developed the difference and the connection between the two kingdoms and the two governances. His basic ideas are summarized in Appendixes III through VII, which had been added in the second edition.

The significance of Johannes Heckel's work can be judged only when it is placed in the wider context of the history of the church. It is one of the tragic characteristics of the history of the church that Luther's juristic-theological positions[1] could be unfolded only incompletely in the development of evangelical ecclesiastical law. Already in the sixteenth century the evangelical churches were subordinated to the ecclesiastical governance of the governmental authorities and their determination of the confessional status of their territories. In the battles of the Age of Confessionalization the evangelical churches felt dependent on the protection and the organizational power of the territorial state *(cuius regio — eius religio)*.[2] Although the constitution of the Old Empire guaranteed legal equality to estates of different religious convictions and thus secured the external existence of the evangelical churches, yet these churches were secularly fenced in and dynastically politicized. In this way the spiritual foundations of evangelical ecclesiastical law were obstructed to a large degree, and this down to the twentieth century; at first the structures of the authoritarian monarchic state were superimposed upon these churches; later they were reshaped by the secular legal ideas of the Enlightenment and of the secular constitutional state. Only the confrontation with the totalitarian movements of the twentieth century made the evangelical churches in a sudden, dramatic way aware that evangelical ecclesiastical law must be built on the foundations provided by the theology of the Reformation. Through difficult external and internal upheavals, experienced first in the struggle with National Socialism, and then in the defense against the power of Communist ideology, the evangelical church gained two insights: existentially seen, the church's external legal form rests on the church's confessional basis; the external form of the church in the world has to be in line with the spiritual essence of the church, which justifies, determines, shapes, and limits that form.

Conscious of the scholarly legacy of Johannes Heckel, I as editor of

Preface

the second edition of *Lex charitatis* am grateful to the colleagues of Valparaiso University, Gottfried G. Krodel (emeritus of the Department of History and of Theology), Jack A. Hiller (emeritus of the Law School), and the late Henning F. Falkenstein (professor of German), to have envisioned this English translation of *Lex charitatis* and undertaken the difficult task of creating the text. I also extend my thanks to all who made this project financially possible. May *Lex charitatis* help the church and society of our days, which are increasingly challenged by the secularization of spiritual life, in the commitment to, and the service of, the truth and promise of the gospel!

MARTIN HECKEL
Tübingen, Reformation Sunday 2009

From Martin Heckel's Preface of the Second German Edition of Lex charitatis, 1973

Lex charitatis, Johannes Heckel's main work on ecclesiastical law, which for many years has been out of print, is now presented in a new edition. The text has remained unchanged, but the scholarly apparatus has been expanded with the sometimes extensive additions found in the author's desk copy.

In the ten years which Johannes Heckel was granted to live after the publication of *Lex charitatis* in 1953, he continued to pay close attention to the lively discussion on Luther's doctrine of the church, of law, and of the two kingdoms, and he critically evaluated the approval of his work and the questions addressed to it. The response of the scholarly community to his work confirmed for him the value of the positions he had developed. Therefore he did not envision basic changes for a new edition. He did envision, however, the expansion of some parts, especially those dealing with the reformer's understanding of a correct church ordinance and with the membership of a Christian in the church in the world (below, 471n. 7). These new materials were to continue and expand his earlier work on the young Luther, especially *Initia iuris ecclesiastici Protestantium.*[1] It was not possible for him to complete these materials and incorporate them in a new edition of *Lex charitatis.*

Therefore in this second edition I added to the original edition of *Lex charitatis* with the author's two appendixes (dealing with the right of resistance to the emperor and the *cura religionis* of the evangelical prince) some of the author's other works as a supplement. *In the Maze of Luther's Doctrine of the Two Kingdoms* (Appendix III), published in 1957,

Preface of the Second German Edition

is important for the controversy on *Lex charitatis*; here the author clarified his position and secured it over against his critics. "Church and Ecclesiastical Law in the Frame of the Doctrine of the Two Kingdoms," the last of the author's works, published in 1962 in Kanonistische Abteilung of *Zeitschrift der Savigny-Stiftung für Rechtsgeschichte*, is a summarizing presentation of Luther's thinking on ecclesiastical law (Appendix IV). "The Unfolding of the Doctrine of the Two Kingdoms as a Doctrine of Kingdoms and Governances," published in 1959 in *Evangelisches Kirchenlexikon*, is important for the stringency with which the author reduced complicated abstract reasoning to an uncomplicated presentation (Appendix V). I added this concise text and the author's two announcements of three of his publications (Appendixes VI and VII) to the former two titles because in these texts the author enables the reader to enter the many-threaded studies of the sources, studies which because of their difficult conceptual frame are sometimes not an easy read for theologians and jurists. . . .

Introduction

Johannes Heckel (1889-1963) was a distinguished member of the Faculty of Law at the University of Munich and a member of the Bayerische Akademie der Wissenschaften, philosophisch-historische Klasse (and for many years its secretary). In addition to scholarship, he was involved in the legal affairs of the evangelical churches in Germany.[1] On November 16, 1951, he presented *Lex charitatis. Eine juristische Untersuchung über das Recht in der Theologie Martin Luthers* to the Akademie. The book was the result of research in the history of law, especially ecclesiastical law, and in Luther's thought, spanning over forty years.[2] When it was published in 1953 it made headlines in terms of both approval and controversy,[3] and it has retained an important place in the scholarly debate.[4] Shortly after the publication, Franz Lau, one of the distinguished Luther scholars of the last century, wrote:

> In the future, Heckel's book will probably be considered to be one of the most significant and important Luther studies produced in our years. It is beyond imagination how someone who is not a member of the theological guild but is a legal scholar has mastered Luther's writings and the secondary Luther literature.... Only with the highest admiration can one observe how a "layman" has penetrated Luther's way of thinking..., and has done it in a way which many other Luther scholars were unable to accomplish, and this includes theologians.... Every theologian ... can approach Heckel's book only with feelings of inferiority unless he has mastered jurisprudence, as the

Introduction

jurist Heckel has. It is no wonder that Heckel is being applauded and praised, but that the discussion with him will not get off the ground easily. In any case, it is a risk to enter into controversy with a scholar for whom . . . it will not be easy to find a match.[5]

In short: After Heckel had dealt[6] with the scholarly debate about 'Luther and law' and formulated the problem as it emerged from this debate, he concentrated on two major topics: "The Basic Features of Luther's Doctrine of Law," and the question how, according to Luther, law structures the existence of a Christian in this world. In the first topic he developed Luther's systematics of law as a theology of law *(Rechtstheologie)*. In connection with the second topic he developed the legal nature of the church in the world and a Christian's legal position in it. Then he dealt with marriage. Finally, he focused on a Christian's position in society and the state. The materials which he presented in this last section for Luther's position on a Christian's right and duty to resist a governmental authority, even with force, created for many readers an image of Luther which in part was totally new when compared with the Luther image of the first half of the last century.

Jack Hiller of the Valparaiso University School of Law discussed the book with me and raised the question whether I would be willing to help in producing an English edition of it. He felt that an English text would give Luther the place in American jurisprudence which he deserves, and which, if not missing, was surrounded by strange ideas and misunderstandings. I knew Heckel's work since my student days, and I had learned from it for my work on church and state, and on Luther and law. Further, I was aware that the concept, reality, and study of 'ecclesiastical law' were alien to the Lutheran churches of my adopted country,[7] and that an English edition could be helpful to its Lutheran churches. I promised to help, and the idea was born to publish an English edition of *Lex charitatis*.

Martin Heckel (a distinguished member of the Faculty of Law at the University of Tübingen, a son of Johannes Heckel and the administrator of his scholarly estate) enthusiastically supported our intention. Through him we were able to secure the cooperation of Verlag Böhlau, Cologne, the publisher of the second edition of *Lex charitatis*. Jack Hiller was able to gain our colleague Henning Falkenstein (professor of German) for the project. He and I prepared an English version of the text only, and then we merged both versions in a first draft. Section by

Introduction

section Jack Hiller corrected our text in terms of English legal writing. In this process our draft was cleaned up. When Henning Falkenstein unexpectedly died in September of 2002, we had a tentative version of the text. In the meantime I had started the work on the notes. As that work slowly progressed, our tentative version was revised in light of the materials in the notes and through Hiller's scrutinizing the text. This work resulted in a new draft. In consultation with Martin Heckel, and under the watchful eye of Jack Hiller as *peritus* of English legal writing, I developed this draft into the final version.

Translating *Lex charitatis* was not an easy task. There were long sentences with interdependent clauses. The book was an Akademie Abhandlung. Therefore the author had the luxury of writing for the specialists among the specialists. We had to deal with this situation inasmuch as jurists had to be made familiar with Luther's theological thinking and vocabulary, and theologians had to be made familiar with juristic thinking and vocabulary.[8] There were adjectives made up of a noun and an adjective,[9] for which a way had to be found to express them in English. We had to deal with the terminology (especially the juristic one). This situation was complicated in three ways: Sometimes a current English term can have a meaning which does not correspond to Luther's German or Latin equivalent; at Luther's time the meaning of some terms was not as fixed as it is today; Luther was not consistent in his terminology.[10] Further, there were words or phrases which have a specific meaning for Luther,[11] or which Luther used with a variety of meanings which to the present-day reader appear to be different,[12] or of which the meaning in Luther's use is not always as clear as one wishes.[13]

We tried to be faithful to Heckel's text, but we also tried to make Heckel — and Luther — speak English. Since neither Heckel nor Luther was 'politically correct', we retained their way of writing. In the text we handled the author's use of square brackets, parentheses, ellipses, and emphases (italics) as we felt it necessary; for emphases in the texts cited we used italics. In a few places we did not follow the author's paragraphing of the text; sometimes it would have created a connection which in the English version would have read awkwardly. Throughout the text and the notes, we adjusted the numbering of biblical passages to that of the NRSV, we corrected the few pesky mistakes which we found (and made some!), and we used pointed brackets for our materials.[14]

Introduction

The scholarly apparatus presented special problems. Regarding the form of the notes and of the Back Matter, the reader familiar with *The Chicago Manual of Style,* for instance, will find that we did some things differently, and purists might fault us for this.[15] We had to use the author's use of "ff." — anything else would have meant outguessing him. In order to be consistent, "ff." is used in the notes, when necessary, but it is not used in the indexes. We eliminated the titles of series, and we did not give the full citation of titles each time when they were used for the first time in the notes of a chapter. In order to enable the reader quickly to find the full citations, we listed all titles as short titles, followed by the place of their full citation. That list, together with the list of the titles of the cited Luther texts, replaces the bibliography. Purists in Canon law will fault us for having added the number of the volume and of the column in Friedberg's edition of the *Corpus iuris canonici;* we felt that this would help in finding the citations, especially since there is a difference between Heckel's way of citing (which we retained) and that of the jurists' *Bluebook.* Finally, some of the older collections of essays do not give the name of the editor.

The first edition (1953) of *Lex charitatis* with Appendixes I and II has 1519 numbered footnotes. That number is incorrect because Heckel added lower case letters to some numbers in order to create additional notes; for instance, to note 1169 on page 144 he added letters (a) through (r). In the second edition (1973) this numbering of the notes has been retained; in some cases the text of these notes has significantly grown through the additional materials which (in preparation for a new edition) Heckel had written in his desk copy, and which the editor of the second edition reproduced. In our version all notes of the second edition with all the references to the primary and secondary materials have been reproduced. But not all the cited texts are translated. In some cases, these citations are cumulative, and the individual texts do not bring anything that is new (or in our judgment important for the author's text); in such cases one or two of the cited texts which best substantiate Heckel's position are translated, and the remaining references are listed. In other cases, an English version of the citation has been given already in the text itself. Again in other cases, the author cited only one or two words as documentation for his text; in order to present a readable English text, it would have been necessary to use more text than we felt was justified. But *all citations* from Luther (translated or not), all citations from other primary materials (translated or

Introduction

not),[16] and all citations from, or references to, the secondary literature are listed at their appropriate place; in a few cases we have summarized the cited text.

Luther's writings are cited according to the Weimar edition.[17] For the creation of the English versions of Luther's (sometimes ponderous) titles we consulted Kurt Aland, *Hilfsbuch zum Lutherstudium,*[18] and *Luther's Works.* American Edition. We added a list of the titles we use, in which each title is preceded by the appropriate number in Aland's *Hilfsbuch*[19] and followed by the number of the volume and of the first page of the text in the Weimar edition. Sometimes the dates added to the titles designate the date when Luther wrote a text, or preached a sermon, or delivered a set of lectures, other times when the text was published. With a few exceptions we used the dates given by Heckel. In the references to the Weimar edition the last numeral listed designates the line on the page where Heckel's citation begins, or where the center of his argumentation is located. Sometimes we adjusted this line number to match our text. All translations are ours unless we used an available English text; the appropriate references to used English texts, or to English texts which were available to us, are given in pointed brackets, following the location in the Weimar edition. In our translations we retained Luther's parentheses and quotation marks, or lack of quotation marks. We checked all citations and references as much as was possible; there were some titles ('old' books, journals, newspapers, collections of essays) which we were unable either to locate or have available through interlibrary loan.

In some of the notes we rearranged the sequence of the cited texts in order to present a most striking text before other materials, or in order to avoid the need for repeating bibliographical information. In many of the citations from the Luther texts, Heckel heavily used square brackets (sometimes parentheses) and ellipses. When we used an available English text for Luther's German or Latin text cited, we had to follow the spelling and use of square brackets as we found them in that English text and ignore Heckel's square brackets. What should be done with them? Further, there were instances when we felt that some materials had to be added to the cited text by placing them in the pointed brackets which we use for our materials. We, too, had to use ellipses in our version of the cited texts. What should be done with the author's ellipses? In order to avoid the need to use additional typographic marks in the notes to differentiate between Heckel's version and our version,

Introduction

we used pointed brackets only unless an available English text demanded square brackets. Therefore with apologies to the author, now some of the materials in the notes in pointed brackets may be his or ours, and this applies also to the ellipses.

Some of Heckel's citations were rather brief. In order to place such brief citations in their background or context, it was necessary to use more text of the source (either translated or summarized) than Heckel had presented. Sometimes such additional materials are not placed in pointed brackets.

At the beginning of the work, Jack Hiller and I decided that in order to be faithful to the book we would not update the secondary literature, even if now some of it is outdated. We have added a few references to secondary materials, which might be helpful for a first orientation.

Many colleagues have enthusiastically and unselfishly helped Henning Falkenstein and me in the preparation of this English edition. It was *Jack Hiller* who initiated this project. With a deft hand he directed the externals and internals of our work. With invincible optimism he encouraged me when I despaired of ever finishing the task, or when illness, surgeries, or deaths interrupted the work; he established the contacts with bilingual jurists in Europe; he read our texts over and over again; he never tired of arguing with me the subtleties of the text, and he patiently listened to whatever argument I presented to him. To the end of his life in November of 2009 his dedication to this project provided the encouragement and energy to bring, finally, the English version of *Lex Charitatis* to the scholarly public. From the beginning *Martin Heckel* supported our work. Especially during the last phase of the work he put much time and energy into patiently dealing with the questions I sent him, and sometimes his answers were what as students we called a *privatissimum*. The bilingual jurists *Heinrich Scholler* (Munich), *Bernhard Großfeld* (Münster), and *Rodney Batstone* (London) helped us find appropriate translations for juristic terms. *Martin Brecht* (Münster) made available to me his inexhaustible theological and bibliographical knowledge on Luther and his times. My former student *Timothy Dost* (St. Louis) did xerox work for me at the library of Concordia Theological Seminary, and my young friend and fellow Reformation historian *Christopher Brown* (Boston) provided valuable information about citations from Augustine. Our colleague *Forest Vance* (†) supplied the translations of Swedish texts. Our colleagues in the Department of Foreign Languages, *Randa Duvick* (French) and *Mark Farmer* and *Michael Kumpf*

Introduction

(Classics), checked the translations of some difficult passages. Over a long period of time, *Walter Keller* (Theology) made available to us many volumes of his *Luther's Works,* and the rich library of *Dale Lasky* (Theology) was always open to me. *Susan Wanat, Marcia Andrejevich,* and *Ruth Connell,* our inter-library loan librarians, with great patience and skill filled my many requests, a task which sometimes was frustrating, notwithstanding the wonders of bibliographical work in the electronic age. To all who assisted us in this project I extend my sincere gratitude. Notwithstanding the help I received, *errare humanum est!* Whatever mistakes are in this English version of *Lex charitatis,* they are mine.

Over many years the Valparaiso University School of Law was the home of this project. When we started, *Edward Gaffney* was the dean. He, together with *Bruce Berner,* and also *Richard Baepler* (then the provost of the university, now emeritus of theology and law), was convinced that the law school of a university in the Lutheran tradition ought to produce an English edition of what has to be considered the standard work on Luther and law. From the very beginning these colleagues endorsed our project and strongly supported our work. Now that the work has been completed, *Jay Conison* is the dean; he has encouraged and supported us in the final phase of our work, and he has secured the finances for the publication of this English edition of *Lex charitatis.* I join Martin Heckel in thanking Dean Conison for his interest and support.

We are honored, and we appreciate that Professor *John Witte, Jr.* (Emory University) accepted the manuscript for the *Emory University Studies in Law and Religion.* It is our hope that this English version of *Lex charitatis* will secure Luther's position in English-speaking jurisprudence, will clarify Luther's contribution to socio-political issues, and will help the Lutheran churches in our country in their necessarily ongoing efforts to shape their legal existence in accordance with the gospel and the foundations which Luther provided.

GOTTFRIED G. KRODEL
Valparaiso, Indiana, Reformation Sunday 2009

Abbreviations

The abbreviations follow Siegfried M. Schwertner, *International Glossary of Abbreviations for Theology and Related Subjects.* 2d ed. Revised and expanded. Berlin, New York, 1992, with the following additions or modifications:

BC	*The Book of Concord. The Confessions of the Evangelical Lutheran Church.* Translated and edited by Theodore G. Tappert et al. Philadelphia, 1959.
BC	Kolb-Wengert ed., *The Book of Concord. The Confessions of the Evangelical Lutheran Church.* Translated and edited by Robert Kolb and Timothy J. Wengert et al. Minneapolis, 2000.
BLD	*Black's Law Dictionary.* 4th ed. St. Paul, 1951.
Friedberg	*Corpus Iuris Canonici.* Edited by Emil Friedberg. Leipzig, 1879. Reprint, Graz 1959. 2 vols.
LW	*Luther's Works.* American Edition. Edited by Jaroslav Pelikan and Helmut T. Lehmann. St. Louis and Philadelphia, 1955-86. 55 vols.
NRSV	New Revised Standard Version of the Bible.
Vulgate	*Biblia sacra iuxta vulgatam versionem.* Edited by Bonifatius Fischer, OSB, et al. 2d ed. Revised. Stuttgart, 1969. 2 vols.

WHICH CONCEPT 'LAW' DID MARTIN LUTHER AFFIRM?

This is *the* question of all questions which connect Protestant theology and jurisprudence. Its significance reaches far beyond Lutheranism, at least in those topics where the Wittenberg reformer influenced the Swiss reformers. Furthermore, the question is not restricted to religious matters; it also branches out to all fields of secular life which ever have been influenced by Luther's theology, or which today are still influenced by it. Luther's understanding of law confronts the historian studying Luther's position on the so-called *corpus christianum* (Christian body), the politician dealing with Luther's opinion of the Christian state, the philosopher of law studying Luther's concept 'natural law', and the canonist studying Luther's doctrine of the church and of eccle-

---

I gratefully acknowledge the support of my research in ecclesiastical law which I have received from the Evangelical Lutheran Church of Bavaria, its bishop, Hans Meiser, its governing council, and its Munich deanery. For scholarly conversations I am very much indebted to Professor Ernst Kohlmeyer (Schönau, near Berchtesgaden). On the occasion of his seventieth birthday, I dedicated to him some of the following materials with the title "Naturrecht und christliche Verantwortung im öffentlichen Leben nach der Lehre Martin Luthers," in *Zur politischen Predigt. Aus der Vorbereitungsarbeit des Ev.-Luth. Dekanats München zur Tagung des Lutherischen Weltbundes in Hannover 1952*, ed. by Evangelisch-Lutherisches Dekanat München (Munich, 1952), 35ff. With the title "Das natürliche Recht und das göttliche Recht bei Martin Luther" I presented other materials of the following study to a conference of historians of law which took place at Schloß Traunsee (near Gmunden) on September 1, 1951. And a synopsis of the book I presented to a conference of the Luther Akademie which took place in Goslar on August 4 and 5, 1952.

siastical law. The question is, of course, especially important for Lutheran theology since all of Luther's main doctrines include a legal aspect. One has to remember only his theology of law, his doctrine of the two kingdoms (the kingdom of God and that of the prince of this world), and his statements about the two governances *(Regiment)*, the spiritual and the secular. This legal aspect is even more relevant for the Fall of man, which Luther understood as the spiritual breaking of law *par excellence*, and for justification by faith, which he understood as the restoration of the spiritual legal relationship existing between the Creator and his creature. Even Luther's terminology shows that in connection with these topics not only theological questions but also legal ones have to be answered. One cannot possibly grasp the legal significance of these topics without knowing Luther's understanding of law.

One would think that Luther's concept 'law', the main and central legal question of the Reformation, has been clarified. History and legal history of Lutheranism have always been rich in paradoxes, and out of this tradition a surprising discovery comes: the question of Luther's concept 'law' has not yet even been properly approached! Of course, generations of scholars have devoted their work to Luther's ideas which are relevant for this question, and they succeeded in theologically and juristically solving many detailed problems.[1] Yet whenever scholars were confronted with the central issue, Luther's concept 'law', their results hardly corresponded to their expectations. According to theologians, philosophers, and jurists there always remained "a remnant of basic vagueness"[2] so that contradictory opinions never ceased to exist. One was not even able to agree whether, in the final analysis, the uneasiness resulting from this situation did not originate in Luther himself, that is, in his contradictory statements about law and right. Even if such doubts could be removed, the fact remains: if Luther had a clear concept 'law', it still remains to be discovered.

What is the reason for this situation? "Scholarly controversies," said Nicolai Hartmann, "prove that a question is alive and that there are new perspectives."[3] Regarding Luther's concept 'law' one is tempted to assume the opposite. Apart from few exceptions, the question is not alive in the scholarly debate of the past, and this is not by accident.

PART ONE

The Present Interpretation of Luther's Idea of Law in the Context of Its Theological Origin and of the Main Stages of Its Development

CHAPTER 1

The Problem

According to the prevailing Protestant position, the Reformation was a struggle for the freedom of faith against the sovereignty of law in the church. Seen from a higher perspective, this is the same as the struggle for the righteousness of God *(iustitia dei)* against the justice of the jurists *(iustitia iuristarum)*.[1] As a result, the theological treatment of law, the term which in theology is used to deal with juridical topics, is totally removed from the doctrine of law found in jurisprudence. Instead of converging, theologians and jurists strictly separate the subject to be investigated in each discipline. Theologians and jurists together are convinced of the correctness of this method, and they mutually suppport each other. This is most obvious in their positions on *the* problem in Luther's doctrine of law, divine law. Because of its decisive significance for our work, we have to sum up, be it ever so briefly, the relevant research on this subject; this will enable us to evaluate the usefulness of the method used in the past and to gain insights for what perhaps may be a necessary new approach to the problem.

§ 1. The Present Situation in Research

Jurists dominate the scholarly discussion on *divine law*. Christian Thomasius,[2] a famous jurist, began a campaign against it, and a second, equally famous jurist, Rudolph Sohm, concluded this campaign. For the history of ideas it would be instructive, and for theologians and jurists alike it would be rewarding, were one to investigate the reaction to Thomasius, and also when and for what reasons the concept 'divine law' disappeared from Lutheran theology, jurisprudence, and legal practice.

No branch of jurisprudence can be more interested in this task than ecclesiastical law, and no branch is more called upon to be engaged in this task. In every other field of law, divine law can either be rejected with the help of an exclusively secular jurisprudence, or it can be sidetracked to a large degree by a positivist theory of law — not so in ecclesiastical law! Here not only the legitimacy of individual commandments or actions is at stake but the very existence of law itself. If the church, for reasons of faith, does not acknowledge the existence of divine law, how could it justify a man-made law for its communal existence in the world? For this reason ecclesiastical law has to deal with divine law. In light of this situation it is understandable that ecclesiastical law became the bastion of divine law when in every other field of jurisprudence it succumbed to the attacks started by Thomasius.

Even this restriction of divine law to ecclesiastical law did not remain unopposed. Let me mention just one name in this scholarly battle, which marks the end of the earlier debate as well as the beginning of our current one. Who else could it be but Rudolph Sohm? He lives in the history of Protestant ecclesiastical law as the creator of a great truth and an equally great error — an error which nevertheless was fruitful because it still contained some truth. His lasting achievement was a new concept which he introduced into the previous discussion about the relationship between church and law. This concept was the kingdom of God.[3]

For centuries, Protestant ecclesiology had used the Christian congregation as the starting point for making the transition from the concept 'church' to the concept 'man-made ecclesiastical law'.[4] Justification for this argumentation was derived from the confessional writings of the Lutheran church; yet neither were they completely used[5] nor was their original meaning totally understood. In the 1840s[6] two forms of the church were differentiated, and in each was present a totally different position on law: the church of faith, the invisible church *(ecclesia invisibilis)*, which, because of the demands of dogma, is free from law, and the church of law *(ecclesia visibilis)*; because of empirical necessities, that visible church is constituted as a legal association.[7] Zwingli was the first to make this differentiation; Melanchthon introduced it

The Problem

into Lutheran ecclesiology, and Lutheran Orthodoxy developed it further. This interpretation, or rather new interpretation,[8] of classical concepts of the ecclesiastical law of the Reformation opened a new chapter in the history of Protestant ecclesiastical law. Positivist ecclesiastical law took control of the visible church[9] just about at the time that Positivism in public law began to control the law of the secular commonwealth.[10] Positivism succeeded in public law, but it did not gain much credibility in ecclesiastical law. Scholars were unable to eliminate the glaring contradiction that exists between one form of the church, in which law is detested, and another one, which demands law;[11] their logic and theology[12] obviously suffered from inconsistency.[13]

Here Sohm made his move.[14] With amazing intuition he more sensed than realized that the concept 'kingdom of God' was one of the strongest roots of the doctrine of law developed by the Wittenberg reformers, especially Luther. This concept, he believed, was the only basis for a doctrine of Lutheran ecclesiastical law. Who could possibly discuss the legal community of Christ's disciples before clarifying the legal relationship between the master and his disciples, between the king of Christ's kingdom and the Christians? This question is both a theological and a juristic one, and it is beyond the church in a legal sense. Emanuel Hirsch called the concept 'kingdom of God' the restless element in the history of the modern doctrine of the state.[15] Since Sohm, the kingdom of God has been such an element of restlessness in the theory of Protestant ecclesiastical law as well.[16] This was Sohm's lasting achievement. He has shaken the self-sufficiency and self-confidence of juristic Positivism in Lutheran ecclesiastical law. He only shook them, however; he did not dispose of them. A necessary consequence was the problem 'law' in the kingdom of God, that is, the problem 'divine ecclesiastical law'. And it had to become the chief part in the doctrine of Lutheran ecclesiastical law, though until now its significance has hardly been recognized. In any case, Sohm passed over it without much ado. Because of his theological framework he saw no need to deal with the problem 'divine law'. His theses were simple and, therefore, captivating: Law is hostile to the kingdom of God, a kingdom of freedom and love; law resides in the world, that is, among mankind which had fallen from God and declared its independence from him; the church is the manifestation of God's kingdom on earth and, therefore, has nothing in common with law. "Ecclesiastical law contradicts the essence of the church."[17]

This ended all discrepancies among the previous positions on the relationship of church and law. It was a terrible end for the discipline of ecclesiastical law, and its representatives desperately tried to fight this death sentence. But those who agreed with Sohm's statements about the characteristics of God's kingdom on the one hand, and about the nature of law on the other, could not possibly reject his conclusions. Therefore all attempts to prove him wrong failed.

Unlike the scholars of ecclesiastical law, the majority of evangelical theologians gratefully accepted Sohm's theses because they gave the problem 'law' its proper place in the theological system. Instinctively, theologians had always disliked any kind of spiritual law,[18] even when it was cloaked in Protestant thought; now they seemed to be fully justified, and this through the work of an eminent jurist. They no longer had to deal with a spiritual law. Law was no longer a topic in the faith, and faith no longer a topic in law. Spiritual law was now a concept without any significance for Salvation; it was contrary to faith and, therefore, an illegitimate concept, a symbol of the intrusion of the world into God's kingdom. Theologians withdrew to an area which was free from law, and thereby they thoroughly alienated themselves from law.[19] Whenever they dealt with law, they worked with a concept 'law' which originated outside of their area, that is, the law of the world.

To that same area outside of theology Sohm exiled ecclesiastical law. He never doubted or even reinterpreted the secular concept 'law'. On the contrary! He exposed ecclesiastical law as a law originating in the wrong place, namely, the church. As a result, ecclesiastical law lost whatever special status it had had within general jurisprudence. The venerable term *ius utrumque*[20] was unmasked as a lie. Ecclesiastical law was nothing other than secular law for religious matters,[21] whether it was written by a secular governmental authority or the autonomous association of Christians.

Of necessity, Sohm's theological and juristic starting point caused the denial of the existence of divine law and, therefore, also of man-made ecclesiastical law. In light of Luther's theology, such a denial is contestable from the start. One has to remember only Luther's ‹free› translation[22] of Psalm 99:4, a passage which is famous in the history of law: "In the kingdom of this king one loves the law."[23] Of which law did the psalmist speak? The law of fallen mankind, or the divine law of Christ's kingdom? Further, the authors of the confessional writings of the Lutheran church frequently mentioned divine law. Certainly, this was not the divine law of the canonistic doctrine of law.[24] Yet by no means can one deny that they intended to make statements about law.[25] These samples compel us to conclude that Sohm's theory, too, is flawed. From Luther he took only the concept 'kingdom of God', but he combined it with the concept 'law' of a much later period without realizing that Luther would not agree with that period's secular concept 'law'. In short: He failed because he ignored divine law;[26] he never found the key to Luther's concept 'law'. He made the mistake of "brewing together faith and reason," to use Luther's words.[27] Yet even this negative result was valuable for further research; it warns us not to date our present concept 'law' back to the thoughts of the Wittenberg reformers, and it challenges us to develop their concept 'law' on the basis of their understanding of faith.

Fortunately, soon after Sohm's battle cry against ecclesiastical law scholars of historical theology began to investigate *biblical natural law*, another main concept[28] in Luther's doctrine of law. There was hope that this concept might shed more light on the relationship of faith and law than positive divine law[29] had done before. For a long time Protestant textbooks of ethics had not contained a chapter on natural law.[30] It emerged again at the turn of the nineteenth to the twentieth century, when social questions demanded answers. At the same time, Leo XIII vigorously revived the Roman Catholic doctrine of natural law, and this forced Protestants to reflect upon their own position critically. When scholars of historical theology traced the Protestant doctrine of natural law back to Luther,[31] they, surprisingly, arrived at two rather different results. One could be called traditional, the other idealistic.

According to the first, Luther maintained a patristic-medieval concept of natural law, which he derived from the theological tradition. In the original revelation, God communicated 'absolute natural law' to human reason. After the Fall of Adam, that law was adjusted to man's sinful condition; it became 'relative natural law', and it has remained valid in the world ever since. In this way, divine dignity of origin was given back to the law of the world, its beginning being traced back to the Original Status of the Creation. Therefore it retains its validity even after the Fall, as Scripture testifies. Luther was understood as being under the spell of the natural-law theories of the pre-Reformation era. Whether these theories have been correctly understood does not concern us at this point. In any case, ‹in this thesis regarding Luther's supposed affirmation of pre-Reformation natural-law theories› not the reformer but the medieval man Martin Luther is the center of the argument. The thesis was first developed in 1901 by the French theologian Eugène Ehrhardt,[32] and its historical orientation led to its success in Germany. Max Weber,[33] and especially Ernst Troeltsch,[34] Günther Holstein,[35] and others supported it. Among jurists it may even today still be considered the dominant thesis.

The Luther expert Karl Holl, however, strongly opposed this thesis precisely because of its medieval, repristinating character.[36] In connection with this thesis, he understood Luther as the great innovator, as he did in connection with other topics. According to Holl, Luther was "the first to cut a breach into the idea, handed down from antiquity, that all nations have the same natural law."[37] Whenever Luther spoke of natural law, he did not deal with matters of law but rather with the Christian commandment of love as a moral norm. In short: According to Holl, Luther did not recognize natural law. Thus theology and the legal concept of the world remain dissociated, as described above.[38] "The question whether natural law can exist concerns jurists," argued one of the most recent authors dealing with our subject;[39] therefore theologians are not responsible for finding an answer to the question.

For the time being, the question how the controversy among Luther's interpreters has to be decided will be postponed. At this point it is important to see where they agree rather than disagree. They all are convinced that law has a secular quality. Some ascribe a thin halo of original holiness to law, others do not. But they are absolutely certain that according to Reformation principles a spiritual law cannot exist. They only cannot agree, however, whether Luther's position on natural law was a remnant of medieval theology, which was contrary to these principles, or something else, perhaps just a moral lecture in which the author used legal terminology.

This is the situation in research today. Scholars have come considerably closer to Luther's view of law. They are no longer satisfied with an abrupt confrontation of God's kingdom and the kingdom of the world; they see God's will for law[40] at work also in the kingdom of the world. Nevertheless, the point which is decisive for our work remains: all law is secular.[41] Therefore the author of the most recent study in the field of legal philosophy, which offers the deepest insights in Luther's thought, summarized: "Luther left all law, including ecclesiastical law, to the world. But this does not mean that he desacralized it, that is, completely secularized it, as the Neo-Protestants did later. For Luther law was simultaneously both secular and sacred."[42]

The Problem

However, if one uses this secular concept of law to interpret Luther's diverse statements about natural law, one soon is lost in a jungle of incomprehensible and incompatible assertions. Even if one grants Luther a truly immense freedom in the use of legal terms, even if one willingly accepts his serious or playful paradoxical theses, one cannot help thinking that a great mind is leading one astray into impenetrable underbrush. The most recent careful analysis of Luther's individual statements on natural law confirms this. Writes Hans Liermann, one of the experts on Protestant ecclesiastical law of our time:

> If one approaches the complex of questions on Luther and natural law without any bias, one realizes the futility of any attempt to extract any system of legal philosophy from Luther's writings. In terms of legal philosophy one could call Luther a naive proponent of natural law, who uses natural-law phrases whenever they are convenient, now this way, now that way, as they flow from his pen. One cannot claim for him any consistency in legal philosophy. The more one tries to decipher and interpret his contradictory statements, the more contradictory they become, and the more unclear becomes the picture of the situation in the history of ideas — what really happened. Therefore it is better to admit frankly that one cannot at all use his writings for the problem productively. This statement does not minimize his religious genius. His greatness lies in a quite different area.[43]

This carefully reasoned and concise judgment deserves our attention. By summarizing the previous efforts to interpret Luther's concept 'law', this judgment presents a blank in matters of legal philosophy. Similar statements had already been made a hundred years ago. "Luther had various thoughts about law," one reads, but he never treated them in a scholarly way.[44] In spite of intensive inquiry,[45] a clear concept 'law' was never discovered in Luther's writings.[46] Does this lack of a clear concept 'law' not fully agree with Luther's antagonism to jurists? How comforting it is for those in the legal profession to know that the reformer's own uncertainty about the nature of law was the reason for his crude invectives against the 'noble servants' ⟨of law⟩!

But alas! This asserted failure of the reformer has a much more serious side. It does not reflect Luther's inadequacy as a jurist — that would be rather insignificant — but his inadequacy as a theologian. For proof one has to remember only the religious and legal situation at the beginning of the Reformation.

In the medieval church, faith and law were integrated and supported each other. Whoever had developed a new concept 'faith', and with it a new concept 'church', could not continue to be burdened with the traditional concept 'law'. Therefore Luther could not "naively"[47] adopt the medieval natural-law formulas.[48] *The reformation of the church involved a reformation of the idea 'law'*,[49] if I might be allowed to use this phrase. And for this reformation the problem 'natural law' was theologically and juristically crucial. Had Luther treated this problem with cool indifference, had he even rejected it,[50] he would have to be accused of blindness in legal matters, which one could ascribe only to a theological bungler.

"It is unfair," Melanchthon, the second of the Wittenberg reformers, wrote, "to ascribe errors to the discipline, which have their roots in the weakness of the teachers."[51] At the beginning I stated that the question of Luther's concept 'law' has not yet even been properly approached.[52] This is confirmed by the survey of the previous research, which brought us to a disappointing result. Our consideration of natural law showed that there were two reasons for this failure. One concerns terminology; Luther used the vocabulary of medieval theology, <but> no one saw that his concept 'natural law' had a new content.[53] The second reason concerns method; scholars dealt with the wrong Luther, questioning him as a philosopher of law; as his profession required, he answered, however, as a theologian. Both reasons together are the source of the confusion.

§ 2. The New Formulation of the Problem

Luther's doctrine of law is part of his theology and, therefore, a *theological doctrine of law*.[54] Luther developed it as a teacher of Holy Scripture,[55] and he claimed to be heard among Christians only in this capacity;[56] his charge as a teacher did not go beyond the Christian community. Therefore, unlike philosophers or philosophers of law, he did not address all mankind[57] but only Christians.[58] He started from the law of Christians, that is, Christ's law,[59] the law in the kingdom of Christ the king. In a condensed theological formula, in the doctrine of justification by faith alone he dealt with the legal communion between Christ <and his

followers>. Therefore the question of Luther's concept 'law' is synonymous with the more specific question: which concept 'law' does the doctrine of justification presuppose?[60] This "chief article"[61] of Luther's theology is the only basis for understanding his doctrine of law.[62] Only a concept of law which is connected with the doctrine of justification may be considered to be genuinely Lutheran. All of Luther's statements about law, especially those about natural law, have to be measured and interpreted in the light of this doctrine.

In opposition to the theology of glory in medieval Scholasticism, Luther characterized his theology of justification by faith alone as theology of the cross.[63] His statements about law, therefore, may be called *legal doctrine of the theology of the cross*. "The cross of Christ is the only doctrine <in> the words of God." This sentence from Luther's second lectures on the Psalms (1518-21)[64] also applies to the Word of God as law *(lex)*. If I am not mistaken, such a coordination of theology and jurisprudence opens for the theologian as well as the jurist an entirely new view of our problem.

Until now the topic 'Reformation and law' has not contributed much to Lutheranism's self-understanding. The topic has been treated in a somewhat disparate way because it lacked a central, simultaneously theological and juristic concept. When one focused on this topic, the central concern of the Reformation was treated only indirectly, namely, whenever different opinions about 'spiritual law'[65] were rejected. Except for this, the materials presented under this topic dealt with the impact of the Reformation on an area of life which was beyond religion, that is, on life in the world with its tensions between faith and law.

Even the discussion of justification and law begun by Karl Barth in 1938[66] remained within these boundaries. With carefully reasoned acuteness Barth criticized those theologians who were content with placing justification and law side by side. To replace this juxtaposition he posed the question: "Is there a relationship between the reality of the sinner, once and for all justified by God in Jesus Christ through faith alone, and the problem of man-made law? Is there an inner, a necessary relationship, a relationship through which man-made law together with divine justification would in some way become part of the Christian faith and Christian responsibility and, therefore, also of Christian confession?"[67] Barth did not find a satisfactory answer to his question in the writings of the reformers. For him, the reformers demonstrated, of course, that the two areas could exist side by side without contradiction, but the reformers were not theologically interested in demonstrating that justification and law are internally connected. Therefore the question remains open whether the reformers based law on justification by faith, and political freedom on Christ's authority, or whether the reformers secretly used a different basis and merely attached the idea of man-made law to the recognition of divine justification instead of connecting the two essentially. Barth was correct when he warned us not to take this gap in the teachings of the reformers lightly.

But does this gap exist? Or is it only the result of a wrong formulation of the question? Before any decision about the relationship between justification and man-made law in Luther's teachings can be made, the legal concept involved in justification has to be clarified. It is precisely this concept, however, which until now is shrouded in impenetrable darkness.

It is our task to eliminate this oppressing ignorance and finally provide the topic 'Reformation and law' with its true, spiritual center. It is called spiritual law *(lex spiritualis)*. Spiritual man is the guiding principle for Luther's anthropology, the spiritual kingdom for his kingdom doctrine, the spiritual church for his ecclesiology,[68] and the spiritual law for his doctrine of law. One follows from the other, one refers to the other, and none exists without the other.

Thus far it was impossible for scholars to acknowledge such a concept of spiritual law as *the* legal concept of Luther. They were aware of Luther's protest against spiritual law[69] and its philosophical-theological foundations. They overlooked that in his theology faith and law were inseparably connected, as they were in the theology of the Middle Ages. One example from many may demonstrate this: ". . . there is no difference," said Luther in a sermon of April 1516,[70] "between not believing in Christ . . . and acting, speaking, ⟨and⟩ lusting against God's law, [that is,] natural law, . . . both are the same and have to be the same."[71] Luther did not attack spiritual law because he rejected a law which was normative for faith. On the contrary, he took such a law for granted. He attacked spiritual law because he wanted to liberate the true spiritual law from the oppressive frame of a false spiritual law.[72] For this reason the reformers wrestled with law.[73]

This observation quickly settles the previous differences of opinion about Luther and natural law. As was the case with his theology, so in his statements about natural law Luther was not under the spell of pre-Reformation doctrines. Also, he did not interpret natural law as a mere moral norm; for him natural law was the elementary form of spiritual law. And finally, he was not a naive proponent of natural law, who used the traditional natural-law formulas because they came to his mind. He used them but made them "transparent" for a new content,[74] and thus he gave them a new, precise meaning. — What was this meaning?

CHAPTER 2

The Theological Origin of Luther's Doctrine of Law and the Development of Luther's Doctrine of Law

§ 1. The Sovereignty of the Divine Law

Luther's doctrine of law is not the result of philosophical or theological speculation. Of course, as a member of the *via moderna* Luther was in the midst of the scholarly enterprise of his time, and already as a young professor he passionately participated in scholarly controversies.[1] His understanding of law owed much to the scholarly world of his day. But, like his dogmatics, the nucleus of his understanding of law was not shaped by the philosophy and theology of his day. Decisive for Luther was a religious illumination, the Revelation of the gospel. It gave the teachings of this original and willful thinker inner unity, mysterious depth, and rousing momentum, in spite of some unbalanced formulations in his theories. He felt that this Revelation was not only his personal experience but universal, for all of Christendom valid knowledge,[2] revealed to him by God,[3] and he understood himself as being moved by God to interpret this Revelation as a theological teacher.[4]

The daily experienced driving and oppressing anxiety in the life of the young Luther[5] was the perfection of the Christian. His whole mind aimed at it, and with burning longing his fiery soul craved it. He entered the Augustinian Order so that he could participate in that status of a perfect Christian, and he meticulously obeyed the rule of the order so that he might reach the perfection appropriate for that status. His efforts led him, however, to a legal question, which would become fateful for his life and teaching: What is the righteousness which is valid before

God? (Romans 1:17.)[6] As he was pursuing this serious question and enduring its weight,[7] he was confronted with God's law, and this confrontation almost shattered the monk and theologian. The *sovereignty of law* appeared before his soul[8] not as a benevolent order but as an extremely terrifying[9] majesty.[10] He always remembered these hours.[11] The domination of law (Romans 7:1; Vulgate), or as he expressed it later in an immensely paradoxical phrase, "the utmost tyranny" of the divine law,[12] became for him *the* mark of man's existence. In a terrifying way man must become aware of three characteristics of this divine law:

First: Divine law is a law of universal righteousness *(lex iustitiae universalis).*[13] God's righteousness demands the entire heart of man[14] and gives just one choice to man: everything or nothing![15] Obedience to God[16] is as indivisible as faith.[17] Even the smallest trace of egocentric love of the law[18] jeopardizes the entire law.[19]

Second: Because of its strictness, divine law is for natural man[20] a law which he is unable to obey *(lex impossibilis).*[21] It demands of man the impossible, because man cannot escape from himself; but in order to fulfill the law he would have to be "outside" of himself.[22]

Third: Divine law is a spiritual law which outlaws[23] sinful man as God's enemy[24] *(lex maledictionis spiritualis).*[25] It does not prosecute individual transgressions[26] but rather the criminal, rebellious thinking and desiring[27] of the offender.[28] It does not condemn sins,[29] be they mortal or venial,[30] but the sinner. This meant for Luther that this law condemns Original Sin[31] which creates sins like evil fruit.[32] In his heart[33] man is always opposed to fulfilling the divine law.[34] But even man's smallest and most secret notions of disobeying God's law[35] are punished immediately, and with the most severe punishment,[36] as spiritual *lese majesty*. And the punishment is spiritual death.[37] This strictness of the law becomes understandable if one keeps in mind the significance law has in the cosmic battle between Satan and God for the dominion of the Creation.[38] In this horrible battle it is not even possible to remain neutral.[39] If one does not obey the law unconditionally and in every detail, one is a rebel[40] and an ally of the devil. If one despises God's existence, one loses one's own. The degree of severity in this rebellion against God does not make any difference, for God's court is very sensitive; what appears to be insignificant in the eyes of man is significant for God.[41]

What should man think of such a law? It is futile for the psalmist to praise that man as blessed who delights in God's law (Psalm 1:2) be-

The Present Interpretation of Luther's Idea of Law

cause from this delight comes Salvation.[42] ⟨This is the reason for this futility:⟩ Human reason[43] has no insight into the meaning of the law, and human will has not the smallest propensity to fulfill it. What could be more absurd[44] than a law that demands the impossible and at the same time, under penalty of death, commands that it is acknowledged as being impossible to be fulfilled? What could be more repulsive than a law that punishes, relentlessly[45] and with the same cruel punishment, the lawbreaker and, even worse, also natural man who wants to obey the law?[46] Such a perverse law and its author[47] can only be cursed,[48] hated,[49] and fled from.[50] But this is the horrible situation: the law accompanies you everywhere,[51] it always stands before you[52] because it is engraved in your heart. In this living presence the divine law reveals its nature and name: *it is the divine natural law.*[53]

Let us pause for a moment. What a rift is opening up! On one side is Luther's horror[54] of the divine natural law, experienced in most terrible *Anfechtungen,*[55] and on the other side is the enthusiastic praise by theologians and philosophers of his day for the same law as the most perfect one. In light of his spiritual experience, this praise disintegrated for Luther as a delusion created by human reason. "Do not enter into judgment with your servant" (Psalm 143:2) prays the frightened heart.[56] But how can God positively react to this pleading without compromising his righteousness, that is, without contradicting himself[57] and becoming untruthful?

Luther was frequently and justly criticized for his sweeping, disdainful statements about Scholasticism, and the gaps in his knowledge of it have been demonstrated. Yet all the human wisdom would not have helped him in his desperation about the divine law, just as the church's means of grace did not help him in his pangs of conscience, in spite of his daily Confession.[58] In light of this situation, the full meaning of a passage in his lectures on Romans (1515-16) becomes clear: "We babble a lot about natural law."[59] With this half melancholic and half derisive statement Luther bade farewell to the natural-law doctrine of his time.

But what did Luther have to offer as a replacement of this doctrine? From the beginning[60] he felt that the problem 'law' was a main topic in his theological work. How could a scholar educated in medieval theology have thought otherwise?[61] Divine natural law, divine positive law, and man-made law, the three central concepts of the medieval doctrine of law, were second nature to all clergy. Every priest had to deal with

The Theological Origin of Luther's Doctrine of Law

them constantly, especially in pastoral care, and there particularly in the confessional box. Knowledge of law was, therefore, part of the scholarly ABC of every clergyman. Luther could not have avoided coming to terms with the traditional idea of law — to the contrary, he was pushed into doing so. Consequently, in the future one may no longer argue that "in Luther's central religious concern the problems connected with natural law . . . were very much peripheral."[62] Luther considered[63] 'law' one of the most difficult topics in his discipline,[64] and a topic on which one has to work constantly.[65] "The question of laws is the most difficult of all questions," he wrote in 1530,[66] "many have wrestled with it in different ways, but no one has ever solved it."[67]

Luther's doctrine of law is a doctrine of ecclesiastical law in the best sense; his doctrine of natural law is part of it and ranks second; his doctrine of the church and its inherent law is the center and highlight. This may sound strange in light of Sohm's thesis about the inconsistency between the essence of the church and ecclesiastical law[68] — but there is no doubt possible. The church and its law — these were the two main theological-juristic problems which already occupied the young Luther in his first lectures on the Psalms,[69] and throughout his life they never lost their significance. The two problems, that of the church and that of the law, may not be separated. True knowledge of the law can be found only in the church and through the church. If one does not listen to the voice of the church one will never gain insight in the essence of law. The final decision about the meaning of law is not established in secular legal philosophy, valuable as its doctrines may be, but in the Christian faith. On this point Luther fully agreed with his scholarly predecessors and contemporaries.[70] But he differed from them all the more when he resolved these two main problems. That solution was not given to him at once — many years he struggled for it. It will be easier to understand his thoughts if we trace their gradual development.[71]

§ 2. The Development of Luther's Doctrine of Law

Let us begin with Luther's first lectures on the Psalms (1513-15). Already here new ideas emerged, though Luther still expressed them in statements which sound very conservative. But his position on the problem 'church' clearly shows this new way of thinking. The universal church *(ecclesia universalis)*, that is, the external church with its legally constituted components, the particular churches *(ecclesiae particulares)*, loses its position as the starting point for ecclesiology; it is replaced with the spiritual church *(ecclesia spiritualis)*, the communion of the true believers.⁷² And that spiritual church determined Luther's statements about the essence of the church, even when he expressed his ideas in traditional materials. This marked a radical change from the canonistic teachings of his time.

In connection with this change, Luther was treading a new path also in his doctrine of law.⁷³ When the Scholastics thought about law, they followed the sequence of God's dealings with and for man. They concentrated on natural law first; then they turned to the Decalogue, and they concluded with Christ's law. Not so Luther! What in Scholasticism was the final point became Luther's starting point. He brought the separation between faith and knowledge, taught by the Nominalists, to its logical conclusion. In order to recognize the divine will for law, that is, the divine law *(lex divina)*, one has to go back to that divine Revelation of which the transmission is not falsified or even only dimmed by human and, therefore, sinful reason *(ratio)*. This Revelation is the law of Christ *(lex Christi)*. Its command to love God perfectly requires more than an external behavior, regulated by law; it requires conformity *(conformitas)* of the will with Christ.⁷⁴ Such a will is "spiritual,"⁷⁵ because this conformity is established in an act of spiritual love *(actus charitatis spiritualis)*.⁷⁶ Therefore Christ's law is called spiritual law *(lex spiritualis)*. It will develop into the organizing concept of Luther's doctrine of law, which at the time of his first lectures on the Psalms was still in the beginning stages. His thoughts about natural law demonstrate this⁷⁷ — he had not yet discovered any new problems regarding natural law.⁷⁸ One receives a similar, overall impression of old and new ideas being side by side when one considers his theology of that period.⁷⁹

In Luther's lectures on Romans (1515-16) there is a greater theological and juristic unity. His doctrine of Original Sin and of the total spiritual perversion of human nature is clearly developed, and in the doctrine of law the contrast between divine and human righteousness emerges with precision. Consequently, the concept 'divine law' is radically spiritualized,⁸⁰ and we will have to deal with this later. This result is a first step beyond the first lectures on the Psalms. A second step is the result of the identification of divine law, or Christ's law, with the divine natural law.⁸¹ In this way the doctrine of divine law is expanded to a ⟨new⟩ doctrine of natural law. Finally, and this is a third step: from now

The Theological Origin of Luther's Doctrine of Law

on[82] Christ's kingdom is identified as the realm in which the spiritual law is valid,[83] and Christ's kingdom is placed in clear opposition to the kingdom of the world, in which the law of the world *(lex saeculi)* rules.

With these three steps, the lectures on Romans guided the further development of Luther's idea of law. The foundation, which Luther built in these lectures, was solid enough to withstand all future blows, especially those by the peasants, the enthusiasts (from 1525 on), and the antinomians (from 1537 on).

As early as 1516 Luther had created a new version of the topic 'natural law', the first of the three topics in the medieval doctrine of law (natural law, divine positive law, man-made law). A short time later, the selling of indulgences[84] led him to the second topic, divine positive law.[85] As a result of the posting of the theses on October 31, 1517, the controversy on the law of the sacraments developed first; in the main it was completed in 1520 *(The Babylonian Captivity of the Church)*. In addition, beginning with his *Explanations of the Ninety-five Theses* (1518), and ending with his *The Papacy at Rome* (1520), Luther thought about the relationship of the divine to the man-made constitution of the church. This topic also touched man-made law, the third topic of the medieval doctrine of law. From 1518 (second lectures on the Psalms) to 1523 Luther dealt with it from various viewpoints. <In this connection the following topics are important:> The call of Christians in the office of governmental authority to reform the man-made order of the church (*To the Christian Nobility*, 1520); the mutual relationship of the divine law of the Christian estate with the man-made law of this world (*On Christian Freedom*, 1520); the range of the legal authority of the church (*On Monastic Vows*, 1521), and the range of the secular legal authority (*The Estate of Marriage*, 1522); the God-given duty of a Christian to create and implement law in the secular commonwealth (*On Secular Authority*, 1523). As Luther was developing his doctrine of law, he perfected its constitutional-law layout by describing the divine governance in both kingdoms. On that basis he returned again to the discussion of natural law and dealt with its connection with the two kingdoms more precisely than before. In 1525 he had essentially completed this tremendous work.

PART TWO

The Basic Features of Luther's Doctrine of Law

———◉———

SECTION ONE

THE BASIS OF LUTHER'S DOCTRINE OF LAW:
THE DOCTRINE OF THE TWO KINGDOMS

———◉———

CHAPTER 3

The Origin of Luther's Doctrine of the Two Kingdoms

Having surveyed the gradual development of Luther's doctrine of law, we shall now attempt to present its basic features systematically. Luther's starting point[1] was the existence of two kingdoms[2] — the kingdom of Christ and the kingdom of the world[3] — and their legal relationship with each other. For this idea Augustine's *On the City of God*[4] has become the model in the western world. Luther's understanding of law was based on Augustine's basic concepts. Of special importance for Luther was Augustine's idea that the essence of each kingdom is determined by a different kind of love,[5] the kingdom of Christ being dominated by the love for God *(amor dei)*, the kingdom of the world by the love for self *(amor sui)*.

Luther, however, saw the contrast[6] between the two kingdoms and its effect on man more precisely than Augustine[7] and the Scholastics,[8] who followed Augustine, had done. The reason for this was Luther's anthropology,[9] more specifically, his understanding of the essence of Original Sin.[10] According to Luther, Original Sin completely destroyed the spiritual part of the human nature, that is, that part which is oriented toward God;[11] it left undisturbed only the corporeal part, that is, that part which is oriented toward the Creation.[12] Following the theologians of the *via moderna*,[13] Luther regarded the will as the noblest faculty of the soul.[14] After Original Sin, the will is completely turned away from God *(voluntas aversa)*,[15] and that will also forces reason into the wrong direction.[16] Therefore man no longer has a *synteresis theologica*;[17] ⟨that is,⟩ not a spark of the divine spirit is left in man's will and reason.[18] Natural man is not open to God's Spirit (1 Corinthians 2:14); he is spiritually dead, as alive as he might appear corporeally, that is, in his relationship with the Creation.[19] In this condition of total spiritual perversion of his originally good nature, man is called corporeal or carnal man, and 'flesh', not 'spirit', characterizes the aeon in which he lives.[20]

CHAPTER 4

The Kingdom of the World

In a succinct sense, corporeal man is external man *(homo exterior)*.[1] He concentrates only on the external appearance of the Creation. About God he knows[2] only a few generalities,[3] abstracted from the created world;[4] for instance, there is a mighty, wise, just, benevolent, merciful, mild deity as the supreme being. As natural man,[5] he knows, however, nothing about God as a person and about God's will for man;[6] to have this knowledge it would be necessary that the intellect and will are oriented toward God.[7] "The participation in the direct vision of <God's> essence, which a pure spirit possesses,"[8] is denied to natural man. The power of his soul does not reach beyond the Creation.[9]

The world, together with man as the crowning glory of Creation, is natural man's measure of all things,[10] including his notion of God. His natural theology[11] is thoroughly anthropomorphic. The relationship of God with man, which was present in the Original Status, is reversed. Man places himself above God; he creates an image of God which is equal to that of man.[12] God becomes the image of man[13] instead of man being the image of God. In this way, man changes the Creator to a creature, and God becomes a part of the world. Deification of the world and idolization of self[14] — that is the pseudo-religion of natural man who fancies himself to be all-knowing[15] and not in need of learning anything.[16] He is his own "God and Savior."[17] If this natural man is confronted with the Creator in all his majesty, he considers him to be the devil.[18]

According to Holy Scripture, all who think this way, the ungodly people *(impii)*, form a family;[19] because of their worldly way of thinking they are simply called the world.[20] Yet since alongside that family there also lives on earth the family of the God-fearing people *(pii)*,[21] Luther occasionally called that ungodly crowd the "earthly world"[22] in order to differentiate it from the "spirtual"[23] or "heavenly world," the congregation of the believers on earth.

'World' is therefore a personalistic concept.[24] The same is true for the concept 'kingdom of the world', of which the essence is identical with the concept 'world'. 'Kingdom of the world' also does not designate primarily an institution[25] but designates a group of persons, a "crowd,"[26] a "people"[27] personally ruled[28] by the head[29] of this communion.[30] This understanding agrees with Augustine's view,[31] with medieval theology,[32] and with the medieval doctrine of the state.[33] One may not at all approach Luther's statements either about the kingdom of Christ or the kingdom of the world with the concept 'kingdom' as developed in the modern doctrine of the state. On the basis of such a modern concept one would understand 'kingdom' as an institution of the highest rank, which regulates and protects human social life within a certain geographic area controlled by this institution;[34] in whatever way one might assign a specific content to this innerworldly task, this institution manages it by means of a huge apparatus of offices and competencies. Luther's theological concept 'kingdom' is different![35] Certainly, he, too, was unable to dispense with offices,[36] but they were unimportant. Essential for him was the personal connection *(influxus voluntatis)* of a head and its mystical body.[37] In the kingdom of the world the devil is the head because he owns the world;[38] those who are not Christians[39] are the body, the "Babylonian body of the devil" *(corpus diaboli Babylonicum)*,[40] regardless whether they are heathen, or Jews, or baptized nominal Christians[41] who live in "God's land," but as heathen.[42]

To this non-spiritual and therefore devilish[43] nature of the kingdom of the world[44] corresponds its governance *(Regiment)*.[45] In agreement with the older legal language, this term is often used as a synonym for kingdom *(Reich, regnum)*.[46] This governance is the sovereignty of wickedness *(saeculum malitiae)*,[47] regardless whether one thinks of the rulers, or the subjects, or the way in which the rulers act. The first characteristic of this sovereignty is the prevailing love for self;[48] it may range from hypocrisy, the best shade of spiritual self-deception, to crime, the most ruthless assertion of egotism. The second characteristic is legal inequality among the members of this kingdom *(differentia personarum)*, which is the result of that egotism.⁴⁹ The third characteristic is the governance by reason *(regnum rationis).*⁵⁰ It is directed by nothing other than worldly usefulness and legal considerations; through laws, coercive actions,⁵¹ and penalties this governance by reason establishes a makeshift order⁵² and protects it by means of the secular sword.⁵³ The fourth characteristic is the insufficiency of this makeshift order because it is restricted to the external state of affairs;⁵⁴ therefore it is unable to deal with the roots of evil, which rest in the heart.⁵⁵

CHAPTER 5

The Kingdom of Christ

Man is born[1] into this kingdom of spiritual death and servitude to Satan,[2] the lord of the world.[3] In spite of the continuing presence of Original Sin, Christ snatches[4] those who believe in him away from the devil's tyranny, and in Baptism he incorporates them into his kingdom, *the kingdom of grace.*[5] In all its parts the constitution of this kingdom is the exact opposite[6] of the kingdom of the world.[7] Only sincere Christians are members of this kingdom of grace;[8] these are the *believing baptized,*[9] while the heathen are excluded, even if they call themselves Christians.[10] These believing baptized are the mystical body of Christ *(corpus Christi mysticum),*[11] the "Christian being,"[12] the "Christian"[13] or "spiritual estate,"[14] the spiritual[15] or heavenly world. Therefore they are called spiritual people, or according to 1 Corinthians 15:48f., heavenly people.[16] They live with Christ their head, and through him with one another in the closest spiritual communion.[17] On earth they are a very small minority,[18] and in addition they are dispersed throughout the world.[19]

Christ's governance over the souls[20] of his disciples is, therefore, purely spiritual,[21] heavenly,[22] inward,[23] and hidden.[24] His sovereignty is directed to believing hearts;[25] in this way this sovereignty is exclusive[26] and personal in the highest sense possible.[27] In Christ's kingdom there is no room for a human governmental authority,[28] neither a secular nor a spiritual[29] one, and this is the reason: no authority *(potestas)* can extend beyond the cognitive capacity of the individual who holds it,[30] no man can see into the heart of another — only Christ is able to do this.

The Kingdom of Christ

When Christ uses people as *instruments of his governance,* they are only messengers; they have no authority to act as they see fit, as secular potentates can do. When, for instance, these messengers exercise jurisdiction in Christ's name, their sentence is valid only if it is in agreement with Christ's — if not, their sentence is invalid.[31]

The *means of Christ's governance* are exclusively spiritual.[32] His kingdom exists only by means of the Word and the Spirit.[33] The law, valid in this kingdom, is a spiritual law, that is, the gospel.[34] His Word[35] is the spiritual sword (which he wields and allows to be handled by the office of preaching), and there is no room for the secular sword;[36] it has no competency in Christ's kingdom, because Christ's governance is to be implemented in truth, meekness, and spiritual righteousness *(in veritate, mansuetudine, iustitia spirituali)* and not according to the ways of external power *(in divitiis et tyrannide)* and corporeal justice.[37] "Christ's sovereignty does not become real in a theocracy, which forces everyone to succumb to Christ externally, but rather on the cross."[38] True peace is found in voluntary submission to the cross.[39] Precisely because Christ excludes power and force from his kingdom is it an eternal kingdom,[40] incomprehensible as this is for someone who bases his judgment on social experiences in the world.

Finally, the *relationship of the citizens of Christ's kingdom with one another* is spiritually regulated. "Harmoniously and without the support of any external thing, they will go into the kingdom of the heavens by the grace of the Holy Spirit only, not in worldly tumult with chariots and horses."[41] Instead of the egotism of the children of the world, *Christian brotherly love*[42] rules among the citizens of Christ's kingdom as the noblest guideline[43] of the responsibility for each other. The inequality among men, existing in the heathen society, makes way for the *equality in the Christian estate.*[44] Coercion, characteristic of Satan's rule, is unknown among Christians.[45] They enjoy the freedom of God's children, the "freedom of a Christian."[46] Christian brotherly love, Christian equality, and Christian freedom — these are *the three divine*[47] *basic rights,* which govern the external life of believing[48] Christians. Compared with them, the basic rights in secular dominions are only distorted silhouettes. Already the reversal of the sequence 'brotherly love, equality, freedom' to 'freedom, equality, brotherhood' demonstrates the contrast between a spiritual and a secular understanding of social life.

Corresponding to this contrast are the different ways of implementing these three basic rights of believing Christians. Not the secularly inclined reason, "worldly wisdom," is at work in the kingdom of Christ, but "Christian wisdom,"[49] the "Christian and free reason,"[50] that is, reason illuminated by faith.[51] That reason is called Christian because it obeys Christ's law, and it is called free because it is motivated not by coercion but by the free impulse of the heart. But only the believing Christian is qualified to live in this way.

Does all of this mean that God completely deserted the kingdom of the ungodly and abandoned it to its autonomy?[52] Not at all! God's omnipresent sovereignty is not restricted to the kingdom of grace — *God also rules in the kingdom of the world.*[53] In spite of falling away from God, mankind is unable to withdraw itself from God's power;[54] God remains its "lord and head,"[55] and man cannot escape God's hand.[56] But mankind experiences this kingdom of God as a kingdom of divine wrath.[57] Servitude to the devil is God's punishment of man's rebellion, for the psalmist says: ". . . with the pure you show yourself pure and with the crooked you show yourself perverse."[58] *God's nature and being does not change!*[59] But when God's efficacious Word meets a heart filled with hate for God, it turns this hostile ⟨heart and⟩ will[60] back against the person who creates such a will;[61] ⟨that is, God's efficacious Word⟩ changes that hostile will into a curse[62] for the creator of that will.[63]

Because of this sovereignty of the divine wrath, the kingdom of the world is called God's kingdom at the left, in contrast to the kingdom of grace, God's kingdom at the right.

CHAPTER 6

The Kingdom of God at the Right and at the Left of God

―――――◆―――――

Today the origin and meaning of this title are no longer understood by everyone. At the present, therefore, the doctrine of the two governances, rather than the doctrine of the two kingdoms, is often designated as "the key to Luther's view of world and society."[1] With the doctrine of the two governances, so one says,[2] "Luther wants to clarify the fact, which is foundational for the ⟨Christian⟩ world view, that God rules the world in two different ways and with two different means: with the governance of the Word on the one hand, with the governance of secular power wielded by the governmental authority on the other." The core of this argument is correct, no doubt.[3] The argument is weak, however, because it oversimplifies the problem and, therefore, grasps only a part of it. According to this argument, the world, with which the two governances are connected, is "one and the same world of God's Creation."[4] In order to evaluate all aspects of the connection between the world and God, one has to consider, however, also the connection between the world and Redemption and Sanctification ⟨and not only with Creation⟩. Each member of this triad has to be considered equally. Otherwise one cannot place the law of the church in the world in Luther's legal system, and in Luther's legal doctrine this law is an important part of the earthly legal order.[5]

Let us disregard this last point. Nevertheless, because it deals only with God's external rule,[6] Luther's doctrine of the two governances is in no way a comprehensive description of God's rule over the world.[7] In the kingdom of grace, this rule is implemented by the church's preaching office through the preaching of the Word and the administration of the sacraments; in the kingdom of divine wrath, it is implemented by the *politia*[8] through the sword of the secular governmental authority. But God's rule as a whole extends in both kingdoms much farther. Luther did not discuss this in his statements about the governances; it was always on his mind, of course, and he also mentioned it when appropriate. Regarding the kingdom of grace, one has to remember only the situation of those Christians who are prisoners of an unbelieving enemy and in this situation have to forgo the comfort of the church; yet they are under the protection of Christ's rule. And in the kingdom of wrath God's rule is primarily implemented through the *spiritual judgment and punishment*[9] of the sinner, while the secular governance is able to punish only transgressions of the corporeal legal order. *The doctrine of the governances, therefore, is only the earthly side of the divine rule over the world, and it receives its significance only when it is connected with the two kingdoms.*

On the basis of its presuppositions, the presently prevailing description of the governances doctrine should arrive at the same conclusion. In that description, the spiritual governance is defined as 'kingdom of listening'.[10] This cannot mean the physical listening to God's Word but has to mean the spiritual listening, that is, the listening to God's Word in faith.[11] Only spiritual people are capable of such a spiritual listening. Therefore only they are under the spiritual governance, or to say it differently, the spiritual governance belongs to Christ's kingdom. The 'kingdom of listening' may not simply be equated with the world — it has to be equated with Christ's kingdom in the world (or with the church).

Finally, and above all else: only the consideration of the eschatological drama,[12] which takes place[13] in the battle between the two kingdoms,[14] can prevent a "dilution"[15] (to use Nietzsche's word) of the governances doctrine and protect us against the dangerous error that a Christian may be a citizen of two kingdoms,[16] and in fact, has to be.

The image of the kingdom of God at the right and at the left of God[17] is derived from Psalm 110. The kingdom at the right is the kingdom of grace. Christ rules in it until Judgment Day "according to his humanity";[18] then he will turn it over to the Father, and thereafter the kingdom of glory begins. God's kingdom at the right embraces the inner, spiritual people, that is, Christ's disciples. The outer, corporeal people, that is, the ungodly, belong to God's kingdom at the left. On the

The Kingdom of God at the Right and at the Left of God

Day of Judgment, Christ as the judge of the world (Matthew 25) will invite his "sheep at the right" to enter the kingdom of glory and consign "the goats at the left" to the eternal fire.

Until that day, God's kingdom at the left will be preserved by the Creator so that mankind may not be totally destroyed by the devil but through the church is gained for Christ by the preaching of law and gospel.[19] This patience reveals God's wrath as wrath of mercy,[20] that is, as love hidden in strictness, as "wrathful love."[21] Therefore the world has two qualities: it belongs to the devil, who tries to destroy it, and yet at the same time it belongs to God, through whose will it exists in the first place and continues to exist.

Secular governmental authority[22] acts as the tool[23] of God's punishing and preserving rule. If one disregards the *cura religionis* of a Christian governmental authority,[24] the main task of the secular governmental authority is to "create and implement law," "protect people from violence and harm, and fight crime so that peace is preserved in the land."[25] As for the Middle Ages, so for Luther the center of the government was the office of the judge.[26] Acting against the evil ones,[27] and with legal means assisting the godly (that is, those who according to earthly standards are righteous), governmental authority is a wall of protection built by God[28] against the chaos among people,[29] which Satan promotes with cunning and force.[30] As an institution, governmental authority proves that the devil is on the loose in the world *and* that God does not surrender mankind to the devil's tyranny but counteracts it constantly.[31] *Therefore God is present also in the office of the secular governmental authority — provided* it observes the limits (still to be discussed in detail) set up by the Creator for the implementation of the tasks of its office.

In the kingdom of wrath God rules mankind externally in a different way than in the kingdom of grace: his rule fits the non-spiritual corporeal legal ⟨quality of⟩ the kingdom of the world. Therefore Christ does not charge secular governmental authority with caring for souls;[32] it is only to protect body and property, and the legal validity of its commandments does not depend on its will to fulfill Christ's will. This is the meaning of Luther's statements that secular governmental authority rules with God's secret[33] counsel but without God's Word,[34] and that the secular kingdom exists and functions on its own, without God's kingdom.[35]

It would be difficult to describe the differences between the rulers, the ruled, and the ways of ruling in both kingdoms in a shorter and clearer way. In one kingdom God's Word is valid, in the other one it is not; there it is acknowledged and obeyed, here it is despised. Since God's Word brings life to receptive hearts, God's kingdom at the right is the "land of the living"[36] (Psalms 27:13, 142:5), God's kingdom at the left is the "<land> of the dead."[37] In their essence there is no likeness between both kingdoms,[38] and *analogia entis* is impossible. Rather, between both kingdoms a deep chasm is fixed, and no Christian philosophy and no theology can bridge it, not even with the narrowest footbridge.

SECTION TWO

LUTHER'S DOCTRINE OF LAW

CHAPTER 7

The Connection of the Doctrine of the Kingdoms with the Doctrine of Law

Luther's doctrine of law has to be evaluated in light of the two kingdoms and their relationship with God and the devil. This provides the only appropriate key for understanding the characteristic features of his legal doctrine. Conversely, only Luther's doctrine of law gives a totally clear picture of the structure of the two kingdoms. Thus far scholars — at least if one considers the jurists[1] — have not acknowledged the significance of this connection of Luther's doctrine of the kingdoms with his doctrine of law.[2] If both are placed side by side, however, their inner unity becomes obvious. This can be demonstrated by considering two points.

The two kingdoms are eschatological and personalistic entities. Likewise, Luther's doctrine of law also is shaped by the seriousness of the Last Judgment;[3] it stands in the shadow of the Day of Judgment, and from this day all law receives ultimate meaning. Now only a believer knows what law truly is; on the Day of Judgment this will be revealed to everyone. Therefore for Luther divine law primarily is not the divine ruler's eternal plan for governing the world, as Thomas Aquinas described the eternal law. Rather, it is a legal order, that is, a will for law; in the service of righteousness that will issues commands, and in the administration of justice it is verified.[4] In fact, one has to add: divine law is *the* legal order in the absolute sense. At the end of the world God will judge according to this legal order, and this fact, in turn, shapes all other legal orders. *Therefore one may call Luther's doctrine of law eschatological.*

This first connection between Luther's understanding of law and his doctrine of the kingdoms is important especially for the theologian. One has to add a second connection, which in terms of the systematics of law is especially important for the jurist. This connection deals with Luther's position on *natural law* and leads straight into the very center of his legal thinking. The reformer mentioned natural law relatively seldom. Therefore one expects that it did not play a major role in his doctrine of law. This is not the case, however. Luther's doctrine of law profited from his critical engagement with the medieval theological and canonistic discussion of the topic 'natural law'. Having said this, we are at once confronted with a structure of the Reformation doctrine of natural law which is new and incompatible with that of the Middle Ages. Since there are two kingdoms, there are also *two kinds of natural law,* and each kind is the basic law[5] of the kingdom to which it belongs. This dualism,[6] which is the result of the function natural law has in the constitutional law of each kingdom, is the central theological position of the reformer's legal doctrine. And that position also influences his discussion of the divine positive law. This dualism is not a mere juxtaposition of heterogeneous laws; it is transcended in the unity of the divine will for law,[7] just as the two kingdoms exist under the one rule of God.

The clarity and consistency in this outline of the topic 'natural law' cannot be denied, not even by those who object to its theological presuppositions. What is true for the great theological systems of the Middle Ages is confirmed here: every profound theological system has to generate its own doctrine of law; therefore the originality and strength of such a system can also be discovered by focusing on its presentation of law.

Now, finally, the way is open to arrive at a sound judgment regarding not only the similarities between Luther's doctrine of law and the juristic-theological positions of the Middle Ages,[8] but also the differences[9] and their necessary reasons. However, the present disquisition does not deal with the details in this comparison. Its foremost objective is to unfold Luther's thoughts and bring them to the attention of those theologians and jurists who study the history of natural law. Natural law apparently was the reason[10] that a consistent concept 'law'[11] could not be found in Luther's thought.[12] Again and again the question was asked[13] whether a theologian who affirms the total spiritual perversion of human nature can also affirm natural law without contradicting himself. Luther gave a decisively positive answer! But his positive answer was at once negatively qualified. This requires an explanation.

The Connection of the Doctrine of the Kingdoms with the Doctrine of Law

"It is to be noted first," so begins Luther's classic exposition on the duality of law,[14] "that the two classes of Adam's children — the one in God's kingdom under Christ and the other in the kingdom of the world under the governing authority ... — have two kinds of law. For every kingdom must have its own laws and statutes; without law no kingdom or government can survive, as everyday experience amply shows." The legal order which is characteristic of Christ's kingdom is present in the divine natural law. This is the law which God issued for all mankind and which is to be obeyed by everyone. No other law can compete with this universal claim of validity, and God has never again given a commandment that has the identical universality.[15] For this reason it is called *the* divine law *(lex divina)*.

At once, however, the contrast between the two kingdoms makes a restrictive explanation necessary. There is a fundamental difference between law in the kingdom of the world and the divine natural law. Of course, that law is also effective in the kingdom of the world, just as God's omnipotence is universally effective. But in the kingdom of the world the divine natural law is not law for man because all law lives from the strength of love,[16] as Luther taught (following St. Augustine).[17] Love provides law with an ontological basis,[18] namely, God, who is love.[19] Consequently, the divine law is a binding law only if the will of the recipient of this law affirms it as being binding;[20] only through this inner consent is it acknowledged as law and as truly valid.[21] Otherwise it is reluctantly endured as a coercive command and will not have durability.[22] This unity with God's will for law, established through an act of spiritual love,[23] exists only in Christ's kingdom, however. In the kingdom of the world, on the other hand, hatred for God prevails;[24] therefore it is impossible that here the divine law is valid as law. Pure law, true law, exists only in the kingdom of grace.[25] In the kingdom of the world man annulled the validity of the divine law for himself by refusing to acknowledge it.[26]

One has to remember this contrasting of the law in Christ's kingdom to the law in the kingdom of the world in order to understand the *first methodological characteristic of Luther's legal doctrine: Luther thinks in contrasts.*[27] One may compare God's law with man's law, but only as mutually exclusive opposites, like God's holiness and man's corruptness. Luther criticized previous scholars working on our subject for having replaced this contrasting method with a harmonizing one. They humanized the divine natural law[28] and subordinated it to human reason,[29] although divine law is beyond reason;[30] they inferred divine righteousnesss from earthly righteousness.[31] Such a method is typical for a beginner in theology,[32] for the theologian who deals with sensual and symbolic theology,[33] who is stuck with the form *(figura)* of law and does not advance to its substance *(res)*. Instead, one has to start with divine righteousness as it is manifested in the divine law, and only then proceed to human righteousness and earthly law.

Such an approach very soon shows, however, that man is not capable[34] of grasping the essence of divine righteousness by means of his natural abilities, and that the Revelation in Christ is the only access to it. Only Christ's law *(lex Christi)* grants the right understanding of God's law.[35] This exclusive turning to the Revelation in Christ[36] is *the second methodological characteristic of Luther's doctrine of law.* The first characteristic is shaped by Luther's awe of God's absolute sovereignty, the second by his faith in God's condescension in Christ. *For this reason, Luther's doctrine of law is Christ-centered.*[37]

CHAPTER 8

The Divine Law in the Status of the Incorrupt Nature

§ 1. The Divine Natural Law

On the basis of Christ's law, let us now attempt to develop those characteristic features of the divine natural law[1] which are most important for a juristic disquisition.

As the *first characteristic feature of the divine natural law* we note: *Divine law is law-creating will.*[2] God's will is law! Even man-made law is commanding will. But how pitiful does it appear when it is compared with the majestic divine will for law.[3] That will confronts man as the 'governing world principle',[4] a truly sovereign will,[5] incomprehensibly free because of its sublimity.[6] In an absolute sense that will is responsible to nothing,[7] no legal standard controls it,[8] but it is the standard of all legal matters.[9] Nothing is righteous unless God wills it to be.[10] To ask for the reason of the divine commandment is futile and blasphemous.[11] There is no theodicy.[12] God's "will is impenetrable and beyond comprehension."[13] God as such *(deus nudus),*[14] that is, whatever is specifically divine in God — as, for instance, his being beyond time prior to the Creation of the world — is totally incomprehensible for man. God reveals himself only 'wrapped' *(involucra)* in his Word and work because only these are somewhat comprehensible.[15]

This does not mean that the will of the 'hidden God'[16] is irrational![17] But human reason does not soar to the height of the divine reason[18] ⟨and, therefore, is unable to understand the divine reason⟩. Participation in the eternal law, an idea which we find in the Thomistic doctrine of natural law,[19] is impossible for man. God's will seizes upon man, but not vice versa. For natural man this incomprehensibility of the Creator results in one paradox[20] after another.[21] Man sees differences and contrasts, but in God, the supernatural, impenetrable essence,[22] they are one.[23] Even though the divine law is supreme love, wisdom, righteousness,[24] and order, for natural man it is cruelty, foolishness, injustice, and arbitrariness.[25] Even though the divine natural law in itself is unchangeable[26] and eternal,[27] in its impact on man it changes constantly according to man's attitude toward God; therefore it appears to man as the most changeable thing that can be imagined.[28] Even though the divine law is revealed, for natural man it is totally hidden;[29] even for those who are illuminated by God's grace, the divine natural law is as inexhaustible as the sea,[30] because the statement "each passage of Scripture can be understood in infinite ways"[31] is valid even for the revealed Word.

No part of Luther's doctrine of law is closer to the thoughts of the great medieval theologians[32] and their successors[33] than this description of the divine natural law. Some phrases seem even to be taken directly from their writings.[34] Yet this similarity exists only on the surface — the same words have an entirely different meaning. Those medieval scholars affirmed the light of reason and free will as remnants of the originally good nature of man, small though they might be. In their system, God and natural man are on the same level in these remnants — in contrast, an abyss opens up for Luther. Therefore Luther was able to adopt from his teachers only those thoughts which were compatible with his basic theological doctrine of the total spiritual corruptness of human nature, and whatever he did adopt has to be constantly connected with his anthropology. One may not interpret Luther as a disciple of Scotus or Occam[35] — but one may also not underestimate the influence of Nominalism on his thinking. This influence is evident especially in the voluntarism found in Luther's legal doctrine and in that of the Nominalists. On the basis of this voluntarism there existed for Luther an affinity (unknown in Thomism) in legal-technical terms between the divine natural law and the divine positive law because the divine natural law is just as much a revealed divine statute *(statutum)*[36] as is the divine positive law; both laws differ only in the way in which the will for law is promulgated.[37] The divine positive law is "set in a corporeal, external thing";[38] on the other hand, according to the testimony of Scripture, the divine natural law is written into man's heart.[39] With this statement we have arrived at the *second characteristic feature of the divine natural law.*

This feature is a *radical spiritualism* which, however, is controlled by Scripture.[40] This spiritualism is the specific characteristic of Luther's legal doctrine. *The divine law is spirit,* God's spirit, nothing but divine spirit. What a difference from man-made laws! They are external norms for external conduct. But God does not command anything external;[41] in fact, his commandment itself is nothing external at all. Man-made laws deal with the corporeal life in the kingdom of this world, God's law deals with the spiritual life in God's kingdom. Man-made laws belong to the orders of the corrupt nature, God's law belongs to the incorrupt nature. According to God's judgment, therefore, man-made laws are dead law — we still have to deal with this — but God's law is living law in the land of the living. This means: God's law not only is life but also generates spiritual life. This law begins to exist for man only at the moment when he 'lives out of God', only at the moment when God enters man's life and generates spiritual life in him. It is not even present outside of such an existence "in spirit and in truth" (John 4:23).[42] Even the Decalogue, even Christ's law does not have divine quality when it is understood as external norm.[43]

All this sounds very strange in comparison with the understanding of natural law prevailing among us jurists. That understanding is shaped by the statements of medieval canonists about the divine positive law, and this for the following, valid reason: In the Decalogue the natural law was repeated and elucidated through the divine Revelation; in terms of their content, the Ten Commandments are natural law; in terms of their form they are positive law;[44] therefore the Decalogue, that is, the divine positive[45] law, is the starting point for the juristic discussion of natural law. Protestant legal doctrine of later years proceeded in the same way when it adopted parts of the canonistic concept 'law'.

Luther's legal thinking, however, was entirely different. For him the divine natural law — not the divine positive law — was the key for understanding the essence of divine law.[46] In the divine natural law no external sign *(signum)* detracts from the substance *(res)*,[47] because that law is not written down but is found in man's heart; here the divine command exists as the Creator's <ceaselessly active,> living Word.[48]

In spite of his view of the divine natural law as statute,[49] Luther did not recast the doctrine of natural law in positivist terms, as the Scholastics after Occam came close to doing in their doctrine of voluntarism.

Instead, a strong element of mystical meditation was present in his thinking.[50] Therefore the spiritual nature of the law does not tolerate any externalizing interpretation of its corporeal testimony in Scripture.

This observation is valid for the divine origin of the spiritual law. By itself, tracing the proclamation of the divine will for law back to a certain moment in history is not important. Of course, there is no divine law[51] without a divine statute *(sine certo Dei decreto).*[52] The proclamation of such a statute has to be reported in Holy Scripture[53] as a historical event, or it has to be demonstrated through miracles that this proclamation is God's action,[54] and one has to be able to verify the divine quality of such miracles on the basis of relevant passages in Scripture.[55] Luther's spiritualism is firmly tied to the "external" testimony[56] of Scripture, and it is at this point that Luther's spiritualism differed from that of the enthusiasts and their claim of an 'inner light'.[57]

Luther also differed from any normativism. God's living Word *(viva vox Dei)* can never become 'letter' *(litera),*[58] even when God's Revelation is wrapped in the language of man and adopts the form of an objective norm. Compared with the divine will for law, this form is only the breath of the Creator's address of man, which never can be separated from the always active God.[59] On the other hand, once man-made law has been promulgated, it is detached from its creator and exists on its own.[60] A well-known phrase illustrates this: we speak of the *spirit of the law,* and we derive this spirit from the objective legal norm. But the spirit of the divine law is the Holy Spirit. The divine law is born from this spirit, is tied to this spirit, and is spirit-generating.

Therefore the divine will for law, expressed as commandment, has to be understood as God's creative speaking into[61] man *(verbum),*[62] as a manifestation of God's power[63] which ceaselessly[64] creates spiritual life in man, in short, as an "active word."[65] Divine law, expressed as such a word, can be grasped only in a spiritual experience.

The goal of the divine law, therefore, is neither the creation of an externally verifiable conduct of man[66] — earthly law has to be content with this[67] — nor the creation of an external *and* internal conduct,[68] as the Scholastics taught.[69] The only goal of the divine law is the creation of a God-formed[70] will,[71] or, and this would be the same, the perfect love[72] for God's law.[73] Such a love exists only in a "pure heart"[74] in which God acts rather than that that heart acts on its own.[75] From this follows that the divine natural law claims man himself; it does not demand certain actions or omissions, it claims man for itself, not only an

The Divine Law in the Status of the Incorrupt Nature

action of man.[76] It claims man as a person in the innermost center of his being. The divine natural law does not address man as a natural being or a moral person,[77] but rather as a religious being, that is, as man whose heart is seized by God's spirit. It addresses the spiritual[78] or internal man.[79]

God created man as such a being in the Original Status. There man possessed the right reason and the good will toward God,[80] and there existed conformity of will between the creature and the Creator. On the one hand, without this conformity the spiritual law cannot be understood,[81] much less be obeyed;[82] on the other hand, this conformity guarantees the fulfillment of the spiritual law also in man's external life,[83] as it is appropriate for the harmony between the spiritual and the corporeal elements in man's existence in the Original Status.[84]

If one pulls all this together, then the divine natural law is a purely spiritual law,[85] regardless whether one considers the legislator, the content, or the recipient of this law.

As the *third characteristic feature of the divine natural law* we note: *The divine law is the order of divine love.* Love *(charitas)*[86] is the essence of this law. God is love, and so is man's pure incorrupt nature[87] on which the divine natural law was engraved in the Original Status. From God's love for man[88] grows man's love for the divine law *(dilectio legis)*.

Love does not tolerate any coercion. Therefore the divine natural law is valid only when it is obeyed joyfully and voluntarily.[89] On the basis of this quality, it is the *order of spiritual freedom,* and Luther called it law of freedom *(lex libertatis)*. Nevertheless, the divine natural law remains a commandment, and it may not be reduced to a mere exhortation.[90] Yet this law grants the "spirit of freedom"[91] both in man's relationship with God and with his fellowman.

From this spirit of freedom comes, first, the freedom to obey the divine natural law; it is not experienced as an oppression,[92] but it is obeyed with joy, as if it were no law at all *(lex vacua)*.[93] If one looks ahead to the Christians, then it is clear that this spirit of freedom, second, grants freedom from the self, purges the heart of egotism, and makes man willing to serve his neighbor.[94] Third, through man's awareness of being safe in God's love, this spirit of freedom protects man from all fear of man; or in other words, it creates the only true perception of freedom in the world.[95]

The *fourth characteristic feature of the divine natural law* is its quality of being the *order of God's faithfulness toward man and vice versa.*[96] As such, the divine law obligates man as a whole to God and, conversely, assures man of God's grace. Such a relationship of faithfulness demands total surrender to God's will. External legal formalism,[97] or obedience to the law based on moral motives,[98] is not enough; obedience 'with all your heart' is needed. Therefore no definite areas can be fenced off as being 'spiritual' or 'carnal'.[99] Luther used both terms to describe man's 'character',[100] <that is,> man as he turns toward or away[101] from God,[102] or, and this would be the same, toward or away from the law of the Spirit.[103] This exclusively personalistic instead of material understanding of the concept 'spiritual'[104] marks the great difference which exists between Luther's concept 'spiritual' and that of the medieval church.

Now the abundance of associations which we find in the *fifth and last characteristic feature of the divine natural law* is clear. And that feature is the *universality*[105] *of the divine natural law,* which was mentioned above.[106] Natural law is *the* universal law; as such it shows that spiritual law alone has the full meaning of the term 'universal'. It is universal because of its Creator,[107] the Lord of all;[108] it is universal because of the spiritual universality of its commandment;[109] it is universal because of the people it addresses, that is, all of mankind in the status of the incorrupt nature; it is universal because of the power of its effectiveness,[110] which grasps man totally, his spiritual but also his external existence; it is universal in terms of time because it lasts eternally; finally, it is universal because it comprises all law valid before God and is therefore exhaustive.[111] Regardless how it is approached, divine natural law always is the model for every law, a model to which no law can live up; it is perfect law *(lex perfecta).*[112] For us this perfection is as difficult to imagine as is original righteousness.[113]

How is such a perfect law promulgated? Nowhere in Luther's legal doctrine does his method of thinking in contrasts[114] become more dominant, and nowhere is his voluntaristic interpretation of the powers of the soul[115] more purely manifested than in his answer to this question. In earthly legislation, reason, judging on the basis of external, sensory perception, is the absolutely necessary mediator in the discovery of law.[116] In connection with the promulgation of the perfect law, Luther did not even mention reason. In this promulgation there is no formulation of an idea for legislation, much less a written or oral fixation.[117] This promulgation takes place in the heart[118] of man as the divine will penetrates[119] the human will. For the heart, into which the nat-

The Divine Law in the Status of the Incorrupt Nature

ural law is being inscribed, is the seat of the will.[120] The lack of any mediator of the will between the Creator and his creature[121] guarantees that the divine natural law is impressed upon man's heart in its original clarity and purity. That law is Word of God *(verbum)*, not mere speaking of God *(locutio)*.[122] This unmediated promulgation[123] in the human heart[124] is the procedural-law mark of the spiritual law, by which this law proves itself to be internal law *(lex interior)*.

Man does not actively cooperate in this promulgation. All striving for God is in truth a stormy movement, a rapture initiated by God.[125] On man's part there is a "resting" of the will,[126] a *mera passio voluntatis*,[127] ⟨and⟩ there is no free will at all.[128] Again[129] we hear the voice of Mysticism: God's people are "empty, resigned people, who have an empty will and do not hang on anything except the will of God alone, that is, they ... are satiated and content with God's will as it is."[130] Their "will and desire are drowned in God's will; outside of this will they neither are concerned with, nor know of, anything; they have disappeared in this will and, as Abraham did, they came forth freed from all things so that they value nothing other than God."[131]

The promulgation at once makes the law effective because the divine natural law is a powerful law *(lex vehemens)*. As soon as it reaches its recipient, it has an irresistible force *(vis legis)* and, therefore, in the status of the incorrupt nature it is at once valid.

According to Luther, this being at once valid does not complete the legislation, however. Following the *Decretum Gratiani*,[132] recipients of law are for Luther not only passive participants ⟨in the legislation⟩. Rather, as legal associates[133] they actively participate in the creation of law by implementing the law, or rejecting and thus nullifying it. At this point, too,[134] there is a fundamental difference between the divine natural law and earthly law: man does not implement the divine natural law, but God implements this law in man.[135] Promulgation, being valid, and implementation of the law are one. God's Word is God's action;[136] "he speaks, and it happens" (Psalm 33:9).

This concludes the survey of those characteristic features of the divine natural law which in modern legal doctrine would be called personalistic, formal, and procedural. Now, and only now, is it possible to deal with the substantive content[137] of the divine natural law. Contrary to the situation in an earthly law, person, form, procedure, and content cannot be separated in the divine natural law. If one knows one link in this chain, one knows also the others; none may be ignored in the discussion of natural law; each of them has its place in the whole picture of law.

Like any law, the divine natural law demands a 'work', yet — and this is characteristic of the divine element of this law — not a work which can be accomplished through earthly strength, but a divine work,[138] that is, a work which only God himself is able to give. And this work is the love for the Creator during man's life in this world and, therefore, in his relationships with the world.[139]

The divine natural law is valid only when it meets a God-formed will;[140] that law claims nothing but "the bottom of the heart";[141] therefore in this heart 'shall' and 'being' coincide;[142] in other words, the content of the divine natural law is a given of man's nature.[143] Natural law is *lex connaturalis*.[144] It tells man: "Dwell in that love which God has given you together with your existence! Affirm the spiritual estate[145] into which you were called[146] when you were born!" The divine natural law, therefore, determines man's estate. If the comparison is allowed: *The divine natural law is the law of citizenship and of man's estate in God's kingdom at the time of the incorrupt nature.* This understanding inevitably and at once leads to a commandment for living in this kingdom and estate: "Lead a righteous life, that is, a life appropriate to your spiritual estate! Make an effort to use the creature correctly, that is, spiritually for the glory and honor of God!"[147] Thus natural law is the divine order of life for spiritual man.[148] The two dimensions of the divine natural law, the personalistic and the substantive one, are the nucleus of Luther's preaching on the law of estate and of vocation.[149]

The existence of spiritual man is filled with the communion with God, and this communion is proven in man's living in the Creation, especially in the communion with man.

The relationship with God is marked by the surrender of man's will[150] to God's will, that is, by the unconditional and total acceptance of God's sovereignty.

For man's conduct toward his neighbor, Christ equated the divine commandment of love with the Golden Rule:[151] "All things that you want people to do to you, do also to them" (Matthew 7:12, Luke 6:31). The Golden Rule is an especially popular expression of natural law and serves as the legal basis for the communal life of Christians. Canon law, therefore, equated the Golden Rule with the divine natural law.[152] Luther, too, frequently followed this traditional usage, but regarding the subject itself he again went his own way. In itself the Golden Rule is not a spiritual law.

The Divine Law in the Status of the Incorrupt Nature

This is proven, first, by its content: it commands an external 'work' ("*do also to them*"); and second, by the reference to the *I* as the standard for conduct ("*you want* people to do *to you*"); in the status of the incorrupt nature, such an instruction would have been completely unnecessary and unthinkable. Therefore the Golden Rule belongs to the status of the corrupt nature, that is, the kingdom of the world. Christ interpreted it spiritually, however, that is, the way in which Christians are to use the Golden Rule. This interpretation incorporates the Golden Rule into the kingdom of Christ, so to speak. Therefore one may state: The spiritually interpreted Golden Rule is that version of the divine natural-law commandment to love the neighbor which in the status of the corrupt nature belongs to the kingdom of Christ. This version accommodates the Golden Rule to the spiritual legal situation of man who, as a result of the Fall, is dominated by egotism and who, in spite of his Redemption by Christ, still has to fight that egotism. According to Christ's interpretation of the Golden Rule, that man is challenged to place this egotism totally in the service of his neighbor; this means, he is to put himself in his neighbor's position, and in this way to subordinate his own well-being to that of his neighbor; he may not think that the divine natural law is fulfilled as soon as his and his neighbor's well-being are placed on the same level.

This suffices for the divine natural law as law of love *(lex charitatis)*.[153]

§ 2. The Divine Positive Law

In addition to the divine natural law there is the divine positive law.[154] God instituted it after the creation of man[155] as "an external thing wrapped in God's Word," as Luther said.[156] Man cannot rationally explain why God chose this particular way of proclaiming his will.[157] Therefore, especially in light of this situation it becomes clear that this law is 'positive'.

Until now the understanding of the divine positive law has been under the same unlucky star as that of the divine natural law. One has not recognized that both laws are spiritual laws — not 'spiritual law' in the medieval sense, but in the sense of Luther's understanding of the concept 'spiritual law'.[158] Divine natural law deals with the spiritual existence of the individual spiritual man in his relationship with God and neighbor ("you shall"); divine positive law deals with the order (institutions) of the spiritual communal life ⟨of the spiritual man⟩.

God provided two legal institutions for the structure of this spiritual communal existence, church[159] and[160] marriage;[161] the former for the promotion of the internal and the external communal life in relationship with the Creator *(cultus dei)*, the latter for the God-oriented relationship of people of different sexes with each other. As in the case of the divine natural law, so in the case of these two institutions, the outer appearance, that is, the legal form of the two institutions, which can be discovered by reason, is only a vessel for the intentions of the Spirit, only a sign for what purpose these institutions should be used according to God's commandment. Only when they are used spiritually *(usus spiritualis)* are these institutions divine orders.[162] Nevertheless, one may not ignore this outer appearance of the orders of the divine positive law. One can differentiate their spiritual and corporeal elements, but one may not separate them. It is the fundamental error of natural reason to see only one quality and never their simultaneity; from this follows that natural reason pulls the spiritual into the realm of the corporeal or vice versa.[163]

There is another characteristic common to the divine natural and the divine positive law: God implanted in man's heart the impetus to fulfill the divine positive law. Regarding the external worship of God, "there has never been a people so wicked that it did not establish and maintain some sort of divine worship."[164] And regarding marriage it has to be pointed out that the phrase "grow and multiply" (Genesis 1:28) is "not a commandment but rather more than a commandment, namely, a work of God, . . . it is implanted nature, . . . it is nature and not arbitrariness."[165]

There was no need for God to institute additional forms for the communal existence of the family of man.[166] Man's existence in the church, which is both spiritual and corporeal,[167] and in the *oeconomia*,[168] which also is spiritually and corporeally perfect,[169] would have been sufficient for obeying the divine natural law;[170] man's communal existence would have taken the form of a family communion,[171] in which the members were devoted to God and to each other in fervent love.

§ 3. Summary

In the status of the incorrupt nature, the spiritual and the corporeal elements exist in a harmonious order. The same is true of the law appro-

The Divine Law in the Status of the Incorrupt Nature

priate for this status: as divine natural law it regulates the spiritual existence of sinless man; as divine positive law it provides the church and marriage, the two institutions for the spiritual communal life in the Original Status.

Commandment and institution are the two forms in which the divine law appears; they complement each other and make up the whole of the spiritual order of the divine law in a wider sense.[172] This divine law is identical with divine love and, therefore, is spiritual; it grasps the total inner life of spiritual man, and through it also his total outer life; consequently, it is exhaustive.[173]

Therefore *Luther's concept 'law' is spiritual.* The reformer understood law as participation[174] in divine love.[175] For him, man's conduct is legitimate when it is shaped by a God-formed will, that is, by perfect love for God; legitimate is an institution which God has founded for the common promotion of this will for love in the relationship with the Creator or with a fellow human being of the other sex.

It is impossible to integrate such a spiritual concept 'law' into the categories of the secular philosophy of law. It would be easier to do this with the concept 'law' maintained in the Roman Catholic legal doctrine. Luther's concept 'law' is closer to that Roman Catholic concept than one has thus far assumed — nevertheless, there is an enormous difference between the two concepts.

Luther was thoroughly aware of the revolutionary consequences[176] his understanding of law had for the philosophy and theology of his day. The legal doctrine needed, he said, another, new theological grammar;[177] its most important paragraph would be the teaching of the absolute contrast that exists between the spiritual and the corporeal law, or in other words, between the heavenly and the earthly[178] righteousness.[179]

How can one explain the origin of this contrast? What are the consequences of the origin of this contrast? Neither a philosopher nor a jurist has the key for answers to these questions — a Christian has it.[180]

CHAPTER 9

Human Law in the Status of the Corrupt Nature during the Age of Unwritten Law

―――⦿―――

§ 1. The Substantive Secular Natural Law

The[1] Fall caused human nature to lose its harmony of spirit and body — it split apart.[2] The concept 'righteousness' also split apart. This schism is the legal mark of the aeon of the corrupt nature.

"There are two kinds of righteousness" — these are the opening words of this aeon's history of law.[3] Now righteousness according to the spirit, which was supreme in the status of the incorrupt nature, is confronted with righteousness according to the flesh, which challenges righteousness according to the spirit on all fronts.[4] The spiritual ‹divine› natural law runs head-on into its opposition,[5] the *secular natural law*.[6] It is called secular because its constitutional-law place is in the kingdom of the world. One could also call it human natural law because man discovered it.[7] Nevertheless, it is appropriate to call it *natural* law[8] because the divine will for law remains inscribed in the heart even of sinful man as divine natural law; as a result of the Fall, man no longer succeeds, however, in grasping its spiritual meaning.

The light of the spirit was extinguished when man lost the quality of spiritual man.[9] Only the deceptive light of nature[10] still renders a blurred image of God, into which man ‹now› interprets his own features.[11] In his spiritual blindness[12] man deals in an identical way with the divine will for law, which he no longer recognizes.[13] Even more dangerous is the fact that the dominant power of his soul,[14] the God-formed will, changes into the opposite, the hate for God,[15] and this means the hate for the divine natural law.[16] With his natural abilities man is absolutely no longer able to love God the way God requests,[17] or, and this would be the same, man can no longer think and act correctly in the divine sense. He no longer 'has'[18] God as a person. In the status of the corrupt nature man does not have a free will in his relationship with the Creator.[19]

This seems to be a devastating judgment about all law on earth. How can it claim to be law since it owes its existence to human arbitrariness? But in spite of his breakaway from the Creator, man is not totally rejected by God. Divine mercy left man an inborn notion of what is law,[20] and this notion still includes the obedience to the divine natural law as the goal of man's conduct.[21] This is natural man's divine 'dowry', which makes him aware of what is right and moral.[22] Weak, dim, and crude as this knowledge of the divine natural law is,[23] nevertheless all creation and implementation of law on earth take place according to a God-given path and in the direction which God has determined,[24] that is, toward the divine law.[25] There is absolutely no human law without this connection with the divine law. Man does not establish this relationship, however, but God's will pulls man into this order. Man does not recognize this action of God. Yet in man's conscience[26] God calls man to order whenever man creates and implements law.

Medieval theologians raised the daring question whether there is a natural law "even if . . . God does not exist, which is imposssible."[27] They gave an affirmative answer. For them this question was a fruitful hypothesis in terms of method, even though in terms of faith it was an impossibility. For the legal philosophers of the Enlightenment this hypothesis became the necessary basis of their thinking, and it resulted in the proclamation of the autonomy of natural law. There was not the slightest trace of this in Luther's thinking. He judged and condemned man's attitude toward the spiritual ⟨divine⟩ natural law as being autocratic. Nevertheless, he also always affirmed that "natural law (understood as secular natural law) . . . cannot be separated from divine natural law."[28] When man ignores this God-ordered connection, he is outside of law. Therefore Luther may not be held responsible for the secularism in the doctrine of law.[29]

Yet when man interprets the divine natural law, inscribed in his heart, he no longer views it with the eye of the spirit but in the light of this world.[30] This means: man no longer relates that law to eternal blessedness, but he relates it to human happiness.[31] "A person's character determines how he judges."[32]

Instead of divine righteousness, human righteousness is now elevated to the supreme position in the order of law[33] on earth, and it is even declared to be divine.[34] Man is not even aware of the enormity of this error.[35] He believes that he is truly searching for God when he attempts a rational interpretation of the divine natural law.[36] But precisely this confidence in his own ability to rethink God's thoughts proves man's arrogance, that rebellious attitude which is his first[37] and fundamental sin.[38] God, therefore, allows man's *ratio,* one of God's noblest gifts to man,[39] to become man's whore;[40] she seduces man to turn his back to God[41] and to find the meaning of the divine law in the Creation instead of listening to the voice of the Creator. Consequently, man remains stuck in the external, non-spiritual world; instead of seeing God as a person, he sees only the work of God's hands.

But even in this situation man creates great things. For the noblest minds of mankind — "the sound heroes and miracle workers,"[42] "the heroic and exceptional men"[43] who do not speak and act "*sine afflatu,*"[44] that is, "without a special inspiration from God"[45] — dedicate themselves to the corporeal interpretation of the divine natural law. Their words of wisdom have the authority of being essentially correct, and therefore they are able to convince also those who are intellectually not very gifted.[46] Their wisdom, therefore, is the norm for everyone. This "law of the heroes,"[47] more exactly, this version of the secular natural law, originates in the human genius;[48] it is the result of the infralapsarian interpretation of the divine natural law[49] by natural man instead of spiritual man.

In the world, the secular natural law is highly esteemed as the masterpiece[50] of jurisprudence and morality on earth, and this with good reason.[51] It is indeed a precious jewel.[52] Its moral basis is the awareness of mankind's solidarity and mutual responsibility as a body whose members are called[53] to serve one another[54] according to their respective talents; its goal is the "common welfare";[55] its model is "the irreproachable man,"[56] that is, the "man who in the judgment of the world is upright";[57] its motto is "to each his own"![58] The spirit of this secular natural law[59] is the universal love for man,[60] which is normatively expressed in the corporeally understood Golden Rule: "All things that you want people to do to you, do also to them."[61] This means in the interpretation by natural man: love your neighbor not less than you love yourself! Therefore, according to Luther, the secular natural law is altruistic,[62] though it includes, of course, the inevitable minimum of love

Human Law in the Status of the Corrupt Nature

for self, without which natural man is unable to exist.[63] At this point, too,[64] a deep rift separates Luther from the interpretation of natural law in the Enlightenment; here the *I* is moved into the center of the system;[65] Luther, however, started with the body of mankind,[66] in which the individual is a member of the body.[67] In contrast to the individualistic concept 'law' developed in Rationalism, Luther's concept 'law' might be called a membership concept.[68]

The regulating principle[69] for the legal life in the kingdom of the world is the corporeally understood Golden Rule; it has ruled in this kingdom since the Fall, and it will assert itself until the Day of Judgment.[70] By drawing conclusions from this original natural law, man gains supreme legal maxims,[71] which also are called ‹secular› natural law. We shall call them derived ‹secular› natural law. Luther called them "universal natural laws,"[72] and he ascribed to them validity also for "heathen, Turks, and Jews";[73] because of this extended validity, claiming all mankind, one could call them heathen natural law provided that the word 'heathen' may be used summarily for all kinds of non-Christians. This natural law is not connected with the kingdom of Christ;[74] yet modern man, caught in a secularized culture, tries — justifiably from his viewpoint — to understand this secular natural law as an expression of a "Christianity of attitude and action."[75]

To this day, the Decalogue is the model[76] for the secular natural law[77] in terms of substantive law.[78] To be more precise one would have to say that the Second Table[79] is this model, for natural man, who idolizes himself,[80] is unable to obey the First Table,[81] not even corporeally,[82] so that its commandments[83] are meaningless as law.[84] As a source of law,[85] the Second Table is the Magna Charta of mankind. Its formulation shows that Moses was mankind's most ingenious legislator; to this day no one has equaled his strength and certainty in the finding of law.

Because of their inner power[86] and the unique authority of Moses, their editor, Luther usually equated the commandments of the Decalogue with the derived secular natural law.[87] In the following we shall ignore that occasionally Luther derived additional norms[88] from the commandments of the Decalogue, which he also called secular natural law. Noteworthy is, however, that in terms of their rank in law he saw no differences between these additional norms and the Decalogue, and this for a good reason: for him the Ten Commandments had the same legal quality as those additional norms; they all are human law.

The Basic Features of Luther's Doctrine of Law

God may not be considered to be the legislator of the prescriptions in the law of Moses. One has to remember only the crude[89] and externally oriented content of some of these norms, their multiplicity,[90] and their restriction to the prohibition of the worst corporeal crimes.[91] How little does all this correspond to the infinite subtlety of the divine spiritual righteousness! The prescriptions of the law of Moses are not divine law, divine directive,[92] if they are understood literally, that is, as norms according to the doctrine of human law.[93] They are only the pale reflection of the divine natural law in a clouded human mirror. In comparison with the medieval doctrine of natural law, this evaluation is revolutionary, not only in relationship to Thomism but also to Scotism and Occamism.[94] Thomas had included all of the Decalogue in the natural law in the strict sense,[95] Scotus had included at least the first two commandments (in a negative interpretation to mean the prohibition of the hate for God),[96] and Occam had interpreted the Decalogue still as a positive divine decree.[97] Luther, however, excluded the law of Moses, understood as the quintessence of the highest norms for the corporeal life, from the divine law and lowered it to the realm of human law.

At this point there is a sharp difference between Luther's concept 'natural law' and that of the Middle Ages, and his concept already points in the direction of the future secular philosophy of natural law. In that philosophy, too, human reason is able to recognize the secular natural law, which also is beyond positivism,[98] and is directly binding. But the similarity does not reach further. Rather, the rationalism of the secular natural law in Luther's thinking and that of the Enlightenment have opposite value presuppositions. For the thinkers of the Enlightenment the light of reason was the beginning of all wisdom, but for Luther it was the epitome of foolish self-confidence.[99] In the Enlightenment natural law was something innerworldly, for Luther it was related to God because it was connected with the divine natural law.

In the natural law doctrine of the Enlightenment there is, therefore, no possibility that a superior power would break the natural law. On the other hand, for Luther the secular natural law is at the Creator's disposal who, according to the biblical records, repeatedly broke it. Those legal acts of God which cannot be explained rationally — the special mandates, privileges, exceptions, and dispensations enacted by the divine majesty[100] — demonstrate that the warp and woof in the norms of the secular natural law are just a toy in the hands of the Almighty; with death[101] and devil he enacts his lofty spiritual game in a way which is often horrifying beyond all measures but always leads to the Salvation of the believer. God has reserved such acts of majesty for himself,[102] and man may not appeal to them unless a divine miracle authorizes him to do so. For man, the secular natural law is *the* human law;[103] he is not permitted to jeopardize the sovereignty of reason inherent in natural law — natural law is indispensable for man.[104]

These materials provide the basis for dealing with the connection between the secular natural law and history in Luther's thought.[105] The historical aspect of law occupied Luther intensely and early on in his life, and there was hardly one among his contemporaries who could rival him in this matter.[106] His reference to the sound heroes and miracle workers,[107] who for him were the movers in the existence of nations, proves how seriously he thought about the irrational element in history. Those unique men he considered to be the true experts of the laws of a commonwealth's growth and existence.[108] For the well-being of a commonwealth these men promote these laws, even in opposition to the positive law: "Indeed they overcome the laws, but they do not destroy the commonwealths."[109] From this position their relationship with the secular natural law has to be clearly differentiated, however. God frequently places the person of these unique men under a law of exemption, but God does not charge them to abolish the secular natural law in a way that would be effective for others. On the contrary! Their most important task[110] is to secure the appropriate authority for the secular natural law in the order of human society and shape the specific historical form of the positive law in accordance with this authority.[111] One is tempted to rephrase Luther's statement, mentioned above, as follows: "They break the laws, but not *the* law (that is, the Decalogue)." That and how they succeed in such a renewal of the legal life is the secret of the gifts bestowed upon them by God. Concretely formulated: the secular natural law itself is not irrational; through God's intervention, the process in which this secular natural law becomes the positive man-made law is irrational.

History reveals its power already before history begins, that is, when supreme legal maxims are derived from the Golden Rule. Luther saw degrees[112] in the perfection of the perception and formulation of the commandment to love one's neighbor, which were conditioned by individuals and circumstances of time.[113] These degrees depend on the level of the feeling for what is right, which is alive in a given period of mankind's history. How much stronger do human deficiencies become noticeable in the subsequent formulation of the derived secular natural law as positive law.[114]

Nevertheless, the original secular natural law remains unchangeable, just as does human reason.[115] This original secular natural law is the "chief law, rule, and standard"[116] of all other laws. In it originate the moral power and the obedience-demanding force inherent in all positive law.[117] For two things must work together for the positive law to emerge and its validity to be secured when it is implemented: First, the internal force ‹of positive law›, which originates in ‹its› obedience to the secular natural law, and second, the external commandment backed by the power of the secular governmental authority.[118] Unfortunately, these two elements of the earthly legal commandment are usually not simultaneously present, and the interaction of law and power is not fully harmonious. On earth only the secular natural law is "healthy law";[119] compared with it, all realizations of the secular natural law in positive law look sickly, like "vain patchwork and beggary."[120] Only "what happens through the strength of nature turns out to be healthy even without laws, or even contrary to all laws."[121]

There is no sadder indication of the atrophy of a vivid feeling for what is right in a nation than the "legal wilderness"[122] of the positive law. For "experience, all chronicles, and also Holy Scripture teach us that fewer statutes make better law, . . . and there has never been a community well ruled for any length of time which had many laws."[123] This statement is valid not only because of the tension between the schematic generality of the law[124] and the concrete legal situation of an individual case but also because of the promotion of legal particularism. "The result of many laws is . . . the emergence of many sects and divisions within the community; one adopts this way, the other that way, and in each person grows a secret, false love for one's sect and hatred, or rather contempt and disregard for the other sects so that brotherly, . . . universal love perishes and self-serving love grows abundantly."[125] The ideal[126] would be sensible rulers who rule according to the secular natural law only.[127] But in a hundred years there is hardly one who has the secular natural law in his head.[128] Therefore the world cannot exist without the positive human law;[129] it is a stopgap only, and in comparison with experience gained from history, it has little value for good government.[130]

Nevertheless, in the process of enacting laws the highest degree of caution is necessary. One should write down and organize only the well-rooted legal custom, and one should not with "powerful words" issue prescriptions which are not obeyed, because "prescribing and obeying are far apart."[131] Further, one has to pay strict attention that positive law does not transgress the limits set up by the secular natural law but stays "within the natural-law neutrality."[132] The "written law flowed from the secular natural law as the fountain of law."[133] Therefore all other human statutes lack the necessary minimum of justice without which the positive man-made law cannot exist. Man-made commandments and prohibitions which do not in one way or another agree with the standard of universal love for man are not law and are contrary to law,[134] even when they are dressed up as universal laws.[135] If such commandments and prohibitions are executive pronouncements of a tyrant,[136] they do not justify the duty of obedience, in fact, they may not be obeyed. In this way, the secular natural law is a permanent warning signal for the legislator. It reminds him that his authority is a law-bound authority, and only as such is it legally valid. The secular natural law[137] is the master of the positive law, not a governmental authority, which is only its servant.

A governmental authority has to demonstrate this understanding of its office[138] especially whenever in an individual case there is a possibility that, because of the fixedness of its norms,[139] the positive law clashes with justice.[140] In such a situation only the consideration of the natural-law principle[141] 'equity' can prevent the "clearest law" from deteriorating into the "clearest injustice."[142] Therefore, dependent on the circumstances of the individual case,[143] enactment and implementation of law have to be flexible enough to accommodate equity (*epieikeia*),[144] that "miracle of the jurists."[145] God himself made this order[146] by first appointing the governmental authority, and only then allowing laws to be given. The judge, the embodiment of the governmental authority, is to be the living law, or rather the soul of the law. While duly respecting the law, in his office he has to be superior to the law; he <may> not play the laws off against what is right, as the *Buchstabenjuristen*[147] do, or let this happen. Therefore by granting a dispensation in cases of need, the rule of the common norm[148] should be protected against unbearable severity,[149] and thus its legal value be maintained. Of course, a highly developed sensitivity for what is right and much experience in handling the law are necessary for this art of using the law so that in the name of equity not the exact opposite might be achieved.[150]

Luther praised Roman law as the model for human legislation.[151] He did not always do this, however. In his earlier years he thought Roman law should be used in Germany only in a pinch because it was "elaborate, it was imported," and it presented a burden to people; therefore it was reasonable for him that Roman law should rank below a territory's "own short laws."[152] After the Peasants War, and in view of the increasing religious tension among the estates of the Empire, he abandoned this desire for such a thorough legal reform. Now he saw greater value in the positive law[153] for the stability of a commonwealth than in earlier years, and in order to avoid a revolution, he rejected any challenges to Roman law, which had been introduced into Germany.[154] He argued that, in spite of its foreign origin, and in spite of lacking authority in day-by-day legal affairs, Roman law was excellent when compared with other legal systems, and that the world would no longer have men with such wisdom in secular governance as the Romans were.[155]

Luther's growing esteem for the "universal book-law"[156] was only relative, however, when compared with his esteem for the secular natural law, and an unsurmountable barrier separated him from the feeling for law of his contemporaries. He was horrified when he observed the self-reliance[157] with which the worldly saints,[158] and especially the jurists,[159] appear before God's throne of judgment, trusting their rational concept of law and thinking they could earn divine righteousness through their earthly understanding and handling of the law.[160] What a dangerous folly[161] to believe that earthly law is God-like! In God's judgment,[162] law which has a non-spiritual goal and, therefore, is fragmented into a multitude of external prescriptions,[163] does not even deserve the name law.[164]

Such a law clearly shows the traces of perversion. Consider only the corporeal understanding of the Golden Rule! Without man being conscious of it,[165] the very nucleus of the Golden Rule's magnanimous altruism grew from love for self,[166] not love for God. Before God, all legal actions shaped by this perversion become sin, even if according to human standards they would be most praiseworthy. The relationship of this kind of legal action to true righteousness is like the relationship of "a play-penny or a counterfeit gulden"[167] to a "genuine gulden."[168] In short: If in relationship with God one relies on the secular natural law, one trusts a counterfeit spiritual law created by reason.

This removes the uncertainty whether in Luther's doctrine of law we find an absolute and a relative natural law;[169] the former would designate the divine natural law and the latter the secular natural law. Obviously, it is impossible ⟨to affirm the presence of this absolute and relative natural law in Luther's legal doctrine⟩, just as it is impossible to place God, the source of the divine natural law, opposite Satan, the instigator of the misinterpretation of this divine natural law in the secular natural law, as if they were an absolute and a relative demon.

Now the difference between Luther's doctrine of natural law and that of the Middle Ages is clear. In Luther's theology faith and reason diverge, and Nominalism is partially responsible for this. In Luther's doctrine of law the spiritual ⟨divine⟩ natural law of the kingdom of God and the non-spiritual[170] secular natural law of the kingdom of the world[171] diverge. But this world stands under the harsh judgment: "... the letter has vanity, not truth, nor does it quicken, but it kills in its way."[172] This raises again the question about the meaning of human law.

We said above[173] that the legal life on earth is not outside the connection with God. Now the issue is the implications of this connection for the Salvation of man's soul. Does not the term 'letter' indicate that, according to God's judgment, sin is attached to human law? In other words: does that connection of earthly law with God not result in spiritual disaster for man?

This question cannot be answered with a simple yes or no.[174] First the meaning of 'letter' has to be clarified. In 'law of the letter', 'letter' receives its meaning from the opposite, that is, 'law of the spirit'. For 'law of the spirit' is decisive that the receiver of the commandment has a God-formed will; for 'law of the letter' a will suffices which obeys the secular natural law and the positive law determined by it. The standard for 'law of the letter' is human righteousness; the law of the letter has to be content with the externally ascertainable fulfillment of the law[175] because no man can see what is in another man's heart. Therefore this externally ascertainable fulfillment of the law is restricted to prescribing external works. Luther placed the stigma 'letter' on all creation and use of law which has to make do[176] with such an external righteousness.

These observations provide the correct understanding of the judgment that human law is 'letter', mentioned above. With this term Luther did not characterize the objective legal order as such. He did not doubt at all that this order was necessary for mankind and was God's good gift.[177] The question is not whether 'law' as the divine order of the earthly communal life is good,[178] but whether 'law' is salutary for my relationship with the Creator; important is not the corporeal benefit of law but its spiritual value for me. And on that issue 'law' is silent[179] (of course, we presuppose that its positive expression, evaluated with the standard set in secular natural law, can actually claim the quality of law). Therefore one has to consider the individual and find out with what spirit he creates and implements law.[180] The degree of practical usefulness or the moral value of a norm[181] does not determine whether or not earthly law is 'letter', but the use of the norm does — not law, but the use of law.[182] Decisive in this connection is whether that use of the law is spiritual or carnal;[183] this means whether in his actions man is illuminated by the Holy Spirit or follows the spirit of the world. In other words: only a spiritual man is capable of the spiritual use of the law, only a carnal man is capable of the carnal use of the law.[184] This result is very important for understanding many of Luther's statements which are constructed with the word 'spiritual' or 'Christian'[185] (to anticipate materials to be developed later); one only has to remember expressions such as 'spiritual' or 'Christian estate', 'Christian marriage', 'Christian school', and last but not least 'Christian governmental authority', with which we will have to deal especially.

In all his actions a spiritual man follows God's will for law. In what way does he find this will in the secular law? In other words: *what is the divine meaning of law in the kingdom of the world?*

Let us remember the twofold nature of this kingdom![186] It is both the land of the dead and God's kingdom at the left. Human law also has this twofold nature.

We begin by considering the first characteristic feature of the kingdom of the world just mentioned.[187] Here we are confronted with a truly desperate situation. As rebels against God's sovereignty the members of this kingdom are banned from the legal communion with God, they are spiritually excommunicated. Therefore no spiritual law exists for them,[188] only an unbearable[189] coercion and ban. The divine natural law functions not as law of love *(lex charitatis)* but as law of wrath and death *(lex irae et mortis),*[190] for the psalmist says: "With the pure you show yourself pure; and with the crooked you show yourself perverse." (Psalm 18:26.)[191] God relates himself to man in the way in which man relates himself to God.[192] This does not mean that God's will changes! His "nature and being" remain eternally the same.[193] What appears as being changeable in God is an event outside of him;[194] that is, the impact of the never-changing divine willpower on man's heart changes, depending on whether that heart is turned toward or away from God.[195]

Human Law in the Status of the Corrupt Nature

To illustrate this idea, Luther liked to use the image of the different impact a sunbeam has on mud or on wax: mud hardens, wax softens, but the nature of the sunbeam does not change.[196] This situation is also true for divine love. Since it is the basis of all that exists, death occurs whenever this life-giving love *(charitas vivificans)* is not at work. If this fact is applied to man's spiritual legal relationship with God it means: as soon as man breaks away from God he loses the spiritual status[197] which has its basis in his participation in divine love. The mutual spiritual legal relationship between him and the Creator is destroyed, and God's spirit recedes from him.[198] Deserted by God *(desertus)*, man falls into the abyss of wretched separation from God.[199] Since he is now spiritually unprotected, the fury of evil, present in the creatures fallen from God, gains power over man already in this life, and this reveals God's wrath. God's wrath does not describe a psychological fact but an ontological one, which at the same time is a legal one. And this fact is man's existence outside of God's grace *(extra gratiam Dei)*. Expressed in terms of Canon law: the law of wrath and death as spiritual criminal law[200] hits the sinner with the punishment of spiritual death, and this punishment is pronounced in an all-encompassing verdict *(poena latae sententiae)*. Since in the divine law the commandment and the giver of the commandment cannot be separated, what we just said can be rephrased as a personalistic statement[201] about the law of wrath: The law of wrath implements the office of spiritually punishing[202] the sinner; it accuses the sinner, convicts him, and sentences him[203] to the expulsion from the land of the living into the land of the dead.[204] No one can evade this judicial process.

When sin came into this world the horrible period began in which the divine law rules in an absolute way, demanding the above mentioned flawless righteousness, which is beyond all human capability, and condemning man to spiritual destruction each time that the human heart resists the divine commandment.[205] Luther called this demand and condemnation the proper or theological use of the law *(proprius sive theologicus usus legis)*,[206] "the noblest office . . . of the law."[207]

The spiritual curse of the law of wrath seizes upon all human law[208] in the kingdom of the world and impresses upon it[209] those characteristics which since then are typical for a law, that is, gravity and severity, coercion and punishment.[210] Every human law reflects the divine wrath, and every governmental authority is its tool. Therefore, as Luther said, human law is "very much the same as punishment."[211] This is *the first spiritual characteristic of human law* as the prototype of law in the kingdom of the world.[212]

No one is able to love such a law with all his heart. Natural man feels compelled to flee from the wrath of God.[213] Therefore everyone would prefer freedom to law,[214] were this possible.[215] No one obeys the law only for its own sake. Only the fear of punishment or the prospect of reward makes one obey and, therefore, no earthly law exists forever.[216] The hidden reason for this transitoriness is man's hatred[217] for the trace of the spiritual coercion by the law of wrath found in human law; before God, therefore, every act of implementing law accuses man of lacking voluntariness.[218]

As a result of this situation, legal life in the world appears in an eerie twilight. In order to preserve peace on earth[219] and corporeal freedom,[220] man is busy setting up a legal order secured by individual laws, which is never secure.[221] In truth, however, he only increases the slavery of the law of wrath and intensifies the danger of spiritual chaos.[222] For, according to the Apostle Paul, each law is an "opportunity to sin" (Romans 7:8, 11), stirs up sin and reveals it.[223] The multitude of laws is in inverse proportion to the presence of faith among a people.[224]

This, finally, fully explains the already mentioned[225] aversion which especially young Luther had to the making of laws in a secular commonwealth. This aversion was motivated by natural-law considerations, that is, his dislike of the excessiveness in the coercive quality of law and of the diminishing of the voluntary universal love for man[226] in the public and the private domain. More important, it was motivated by the intense worry about the disastrous influence of law[227] on man's relationship with God.[228] On this point, like it or not, one is confronted with the statement: "The best of laws does not liberate from God's condemnation."[229]

Yet Luther's doctrine of law does not end in such a negative way. In spite of man's Fall, the kingdom of the world remains God's kingdom, that is, the kingdom of God at the left.[230] The divine will for law does not deny its quality of love, not even in a world that turned away from God. The rod of divine wrath is simultaneously the rod of divine mercy,[231] the law of wrath is simultaneously the hidden[232] law of love *(lex charitatis latens)*.[233] Human malice forced the divine will for law, against its essence (so to speak), to be active in the sinful world as wrath.[234] With this meaning in mind, Luther placed the law of wrath on the one side in opposition to God on the other side, almost like two antagonists.[235]

Human Law in the Status of the Corrupt Nature

Through punishing, the law of wrath does its proper work *(opus proprium)*, which for God is an alien work *(opus alienum)*;²³⁶ he undertakes it only in order to complete his proper work,²³⁷ and that proper work is the restoration of divine love which had vanished from the world of sin.²³⁸ When the law of wrath is used for this task, it enacts its alien work.²³⁹

If one understands the law of wrath in this way, then it becomes the spiritual antidote of the spiritual and corporeal decay of mankind. It fights, first, the power of sin in man's heart by driving him to the recognition of sin;²⁴⁰ in doing this, the law of wrath implements its office²⁴¹ of penance within the process of Salvation worked out by Christ. This is nothing other than the theological use of the law²⁴² serving Redemption. Second, the law of wrath opposes the devil's destructive power in the external life; to human law the law of wrath grants the characteristic of being an external force of order to deter the evil and protect the righteous.²⁴³

The law of wrath performs this service for the corporeal well-being of mankind as hidden law of love, regardless whether man opens or closes his heart to the spiritual exhortation to repent. As "the sun always shines even if a blind man does not see it, so the Word of God is always salutary, even when it is poison for the godless and fatal news bringing death to them."²⁴⁴ Through human law, God preserves mankind from the corporeal doom to which the devil wants to lead mankind through the slogan 'might makes right'.²⁴⁵ Positive human law with its natural-law gravitation toward order becomes the tool of the divine will for preserving mankind.²⁴⁶ "Where there is law, there is no longer the world or the governance of the world at work, but God himself."²⁴⁷ Luther called this office of the law of wrath, which is to preserve mankind, the political or civic use of the law *(usus politicus sive civilis legis)*.²⁴⁸ This office grants *the second spiritual characteristic to positive human law:* in addition to being *Strafrecht* <criminal law>, it is also *Zuchtrecht* <law of disciplining>.²⁴⁹

Every law in this world is the result of a double effect of the divine law.²⁵⁰ These effects are not unrelated; they owe their offices to the same divine will for law, and they have the same²⁵¹ divine goal,²⁵² that is, the restoration of spiritual legal peace with God. Corporeal law is able to serve this purpose only indirectly by securing external peace in the secular commonwealth, and that peace paves the way for the proclamation of the gospel.²⁵³ The political or civic use of the law, therefore, ranks much lower *(rudis,*[254] *infimus*[255] *usus)* than the theological use[256] — it is only a "crude, carnal example"[257] of the theological use.

Nevertheless, God wills that even in this modest position earthly law is a part of the constitution of his kingdom at the left.[258] Therefore ignoring the law is identical with becoming guilty before God. If one does not even meet the requirements of the secular natural law, that is, corporeal righteousness, how can one take seriously the commandment of the divine natural law, that is, spiritual righteousness?[259] He who despises earthly law and is judged according to the standards of righteousness valid in God's kingdom at the left is not at all equal to him who favors the law. God left man the free choice to accept or reject the secular natural law and the positive human law derived from it. In this sense, man does have a free will in his relation to the (transpositive and positive) human law, just as he has a free will in his relation with the Creation on the whole.[260] But whoever uses this free will in opposition to God's will of preservation is hit by the law of wrath as a destructive commandment *(ira severitatis).*[261] Externally this is obvious from the fact that God lets a corporeal punishment follow a corporeal crime. Conversely, he who according to secular standards is righteous experiences that God rewards him with temporal blessings.[262] Therefore the right use of the law begins already in this world;[263] here God teaches man an introductory lesson[264] for understanding divine righteousness.[265]

In this lesson man has to learn two things about the relationship of the spiritual to the corporeal righteousness; one is labeled 'no longer', and the other 'not yet'. Regarding the former: the civic or political use of the law makes clear that the natural-law barrier for human law also marks the boundary to which the divine will for law, manifested in the divine natural law, extends in its widest expansions; wherever the universal natural-law commandment to love the neighbor is no longer heeded,[266] there divine love, that is, divine righteousness, also is no longer alive.[267] Regarding the latter: the civic or political use of the law opens man's eyes to the insufficiency of earthly law[268] in spite of the fact that it is connected with God. Earthly law comes into existence when God acts "by means of the creature."[269] Since "the creature's will[270] flows into God's action," earthly law is "not only God's own work."[271] This explains that earthly law is seldom to the point and clings to externals, to mention just a few things.[272] From this deficiency of human law follows that not even the most conscientious use of human law is able to measure up to obeying the commandments of the divine universal righteousness. Above we stated[273] that a culpable breaking of earthly law, which is legitimate in terms of the secular natural law, evokes God's wrath and bars the entry to the kingdom of heaven. Now we have to add: even the meticulous obedience of human law is unable to open the entry into the kingdom of heaven.[274] These spiritual weaknesses of human law and of its use by man signal that beyond the corporeal righteousness has to exist a higher, perfect, true righteousness. Earthly law certainly is essential for the preservation of mankind[275] and of highest value for the preaching of God's judgment and mercy, but its use contributes nothing to the building of God's kingdom at the right.[276] Spiritually seen, earthly law is "beggary."[277] "The (spiritual) law condemns the (corporeal) law."[278]

These materials describe the extreme degree of closeness but also the total distance between the divine natural law and the secular natural law, and the human positive law derived from it.[279] Closeness and distance belong together. <Obedience to> the transpositive[280] and the positive human law creates external peace,[281] but obedience to the divine natural law gives the true, divine peace of the heart. <Obedience to the transpositive and the positive human law and obedience to the divine natural law> are related to each other like sign *(signum)*[282] to reality *(res ipsa)*.[283] Thus external legal life becomes the vessel *(calix)* of the spiritual[284] legal life and points to it.[285] This is *the third spiritual characteristic of human law* in God's kingdom at the left.[286]

All three characteristics show that the secular law also fulfills a spiritual task, and this in spite of its corporeal nature, through which it is turned away from God. Only a spiritual man is able to recognize this task, while it is hidden[287] from a natural man.[288] Nowhere did Luther describe the secret activity of the heavenly righteousness in the civic righteousness better than in his interpretation of the Decalogue in *The Large Catechism.*[289] He made two points. First: the spiritual understanding of love for God and love for the neighbor, that is, of the divine natural law, which he derived as hidden spiritual law from the First Commandment understood as an external natural-law norm;[290] second: the spiritual use of the secular natural law as that law is set forth in the remaining commandments, especially in those of the Second Table.[291] A spiritual man,[292] therefore, sees in the secular law also a "divine external order,"[293] and he uses the secular law according to these two qualities.[294] Luther could therefore summarize: "God himself is the creator, lord, master, promoter, and rewarder of both kinds of righteousness, the spiritual and the corporeal."[295]

This concludes our survey of the <substantive> secular natural law and of the positive law derived from it.

§ 2. The Institutional Secular Natural Law[296]

What happened in the kingdom of the world to the institutions of the divine positive law after the Fall?[297] Their history confirms the knowledge which Luther had gained from studying the divine natural law and the secular natural law. Those institutions experienced the same secularization and externalization[298] as did the divine natural law in its infralapsarian misinterpretation.[299]

This is true even for the *church*.[300] In fact, the church shows this secularization in the most horrifying form. The true church, which exists in accordance with God's Word and believes God's promise of the Redeemer, is confronted with the "church of the evildoers" (Psalm 26:5; Vulgate).[301] This is the devil's church,[302] in which is preached not only contempt for the divine natural law but also for the secular natural law, and in which people act accordingly.

This church of the devil was founded by Cain the fratricide. He founded a city for the sole purpose of gathering in it his descendants around himself[303] in a church of hypocrites.[304] Therefore the first political commonwealth was founded not for political reasons, for instance, the need of protection against earthly enemies,[305] but it was founded for a religious reason of horrifying magnitude, that is, the declaration of war on the God proclaimed by Adam. That God was totally to be excluded from this new state. "Good riddance of the father <Adam> and his church"[306] was the supreme governing principle of Cain's commonwealth. An absolutely worldly state was founded — the first in the history of mankind and, therefore, trendsetting for the kingdom of the world!

This state is centered in a 'world'-religion and a 'world'-church organized for the practice of this religion. Therefore the supreme power of the state and the supreme power of the church are united; the head of the 'world'-church is also the political ruler. This concentration of all spiritual and all secular[307] power in one person assures the unrestricted sovereignty of the hate for God. In such a state there is no public or private area in which the true worship of God is even tolerated, not to mention recognized as being valid. Disguised as church,[308] and with the rage of religious fanaticism,[309] the state persecutes the godly, condemns them as heretics, and murders them as enemies of the state.[310] Oppressed by this anti-godly state-church, the true church exists only as hidden[311] and oppressed church *(ecclesia latens et pressa)*. In the fire of *Anfechtung*[312] "the little church of the few souls"[313] often shrinks to one person.[314] Yet God again and again gathers a group of godly people for this little church, renews its worship,[315] and finally gives it a home among the Jewish people.

After a blessed beginning among the Jewish people, religion was secularized. No longer did the people understand the spiritual meaning of the divine commandment, but they embraced a legalistic piety, which focused on external works. Only few remembered that faith in the God-promised Redeemer was important, not works. No schism occurred in the church, but within the worshiping community tensions arose between those members of the church who thought in spiritual categories and those who thought in carnal categories. The two forms of the church, the spiritual and the corporeal one, were no longer in harmony.[316] The official church embraced a secularized concept of God and of righteousness, and the true church became "the hidden and dispersed church *(ecclesia abscondita et dispersa).*"[317] At times the true church disappeared so much from the public ecclesiastical life that even a prophet like Elijah lost sight of it. Now the fate of the true church became even worse than when it existed among the heathen. It was persecuted in order to serve God,[318] and the actions against the prophets were indicative of this situation.[319] Their spiritual interpretation of God's Word was understood as blasphemy[320] and instigation of revolt,[321] and it was punished accordingly. The official church and its ally, the state, attacked God's messengers[322] and annihilated them.

Summing up: after the Fall, the church in the world is thrown into a threefold battle; it is persecuted by those who have power in the *politia;* it is suppressed by the church of the hypocrites, which is organized as a counterchurch; it is harassed by the unbelievers within its own ranks.[323] All of this creates a sharp contrast between the church's corporeal form in the world of sin and the church's spiritual form of existing, which befits it as a community of Christ's kingdom. In the continuing battles with its opponents, the existence of the true church is not endangered, however, but strengthened. Therefore until the end of all times the church in the world remains a permanent institution[324] of the divine positive law.

The church in the world is the only institution of this nature. In the status of the incorrupt nature *marriage* also was a part of the divine positive law.[325] As a result of sin, marriage forfeited, however, its quality of a spiritual institution. Yet even now God does not abandon marriage,[326] but it becomes an "external, corporeal thing,"[327] and the estate of marriage becomes a "worldly affair"[328] and "worldly estate."[329]

In the aeon of the fallen world, marriage shares the fate of the divine natural law. Married life is corporeally interpreted. Thus marriage moves from the legal realm of God's spiritual kingdom into that of the kingdom of the world.[330] As a public estate, marriage becomes a part of the legal order of the kingdom of the world,[331] and the secular legislator[332] and judge have legal competency for marital matters. This applies also to the marriage of Christians.[333] Contrary to the legal interpretation by the medieval church, marriage is not a sacrament. Therefore there is no divine positive law for marital matters, and the church does not have jurisdiction over marriage.

In the kingdom of the world, marriage is significant in a unique way: it is the mother of all legal institutions on earth. The spiritual kingdom of God can exist without the institution of marriage,[334] of course, but not the kingdom of this world. A marriage blessed with children is the primeval commonwealth in the same way that the secular natural law is the primeval law of mankind, and between both exists close legal affinity. In the following, therefore, we differentiate between marriage according to the substantive secular natural law and marriage according to the institutional secular natural law.[335]

In Luther's discussion of the essential features of marriage according to these two kinds of law we find a surprising similarity. The first characteristic of marriage is the spiritual perversion, which also afflicts the substantive secular natural law. Because of its compulsory quality, the substantive secular natural law differs from the voluntary law of love in Christ's kingdom; similarly, after the Fall, in marriage the voluntary recognition of the male as "the more distinguished part of the human nature"[336] is replaced with the power claimed by the head of the family,[337] and the equality existing between the spouses changes into inequality — the *Hausregiment*[338] emerges. The substantive secular natural law is the ideal human law; similarly, marriage and family are the best possible forms of an earthly communion of love; in no other setting than in marriage is caring for one's neighbor stronger than human selfishness.[339] Finally, the substantive secular natural law as well as marriage,[340] and the secular governance derived from it,[341] are transpositive orders which support each other. Man did not invent them, but God gave them to man beforehand. They not only exist as God-created orders but they also are to be used by man as God-created orders.[342]

In its essence, marriage is, therefore, beyond man's legal manipulations.[343] Luther emphasized this by calling marriage "something naturally necessary,"[344] "a divine work,"[345] "a divine and blessed estate,"[346] "a divine and natural order,"[347] "a work ... planted by God ⟨in man⟩."[348] As a safeguard of public and private morality,[349] marriage deserves the highest respect,[350] and it is removed from man's "arbitrariness."[351] These thoughts explain Luther's position on the impediments of marriage[352] and on celibacy,[353] among other topics.

The *transpositive law for marriage* prohibits man from creating rules to allow or prohibit marriages. For Luther the impediments of marriage[354] were established by God himself, and he condemned the man-made prohibitions of marriage as being anti-godly.[355] Nowhere did Luther follow Canon law terminology as strictly as in these statements. Yet they easily fitted in his new understanding of law and confirmed it. Just as Moses, commanded by God, wrote down the substantive secular natural law in the Decalogue,[356] so upon God's instruction he also wrote down all the impediments of marriage;[357] in this way he authentically explained the corporeal nature of marriage. For Luther these sections of the Mosaic legislation were definitely a part of the transpositive marital law.

We see the same incorporation of traditional legal thinking in a new legal system when Luther dealt with monogamy[358] and the indissolubility of the marital union.[359] The Creator bestowed both qualities upon marriage, and the secular legislator has to act accordingly. Luther never doubted this, just as his theological opponents never did. Yet this does not eliminate a question. Moses is respected as the model legislator; in his marital law he allowed polygamy,[360] and he saw a possibility for divorce;[361] if he did this with God's permission,[362] may one then consider monogamy and the indissolubility of the marital union parts of the transpositive marital law?

Medieval theologians solved this problem by differentiating between two classes of natural-law prescriptions for marriage.[363] The first class ('primary commandments') is the result of the essence of marriage itself, is universally binding, and there are no exceptions. The second class ('secondary commandments') is derived from the first, yet not as a stringent conclusion but only as a rule which is most appropriate for the purpose of marriage. Therefore this rule may not claim universal validity. Rather, on the basis of a legal exemption this rule may be ignored or broken. In general, the commandment of monogamy and the indissolubility of the marital union were considered to be parts of this second-class natural law and, therefore, to be open for dispensation.

This is as far as Luther followed the Scholastics. He moved far away from them when he discussed the competency for granting such a dispensation. The Scholastics assigned this competency to God exclusively,[364] and they understood such a dispensation as a change in the second-class secular natural law enacted in the divine positive law. Luther saw the legal situation quite differently. He also regarded monogamy and the indissolubility of marriage, the qualities of marriage we are discussing here, to be matters of the second-class institutional secular natural law. Therefore polygamy[365] and the possibility of divorce among the Jews,[366] as described in the Old Testament and practiced also among heathen, cannot be a part of a model for a well-organized commonwealth. The precedents described in the Bible only demonstrate that dispensations can be made in matters of the institutional secular natural law. The commandment of equity is a part of the Decalogue's substantive secular natural law and permits a dispensation in case of need. This applies also to marital law, and secular authorities have the competency to grant such a dispensation.[367] Their decisions will deal with borderline cases; therefore they will make use of the pastoral counsel given by theologians. The juristic starting point for a brief issued in such a case by theologians shows how necessary this counsel is.

As is known, Canon law differentiated between a true and legitimate marriage and a legitimate but not true marriage.[368] The first is a marriage of believers, the second a marriage of unbelievers. Luther also started with this differentiation. But contrary to Canon law, for him the decision who was a believer or unbeliever depended not on the membership in the community of the baptized but on the membership in the community of believers; decisive for him was not the membership in the universal church but in the spiritual church.[369] This position agreed with his doctrine of the kingdoms and of the church. If one adds the already mentioned lack of the sacramental quality of marriage,[370] then the outline of a Christian marital law is totally changed in comparison with that in Canon law. This will have to be discussed in greater detail later on.[371] Now we will deal only with those questions which are connected with a dispensation from the secular natural law concerning the estate of marriage.

A theological brief on marital matters has to start with the difference between Christians and non-Christians ⟨just mentioned⟩. Therefore its authors have to be extremely restrained regarding the non-Christians.[372] They do not belong to the church, even if as baptized people they cannot be separated externally from the church. Only to the extent that the legal situation of these non-Christians is based on the secular natural law is the magisterial office of the church authorized to speak.[373] Otherwise this office must leave decisions in matters of the marital law for non-Christians to the discretion of a governmental authority. Occasionally Luther did go further and recommended that for non-Christians the Jewish divorce law be incorporated in the marital law of the *politia*.[374] This recommendation was, however, not a statement of the magisterial office of the church but Luther's personal opinion. The situation was different in the case of a theological brief for dealing with Christian marriages.[375]

Let us first consider *divorce*. Since God instituted marriage, it is no "additional, pert, human property, which one does not need or without which one could ⟨easily⟩ get along."[376] Beyond the limits set by the secular natural law outlined in Holy Scripture, earthly legal authorities may neither permit nor prohibit a marriage. This is true also for divorce. There is no substantive law for divorce.[377] Regarding divorce, Christians have to follow Christ's and St. Paul's interpretation of Holy Scripture (Matthew 19:8f., 1 Corinthians 7:9ff.).

In the New Testament we find three reasons for divorce: Adultery,[378] which Luther most severely condemned as "the greatest robbery and theft";[379] malevolent desertion;[380] the *privilegium Paulinum*,[381] that is, the divorce of a Christian married to a non-Christian if the latter intends to force the former into a godless life. This list is complete as far as the standard for the moral and religious weight of the transgression is concerned, and this standard may under no circumstances be weakened. But it is not prohibited to extend this list by analogy to other, equally weighty offenses against a marriage.[382] Luther had to accept this, although since his early days he had been an outspoken opponent of divorce.³⁸³ In case of such an offense, a Christian may not be denied a divorce. Of course, a true Christian, that is, a member of the spiritual church who is thoroughly grounded in the faith, would forgive even the most severe transgression of a spouse.³⁸⁴ God does, however, not expect a weak Christian to continue living in a shattered marriage and forego a second marriage.

To these concrete conditions for granting a divorce have to be added legal proceedings created by a governmental authority,³⁸⁵ since marriage is "organized by secular governmental authority";³⁸⁶ therefore neither partner is at liberty to deal with marriage as he or she wishes. In this context it is necessary for governmental authorities to initiate preventive measures against frivolous divorces; for instance, enforcing a waiting period before a second marriage can take place³⁸⁷ should make spouses think twice before running away.

Polygamy was a considerably more difficult exegetical problem for Luther than divorce. In the New Testament he did not find a statement by Christ or the Apostles against it. The patriarchs of the Old Covenant practiced polygamy, and yet they were God's and Christ's priests and prophets.³⁸⁸ Their conduct cannot be explained with sexual licentiousness.³⁸⁹ Rather, there was something "behind" their conduct,³⁹⁰ namely, a spiritual meaning; at least this is true in the case of Abraham;³⁹¹ he was a "true, even perfect Christian and lived the most evangelical life in God's Spirit and in faith."³⁹² According to the Apostle Paul,³⁹³ one has to see in the stories of Abraham and of the other patriarchs a God-willed "metaphor" *(figura)*³⁹⁴ of a future event in Christ's kingdom.³⁹⁵ Therefore these forefathers were not reprimanded in the New Testament, and their polygamy was not identical with living in a sinful estate;³⁹⁶ this has to be carefully considered. Yet on the other hand, among Christians polygamy could not have the meaning of a metaphor. In addition, the substantive secular natural law, which Christians are to obey in an exemplary way, opposes polygamy. More important, in the New Testament there is no "specific Word of God"³⁹⁷ which would permit one to imitate the example of the patriarchs. There only remains, then, to follow the institutional secular natural law and to implement it strictly in the positive law as prohibition of polygamy. There is one proviso, however: a legislator is not prevented from granting a dispensation in the case of extreme need, such as a married woman getting leprosy,³⁹⁸ or certainly when the wife consents that the husband takes a second wife, as in the example of Sarah.³⁹⁹

Human Law in the Status of the Corrupt Nature

Luther had presented this line of thinking[400] in the 1520s,[401] and already then he caused a great sensation. And in 1531, in connection with the divorce of Henry VIII, he stated that he would rather approve bigamy than divorce.[402] Then, in 1539, he again faced the same problem as a practical case, now dangerously intensified. This was the question: may a Christian, motivated by pangs of conscience, on his own authority transgress the prohibition of bigamy, decreed in the Imperial law, and yet not commit an injustice? Landgrave Philip of Hesse asked the question. The answer was the often-quoted confessional dispensation[403] granted to him by the reformers, because he had claimed to be in a situation of spiritual need. ‹For the reformers› the issue was the power of Confession[404] — not the secular ‹Imperial› marital law, to which the dispensation granted as a confessional counsel did not extend; therefore one may ignore the case at this point. Luther, by the way, learned his lesson from the sad experiences which he had at that time because of his pastoral leniency.[405] When in the section of his lectures on Genesis which has to be dated after 1540[406] he dealt with the bigamy of Jacob, he emphatically warned his audience not to follow the example of the patriarch,[407] and he mentioned not one word about the possibility of a dispensation.

Let us now turn to the *role of marriage in the area of public law;* in this connection we understand marriage as a legal relationship set up in the institutional secular natural law. The domestic governance of a father is the first legally organized power relationship[408] on earth. Here originates the total order of offices and estates in the *politia;*[409] therefore marriage becomes the source of the *oeconomia* and *politia*.[410] The civic order in a state, even more, the civic order among mankind, is derived from this source.[411] Therefore Luther's concept 'marriage' became the nucleus of his concept 'state', with marriage being understood as an infralapsarian institution to be managed according to the secular natural law.[412] For only since the Fall is there power over life and death on earth,[413] only since then is there governmental authority.[414] Because this authority has the competency of punishing, its symbol of office[415] is the sword.[416] As mentioned above,[417] its task is to preserve peace in the kingdom of the world; it is to protect the good and punish the evil.[418]

The office of governmental authority is governed by the earthly common good, as are the secular natural law and the positive human law. The spiritual verdict about them is identical. If one compares the office of governmental authority with the pastoral office,[419] then one has to affirm that before God "governmental authority is not very important."[420] Because a governmental authority does not assist anyone in reaching Salvation, "there is no way that its importance could be compared with that of the spiritual office of preaching."[421] When viewed from God, princes have the lowest rank in the hierarchy of offices.[422] The secular kingdom deals with "evildoers and crooks," and by necessity even the best of princes is a "host of crooks"[423] and "God's hangman and warden."[424] There is nothing for a prince to rule in Christ's kingdom, and woe unto him when he transgresses this limitation of his competency![425]

Nevertheless, the office of princes, though it is to function in the kingdom of Satan,[426] also serves in God's kingdom at the left. And this service is the second highest and most useful service[427] after that of preaching.[428] No doubt, peace[429] and security, and the orderly handling of the law[430] are precious works of divine mercy and goodness.[431] Secular governance is the "cornerstone, rock, and foundation"[432] of a people and country; it turns wild animals into human beings and prevents them from again becoming wild animals.[433] Through this, governmental authority demonstrates that it is "a necessary office and estate."[434] It is an institution which emerged from marriage and which was founded by God himself.[435] Governmental authority is one of the three basic, visible estates of the human communal life, ranking between the domestic and the ecclesiastical governance.[436]

Therefore *God is present also in the secular governance.* By his commission,[437] governmental authority is in the first place the executor of the divine punishment in the kingdom of the divine wrath *(vindex Dei in iram)*;[438] secondly, it is the tool of God's merciful love;[439] and thirdly, it is the mask *(larva)*,[440] viceroy,[441] and officer[442] of the divine governance over the world in God's kingdom at the left. This threefold connection with God makes governmental authority "God's own work, order, and creature,"[443] a "useful and glorious divine order."[444] And the secular estates are "divine estates"[445] provided they stay within their boundaries drawn by the institutional secular natural law. The commands of a governmental authority claim the obedience of all people,[446] not only because they are backed by external power but also especially because of their spiritual meaning, which <only> a Christian recognizes;[447] their connection with God's holy will for law[448] makes these commands holy.[449] Viewed from the institutional secular natural law, the law enacted by a governmental authority is "a shadow and sign of the hidden righteousness."[450] In a way unknown to his contemporaries, Luther religiously glorified the claim of validity inherent in such a law and, therefore, the legal power,[451] the authority,[452] and the honor[453] of secular governance.[454] Conversely, because of its high moral and religious significance, the office of governmental authority demands from its holder a strong awareness of the responsibility for the common good.

In order to generate this awareness, Luther drafted a kind of *Fürstenspiegel*.[455] ⟨He justified his efforts by arguing that⟩ it is the task of a preacher[456] "to inform and instruct all estates how to conduct themselves in their offices and estates so that they act correctly before God," because "temporal peace, the highest good on earth which contains all other temporal goods, is actually a fruit of the preaching office."[457] According to this instruction, the head of the *politia* has to implement the duties of his vocation *(Beruf)* conscientiously, without self-interest, "carefully,"[458] for the best of his subjects,[459] with justice[460] and equity[461] for all, with appropriate severity[462] toward transgressors, with mercy[463] toward the weak,[464] and with mercy toward the remorseful as far as the common good allows. Only then will "the actions of a governmental authority be carried out in love"[465] (that is, they will agree with the secular natural law) and have durability.[466] Because of this God-created design, every worldly commonwealth is "a community of God"[467] in spite of its worldliness, and no one may undermine the natural-law basis of this community.

A subject does not have the right to disobey secular governance when the office of governmental authority is being misused;[468] "misuse does not destroy[469] the office."[470] Therefore rebellion is the supreme crime in the *politia*.[471] Rebellion jeopardizes the existence of a commonwealth because it attacks the head[472] of the commonwealth; it threatens not specific laws and institutions, but it turns against the secular natural law itself.[473] That is, rebellion turns against God, who instituted governmental authority.[474] The result is the intermingling of the two kingdoms. Therefore everyone, regardless of his occupation[475] and without being called upon,[476] has to fight against rebellion, even at the risk of his life.[477] One should rather let oneself be killed than let oneself be forced to join in a rebellion.[478]

With this argumentation a governmental authority is not granted a license for misusing its office — it will not escape its punishment. God has reserved for himself the authority to punish a governmental authority;[479] he wants to be its judge and master;[480] he pushes the mighty from their thrones and tears them up by their roots, destroying their names and their memory.[481] Therefore subjects are prohibited to ignore the commands of a governmental authority whenever these commands are not legitimate.[482] Yet the obedience of subjects is limited by the natural law.[483] Luther dealt with the details of this issue in connection with a Christian's right of resisting the government. We shall return to it below.[484]

CHAPTER 10

Written Law

———⊙———

Now we have to deal with that period in the history of mankind which began with the Sinai legislation. Then started a new epoch in the age of the corrupt nature. Until then there had not been a written secular natural law authorized by God. People lived in the age of unwritten law.

During this age, man's originally excellent disposition deteriorated more and more. The apostasy from God caused the rapid decay of man's corporeal and spiritual powers, and with it also of his moral self-discipline. Not only did the divine natural law vanish in impenetrable darkness but also the secular natural law became shrouded in mist.[1]

God intervened. In a new legislative act[2] the divine natural law was renewed, that is, it was again proclaimed, <now> to the chosen people. The result was the Decalogue,[3] with which the age of written law began.

The Decalogue repeated the divine natural law in the form of positive law. That law was divided in individual norms, and it was enclosed in the great codification of Moses, of which the Ten Commandments was the nucleus.[4] Is this situation consistent with the essence of the divine law as presented above?[5] Apparently there are considerable tensions at this point. They forced Luther to differentiate between *three characteristics of the Decalogue*.

First: the Decalogue is a part of the Jewish national law, something like the *Sachsenspiegel* of the Jews.[6] Therefore the Decalogue is of no concern to other nations.[7] It was promulgated by Moses as the ruler of the Jewish people.[8] Moses acted, of course, in obedience to a divine command,[9] yet the claim of the formal validity of the Sinai legislation was based on the governmental office of Moses. For this reason, the Decalogue, which is a part of this legislation, also is positive human law. In terms of the ethical value, however, Moses' codification is not simply a parallel to the law of other nations.[10] As a secular law, Moses' law has superior features. Therefore in earlier years Luther recommended that certain legal materials of Moses' code be included in the local law.[11] After his clash with the enthusiasts, and motivated by the concern for the orderly conduct of local legal matters, he advised against such an inclusion.[12] He was especially worried that such a partial reception might promote the superstition that the Sinai legislation was the divine paradigm for the constitution of a *politia* and, therefore, would obligate Christians to imitating it.[13]

Nevertheless, the Decalogue is binding for all mankind, not as positive law but only insofar that transpositive law is expressed in it. This brings us to the *second characteristic of the Ten Commandments:* they communicate the secular natural law[14] to us[15] — Moses merely translated and explained it.[16]

This becomes clear when we look at the genesis of Moses' law. That genesis lacks the directness of a divine promulgation, which is characteristic of the spiritual law.[17] No sinful man, and therefore also not Moses, is capable of standing face to face with God.[18] Therefore the divine will for law was proclaimed to the Jewish people by two mediators; first by the angels[19] to Moses, and then by Moses to the assembly of the people. This interposition of two mediators weakened the force *(vis)*[20] of the law in such a way that man could endure the law. Yet as a sinful man, Moses received and passed on the divine Word in the spirit of fear and not of freedom.[21] As a result, that Word lacked the life-giving force of mercy *(vis)*,[22] which is inherent in the divine Word and makes the divine natural law easy <to obey>. Therefore the old law[23] was heavy, oppressive, and incapable of creating delight in the law in man's heart;[24] it also lacked the clarity[25] which is appropriate for the spiritual law. In the Ten Commandments the divine legislator spoke through a mask.[26] The inner power[27] of the spiritual law[28] did not become effective in the commandments, only the power of the human[29] secular natural law.[30] In other words: in Moses' work[31] God's Word was changed into the words of man;[32] the divine <natural> law became a transpositive human law.[33]

Only a spiritual man would be able to discover in this transpositive law God's hidden will for Salvation, God's veiled Word,[34] as that will functions in the plan and enactment of Salvation;[35] only a spiritual man would be able to value the Decalogue as hidden spiritual law *(lex spiritualis latens),*[36] and only he could use law theologically.[37] This is the *third characteristic of the Decalogue.*

All other people do not know how to deal with law correctly.[38] They are divided in two groups. Directed by priests,[39] the large crowd of people[40] equates the external law of Moses[41] with God's internal law.[42] They believe, therefore, that God recognizes the human secular natural law as the standard of the heavenly righteousness.[43] As a result, righteousness based on the law and on works[44] now dominates more than before, ⟨and⟩ people intend to earn the spiritual righteousness before God by means of the strictest obedience to the Ten Commandments.[45] By supporting this effort with God's explicit command,[46] man creates a false spiritual security; that security is more dangerous[47] than was man's reliance on his natural morality in the age of the unwritten law.[48] Through this perverted thinking, the law of Moses educates only hypocrites.[49] On the other hand, those[50] who have a notion of the seriousness of the divine will for law expressed in the Decalogue are pushed into despair and hate for God; they are unable to believe that God might have the will to save such reprehensible creatures as sinners are.[51]

In summary: In spite of the promulgation of the Ten Commandments, the infralapsarian misinterpretation[52] of the divine natural law was not eliminated.[53] As a result, the divine natural law as law of love *(lex charitatis)* continued to be hidden from the world — if one disregards the few who believed in the promise of the future Redeemer — and it continued to function as law of wrath.[54] Through the repetition of the divine natural law, the sovereignty of the law of wrath did not lose any of its horror[55] — to the contrary, the misuse of the Decalogue increased this horror. "The stone tables, ⟨that is, the hard hearts of the people of the law,⟩[56] only serve[57] written letters,[58] but they do nothing ⟨for Salvation⟩."[59]

CHAPTER 11

The Law of Christ

———◆———

The misuse of the written law[1] caused God to repeal "his own law, which he had sent down from heaven."[2] To accomplish this, God sent his Son into the world. Christ restored[3] the true meaning to the divine natural law and thus its true goal.[4] He is the light of the world.[5] God's Son had the immediacy of the nearness to God which Moses, the mediator of the law, did not have. Therefore the interpretation of the divine natural law by Christ,[6] "the spiritual teacher of the whole world,"[7] that is, "the teacher of divine righteousness,"[8] is authentic.[9]

Yet mankind would not be helped at all through a mere interpretation of the divine natural law. Natural man[10] may be confronted with the unadulterated meaning of the divine natural law, but that meaning will not enter[11] his heart.[12] Christ's interpretation is spiritual, as it is appropriate for the spiritual law,[13] with which this interpretation deals. Natural man, however, does not have the capability, that is, the spiritual faculty of understanding[14] and the spiritual disposition of the mind, for receiving this spiritual law. He would interpret Christ's word in the same secular way[15] as he had interpreted the divine natural law, that is, in the sense of the secular natural law and its idea of what man is.[16] Luther believed that he found significant proof for this situation in the philosophy and theology of his day. In one word: natural man does not listen to God.[17]

Because of this spiritual incapability,[18] the main task of Christ, his proper work *(opus proprium)*,[19] was not the interpretation of the divine natural law but the rebirth of man *(regeneratio hominis)*,[20] the creation of man as a new creature, the restitution of the image of God.²¹ Only when this is accomplished will the divine natural law again receive its authority *(potestas)*.²²

Christ's third task, most closely connected with the first two,²³ was the establishment of the spiritual church,²⁴ and together with it at the same time²⁵ the establishment of the corporeal existence of the church.²⁶ In this spiritual church the Holy Spirit continues the Lord's work of Salvation in the period between the Ascension of the resurrected Christ and his return.²⁷ In this way the Holy Spirit secures the knowledge of the divine law, because outside of the church there is no true knowledge of God and his will for law,²⁸ and, therefore, no Salvation.²⁹

The communal life³⁰ of the spiritual church is the worship of God. For this communal life Christ mandated the proclamation of the Word and instituted two sacraments: Baptism, the sacrament of the Christian estate,³¹ and the Lord's Supper, the sacrament of the unity of the church, in which Christ unites himself with the members of his mystical body.³² To this spiritual church Christ gave the Power of the Keys.³³ Further, for the preaching of the Word and the administration of the sacraments he established in this church the public ministry *(ministerium publicum)*³⁴ of the Word,³⁵ the *only office* of the divine positive law set up on earth.³⁶

This entire constitution was the result of a legislative act³⁷ by Christ. It is the only time that Christ acted as legislator,³⁸ and the result was the divine positive law of the spiritual church *(ius divinum positivum*³⁹ *ecclesiae spiritualis)*.⁴⁰ The spiritual church does not have any other law, and this law is not connected with any other church than this spiritual church. Yet wherever this divine positive law is implemented as commanded by Christ, there exists the spiritual church, no doubt, for God's Word does not return empty to God ⟨Isaiah 55:11⟩.⁴¹

This divine ecclesiastical law of the New Testament has the same spiritual quality⁴² as the divine positive law of the Original Status.⁴³ The divine ecclesiastical law of the New Testament can be recognized externally, but — comparable with the divine natural law of love — it creates spiritual life only when it is spiritually used, that is, when it is used in faith;⁴⁴ on the other hand — in analogy to the divine natural law as law of wrath and death — it brings judgment to the unbeliever.⁴⁵

After this insertion let us return to *Christ's main task*.⁴⁶ Luther described it as a "changing *(transmutatio)* of the old man, a son of the devil, into the new man, a son of God."⁴⁷ In the frame of the present disquisition in jurisprudence we cannot deal with the details of this rebirth. It takes place through the preaching of law and gospel in the justification of the sinner by faith alone. Only *the legal results of this rebirth* are important for us.

In faith, justified man is united with Christ,[48] and, as a member of Christ's mystical body,[49] he participates in Christ's righteousness.[50] Faith and only faith is essential.[51] "Faith is the mother *(creatrix)* of the divine quality *(divinitas)* not in God's being *(substantia)* but in us."[52] Faith is the only way[53] to God,[54] but it is also the straight[55] and short[56] way. That way demands nothing[57] but the turning of the will to God, which is brought about by the Holy Spirit.[58]

This renewal of the mind fundamentally changes man's spiritual legal status;[59] man[60] is saved from the servitude to Satan in the kingdom of the world and placed in the kingdom of grace, that is, the kingdom of Christ.[61] *Man changes his citizenship. He receives a new personal status, which Luther called the Christian estate.* This development led the reformer to two most important questions. First: which law is valid for the Christian estate? Second: how is this law implemented in the Christian estate? The first question deals with the status, the second deals with the life of a Christian.[62] Status and life are inseparable; therefore Luther sometimes called both of them with one word, *Christentum*.[63]

Let us first deal with the law of the Christian estate. At once we are struck by the sharp contrast which exists between the previous estate-law of the sinner and the estate-law of the Christian. For the sinner the law of wrath and death is the law of citizenship and estate, and that law marks him as spiritually dead.[64] This sovereignty of law with its horrible spiritual curse and coercion has now come to an end, because in Christ's kingdom reigns the freedom of God's children.[65] The sovereignty of the law is succinctly expressed in the Decalogue. Therefore, as mentioned above,[66] Luther was able to say that Christ abolished the law of Moses — not only the ceremonial and judicial laws, as the Scholastics assumed,[67] but also the moral law, the Ten Commandments,[68] for it is written: "The law is not placed upon the righteous one."[69]

This sentence forces us, however, to understand the statement about the abolishing of the Decalogue in a restrictive sense *(relative)*.[70] Only the sovereignty of the law is abolished. For the Christian the legal relevance of the law as such is not abolished. Only with great reservations[71] may a Christian be called righteous *(iustus)*. Throughout his whole life[72] he is afflicted with Original Sin as with a sickness,[73] and this in spite of his Baptism.⁷⁴ Sin has lost its power only over the justified, and this also caused the downfall of sin's spiritual antitype, the sovereignty of the law.⁷⁵ But the battle between Christ and Satan about man and in man will never end; during his pilgrimage on earth,⁷⁶ therefore, a Christian will never escape the battle with Original Sin.⁷⁷ Only through prayer, through the prayerful confession of his spiritual corruption,⁷⁸ does he even have a chance of surviving in this battle. Yet while on earth, he can never reach⁷⁹ perfection.⁸⁰ The tension in a Christian between his spiritual status and his sinful condition will never end in this world. His whole life, therefore, has to be a life of ongoing repentance,⁸¹ and the spiritually understood Decalogue⁸² is the *Bußspiegel*⁸³ for recognizing sin <and therefore the guide for such a life of repentance>. Even in the status of rebirth the law of Moses retains its validity as the accuser of the sinner.⁸⁴ That law, however, lacks the power to execute the justified with the punishment of spiritual death⁸⁵ because Christ has taken the guilt and punishment upon himself and atoned for them.⁸⁶

The old law, sovereign lord in the kingdom of wrath, is replaced by the new law *(lex nova)*, the *law of Christ (lex Christi)*.⁸⁷ How does one have to understand this term? A comparison with the divine natural law shows that the content of Christ's law and that of the divine natural law is identical.⁸⁸ In a strict sense, Christ's law is not law at all.⁸⁹ It is the divine proclamation⁹⁰ of the divine meaning of the divine natural law; that meaning was hidden in the Decalogue,⁹¹ and now it is again brought out into the open.

For this reason Christ's law is called new law. This title is appropriate also for another reason. Insofar as the recipient of this new law is concerned, this law is spoken in a legal situation which is new when compared with that in the Original Status. As mentioned above,⁹² already the form of the Christian command of love demonstrates the fundamental change in the personal presuppositions for the implementation of this law, which had occurred in the meantime: only a righteous <spiritual> man *(homo iustus)* can fulfill a spiritual law.⁹³ This is the opposite of the situation in secular laws; here a man is called righteous if he obeys the law. A spiritual law, however, can be obeyed only by a righteous <spiritual> man. This was the case with the recipient of the divine natural law in the Original Status. He possessed the original righteousness *(iustitia originalis)*; the justified sinner, however, does not.⁹⁴ By his own strength man is unable to acquire a new righteousness before

God;[95] if he looks at himself, he does not find anything spiritual in himself; only in the communion with Christ is he holy *(sanctus)*.[96] Therefore he is described as being simultaneously sinner *and* righteous *(simul peccator et iustus)*.[97] His righteousness is righteousness originating outside of man, foreign righteousness *(iustitia extra nos, iustitia aliena)*,[98] or passive righteousness *(iustitia passiva)*,[99] that is, it is Christ's righteousness.[100] Because this foreign righteousness is given only to the believer, it is righteousness of faith *(iustitia fidei)*. "By divine action righteousness is created from faith in the heart and God's imputation."[101] In fulfilling the law, faith is, therefore, the *causa efficiens*,[102] and, following the Apostle Paul,[103] Luther also used the term 'law of faith' *(lex fidei)* for Christ's law.

In the development of this personalistic aspect[104] *of the divine natural law as law of faith Luther's doctrine of law culminates,* just as justification by faith alone is the central dogma of his theology. Compared with the Middle Ages, the emphasis in the theological view of the divine natural law is shifted from the material to the personalistic aspect, from doing to believing.[105]

In the comprehensive concept 'divine natural law', understood as law of love *(lex charitatis)* with its two commandments, love God, love the neighbor, Luther differentiated between the law of faith and the law of love in the narrow sense; now the law of faith is identical with the commandment to love God, the law of love is identical with the commandment to love the neighbor. Then Luther contrasted this law of love in the narrow sense to the law of faith. On the basis of this contrast he argued that the law of faith takes priority over the law of love; the law of faith may not be compromised by the law of love[106] because "faith is the actor, love is the action."[107]

<Now we can understand why> the scholarly interest of Lutheran theologians focuses primarily on the law of faith — <it is *the* theme of their work>. Consequently, the connection between the law of faith and the divine natural law as *lex charitatis* comprehensively understood is neglected[108] <so that> finally this connection is no longer mentioned in theology; in fact, theologians are no longer even aware of it. The result is the problem which confronted us again and again at the beginning of this disquisition: one no longer knows how to incorporate the divine natural law into the totality of the reformer's theology, and the law of faith no longer provides a theological and legal access to the divine natural law.

The Law of Christ

Luther himself, apparently, may not be held responsible for this situation[109] — he took this connection ‹between the law of faith and the divine natural law› for granted. For him only two statements are made about the same subject when one calls the divine natural law in Christ's interpretation law of love (in the comprehensive sense) *or* law of faith. That one can make both statements is the result of different viewpoints, namely, whether one focuses on the Original Status or the status[110] of the Christian.[111] In the reformer's opinion both statements agree in content. Therefore, following the Apostle Paul (Romans 13:10), he could say that "love is the fulfilling of the law," and he could also say that "faith fulfills the law."[112] In both cases we have the same law; as Christ's law it is proclaimed to the fallen world[113] and is effective only for a believing Christian.

In summary: As in the kingdom of the world the law of wrath is the law of citizenship and estate of Satan's servants, so in the kingdom of grace the law of love *(lex charitatis)* is the law of citizenship and estate of God's children; for Christians that law of love is normatively interpreted as law of Christ, that is, as law of faith when Christ's law is understood as the law of the Christian estate.

Having surveyed the law of the Christian estate,[114] *we now have to deal with its implementation in the existence of a Christian.*

As soon as through faith in Christ[115] the turning of the will toward God is given to man, he is again listening to God,[116] and, therefore, in his reason the light of grace flares up.[117] When he views the Incarnation and the suffering of Christ,[118] he understands[119] the spiritual meaning of Christ's law[120] with its two absolutely positive[121] demands: first, the commandment to love God perfectly, a love which is greater than all things,[122] even man's greatest treasure, his love for himself;[123] second, the commandment to love the neighbor perfectly,[124] a love in which man's love for self[125] is totally changed[126] into the denial of self[127] and into selflessness. With this understanding of the divine law the Christian has a big advantage, even over Moses. Therefore Luther exclaimed triumphantly: ". . . having Christ, it will be easy for us to create laws and judge all matters correctly. In fact, we shall make new decalogues, . . . and these decalogues will be brighter than Moses' Decalogue, just as Christ's countenance is brighter than that of Moses."[128]

The more fervent a man's faith becomes, the more divine and all encompassing[129] the Christian commandment of love[130] becomes for him. Therefore, depending on the strength of faith,[131] there are degrees of perfection[132] in the perceiving and fulfilling of Christ's law,[133] or in other words, man grows toward the fullness of Christ.[134] The commandment of Christian love of the neighbor[135] may serve as an example. The lowest degree of perceiving and fulfilling this commandment is the literal implementation of the spiritually understood Golden Rule.[136] It obligates a believer to helping[137] a neighbor in need[138] by using all personal means. Such help is to be given not only for the sake of the corporeal well-being of the neighbor but also, and especially, for the sake of his soul's Salvation.[139] Luther called the highest degree "Christian law."[140] Its essence is, in accordance with Christ's example, the willing acceptance of the injustice inflicted on me by others, and this essence is most perfectly embodied in the love of my enemy.[141] This Christian law of the cross bearer is the estate privilege of a Christian.[142] By using it, a Christian becomes Christ for his fellowman.[143] Such a level of attitude is rarely reached, however. "A Christian is a rare bird,"[144] for an externally ideal conduct does not suffice ⟨for implementing this estate privilege⟩; whatever one does has to come from the heart,[145] and it has to be done joyfully and voluntarily.

The Christ-formed will,[146] therefore, is crucial for the fulfilling of the commandment of Christian love. Without it, even the best deed is vanity[147] in God's eyes, fruit of sin,[148] and has no value before God.[149] Through good works a Christian is not able to gain God's approval, or even contribute anything to gaining it. This insight is humiliating, but at the same time it liberates man from the pressure to which the soul is exposed by the perception of the spiritual insufficiency of all human efforts. This was for Luther the *evangelical freedom of conscience.*[150]

Yet to deny the significance of good works would be totally wrong, for faith without works is dead.[151] Works are faith incarnate, so to speak.[152] Faith, therefore, is the "chief work,"[153] "the working master and captain in all works."[154] As a good tree has to bear and does bear good fruit, so faith has to bear good fruit. Good works demonstrate the vitality of faith. In good works, man, God's coworker,[155] cooperates with the Creator as the Creator's tool. Therefore the doctrine of good works has to avoid two errors[156] — a difficult task indeed:[157] it has to eliminate the confidence that good works earn merit before God,[158] and at the time it has to fight vigorously quietism which shies away from action.[159]

Thus far we have described the life of a Christian as it should be conducted in believing obedience to Christ's law. But man is at the same time a sinful *and* a righteous person. Therefore we have to concentrate now on this first quality of his being.[160]

The power of evil, existing in man's flesh and never resting, is constantly rebelling against the Creator. A non-Christian is simply caught in the web of that power because no one is able to resist it in his own strength. A Christian, on the other hand, fights this power with the weapon of prayer,[161] with which he implores God for help. In this way a Christian exists in an ongoing battle with himself.[162] Yet this active resistance of the devil in man's heart is, however, a willing enduring *(passio)* of the Holy Spirit's action against the old man by means of the law of wrath. A Christian places himself in the service of the law of wrath against his evil self; he does this because he knows that the dying of the old man is simultaneously the becoming healthy of the new man, a process effected by Christ.[163] When this working of a Christian against his old self consists of corporeal self-discipline Luther called it "ruling the body."[164]

Now the picture presented in Luther's statements about man's twofold qualities, righteous and sinful, is complete. For the interpreters of the reformer's thought these statements created considerable difficulties,[165] ⟨and this for the following reason:⟩ At one time Luther called justified man totally righteous and totally sinner *(totus iustus et totus peccator)*, yet at another time he called justified man partially righteous and partially sinner *(partim iustus, partim peccator)*.[166] The contradiction in these two statements, which seem to be irreconcilable, is eliminated if one considers our twofold view of a Christian, the one according to his estate, the other according to his life.[167] The first statement deals with a Christian according to his status in the kingdom of Christ; it describes his connection with Original Sin *(peccatum originale)* and with Redemption. The second statement deals with a Christian according to his life; it presents him in his battle of Sanctification, that is, in his spiritual battle to resist the temptation to sin *(peccatum actuale)*.

In this battle a Christian easily and frequently experiences defeat because Satan succeeds in bringing about a victory of the flesh over the spirit. To accomplish this, Satan chooses two points of attack. The first is man's will; through its innate egotism it is to be lured away from God. The second is man's intellect; its judgment about good and evil is confused through devilish trickery so that the misled will can be totally confounded. If in one or the other case a Christian "consents to sin,"[168] he at once loses his citizenship in the kingdom of Christ. He again becomes a serf in the kingdom of the world, and the sovereignty of the law of wrath with its consequences of spiritual and corporeal punishments is activated.

Even if God keeps a Christian from apostasy, because in faith a Christian resists temptation, a Christian's situation remains most deplorable. All his efforts to obey God are opposed by his sinful disposition; it restricts his power of will and intellect in such a way that he never reaches the goal which God has set up for the spiritual man. A Christian always carries within himself the awareness of the tension between what he should be and what he is,[169] and this awareness is like a wound which will heal only in the world to come. In his relationship with God, man's shortcomings in meeting the demands of the divine will for law are charged to him as guilt *(reatus)*. <When> he, with a repenting heart, confesses the severity of that guilt to God, <he> testifies that he does not consent to <his> sin; <therefore,> for Christ's sake, he is not held accountable for that guilt, <and> he does not lose his citizenship in God's kingdom <at the right>.[170]

These observations enable us to deal with the erring conscience, a topic frequently discussed in medieval theology.[171] For Luther this topic[172] became a simple problem. Each error in perceiving the divine will for law, whether it is an *error vincibilis* or *invincibilis*,[173] originates in the spiritual perversion of human nature and, therefore, is sin. The only question is whether God charges this sin to the sinner. It is always charged to a heathen, who lives outside of faith. <Further,> no one may defend himself with the arguments that with his natural strength he did everything that was possible, and that God could not demand something that is impossible for man to do.[174] For a Christian it is decisive that his decision is based on obedience to the divine natural law, that is, that his decision 'flows' from love for God and the neighbor, or in other words, that his decision as a deed of love is a fruit of faith.[175] To use Luther's phrasing: only in the presence of man is the *conscientia activa* sufficient, in God's presence all depends on the *conscientia passiva*.[176]

Before we turn in Part III to the most important practical consequences which the presented materials have for the legal existence of mankind, let us summarize those results of our work which will be relevant for this topic.

One has to start with the *eschatological dualism in Luther's doctrine of natural law,* and one has to differentiate between the divine natural law, the legal order of Christ's kingdom, and the secular natural law, the supreme legal order of the kingdom of the world. The divine natural law was spiritually interpreted by Christ, the secular natural law was written down by Moses in the Decalogue, which in terms of substantive law is exemplary until today. Both legal orders are united in the divine will for law. That will is active in the two kingdoms in different ways, however: as spiritual law of love *(lex charitatis spiritualis)* in the kingdom of Christ, as law of wrath and death *(lex irae et mortis)* in the kingdom of the world.

The *divine natural law* with its commandment of God-formed love for the Creator and for the neighbor is the *standard for a Christian*[177] in his private and public life; it is the source of law for a Christian,[178] and, although totally clear,[179] only he is able to understand it;[180] therefore it is valid only for him.[181] There is, then, only a *Christian* natural law;[182] its fulfillment is possible only in faith, and that fulfillment provides the good conscience before God.[183]

The *standard for the conduct of a non-Christian is the secular natural law*.[184] This law demands universal love for man, a love which is to be practiced as much as it is possible for natural man; its fulfillment provides the good conscience before man.

The *two families of mankind,* the children of the light and the children of the world (Luke 16:8),[185] strictly adhere to the statutes governing their spiritual personality.[186] Neither shares the law of the other,[187] each acts according to the law of its own estate: a Christian obeys the law of the Christian estate,[188] a non-Christian obeys the law of the heathen estate.[189] No one is a citizen of both kingdoms,[190] <and> there is no legal order above them, which would be common to both of them.[191] Yet a Christian is also responsible for the secular law nevertheless, and this for the following reason: in spite of its non-spiritual goal, secular law serves God's will for law,[192] <but does so> in a hidden way, which only a Christian is able to recognize.[193]

PART THREE

The Existence of the Christian in the Legal Structures of This World

CHAPTER 12

The Christian as a Member of the Church in the World

If[1] one views the legal structures in which a Christian exists in this world in light of the principles thus far developed, one is confronted with two facts which have to be clearly separated: the communal life of Christians with one another on the one hand, the coexistence of Christians with non-Christians on the other. First it must be stated, however: in every situation of his life a Christian acts in accordance with one uniform standard, that is, Christ's commandment, which excludes all other standards.[2]

The communal life of Christians takes place in what Luther called "the Christian body."[3] Here are no legal problems as they are defined in secular law;[4] all actions[5] are governed by the commandment of Christian brotherly love,[6] and that love excludes any laws and claims.[7] All actions of Christians are directed toward "one community ⟨and⟩ the strengthening of body and soul."[8] A Christian is a servant of all things and subject to all people.[9]

Christian brotherly love is the *first* and highest ranking[10] spiritual *basic right*[11] in the external communal life of Christians with one another. That love serves the neighbor, especially fellow Christians, ⟨particularly⟩ whenever those whom God has called to such service in the first place do not meet this call.[12]

The *second* spiritual *basic right* is *Christian equality*.[13] In Christ's spiritual governance[14] all differences of estate,[15] rank,[16] and works[17] disappear.[18] How could there be any kind of lordship among Christians when, following the example of Christ, the only master of Christians,[19]

The Existence of the Christian in the Legal Structures of This World

everyone has to consider himself to be the least among his brothers?[20] From the Christians' sharing one faith *(communio fidei)* follows their sharing one law *(communio iuris);* all of *Christ's disciples live according to one common law (ius commune Christianorum).*[21] There are no privileges or exemptions[22] among Christians. There is only *one spiritual*[23] *estate,*[24] the Christian estate;[25] it is set up in the divine positive law,[26] and it is the only estate of this kind.[27] Roman Catholic doctrine differentiated between ⟨the estate of the⟩ clergy and ⟨that of the⟩ laity, and this differentiation was derived from what was considered to be divine positive law. Attacking this doctrine, Luther called the Christian estate the universal priesthood of believers,[28] a formula reminiscent of Canon law.[29] The significance of this formula[30] as a positive-law principle for the organization of the institutional church is mostly overvalued.[31]

The *third* spiritual *basic right* in the communal life of Christians with one another is *Christian freedom.*[32] This is the exemption from the sovereignty of the law of wrath,[33] while a Christian lives on earth, and, therefore, from the sovereignty of the law's earthly coercive force.[34] By following Christ's example,[35] a Christian is a free lord over all things and subject to no one.[36]

"The church in the world"[37] — the church on earth,[38] Christendom, all of Christendom or universal Christendom, universal church *(ecclesia universalis, ecclesia universa, tota ecclesia)*[39] — shows what a commonwealth based on the Christian estate has to be. That church in the world exists in the Christian "assemblies"[40] or congregations *(ecclesiae particulares, singulares, partiales)* of the "Christian people,"[41] or of the "church-people,"[42] or of the "ecclesiastical body."[43] *"The churchly commonwealth (respublica ecclesiastica)*[44] *is organized by only one law, that of love"* — this is the central statement in the constitution of the church on earth.[45] Therefore the creation and implementation of man-made ecclesiastical law are matters of man's obedience to the divine natural law.[46] Serving brotherly love for fellow Christians,[47] and acting on the basis of their legal equality,[48] the believing members of the church are to create human ecclesiastical law[49] voluntarily.[50]

Do their efforts succeed in the church? That is an important question. The church on earth resembles a hospital or convalescent home.[51] Therefore its legal order is never perfect; nevertheless, that order has to be endured patiently for the sake of the weaker brothers. This defect is inevitable. Yet this cross[52] by no means legitimates the existence or a particular form of the man-made ecclesiastical law in the church.

Rather, this cross challenges the believing members of the church to reform that law in the spirit of Christian brotherly love <and> in accordance with the true spiritual requirements of the ecclesiastical communal life.

Such a reform becomes mandatory in two situations: ecclesiastical law and its implementation are contrary to the divine positive law[53] (for instance, in matters pertaining to the proclamation of God's Word and the administration of the sacraments);[54] ecclesiastical law and its implementation do not agree with the three spiritual basic rights of the Christian estate. This second situation occurs, for instance, when one particular church[55] claims to be lord and head of the remaining churches, because in their relationship with Jesus Christ, the one and only head of the universal church, all churches have equal rank;[56] or it occurs when higher church officials, claiming the supposed divine institution of their <administrative> office, demand obedience regulated by Canon law,[57] a demand which would be spiritual tyranny because it lacks any legal basis whatsoever. When in cases like these the members of a particular church and their shepherds do not comply with the demand of the true Christians for a change in the corrupt ecclesiastical law, then the only recourse true Christians have is the separation from that institution, which has become a hypocritical church; the degree of separation is determined by the degree[58] in which that institution has lost the spiritual connection with the universal church and has become 'world'.[59] Such a separation is not a secession from the church; on the contrary, it is the remaining of the 'healthier' *(sanior)* particular church with the universal church.[60]

Only refusing to obey the ecclesiastical authorities of a degenerate particular church is not sufficient. The true Christians have to join together in a congregation which organizes its legal existence according to Christ's plan,[61] and which, therefore, Christ can accept as his church. In this way active spiritual resistance occurs within the church on the basis of the divine positive law, and this resistance extends into the church's external communal existence.[62] These experiences within the institutional church shaped Luther's thinking about the right of resistance. By comparing *ecclesia* with *politia* and contrasting them he developed his position on the right of resistance also in the secular realm.[63] But the doctrine of resistance unfolded its real strength within the church, and here it resulted in the creation of a new ecclesiastical law. According to Luther, there is no divine positive law for a hierarchy of orders or jurisdictions. Therefore the divine natural law is much more important for the creation of ecclesiastical law than it is in the Roman Catholic Church — it is the foundation of the whole man-made order of the church.

These are the main topics in such an order: Congregational worship (orders of divine services);[64] *diaconia* in a congregation, especially the care for the poor;[65] the educational system; the office and estate of the servants of the church, that is, of those members of the church who are called into the ministry of the Word;[66] the participation of the members of the church in the publicly administered ecclesiastical discipline;[67] the organization of supervision in the church[68] and of the governance of the external, temporal affairs of the church.[69] The purpose of this man-made order[70] is educational in nature[71] so that man-made ecclesiastical law tends to be similar to the laws for parents and schools.[72] The prescriptions of this man-made ecclesiastical law are to guarantee the smooth conduct of the ecclesiastical affairs of Christendom;[73] they are to make it easier for Christians to carry out the spiritual tasks which are determined by the divine positive law.[74] If this purpose can be accomplished in some other way and without endangering the Salvation of one's soul or that of the neighbor, these prescriptions may be ignored;[75] man-made ecclesiastical law is not "necessary law."[76] Administered in such a spirit of freedom, man-made ecclesiastical law is to guarantee that congregations are supplied with the Word, that unity among them is strengthened, and that they are protected against turmoil. In all these facets, the universal church, when it creates its law, is bound by the divine natural law as it is interpreted by Christ;[77] this is the limitation of the church's legal authority. Outside of Christ there is no law in the church whatsoever, neither a divine nor a man-made law.[78]

The creation of law in the universal church is a public process within the church,[79] and it is conducted according to rational considerations.[80] Reason is illuminated by faith, however;[81] therefore it is not dominated by the coercive force of the law of wrath, and — in contrast to the natural reason of the carnal man — it is called "the Christian and free reason."[82] As an external work, man-made ecclesiastical law belongs to the realm of reason, but it is not a part of the kingdom of reason,[83] that is, the kingdom of autocratic reason, which is identical with the kingdom of the world.[84] Rather, as a work of faith,[85] that law is connected with the kingdom of faith.[86] Man-made ecclesiastical law exists in this world, and in that sense it is worldly.[87] That law is, however, not of this world, that is, it is not submissive to this world. Man-made ecclesiastical law,[88] or "the order of the Christian community,"[89] as Luther called it sometimes, is based on the three spiritual basic rights of the Christian estate,[90] and, therefore, it is different from all other law on earth.[91] According to Luther, there is, then, *ius utrumque*,[92] the ecclesiastical law and the secular law, and the specifics of each law are a mark[93] of the commonwealth which it serves.

The two laws are fundamentally different. Ecclesiastical law deserves its name only when the promulgation and implementation of its decrees are spiritual acts of love. The norms are not important — important is the activity of the legal mind which is guided by faith. Only a believing Christian is capable of judging whether such an activity is a spiritual act.[94] "The spiritual man judges all things." (1 Corinthians 2:15.) This statement of the Apostle Paul, which in the history of ecclesiastical law had major consequences, constantly exposes man-made ecclesiastical law to the judgment of the members of the spiritual church.[95] Only they who know of God's will for law are capable of judging the legitimacy of this ecclesiastical law, and their standard for judging is the divine positive law and the divine natural law. Both are the basis for the legitimacy of man-made ecclesiastical law in the same way that the secular natural law is the basis for the legitimacy of the secular positive law. The sum of norms may be called ecclesiastical law only if that law has grown from the spirit which rules the spiritual church, and if that law is implemented in that spirit. The situation is identical in the relationship of the universal church with the spiritual church; if one thinks of the former without also at the same time thinking of the latter, then the concept 'church' is a "blind word."[96] If one separates the ecclesiastical law from the divine law, ecclesiastical law becomes a dead letter.

Secular law has a totally different character. On the basis of external standards, any knowledgeable person can determine whether this secular law agrees with the secular natural law; provided that the norms have that minimum of internal authority, they are already law in the eyes of man. A Christian is confronted with this secular positive law as soon as he enters the legal realm of the *oeconomia* and of the *politia*. Let us begin with the former.

CHAPTER 13

The Christian in the Estate of Marriage

———⋅◉⋅———

We have seen that in the status of the corrupt nature marriage is a secular matter.[1] This, according to Luther, Christ did not change for his disciples; he did not elevate marriage among Christians to a sacrament,[2] and he did not assign spiritual quality to marriage. Luther did not find a divine positive law for marriage in the New Testament. Nevertheless, he clearly differentiated between a Christian and a heathen marriage. The decisive criterion for this differentiation is the shaping of the married life by God's commandment, that is, the spiritual use of marriage, or in other words, the implementation of the law of the gospel in the estate of marriage.[3] Only believing Christians are able to implement that law. Their marriage is a corporeally living together in faith. Luther called it a "spiritual"[4] and "blessed"[5] estate, even the "most spiritual"[6] of all estates. With this description he intended to say that from no other estate comes such an abundance of spiritual blessings as from the marriage of Christians,[7] regardless whether one considers the relationship of the spouses with each other or the family community of parents and children. But even the marriage of the most perfect Christians does not achieve the spiritual purity which marriage had in the Original Status;[8] concupiscence of the flesh cannot be avoided in married life. God mercifully ignores this weakness,[9] however, because he has established marriage, and he accepts a marriage lived in faith as a service to[10] himself.

Marriage is an external ⟨secular⟩ community of people living together; therefore a Christian's duties in marriage and family and their fulfillment are mostly identical with the corresponding demands found

The Christian in the Estate of Marriage

in the secular natural law. Christians fulfill these duties in obedience to the divine natural law. The practical consequence of this situation emerges especially in times of *Anfechtung*.[11] When the secular natural-law commandment of love will not do and only the power of Christ's law will meet the demands of the circumstances,[12] then faith reveals its true strength, ⟨and this⟩ also for a non-Christian. Above we mentioned already how a true Christian[13] would act when, for instance, a marriage is in danger of breaking up because of a severe transgression by one spouse.[14]

Therefore the weight of the demand to fulfill the duties of marriage is different for Christians and for non-Christians, even though the duties themselves are identical. There are some duties which pertain, however, only to Christians, or at least only Christians are able to fulfill them in a God-pleasing way. One of the most important of these specially Christian duties is the Christian education of children.[15] When parents instruct their offspring in the Christian faith, they practice the universal priesthood of the spiritual church, and they do this long before the corporeal church can take care of the religious formation of children through its servants. In this way, marriage, which for non-Christians is only the source of the *politia*, is for Christians also a "nursery" of the church.[16] Therefore among all secular estates marriage has a unique significance.

A Christian husband should affirm this connection of church and marriage already at the wedding ceremony. According to divine law,[17] that is, according to the institutional secular natural law, the husband's estate is a public estate. This he has to affirm before the Christian congregation in a public statement concerning his will to get married; who ignores this duty is in danger of offending the Christians living in a particular location. A church wedding, therefore, is self-evident for a marriage of Christians; this is not a necessary law but a consequence of the duty of Christian brotherly love within the institutional church.

This raises the question whether ecclesiastical prescriptions for the marriage of Christians are permissible and what their legal nature would be. Let us state at the outset that a substantive ecclesiastical law regarding marriage does not exist ⟨for two reasons:⟩ "because weddings and the married estate are worldly affairs, it behoves those of us who are 'spirituals' or ministers of the church in no way to order or direct anything regarding marriage";[18] and because the corporeal church does not have legal authority over believing Christians — the spiritual man is

The Existence of the Christian in the Legal Structures of This World

judged by no one <1 Corinthians 2:15>. The corporeal church has not even the authority to prescribe an impediment of marriage[19] in the case of a Christian intending to marry a non-Christian; to prescribe such an impediment would restrict the spiritual freedom of that Christian. In view of this legal situation, ecclesiastical prescriptions for a Christian marriage are now usually not called evangelical marriage law but evangelical wedding law.[20] But just because we have a term does not mean that we also have a homogeneous body of law. Luther strictly differentiated between two groups of presciptions. One is a part of the so-called autonomous ecclesiastical law,[21] that is, that ecclesiastical order which the church in the world, motivated by Christian brotherly love, creates for its members. Here one would have to list, for instance, rules for the preparation of the performance of a wedding and for its actual performance.[22] In the second group the legal materials have quite a different quality. Here the church in the world acts as the servant of the spiritual Power of the Keys, which is entrusted to the spiritual church. Legal actions in this legal realm may claim validity only when they agree with the divine positive law. Such actions are to be considered to be a part of the heteronomous ecclesiastical law.[23] Their content is the administration of ecclesiastical discipline against public sinners within the institutional church, and the most powerful means the church has in such a case is excommunication.[24] Luther wanted it used, for instance, against those who are Christians in name only and divorce their marriages for other reasons than those allowed in Holy Scripture.[25] Because of their heathen conduct in public, they exclude themselves from the spiritual church and live in a "condemned estate."[26] The church informs them of this situation point blank by separating itself from them.

CHAPTER 14

The Christian in the Politia

§ 1. The Spiritual Basis of the Christian's Freedom in the *Politia*

We leave the law of the *oeconomia* and turn to Christians living in the *politia*. *Politia* is the legal form of the human community. This community is oriented toward earthly goals, and, therefore, it is the secular and world-wide counterpart to the universal church.[1] The universal church is organized as a multitude of particular churches, which under Christ's spiritual governance are united in faith and love. Likewise, the *politia* is divided in a multitude of kingdoms, principalities, and cities (collectively this multitude is sometimes called *politiae*).[2] Yet because of the egotism of rulers and ruled (which prevails among and in them) these political units are far removed from being internally united, even when they are united under the external governance of the emperor.

In the *politia* a Christian is confronted with doctrines of philosophy, of state, and of law[3] which are totally alien to his thinking, for he finds himself in the kingdom of reason, or the natural kingdom — a kingdom which is far removed from God. A Christian is not subordinated[4] to the law created by reason in the *politia*, the *politica iustitia*.[5] He lives in the secular commonwealth not as a citizen but as a foreigner;[6] this means, Christ has "pulled him out" from under the sovereignty of the law which is valid in this commonwealth — he is exempt from this law.[7] Therefore precisely in the kingdom of the world a Christian is a free lord of all things and subject to no one.

The Existence of the Christian in the Legal Structures of This World

§ 2. The Christian as a Legal Associate in the *Politia*

This[8] spiritual freedom of Christians does not cause any difficulties for their living together with non-Christians who have the same rank in secular law as they do. In the civic life there are no essential differences between Christians and non-Christians, if one disregards the article of the cross.[9] The demands of the divine righteousness, that is, of the divine natural law,[10] are much more important than the demands of the earthly righteousness, which are fixed in man-made law.[11] If a Christian suffers an injustice from a non-Christian, he has to confront the non-Christian and point out the divine punishment for such an injustice.[12] This is a Christian's active spiritual resistance to someone else's sin. But aside from this, it is his 'Christian law'[13] to endure that injustice,[14] because a Christian uses the things of this world as if he were not using them.[15] In matters of faith, however, the situation is totally different — here yielding is out of the question.[16] But the resulting conflict would be beyond the competency of the members of the *politia*[17] who have the same rank in secular law. Therefore we may now exclude such a situation from our consideration.

In temporal ‹secular› matters a Christian is allowed to fight an injustice only if the public good demands it. An example would be severe crimes.[18] In such a situation a Christian has not only the right but also the duty to demand that the governmental authority act. He may use self-defense only when in cases of imminent danger a governmental authority cannot be called upon to act; an example would be robbery on a deserted street.[19] A Christian should always seriously examine himself, however, whether his actions are motivated entirely by the concern for the common good and not by selfish reasons.[20] When in doubt, he should rather let go of his temporal possessions.

In summary: In the legal realm of the *politia*, obedience to the divine natural law is far superior to obedience to the positive man-made law.[21] This principle excellently describes the role of a Christian as a private person, or as a legal associate in the *politia* with the same rank in secular law as other members of the *politia*.

The Christian in the Politia

§ 3. The Christian as a Subject in the *Politia*

More complicated is the answer to the question whether a Christian as a subject ⟨in the *politia*⟩ has the duty of obeying the commandment of the secular governmental authority. A Christian knows the spiritual meaning of the office of governmental authority,[22] and he knows that God ordered him[23] to support this office with his body and possessions.[24] Because of his exempt status in the kingdom of the world,[25] he is not directly obligated to obey the commandments of secular governmental authority.[26] Therefore his obedience is voluntary. Christians are not subjected to the coercive force of the secular law. Yet the duty to love the neighbor, derived from the divine natural law,[27] obligates them to respect the positive man-made law, and for the fulfillment of this obligation they are responsible to God.[28] A Christian knows that a culpable transgression of a legitimate command of a governmental authority would not only result in temporal punishment but also, and especially, evoke God's wrath[29] and endanger the Salvation of the soul. Therefore he obeys earthly law much more conscientiously than a heathen.[30] For this reason, being a Christian provides the strongest support for a secular commonwealth.[31] One may not understand this the way some medieval thinkers did; they believed that legitimate sovereignty could exist only within Christendom[32] — such legitimate sovereignties existed already before the birth of Christ; but one should understand this in the sense that the best protection against rebellion and disobedience exists wherever the subjects are Christians.

The responsibility to God is the reason for a Christian's voluntary obedience to the secular law, but that law[33] also limits the duty of that obedience. Luther described this limit in different ways, for instance, as divine mandate,[34] as God's Word[35] or commandment,[36] as righteousness and truth,[37] as prohibition to commit an act toward God ⟨or⟩ man that would be unjust,[38] etc. These formal and material elements identify this limit with the institutional and the substantive secular natural law.[39] As transpositive universal human law obligating everyone, it applies directly not only to governmental authority but also to subjects. Therefore each individual is responsible for deriving this limit from the secular natural law.[40] No command of a governmental authority can release anyone from this duty,[41] which is rooted in transpositive law. Honoring God is more important than honoring the human office ⟨of governmental authority by obeying it⟩. No servant of God may let himself be turned into a servant of sin by a governmental authority. This applies especially to the incumbents of lower governmental offices when their superiors demand them to implement commands which contradict the secular natural law. In such situations the demand of the more important obedience to God takes precedence over the hierarchy of the secular offices.

Luther saw the major danger for governmental authority to transgress its competency located in the area of the institutional secular natural law. This would be the case whenever in its relationship with the church, or with marriage, secular governmental authority ignores the God-given limits of its office. Let us begin with the relationship between governmental authority and church.

Governmental authority is entrusted with the promotion of the temporal well-being of man[42] — it is not charged with caring for the Salvation of man's soul. In Luther's blunt language: it is not proper for governmental authority to change from hangman to shepherd.[43] If a governmental authority nevertheless dares[44] to rule souls,[45] if, for instance, it prohibits the teaching of pure doctrine,[46] or if it interferes with the ecclesiastical governance of the office of public ministry[47] by ordering, for instance, that someone be excommunicated,[48] the commandment of that governmental authority is void because of its absolute incompetency in these matters.[49] To resist such actions[50] is not only permitted but absolutely commanded.[51] Such actions change the border between the legal orders of the two kingdoms,[52] and to change this border is prohibited to man.[53] Occasionally Luther expressed this idea in the argument that obedience to the First Table of the Decalogue has to have priority over obedience to the Second Table.[54]

Even in such a case of resistance, the office of governmental authority may not indiscriminately be ignored — it still deserves respect.[55] One may not treat a prince who transgresses the competency of his office as if he were a private person.[56] The misuse of the office makes the action of a governmental authority defective, but the action nonetheless retains the quality of an action by a governmental authority.[57] This determines the kind and degree of resistance. In resisting, the "difference between thing *(res)* and person"[58] has to be observed. The resistance has to be shaped in such a way that the power of governmental authority to issue commands is acknowledged, while at the same time the attack on the soul by the unlawfully acting incumbent of the office is rejected. A governmental authority has to be publicly informed of both actions.[59] Silent disobedience, therefore, is not sufficient.⁶⁰ A governmental authority has to be clearly instructed about its error in law, and it has to be admonished to obey God's order.⁶¹ But resistance may not go beyond such a remonstrance, that is, a courageous affirmation of the law⁶² and a warning of the coming divine judgment and punishment.⁶³ In this sense, resistance is spiritually active but corporeally passive.⁶⁴ Yet in such a conduct, resistance extends as far as sacrificing one's life,⁶⁵ and it is absolutely uncompromising.⁶⁶

The same principles are to be used when a governmental authority issues orders which violate the nature of marriage, for instance, when it compels a man or a women to marry contrary to their wills.⁶⁷

An infraction of the substantive secular natural law by a governmental authority creates a similar situation. Taken by itself, even an unjust command of a governmental authority to do this and not to do that in temporal ‹secular› matters has to be obeyed.⁶⁸ But when such a command orders an action against God or man which according to the secular natural law is prohibited — in practical terms, if the intention of the command is to force a subject to act against the Ten Commandments⁶⁹ — then such a command is no longer law,⁷⁰ and under no circumstances may it be obeyed.⁷¹ A command of a governmental authority is not legally binding if it contradicts the secular natural law.⁷² But aside from the duty to remonstrate, only passive corporeal resistance⁷³ is permitted,⁷⁴ and this for the same reasons as mentioned above, in connection with resistance in matters of the institutional secular natural law.⁷⁵ But that kind of resistance will be pursued to the final consequences.

The case of war⁷⁶ illustrates the situation. Under no circumstances may a Christian participate in a war of which he is convinced that it is unjust.⁷⁷ Only a war of self-defense⁷⁸ is just, that is, a war which is forced upon someone.⁷⁹ "Who starts a war is unjust."⁸⁰ Refusing to serve in an unjust war is a duty to God, which is derived from the substantive secular natural law (Fifth Commandment!). Such a decision may be made, however, only after the legal situation has been examined conscientiously, and this includes the examination of one's own ability to reach a correct judgment! As long as a subject is unable to arrive at a decision which is free from any doubt, he may not refuse to participate in a war.⁸¹ At whatever decision he arrives, he, and he alone is responsible for his decision, and no one can assume this responsibility for him. There is no blind obedience in Luther's doctrine of law. A very impressive example of this line of thinking is Luther's threat to issue a public protest if his elector would wage an unjust war.⁸²

The Existence of the Christian in the Legal Structures of This World

§ 4. The Doctrine of the Tyrant

All cases discussed thus far deal with the illegal actions of a legitimate governmental authority. It is legitimate because it obtained its office either directly from God,[83] or indirectly from man through a secular legal system. By misusing the office through the violation of the secular natural law, the incumbent of the office becomes a secular tyrant. This is the type of tyrant which in the literature of the Middle Ages is called *tyrannus quoad executionem*.[84] Luther knew also of the *invasor*,[85] that is, the usurper of governmental power, the *tyrannus quoad titulum*,[86] mentioned in the medieval doctrine of law. According to the secular natural law,[87] a subject has the duty to obey the command of governmental authority. It is to be taken for granted, therefore, that he assists the legitimate ruler against the usurper so that there is no need to discuss usurpation in the following materials. One has to obey the usurper only if, with God's permission, he definitely possesses the governmental authority.[88]

It seems that these ideas do not go beyond the Middle Ages.[89] Yet the situation changes[90] if these ideas are based on the doctrine of the two kingdoms and their legal orders. In this connection two points have to be made.

First: The question whether resistance is permissible arises anew, and for a Christian the answer is different from that for a non-Christian. Secular natural law does not require a non-Christian to ignore his personal welfare when dealing with his neighbor; he may claim for himself the principle 'suum cuique';[91] if his neighbor ignores this principle, he may defend himself. Of course, the principle 'vim vi repellere licet'[92] applies at best to a situation in which persons have equal legal rank.[93] It does not apply to a situation which might develop between subjects and a governmental authority. Even then, however, a governmental authority may be passively resisted in an effort to oppose its attacks on life and property, with which it defies the secular natural law. The situation is totally different for a Christian. For his own sake he may never attempt to avoid an unjust act directed at his life or property. He may resist governmental authority only if he is forced to commit an unjust action against God or his neighbor — but then resistance is commanded.[94]

Second: For the punishment of the crime of tyranny the new insight in the relationship of the church (spiritual and universal) with the *politia* becomes effective. The judicial authority of the church is purely spiritual. The church can condemn certain actions of a secular governmental authority as sinful, and it can decide that, because such actions violate the institutional or the substantive secular natural law,[95] they are not binding the people. Further, the church can use ecclesiastical discipline against an incumbent of the governmental office provided that he has been baptized, and in an extreme situation the church can excommunicate him. But the church may not ascribe to itself any authority to rule in the *politia;* it may not even claim an extraordinary sovereign right of interference in order to oppose sin. Therefore the church is not permitted to touch the organization of the *politia*. The church may only voice opposition to the usurpation of the office and the misuse of the office which violates the secular natural law, and it has the duty to do this. The church is prohibited, however, to depose an incumbent of the governmental office because of his sin. This does not change even when a baptized ruler is a heretic. Neither the church[96] nor the subjects may use a violation of the faith as pretense for declaring an incumbent of the governmental office deposed. God has reserved for himself the authority to judge a tyrannical prince. A direct or indirect authority of the church in temporal matters no longer exists.[97]

This position certainly marks an important structural shift[98] in the doctrine of tyranny. This shift, however, does not yet at all explain the center of Luther's doctrine of the right of resistance, ⟨and this is the reason:⟩ *The passive quality of the corporeal disobedience,*[99] *which characterizes Luther's position, is accompanied, even dominated, by a most intense spiritual activity, the call on God in prayer.*[100] God, the overlord and supreme judge of secular governmental authority, in his way is to make an end to tyranny as it deserves. In the discussion ⟨of Luther's position on the passive quality of the corporeal disobedience to a governmental authority⟩ one has to concentrate on prayer, the spiritual weapon of a Christian, and on the use of the power of prayer against the power of injustice.[101] Only if one does this will there be a chance of grasping the reformer's position, only if one does this will the reformer's warning of the tyrant having to face God's punishment have the weight it deserves. ⟨In this intense spiritual activity⟩ a Christian does not speak for himself,[102] but he speaks as a servant of ⟨God's⟩ law of wrath,[103] and he speaks because of his responsibility for the Salvation of his neighbor.[104]

This position was the result of Luther's conviction that tyranny was not only the battle of human injustice against the human transpositive law and the positive law corresponding to it. For him, tyranny was also, and especially, Satan's attack on the basic order of God's kingdom at the left, that is, it was a spiritual battle. And in this battle between God and the devil a Christian is not permitted to remain passive. "Resist the devil," Scripture commands (James 4:7b). Therefore a Christian must oppose Satan's attack with the power of prayer. This is a Christian's true resistance to the injustice in this world, and it is an active spiritual resistance, "a spiritual war."[105] By appealing ⟨in prayer⟩ to God's court, a Christian, so to speak, issues an indictment of the spiritual transgression of law, which is being committed against God's order. Then he has to wait for the verdict of the divine court.[106] It would be a lack of faith were he to act by fighting the tyrant and thus encroach on that verdict.[107] Passive corporeal disobedience is, then, nothing other than the consequence of the case against tyranny being in God's court for judgment; in other words, it is the corporeal result of the active spiritual resistance in prayer.[108]

Yet surprisingly enough, *Luther also knew a case of active corporeal resistance,* or more precisely, *of resistance with ⟨armed⟩ force.* This is hardly mentioned in previous accounts of Luther's position on the right of resistance.[109] Therefore the opinion became prevalent that Luther permitted only passive corporeal disobedience. This case is quite exorbitant. On top of this, it is wrapped in such concrete and unusually violent polemics that the view for the natural-law materials contained in this polemics is obstructed. The case adds one most interesting type of tyrant to the usual presentation of Luther's doctrine of the tyrant, and it shows that, in addition to the spiritual tyrant in the universal church,[110] Luther knew of not only one, but two kinds of secular tyrants in the *politia*.

The first kind is represented by those villains who sometimes rule one or the other of the units in which the *politia* is organized.[111] Since their despotism is more or less limited in terms of space and actions, we will call them petty tyrants *(tyranni particulares)*. Our previous presentation of the right of resistance dealt with them.[112] Those fellows are relatively harmless if one compares them with the other kind of tyrant.

When in 1529 the danger of the Turkish invasion of Germany increased,[113] Luther was haunted by the horror created by the second kind of tyrant. When in 1539 he was confronted with the imminent danger of a religious war against the evangelicals, he clarified the religious[114] and the political atrocity of this second kind of tyrant in theological and juristic terms. Since the days of Nimrod, the great persecutor[115] of mankind, one is again and again confronted with this second kind of tyrant. He is the grand or world tyrant *(tyrannus universalis)*.[116]

The Christian in the Politia

There is an enormous difference between this grand tyrant and the petty tyrants! The reason for this is not only the grand tyrant's unlimited craving for power over land and people but also especially the revolutionary, all-encompassing dimension of his governing principles. He is not content with egotistically transgressing the institutional or the substantive secular natural law in individual instances ⟨as is the petty tyrant⟩.[117] The grand tyrant's slogan is not that of the petty tyrant, "might makes right";[118] through it, the authority of law, by which actions are made legitimate, is at least still acknowledged, granted, reluctantly. The slogan of the grand tyrant is: "The sovereign's power is law," man's will is law![119] The deification of man's will for power differentiates the grand tyrant from the petty tyrant; he only occasionally takes the liberty of disobeying the secular natural law, the grand tyrant does not even acknowledge the existence of the secular natural law.[120] For him exists no law which God gave to man, no two kingdoms according to God's will. For him exists only his own kingdom,[121] which he strives to extend over body and soul.[122] Totally aware of what he is doing, he places himself outside of all law connected with God,[123] and above it.[124] For this reason, he loses any status in law,[125] be it in divine or human law, ecclesiastical[126] or secular law.[127]

In eschatological terms such a product of hell is "the lawless one" (*anomos*; 2 Thessalonians 2:8).[128] Therefore God has outlawed him. God's sentence of condemnation is corporeally visible in the actions of this lawless one,[129] and that sentence demands that everyone executes it immediately.[130] One has to put an end to this criminal as if he were a wild beast,[131] and one has to fight his helpers as one fights robbers[132] or foreign enemies,[133] such as the Turks for instance. Because this enemy is so horrible, Luther used words of horrible passion to call everyone to battle[134] and strictly to reject any delay.[135] In such a situation even commandments to the contrary, issued by one's own governmental authority, are void;[136] if it opposes this battle,[137] it has to be ignored.[138] The people[139] have the right and duty to rebel against a governmental authority which supports the grand tyrant. At this point the positive public law is at an end; "necessity has no ⟨positive⟩ law."[140] Until the time that the danger has passed only the secular natural law rules. This means that, when the supreme government of the state breaks down, the incumbent of each lower office, in hierarchical order down to the ordinary man, has to take the initiative.[141] Even a subject could, therefore, find himself in the situation of being forced to as-

The Existence of the Christian in the Legal Structures of This World

sume functions of sovereignty for the benefit of the endangered commonwealth. "When the magistrate does not function, the common people *(plebs)* are the magistrate."[142]

§ 5. The Christian in the Office of Governmental Authority[143]

It is a rare exception for a Christian to function in the sovereign way just described. May in normal circumstances a Christian assume a task of governmental authority? May he accept an office of governmental authority?[144] May he even apply for it? Because he is a foreigner[145] in the kingdom of the world, one might think that he should withdraw from secular affairs. Already in Luther's days the opinion was expressed among evangelicals that God wanted the Christians to withdraw from the *politia*. The reformer, however, condemned this position as heresy.[146]

Luther tried to explain his position with a very traditional sounding distinction: During his life on earth, *a Christian is in two relationships, one with Christ and the other with the world; he is at the same time a 'Christ-person' and a 'world-person'*, he has a twofold office, and he has to do justice to both offices.[147] 'Maintaining two persons' was a formula which had been used already in the Middle Ages. In Luther's theological system the formula has weight only in polemics; therefore it has often been misunderstood.[148] The formula expresses the tensions which exist between the structure of the kingdom of Christ and that of the kingdom of the world;[149] and it explains these tensions as being insoluble for a Christian who serves in an office of governmental authority. This does not show, however, how a Christian may enter such an office in the first place without denying his Lord.[150] ⟨In order to enter such an office and not deny his Lord, a Christian⟩ may not enter into any kind of spiritual legal relationship with the kingdom of the world, may not succumb to the spirit of the secular law,[151] and may not abandon his Christian freedom.[152]

Accepting a secular office is, therefore, possible for a Christian only if it has a hidden spiritual legal quality in spite of its obvious secular quality. That, indeed, is the case, because God implements his governance in the kingdom at the left through offices.[153] A Christian may serve in governmental offices only if they function within the limits of the secular natural law,[154] or in Luther's words, as long as "they function in love."[155] Then through the secular natural law the office is connected with the divine natural law. If a Christian implements the duties of his office with this understanding in mind,[156] he is able to serve God[157] — and he should do so. When he does, he fulfills his divine vocation[158] in the world, namely, to be God's co-worker;[159] he assists in the implementation of the divine natural law,[160] which in a mysterious way is active in the secular law. This is confirmed[161] in Holy Scriptures: "In the Old and the New Testament there is no one a saint who has not been something either in the *oeconomia* or the *politia*."

No one is better qualified ⟨for a governmental office⟩ than a Christian. "The handling of the sword and the use of power, special services to God, are due to the Christians before all other people on earth." "Natural man ⟨does not handle the sword the way a true Christian does⟩."[162] Offices in the *politia* require, of course, natural talents, especially earthly wisdom, knowledge, and experience.[163] Because of the "divine law,"[164] that is, the God-created design of the *politia*, those talents are more important than others, even the moral capacity *(bonitas)*[165] which is aware that a ruler is not the lord but the servant of his subjects.[166] Because secular offices have such a rational quality, the appointment to an office should preferably be by direct election from the most competent and experienced citizens, and not by the law of hereditary succession, as it has been the custom in Germany.[167] Being a Christian does not endow someone with those qualities necessary for a ruler; on the contrary, non-Christians are often better rulers.[168] Yet the God-willed use of a Christian's natural talents is strengthened by his spiritual qualities; his natural reason is illuminated by faith so that he recognizes God's commandments, and his heart is filled with the desire to fulfill them. All of a Christian's actions, including those in an office of governmental authority, 'confess'[169] the divine will for law before men.

No one has such a profound insight into the God-created disposition of man for the social and political life,[170] no one knows the law of the *politia's* existence — that is, harmony[171] based on the secular natural law — as thoroughly as he who also knows the essence of the unity in the spirit based on the divine natural law.[172] No one is able to fulfill the commandment to love the neighbor as unselfishly[173] as he who is willing to dedicate his life to the spiritual love of the neighbor.[174] No one implements the duties of the office held by a *persona publica*, a "public person"[175] — that is, a public office — with such great responsibility and, therefore, also careful observation of the limits of his vocation[176] as he who knows that he not only owes obedience to the secular governmental authority because of the secular natural law but also is directly obligated to God[177] because of the divine natural law[178] and, therefore, prays for God's help when he implements the duties of his office.[179] Finally and most importantly: no one but a Christian knows of the spiritual meaning of human law as a part of the implementation of the divine plan of Salvation and, therefore, is able to organize his private and official conduct according to this knowledge.[180] For instance, a Christian prince will subordinate the implementation of his duties as a ruler to God's commandments, and in doing this he is motivated by reasons[181] which a heathen ruler does not know; and further, he will undertake tasks which are alien to a heathen.

To begin with the first point: A Christian prince will order the law of the *politia* to be examined whether it corresponds to the principles of the secular natural law; only if it does correspond will his Christian subjects be able to use the law of the territory as service to God,[182] that is, in believing obedience to the Creator.[183] A Christian prince will eliminate all commandments, prohibitions, permissions, laws, and institutions of the secular law if their implementation, or a Christian's recourse to them, or their use is not permitted to a Christian. A commonwealth of such a design is by no means Christian[184] — it does not lose its secular nature. It is, however, a commonwealth which is suited for a Christian's service in a secular office, and, therefore, in Christian understanding, it is a well-ordered commonwealth.[185]

<To continue with the second point:> A Christian prince does not only care for the well-being of the secular commonwealth but also for the well-being of the church.[186] Below we shall deal with the content, the place in history, and the legal basis of this *cura religionis*.[187]

Only Christians[188] have the knowledge of the spiritual and secular nature of the governance implemented by governmental authority and of the abundance of the religious and political tasks of governmental authority. Therefore the world cannot do without Christians. They are, as it were, the good conscience of the world, the best qualified candidates for the political governance. The office of governmental authority "belongs to, and benefits the Christian congregation,"[189] because *the ideal ruler is a Christian endowed with the gifts of natural prudence.*[190] Christians, therefore, may not hesitate to serve in the office of governmental authority;[191] faith demands their engagement in public life as an excellent "occasion for practicing faith and love."[192]

Motivated by love for his neighbor, a Christian assumes the tasks of public service. He also takes upon himself a burden,[193] which puts the strength of his faith to the hardest tests and requires of his self-denial the greatest sacrifices. Nowhere is the atmosphere as polluted with the infectious poison of the kingdom of the world as in the public life of the *politia*,[194] and nowhere is a probable defeat by the spirit of this world's law as great as in the public life of the *politia*.[195] Power is not evil in itself.[196] In secular life it elevates man above his equals, however, and this increases the temptation to misuse the office of governmental authority corporeally or spiritually.[197] A host of dangers, fatal for the soul, is lurking here. They range from the tyrant's large external infractions of the secular natural law and of the positive man-made law, to cunning methods used to misuse the office, such as selfish implementation of the duties of the office instead of its proper use, which would benefit the subjects; they range from blasphemous arrogance to spiritual self-satisfaction, which before God takes pride in the meticulous implementation of the official duties.[198] Worst of all: to no one is the devil more hostile than to a Christian ruler.[199] Indeed, a Christian prince is "venison in heaven."[200] In light of this situation, Luther recommended to Christians ⟨the service in⟩ the estate of governmental authority with its high demands[201] as a God-pleasing work,[202] but he also in a most sober way presented to them the political and spiritual dangers[203] to which that estate exposes them.[204]

The legal situation in which a Christian finds himself in the office of governmental authority is indeed very odd. The obedience to the law of love, that is, the commandment to love the neighbor, makes that Christian a servant of the law of wrath[205] and puts the sword in his hand.[206] Even more: he knows very well that the secular law is spiritually deficient, but he has to guard and develop it for the protection of the external legal peace. He may not fall prey to the delusion that the constitution of Christ's kingdom could be transferred to the kingdom of the world.[207] A Christian in the office of governmental authority does not create or implement 'Christian' law[208] for Christian law exists only in Christ's kingdom. The *politia* has to function according to the order of the kingdom of the world.[209] If we disregard the exceptions discussed above,[210] then in the kingdom of the world the following statement is in force: "The works of a wicked man are very similar to the works of a godly man."[211] Therefore Luther could say that a Christian has to act as if there were no God,[212] and as if he had to save[213] and rule himself.[214]

The Existence of the Christian in the Legal Structures of This World

The standard for acting in this situation is the secular natural law and, insofar as it leaves room for a ruler's discretion to create and implement law, the common good. In serving the common good, a Christian is not required to do anything beyond what he is able to do according to his natural talents. *Facere quod in se est* is sufficient for acting in the kingdom of the world, although, in contrast to the teachings of the Scholastics, it is totally insufficient for acting in Christ's kingdom.[215] Yet if someone strives to be God's official in a secular office and does the best that he is able to do, he meets his responsibility before God.[216]

§ 6. Luther's Doctrine of the 'Christian Body' Especially in *To the Christian Nobility of the German Nation*

The difference in the structure of the two kingdoms can be found in every detail of Luther's doctrine of law. Did Luther in *To the Christian Nobility of the German Nation*[217] not speak of a 'Christian body'[218] in which supposedly the ecclesiastical authority and the secular yet Christian governmental authority cooperated harmoniously and supported each other? What gives us the right to apply the phrase 'Christian body' to the community of believing Christians, as we did above?[219] Does one not have to assume that in principle the reformer affirmed the medieval ideal of a spiritual-secular commonwealth?[220] Was his new construction of this kingdom of Christendom not simply a redesigning of the old building while retaining the same floor plan? And in this redesigning did he not simply eliminate the superiority of the ecclesiastical authority over the secular, place both on the same level, and make each independent from the other?[221] — To this day the controversy has not been settled whether Luther affirmed[222] the idea 'corpus christianum'.[223]

In general, the argumentation is based on Luther's *To the Christian Nobility* (1520). In this book Luther used 'Christian body'[224] or 'the whole body of Christendom'.[225] With these terms he adopted the language of medieval canonistic and other writings.[226] Here phrases like *totum corpus ecclesiae* (the whole body of the church),[227] or *corpus universitatis fidelium* (body of the totality of believers),[228] or *corpus reipublicae christianae* (body of the Christian commonwealth)[229] were quite common. One may not take such phrases out of the theological context, however, and discuss them by themselves. To argue ⟨on the basis of Luther's use of such phrases⟩ that there was a continuity between

The Christian in the Politia

the Middle Ages and Luther would be rash; in later years he expressed his ideas in ways which were quite similar to those he had used in *To the Christian Nobility* of 1520, and in these cases it is impossible to use the Middle Ages as a key of interpretation.[230]

The main topic of *To the Christian Nobility* is the correct constitution of the Roman church, a particular church within the universal church, or as Luther also said,[231] "Christendom,"[232] or "all of Christendom."[233] For Luther, the order of the corporeal church[234] is the result of the connection of the corporeal church with the spiritual church. This spiritual church is a *corpus aequale*.[235] It consists of all those whom the Holy Spirit has touched in Baptism and who in faith[236] preserved this baptismal consecration[237] to be spiritual persons.[238] By divine positive law they all have the same rank in law and are members of the truly "spiritual" or Christian "estate";[239] they form a body which is spiritually directed by the true Christians;[240] and they are the true representatives of the universal church, that is, the church in the world.[241]

In the Middle Ages, the universal church was identified with the clergy, the spiritual estate according to Canon law.[242] Luther picked up this idea but developed it. Because of the nucleus of true Christians[243] existing in the universal church, he, using the trope synecdoche, equated 'universal church' with 'Christian estate'; this is indicated by the title of the little book: *To the Christian Nobility . . . for the Improvement of the Christian Estate*.[244] When Luther made statements about the correct structure of the universal church and its parts (the particular churches), about the need to reform the universal church ‹in one particular church, the Roman church,› and about the right to make such reforms, he always focused on the true Christians, the spiritual people in the church. As the important part, they are the Christian body,[245] ‹or› the Christian church[246] corporeally existing. The remaining members of the church are either weak Christians or lip-Christians. Because the Holy Spirit has at least started to work in the weak Christians, they will subordinate themselves to the judgment of the true Christians[247] who, as spiritual people, judge all things and are judged by no one.[248] These weak Christians are the beginners in the faith and willingly follow the advanced Christians; Luther, therefore, saw no need further to deal with them. The lip-Christians, on the other hand, have no right of citizenship[249] in the church whatsoever.[250] Therefore they have no right to participate in the discussion about the reform of the church.[251] This right belongs only to the "faithful members of the whole body,"[252] both

The Existence of the Christian in the Legal Structures of This World

as one unit[253] and individually. All these ideas are the necessary consequences of the ecclesiology, which the reformer had sketched as early as 1517.

These observations refute the previous interpretations of Luther's statements mentioned above.[254] They have one error in common: their authors no longer are aware of the concept 'universal church',[255] and this to such a degree that someone could even argue that Luther "fought against it."[256] Yet the truth is that the concepts 'universal church' and 'spiritual church' *(ecclesia universalis, ecclesia spiritualis)* belong to the chief parts of Luther's ecclesiology; it is incomplete and incomprehensible unless one always simultaneously focuses on these *two forms* of the *one church* of Christ,[257] <the universal church (as it exists in particular churches) and the spiritual church>. The tension between the hidden church *(ecclesia abscondita, ecclesia spiritualis)* and the manifest church *(ecclesia manifesta, ecclesia universalis, ecclesiae particulares)*,[258] or more correctly, between the immaculate church *(ecclesia)* and its maculated earthly appearance *(facies ecclesiae)*,[259] occupied Luther from the time of his first lectures on the Psalms (1513-15) until the end of his life. In *To the Christian Nobility* this tension caused him to search for the law of the 'heavenly' kingdom of holy Christendom,[260] that is, of the universal church. This universal church has to organize itself according to the heavenly, that is, the divine legal order of the spiritual church,[261] in which the saints[262] are the called spokesmen.[263] Therefore the concept 'Christendom' or 'Christian body' may not be applied to the mystical body of the true believers[264] without at once considering their position and task in the institutional church. On the other hand, the concept 'Christendom' or 'Christian body' may not be understood as designating the totality of those who are baptized without at once considering those who are the spiritual estate only because they, guided by the Holy Spirit, in faith preserved their spiritual status after they had been baptized. And finally, it is inappropriate to consider the concept 'Christendom' or 'Christian body' to have many meanings;[265] supposedly at one time it designates the totality of the believing Christians, and at another time it designates the totality of those who have been baptized. This concept always designates the body of the true Christians within the community of those who have been baptized. If we consider 'Christian body' or 'Christendom' in terms of ritual tasks and organization, then 'Christian body' or 'Christendom' is nothing other than the church in the world.[266] Therefore the

The Christian in the Politia

concept 'Christian body' or 'Christendom' reveals its true meaning only if within the one concept both forms of the church in the world — that is, the church as spiritual church and the church as universal church — are differentiated and at the same time seen as one unit, because both forms belong together.[267] In this way, 'Christian body' can be defined by beginning either with the spiritual church or the universal church. *Christian body is the community of believing Christians (ecclesia spiritualis)* when by the divine law of the Christian estate,[268] which belongs to that community, that community exercises legal authority in the universal church, and *Christian body is the universal church* when through its believing members that church is connected with the spiritual church personalisticly and voluntarily.

Let us now test this suggested interpretation and see whether it agrees with the details in Luther's *To the Christian Nobility!* According to Luther, the Romanists erected *three walls*[269] in order to prevent the Christian laity, especially the Christian nobility, from taking steps toward a reform of the church which is obedient to Rome, ⟨a particular church within the universal church⟩.

The *first wall* is the *exemption of the clergy from secular authority.*[270] As Luther tells us, the reason for this exemption is the difference between the estate of the clergy and the estate of the laity, supposedly established in divine positive law; therefore by divine law the universal church is a *corpus inequale,*[271] and it is not permissible that secular authority rule over the spiritual.[272] According to Luther, this thesis is wrong from the beginning, because in the universal church there is only one sacramental ⟨spiritual⟩ estate established by Christ,[273] the estate of believing Christians. All differences between estates in the church are based on man-made law and are in reality only differences in man-made commissions for offices.[274] Such commissions are not different from those for secular offices held by Christians; they, too, are awarded according to man-made law. Servants of the church, therefore, are not able to claim divine law when they insist on being exempt from secular authority. By divine law is the spiritual use of all vocations, however, be they ecclesiastical or secular, so that they are a service of Christian brotherly love, that is, the implementation of Christ's law for the "promotion of body and soul."[275] In fulfilling this task, each vocation has the same spiritual dignity; and in fulfilling this task, Christians prove that they belong to a legal community of the divine law, that is, Christ's mystical body. In this understanding and implementation of

The Existence of the Christian in the Legal Structures of This World

their vocations, Christians are connected with one another in a similar way that limbs of a natural body are connected.[276]

This is the meaning of Luther's famous statements about the position of secular estates in Christendom. For instance: Luther said that the incumbent of a secular governmental authority has become "a member of the Christian body"[277] because he has Baptism, faith, and the gospel in common with the clergy.[278] This does not mean that this secular estate as such, ⟨that is, governmental authority,⟩ is declared to be a member of the Christian body.[279] Rather, it is the 'true' Christian who is in the office of governmental authority who is declared to be a member of the Christian body. Only of him can one affirm that he belongs to the spiritual estate, although he has to be engaged in a "corporeal work";[280] that is, he has to implement the duties of an office in the *politia,* which deals with the temporal well-being; he does not have to implement the duties of a spiritual office in the universal church, as the clergy has to do. When a believing Christian conscientiously implements the duties of his office[281] in the governmental authority, he is useful to the Christian congregation; then it does not have to suffer from the conniving of evil persons. The Christian congregation even "owns" him,[282] that is, the congregation has a claim on this member to implement the duties of his office in this conscientious way; 'owning' should be understood as being responsible for the implementation of the duties of the office in this conscientious way, and therefore as a legal claim of the Christian congregation for protection by the office of governmental authority. Christendom, therefore, will not at all obstruct secular governmental authority when it implements its official duties. There exists no *privilegium fori* or *immunitatis* for the human vocational estate of the clergy.[283]

It is another question whether the divine ⟨spiritual⟩ estate of true Christians would not justify an exemption from secular authority. It is easy to answer this question if one considers that each true Christian, motivated by Christian love for the brother,[284] voluntarily assists his fellow Christian who holds an office of governmental authority, and voluntarily affirms that office's authority to use the sword. Thus the power of secular governmental authority "permeates the whole body of Christendom";[285] in practical terms this power is not obstructed by the spiritual estate of the true Christians. This is as far as Luther went in *To the Christian Nobility.* But he did not come to terms with the whole scope of the problem, for in Scripture is written: "The law is not given to a righ-

The Christian in the Politia

teous person." (1 Timothy 1:9.) Luther was aware of this situation, and therefore he returned to this problem in *On Christian Freedom*.

The *second wall* of the Romanists[286] is *the claim that ⟨only⟩ the pope interprets Holy Scripture authoritatively*. According to Luther's judgment, the qualification for such an interpretation is not derived from membership in the universal church, an externally recognizable community of human law,[287] or from having an office in it.[288] Rather, it is derived from membership in the spiritual church, that is, in the church of the divine positive law. Consequently, only the true Christians — each one of them — have the right to interpret Holy Scripture authoritatively.[289]

The *third wall*[290] is *the pope's claim that only he may convene a general council and that he is superior to it.* In contrast, Luther assigned the right and the duty to start reforming the corrupt man-made ecclesiastical law to each faithful member of the whole body,[291] that is, to each true Christian, and he thought that especially Christians in the office of governmental authority were called to this task.

These materials show that Luther's book is an important contribution to the ecclesiology of the Reformation. They also show that the book may not be understood as a draft for a "Christian order of society."[292] The concept 'Christian order of society', or the ideas corresponding to it, was far from Luther's mind — he stayed with the traditional, medieval categories 'universal church' and 'politia'. By placing the structure of the universal church under the control of the spiritual church, he gave, however, to the universal church a legal basis which was different from that of the secular commonwealth. The law of the universal church and the law of the *politia* have different roots and, therefore, different qualities.

This result has far-reaching consequences for understanding the external order of mankind. External Christendom, the universal church, can no longer be used as the center around which the legal existence of the human community is organized. The medieval *respublica christiana* no longer exists,[293] and even in later years Luther did not again think in terms of this medieval *respublica christiana*.[294] Especially his doctrine of the three hierarchies[295] may not be interpreted as if he again affirmed this idea. According to this doctrine, God established three "holy orders,"[296] the office of priest, the estate of marriage, and the secular governmental authority; through them God rules the world. Luther turned this doctrine against the special religious value which the clerical and the monastic estate had in the medieval church. He emphasized that in the three hierarchies a believing Christian is able to perform holy works equal to those done by the clergy and monks — and he should do so.[297] In other words: for Luther there exist no degrees of ‹spiritual› perfection between those three estates. Based on the doctrine of the three hierarchies, Luther evaluated the spiritual quality of service in the universal church and in the *politia* (including the *oeconomia*), but he said nothing about the organizational relationship in which the three hierarchies exist with each other. The doctrine of the three hierarchies does not at all presuppose the concept 'Christendom' as an entity that encompasses both the state and the (visible) church.[298] The constitutional law of the universal church is determined by the connection of that church with the kingdom of Christ; the constitutional law of the *politia* is determined by the tasks the *politia* has in the kingdom of the world. This difference may not be bridged by a higher concept. Therefore it was far from Luther's mind to replace the pope's monarchy with a dyarchy of the secular and of the ecclesiastical authority.[299] His doctrine of the two governances is terribly misunderstood in the following argument: Luther declared secular governmental authority to be the "indispensable member of Christendom,"[300] that is, a member "of the kingdom of God (Christ's kingdom, kingdom of heaven), which is ‹present› in the world."[301]

Luther also did not elevate the spiritual church to be the spiritual center of the "Christian social organism."[302] "With its power of life" the spiritual church supposedly "penetrates" this organism, and in this way shapes it into the "body of Christendom."[303] How should this come about? Christ's mystical body has no other power of life than that of the Holy Spirit, and that power is received in faith; who does not believe does not share in this power, even if he has been baptized. The spiritual church has nothing in common with nominal Christians.[304] They and the spiritual church do not form a body because a body is nothing without a head, which provides the power of life. This idea was well-known in medieval theology, and Luther affirmed it.[305] The head of the spiritual church is Christ, the head of the unbelievers is the devil. Therefore, according to Luther, one cannot construct the Christian quality of the human social organism on the foundation of external Christendom with its mixture of believers and unbelievers. Certainly, a governmental authority is not Christian "under any circumstances"[306] just because all its actions take place within a Christian frame, that is, within "external Christendom"; and a governmental authority is not Christian just be-

The Christian in the Politia

cause at one time it acts "within this universal Christian frame as a member of the whole Christian body, that is, of Christian society," and at other times it acts as *praecipuum membrum ecclesiae*,[307] that is, as the "chief functionary"[308] of a territory's organized church. This "universal Christian frame" did not exist for Luther. The eschatologically-based contrast between the two kingdoms and their law makes it impossible to understand church and *politia* as a homogeneous body, built on one law.[309]

Consequently, the title 'Christian' connected with external Christendom does not provide a legal basis for explaining the Christian quality of the office of governmental authority,[310] in the same way in which a governmental authority is not Jewish or heathen just because it deals with Jews or heathen. It is also impossible to explain the Christian quality of a governmental authority in terms of the content of its actions; for instance: the incumbent of a governmental authority may not be called Christian because and whenever he cares for the Christian church — he is just as Christian when he rules the secular commonwealth. Rather, the only decisive factor in explaining the Christian quality of a governmental authority is the membership of the office's incumbent in the spiritual church[311] — this alone determines the quality of his actions.[312] That always was Luther's position, and there is no difference between statements he made in *To the Christian Nobility* and those he made in later years. In the strict sense, only a true Christian can be called a Christian governmental authority; *important is not the holding of the office, but the performance of the duties of the office.*[313] Governmental authority has to establish its Christian quality through its actions; based on the kingdom of Christ,[314] it has to act for the kingdom of the world, and conversely, it has to relate all its actions in the kingdom of the world to God.[315] Actions of a governmental authority, which are legitimate in terms of the secular natural law, may be called Christian only when they also[316] are a service of faith to the divine natural law,[317] that is, to Christ's law.[318] This alone provides a good conscience before God and at the same time before men.[319] "Then governance functions according to, and originates in, a sensitive, pure, upright heart, a pleasure to God and the world."[320] God is pleased because "everything is done according to God's Word and for God's sake"[321] so that the spiritual law of love is in action; the world is pleased because it experiences that all actions of governmental authority are directed toward the "benefit, honor, and well-being of others"[322] so that in this way the secular natural-law commandment of universal love for the neighbor is fulfilled.[323] A ruler who organizes his office in such a way that "it functions in God's spirit and also serves the neighbor" rules "in God's kingdom."[324] Important, therefore, is not the institution[325] but the person;[326] important is not the person's external actions but his God-formed will motivating his actions.[327] Such a "believing governmental authority"[328] rules "in the spiritual estate"[329] and, therefore, is Christian.

Now we are able to answer Barth's question[330] whether in the teachings of the reformers human law was a topic of the Christian faith and, therefore, also of Christian confession. Using almost the same words with which Barth asked his question, Luther answered affirmatively; this proves that he would have considered Barth's question theologically justified: "Secular order is an external matter and does not strengthen faith, and it is also an article of faith because of the Word on which it is based, Romans 13‹:1›."[331] This statement is not positivist reasoning by citing a passage from Scripture, but it is the result of the understanding of faith and law as developed in "the purest theology, ‹that is, the theology› of the cross."[332] This theology leads man, who wants to have a clear picture of the order of the world, to the only adequate doctrine of state and society, that is, *the Holy Spirit's doctrine of state and society.*[333] In that doctrine we find what human doctrines about this topic are unable to present, regardless whether they are developed by jurists or philosophers. Of course, those doctrines are valuable; whoever wants to be informed about the substance and form of the *politia*,[334] or about mankind and its place in the secular commonwealth, has to consult these documents of human wisdom and experience. The value of these contributions to the efforts of shaping the best of possible states has to remain undiminished! Yet the result of all those human efforts, impressive as they are, ultimately is nothing but miserable patchwork because it lacks what is most important, that is, the orientation toward God in Christ.[335] At this point the divine doctrine of state and society begins. In four chapters it deals with its topic, ‹the *politia* oriented toward God in Christ›.

In the first chapter God is presented as *causa efficiens et finalis mundi.*[336] In the second chapter the *ordo naturalis mundi*[337] is explained as the legal order of God's kingdom at the left; this order is fixed by God in the secular natural law, and this order establishes man as *minister et cooperator Dei.*[338] In the third chapter the *regnum Christi in mundo,* that is, God's kingdom at the right, is used to demonstrate how in the *politia*

The Christian in the Politia

the secular natural law should be used in a divine way, namely, by obeying the spiritual <divine> natural law.[339] In the fourth chapter the personalistic prerequisite for this obedience is developed, that is, *iustificatio sola fide*. Thus the connection between justification by faith and law in Luther's thought is established. Only a justified person has the insight[340] into the spiritual foundations of the secular legal order and affirms them.[341] Only he sees in the *politia* a "community of God."[342] Therefore only a justified person has the spiritual ability and authority[343] to implement man-made law and political authority according to the divine natural law. A natural person,[344] on the other hand, can at best act according to the human secular natural law. The *usus legis spiritualiter et corporaliter legitimus*[345] is possible only for a justified person.

§ 7. Retrospect

We are at the end of the presentation of Luther's doctrine of law and are looking at the practical consequences of that doctrine once more. The legal existence of a Christian in the world has two different forms, depending on whether he deals with Christians or non-Christians.

Among Christians rules only the divine natural law as Christ's law. A corporeal association organized on this legal basis exists in particular churches of Christendom — and only there.[346] The legal existence of these particular churches is governed by the divine law, either the divine positive or the divine natural law — the latter when a Christian congregation[347] creates human ecclesiastical law; this[348] Christian law is shaped according to the law of love *(lex charitatis)*.

The secular law of the *politia* is quite different. A Christian is not subject to the coercive force of this secular law. Christ's law instructs him, however, to obey this secular law voluntarily for the sake of the love for the neighbor. Thus the Christian becomes involved in the contrasts and tensions which exist between the divine natural law and the secular natural law, and between the secular natural law and positive man-made law when it is in opposition to the secular natural law. When he is able to act freely within the realm of the secular law, he has to act according to Christ's law. When a governmental authority makes demands on him as a subject, its authority to command is limited by the institutional and the substantive secular natural law. When a governmental authority commands him to violate this secular natural law in his relationship with God or his neighbor, he has the right and the duty to remonstrate and disobey the commanding tyrant. This disobedience develops into armed resistance to the grand tyrant; he rejects the God-ordained separation of the two kingdoms and their respective law on principle and replaces the divine will for law with his will for power. In every form of resistance a Christian is exclusively guided by obedience to God and love for the neighbor, and this is different for the non-Christian. For a Christian the issue in resistance is not to defend himself against the threat of personal injustice but to defend the order of God's kingdom at the right and at the left. The same concern for the well-being of the neighbor also decisively answers the question whether a Christian may and should hold an office of governmental authority. The duty of a Christian to serve in such an office has to be affirmed emphatically. Serving in a secular office, a Christian not only serves his fellowmen, as he is obligated to do according to the secular natural law, but, more important, he also fulfills a commission issued by the divine natural law. Only a Christian can fully do justice to the spiritual meaning of this commission; the care of a Christian ruler for the church of his territory demonstrates this in a special way. A commonwealth governed by a true Christian is in good order when the ruler has those natural qualifications for ruling which his office demand; the commonwealth retains, however, its secular character — *a 'Christian' state does not exist.*[349] Even for a Christian in the office of governmental authority the secular natural law is the supreme standard for governing. This answers the highly controversial question whether Luther envisioned the order of society to be a Christian social organism, a 'Christian body' *(corpus Christianum),*[350] which would combine church and *politia* in one unit. One may not understand Luther's doctrine in this way, because for him law in each of the two kingdoms had a different quality, and both laws had to be strictly separated.

WHAT HAPPENED TO LUTHER'S DOCTRINE OF LAW?

The controversy about the *corpus christianum* in Luther's thinking[1] deserved special attention because it is typical of the problems which his doctrine of law posed for the generations that followed him. On the one hand, one recognized that his doctrine of law was deeply rooted in the theological-juristic teachings of the medieval church. On the other hand, one sensed the bold change that these teachings underwent. Yet one was unable fully to do justice to Luther's own, original contribution to the doctrine of law. That contribution was the incorporation of the tradition in a totally new system of law, and that system was the result of a new understanding of faith.

How should it have been otherwise? Already in Melanchthon's case[2] it is sometimes difficult to recognize how close he was to Luther.[3] Melanchthon was more interested in the world, its law and its political structure, and the continuity of its philosophical education and political history. How much space did he give in his lectures to external discipline *(disciplina externa),* and how much ethical weight did he assign to it! How tenaciously did he hold on to the concept 'respublica christiana' as the politically organized Christendom,[4] as long as there was even the slightest hope that the secular unity of Christendom could

---

A literal translation of the title would read: "The Fate of Luther's Doctrine of Law." The following materials justify the replacement of this rather weighty title with our simple version.

help bring about a new religious ⟨churchly⟩ unification! With what skill did he adjust the political wisdom of the past to the demands of the new situation when he developed the legal materials for the guardianship of Both Tables *(custodia utriusque tabulae)*[5] or for society *(societas)*![6] Nevertheless, in Melanchthon's work, at least in that of the young Melanchthon, the basics of Luther's doctrine of law were still very much present. Because of its usefulness for teaching, its systematic unity, and its juristic precision, Melanchthon's doctrine of law may be considered an excellent introduction to the legal materials of Luther,[7] the other and greater reformer, and this in spite of the specific materials which are typical of a Humanist and a conservative politician.

Since the turn of the sixteenth to the seventeenth century Melanchthon's legal doctrine was, however, no longer viewed in the frame of this connection with Luther's doctrine of law. This documents the strength of a new feeling for law, which was making headway. The main characteristic of Luther's doctrine of law is the duality in the concept 'law', the spiritual law and the secular law, with the former ranking before the latter. Now this understanding made way for a monistic understanding of law, which Luther would have called secular. No longer the theologian but the philosopher interpreted law. In this interpretation the *politia* replaced the church as the organizational center. In order to be able to claim the title 'law', all law has to have the same essence as the law of the *politia*. That principle was applied even to the divine law. Its existence was not at all denied, but divine law lost its spiritual dynamics, vitality, and fullness which, according to Luther, are characteristic of the divine commandment. The divine law became the norm of norms. Of course, one considered this norm to be far superior to human norms because it regulated not only the external conduct but also the internal life of the believers. Nevertheless, divine law was now a commandment which essentially was identical with human norms.

Thus the philosophical idea of law dominated all law.[8] Whatever did not agree with this idea — for instance, the divine law concerning the sacraments, or the man-made liturgical order — was considered to be a part of the non-legal makeup of the church, while the church itself was absorbed into the legal order of the state. The famous statement of Bishop Optatus of Milevis became valid again: "The church is in the state."[9] Ecclesiastical law became a part of the law of the state, and he who had the authority to create and implement law in the state had the same authority also in the church.[10] The state made ecclesiastical matters its business, and did so in two, interconnected ways: the state legally incorporated the church in its order, and the state subordinated the ethos of the state to the religious mission of the church.

At this point the ideal state of the *respublica christiana* was renewed.[11] This ideal state was, however, no longer identical with the *respublica christiana* of medieval teachings about state and church; it was not vibrant with the spirit of the so-called *corpus christianum* of the pre-Reformation period; it did not even have anything in common with Melanchthon's universally perceived *respublica christiana,* because this new ideal state was developed within the frame of individual states; and it was far removed from Luther's idea of law.

Protestant Humanism created this ideal state. In it, ideas of Christian late antiquity became again effective by being merged with the religious energies of the Reformation. For the construction of a new political system and a new system of ecclesiastical governance one took from the Reformation some most useful legal concepts and principles of governing. One has to mention only the idea of the Christian prince, modeled according to Luther's Christian governmental authority, or the incorporation of Melanchthon's materials for the *cura religionis* of the godly magistrat in the law of the state's sovereignty as the most important regale.[12] Even Canon law was attractive, and one was quite willing to use it as long as evangelical dogmatics permitted it somehow; after all, jurisdiction according to Canon law and jurisdiction according to secular law have the same root in Roman law.

These materials were skillfully used for the development of 'the Protestant idea of state', and in this idea they were pulled together in a unified system. This idea dominated the legal situation in the Lutheran territories of Germany for centuries. The *landesherrliche Kirchenregiment* demonstrated that this idea was compatible with Lutheranism's understanding of the faith. But this restrained judgment did not satisfy those who represented the dominant praxis and theory. They projected their ideas, derived from Protestant Humanism, into Luther's writings; living proof of this is the fact that still today some people tenaciously affirm that Luther maintained the concept 'corpus christianum'.[13] Yet as far as the relationship of the church with the *politia* is concerned, this Protestant idea of state did not grow from the reformer's theology and doctrine of law. One may even argue that precisely this independence of the Protestant idea of state from Luther

What Happened to Luther's Doctrine of Law?

made it possible that this idea prevailed so long without the theological controversies among Lutherans having any significant impact on it.

From the very beginning this Protestant idea of state was tied to monarchy. With the disappearance of monarchy, this idea also disappeared. Now Lutherans were faced with the difficult task of finding a theological and a juristic solution of the problems created by this new situation.[14] All efforts in this connection lead to Luther's doctrine of law, and they demand a critical position on it.[15] In the process of developing such a position, the materials dependent on the circumstances of Luther's time have to be separated from those which have lasting significance. Yet access to Luther's doctrine of law is almost blocked. It will again become open only if his statements concerning law are interpreted in the frame of his theology, and if in this way his understanding of law is established. To show the way for this undertaking was the goal of the present vade mecum for the reformer's doctrine of law.

APPENDIX I

Luther's Doctrine of the Right of Resistance to the Emperor

Johannes Heckel added Appendixes I and II to the original edition (1953). Martin Heckel, the editor of the second edition (1973), added Appendixes III-VII. See also above, xivf.

Luther's position on the right to resist[1] the emperor[2] has been repeatedly and thoroughly studied.[3] Yet in terms of theology and jurisprudence this topic is not yet completely clarified.[4] Therefore the impression could develop that difficult, inner struggles caused the reformer to "twist and turn"[5] in his position on this topic. In reality, his position was more uniform[6] than it might appear in light of this impression.

In all stages of his thinking about this topic, Luther was concentrating on the same question, that is, how the controversy between the head of the Empire and the evangelical princes had to be judged according to the law of each of the two kingdoms. This question determined, first, the competency of theologians to speak in this matter;[7] their authority was restricted to the situation when the divine natural law and its traces in the secular natural law were at stake.[8] This question determined, secondly, the decision whether in principle active corporeal ⟨armed⟩ resistance to governmental authority was at all permitted, and whether a Christian in the office of prince may use this right. This question determined, finally, whether the right of resistance may be claimed in a concrete situation. ⟨Throughout his life,⟩ this question and the three situations derived from it were the legal basis of all that

Appendix I

Luther said on this topic. As time progressed, he developed, however, from this basis different ideas about armed resistance to the emperor, and we can distinguish *three lines in his thinking;* they overlapped in terms of material and chronology, but juristically they were distinct from each other. The first line evolved between 1522[9] and 1530, the second after 1530, and the third was completed around 1539.

In the *first line of thinking Luther dealt with an illegitimate command of a legitimate governmental authority,* if the situation was judged by the secular natural law. Luther precisely differentiated between the content of the command, which by the standards of the secular natural law was invalid, and the official authority of the command. The emperor's intended suppression of the true ‹Christian› doctrine opposed God's holy will;[10] therefore military service in a religious war against the evangelical estates of the Empire had to be refused.[11]

This refusal to obey the emperor's command is not rebellion[12] but a duty toward the divine overlord of the emperor; therefore it does not violate the secular natural law but rather obeys it. Yet one may not exceed passive disobedience. All reasons derived from secular natural law, which the jurists cite to justify active disobedience, accomplish nothing. Invalid is the argument that the emperor has broken his oath of fidelity[13] so that the feudal-law bond between the evangelical princes and the head of the Empire is dissolved automatically; according to Luther, the emperor remains the secular head of the Empire as long as he has not been deposed in due process.[14] Invalid is also the argument that the Protestants are denied a hearing which is guaranteed by law;[15] the diet, ‹the place for such a hearing,› would condemn the confessors of the gospel anyhow.[16] And useless is the natural-law permission of armed resistance; the principle 'one may fight force with force' *(vim vi repellere licet)* is valid only for those of equal rank in law,[17] if it is to be valid at all.[18] Therefore active corporeal resistance cannot be justified on the basis of the secular natural law.[19] And even if it could be justified, this would not at all provide a Christian in the office of prince with sufficient authorization for engaging in such resistance;[20] when dealing with a legitimate governmental authority, a Christian in the office of prince has to follow not the secular natural law but the divine natural law, and this law does not include the permission of active corporeal resistance.[21]

In the *second line of thinking Luther concentrated on the positive public law.*[22] According to the information the jurists provided to Luther, there was a law which authorized armed resistance of the Imperial estates if the emperor violated the Empire's constitution.[23] Since in terms of the secular natural law one could not object to such an arrangement,[24] the theologians had no authority to speak.

Again,[25] it is a different problem, however, whether a Christian prince may use this positive-law authorization, or rather does not have to entrust the protection of the true church to Christ, the divine "guardian of the church" *(custos ecclesiae).*[26] Luther was very cautious at this point. He warned not to trust human power, but aside from this, he left the decision to the consciences of the princes.[27] This meant: God does not prohibit active corporeal resistance as an institution of the positive public law.[28] The decision to engage in such a resistance, however, may not be justified with a supposed necessity to protect the church ⟨and the believers⟩ with secular means;[29] political reasons would be the only acceptable justification; they are not connected with being a Christian,[30] and, therefore, they could also motivate a non-Christian to act. Being a Christian is not a public-law title for a prince to proceed against the emperor with arms.[31] Therefore every evangelical governmental authority has to decide whether to engage in active corporeal resistance and be personally responsible to God for this decision. To make a mistake in such a decision would still be more tolerable before God than the insistence on a right of resistance supposedly based on the secular natural law. At least such a wrong decision would demonstrate a Christian's will to entrust his action to God's guidance.[32]

Luther developed the thoughts presented thus far on the basis of a legitimate governmental authority issuing an illegitimate command to its subjects. At this point began the *third line of his thinking on resistance. Did this situation exist when the emperor made war against the evangelical princes for the sake of religion?*[33] This was Luther's new question. It shows that he now had a better understanding of the public-law structure of the Empire than earlier. Further, Luther's membership concept of law[34] became now more effective in practical matters than earlier; then, so it seems, the structure of the *politia* as a sovereign entity opposed this concept.

The reformer cleared the way to a new solution of his task with remarkable thoroughness. His starting point was the dualism[35] in natural law. ⟨According to Luther,⟩ every Christian is obligated to obey the secular natural law,[36] but the divine natural law has precedence;[37] the duty to be faithful to Christ in his kingdom ranks higher than any duties to obey the order of the kingdom of the world. Based on this principle,

Appendix I

Luther discussed the right of active corporeal resistance, using three specific cases: First, resistance to the robber who takes away one's property by force; second, the conduct of a subject toward his territorial governmental authority which, contrary to law, inflicts evil upon him;[38] third, the legal situation of the Imperial estates, especially of the electors, when the head of the Empire makes war against them for the sake of religion. Luther started at the lowest level in the structure of a commonwealth, then related that level to the next higher level, and ended with the discussion of the relationship of this higher level to the highest level.[39] In each of these three cases the situation in law was different.

In the *first case, the attacker and the victim have equal rank in law. The victim is a private person;* as a Christian he does not cling to his earthly goods and, therefore, yields to the attack of the robber, though he threatens the robber with God's punishment. Now a new idea[40] appears: *The victim is also a citizen, ⟨a public person,⟩* and each citizen shares in the responsibility of maintaining the legally established peace within the secular commonwealth; that is, he has a public function,[41] and, therefore, he participates in the office of governmental authority as its member.[42] When the situation is viewed in this way, then the fight against the robber is not only a subject's right but his duty;[43] this consequence is the result of the subject's natural-law position vis-à-vis governmental authority. Therefore, *among people of equal rank in law, active resistance to the illegal action of stealing property is commanded.* It does not make any difference when the robber justifies his action with supposed religious reasons.[44]

The situation is different in the second case: a legitimate territorial governmental authority persecutes evangelical Christians for the sake of their religion. Maintaining peace is the noblest task of a ruler,[45] and every subject has to support him in this task; under no circumstances may a subject obstruct him.[46] *Therefore the right of active corporeal resistance to governmental authority does not exist, not even in the case of religious persecution.*[47] It is true, a secular governmental authority has no right to issue commands in matters of faith;[48] therefore disobedience to its illegitimate command does not violate the secular natural law.[49] When that governmental authority proceeds with force against body, life, and property of an evangelical Christian because he disobeys that illegitimate command, he has to yield to it,[50] but he may escape from the power of that authority by fleeing or emigrating.[51] A Christian has to accept this legal situation. The Christian estate, ⟨that is, being a Christian,⟩ does not grant any jurisdictional competencies in the secular commonwealth.⁵² Among them would be the right of active resistance to the governmental authority, because that right presupposes the competency to be the judge of the governmental authority; ⟨therefore that right does not exist⟩.

⟨The jurists took up the idea of being a Christian and argued:⟩ All Christians are equal before God, and all have the same duty to serve the Creator with all their strength. From this basis they derived consequences for public law.⁵³ Luther did not agree with them, because this argumentation resulted in the mixing of the two kingdoms; a spiritual basic right⁵⁴ would be transferred into political life.

Nevertheless, Luther arrived at granting an evangelical prince the right of active corporeal ⟨armed⟩ resistance to the emperor ⟨when he discussed *the third case, that is,*⟩ *when the emperor would make war against an evangelical prince for the sake of the prince's faith.* That certainly was a surprising change. In earlier days Luther simply had applied the law of a territorial subject's duty to obey his territorial lord to the relationship between the Imperial estates and the emperor.⁵⁵ Now he abandoned this position. The statements of the jurists⁵⁶ about the estate structure of the Empire⁵⁷ had produced results. They convinced Luther that the positive constitutional law of the Empire did not allow one to equate the relationship between an elector and the emperor, the head of the Empire, with that between a subject and his territorial lord.⁵⁸

It is noteworthy that Luther used legal ideas of the conciliar theory to clarify for himself an elector's position in the governing of the Empire. Electors were the parts of the Empire *(partes imperii)*;⁵⁹ because of their official responsibility *(in partem sollicitudinis)*,⁶⁰ they, together with the emperor, were called to govern the Empire.⁶¹ The situation was similar to the conciliar understanding of the role of bishops, which Luther⁶² affirmed: Together with the pope and under his guidance, the bishops rule the church; by divine positive law the pope and the bishops have equal rank in the church's hierarchy; each bishop is appointed to take care *(in partem sollicitudinis)*⁶³ of his diocese.

⟨On the basis of these materials, Luther argued:⟩ Apart⁶⁴ from certain prerogatives of the emperor,⁶⁵ he and the electors have the same rank in law.⁶⁶ Therefore any coercive action of the emperor against the Imperial estates, at least insofar as the electors were concerned, would be not an administrative enforcement (a police action), but it would be a war, or war-like, public-law execution. The public law of the Empire, however, in no way authorizes such an action of the emperor, either the substantive public law or the law of procedure. ⟨Therefore the war against the evangelical princes for the sake of their faith, planned by Emperor Charles V, would be an unjust war,[67] and the evangelical princes would have the right and duty of armed resistance. A combination of arguments derived from the substantive and the procedural law of the Empire would justify their action. We deal first with the substantive law.⟩ In religious matters, the institutional secular natural law, ⟨which controls the positive law[68] and thus the substantive public law, in which the emperor's competencies are fixed,⟩ does not grant any power of commanding to the emperor. ⟨If the emperor issues the Imperial ban against the evangelical princes because they do not comply with his order to suppress the preaching of the gospel, and then makes war against them to enforce the ban, he transgresses his competency. That is, the emperor violates the basis of the substantive public law in the institutional secular natural law. On the other hand, the princes who resist him with force obey the transpositive institutional secular natural law. Their resistance is an effort to restrict the emperor's competency to secular matters, and⟩ in secular matters the princes obey him ⟨so that he has no reason to make war against them. Now we turn to the procedural law of the Empire. According to that law,⟩ the emperor's unilateral action against the evangelical princes is also to be resisted. Only together with all the electors could the emperor decide on a legal action of such revolutionary consequences as issuing the ban against an elector and making war against him to enforce the ban. Such a decision has never been made, and never will be made. The emperor's planned religious war is, therefore, nothing other than a despicable raid against the evangelical princes for depriving them of their possessions.[69] Anyone who turns a body politic into a den of robbers[70] has to be treated as a highway robber,[71] ⟨and⟩ the princes must oppose him with active corporeal resistance. Already the Second Table of the Decalogue makes that resistance legitimate,[72] and the institutional secular natural law, which charges the Christian prince with the *cura religionis*,[73] makes it even more so. It is obvious that Melanchthon's tireless propaganda for the guardianship of Both Tables[74] as a divine charge of governmental authority had its positive effect on Luther.[75] Finally and most important: The emperor's planned religious war is truly monstrous, and it is beyond any juristic label. Religion is not the reason for this war — how could a Christian emperor kill the confessors of the true Christian faith for the sake of Christ? Nor is law, or the ⟨well-being of the⟩ Empire, the reason. The commander-in-chief in this war is the archenemy of law, of the Empire, and of religion — the pope.[76] With words of terrible passion, Luther hurled his juristic and theological anathema at the pope, and he hurled the same anathema at the pope's soldier,[77] the emperor. Like Nimrod,[78] pope and emperor try to spread a new, God-opposing *politia*[79] all over the world. As usurpers of a God-hostile sovereignty over the world, pope and emperor condemn themselves to annihilation.

APPENDIX II

The Cura Religionis *of the Evangelical Prince*

Nothing demonstrates the difference between the government of a heathen and a Christian better than the *cura religionis*.[1] It is surprising that Luther called it "the spiritual governance" of the secular governmental authority,[2] or spoke of the governance of governmental authority in "the spiritual estate."[3] With such phrases he described the caring of a governmental authority for the church in its territory. This caring proves that a true Christian, that is, a member of the spiritual estate,[4] occupies the office of governmental authority and administers it in obedience to God; in other words, he implements his secular governance for the good of the church in a spiritual way, as a Christian governmental authority should. A heathen ruler is incapable of this caring for the church in a God-pleasing way; either he is blind and does not see the tasks necessary in this connection, or if he does see them he attempts to fulfill them in a way that is contrary to God's will. In contrast to such a heathen ruler,[5] a Christian ruler knows the "law of the gospel."[6] Therefore he not only sees in the *cura religionis* the most important task of governing, but he also knows how to undertake this task in the right way.

The *cura religionis* consists of *two major duties:* The positive caring for religion on the one hand;[7] the elimination of defects in a territory's public religious system on the other, and, in preparation for this project, the visitation of the congregations in the territory.[8] The first duty results, for instance, in the care for the appointment, protection, and maintenance of the servants of the church;[9] in the following we shall not deal with these matters. Fulfilling the second duty results in the fight against publicly taught false doctrine[10] as the crime of blasphemy.[11] It results also in the competency to reform the man-made ecclesiastical law of the territory's particular church when the following three conditions exist: that law violates the three spiritual basic rights[12] of a well-ordered church;[13] contrary to Christ's will, that law turns that particular church into a *politia* with the spiritual title 'church'; the church[14] does not have the strength to get rid of this monstrosity. A prince who cares for the church in this way remains within the competency of secular governmental authority. One is tempted to argue that in this *cura religionis* the secular and the spiritual governance are intermingled. This argument would be wrong, because caring for a territory's public religious system is the noblest task of a secular governmental authority.[15] Further, a prince does not encroach on the spiritual governance when he, as a member of the ecclesiastical body, gives brotherly aid in the creation and implementation of ecclesiastical law.[16] Yet in doing this, he has to adhere strictly to the divine positive law of the spiritual church. Therefore he may not give any orders to the representatives of the ministry of the Word when they preach God's Word and administer the sacraments in accordance with Scripture.[17] In fact, he has to guard against using the power of governmental authority in the church,[18] because the spiritual church, and therefore the institutional church, has only one governmental authority, that is, God in Christ. No one may impose ecclesiastical law made by governmental authority on the Christian congregation. *Luther was not one of the ancestors of the landesherrliche Kirchenregiment.*[19]

Luther also was not an heir of the medieval doctrine of a prince's *advocatio ecclesiae*.[20] This seems to be a risky argument. Luther, it is true, used strong words when he opposed the emperor who, claiming to be the secular head of Christendom, set himself up as the protector of the faith and the church.[21] Yet he also demanded of the evangelical princes to implement the *cura religionis* in order to demonstrate their faith; and he pointed out that the church has to expect a godly prince to defend and protect it.[22] This line of arguing does not suggest clarity in principle but rather opportunism in ecclesiastical affairs. Therefore in recent scholarship this situation has been evaluated in different ways.

When implemented, the *cura religionis* was very close to the medieval *Kirchenvogtei,* but its legal basis was different nevertheless. ‹In medieval society› the *advocatio ecclesiae* was due to a secular prince within the church,²³ ⟨that is, the universal church⟩. Two legal titles had to coincide: a spiritual one, that is, membership in the universal church,²⁴ and a secular one, that is, the legitimate holding of the office of governmental authority. In the medieval *advocatio ecclesiae* both titles were merged in a unified institution, as it was appropriate for the spiritual-secular empire of Christendom.

Luther, too, affirmed that for the ⟨legitimate⟩ implementation of the *cura religionis* a spiritual legal title and a secular legal title had to coincide. For him these two titles only cooperated with one another, however; they were not absorbed into a higher, homogeneous term, just as the church and the *politia* did not penetrate each other in an organization which transcended both. This was the first difference between Luther's position and that of the Middle Ages, and it was based on his doctrine of the two kingdoms. The second difference grew from the reformer's ecclesiology; here membership in the universal church by itself was not at all a title of spiritual law.²⁵ Unlike the followers of the papacy, Luther understood the universal church not as a spiritual, that is, divine communion, but as a human communion.²⁶ Membership in this communion, that is, external Christendom, did not enable someone to know what is the true doctrine and the well-being of Christ's church in the world; only membership in the spiritual church, that is, internal Christendom, does this. According to Luther, the spiritual legal title was membership in the spiritual church; without this title a prince was unable legitimately to implement the *cura religionis* with the goal of reforming the corrupt ecclesiastical law. This title belonged to all believers in the universal church — but only to them. It also belonged to the ⟨believing⟩ Christian in the office of governmental authority; for reasons of order, he, before anyone else, was called to use this title.²⁷

This believing Christian in the governmental office may act in ecclesiastical matters, however, only if and when the church's constitution does not work. This situation occurs when the ecclesiastical officials, who in the first place are called to remedy defects in the church, misuse or neglect their office. Then ⟨a believing prince acts on the basis of⟩ an inner-churchly emergency law,²⁸ which belongs to all believers. The use of this law is grounded in the spiritual church, and the incentive to use this law is spiritual, that is, Christian brotherly love. A Christian dedicates all his ability and means to the service of this love, and, therefore, also the power of the governmental office. A prince may use the authority of his office, however, only in such a way that the particu-

The Cura Religionis *of the Evangelical Prince*

lar church <of his territory> is liberated from the oppression by a law which is no longer churchly so that that liberated church is enabled to reorganize itself according to the three spiritual basic rights.[29]

Having surveyed the legalities of the *cura religionis,* we are able to take a position on the most important interpretations found in recent scholarship. Sohm and Holl are its outstanding representatives.

According to Sohm,[30] a prince is not only an individual within Christendom, which is ruled by the ecclesiastical authority, but also the representative of the power of governmental authority. As such he is the *praecipuum membrum ecclesiae* (foremost member of the church) and has the *ius reformandi* (right to reform) in the church, a right which is endowed with the power of coercion <for enforcing the prince's command>.

The starting point in Sohm's argumentation was correct, but his subsequent ideas were not. He overlooked that the Christian <spiritual> estate, on which the church's constitution is based,[31] is incompatible with the presence of the secular governmental authority's governance in a particular church. That Christian <spiritual> estate, therefore, does not permit that in the church a Christian prince has the authority of commanding. A prince may not enforce his authority in the church on earth in an authoritative way, that is, as the power of the sword. Sohm failed to understand Luther's concept 'church'. So far Holl's critique of Sohm was justified.

Yet Holl also did not present a clear picture of Luther's position when he discussed the reformer's doctrine of the state, or to be more precise, his concept 'Christian governmental authority' *(christliche Obrigkeit)* and its relationship with the church. Holl[32] clearly differentiated between a Christian as a person and the office of governmental authority; the substance of this office was not altered when its incumbent affirmed Christianity:

> When the church itself does its duty, then a Christian prince is in the church nothing other than another Christian. His office is outside of "Christendom." The fact that in addition <to being nothing other than a Christian> he is also a prince becomes significant only at the moment when the church does not do its duty (or is unable to do it). In that situation it becomes important that <the office of> secular authority *is more involved in preserving the order of the world,* which has its goal in the (invisible) church, *than any other office* (except the spiri-

Appendix II

tual office of public ministry). For the activities ⟨of secular authority⟩ are "the most important work of reason," ...

The legal title authorizing governmental authority to act in ecclesiastical matters is, therefore, purely secular; it is the concern for the secular common good, or in other words, the political interest in a well-ordered church. This is a totally modern idea. It emerged from the problems connected with the modern Protestant *Kulturstaat*[33] and its relationship with the church. In such a state the church is understood as an important component in the organization of the civic commonwealth. In an emergency situation, ⟨the representative of the⟩ state as the protector of the public order[34] feels authorized also to see to it that in ecclesiastical matters all things are in good order. His spiritual qualifications are unimportant;[35] his evangelical confession is sufficient.[36] Membership in external Christendom makes the incumbent of the governmental office into a *christliche Obrigkeit.* He is a Christian, that is, a member of the (visible) church,[37] and "in addition he is also a prince." It is easy to see here the image of the German evangelical prince of the era of the *landesherrliche Kirchenregiment.* Holl was very careful to paint this image in colors taken from Luther's palette — indeed, he came closer to the right shade than his predecessors — but he accomplished only a distant resemblance of the model Luther had created. *In the phrase 'christliche Obrigkeit' the adjective was important for Luther, for Holl it was the noun.* 'Christliche Obrigkeit' was for Luther a theological concept, for Holl a political concept. Therefore Holl was able to assign a *political emergency law applicable to the church* ⟨*from outside of the church*⟩.[38] Luther, on the other hand, thought of a *spiritual emergency law* ⟨*created*⟩ *within the church* ⟨by certain conditions⟩. Holl's reference to "the most important work of reason," which the governmental authority undertakes, marks the difference between both positions in a significant way. For Luther the decisive mark would be missing in this phrase, that is the fact that the reason of a *Christian* governmental authority is illuminated by faith.

APPENDIX III

In the Maze of Luther's Doctrine of the Two Kingdoms

Johannes Heckel, *Im Irrgarten der Zwei-Reiche-Lehre. Zwei Abhandlungen zum Reichs- und Kirchenbegriff Martin Luthers.* Theologische Existenz heute. Eine Schriftenreihe, ed. by Karl G. Steck and Georg Eichholz. Neue Folge 55 (Munich, 1957), 3-39. For the second title, see below, 466, n. 92.

The presentation of Luther's doctrine of the two kingdoms by some evangelical theologians resembles an elaborately planned maze whose creator lost the design while working on it; therefore whoever follows the creator is lost in this maze. In light of this situation, those engaged in Luther research today prefer to follow the apparently clearer doctrine of the two governances; they deal with the kingdom doctrine only to the degree that it is connected with the doctrine of the governances. And those engaged in jurisprudence, almost without exception, avoid dealing with the kingdom doctrine, and when they concentrate on a theological-philosophical concept 'kingdom' they do not deal with Luther's two kingdoms.

Yet Walther Schönfeld stated correctly that "the differentiation between the two kingdoms is the alpha and omega" of Luther's doctrine of society.[1] Whoever deals with the relationship between theology and law in the reformer's thought, time and again will be drawn into that maze mentioned above. Therefore it is necessary to approach the kingdom doctrine in a new way, that is, its legal content has to be examined.

Appendix III

'Kingdom' is not only a theological but also a legal concept. In the thought of an author trained in late scholastic theology, as Luther was, 'kingdom' has a clear legal profile. Not much attention has been paid to this fact in the available theological presentations of Luther's thought. Therefore one may hope to gain new results by using juristic methods, especially those of the history of law.

Guided by such considerations, I began my book on Luther's doctrine of law, *Lex charitatis,* with a sketch of the reformer's kingdom doctrine. Luther's doctrine of law and his kingdom doctrine complement each other in such a way that one is constantly connected with the other; both can be understood, therefore, only on the basis of this connection. That sketch was restricted to what was absolutely necessary because the central theme of the book was not the reformer's kingdom doctrine but his doctrine of law.

Discussing the book, theologians have suggested that Luther's usage of the word 'kingdom' should have been "still more clearly" unfolded.[2] The following article picks up this suggestion.[3] I also intend to defend the kingdom doctrine presented in *Lex charitatis* against its critique. The "remarks" made by Paul Althaus in "Die beiden Regimente bei Luther. Bemerkungen zu Johannes Heckels 'Lex charitatis,'" *Theologische Literaturzeitung* 81 (1956): 129ff., may be considered to be representative of this critique. Althaus repeated his critique and made it more explicit in "Luthers Lehre von den beiden Reichen im Feuer der Kritik," *Luther Jahrbuch* 24 (1957): 40ff.

I

Althaus started his critique with a fanfare: *Lex charitatis* "demands and deserves the full attention of theologians" because it is not only a work in the history of law, but it also contributes to the present discussion on the correct theological rationale for law and state. He proved this by arguing that in this book Luther "is presented as the main witness for Barth's christological rationale for law and state." Therefore, according to Althaus, the necessary debate on *Lex charitatis* would have to "zero in" on the question who in the controversy on the rationale for law and state between Barth and Althaus, and their supporters, may claim Luther for himself.[4]

I am a jurist, and I am far removed from making a judgment

whether and to what degree my book is significant for the controversy among representatives of the present different theological schools. In any case, if the debate on *Lex charitatis* would "zero in" on this issue, I would have to consider this a shift in the approach to my subject and a narrowing of my topic. What does *Lex charitatis* have to do with that controversy among the representatives of different theological schools?

I restricted myself to emphasizing Barth's unquestionable merit for shaping the problem 'justification and man-made law in the thought of the reformers'.[5] Barth picked up a question which already Luther felt to be important. Indeed, Luther answered it affirmatively, using almost the same words Barth used when he asked the question. However, I did not even touch Barth's solution of the problem 'faith and law', and I did not deal with the relationship of Barth's pertinent dogmatic positions to those of Luther. Others may decide whether Luther was a crypto-Barthian of the sixteenth century, or whether Barth is a latent Lutheran of the twentieth century. Why should these questions concern *Lex charitatis*?

II

Althaus found many points to criticize in the kingdom doctrine presented in *Lex charitatis*. This is the main defect of the book: There is no sufficiently precise differentiation between the kingdom of Christ and the kingdom of the world (in the sense of Satan's kingdom) on the one hand, and, on the other hand, Christ's governance and the secular governance are not sufficiently precisely kept apart when they are seen in juxtaposition.[6]

What is the true situation? Let us first consider the position developed in *Lex charitatis*, and then the argumentation of Althaus.

III

According to *Lex charitatis*, the central concept of the reformer's kingdom doctrine is the kingdom of Christ *(regnum Christi)*; therefore this doctrine is Christ-centered.[7] Luther differentiated between the kingdom of Christ, which is based on Christ's being the head of the church,[8] and that kingdom which consists of Christ's sovereignty over the created world.[9] In line with these two aspects of the kingdom of Christ, Luther divided his kingdom doctrine into two sections. The first one deals with the kingdom of Redemption and Sanctification in the "kingdom of grace,"[10] the second one deals with the kingdom of the divine omnipotence over the Creation.[11] Each section has its own concept 'regnum' or 'kingdom',[12] which, in turn, branches out into various directions.

IV

In developing his kingdom doctrine, Luther's starting point was not the divine sovereignty over the world but the kingdom of grace. Since this is of fundamental significance we use *Basic Meaning of the Kingdom Doctrine* as the title for the first section of Luther's kingdom doctrine. Terminologically this basic meaning is characterized by the equation of kingdom *(regnum)* with mystical body *(corpus mysticum)*. In the kingdom of grace Christ rules as head among his disciples, the members of his mystical body, "according to his humanity."[13]

This body has three features, and in each case 'kingdom' *(regnum)* has a different meaning. 'Kingdom' designates, first, the royal dignity of the head *(rex);* second, the governance of the head as its life-giving impact[14] on the members of the mystical body *(influxus capitis in membra);* and third, the royal people of believers, who voluntarily follow their head, that is, "Christ's people" *(populus Christi)*,[15] or "church people" *(populus ecclesiasticus)*,[16] that is, the true church *(ecclesia vera)*, or the ecclesiastical body *(corpus ecclesiasticum)*.[17] These three statements about Christ's kingdom always have to be seen together.

Christ's kingdom is opposed by another kingdom, the kingdom of the world *(regnum mundi)*. In this connection, 'world' designates mankind alienated from God. Here, too, we find a mystical body with a head, Satan, and also the three features described above: the power of the prince of the world *(princeps mundi)*, the governance of the devil, and the people of the devil, who follow their head, that is, the world or the Babylonian body *(mundus, corpus Babylonicum)*.[18]

Both mystical bodies are locked in a fierce battle between their heads and members, and this battle will never end prior to Judgment Day. This battle takes place in everyone's heart.[19] It also takes place externally in the human communal life, either between persons,[20] or within the orders of society, or between the orders of society.[21]

In the Maze of Luther's Doctrine of the Two Kingdoms

V

Now we move to the second section of the kingdom doctrine, that is, Christ's kingdom as sovereignty over Creation. It seems that now 'kingdom' is not connected with a body. Kingdom is lordship (*dominatio* in the sense of governing).[22] Therefore we use *Doctrine of the Governances* as the title for this second section of the reformer's kingdom doctrine. In this context, kingdom *(regnum)* designates, first, the position of authority[23] over those who are subjected to that authority, though that position does not depend on the subjects' affirming it; second, the implementation of that authority over these subjects; and third, the totality of those who are subjected to this authority. Christ's kingdom, therefore, extends not only over his people but also over his enemies.[24] Conversely, the kingdom of the devil extends not only over those who follow him. It extends also over Christ's disciples, because at one time they belonged to Satan's kingdom, and, therefore, they remain susceptible to sin *(simul iustus, simul peccator)*.[25] For instance, in the exposition of the Second Petition of the Lord's Prayer[26] Luther could write that all people are "a part of the devil's kingdom" yet "with a difference": the godly people are a part in such a way that they resist the devil and do not let sin rule them, the followers of the devil are a part in such a way that they lust after every evil desire.

The implementation of the divine governance over world and mankind takes place through the Word in an ongoing Creation *(creatio continua)*. It concentrates on man's heart; it is *verbum dei in nos* and not *ad nos*.[27] Only a fraction of the people accepts this message in faith and turns to God. The others turn away from God and close their hearts to him. The former accept God's commandment spiritually *(spiritualiter)*, the latter hear it only corporeally *(literaliter)*[28] or carnally *(carnaliter)*. Both groups of people live accordingly.[29] Therefore the divine Word has a dual effect[30] ⟨resulting in the two groups of people⟩. The first group is internally grasped by God's governance, the second is externally grasped,[31] and the essence of the governance corresponds to this situation. The governance over the first group is spiritual, internal, because the members of that group obey God in faith, and the external life of these true Christians conforms to their God-formed will. The situation is totally different when one considers the second group. Since its members do not receive God's will into their hearts, they at least have to be kept in check through external coercion.

Appendix III

Above we stated that it seems that in the doctrine of the governances 'kingdom' is not connected with a body.³² Now it is clear that it is connected with a body after all, and also to what extent it is connected with a body. As head of his mystical body, Christ implements God's sovereignty over the believers. God's sovereignty over the unbelievers hits the Babylonian body <of the devil>. In the first case, God's governance extends over a mystical body which is turned toward God; in the second case God's governance extends over a mystical body which turns its back to God. Therefore in the doctrine of the governances the idea of a body is also present in the concept 'kingdom' when it is understood as lordship *(dominatio)*.

All of this was so obvious for Luther that, without thinking twice, he interchanged the terms 'kingdom' (*regnum* as *corpus*) and 'governance' (*regnum* as *dominatio*), even using them with a double meaning. A striking example for the first usage is a passage in which he dealt with the spiritual kingdom (*regnum* as *corpus*) and called it 'governance'. A proof for the second usage is a passage dealing with the secular governance (*regnum* as *dominatio*), which Luther called 'kingdom'.

The first passage³³ reads:

<The first of the three governances on earth which God established is> his heavenly kingdom, that is, his divine Word and service;³⁴ here he rules consciences and souls through the sermon, Baptism, or the Lord's Supper. <Therefore> it is only right that this kingdom is called and shall be called "Christian or divine governance," because here God himself is the lord and prince, and all of us, who are baptized and called to listen to his Word, or called to the office of baptizing, preaching, comforting, admonishing, etc., are his court people.

The second passage³⁵ reads:

All who are not Christians belong to the kingdom of the world and are under the law. There are few true believers, and still fewer who live a Christian life, who do not resist evil and indeed themselves do no evil. For this reason God has provided for them a different <governance> beyond the Christian estate and kingdom of God. He has subjected them to the sword so that, even though they would like to, they are unable to practice their wickedness, and if they do practice it they cannot do so without fear or with success and impunity.

VI

According to these materials, in Luther's thinking the basic meaning of the kingdom doctrine and the doctrine of the governances are one unit. Both are oriented toward typical figures of people: on the one hand, toward true Christians, who not only listen to the Word but also act according to it, and, on the other hand, toward non-Christians, who enact their hostility toward God also in upsetting and destroying the God-willed external order of the communal life. These are the two 'crowds' within mankind, who oppose each other, and among whom faith or unbelief and the corresponding external life are one. But it also happens again and again that Christians succumb to the devil's seduction and act against the external order of the communal life as the members of the devil's body do.

This situation causes serious problems for those presently enagaged in Luther research, and these problems are frequently used to attack the now proposed unity existing between the basic meaning of the kingdom doctrine and the doctrine of the governances. Yet for the reformer the legal situation was quite simple.[36] Whenever in their actions Christians surrender themselves to Satan's governance, the divine opposition against acts of hostility toward God is automatically effective against them; that is, they are exposed to the coercion enacted by the secular governance. In his external life *(vita)* the fallen Christian has acted against God, and for this he has to endure the legal consequences. From this situation one clearly has to differentiate the question whether that Christian through honest repentance asks God for forgiveness of the disruption of his Christian estate *(status)* by his sin, or whether he lets sin rule his heart. The answer to this question determines whether from now on he will belong to Christ's body or the devil's body. Yet these external actions of a Christian do not at all change the layout of the doctrine of the two kingdoms; therefore in the following materials they will not be mentioned again.[37]

VII

For both kinds of governance God established offices administered by people, who are his tools. For the spiritual governance God established

Appendix III

the preaching office, for the secular governance he established the office of governmental authority.

For the doctrine of the governances it is characteristic that Luther used the phrases 'spiritual governance' and 'secular governance' both for the divine sovereignty over the world (which for believers or unbelievers has different effects) and for the offices established among mankind for the implementation of the governance. For Luther, God's sovereignty over the world and the offices which implement that sovereignty were one.

The usage of these phrases in this sense confirms our position that the basic quality of the reformer's doctrine of the governances is personalistic. For him governance is the impact of a ruler on a body, that is, on a group of people which is formed by their connection with a specific head. Therefore Christ's spiritual governance is the impact of the head on the members of his mystical body.[38] And the spiritual governance of the preaching office is the ruling, that is, shepherding, this group of people, Christ's sheep. Secular governance, on the other hand, is established for implementing the authority of the world's divine sovereign over those whose actions demonstrate that they are tools of the devil, in other words, over the devil's body; secular governmental authority forces the members of that body to live harmoniously within society.[39]

Christians have to serve also this secular governance — but this is a different problem. Their spiritual relationship with the secular governance is totally different from that of non-Christians with that governance; later on we shall separately deal with the reason for this.

VIII

This personalistic quality of the doctrine of the governances — and nothing else — explains the differences between purposes, offices, competencies, and means of action of the two respective governances. Yet until now one has attempted to understand the essence of the governances on the basis of secondary criteria. Of course, such an approach led only to partial results; they did not produce a unified picture, even though details in these results might have value and be correct.

Especially the proper meaning of 'secular' as used in the doctrine of the governances is frequently no longer understood. Althaus, for instance, equated[40] 'secular' with 'temporal' or 'corporeal', and he understood secular governance to be the order of the temporal, corporeal conditions of life. This is true to a certain degree. Luther, too, often used 'secular' in this way. In order to understand the implications of such statements one has to pay attention to their context, however. For instance: Luther described the order of the divine world governance in the three hierarchies,[41] and he instructed a Christian that God claims him as co-worker in the secular governance. In this connection it suffices to outline the material tasks of the secular governance, that is, its care for peace established by law; the connection of the doctrine of the kingdoms with the doctrine of the governances will automatically establish the group of persons to be covered by this secular governance.

As we have seen,[42] the divine world governance has three individual characteristics: the authority of the sovereign, the people over which he rules, and the quality of the rule; that quality, in turn, is determined by the attitude which those have toward their lord who are the object of this divine governance. Therefore one cannot discuss the spiritual or the secular governance without also considering at the same time the people who are ruled. In his definition Althaus did not do this. For him governance is not connected with persons (that is, it is not a governance over a people); it is connected with things (that is, it is an order of temporal affairs). Luther proceeded quite differently! He looked first at people, and then the order was determined <by the essence of this people> — and not the other way round! In short: In the doctrine of the governances the terms 'spiritual' and 'secular' are connected with those who are the object of the divine governance.

By means of the preaching office, the divine governance constantly addresses all people. Preaching law and gospel, the incumbent of this office proclaims the will of God to all people and exhorts them to obey God. Only a fraction of the people responds positively to this proclamation. Again and again a division occurs among the people.[43] Only the spiritual, internally-orientated, believing people make room for the Word in their hearts. Only in them can Christ live and organize his spiritual governance, because it is essential for that governance to exist in the heart of a person. Therefore the three concepts 'spiritual kingdom', 'spiritual people', and 'spiritual power'[44] belong together. The opposite is true for God's governance in the kingdom of the world. Here his governance is recognized as something external only, because people are blind to the spiritual meaning of God's governance. This is the case with the children of the world, the *homines mundi* or *saeculi*;[45] they understand only temporal things, for them the divine governance is only the order of the external human communal life.

The use of 'spiritual' or 'secular' is, therefore, determined by the spiritual status of the subjects of the respective governance.[46] Luther's use of the term 'kingdom of the world' for both the devil's body and the secular governance over this body was not arbitrary but had a theological basis.[47] Of course, Luther did not mean to say that both were identical! Rather, his use of the same term <'kingdom of the world'> indicates that God established the 'kingdom of the world' (that is, secular governance) for the 'kingdom of the world' (that is, the <world->people who do not have faith).

Only these observations help one understand Luther's harsh verdicts about the office of the secular governance, about the low rank of the secular governmental authority within the frame of the God-established order of offices,[48] about the spiritual corruptness of the subjects of the secular governmental authority,[49] and especially about the spiritual insufficiency of the secular power active in the secular governance in comparison with Christ's power.[50] Only Christ's power is true power in the sense of the divine will for Salvation *(potentia salvandi)*; the power of the secular governmental authority, however, is an evil power *(potentia perversa)* which at best can accomplish the destruction of the corporeal existence *(potentia nocendi)*[51] <of evil>.

Yet in other passages Luther highly praised the secular governance. These passages, too, can be correctly understood only when they are connected with the body of the devil. The office of the secular governmental authority is precious because without its activities mankind would succumb to the attacks of God's enemies. In this context belongs also the fact that Luther called the spiritual governance God's kingdom at the right, and the secular governance God's kingdom at the left. Luther derived this usage from the allegorical exegesis of passages in the Psalms, in which 'right' or 'left' designates the location of God's grace or God's wrath.

IX

This understanding of the concept 'secular governance' needs a careful definition of the relationship Christians have with the secular governance. Luther supplied it in a negative and a positive way.

In the Maze of Luther's Doctrine of the Two Kingdoms

Luther stated, first, that a Christian is "pulled out" from under the secular governance.[52] This means that God did not establish the secular governance as a commanding authority over Christians; it does not have authority over them, either in matters of the spiritual or the corporeal life, either in their relationship with God, or in their relationship with their fellowmen. On this Luther has always been clear. Since this topic is important, I shall add a few passages to those mentioned in *Lex charitatis*. In *Sermons on the First Epistle of St. Peter* (1523),[53] we read:

> ... there are two kinds of ‹governance› in the world, just as there are two kinds of people, namely, believers and un-believers. Christians let the Word of God rule them; for themselves they have no need whatever of the secular ‹governance›. But non-Christians need another ‹governance›, namely, the secular sword, because they refuse to be guided by the Word of God.... Christ has entrusted the wicked to ‹governmental authority› to be ruled as they must be ruled. But the pious He keeps for Himself and rules them Himself with his Word alone.

In a June 18, 1524, letter to Duke John Frederick of Saxony,[54] Luther wrote: "... secular laws are external matters, like food and drink, clothing and housing; therefore they are of no concern to Christians who are ruled by God's Spirit according to the gospel." The reformer picked up this idea in *Whether Soldiers, Too, Can Be Saved* (1526)[55] when he wrote: "We Christians have nothing to do with your governance."

A definition of secular governance, in which the personalistic aspect of its competency is ignored, and in which secular governance is understood as the order of the temporal life,[56] does not do justice to these and similar statements of Luther. This has grave consequences; not only does one not understand the foundation of an evangelical doctrine of the state, as Luther presented it in *On Secular Authority* (1523),[57] but one also does not have at all any access to Luther's doctrine of society and of law; they seem to present an insoluble riddle.

Yet Luther's thinking was quite uncomplicated. ‹For instance, when› he dealt with the *privilegium fori* of the clergy,[58] he saw in it a correct principle, but he rejected its implementation set forth in Canon law. For Luther, freedom from secular authority[59] did not belong to the spiritual estate as it was defined in Canon law, that is, the clergy — they were for Luther only an occupational estate[60] in corporeal Christendom

— but to the spiritual estate as it was defined in divine positive law, that is, the Christian estate of internal Christendom, <or> the true disciples of the Savior. They, and only they, are the true 'spirituals',[61] the spiritual people of whom the Apostle Paul says in 1 Corinthians 2:15: "They judge all things, <but> they are judged by no one."[62] Though they are still tied to sin *(simul iusti, simul peccatores)*, they are no longer *perversi* but *conversi*.[63] Their spiritual legal status is in the kingdom of grace, not in the kingdom of the world, and in the unity with Christ they are enjoying the freedom of a Christian. They have this freedom, however, only when their external lives correspond to their Christian estate, that is, when they fulfill those duties which God has imposed on them for their conduct in the relationship with the secular governance. If they fail to do so, they are subjected to the secular governmental authority's power of the sword.[64] This raises the question: How do Christians have to relate to the secular governance?

X

The exemption of Christians from the secular governance means that as members of the kingdom of grace Christians are not subjected to the coercive power of the secular governmental authority. From this one may not conclude, however, that they have nothing to do with the secular governance, either that they have to flee from it, or that at least that they need not pay attention to it. Christian faith does not reject the secular governance — quite to the contrary! In obedience to Christ and his spiritual law of love *(lex charitatis spiritualis)*,[65] a Christian is obligated to serve his fellowmen in every possible way, that is, serve in all institutions established by the Creator for the preservation of the family of man.

For this reason, the secular governance is just as binding for the Christian as it is for the non-Christian, but the title of spiritual law is different: the non-Christian obeys the secular governance because God forces him to do so,[66] the Christian obeys because Christ gives him the freedom to do so.

This difference is decisive for a Christian doctrine of kingdom and of law. A Christian's due is to subject himself voluntarily to the secular governance and responsibly participate in its tasks; this is true even when he, a member of the kingdom of love and grace implementing actions of the kingdom of wrath, is exposed to the most difficult tests of his faith, that is, the denial of self.[67] This is the positive side of the relationship of a Christian with the secular governance. The Christian estate is not an obstacle for the positive law of the state to engage a Christian as a member of the body politic.[68] In a famous passage in *To the Christian Nobility* (1520) Luther went so far as to state: "The office ⟨of the secular authority⟩ ... belongs ... to the Christian congregation."[69] The meaning of this surprising statement becomes clear when one considers the mutual relationship of the two governances with each other. They do not exist only side by side, but they have an identical goal; both serve the divine plan for man's Salvation.

XI

To implement this plan, God provided two commonwealths on earth. One is to serve the gathering and preservation of Christ's mystical body through the Holy Spirit. It is called church in the world, churchly commonwealth *(respublica ecclesiastica)*, or church.[70] In it is located the preaching office. The other one is the organized world without faith and grace, which exists under the secular governmental authority. It is called *politia* or political kingdom *(regnum politicum)*,[71] and it is managed by the secular governmental authority. Through that authority God protects the external peace established by law from being destroyed by the Babylonian body[72] in order to gain it for the ecclesiastical body through the preaching of the Word; the external peace in the *politia* makes the work of the preaching office easier.[73]

Let us pause in our systematic presentation in order to augment it by considering the place of Luther's doctrine of society in the history of ideas. The upheaval which came from the religious and political nucleus of Luther's doctrine of society can hardly be overestimated. Until Luther's time one thought that Christendom had been sheltered in a spiritual-secular kingdom, the Christian commonwealth *(respublica christiana)*; as *one body* it was to fulfill its religious mission under the guidance of the spiritual governmental authority,[74] and its political mission under the guidance of the secular governmental authority, the latter acting with the spiritual governmental authority in unanimity. In Luther's doctrine of society, this one spiritual-secular kingdom was split into two commonwealths, the church on earth and the state; the

Appendix III

one body was replaced by two bodies, and each had a fundamentally different structure. No one before Luther had ever separated the spiritual and the secular sphere so clearly, and no one before Luther had drawn organizational consequences from this separation so strictly to the effect that both spheres may not be intermingled. This separation shaped not only the church in the world but also the state. In fact, it was only now that the state was theologically understood as a commonwealth with its own secular legitimacy, which had its basis in God's secret plan; therefore it did not need to be confirmed by the church, as such a need was suggested, for instance, in the medieval dictum: "Outside of the church there is no empire."[75] It was Luther, and not a political philosopher, who discovered the problems in the relationship of the church with the state; his religious vision brought them to light. Therefore only his doctrine of the two kingdoms is the correct criterion for fixing the place of the Reformation in the movement of the religious and political ideas from the Middle Ages to the Enlightenment, a place which is connected with both periods. Luther affirmed one theological idea of the medieval doctrine of society: in spite of its worldliness, the state, consciously or not, serves the divine plan of Salvation, yet only on the lowest level, that is, that of external order.

XII

Because of this goal, ⟨the implementation of the divine plan of Salvation,⟩ both governances are violently opposed by the devil and the members of his Babylonian body.[76] This statement brings the doctrine of the governances back to the first section of the kingdom doctrine; both governances are entangled in the eschatological battle between the two kingdoms, discussed in that section.[77]

The devil uses his power to create chaos against the divine world order in many ways.

First: The devil causes people to blur the border between the two governances, to exchange the respective legal orders, to transfer the basic organizational principles of one kingdom into the other, or even to place themselves above both governances. For instance: Christendom is proclaimed as a holy empire,[78] as one body. In this one body, a spiritual head, claiming the authority of his ecclesiastical office, interferes in the secular governance, or ⟨conversely,⟩ a secular head, calling himself defender of the faith, persecutes true doctrine. Further, the constitution of the secular governmental authority is transferred from the secular kingdom into the church on earth in the form of a hierarchy; it demands obedience regulated by Canon law, even though the order of the church should be governed by the principles of Christian brotherly love, Christian equality, and Christian freedom.[79] Or, these spiritual ‹divine› basic rights of the church on earth are transferred into the secular commonwealth (as the enthusiasts and peasants did), and they are used to start a revolution against the secular governmental authority.

Second: Within the sphere of each governance Satan seduces those who have offices to misuse their positions, and he seduces the subjects to an anti-law obstinacy. The result is ecclesiastical and secular tyranny,[80] and rebellion in state and church. The perversion reaches its epitome in the apocalyptic world tyrant;[81] in order to unite all power over souls and bodies in his hand, he destroys both governances by destroying their offices (the preaching office, the office of the secular governmental authority, the office of the domestic governance). In one sentence: Each divine commandment is opposed by a man-made countercommandment inspired by the devil, each institution established by God is opposed by a satanic counterinstitution, each divine use is opposed by a devilish misuse.

Against these perversions the ecclesiastical body enters the arena of history and implements the Christian's duty of resistance. Therefore Christians are the most conscientious defenders not only of the church in the world but also of the state.

XIII

The battle between the two mystical bodies and their heads shapes the people in each governance (the members of the *politia* and the members of the church in the world) in such a way that in the political commonwealth alongside the non-Christians also Christians actively work at shaping the communal life, and that in the ecclesiastical commonwealth, in addition to true believers, are also baptized unbelievers. For the doctrine of the state this situation creates the problem of the Christian state, which we are only mentioning.[82] For ecclesiology this situation creates the problem of the spiritual meaning of the corporeal, institutional church.

Appendix III

This is one of the most difficult problems in evangelical ecclesiology. One answer, still presented today,[83] claims that the corporeal church is a mixed body *(corpus permixtum)* of baptized believers and baptized unbelievers. With this formula one intends to find a basis for demonstrating that man-made ecclesiastical law has the same quality as the law of the secular commonwealths; they, too, are mixed bodies of those who obey and those who violate the law. In the same way in which one cannot eliminate coercion and punishment from the secular commonwealth, so they cannot be eliminated from the church; therefore the church has to have a 'secular' ecclesiastical law.[84]

Those who present this answer assume that they follow Luther because, supposedly, he, too, considered the corporeal church to be a mixed body. There might be some value in this understanding of Luther. As is known, the formula[85] originated with St. Augustine. He developed the doctrine of two cities, the city of God and the earthly city. That doctrine was the basis of Luther's doctrine of the two kingdoms.[86] Is it, then, not possible that Luther also adopted from Augustine the concept 'mixed city'?[87] Indeed, Luther did not at all hesitate to use the terms 'intermixed church' or 'mixed church.'[88] Nevertheless, this line of thinking would not do justice to Luther's position. In the development of his Augustinian starting point for the doctrine of the two kingdoms Luther was more precise than his famous patristic model.

If one views the formula 'mixed body' in light of Luther's theology, then the use of the formula is either a return to Scholasticism or a borrowing from the modern public corporation law.[89] The Scholastics taught that in the mystical body of Christ next to living members could also be dead ones; they do not belong to the body of Christ *in actu,* but they belong nevertheless *in potentia.*[90] Luther fought this idea passionately. For him the church can only be a "living body,"[91] and Christ is not "the head of an evil community."[92] About "the godless and the evil ones" one has to say: "They do not belong to the body of the church."[93] Therefore the formula 'mixed body' is misleading. If it is used as a concept of the secular corporation law, then a sociological meaning of the term 'body' is introduced in ecclesiology; it is useless for our problem[94] because it deals only with the relationship of people with one another and not with their relationship with Christ.

XIV

In reality, the supposed mixed body consists of two bodies, namely, the members of the mystical body of Christ and the members of the devil's body, who form nothing but a "simulated church body."[95] With this situation in mind, Luther examined the corporeal church, using two criteria,[96] that of truth and that of love. When using the first criterion, he observed that within the ecclesiastical commonwealth only believing disciples, in whose hearts the Savior rules, belong to the true church. No one is able to identify these believing disciples in the community of the baptized. Therefore only the second criterion, established by Christ, remains ⟨for finding out who belongs to the church⟩, and that is Christian brotherly love. If one uses this criterion, then each baptized person, who has not excommunicated himself ⟨or herself⟩, has to be considered to be a member of Christ's church. Only if one simultaneously uses both criteria can one correctly understand the corporeal church as "Christian body."[97]

XV

Only if one simultaneously uses these two criteria for examining the corporeal church can one do justice to the reformer's sacramentally shaped[98] concept 'church'. According to Luther, if the corporeal church administers Word and sacraments correctly, it is a sign of the spiritual church. This statement involves three consequences.

First: The corporeal church is only a sign *(signum)* of the true church, but it is not the true church itself *(res)*. Therefore the spiritual church exists in the corporeal church only as "hidden" church *(ecclesia abscondita)*.[99] No person who has been baptized may be denied the quality 'Christian', unless he ⟨or she⟩ has excommunicated himself ⟨or herself⟩. Occasionally Luther called this principle "rule of love."[100]

Second: The corporeal church is the sign of the spiritual church. The latter, therefore, gives life to the former, and alone for its sake is the former called church.

Third: The unity between the spiritual and the corporeal church is created in faith. Through Word and sacraments God addresses people, and a believing heart has to respond to this address. Only a believer belongs legally, that is, by the authority of the divine positive law, to both

Appendix III

the spiritual and the corporeal church. Conversely, the unbeliever is not only an internal enemy[101] of the spiritual church but also of the corporeal church, even though through Baptism he belongs to the corporeal church. In this case, visible membership in the (corporeal) church[102] is only a sham appearance *(species)* to which in truth *(re vera)* and spirit *(in spiritu)* does not correspond a membership in the (spiritual) church.[103] Therefore what appears to man to be legal[104] is not legal before God. Luther called this principle "rule of faith."[105]

To sum up the relationship of the spiritual with the corporeal church: both belong together; one may not be considered without also considering the other; there is a constant tension between them, which can split them.[106] Therefore the church in the world is always attacked from within,[107] apart from the fact that in this life even the members of the spiritual church are constantly exposed to Satan's attacks.[108]

XVI

These materials provide two guidelines for creating an ecclesiastical ordinance.[109] First: Such an ordinance has to make provisions that within the church Christ's command to preach his Word to both kingdoms of people is publicly implemented; especially Christ's spiritual governance over the believers through the preaching of the Word and the administration of the sacraments has to be implemented. Second: The communal life of Christians has to be organized in accordance with the command to love the Christian brothers[110] (a love which simultaneously gives and demands)[111] and show mercy toward others.[112] Only when these commands of Christ are implemented in faith and action is the corporeal church connected with the spiritual church.

This has to suffice for the kingdom doctrine presented in *Lex charitatis*.

XVII

Althaus presented a quite different layout of the kingdom doctrine. He did not start with the eschatological battle between the two kingdoms,[113] but he started with the traditional doctrine of the governances and its main question: What authorizes and obligates a Christian to participate in the secular governance? At this point the center of the discussion is not the church, its spiritual structure and its manifestation on earth, but civic society governed by a Christian governmental authority, or in one word, the 'Christian world'. A Christian's responsibility for the welfare of this Christian world is summarized in one sentence: The Christian is a citizen of both kingdoms. Althaus emphatically affirmed this thesis.[114]

How did Althaus make this thesis agree with Luther's theology?

In his presentation of the doctrine of the governances Althaus observed, correctly, that Luther used a dual concept of kingdom; in this respect Althaus's presentation of the governances doctrine agrees with the kingdom doctrine presented in *Lex charitatis*. The same agreement exists when Althaus connected one concept 'kingdom' with a people, namely, the disciples of Christ or the followers of Satan. For this situation he used the phrase "kingdom in the absolute sense."[115] Logically, there should then also be a kingdom in the not absolute sense. Nowhere did Althaus say how this phrase would have to be understood. Yet in the context of his argumentation this kingdom in the not absolute sense could only be the other kingdom, that is, the secular or the spiritual governance, or more precisely formulated, the *politia*[116] and the church in the world, the ecclesiastical commonwealth. Althaus did not deal with the ecclesiastical commonwealth, but he was very thorough in his treatment of the secular governance, as is traditional and appropriate for the doctrine of the governances. At this point there is a deep discrepancy between Althaus's position and the position developed in *Lex charitatis*.

According to Althaus, God subjected both non-Christians and Christians to the secular governance and incorporated both as citizens in it.[117] In *Lex charitatis*,[118] on the other hand, this equal treatment of the two groups of people is rejected because of their different spiritual status, and a Christian's participation in the secular governance has a different basis.

XVIII

For Althaus, the difference between an absolute kingdom of Christ and an absolute kingdom of the world on the one side, and a not absolute kingdom of Christ and a not absolute kingdom of the world on the other side is the fact that in the kingdoms in the absolute sense all members have the same spiritual status, and in the kingdoms in the not absolute sense all members do not have the same spiritual status. One may look at the situation also differently: In the kingdoms in the not absolute sense all members have the same social status; in the state it is a political status, in the church it is a status in terms of ecclesiastical law. In the kingdoms in the absolute sense such an equality in the social status does not exist. One may ask whether in view of this legal situation[119] it is wise to differentiate both types of kingdom in terms of absolute and not absolute. In any case, conclusions regarding one or the other kingdom, drawn from a comparison of the two, are negative, never positive. If one tries nevertheless to obtain positive statements, one can do this only in an underhand way, that is, with the *quaternio terminorum*.[120] It is often and successfully used in legal and theological argumentation. In the 'chaos of one word'[121] (to use Luther's words)[122] the *quaternio terminorum* pulls together two fundamentally different contents of this one word.[123] This is the argumentation:

1. *A Christian* is a citizen of Christ's kingdom in the absolute sense ⟨that is, he has *citizenship*⟩.
2. *A Christian* is a citizen of the kingdom of the world in the not absolute sense ⟨that is, he has *citizenship*⟩.
3. As an organizational concept, *citizenship equals citizenship*.
4. Therefore *a Christian* is a citizen of both kingdoms ⟨that is, *has citizenship in both kingdoms*⟩.

In this argumentation *it is ignored that citizenship designates in (1) a spiritual relationship, in (2) a relationship in terms of public law.*[124]

XIX

Long ago one could have discovered that the thesis concerning a Christian's citizenship in both kingdoms is illogical had one not placed the divine ruling of the world in a wrong analogy to public law. One interpreted the God-established spiritual and secular governance as ways of governing different areas, "goods,"[125] "aspects,"[126] "spaces,"[127] and "dimensions"[128] of human existence, just as in a state appropriate offices for different areas of social life are organized. In general, these offices are structured according to material and not personalistic criteria, because the people living in a state have the same legal quality, that is, they are subjects of the state's authority. In a similar way one views mankind, or the world, in its relationship with the Creator. According to this view, God created something like two departments for his governance over mankind, one "to preserve the corporeal, earthly, temporal life," the other "to assist man in reaching eternal life."[129] The former, the secular governance, serves the preservation of the world; the latter, the spiritual governance, serves "the Redemption of the world."[130] Law rules in the former, and does so "with power,"[131] in the latter Christ rules through the Holy Spirit. One could continue by saying, the former is an external governance, the latter an internal one. In this way a Christian is subjected to both governances, the secular and the spiritual one.

Did Luther understand the relationship of a Christian with the secular governance in this way? Let us remember, the world in its relationship with God was for him not a uniform body but two peoples or families,[132] and both did not have the same spiritual relationship of subject to Creator. Would God have subjected one just as the other to the same governance, namely, the secular as well as the spiritual? Never! Christians understand God's commandment, and therefore also his will to preserve the world, as spiritual law; it penetrates their hearts, and it governs their relationship with both God and the neighbor. They do not need the state's coercive rules, even if they are issued with the label of the state's "paternal office of caring."[133] Among Christians there is, then, no room for the secular governance alongside of Christ's spiritual governance; there is no necessity for it, not even a possibility. Therefore Christians have been "pulled out" from under the secular governance, that is, they are exempt from it. But the opposite is true for the non-Christians. God's governance touches them only externally, it does not enter their hearts. Therefore they are subjected to the external secular governance, and only to it.

XX

Althaus wanted to substantiate his view with a Luther text from 1539.[134] Here a Christian is called a "citizen of the world,"[135] while in earlier texts the reformer called the Christian a "foreigner" or "guest" in the world.[136] Is it possible that in the period between these texts Luther changed his

Appendix III

position, perhaps influenced by the doctrine of the governances which he developed after the earlier texts? Or do we have here an example of Luther's freedom[137] in his use of theological-juristic formulas?

As is known, Luther often used such formulas only to shape a polemical thesis, nothing more, and the text cited by Althaus is no exception. "Citizen of the world" means that a Christian has to serve the secular governance. Nothing is said about the legal title which obligates the Christian to such service, if the situation is viewed from God. Therefore the quotation from the 1539 text cannot contribute anything at all to support the thesis of a Christian's citizenship in both kingdoms. And this is even more the case if one keeps in mind that, when during the later 1520s and the 1530s Luther discussed the relationship of a Christian with the secular governance, he consistently presented his position of the earlier years. For this I cite a passage in the sermon of November 15, 1528, and a passage in *Notes on Some Chapters of Matthew;* since the *Notes* originate in 1538, they are especially important.

The first passage[138] reads:

> ... there are two kingdoms. ... In one kingdom rules the Word of Salvation .... Christ is king ... of this kingdom. In the other kingdom live the ungodly. ... This kingdom is ruled by princes and magistrates. Their task is to govern and coerce the ungodly with the sword because these people cannot be governed with God's Word. For this task God entrusted the sword and power ⟨to princes and magistrates⟩. ... ⟨The emperor⟩ does not ⟨rule⟩ over Christians but over the ungodly and the violators of God's commandments.

In the second passage[139] Luther commented on Matthew 17:27 ("that we do not give offense to them"):

> This is the reason for obeying the secular magistrate, given by the Lord himself. Therefore it has to be pondered and obeyed as a statement of the supreme majesty, namely, that a magistrate is to be honored, ... so that they cannot accuse Christians of rebellion, as people who do not want to obey ⟨secular⟩ authority but want to create a new civic kingdom. At the same time ⟨the Lord⟩ declares in this statement his kingdom not to be a civic or worldly kingdom, ⟨and says:⟩ "Go now, Peter, and know that we are kings and a king's children in another kingdom. Leave their kingdom to them, in which we are only

guests. Therefore let us pay to the innkeeper what we owe him so that they may not say we live as dishonest people in their kingdom, who eat their goods but do not pay." ... <Christ> says: "We are children of a kingdom, but not of this worldly kingdom."

XXI

Do such statements not suggest that Luther contradicted himself after all? As Althaus correctly emphasized,[140] there are other passages in which Luther based the "secular governance in a wider sense" — that is, the temporal order beyond the state, for instance, <matters pertaining to> the housefather, property, vocation, estates, economy, etc. — on the fact that that order has been established in Paradise. Was Althaus not correct when he considered such statements to support his thesis that not the total secular governance, not even the state in all its features, exists "because of sin"?[141] Let us take a closer look at the role sin plays at this point.

According to Luther, by Creation man is endowed with the gift of creating rational order and of rationally using the works of the Creation to meet the necessities of his life. God preserved this gift in spite of the Fall, but fallen man no longer uses this gift spiritually. That is, man no longer uses this gift to honor the divine Creator, and, therefore, he no longer uses it for the Salvation of his soul and that of his neighbor. He uses this gift corporeally, that is, he uses it as autocratic, earthly creator for his earthly well-being,[142] and he creates all institutions of human communal life according to this standard. As a whole, these institutions serve the corporeal peace of mankind, which has lost sight of the Creator and does not believe in him. When one views these institutions from the Creator's point of view, then it is irrelevant whether they build up society, or protect it by means of punishment and coercion from destruction. Therefore Luther derived the origin of the state from marriage as it existed after the Fall,[143] and he used the sword as symbol for all institutions of the external, infralapsarian life in the *politia*.[144]

In this sense, Luther's statements about Adam's secular governance in Paradise have to be interpreted.[145] Luther's words are not precise juristic statements about the origin of the secular governance. Let us remember that Luther's quotation from Genesis 1:26 and 28 deals with lordship *(dominatio)* over animals![146] Legally seen, there cannot be

Appendix III

a secular governance of Adam in the Original Status at all because in Paradise the two first humans had equal rank in law.[147] Luther used the Genesis passage only in order to differentiate between Christ's spiritual governance in the kingdom of grace and the secular governance, which is active in a kingdom not ruled by the Holy Spirit.[148] This demonstrates once and for all that secular governance exists after the Fall, and it rules in the kingdom of the world.

To sum up: logically the doctrine of a Christian's citizenship in both kingdoms cannot be maintained; it does not have a theological-juristic basis, and it is not solidly supported in Luther's writings.

XXII

After these basic statements we now turn to individual objections raised by Althaus.

The first objection is directed against what Althaus considered to be a "distortion" of the secular governance: ⟨the image of the secular governance presented in *Lex charitatis*⟩ is shaped by St. Augustine rather than by Luther. According to Althaus, ⟨I,⟩ "supposedly following Luther," presented secular governance as "the sovereignty of wickedness," though at another place I added that secular governance is God's establishment, but this happens "only much later."[149]

Here Althaus was the victim of an obvious misunderstanding. First: He did not grasp the systematic structure of the book. According to this structure, the basic meaning of the kingdom doctrine — that is, kingdom *(regnum)* as body *(corpus)* — has to be treated before the doctrine of the governances — that is, kingdom as lordship *(dominatio)* — can be treated.[150] Obviously, one may speak of the secular governance as God's establishment only in the context of the doctrine of the governances, especially in connection with a detailed discussion of the office of the secular governmental authority — that is, "only much later." Second: Althaus did not sufficiently pay attention to the fact that the basic meaning of the kingdom doctrine is determined by the equivalency of kingdom and body, and that this equivalency shapes all details of the concept 'kingdom'. ⟨In connection with these details⟩ the governance which is functioning in the kingdom of the world is described as "sovereignty of wickedness";[151] this obviously means the governance of the head of the Babylonian body, that is, the governance of the devil,[152] and the secular governance is not even mentioned. Thus the base is cut out from under Althaus's first objection. At the same time the value of his most recent contention that in *Lex charitatis* "the two governances are derived from the two kingdoms"[153] is also nullified — this simply is not true.

XXIII

It is only natural that Althaus's misunderstanding had consequences for his subsequent presentation. For instance, he asked whether one may speak of a battle between both kingdoms when one considers God's kingdom at the right and God's kingdom at the left,[154] or he doubted the affirmation that love of self dominates the secular governance.[155] In both cases he incorrectly transferred statements of *Lex charitatis* dealing with the basic meaning of the kingdom doctrine to the doctrine of the governances. Obviously, then, he could find in *Lex charitatis* one "unclarity"[156] after the other and see in the book a documentation for the "confusion in the understanding of the doctrine of the two kingdoms."[157] Again we ask: What does all this have to do with the book?

⟨Althaus⟩ used the same method of arguing when he criticized[158] the thesis of *Lex charitatis*[159] that the legal inequality among the members of the kingdom of the world is the result of the egotism which dominates that kingdom; according to Althaus, this thesis is "only a construct," "which cannot be supported with any Luther text." He argued that superordination and subordination *(differentia personarum)*[160] are, so to speak, technical necessities for God's rule over the world and are not directly connected with sin. I reply: Superordination and subordination as such are certainly not connected with sin, as the constitution of Christ's kingdom shows. Yet in the kingdom of the world they are very much connected with sin. For this reason, Luther traced the historical origin of this legal inequality in the world to the Fall. To demonstrate that the thesis does not deserve the charge of being a construct without a basis in Luther's writing, because Althaus did not find a quotation from Luther in *Lex charitatis,* I now quote Luther[161] at greater length than in *Lex charitatis:*

> ... Eve has been subjected to the authority of the man, she who before was absolutely free and in no way inferior to the man, ⟨and⟩

shared in all of God's gifts. This punishment has been born from Original Sin. . . .

XXIV

Althaus's statements about 'God's kingdom at the right, God's kingdom at the left' as a pair of concepts are especially important.[162] Before all else: At issue are the spiritual and the secular governance. Therefore in *Lex charitatis* both topics are treated in the doctrine of the governances so that the kingdom of God at the right or at the left in the sense of God's governances is not confused with the two kingdoms, the two mystical bodies, ⟨that is, Christ's mystical body and the Babylonian body of the devil⟩. It seems that one has to assume that in Althaus's statements such a confusion has taken place.

Althaus raised four objections to the pertinent theses presented in *Lex charitatis:*

1. According to *Lex charitatis,* the kingdom of God at the left, that is, the secular governance, incorrectly, extends only to the godless, rather than also to the Christians in their external life. For a reply I refer to my statements about the concept 'secular governance'.[163]

2. In reality, God's kingdom *at* the left is God's kingdom *with* the left hand. This is to suggest that the secular governance ranks below the spiritual governance, because with his left hand God gives only temporal, corporeal goods, but with his right hand he gives eternal goods.

3. One may not place God's kingdom at the left as a kingdom of wrath in opposition to God's kingdom at the right as a kingdom of grace.

4. It is wrong to bring Matthew 25 ⟨especially verses 33f.⟩ into the discussion. In this passage the sheep are at the right and the goats are at the left of Christ, the judge of the world. ⟨Supposedly,⟩ Luther did not speak about people standing at the right or the left of the judge, but he spoke about God's action with his right or left hand.

In dealing with these objections, I begin with the third one. The result regarding this objection determines also the answers to the second and the fourth objection.

To 3: Following the Fathers and the Scholastics, Luther used 'right' and 'left' with many meanings. As Augustine had already done, so Luther used them to describe the difference between spiritual and corporeal goods.[164] Again following Augustine, Luther also used 'right' to designate the place of divine favor and Reconciliation,[165] or grace.[166] And he also identified 'right' with Christ, the donor of grace.[167] Where the Son of God is the head of his mystical body, there also have to be the members of his body. 'Right', therefore, designates the place of the internal man,[168] "the son of the right and of grace,"[169] and also of the community of such people, that is, the church.[170]

'Left', of course, designates the opposite of all of this. It stands for temporal goods and the happiness found in them,[171] for the spiritual *Ungnade*,[172] etc. Therefore it was only natural for Luther in allegorical interpretation to connect the left and the right hand of God with wrath and grace.

To 2: The reformer's use of 'kingdom *at* the right and *at* the left' totally agrees with this phrasing. He occasionally used the variant, *with* the left hand. The basic idea, however, is the local meaning, *at* God's right or left; the variant is derived from it, so to speak, because only the use according to the first meaning, ⟨the local one,⟩ is biblical. With this local meaning Luther followed Psalm 110:1.[173] In interpreting this Psalm, he contrasted Christ's kingdom at the right[174] as a hidden, spiritual kingdom,[175] to the kingdom at the left as a visible and corporeal kingdom.[176] As the people[177] of the spiritual kingdom he named the church, and he described the members of the kingdom at the left as people who "seek in all they do their own ⟨advantage⟩, . . . ⟨and the implementation of their⟩ will, without ⟨paying attention to⟩ God."[178] They have no feeling for spiritual but only for moral and corporeal goods; therefore the community of people with such a disposition is the visible, temporal kingdom,[179] that is, the kingdom at the left, or the kingdom of the world.

To 4: Matthew, chapter 25, has to be applied to this situation, there can be no doubt. ⟨Said Luther:⟩[180]

> . . . in the midst between ⟨the church and the world,⟩ . . . stands King Judah, Christ, like the most righteous judge ⟨stands⟩ between the sheep and the goats, having the first ones at his right as the beloved ones set free by his right hand, but the latter ones on his left.

Appendix III

XXV

Is in this argumentation the secular governance not too much seen in the frame of Satan's kingdom? This was Althaus's concern.[181] In his opinion, even mankind fallen from God "experiences" God's almighty sovereignty not only as a kingdom of the divine wrath[182] but also as "God's benevolent action."[183] Really? God's enemies hate him as if he were the devil.[184] Should they then, nevertheless, also acknowledge God as their benefactor? Of course, they, too, experience the secular governance as something good. But they do not connect its institutions and actions with the true God, in whom they do not believe, but they connect it with man's image of man made into an idol.[185] For them, the true God is a tyrant.[186] Only a Christian is able to honor the secular governance as a manifestation of the true God's grace.[187]

XXVI

Thus[188] far I discussed the secular governance in the *politia*. According to Althaus, the competency of this governance extends also to the church in the world. For him the "empirical church," that is, the legally organized church, is a part of the "kingdom of the world."[189] This is logically consistent, no doubt; if one understands the secular governance to include "all that serves the preservation and order of this temporal life," <as Althaus did,>[190] then, among other things, the organization of the corporeal church has to be included in the competency of the secular governance. This conclusion is inevitable if one adopts Althaus's doctrine of the governances. A test case will demonstrate whether his doctrine of the governances agrees with the reformer's position.

It is not accidental that this test case is connected with the legal structure of the corporeal church,[191] because the doctrine of the governances is controlled by the <doctrine of the> church. Christ ruling in his mystical body[192] is the nucleus of the church, and on this nucleus depends the legal structure of the corporeal church. If something is wrong in the connection of church and governance doctrine, then it is proven that something is wrong in the governance doctrine as a whole. Therefore it is necessary to deal with Althaus's thesis[193] further in order to test it by considering its consequences.[194]

XXVII

If one pursues this subject one finds out that there are two ways of doing this. Both lead to a dead end.

The first way is characterized by the fact that the church is really placed under the competency of the secular governance. According to Luther, each governance has its own structural principles, and they may not be interchanged, not even partially. Therefore the church in all its legal aspects has to have the characteristics of that governance to which it belongs. If the church is a part of the kingdom of the world,[195] then it has to have those characteristics which Althaus correctly described as being typical of the secular governance.[196] Then the church is an institution of the secular sword(!), because for Luther the secular sword and the secular governance are identical. The church's constitution is secular law. Those members of the church who are called to issue and implement such a law in synods and through the offices of ecclesiastical administration, of pastors, or of elders act — as far as the preservation of the temporal, earthly life is at issue — as world-persons (regardless whether privately they consider themselves to be Christians). The law for ecclesiastical offices establishes a system of dependences and commands, etc. In short: *The church is a secular association dedicated to the caring for the Christian faith.*

What would Luther say to this understanding of the church and its law? He told his elector in no uncertain terms that the secular governance did not extend to the order of the church; "as secular governmental authority," Luther argued,[197] the elector was not obligated to conduct a visitation of the church ⟨in his territory⟩.[198] Further, the reformer recognized only believing Christians as legitimate incumbents of the ecclesiastical office, and he ordered people to flee from all others as if they were wolves. Finally, he emphatically rejected structuring the order of the church according to jurisdictions as they were fixed in Canon law: "⟨In the church⟩ are no ⟨superiors⟩, because Christ has forbidden their existence."[199] "The gospel and the church do not know of any jurisdictions, which are nothing other than tyrannical inventions of people. ⟨The gospel⟩ knows only love and service, not power and tyranny."[200] All this means that structuring the order of the church according to the principles of the secular governance is totally contrary to Luther's position.

Thus only the second way remains, that is, to shape the constitu-

Appendix III

tion of the church according to the principles derived from Christ's spiritual governance. Then it is impossible for the secular governance to be competent for shaping this constitution. Were it otherwise, the intermingling of the two governances would occur, which Luther fought. In his doctrine of the governances, Althaus was unable to present a way out of this dilemma. The test case demonstrates that his governance doctrine does not have the correct starting point, notwithstanding that it presents many correct details.

XXVIII

We are at the end of our discussion. Althaus charged *Lex charitatis* with a series of mistakes: It has a wrong starting point, namely, the battle between the two kingdoms "in the absolute sense";[201] it lacks a systematic development of ideas; two different concepts of kingdom are confused and confusing; there are mistakes of terminology and content in the doctrine of the kingdom at the right and at the left; the rejection of a Christian's citizenship in both kingdoms is not proven with texts from Luther. I have examined this critique bit by bit and found no reason to correct the reformer's kingdom doctrine presented in *Lex charitatis*.

Althaus's critique should be taken very seriously nevertheless. It is symptomatic of the difficulties which present-day evangelical theologians face when they want to penetrate the reformer's kingdom doctrine and his doctrine of law. In this connection the task is nothing less than dealing with the questions whether Martin Luther recognized the central significance the topic 'law' had for his theology, and whether he mastered this topic. The "noisy controversy"[202] concerning the doctrine of the two kingdoms could lead one to the frightening result ‹that theologians might not be a match for this task›. Our disquisition has demonstrated, however, that the reason for the uncertainties regarding the true meaning and significance of the doctrine of the two kingdoms does not lie in that doctrine itself but in a wrong starting point for gaining an insight into it. First, one has not seen that this doctrine originates in a twofold Christ-centered view. Second, the basic meaning of the kingdom doctrine[203] became imprecise for two possible reasons: its simultaneously theological and juristic content is incorrectly interpreted; it is placed at the periphery of the discussion rather than the center. Third, one has not adequately made allowance for the inseparable connection of this center of Luther's kingdom doctrine, ⟨that is, the basic meaning of the kingdom doctrine,⟩ with his governance doctrine. As soon as these mistakes are avoided, the kingdom doctrine, and together with it Luther's doctrine of law, becomes surprisingly clear. All their foundational concepts form one unit, of which the structure turns out to be so logical that some theologians think it is too good to be true. But since theologians have abandoned the idea that Luther was an unsystematic theological thinker, then one should not hesitate to risk abandoning also the idea that Luther was an unsystematic juristic thinker. To do the latter, one only has to eliminate all sorts of accidentals and draw the legal nuggets from his statements, which juristically often seem to be imprecise. If this is done, it will become clear that the reformer's kingdom doctrine and his doctrine of law in all their major features have one center, Christ's kingdom and its spiritual law, or the law of Christ. The doctrine of justification by faith alone provides the key for unlocking the meaning of the terms 'Christ's kingdom', 'spiritual law', or 'law of Christ'. Based on this doctrine one grasps in Luther's doctrine of society both the spiritual structure and order of mankind in both kingdoms and the spiritual structure and order of the spiritual and corporeal existence of mankind under the two governances, that is, in the church and the state. In this way the reformer's kingdom doctrine, his doctrine of law, and his theology form one unit. Is there a more convincing proof for the authenticity of this image of law ⟨than what is presented in *Lex charitatis*⟩?

APPENDIX IV

Church and Ecclesiastical Law in the Frame of the Doctrine of the Two Kingdoms

---

Johannes Heckel, "Kirche und Kirchenrecht nach der Zwei-Reiche-Lehre," *Zeitschrift der Savigny-Stiftung für Rechtsgeschichte. Kanonistische Abteilung*, 48 (1962): 222-284. Dedicated to Ernst Wolf on his 60th birthday in appreciation of the scholarly stimulation which my Luther research received from his work.[1]

A century ago, Adolph von Harleß wrote regretfully: "We Lutherans will never stop writing and quarrelling about church, ecclesiastical office, and ecclesiastical law."[2] Nothing has changed, though after Rudolph Sohm's attack against ecclesiastical law[3] the number of critics has significantly increased. Yet in the *Smalcald Articles* we read: ". . . thank God, a seven-year-old child knows what the church is, namely, holy believers, and sheep who hear the voice of their Shepherd."[4] Nevertheless, according to one of the most eminent theologians of our time, the problem 'church' "has remained the unsolved problem of Protestantism.... There has never been clarity about the relationship of the church according to faith, that is, the congregation of Jesus Christ, with the one or the many institutions which are called church."[5]

Ecclesiastical law has been most profoundly shaped by this lack of clarity. Of course, the polemic against this law's right to exist was not convincing and had no influence at all on the conduct of ecclesiastical affairs. Today those who conduct these affairs have a more positive attitude toward law, not to say they are more assiduous in matters of law than ever before, at least in Germany. Yet also the defenders of ecclesiastical law did not gain much support. Since both proponents and opponents of ecclesiastical law claim Luther for their positions, we have to go to the sources; that is, using juristic criteria, we have to *examine Luther's thoughts on church and law* whether and how they fit in his "faith-determined world view."[6] Until recently there has been almost no attempt by historians of ecclesiastical law to make such a study — they diligently investigated the reformer's concept 'church' but not his concept 'law'. And apart from a few outstanding exceptions, theologians have not been much help, as Lutheran textbooks of dogmatics show. In view of the present situation in scholarship, the following study has to be restricted to the presentation of those materials which are appropriate for a juristic disquisition of the idea 'law' in Martin Luther's theology.[7]

I

Luther's ecclesiology emerged from his theology of the two kingdoms.[8] That doctrine is "the juristic-theological fundamental formula for the eschatological character of the Christian existence and, therefore, also of the existence of the church."[9] The church in the world is the innerworldly beginning of Christ's kingdom.[10] The Holy Spirit calls people into this kingdom, he gathers them in it, and in it he enlightens, sanctifies, and preserves them in the true faith.[11] Because of this faith-creating and preserving activity of the Holy Spirit, the church is called spiritual church *(ecclesia spiritualis)*.[12] The church as a whole is spiritual, and only what is spiritual is churchly. Spiritual is the head of the church, spiritual is the governance implemented in the church, spiritual is the ecclesiastical people. Let us consider these statements in greater detail.

The head of the church[13] is Christ according to his humanity. From him flows the divine power of life into Christendom because "it is the nature of the head of a body to transmit to the members all its life, mental attitude, and activity." Through this, a Christian receives "the mental attitude, courage, and will which Christ has in heaven." No human being, not even the most venerable incumbent of an ecclesiastical office, may boast of such a power. Therefore it is impossible for the church to have an earthly head,[14] not even a head which is a servant.[15] By the same token, Christ did not appoint anyone to be his vicar.[16]

Appendix IV

Christ, therefore, is the sole owner of the ecclesiastical governance.[17] He implements it in a way which is totally alien to the governance in human associations. By divine love, Christ's ecclesiastical governance is implemented as a shepherd's office; it is the spiritual pasturing *(pascere)* of the little sheep who listen to the Savior's voice. Such a governance is not lordship *(dominatio)*[18] but rather the service of soul-caring. In the church there is not to be any governmental authority, either the secular or the ecclesiastical kind. As the structural principle for the organization of the church in the world the position of superiority *(maioritas)*, found in Canon law,[19] is replaced with ministry *(ministerium)*.[20] For this reason, Luther passionately fought the traditional concept '<clerical> power of jurisdiction' *(potestas iurisdictionis)*, which <supposedly> has its roots in divine positive law. Christ did not invest any human being with such a power or leave it to anyone,[21] not to mention that he would have instituted offices for it. Rather, he reserved the totality of the ecclesiastical governance for himself.[22]

Christ implements his ecclesiastical governance through people.[23] In Baptism[24] he obligates the baptized to be his comrades-in-arms,[25] and he calls them into the ministry of the Word *(ministerium verbi)*; this is a *sacramental call (vocatio)*.[26] Following Christ's command, the Christians in a given locality designate someone from this group of born priests[27] to administer the ministry of the Word as a "public office";[28] that is, they issue an *extra-sacramental call (vocatio)* into the public ministry of the Word,[29] and they do this on the basis of the authority a congregation has to order[30] its communal existence. All of Christ's servants of the Word are only messengers, transmitters, or in Luther's graphic words, "tubes"[31] through which Christ speaks to man.[32] The means and ways through which the Lord implements his ecclesiastical governance are exactly prescribed for Christ's servants, that is, the proclamation of God's Word, especially by means of public preaching, the administration of the sacraments, and the use of the Power of the Keys.

The ecclesiastical people governed by this spiritual governance of Christ are the *baptized believers*.[33] In their relationship with the Savior they all — but only they — are *Christ's mystical body,* and in their relationship with one another they are a *spiritual brotherhood.*[34] This is the only brotherhood which deserves this name before God, and Luther called it true, internal, spiritual Christendom.[35] He found this meaning already in the Apostles' Creed and its definition of the church as communion of saints *(communio sanctorum)*.[36] The church is a faith-community,³⁷ or "the church of faith."³⁸ In the language of the doctrine of the two kingdoms the church is called kingdom of faith *(regnum fidei)*.³⁹ The mark which determines membership in the church is the rule of faith *(canon fidei)*.⁴⁰ No other marks are necessary,⁴¹ especially not the integration of churches ⟨of a given geographic area⟩ in a union, which is governed by a supreme ruler; this is the case, for instance, in the church which is obedient to the Roman church. In contrast to such a union, the members of the church live in a spiritual diaspora, scattered all over the world among Christ's enemies.⁴² The essence of the church is not determined by such a mark of local churches ⟨being integrated in a union⟩. Likewise, it is not determined by a personalistic mark; therefore it is not determined by an uninterrupted succession (beginning with the Apostles) in which the occupants of the ecclesiastical magisterial office function.⁴³ "The church is bound to the ministry,⁴⁴ to the gospel, and not to the ministers."⁴⁵ Churchly rosters do not do justice to such a community of faith. "The church is hidden, the saints are unknown," said Luther in a famous statement in *The Bondage of the Will*.⁴⁶

This hidden church cannot be found if one searches for it with criteria provided by human reason.⁴⁷ Yet it is not a mere idea, a Platonic City;⁴⁸ it is the supreme reality which is beyond all human reasoning, because it is the divine reality, that is, the presence of the Holy Spirit. The activity of the Holy Spirit, and with it the existence of the spiritual church, can be recognized in this world, however. The hidden church has an earthly, visible side *(facies ecclesiae)*.⁴⁹ This aspect of the church means nothing to natural man; he is guided by the dictum: The church is invisible.⁵⁰ In contrast, he who is filled with the Spirit, that is, the believing Christian, perceives this spiritual reality and affirms: The church is visible.⁵¹

Yet even this spiritual man sees the spiritual church only hidden in veils, which totally obscure the essence of the church to the eye of the non-Christian. Therefore *Luther differentiated between two forms or aspects of Christ's church*.⁵² He connected internal, essential Christendom with external Christendom, the spiritual church with the corporeal church, the internal church with the external church.⁵³ Through the rite of Baptism every baptized person is incorporated in the external church. Because of the universal validity of Baptism, this ⟨community of those who are baptized⟩ is called universal church *(ecclesia universalis)*.⁵⁴ As a whole, that church is neither organized nor can it be organized. But within it, local unions are formed, the particular churches *(ecclesiae particulares).*[55] In relationship with one another and vis-à-vis Christ, the head of the spiritual church, all these particular churches are on the same level.[56] The membership and the place in the constitution of a particular church of those who are baptized can be known on the basis of criteria provided by reason. Therefore Luther called such a particular church manifest church *(ecclesia manifesta).*[57]

This twofold view of the church was not new in the history of ecclesiology. It was known during the Middle Ages,[58] yet Luther's view had revolutionary significance. In the traditional ecclesiology the starting point was the universal church; for Luther it was the spiritual church. In later years Luther praised the discovery of the forgotten "form of the Christian church" as one of the greatest blessings of the Reformation.[59] New in Luther's understanding of Christ's church was the emphasis on the spiritual essence of the church as the decisive characteristic of ecclesiology. He was convinced that, in contrast to this emphasis, the traditional understanding of the church suffered from a theologically unacceptable overemphasis of the church's external appearance and, therefore, from a wrong understanding of church and law.

Between the spiritual and the corporeal church exist both an absolutely necessary connection and an irrevocable tension.[60] If this 'simultaneity' is disregarded, the concept 'church' becomes a "blind word."[61] Regarding external Christendom one may make both statements: The church (that is, the universal church) cannot err,[62] the church (that is, the universal church) has the "face of a sinner."[63]

The truth of the first statement is based on the facts that Christ instituted the rite of Baptism as the means of reception into his kingdom, and that he ordered God's pure Word publicly to be proclaimed within the community of the baptized.[64] Even the manifest church is derived from Christ's Word. Therefore both forms of the church in the world belong together; one may not think of one without at the same time thinking of the other. In other words, Christ considers the church according to its spiritual and its corporeal aspect to be his church.[65] This is true, however, only to the degree that in that church Christ's governance is obeyed in faith, or, and this would be the same, that the hidden church[66] exists in the manifest church. That his disciples could tell with certainty whether this was the case, Christ left externally visible marks: the preaching of the Word and the administration of the sacraments according to Holy Scripture.[67] Wherever these marks exist, there the Holy Spirit is at work and builds Christ's church[68] because "God's Word never returns empty" <to God>.[69] These marks, therefore, are efficacious and infallible.[70] They guarantee that in the manifest church the continuous succession of believers *(successio fidelium)*[71] never ends. Through these divine marks the corporeal church points toward the spiritual church and itself has the quality of being a sign <of the spiritual, hidden church>.[72]

The paradoxical quality of the second statement[73] becomes understandable when one considers that according to the doctrine of the two kingdoms[74] Christ's people are included in the eschatological battle[75] between God and Satan.[76] Therefore the church in the world is a "church of fighters"[77] *(ecclesia militans).*[78] With guile and might the evil spirit breaks into the group of Christians and seduces them to sin.[79] The prince of this world celebrates his greatest triumph when he is able to place persons who are Christians in name only in the offices of a particular church; this would have the result that, with the authority of the church, they preach heresies and administer the sacraments contrary to Holy Scripture, or, pretending their spiritual quality, implement a worldly governance.[80]

These nominal Christians and their followers form the devil-church or sham church *(ecclesia diaboli*[81] *sivi simulata)*[82] of the mystical body of the devil.[83] Like the universal church, this devil-church organizes associations <of particular churches> in which the tension between the spiritual church and the manifest church has resulted in a break between the two. As far as the influence of the devil's church extends, such a particular church loses its connection with the spiritual church and, therefore, also with the corporeal church; it becomes a "made"[84] church. <Now> Christ's one church with its two aspects[85] falls apart into "two churches,"[86] the true but oppressed church[87] and the ruling but false church.[88] Because of the continuous battle between Christ and Satan in the militant church, the group of the baptized Christians does not have a uniform spiritual status. Unlike the hidden church, that group is, therefore, not a mystical body, since for the reformer a mystical body is a gathering of people enacted by a head, is filled with his spirit, and is formed in the constant struggle with a counterhead. Such a body[89] does not have a fixed constitution as a modern corporation has. Rather, the gathering is constantly in motion; moved by the Holy Spirit, it is pushed toward Christ, or, seduced by the evil spirit, it is pushed away from Christ. In light of this situation, it is easy to understand that the external, fixed mark of the baptismal rite is not suitable to form the group of the baptized into a mystical body.

Yet to this day the militant church is called a mixed body *(corpus permixtum)*,[90] consisting of baptized believers and baptized unbelievers. This term is borrowed from Scholasticism or adopted from the corporation concept in public law. The Scholastics taught that Christ's mystical body, in addition to living members, has also dead ones; while they are members not *in actu,* they are nevertheless members *in potentia.*[91] Luther vigorously fought this idea.[92] For him, Christ's church is a "living body";[93] the "ungodly and evil ones are not members of the church body,"[94] and Christ is not "the head of any evil community."[95] The formula 'mixed body' is theologically misleading. And if one intends to use it according to the meaning it has in secular corporation law, one would be guilty of a transition to another genus; one would exchange the reformer's theological concept 'body' for a non-theological one, that is, a sociological one.

II

The dependence of the manifest church on the hidden church and the essence of the militant church demand and make it possible to deal with the problem of membership in the church on earth. The solution of this problem is most important for our disquisition; it clarifies who as a citizen of Christ's kingdom is authorized to create human ecclesiastical law; it also clarifies the irregularities which occur in the implementation of this citizenship as a result of the tension between the spiritual and the corporeal church.[96]

Again, two approaches have to be used when one deals with this problem. The first one starts with the spiritual church, and it investigates how membership in that church is related to membership in the corporeal church. Conversely, the second approach starts with the members of the corporeal church, and it tries to find out by what law one may apply the spiritual quality 'Christian' to them.

The first issue, ‹the relationship of membership in the spiritual church to membership in the corporeal church,› is solved with the help of the rule of faith,[97] which is valid for the hidden church. In this connection we find three law-creating situations.[98] Luther clarified them by means of the relationship which exists between soul and body, an image adopted from the traditional doctrine of the sacraments.[99]

Normally, in view of the unity of soul and body, a Christian would belong to both, the internal and the external Christendom. In the case of a *baptized believer* this is true — he has citizenship in both, the spiritual and the corporeal church. In two ways this unity <of citizenship in both churches> can be destroyed, however. <First,> the *excommunication* of a <baptized> believing Christian by the officials of a particular church is a legally invalid act;[100] it does not change the spiritual status of that person — he remains a member of the spiritual church, and *de iure* also of the corporeal church; but *de facto* the illegal verdict of excommunication prevents that person from using his right of citizenship in the corporeal church. He loses the corporeal connection[101] with the corporeal church, he only retains the connection with the spiritual church. Luther compared the victim of an unjust excommunication with someone who has lost his body while his soul continues to live. <Second,> a *baptized unbeliever* has no legal status in the kingdom of Christ and, therefore, also not in the manifest church; that person belongs to Satan's church, the assembly of the spiritually dead, just as a body without a soul has no part in life.

This is the legal situation as seen from the spiritual church. Luther thought about this soon after his struggle against the indulgence traffic had begun.[102] Then he had to face the possibility of a trial for heresy; at that point he was forced to come to terms with the issues whether, and with what legal consequences, he may resist excommunication, or be obligated to do so, and what would be the spiritual rationale for this resistance.

This solution of the first issue is the basis of the solution of the second issue mentioned above <namely, by what law may the spiritual quality 'Christian' be applied to members of the corporeal church>. As the solution of the first issue demonstrated, among those who are baptized are great differences regarding their membership in Christ's kingdom.[103] Yet there is a solid reason not to deny the quality 'Christian' to *any baptized Christian* but to consider him to be a *member of the universal church*. Everyone who is baptized carries the mark of the spiritual church.[104] Of course, no one knows whether the spiritual reality of a baptized person is in line with this mark, or whether he only pretends to be Christ's disciple. Only God has the authority to make a decision in this matter according to the rule of faith, and no Christian may appropriate God's judgment to himself. He has to use another spiritual criterion, provided by the Savior. This is the rule of love,[105] the commandment of Christian love of the brother,[106] which governs the relationship of Christians with one another. Each person who is baptized has to be considered a member of the church — *provided* that he ⟨or she⟩ has not publicly excluded himself ⟨or herself⟩ from the church and, therefore, has been banished from the corporeal church through ecclesiastical discipline. In this connection it cannot be avoided that baptized unbelievers act as if they were members of the church,[107] even though in reality they are Christ's most dangerous enemies. They belong to the church only according to the roster *(numero)* but not according to their spiritual quality *(merito)*.[108] In other words, they are "in the church"[109] but not "of the church."[110] In these cases what *appears* to man to be legal in no way coincides with what *is* legal before God.[111] — This has to suffice for the personalistic structure of the two forms of Christ's church. Each of these forms has its own ecclesiastical law.

III

All law of the hidden ⟨spiritual⟩ church is based on the manifestation of Christ's will, that is, it is divine law.[112] If it deals with the Lord's ecclesiastical governance,[113] it is divine positive law. If it deals with the conduct of the members of Christ's mystical body with one another, obedience is demanded to the interpretation of the spiritual law of love by Christ *(lex charitatis spiritualis)*, that is, the divine natural law. The spiritual church has no other law. This is obvious when one remembers that the church exists only when the Holy Spirit rules in it.[114] Conversely, spiritual law exists only in the hidden ⟨spiritual⟩ church.[115]

IV

Totally different questions are *whether human ecclesiastical law can develop in the manifest church,* and how the binding quality of such a law can be justified. Luther presented the basic ideas for the answers as early as 1520/21. Later on he occasionally dealt with these questions, though he never treated them systematically. His scattered statements are difficult to understand because in most cases he presented them in polemics against Canon law. Consequently they tell us what, according to his opinion, man-made ecclesiastical law should not be rather than what it may be. Only the doctrine of the two kingdoms enables us to grasp what is positive in his statements. Therefore one may state the following: According to the gospel, there are only two kingdoms and two governances, the spiritual and the secular.[116] In the law of Moses, God "placed between these two kingdoms still another kingdom, half spiritual, half secular; it provided the Jews with commandments and external ceremonies, which regulated their conduct toward God and man in the external matters of this world."[117] For Christians this order of the "external spiritual governance"[118] has been abolished. In other words, the law of the corporeal church is not based on the divine positive law.

V

In man-made ecclesiastical law one has to differentiate between two groups of legal acts. The first one consists of acts which implement the divine positive law (proclamation of God's Word, administration of the sacraments according to their institution in Holy Scripture, use of the Power of the Keys),[119] and the second consists of acts which are outside of this area.

To the first group belong the imposing and lifting of excommunication.[120] Excommunication is a "spiritual penalty";[121] it is a penalty for the purpose of improvement[122] (or in terms of Canon law, a *censura*), provided by Christ. In a procedure, for which Christ himself has set up the rules,[123] this penalty is enacted against public, obstinate sinners by the public office of preaching with the consent of the congregation.[124] In its substance, excommunication is proclamation of the Word in the form of a judicial verdict. Christ made the effect of this verdict binding for his kingdom; that is, this verdict excludes the guilty one from the spiritual church and banishes him into Satan's kingdom. Excommunication implements the divine positive law. But this legal act also deprives the sinner of the membership in the corporeal church; therefore excommunication is also a legal event in the area of man-made law. It is such a severe action that it may be imposed only in cases of the most serious offenses against God and neighbor;[125] for instance, the publicly committed vices listed in the Decalogue,[126] publicly taught heresy, se-

Appendix IV

vere public interference in Christ's spiritual ecclesiastical governance by secular authorities. In addition, the condition for imposing excommunication is the obstinate refusal of the sinner to repent.[127]

In all these cases we have a situation which on the basis of the existence of the law itself already results in the loss of membership in Christ's kingdom, ⟨even if the church would not pronounce the verdict,⟩[128] so that only a semblance of membership would exist. But from this internal excommunication, executed by God, the manifest church draws the consequence for its communal life[129] through the external excommunication.[130] Therefore excommunication is the verbal establishment of a prior loss of legal status,[131] combined with the admonition to repent and the promise of divine grace when the sinner[132] turns away from his sinful ways.[133]

The same legal principles govern the readmission into the corporeal church. With the consent of the congregation, the incumbent of the public preaching office readmits the guilty one after he has publicly done ecclesiastical penance; such a readmission results in the restoration of membership both in the spiritual and the corporeal church. This is the correct use of the Power of the Keys.

Yet the tension between the spiritual and the corporeal church[134] can cause mistakes,[135] resulting in a rift in the legal situation existing according to the divine positive law and the legal situation created by man-made law.[136] Luther's own life is an example for this situation; he was excommunicated, even though he preached the pure doctrine of the gospel. Another example would be the readmission of a non-repenting hypocrite into the Christian congregation. In such cases the spiritual status of the persons involved is not changed. The innocent person who has been excommunicated retains the right of membership both in the spiritual and the corporeal church; *de facto,* he is prevented, however, from using this right in the corporeal church. Conversely, the person who is illegally absolved from the excommunication remains outside of the spiritual church and belongs to the corporeal church only by appearance, even though because of the rule of love one may not deny him the use of the right of membership in the corporeal church.

In summary: Excommunication and readmission are acts of Christ's spiritual ecclesiastical governance. The incumbent of the public preaching office, together with the Christian congregation and in strict dependence on God's judgment, has to implement these acts.

The corporeal church has only the office of executor[137] of the divine judgment, it does not have its own authority of jursidiction. Therefore I propose for this implementation of the spiritual Power of the Keys the term 'heteronomous ecclesiastical law'.

VI

Let us now consider man-made ecclesiastical law outside of the Power of the Keys. Here we find that each particular church has its own ecclesiastical ordinance.[138] Luther dealt with the problems raised by such ordinances primarily in connection with the order of worship, using the terms 'ceremonies' and 'traditions'. Both terms have very broad meanings; ceremonies, for instance, include all institutions and arrangements of the corporeal church pertaining to worship, beginning with the church building and ending with liturgies and rites.

A church ordinance serves the external, temporal governance of the church,[139] and it has an educational task; therefore it is related to the law connected with parents and schooling. It is supposed to teach the members of a congregation, especially the young and the simple folk,[140] a conduct which promotes the proclamation of the divine Word as far as man is able to judge. Christ turned the creation of such an ordinance over to his disciples.[141] Therefore we may use for such ordinances the term 'autonomous ecclesiastical law'.[142] The existence of man-made ecclesiastical ordinances does not violate the spiritual law of Christ's kingdom[143] or, and this would be the same, of the spiritual church. But such an ordinance may not claim to be spiritual.[144] For the Christian estate it is unimportant what a church ordinance is like, and Christians do not attribute any spiritual quality to it. They use it indifferently *(indifferenter)*,[145] regardless of its alleged spiritual quality. Therefore it is wrong for Canon law to call itself 'spiritual law'.[146]

VII

The binding quality of a church ordinance is in no part based on any kind of authority to make law granted in divine positive law to those who govern the church. Neither the Power of the Keys nor the shepherding office of the hierarchy[147] includes the competency to issue laws, that is, commandments which bind a Christian's conscience to obedience because of God's commandment to obey the authorities. Therefore it is impossible for a church ordinance to be 'necessary law'. It is valid ⟨and binding⟩ not because a law is needed[148] but because a brother needs a law,[149] that is, because of the concern for a Christian brother's Salvation of the soul. "The ecclesiastical commonwealth is organized by *one* law, that of love."[150] This is the guiding principle of all man-made ecclesiastical law. With this principle, Luther adopted an idea which we find already in medieval canonistic literature,[151] but he gave it a different meaning by connecting it with the spiritual law of the hidden church.

The foundation in the spiritual law of love makes man-made ecclesiastical law, or as Luther said, "the order of the Christian congregation," or "the order of the church," different from all other law on earth.[152] According to Luther, there exists *ius utrumque*,[153] an ecclesiastical[154] and a secular law. In its own way, each law is a sign of the commonwealth which it serves.

VIII

As a result of their examination of the circumstances, Christians decide whether a church ordinance is to be created and what its content should be. Man-made ecclesiastical law, therefore, is a product of human reason,[155] with reason having been illuminated by faith[156] *(fide illuminata)*. In contrast to the natural reason of carnal man, the reason of a Christian is spiritually free *(christiana et libera ratio)*. These statements do not suggest that the Christian status improves or perfects a believer's innate talents. Yet through his faith a Christian has insight in the structure of the divine sovereignty in both kingdoms and of its implementation by means of the two governances; he has the "Christian understanding of law,"[157] and he knows that he is called to serve Christ's royal rule.[158] If one applies these principles to the church, then it is clear that an ecclesiastical ordinance has to be in line with the three spiritual basic rights of the Christian congregation, that is, Christian brotherly love, Christian equality, and Christian freedom.[159]

IX

Who has the competency to enact a church ordinance?

In order to limit in a negative way the people who could be involved, we shall first deal with the secular authorities. God has assigned the preservation of external peace in God's kingdom at the left to them.[160] Therefore they have the sword as the symbol of their coercive rule[161] over body and life. But Christ did not give any office in God's kingdom at the right to them[162] and, therefore, also not in the manifest church. It would be an encroachment on Christ's ecclesiastical governance, or the freedom of a Christian congregation, were one to interject the secular coercive rule into the manifest church; this would mix the two kingdoms and governances. Therefore a church ordinance may not be imposed upon the corporeal church — it has to emerge from within the church. For creating such an ordinance a Christian congregation does not even need the recognition of this right by the secular governance, or its permission; this becomes especially ⟨important⟩ when the church is being persecuted by the state.

Secular governmental authority is restricted to caring for the *pax politica*[163] in such a way that the divine mission of the church is unobstructed in the secular commonwealth.[164] Consequently, the legal situation was different in the case of the opponents and in the case of the proponents of the Reformation. Those rulers who had not yet become convinced of the truth of the evangelical faith may not use their power in an attempt to settle the spiritual battle between the proponents and the opponents of the evangelical confession of faith; they have to be content with the Roman Catholic party "keeping peace and believing what it wants to believe," just as the evangelicals "also believe the truth" (confessed, for instance, in the *Augsburg Confession*), "for even God himself, who is superior to all authority, never wants to use force for bringing someone to faith."[165] That is, Luther demanded an Imperial-law order for equal tolerance in favor of his followers in their relationship with Roman Catholic Christians. His basis was different from the modern idea of tolerance, however; it was the confidence that once tolerated his doctrine would be victorious in the battle of faith.[166] — This has to suffice for clarifying the legal relationship of a Roman Catholic ruler with the particular church of his territory.

Once a secular ruler has been won for the evangelical confession of faith, then to his rights as guardian of the *pax politica*[167] are added the duties[168] which he has as a Christian brother to care for the prospering of the manifest church. Yet even in this situation he does not have sovereign power[169] ⟨in matters pertaining to the church⟩. The *cura religionis*,[170] to which he is obligated as a member of the Christian body, grants him nevertheless a wide range of positive actions in matters of caring for the faith.[171] In an extreme situation ⟨this caring for the faith by a secular ruler as a Christian brother⟩ extends to giving emergency relief[172] for the organization of the temporal, external ecclesiastical governance[173] of a particular church — *if* life in that church has been shattered and the ecclesiastical officers, who are called to enact reforms, do not meet their responsibilities; but even now a ruler may not usurp the spiritual ecclesiastical governance.[174]

Apart from such an exception in which a ruler acts substituting ⟨for the ecclesiastical officers, who are responsible to act but do not act⟩, a church ordinance is created through the harmonious, voluntary cooperation of the Christians of a particular church. Such a consensus of the believers is necessary. The rule of faith and the rule of love[175] determine who the believers are: ⟨all⟩ the baptized decide the church ordinance, but it is binding only if the true Christians[176] do not object to it.

X

Luther suggested that greatest care be taken when one determines the content[177] of an ordinance for the cultic communal life and the time that such an ordinance would be enacted.[178] Such an ordinance should never have the appearance of a sovereign decree, as is the case with secular laws. A regimentation[179] of worship, brought about by decree, would direct the attention of people away from the sermon, the center of worship, and toward the performance of rites; it also would attribute a spiritually binding quality to such rites, which they do not have, and thus make them into traps for consciences.[180] Therefore for the time being one should wait[181] until the evangelical doctrine has been firmly rooted in a congregation, ⟨Luther argued,⟩ and even then one should let customs of worship grow gradually.[182] Then, finally, one should write down the ceremonies. Yet one should present such a text to congregations not as a binding norm, but only as an example, a story, and one should let the congregations decide whether to adopt it.

XI

The pastor[183] of a local congregation initiates the process of creating law in the church, or in the case of larger particular churches the spiritual shepherd[184] does it. Compared with other members of the church, that shepherd has not only the specific knowledge but also a higher degree of responsibility for good order in his diocese; as the incumbent of the shepherding office he has a higher degree of authority. Luther took it for granted that the pastor or bishop, who is called to implement the spiritual ecclesiastical governance publicly, leads in settling matters also of the external temporal ecclesiastical governance. Because of the different legal situations, the tasks in both areas have to be strictly separated, yet in the daily praxis they are closely connected. This connection results in a competency which is a part of man-made ecclesiastical law. But this competency may not be derived from the Power of the Keys or the office of spiritually shepherding, that is, from legal titles in the divine positive law.[185]

XII

A church ordinance is created through an orderly decision of a congregation.[186] The procedure to be used is left to the judgment of the particular church. One possibility would be the legal forms used for the creation of laws in the secular community, and there are no objections to following such procedures.

According to Canon or secular law, transgressions of individual laws result in sanctions. In the case of a church ordinance there are no sanctions if it is violated[187] — a church ordinance is not binding in an absolute sense.[188] For the sake of the fellow Christians one should, of course, do all to conform to it.[189] But when neither the Salvation of the neighbor nor one's own is jeopardized, one may ignore a church ordinance with a good conscience, and when Christian love of the brother demands it, one has to ignore it. The spiritual law of love always takes precedence over man-made ecclesiastical law. If, however, any one of the three spiritual basic rights[190] is not applicable to a situation, then a particular church may discipline a transgressor of its ordinance. But even then the transgressor may not be excommunicated.

Appendix IV

XIII

The law concerning ecclesiastical offices presents greater difficulties to the judgment of the jurist than a church ordinance. Each particular church has offices, and all of them serve the good order of the church's communal life. A particular church creates these offices and appoints persons to them because it is responsible for the Salvation of its members. In doing this, a particular church obeys the law of love, as far as the actions of the church are determined by faith. In that law all ecclesiastical offices have their common foundation, which is to be considered a part of the divine law. These offices differ, however, because different charges are assigned to different offices. There is the office of public preaching;[191] because of the specific legal situation of this office, we have to deal with it separately.[192] There are other offices; for instance, the office of caring for the poor,[193] of instructing pupils,[194] of administering the properties of the church,[195] etc. These offices are additions to the preaching office, but they are not derived from it.

It is up to the judgment of a congregation whether such additional offices are to be established and how their content is to be shaped. But there is *one office* for which a congregation has no authority to decide whether it is needed or what its mission is — both are prescribed for the congregation in the divine positive law. And this is the office of public ministry *(ministerium verbi publicum)*, or the office of public preaching. One may call it *the*[196] ecclesiastical office.[197] For Luther this office[198] was one of the marks of the church since the office of public preaching[199] and the Christian congregation cannot exist without each other. "... externally one recognizes the church by the fact that it consecrates ecclesiastical servants, or calls them, or has offices for which it has to appoint persons, for one has to have bishops, pastors or preachers.... Be certain that wherever you see ⟨such offices⟩, there certainly have to be God's people ... the holy Christian people."[200]

XIV

In the public office of preaching the divine positive law, the spiritual law of love, and man-made law, that is, ecclesiastical law, overlap. This situation has caused many misunderstandings, which in most cases are the result of the same mistake: arguments which originate in man-made ecclesiastical law are transferred to the divine positive law and vice versa. The true legal situation can be briefly presented by focusing on the call into the public office of preaching. Let us assume that a congregation, living by God's Word, calls a believing Christian into its office of pastor.

XV

As mentioned above,[201] one has to differentiate between two forms of the call *(vocatio)*, the sacramental and the extra-sacramental call.

Sacramental is the call into the priesthood through Baptism.[202] Baptism, the bath of rebirth, is also God's call into the ministry of the Word.[203] Everyone who is baptized in faith is spiritually born as a priest.[204] This priesthood is given to such a person because he is a member of the Christian body. From this follows that this priesthood may be practiced only in unity with the Christian congregation. If understood in this way, this priesthood is *ius commune*, a common right held by an individual Christian and at the same time by a congregation.[205] The usual term, 'universal priesthood of the believers', expresses only one side of this legal relationship.[206]

This sacramental call through Baptism is the only form of priestly consecration; it cannot be repeated and it grants a *character indelebilis*.[207] <Thus> Ordination, which according to Canon law is a sacrament, loses its place in divine positive law. It becomes a rite of man-made law which can be repeated[208] and does not create a *character indelebilis*.[209] It does not provide a basis for an estate differentiation[210] between clergy and laity which would originate in the divine positive law. Therefore the canonistic interpretation[211] of the church as an association of unequals[212] is rejected. <Now> all members of the church are legally equal citizens in the kingdom of Christ.[213] Therefore the clergy may not claim privileges <supposedly attached to their> estate, especially not the *privilegium fori* and the *privilegium immunitatis*.[214]

XVI

The extra-sacramental call is the call[215] into the public office of preaching in a congregation.[216] The typical form in which this office is organized is the office of pastor. In terms of substance, employment in the pastoral office adds nothing to the priestly duties and competencies with which Christ charged his people in the sacramental call. The main task in the sacramental call and in the extra-sacramental call is the teaching of God's Word,[217] and in this task all other priestly tasks[218] are contained. Nevertheless, for the employment in the pastoral office the extra-sacramental call has to be added to the sacramental call. The reason for this is the already described quality of the universal priesthood as *ius commune*.[219] It demands the creation of a "common, public office"[220] for preaching before the congregation. In differentiation from the universal priesthood of an individual Christian, this office is called common because its duties are to be carried out "in stead and in the name of all,"[221] or in other words, because the congregation acts through this office.[222] For two reasons the office is called public. First: According to Christ's charge, the teaching of God's Word has to "shine publicly";[223] that is, God's Word has to be proclaimed in public in contrast to a proclamation in the <private> domestic community.[224] According to this understanding of 'public',[225] the administration of the sacraments is to be an action of <publicly> confessing Christ.[226] Second: The office is to be acquired by way of a public call procedure to be conducted before the congregation of believers; only in this way is the office acquired legitimately. Such a procedure is missing in the case of the *Winkelprediger*;[227] they sneak into the office without a public call.

In the procedure of the call into the public office of preaching one has to differentiate between the action of God and of the spiritual church on the one side, and the action of the manifest church on the other. One has to begin with Christ's call into the ecclesiastical office. This is an act of his "eternal ecclesiastical governance."[228] In the manifest church he implements this act either himself, and then makes it known through a miraculous sign — in the following we shall not consider this case — or he has this act implemented through people.[229]

XVII

When the incumbent of the public office of preaching carries out tasks of the spiritual ecclesiastical governance, he acts under the direct order of <Christ,> the head of the church, from whom he derives his spiritual authority; if he uses this authority in accordance with Christ's will, he acts independently from any earthly authority, and even a Christian congregation is not authorized to give any instructions to him[230] — it is restricted to correcting a misuse of the office ⟨when it occurs⟩. Nevertheless, the congregation, too, has a positive role in the call into the public office of preaching. The legal title for this positive role is provided by the quality of the public preaching office as a common office. At this point the office is subordinated to the right and duty of the congregation to care for the good order of its communal life. In other words, Christian brotherly love commands the congregation to charge a qualified person with the public preaching office. In summary: Christ the head and the members of the spiritual church work together when a congregation of believers[231] appoints a believing Christian to the public office of preaching; Christ acts in the realm of the divine positive law (call to service in the spiritual ecclesiastical governance), the Christian congregation acts in the realm of the divine natural law (call into the common office of preaching).

XVIII

Let us now turn to the manifest church. Here the legal acts which take place in the spiritual church are present in a hidden way only. They are "wrapped" in the forms and procedures of the secular communal life in the same way in which the hidden church on earth is "wrapped in flesh."[232]

In the manifest church the actor[233] is external Christendom existing in a particular church; yet what according to God's judgment is the correct use of its legal authority is present only when internal Christendom, gathered around Christ, is active. This incongruity between the spiritual and the corporeal church dominates the call procedure. It consists of a series of acts which follow each other. They begin with selecting the future occupant of the office and determining whether he is qualified for the office.[234] Then follows Ordination, that is, the public[235] confirmation of the legitimacy of the call,[236] conducted in a worship service.[237] This public confirmation is combined with the assignment of the candidate to the congregation which has called him, and with his reception into the ecclesiastical service of that congregation.[238] If for comparison criteria from the secular administrative law were applied to this procedure, one would have to conclude that the ordained person derives the authority of his office from the congregation, or, and this would be the same, receives it from the members of the particular church on the basis of their universal priesthood. The truth is, however, that the content of the spiritual ecclesiastical governance, which the ordained serves, precedes the congregation.

XIX

Therefore one has to concentrate on the spiritual sources of man-made ecclesiastical law in order to understand the true difference between the external and the internal essence of that law, and the mutual relationship between them.[239]

Only if one does this, can one also determine the place of man-made ecclesiastical law in the doctrine of the two kingdoms and eliminate the uncertainty (existing until now) whether that law belongs to the spiritual or the secular governance.

XX

The solution of this problem is simple when one considers acts through which the heteronomous ecclesiastical law[240] is implemented; the correct use of the Power of the Keys is a part of the spiritual governance.

But what is the situation regarding the remaining sections of man-made ecclesiastical law? The reformer's answer is surprising. Repeatedly he called the order of the corporeal church secular.[241] This seems to be a fundamental contradiction of everything that we have thus far said about the autonomous ecclesiastical law.[242] It also seems to confirm the position of those interpreters of the doctrine of the governances who assign the creation and implementation of man-made ecclesiastical law to the secular governmental authorities. Above all, Sohm's famous thesis that the essence of the church is spiritual, but the essence of law is secular, sounds like a modern version of Luther's statement that the order of the corporeal church "is placed outside of the church."[243] Yet such an interpretation of the reformer's ideas is wrong. In our context, Luther used the term 'secular' primarily as polemic against Canon law. According to Canon law, the structure of the corporeal church is based on divine positive law, and, therefore, it is binding for faith. According to Luther, however, no part of the order of a particular church[244] may claim such a quality. This order is created by human reason,[245] and in its totality it is outside of the church, that is, outside of the spiritual church.[246] At this point 'secular' designates 'non-spiritual'.[247]

Yet this negative statement covers only a part of what Luther intended to say when he used the phrase 'secular law' of the church. In order fully to comprehend the meaning of the phrase one has to consult the doctrine of the two kingdoms because it presents the most precise understanding of 'secular law'. Secular law is the order in the kingdom of this world, that is, among mankind which has fallen away from God. That kingdom is created and developed by human reason, and, therefore, it is called the kingdom of reason. The Fall, however, perverted human reason and at the same time weakened its potential. This had disastrous consequences for the law in the age of the corrupt nature; now law is external, corporeal, secular, temporal (that is, without duration), inconstant.[248]

This just mentioned weakness of natural man in the creation of law is present even when man has converted to Christ and has been received by Christ into his spiritual kingdom. Law created and used by believing Christians also has the same external, temporally restricted, inconstant characteristic as the man-made law of the kingdom of reason. This explains why Luther borrowed the term 'secular' from the kingdom of the world and transferred it to man-made ecclesiastical law. We may not be surprised to see that terminologically Luther went even one step further: In order to underscore the difference between the divine law and the man-made ecclesiastical law, he occasionally contrasted the kingdom of faith to the kingdom of the world; and then he assigned both the law of the civic commonwealth and the law of the manifest church to the kingdom of the world. At this point 'kingdom of the world' covers both the law originating in the autocratic kingdom of reason and the law originating in that reason which serves the spiritual church. This terminology, without doubt, makes it difficult to understand the doctrine of the two kingdoms.

XXI

Some matters in the existence of the church (for instance, the management of the church's property) have equivalents in the secular commonwealth, the *politia;* in terms of civic life one could call them the secular matters of the manifest church.[249] In the secular commonwealth the governmental authorities have to regulate secular matters within the limits set by the secular natural law. According to the doctrine of the two kingdoms,[250] these matters are subject to the secular governance. Therefore one might assume that the competency of the secular governance extends also to the secular matters of the corporeal church. Indeed, the prevailing interpretation of the doctrine of the two kingdoms compels one to this conclusion, since here 'kingdom' is understood as 'area' (of eternal goods or temporal matters).[251] This, in turn, leads to the disastrous consequence that the temporal ecclesiastical governance is subordinated to the coercive lordship of the secular governmental authority.[252] The truth is totally different, however. God established the secular governance for his kingdom at the left.[253] The manifest church does not belong to this kingdom. Therefore the church itself has to regulate its secular matters. Yet the spiritual law of love obligates each Christian and, therefore, also the corporeal church to promote the well-being of the secular commonwealth.[254] Consequently, the church has to be concerned to fit the management of its secular matters into the order of the *politia*[255] — *provided* that that order is legitimate if measured with the standards of the secular natural law,[256] and that the care for the Salvation of the members of the church does not demand some other action.

The autonomous, man-made ecclesiastical law has secular features ⟨not only because it regulates the secular matters of the church but also⟩ because it uses many legal forms and procedures which have been developed in secular law, and of which the value has been proven in secular law. Because, and to the degree that, these ⟨materials from secular law⟩ serve the well-being of ⟨the corporeal church⟩[257] and its members, it is not contrary to, but in accordance with, Christian brotherly love to use these materials in the legal order of the church.

XXII

No matter in whatever way one calls the autonomous, man-made ecclesiastical law secular, there remains a big difference between that law and the law which rules in the kingdom of the world. In both cases the basis of legitimacy and, consequently, the claim and extent of validity are different. *There exists, then, ecclesiastical law.* Luther's formula with which he described the church in the world also provides the shortest description of the relationship of that law with secular law: order in the church is "worldly but not of this world."[258]

XXIII

Now the way is open for finding the answer to the question asked above: Where in the doctrine of the two kingdoms is the place for the autonomous, man-made ecclesiastical law?[259] A first step in this direction is the important realization that and why one is unable to master this problem by means of the prevailing doctrine of the governances:[260] it assigns that ecclesiastical law to the secular governance and, therefore, intermingles the two kingdoms.[261] The guiding principle of the secular governance is not the divine natural law of Christ's kingdom[262] but the secular natural law.[263] Serving that secular natural law, secular governmental authority rules with the sword according to the law of wrath,[264] and not with the gospel as the spiritual law of love. Yet the autonomous, man-made ecclesiastical law may also not be assigned to the spiritual governance. That law is not revealed by the Holy Spirit but created by human reason.[265] Of course, that law is connected with the kingdom of faith. In order to deserve its name, ‹ecclesiastical law,› it has to be created and used in obedience to the divine law; but this creation and use take place according to the natural abilities of the believers, and their actions do not proclaim God's Word. Therefore it would also be wrong to derive the creation and use of the autonomous, man-made ecclesiastical law from the universal priesthood of the believers; the creation of an ecclesiastical ordinance is not a part of the authority (and its corresponding duties)[266] granted by Christ to that priesthood. There is no divine positive law which could serve as a legal basis for ‹the autonomous, man-made ecclesiastical law›.

This situation leaves us only one way out: We have to look at a different chapter[267] in the doctrine of the two kingdoms in order to find there the source for man-made ecclesiastical law. Therefore we now turn to the basic meaning of the kingdom doctrine,[268] which leads us to the Christian congregation. According to the constitution of the spiritual ecclesiastical governance in Christ's kingdom, a Christian congregation is not only a community of preachers of God's Word and of listeners.²⁶⁹ Holding citizenship in Christ's kingdom, a Christian congregation is also a community of mutual brotherly love. And in this capacity a congregation creates and uses the man-made, autonomous ecclesiastical law for the religious communal life of external Christendom, that is, for the community of the baptized. This statement is valid with one reservation, however. According to its origin and use, the autonomous ecclesiastical law is part of the church in the world; therefore that law remains caught in the tension between the rule of faith and the rule of love;²⁷⁰ it deserves to be called law of the church only if it serves the correct use of the spiritual law of love. Whoever teaches otherwise has no clear concept of the church; for him 'church' is a "blind word."²⁷¹

XXIV

This qualifying statement about the correct use is a warning sign. It tells us that in its legal existence the corporeal church is constantly attacked²⁷² by the prince of this world's kingdom, and that the church in the world is always in danger of becoming 'world', that is, of falling victim to Satan's governance. The cause for this situation comes in many forms. In Canon law, so tenaciously upheld by his Roman Catholic opponents, Luther found a compendium of the most important degenerations of the church in the world.²⁷³ He made three charges against Canon law: It turned the church, the spiritual kingdom of Christ, into a non-spiritual²⁷⁴ world-monarchy,²⁷⁵ ruled by the hierarchy by means of a host of norms and institutions;²⁷⁶ it abandoned the ⟨legal⟩ equality existing between particular churches in favor of the supremacy of the Roman church;²⁷⁷ it humanized the divine law by deifying the man-made ecclesiastical law ⟨in the medieval Canon law⟩.

Luther also had to experience that even those congregations which sided with him and regulated their legal matters according to the spiritual law of love slid into a morass of difficulties.²⁷⁸ The effort to match the unity in faith, existing among particular churches, with some kind of unity in matters of the external order of the churches easily could result in a forced leveling of differences.²⁷⁹ On the other hand, if the spiritual basic right of Christian freedom²⁸⁰ was used in a wrong way,²⁸¹ the outcome was a miserable particularism in ecclesiastical law.²⁸² ⟨Further,⟩ Christian love of the neighbor commanded people to be patient with those who for the sake of conscience maintained traditional

⟨ecclesiastical⟩ practices until such time that they would have gained better insights through instruction.²⁸³ But what was to happen when from the very beginning obstinate hearts made all instruction useless?²⁸⁴

These problems arose within the manifest church. But the world also caused problems for the church. For instance: The church used secular legal forms.²⁸⁵ How could one prevent that with this use secular legal thinking would penetrate the practice of the church and destroy the spiritual intentions of man-made ecclesiastical law? Even Canon law, so detested by the reformer, again and again demonstrated its power and caused exasperating disagreements, especially in family law.²⁸⁶ There was the pressure of secular governmental authorities; they transgressed the God-established limits of their political office, either in order to suppress the Reformation,²⁸⁷ or zealously to promote it, or ⟨even⟩ to direct it.²⁸⁸ These and many other ⟨problems⟩ were typical of the existence of the militant church.

That church is like a hospital or convalescent home;²⁸⁹ therefore man-made ecclesiastical law is not free from the spiritual diseases of its residents. Yet it would be wrong to underestimate the value of this man-made ecclesiastical law. On the contrary! It is essential as an aid for educating Christians. Its imperfection is a part of the cross which the church in the world has to bear. At the same time this imperfection constantly admonishes the church to use the standard of the spiritual law of love for examining and correcting its law.

XXV

Such a reform becomes necessary when the man-made ecclesiastical law contradicts the divine positive law (for instance, in matters of the sacraments) or is not in harmony with the three spiritual basic rights²⁹⁰ of the Christian estate.²⁹¹ This latter situation occurs when ecclesiastical authorities, claiming the supposed divine foundation of their office, demand obedience regulated by Canon law; such a demand lacks any legal basis and is spiritual tyranny. If in such cases the request of the true Christians for changes in the corrupt ecclesiastical law is ignored by the fellow members of a particular church and its shepherds, then these true Christians have to separate themselves from this institution, which has become a hypocritical church; such a separation is governed

Appendix IV

by the degree[292] in which this institution has lost the spiritual connection with the universal church[293] and has become world. These true Christians do not secede from the church[294] — to the contrary; they are the healthier part *(sanior pars)*[295] of this particular church, who steadfastly remain[296] with the old,[297] catholic church,[298] while the hypocritical church excludes itself from the church.

The same principles have to be used when a minister of the Word does not meet the duties of his office in his teaching or conduct. If in spite of being reprimanded by his congregation he does not improve, one has to separate oneself from him; he has to be chased away like a wolf[299] who has invaded the flock of Christ's little sheep. Since he is an enemy of the true church he has forfeited his office[300] and benefice automatically.[301]

Refusing to obey the ecclesiastical authorities of a corrupt particular church does not suffice, however. People have to join together in a church which organizes its legal existence according to the norms set up by Christ, and which, therefore, he can recognize as his church. On the basis of the divine positive law there exists ⟨the possibility for⟩ active spiritual resistance within the church, which becomes effective in the external communal life of the church. In fact, Luther derived his ideas concerning the right of resistance from his experiences within the church. His position on the right of resistance in the secular realm was the result of the comparison of the church with the *politia* and of their contrast. But the real dynamics of the resistance doctrine developed within the church. Here this doctrine resulted in the construction of new ecclesiastical law. According to Luther, there is no divine positive law for a hierarchy of orders or jurisdictions. Therefore the divine natural law has a much more important role in the construction of ecclesiastical law than in the Roman Catholic church — it is the basis for all man-made order in the church.

XXVI

A church ordinance should deal with the following topics: The religious rites of a congregation (orders of worship); the office and estate of the servants of the church, especially the preachers; the congregational diaconate, especially the care for the poor;[302] the congregational participation in the ordering of the educational system;[303] the administration of ecclesiastical discipline,[304] especially the imposition of <excommunication>,[305] or the denial of a church funeral;[306] the administration of the church's property;[307] the establishment of supervision in the church on the level above the local congregation.[308] All such prescriptions have in common that they are not 'needed' law, and this is contrary to Canon law! Used in the spirit of Christian freedom, man-made ecclesiastical law is to guarantee that congregations are provided with God's Word, that unanimity among congregations is strengthened, and that congregations are protected against disturbances. That same spirit of voluntary[309] and harmonious[310] cooperation is to govern also the relationship of particular churches[311] with each other, and thus create unity in religious rites and legal practice[312] among congregations in a larger geographic area.[313]

The legal authority of the church in the world is limited by the divine positive law and the divine natural law. As developed above,[314] the divine positive law is established by Christ, the divine natural law is authentically interpreted by Christ. Therefore outside of Christ the church in the world has no ecclesiastical law, neither a divine nor a man-made one.

XXVII

Only a believing Christian can judge whether the legal practice of the church agrees with these principles. In the history of ecclesiastical law, the statement of the Apostle Paul, "The spiritual man judges all things" (1 Corinthians 2:15), has had serious consequences; it constantly exposes man-made ecclesiastical law to the judgment of the members of the spiritual church.[315] Only these members, who know of God's will for law, are capable of judging the legitimacy of the ecclesiastical law. Whether the other members of a particular church listen to these members of the spiritual church is another question. It will happen again and again that the 'healthier' part of the church will become the minority. In this situation there is no institution on earth which could determine infallibly which opinion is to be followed — God alone will rescue his church from such pitfalls. With this statement, a church ordinance points beyond itself to Christ, the true guardian of the church *(custos ecclesiae)*.

APPENDIX V

The Unfolding of the Doctrine of the Two Kingdoms as a Doctrine of Kingdoms and Governances

Johannes Heckel's Contribution to "Zwei-Reiche-Lehre" in *Evangelisches Kirchenlexikon*, 3 (Göttingen, 1959): 1936-1945[1]

1.*a*. The doctrine of the two kingdoms is the key to Luther's ecclesiology, his doctrine of the state, and his doctrine of law. *The doctrine of the two kingdoms marks a revolution in the history of the Christian theology of society.* According to medieval theory, God provided a twofold order for ruling the community of baptized Christians: one is to mediate eternal Salvation, the other is to serve temporal well-being. According to Christ's mandate, Christendom is governed in spiritual matters by the clergy so that it forms the universal church *(ecclesia universalis)*. On the other hand, in secular matters Christendom is governed by Christian rulers, and it is called *politia. Ecclesia* and *politia* describe the two separate but coordinated structures of the one spiritual-secular kingdom of Christendom, the *respublica christiana*.

Luther replaced this order with the doctrine of the two kingdoms. He started with Augustine's differentiation between the heavenly and the earthly city, and he used its development in late medieval exegesis, especially in the work of Gabriel Biel. Of the manifold late medieval kingdom doctrine two concepts were especially fruitful for Luther: kingdom understood as lordship over those who are subject to power *(dominatio)*, and kingdom understood as citizenship in a mystical body *(civitas)*. Luther adopted the terminology and the starting point of the late Scholastics, and thus he maintained some continuity with the traditional kingdom doctrine. Yet within the form of this traditional thought pattern he systematically transformed the traditional kingdom doctrine. Characteristic of this process is his Christ-centered thinking. He began with Christ's kingdom *(regnum Christi)*; he precisely differentiated between Christ's kingdom according to Christ's humanity *(regnum Christi secundum humanitatem eius)* — that is, the kingdom of God's incarnate Son or the kingdom of grace — and Christ's sovereignty over the world according to his divinity *(secundum divinitatem eius)* — that is, the kingdom of God's omnipotence. Therefore the doctrine of the two kingdoms is structured in two sections. The first one, which is fundamentally important for the layout of the topic, we call *Basic Meaning of the Kingdom Doctrine,* the second one we call *Doctrine of the Governances.* Both belong together.[2]

b. Decisive for the *basic meaning of the kingdom doctrine* is the equation of kingdom *(regnum)* and mystical body *(corpus mysticum)*. At this point 'kingdom' is a personalistic term which describes a community of persons under one head. In the kingdom of grace, Christ rules according to his humanity in the midst of the congregation of his disciples. Through him and in him they are a spiritual body *(corpus Christi mysticum)*. This body has three characteristics, and each one determines a different meaning of kingdom. Kingdom designates, first, the royal dignity of the head *(rex)*; second, the head's governance as a life-creating impact on the members of the body *(influxus capitis in membra)*; and third, the royal people of believers, that is, Christ's people, or the true church, or the communion of saints, or the ecclesiastical body *(populus Christi, ecclesia vera, communio sanctorum, corpus ecclesiasticum)*. All three characteristics of Christ's kingdom have to be seen together.

This kingdom is opposed by another kingdom, the kingdom of the world *(regnum mundi)*; in this context, 'world' designates mankind alienated from God. Here, too, exists a mystical body under one head, Satan, and again we find the three characteristics described above: The ‹royal dignity›[3] of the prince of the world *(princeps mundi)*, the governance of the devil, and the devil's people. 'World' is, then, identical with 'Babylonian body' *(corpus Babylonicum)*.

c. The *doctrine of the governances* has this same personalistic understanding of kingdom, which is decisive for the basic meaning of the kingdom doctrine. Now *regnum* or kingdom means lordship *(domi-*

natio) over those who are subject to power; it designates, first, a position of power, second, the use of power, and, third, the sum of those who are subject to power.

2.*a.* According to the *first characteristic of the governances doctrine*,[4] there are a kingdom (that is, governance) of God and a counter-governance of the devil. Each extends over all of mankind, with differences: God's governance is irresistible, and, therefore, Christ rules also over his enemies; in faith a Christian is able to resist Satan's governance so that sin does not dominate his heart. Thus already this first characteristic shows that mankind is divided into two bodies.[5]

b. The *second characteristic*[6] makes this division even clearer. God rules mankind through his Word. It is addressed to man's heart, it is 'Word of God into us' and not 'around us'.[7] Only a part of mankind accepts God's message in faith, turns to God, and receives from him the righteousness which is valid before him *(iniusti iustificandi)*.[8] The others turn away from God, close their hearts to him, and are damned *(iniusti non iustificandi)*.[9] The former accept God's commandment spiritually *(spiritualiter)*, the latter listen to it only carnally *(carnaliter)* or literally *(literaliter)*, and both groups live accordingly. God's Word, therefore, divides mankind into two groups <or families>. The first one is internally grasped by God's governance, the second one only externally. This situation determines the quality of the divine governance. The people of the first group listen to God in faith; therefore the governance over them is as a spiritual, internal one, and the external life of these true Christians is shaped by their God-formed will. The situation is different for the people of the second group. Because they do not receive God's will into their hearts, God must use external force to rule them.

If we now reconsider the basic meaning of the kingdom doctrine, then it becomes clear that both, <the doctrine of the kingdoms and the doctrine of the governances,> are a unified whole. As the head of his mystical body, Christ implements God's sovereignty over the believers. God's sovereignty over the unbelievers hits the Babylonian body. In the first case, God's governance covers a body which is turned toward God; in the second case, it covers a body which turned away from God. The unity between the basic meaning of the kingdom doctrine and the doctrine of the governances is so obvious for Luther that he interchanged the terms 'kingdom' (in the sense of body) and 'governance' (kingdom in the sense of lordship), even used each term with a double meaning.

The Unfolding of the Doctrine of the Two Kingdoms

Both bodies are involved in a fierce battle of their heads and members with each other. It takes place in each Christian's heart. It also takes place externally, in the offices and vocations which God has instituted for the implementation of his governance over mankind. Wherever a Christian is, he is attacked.[10] Wherever God gives a commandment or provides an order,[11] there is God's opponent to prevent their implementation. In this way, Luther's theology of society is the doctrine of kingdoms and of law in the theology of the cross *(theologia crucis)*. This battle will not end prior to the Day of Judgment. Therefore the reformer's doctrine of the kingdoms has a most dramatic, trans-worldly and inner-worldly eschatological quality.

c. This quality sheds light on the *third characteristic of the doctrine of the governances,*[12] and also on the basic meaning of the kingdom doctrine. Neither of the two peoples engaged in battle is static. Their membership constantly is in motion, either to Christ (because of the Holy Spirit's work), or away from Christ (because the evil spirit seduces people). Therefore 'body' can be seen only in the process of people being gathered by a head, a process which takes place in a constant struggle with a counterhead. This legal image of the mystical body is totally different from the modern doctrine of corporation or organism.

Excursus

The perception of this ‹ever-present,› restless, spiritual battle between two human armies, each gathered around its own head, has far-reaching consequences for the relationship of Luther's theology of society with that of the Middle Ages.

a. Christ's mystical body and the mystical body of the devil cannot be one legal community before God. Each person has his spiritual legal status either in the one or the other body. No one is a citizen of both kingdoms. Thus the medieval idea that on the basis of divine natural law all of mankind exists in one legal community is nullified. Only the believers have insight into the divine will for law, and only they are willing to obey that will. In contrast, the unbelievers affirm a concept of law which in God's eyes is distorted and perverted. The questions whether and why this concept nevertheless may be called law can be answered only with the help of another theological grammar than the one used in the traditional doctrine ‹of law›.[13] ‹The development of this new grammar› made Luther the founder of a new theological doctrine of law.

Appendix V

b. If the traditional ecclesiology is evaluated in light of the doctrine of the two kingdoms, then it also needs to be fundamentally reshaped. In God's judgment even the community of the baptized is not one spiritual unit. In external Christendom there are in addition to believing baptized also unbelieving baptized. In light of the proclamation of the Word and the administration of the sacraments, which take place in the midst of external Christendom,[14] the community of the baptized is called universal church *(ecclesia universalis)* since God's Word never returns empty to God (Isa. 55:11). Nevertheless, in spite of these sacred marks, ⟨the proclamation of the Word and the administration of the sacraments,⟩ which guarantee the activity of the Holy Spirit within corporeal Christendom, ⟨the universal church⟩ is not a mystical body. Therefore it may not be used as a starting point for ecclesiology. Here, too, Luther had to construct something new.

c. Therefore, obviously, Luther had to reject the idea 'respublica christiana'. The secular organization of mankind ⟨*politia*⟩ has no sacred marks instituted by God's Son which would point toward the Holy Spirit's hidden activity ⟨so that that organization could be called Christian⟩. The much-discussed question whether Luther adopted the medieval model of society, the so-called Christian body *(corpus christianum)*, has to be answered negatively.[15]

3. *Luther's image of the external constitution of mankind is determined by the existence of two peoples who are totally different when spiritually viewed, the Christians and the non-Christians.* The former are in God's kingdom at his right hand, that is, under the *governance of grace*, the latter are in God's kingdom at his left hand, that is, under the *governance of the divine wrath*[16] over sin, a wrath which nevertheless is a wrath of mercy. According to God's will, *both governances have their own order of law, of estate, and of office, and the nature of these orders is determined by the spiritual condition of each of the two peoples.*

a. Let us first consider *law*. In the kingdom of grace the divine will for law is valid as it has been created into man's incorrupt nature in the Original Status, that is, as *divine natural law*. Christ interpreted it authentically as spiritual law of love *(lex charitatis spiritualis)*, that is, as the commandment of perfect love for God and neighbor. It is called law of Christ *(lex Christi);* because this law of Christ can be known and affirmed only by Christians in faith, it is also called law of faith *(lex fidei)*. A totally different situation exists in the kingdom of divine wrath! Non-Christians also have the divine natural law engraved in their hearts, but

The Unfolding of the Doctrine of the Two Kingdoms

they are no longer able to grasp its God-related meaning. Held captive in egotism, they interpret it in such a way that its goal is no longer eternal Salvation but earthly well-being. They change the spiritual law of love into a humanitarian *secular natural law,* that is, the commandment of universal love for man; in its nucleus this love cannot rid itself of egotism. Its briefest version is the Golden Rule, and the Decalogue is its exemplary illustration in terms of substantive law. This secular natural law is the *fountain of all positive man-made law.* Therefore it is a precious jewel. In his mercy God has left this jewel to fallen mankind in order to protect it against self-annihilation. If measured with the standard of the divine natural law, it is, however, only a shadow *(umbra)* of divine righteousness, a "spiritual beggary."[17] This dualism of the divine natural law and the secular natural law corresponds to the division of mankind into God's friends and God's enemies, and it is transcended in the unity of the divine will for law. This will is perfectly manifested in the kingdom of grace, but in the kingdom of wrath it can be grasped only as a pale reflection or in crude examples, for instance, in the prohibitions of the Second Table of the Decalogue.

b. The same dualism is present in the order of *estates* and in the order of *offices* for the two peoples of mankind. Christians exist in a spiritual, non-Christians in a counter-spiritual association of estates. God has assigned an office of governance to each estate: the office of preaching to the Christians, the office of secular governmental authority to the non-Christians.

God implements his sovereignty over mankind through people who are called into such offices, and he does it in two ways: In his kingdom at the right God implements the governance over Christians through the preaching of the Word *(pascere verbo);*[18] preaching is also a missionary work directed at non-Christians in order to bring them to faith (that is, preaching is addressed to both kingdoms or both kinds of people). In his kingdom at the left God lets his governance be implemented through corporeal force *(vis).*

4.*a.* In this governance constitution the totality of Christians is called *church in the world.* For this church one has to *differentiate between a spiritual and a corporeal form.* According to the first form, the church is a communion of faith, and it is called inner or essential Christendom. It is identical with the Savior's disciples; corporeally they are scattered all over the world (diaspora), but they are united in faith *(ecclesia spiritualis)*. According to the second form, the church in the world is the community of the baptized or external Christendom *(ecclesia universalis)*. Both forms belong together in a way which is absolutely necessary for the existence of the church, and we will discuss this <below, in (5)>.

The church in the world faces the *politia*. Luther used this word sometimes with a wide, sometimes with a narrow meaning. The wide meaning covers the totality of the non-Christians under the governance of the secular authority. <In the narrow meaning the word is identical with the state.>

b. The relationship of the church in the world with the *politia* in the wide meaning of the word is not identical with the relationship of the organized church *(Kirchentum)* with the state; nevertheless, it shapes the relationship <of the church with the state> spiritually, <and this for the following reason:> The members of the church in the world and the members of the *politia* create particular associations of man-made law. In the process of their missionary and diaconic mission, the members of the church in the world organize individual churches *(ecclesiae particulares)*.[19] Following Cain's example,[20] the members of the *politia* in the wide meaning of the word organize individual states (*politiae* in the narrow meaning of the word, that is, kingdoms and cities). Into these two types of particular, legally organized associations Luther dissolved the constitution of the one <medieval> spiritual-secular kingdom of Christendom with its universal legal quality. At this point the modern problem 'state and church' appears, not its language but its subject, and Luther was the first to create a theological rationale for it. The differentiation between the two peoples of mankind is the reformer's contribution to the modern public law concerning the church.[21]

5.*a.* The *spiritual church* is for Luther the center of the social order presented above, which is drawn up according to spiritual criteria. The Holy Spirit calls sinners, who are converted through the preaching of the Word, into this church and preserves them in the one true faith. The members of this spiritual community are known only to God; therefore it is called hidden church *(ecclesia abscondita)*. *One has to differentiate between that church and the corporeal community of the baptized*, the manifest or universal church *(ecclesia manifesta, univeralis)*.

In order to determine the legal connection between these two forms of the church in the world one has to start with the hidden church. It is a spiritual congregation; therefore it exists exclusively according to the spiritual, that is, divine law, either the divine positive law (Christ's command to preach the Word and administer the sacraments through the office of public ministry), or Christ's law, that is, the divine natural law and its three spiritual basic rights of Christendom (Christian brotherly love, equality, and freedom).[22] That ‹spiritual› church creates a corporeal association. Christ required the rite of Baptism for admission to the spiritual church, and the fulfillment of this requirement creates the ‹corporeal› community of the baptized. Therefore the existence of the corporeal church is also based on the will of Christ. The two forms of the church in the world, ‹the spiritual and the corporeal,› belong together, and one may not think of one without also thinking of the other. At the same time, however, there is also a tension between them, which cannot be abolished. Luther used images of the scholastic doctrine of the sacraments (sign and reality, soul and body) to illustrate this 'simultaneity'.[23] It is a sign *(signum)* for the existence of the true ‹spiritual, hidden› church *(res)* when ‹and wherever in the world› in the manifest church the Word is preached and the sacraments are administered according to Christ's command.

Luther used the same principle for deciding the membership in the church. Because of Christian brotherly love *(canon charitatis)* no baptized may be deprived of membership in the church — *provided* that he ‹or she› does not exclude himself ‹or herself›. God, however, ‹concentrates on a person's› faith *(canon fidei)*.[24] Therefore a baptized unbeliever has only the corporeal mark of the Christian estate,[25] but his spiritual reality is not in line with this mark (body without soul). He is outside of the spiritual church, and, therefore, he also has no legitimate membership in the corporeal church; rather, he is a member of Satan's hypocritical church *(ecclesia simulata)*. Conversely, a believing Christian who has been excommunicated unjustly remains in the spiritual church, even though he has been deprived of the mark of active membership[26] in the corporeal church (soul without body). The believing baptized who has not been excommunicated is a member of both the spiritual and the corporeal form of the church (soul and body).

b. *All man-made law within the corporeal church has to demonstrate that Christ's law is in action;* this is the consequence of the dependence of the corporeal church on the spiritual church for the legal order of the corporeal church. "The churchly commonwealth is organized by only *one* law, that of love."[27] In differentiation from secular law, man-made ecclesiastical law derives its validity not from the duty of obeying a governmental authority[28] instituted by God for creating law *(ex lege)* but from the Christian brotherly love *(ex necessitate fratris)*. This situation does not diminish the obligation of Christians to obey man-made ecclesiastical law. To the contrary: when the ‹law› of a governmental authority is at an end,[29] then Christian brotherly love becomes even more active.[30] Man-made ecclesiastical law has its own legal basis, and the authority of this law is not derived from the political commonwealth. The value of these two qualities is proven especially when the church is persecuted by secular rulers or harassed by internal disruptions, two situations which are normal for the church in the world as church under the cross. This church itself, attacked as it is,[31] has to organize its legal existence by drawing on the strength of the faith. In this connection the church has to meet two major tasks: In the manifest church Christ's commission to preach the Word and administer the sacraments has to be publicly fulfilled by his servants; the communal life of Christians (worship and charitable actions) has to be shaped according to the requirements of brotherly love which demands both service and discipline (2 Timothy 1:7). In short: All man-made ecclesiastical law has to be created and used as a law of service implementing the spiritual law of love *(lex charitatis spiritualis)*. Only when it is used in this spiritual way is man-made ecclesiastical law a part of both the spiritual and the corporeal church. It is *the* serious question, with which the individual churches *(ecclesiae particulares)* are constantly confronted, whether the ecclesiastical law and its use are in line with such a spiritual use of Christ's law *(usus spiritualis legis Christi)*; man-made ecclesiastical law is not protected against the battle between the true church and the devil's church.

6.a. The essence of the church provides the criteria for evaluating the politia. It is God's order of offices provided for the world without faith and grace. In its origin, this order is similar to the secular natural law, and it goes back to the divine establishment of marriage in the Original Status; therefore it is a 'holy' institution. This order came into existence, however, only after the Fall. Then the perfect spiritual-corporeal love community of spouses changed into a relationship of power, the domestic governance, and from this governance the office of the secular governmental authority is derived. The secular natural law and the secular governmental authority belong together also internally.[32] For, according to the instruction of the secular natural law, a secular governmental authority has to protect the external peace in the human community against disruptions by the evil ones. Therefore the sword is the symbol of its power of coercion and punishment. The external order, which a secular governmental authority secures, also facilitates the service of the office of public preaching which, in turn, admonishes the hearts of people to maintain peace. *In all activities, a secular governmental authority, consciously or not, acts according to God's charge.*

b. The authority of the secular sword does not extend to the members of Christ's kingdom. A Christian remains a sinner throughout his life. For the sake of his faith, Christ has liberated him from being dominated by sin and justified him before God *(simul peccator et iustus).*[33] Therefore the believer is not subject to the governance of the divine wrath; for the execution of this wrath on earth the secular governmental authority has been established. Rather, Christians are pulled out from under it (exempt). Nevertheless, motivated by obedience to Christ's command, love the neighbor, Christians subordinate themselves to the secular governmental authority voluntarily — *provided* it remains within the limits of its competency established in the secular natural law;[34] they even accept secular offices, although in so doing they expose themselves[35] to Satan's most dangerous *Anfechtungen.*[36] This is the legal situation when it is seen from the viewpoint of Christ's spiritual kingdom. Of course, in the *politia* one thinks differently about this legal situation. Because the *politia* can and must take care only of the external order of the communal life, it is not concerned about the spiritual difference between Christians and non-Christians, but it directs its commands equally to both; it understands itself as a political body *(corpus politicum),* and it considers Christians as well as non-Christians to be its citizens. Luther, too, used this line of thinking about the legal situation in the frame of public law in order to impress upon Christians the duty to serve and obey the *politia* on the one hand, the limits of the secular legal authority (the Christian's duty of resistance) on the other hand. The public law concept 'citizenship in the *politia*' has, however, nothing in common with the theological concept 'citizenship in Christ's kingdom'. Therefore both concepts may not be placed under one higher concept, that is, 'citizen of two kingdoms' or of 'two aeons'.

This view of the *politia* completes Luther's doctrine of the kingdoms and of law. *Justification by faith alone is the key for understanding the spiritual structure and order of mankind in both kingdoms, and the*

Appendix V

structure and order of man's spiritual and corporeal existence under both governances (that is, in church and state). All parts of the reformer's doctrine of kingdoms and of law point toward one center, Christ's kingdom and its spiritual law or law of Christ *(regnum Christi, lex spiritualis, lex Christi).*

Excursus

a. Luther's followers adopted only a variation of his doctrine of the two kingdoms. Already Melanchthon emphasized the doctrine of the governances at the expense of the basic meaning of the kingdom doctrine, and in the confessional writings of the Lutheran church that position was affirmed. The Orthodox Lutheran theologians started with these writings and developed the *first post-Reformation form of the doctrine of the two kingdoms as a doctrine of the governances.* Only partially was their model of society in line with Reformation thought. They returned to the ideal of the *respublica christiana,* but they replaced the medieval doctrine of the two authorities with a diarchy of estates. They assigned internal, that is, spiritual matters, to the theological estate of teaching (more precisely, the estate of the preaching office), and they assigned external, legal matters to the political estate, that is, the secular governmental authority of the Protestant confessional state. With the title *landesherrliches Kirchenregiment*[37] especially the care for the legal order of the corporeal church was assigned to the secular governmental authority; man-made ecclesiastical law was controlled by the sovereign authority of the secular governance, though in theory the counsel of theologians and the consent of housefathers (doctrine of the three estates)[38] were to be respected when this care was implemented. Now the state-church system of Marsilius of Padua[39] was revived, but its justification was derived from evangelical theology. Though the doctrine of the governances developed by Orthodox Lutheran theologians was theoretically unbalanced, it remained influential in Germany until the end of the monarchy.

b. In the meantime the idea and form of the state changed. The German Protestant confessional state was replaced by the 'Christian' state, in which legal equality of the confessions was guaranteed. And the governance of the prince was changed through the introduction of constitutionalism. This new situation in public law was reflected in a new interpretation of Luther's statements. The *second post-Reformation form of the two kingdoms doctrine,* shaped by Christoph E. Luthardt, replaced the Christian doctrine of the governances

The Unfolding of the Doctrine of the Two Kingdoms

with the doctrine of the Christian citizen.[40] Now kingdom designated area, sphere of living. In the existence of a Christian are two such areas: the internal kingdom, in which Christ issues instructions for the conduct of his followers, and the external kingdom, in which the secular governmental authority creates law and implements it with coercion. The one is Christ's kingdom, the other is the kingdom of the world. The Christian citizen lives in both kingdoms; as a Christian he lives in the kingdom of the order of grace, as a citizen he lives in the kingdom of the order of law. This juxtaposition of the two kingdoms did not yet present a problem, because one lived ⟨supposedly⟩ in a 'Christian' world and its order of law ⟨supposedly⟩ agreed with the order of grace.

c. The *third and most recent post-Reformation form of the two kingdoms doctrine* does not deal with the connection between the doctrine and its sociopolitical setting. That form is called doctrine of the governances (Törnvall).[41] It takes from Luther's theology of society the correct idea that God rules mankind in two ways: its spiritual existence through the Word, its external existence through the coercive command of the secular governmental authority. Those who affirm this doctrine of the governances are unable, however, to explain why God created such a twofold governance because they do not base the doctrine on the difference between the 'two peoples' of mankind. Therefore they are also unable to answer Karl Barth's question whether there is a connection between justification by faith alone and man-made law.[42] And finally, in terms of the systematics of law they are unable to make full use of Luther's statements about the connection of the spiritual with the corporeal church because they turn man-made ecclesiastical law over to the secular sword. These defects can be avoided only if the basic meaning of the kingdom doctrine and the doctrine of the governances are considered as one unit.

APPENDIX VI

Announcement of Initia Iuris Ecclesiastici Protestantium

―――✽―――

Zeitschrift der Savigny-Stiftung für Rechtsgeschichte.
Kanonistische Abteilung, 37 (1951): 474-479
Announcement by Johannes Heckel of
Initia iuris ecclesiastici Protestantium
Sitzungsberichte der Bayerischen Akademie der Wissenschaften
Philosophisch-historische Klasse, 1949. Heft 5 (Munich: Verlag der
Bayerischen Akademie der Wissenschaften, 1950)[1]

In continuation of my article "Recht und Gesetz, Kirche und Obrigkeit in Luthers Lehre vor dem Thesenanschlag von 1517. Eine juristische Untersuchung,"[2] I turn in the present study to the theses[3] themselves and examine them for their basic thoughts on ecclesiastical law. Until now such an examination of this document of world historic significance has never been undertaken. Notwithstanding that the theses were an epoch-creating document in the history of the church, no one granted them any special significance for the history of Protestant ecclesiastical law. They were considered to be the first public expression of some sort of alienation from the prevailing church doctrine and government. No one, however, asked whether they were not already based on a new concept 'ecclesiastical law'. Apparently there are two reasons for this omission. It is difficult for jurists to free themselves from a secularized concept 'law' and penetrate to the concept 'divine law', which was decisive for Luther — not to mention that Luther has the reputation of not being attuned to matters of jurisprudence so that his writings are not very inviting for a juristic examination. On the other hand, when historians of the Reformation look at Luther, they see the fighter against Canon law, even more, against the justice of the jurists *(iuristarum iustitia)*. This raises the question: May one expect that Luther, the man of protest, had a positive doctrine of law, which would have been important for the beginnings of the Reformation?

The late medieval churchly environment, in which Luther lived, was saturated with concepts of law. One who lived in a church in which faith and law thoroughly penetrated each other certainly was not at all able to engage in theology without constantly taking a positive or negative position on law. Without a new concept 'law' Luther would not have been able to give value to his new concept 'church', and without a new concept 'church' his <new> concept 'law' could not have been maintained. In his theology, the concepts 'law' and 'church' had to be as inseparable as they had been in the theology of the medieval church.

Luther did not reach his new concept 'ecclesiastical law' at once — he had to take *three steps* before he arrived at it.

I

Luther took the *first step* in his first lectures on the Psalms (1513-15).[4] These lectures grant us a glance at his work on the concept 'church', which was very closely connected with his work on the doctrine of justification. His work on the concept 'church' and on his doctrine of justification grew out of his struggle with the sacrament of Penance. Theologically seen, the work on the concept 'church' and on justification belong together because one cannot speak of the righteous *(iusti)* without also thinking of the "company of the upright <in the congregation>." (Psalm 111:1.) Only God knows this association <or congregation> of true believers, natural man[5] does not. Therefore Luther called it the hidden church *(ecclesia abscondita)* in contrast to the organized church *(ecclesia manifesta)*. *This theological distinction between two forms of the church became fundamental for the Reformation,* but it did not contribute anything new to the ecclesiology of Luther's days. Here, in addition to the universal church *(ecclesia universalis)*, that is, the church as a legal community of those who through Baptism were authorized to receive the sacraments, we also find the hidden church *(ecclesia*

Appendix VI

occulta), the community of those who have perfect faith and love; these are the people whose faith has been 'formed' by love *(fides charitate formata)*, and who are known to God only. In the light of Luther's connection with Scholasticism, with which in matters of ecclesiology he became familiar through the doctrine of Penance in the writings of Gabriel Biel, one asks: Was the doctrine of justification developed by the monk Luther[6] already that of the Reformation while his ecclesiology was still that of the Middle Ages, that is, of the Roman Catholic church? To this day this question has never even been asked. Yet it urgently demands an answer since the available scholarship on the origin of Luther's concept 'church'[7] to a large degree is based on shaky, even wrong materials. Now I can make a suggestion only (I am working[8] on a special study): in ecclesiology, the difference between Luther and Scholasticism, that is, his breakthrough to the ecclesiology of the Reformation, is, to be brief, the fact that he made the hidden church the center of ecclesiology, while for the Scholastics the universal church was that center.

What were the consequences of this shift for the church in its two forms, mentioned above? As a result of the close connection of faith and law in the medieval ecclesiastical system this question is not only a theological problem but also a problem in law. In the following I shall deal only with the latter problem.

In the first lectures on the Psalms we find a *first* hint of Luther's view, nothing more. In the midst of much material taken from the canonists, we read: "Before God . . . the entire structure . . . of Christ's church is internal, invisible."[9] If one reads this sentence in the light of Canon law, then it is a monstrosity. Where did this sentence leave the rationale, ⟨supposedly⟩ established in faith ⟨and thus in divine law⟩, for the external jurisdiction of the church *(iurisdictio externa ecclesiae)*? How did Luther understand divine law?

II

In his lectures on Romans (1515-16)[10] Luther prepared the ground for the answers to these questions when he interpreted the divine natural law. This was the *second step* on the way to a new ecclesiastical law. In the context of the theology of justification Luther taught that the *divine natural law* is coordinated with man's spiritual existence, man-made law with man's natural existence. A life is spiritual when it is without any human self-will and totally immersed in God's will so that it concentrates on nothing other but God and clings only to his will.

Unlike man-made law, divine natural law is not addressed to the external but the internal man. For God does not demand a specific external conduct but rather something more, in fact, something which natural man is totally unable to accomplish, that is, a God-formed will. God's law, that is, God's will *(Dei voluntas lex)*,[11] can be fulfilled only by such a God-formed will. According to author, addressee, and subject, the divine natural law is spiritual law *(lex spiritualis)*; it is law totally turned to the internal. The implications of this radical spiritualization cannot be overestimated; for Luther's doctrine of law it had the same significance that justification by faith had for his theology.

III

Luther had progressed to this point when the indulgence traffic brought him into the public arena. This was the *third and last step* on his way to an evangelical ecclesiastical law. The selling of indulgences raised several questions, among which was also one concerning the constitutional law ‹of the church›. It dealt with the authority of the church and reads as follows: May the pope remit penitential works, which are spiritually effective for the life to come,[12] by declaring that the God-imposed temporal punishments for sins are cancelled when specific works are done? Without any hesitation the canonists answered affirmatively and added: "The pope has this authority from God." Not so Luther! For him, the divine law[13] was spiritual law. Therefore a more contradictory legal principle than the assignment of spiritual authority[14] to an external man (that is, the pope) for establishing a constitutive order of the life of an internal man[15] could not be imagined.

When Luther protested, he found himself forced to expand his concept 'law', which had emerged from the personalistic quality of his doctrine of justification, into the realm of the ‹ecclesiastical› organization and institution. Now to the *divine natural law (lex divina),* which is *addressed to the individual believer's spiritual life* in his relationship with God and neighbor, is added the *divine positive law (ius divinum),* which orders *the spiritual communal life of Christ's disciples.* (It is probably no

Appendix VI

accident that in Luther's writings the phrase *ius divinum* now[16] appeared for the first time.) *Christ's disciples live in the hidden church; therefore ius divinum is the law of the hidden church.* This purely spiritual concept *ius divinum* nullified that same concept in Canon law; here *ius divinum* was connected with the internal *and* the external existence of the church.[17] And with the fall of this Canon law concept, the Roman Catholic concept 'church' fell.

The Canon law concept *ius divinum* and the Roman Catholic concept 'church' can exist only together, and they also fall together. Conversely, through the perception of the evangelical concept 'divine positive law' the development of Luther's concept 'church' was for the first time concluded, and this in a final way. Now church and law were also most closely connected.[18] In short: *Protestant ecclesiastical law was born.* The posting of the theses on October 31, 1517, marks the beginning of the Reformation not only in the history of the church but also in the law of the church. This had far-reaching consequences, of which we shall mention only two:

The divine positive law deals exclusively with the hidden church. Therefore the universal church becomes a community of man-made law. The entire organization of the church, including the primacy of the pope, is assigned to this man-made law.

The traditional concept 'ecclesiastical authority'[19] can no longer be affirmed. Until now it united both the spiritual authority of binding and of absolving sinners *and* the authority to rule the church externally. This was for Luther a monstrous mishmash of the divine and the human in the 'chaos of one word'.[20] Therefore he clearly separated the authority of binding and absolving, an institution which belongs to the divine positive law of the hidden <or spiritual> church, from the authority of externally governing the church as a part of the man-made law of the universal church. This was one of the most far-reaching separations of authorities which ever occurred in the history of the Christian world.

IV

When one compares these results with the traditional view of the emergence of Luther's concept 'church', then many details are identical. As a whole, the picture has to be redrawn, however. The chronology is significantly changed, and only now do Luther's central <ecclesiological

Announcement of Initia Iuris Ecclesiastici Protestantium

themes> reach a position of prominence. Therefore in the historiography of church history there are differences between our results and the traditional accounts. The differences are, however, even greater between our results and the traditional theories of ecclesiastical law.

As demonstrated above,[21] Luther knew a divine and a man-made order of the church *(Kirchenordnung).*[22] According to the divine order, the church is restricted to service; it is called to pronounce the divine judgment over man only through the office of the Keys,[23] but it may not undertake any law-creating acts. On the other hand, according to the man-made order, the church creates and controls law, tasks which the ecclesiastical officers perform in cooperation with the members of the church.

Within this layout, ecclesiastical law is created in two ways. The first way leads to the *heteronomous ecclesiastical law.*[24] It is a series of external legal acts in connection with the God-willed use of the Power of the Keys directed at internal man; an example would be the legitimate excommunication. The second way leads to the *autonomous ecclesiastical law.*[25] It is a series of legal acts — based on the consensus of the brothers *(consensus fratrum)* — for the implementation of Christian brotherly love. Therefore Luther wrote in his *First Commentary on Galatians* (1519) in classical brevity: "The churchly commonwealth is organized by only *one* law, that of love."[26]

Since man-made ecclesiastical law is an act of love, it has to be created and used in total freedom. Under no circumstances may it degenerate into a <coercive> law, as we find it in Canon law. Therefore its basis in Scripture is not Romans 13:1 but Romans, chapter 12. Nevertheless, it is genuine law because the divine primeval form of law is an order of love.

The purpose of man-made ecclesiastical law is the strengthening of internal man's growing faith through external means and actions. Only this need of the brother *(necessitas fratris)* substantiates the binding quality of the autonomous ecclesiastical law, not the concern for its supposed holiness.

The man-made ecclesiastical law is created by reason according to expediency. Therefore this law belongs to the kingdom of reason and not faith. It has no spiritual or quasi-spiritual quality, but it has a secular one — not because the secular sword is competent for it, but because it originates in the church in the world.

God's people, that is, the members of the hidden church, are enti-

Appendix VI

tled to create this law. But all human ability to organize is not able to record them in ⟨rosters⟩, not to mention guaranteeing them the leading position in the church. Therefore a makeshift procedure is necessary, a sort of leap from the spiritual into the universal church, and that is Baptism. It incorporates man in the spiritual church, and through this one act man is also received into the universal church. As long as he has not been excommunicated, he is in principle entitled to participate in the creation of law in the church. This is not more than a makeshift, and a dangerous one on top of it. Hypocritical Christians can gain control of the church and create ecclesiastical law which is not in line with its spiritual purpose. Then true Christians will have to resist such a law, but in any case such a law will severely shake the church. Through such shocks ecclesiastical law points beyond itself to God, the only guardian of his church.

V

In the theses and their *Explanations*[27] Luther applied the principles which we have presented to the sacrament of Penance and to excommunication. In this process he almost completely transformed the penitential law of Canon law. He made the deepest cuts in the doctrine of the sacrament of Penance. The concept 'forum internum ecclesiae'[28] is eliminated, and the position of the priest is changed in such a way that he no longer is the minister of the sacrament *(minister sacramenti)*.[29] Regarding excommunication Luther seems to have been more conservative. He accepted a jurisdiction of the church granted in divine positive law. But his differentiation between the divine positive law of the hidden church and the man-made order of the universal church created new legal thoughts, which were no longer in line with Canon law.

APPENDIX VII

Announcement of Lex Charitatis *and of "Widerstand gegen die Obrigkeit?"*

Zeitschrift der Savigny-Stiftung für Rechtsgeschichte.
Kanonistische Abteilung, 40 (1954): 313-321
Announcement by Johannes Heckel of
Lex Charitatis. Eine juristische Untersuchung über das Recht in der Theologie Martin Luthers. Abhandlungen der Bayerischen Akademie der Wissenschaften Philosophisch-historische Klasse, Neue Folge, 36 (Munich: Verlag der Bayerischen Akademie der Wissenschaften, 1953)
and of
"Widerstand gegen die Obrigkeit? Pflicht und Recht zum Widerstand bei Martin Luther." *Zeitwende. Die neue Furche* 25 (1954): 156-168[1]

Lex Charitatis originated in studies[2] of the theological and juristic foundations of Martin Luther's concept 'church' at the time he posted the theses on October 31, 1517. In the process of these studies it became necessary to investigate Luther's idea of law anew. For more than a hundred years this topic has been dealt with, but not much progress has been made. The situation in scholarship is marked by the difficulties which Luther's interpreters have with divine law. When it is the divine positive law *(ius divinum positivum),* one bluntly denied that it had the quality of law (Rudolph Sohm, Wilhelm Kahl). When Luther mentioned

Appendix VII

natural law *(ius naturale),* either the same happened (Karl Holl), or natural law in Luther's thought was considered to be a remnant of medieval ideas (Ernst Troeltsch), or Luther's statements were considered juristically useless because ⟨supposedly⟩ they were not clear.

I

All these interpretations are a failure. They do not connect Luther's theology with his doctrine of law. They are unable to show the connection between justification by faith and man-made law, as Karl Barth pointed out, nor are they at all able to clarify that concept 'law' which is innate to justification by faith. But without this concept the key to understanding the reformer's doctrine of law is missing.

These interpretations failed because the theological-juristic starting point for Luther's pertinent statements was not clear. Indeed, it is not easy to find that point ⟨for two reasons:⟩ Luther's famous or infamous non-juristic and unsystematic way of thinking and working; more important, the difficulty to get to the bottom of the interplay of traditional concepts and their new meanings ⟨which we find in Luther's system⟩. The systems of the patristic Fathers and of the Scholastics, for instance, provided the formal frame for Luther's doctrine of law. But one may never assume that the well-known technical terms still have their traditional meaning! Ideas and concepts which are deeply rooted in history play a powerful role in the history of ideas. If one is aware of this, then one will be amazed to see how little Luther was influenced by such a role, and how with absolute mastery of the materials he used the ideas and concepts of earlier thinkers without first establishing new definitions for them. Let us look, for instance, at the outline of his juristic materials! He used the traditional division of law in divine law and man-made law, subdividing the former in divine natural and divine positive law. With correct logic, and as his predecessors had done and his contemporaries were doing, he selected *natural law as the basis of his presentation.* But he did this from a totally different ⟨starting⟩ point.

II

Medieval theologians started with natural man, that is, man who pos-

Announcement of Lex Charitatis

sessed natural reason. In spite of the Fall, they granted synteresis to that man, that is, a spark of insight in the divine will for law and a faint inclination toward that will. For Luther this was a fundamental error. According to his understanding of Holy Scripture, Original Sin caused natural man to be totally perverted spiritually, that is, in his relationship with God, and, therefore, suffering from blindness. Natural man receives nothing of God's spirit (1 Corinthians 2:14); God remains incomprehensible and beyond penetration. Therefore there is no way for man to recognize divine righteousness, that is, divine law; the light of nature *(lumen naturae)* does not enable man to have this recognition.

III

God, however, has opened an access to himself — faith in Christ's action of Redemption. *Man justified by faith* — and only he! — again knows the divine will for law through the light of faith *(lumen fidei)*. The justified — and only he! — listens to the voice of Christ, the authentic interpreter of the divine natural law. Therefore the law of Christ *(lex Christi)* is the center of Luther's doctrine of law. Law of Christ, law of love, law of faith *(lex Christi, lex charitatis, lex fidei)* are synonyms for the divine natural law when it is seen from different viewpoints. The *first basic characteristic of Luther's doctrine of natural law,* even of his whole doctrine of law, is, then, the fact that it is Christian in the exact sense of the word, that is, *Christ-centered.*

The *second characteristic* is the *voluntaristic spiritualism which is strictly bound to Scripture.* God's commandment is sovereign, law-creating will, and it is spirit; therefore it demands of man to be and to act in the spirit and in truth ⟨John 4:24⟩; that is, it demands a God-formed will, not an external conduct as man-made law does. "God looks at the heart" (1 Samuel 16:7). People who have such a God-formed will exist only in the communion of saints *(communio sanctorum)*. Therefore Luther's thinking about law exists in the legal realm of the spiritual church. His *doctrine of law is churchly* in the sense of the spiritual church *(ecclesia spiritualis)*. This is the *third characteristic* of Luther's doctrine of law.

The *fourth characteristic,* the most surprising one, is connected with Luther's *doctrine of the two kingdoms.* Next to Christ's spiritual kingdom, the communion of believers, exists the corporeal kingdom of

Appendix VII

this world, the totality of non-Christians. Their hatred for God makes them allies of the devil and subject to him. Nevertheless, their kingdom cannot withdraw from God's omnipotence; the divine will for law maintains its sovereignty over this kingdom in spite of Satan's resistance. But in this kingdom God's law *(lex divina)* is active as a curse over sin; it is law of wrath *(lex irae)*, and it gives to all law in the kingdom of the world the quality of severity, oppression, ⟨and coercion⟩. Only indirectly is the Creator's hidden love *(charitas latens)* nevertheless revealed through this law of wrath because only through coercion can order be maintained among sinful mankind. In both respects, the kingdom of the world is called the kingdom of God at the left. Christ's kingdom is the kingdom of God at the right.

The miserable situation which exists in the kingdom of the world is most obvious in its relationship with the divine natural law. Non-Christians are no longer capable of recognizing the divine meaning of this law, even though it is created into them. They interpret it in such a way that its goal is no longer eternal Salvation but earthly well-being. They change the spiritual love *(charitas spiritualis)* into corporeal love *(charitas corporalis)*, the universal love for man. In this way the non-spiritual thinking of natural man creates the idea of a humanitarian *secular natural law.* Its shortest expression is the Golden Rule, and in the Decalogue of Moses its legal substance has been set forth to this day in an exemplary way. Judged by the divine natural law, this secular natural law is, however, only a shadow *(umbra)* of divine righteousness, and, therefore, spiritually seen it is 'beggary'. But since it creates order in the kingdom of the world, it is also an indispensable precious jewel left by God's mercy to fallen mankind. This juxtaposition of ⟨divine⟩ spiritual natural law and secular natural law corresponds to the schism in mankind between God's friends and God's enemies. As a mark of Luther's legal doctrine this schism creates the *dualistic quality of natural law,* though the core of this schism points us back to the one will of God for law.

Let us add a *fifth characteristic,* which especially for jurists is troublesome. In his doctrine of law Luther did not think in terms of legal norms, but he thought in personalistic terms. God's commandment is the Creator's personal address of man; it is not a legal maxim which could be personalized as an autocratically binding norm. Only as the personalistic Creator-word does that commandment have the quality of living law *(lex viva)*, that is, of creating spiritual life in man. The two

Announcement of Lex Charitatis

kingdoms have the same personalistic quality — they are not institutions but families of man. Luther's statements about the legal life in these two kingdoms are also personalistic in a twofold sense. 'Spiritual' and 'secular' designate, first, the place of a legal institution in one or the other kingdom, and second, the use of such an institution by a believer or unbeliever. Marriage, for instance, as an institution of the kingdom of the world is something secular; yet for believing Christians marriage is also a spiritual estate because they conduct their married life in believing obedience to the <spiritual> law of love. The situation is identical when one considers governmental authority; it is something secular and <at the same time it also can be> Christian, etc.

This concludes the survey of the typical features of Luther's doctrine of natural law. They will come up again in connection with the divine positive law of Christ's kingdom, and they also influenced Luther's interpretation of man-made law.

IV

The following picture of man's legal existence emerges. Mankind is not a uniform community guided by natural law, as one assumed in the Middle Ages. Rather, Christians and non-Christians live according to their respective spiritual personal statute.

For the Christian this statute is the divine natural law. For purposes of organization the three spiritual basic rights, Christian brotherly love, equality, and freedom, are derived from it. These basic rights regulate the law which Christians create for organizing their communal life. The communal worship of God is governed by the divine positive law of the New Testament; it contains the establishment of the church on earth, its endowment with Word and sacrament, and the institution of the ministry of the Word *(ministerium verbi)*.

In contrast to this internal, spiritual kingdom of God-formed love, non-Christians live under an external, non-spiritual, coercive governance. It is based on the secular natural law. In terms of organization, it is maintained by the domestic governance, and especially by the secular governmental authority, which is derived from the domestic governance, and both emerged from marriage. In the Original Status marriage was founded by God as a spiritual-corporeal community of love between persons of equal rank in law but of different sex. After the Fall

Appendix VII

it lost this spiritual nature and became the authoritarian community of family law.

Christians have nothing in common with such a secular, coercive law. They are not subject to it, they are pulled out from under it (exempt) because Christ gave them freedom. Nevertheless, they are responsible for maintaining the order created by the secular natural law for the kingdom of the world because God established this secular natural law in this kingdom of the world as the foundation and limitation of human legal authority. Therefore, as God's co-workers, and because of Christian love for the neighbor (that is, in the process of implementing the divine natural law), Christians have to do all that is in their power that that secular natural law is obeyed.

V

This layout of law, structured according to two kingdoms, has to be kept in mind when one considers the different areas of law *(Rechtskreise)* in which a Christian exists on earth. There are three such areas: The order of the church on earth as a community governed by man-made law *(Kirchenwesen)*, the order of marriage, and the order of the secular commonwealth *(politia)*.

Let us first deal with the *church*. To our surprise, the value of Rudolph Sohm's much-attacked critique of previous doctrines concerning the essence of ecclesiastical law is confirmed! In those doctrines, man-made ecclesiastical law *(ius humanum ecclesiasticum)* is not derived from its connection with the spiritual church but from its task of creating and maintaining order in the external structure of the church. Therefore the same legal quality is assigned to man-made ecclesiastical law as is assigned to any other man-made law. Whether man-made ecclesiastical law is autonomously created in a churchly association or prescribed by the state is irrelevant for its binding force; in both cases it is just as binding as are the norms regulating the civic community. If one considers the quality of law, then the church on earth participates in the legal concept of the kingdom of the world, or in other words, the church is an institution of the kingdom of the world. This results in an absurd conclusion: the spiritual church belongs to God's kingdom at the right, the external <organized> church belongs to God's kingdom at the left; the divine will for law is present as law of love in the kingdom at the right ⟨and, therefore, in the spiritual church⟩, as law of wrath in the kingdom at the left ⟨and, therefore, in the organized church⟩! It is Sohm's permanently valid contribution to scholarship to have pointed out that such a position is untenable. Yet his own thesis — ecclesiastical law contradicts the essence of the church — was also a failure; he neither acknowledged that the universal church is 'church', nor was he at all aware of the divine natural law. Therefore man-made ecclesiastical law had for him neither an area to be ordered nor a basis of legitimacy.

This is the true situation. In the organized church the commandment of the divine natural law to love the brother *(charitas fraterna)* necessarily results in the creation of man-made ecclesiastical law, and it determines the quality of that law ⟨for the following reason:⟩ every legal act ⟨in the organized church⟩ has to be an act of spiritual love *(actus charitatis spiritualis)*, which is governed by the three basic rights existing in Christ's kingdom. The sum of norms has no spiritual quality; only the spiritual use of the law *(spiritualis usus iuris)* by true Christians, the true representatives of law *(Rechtsträger)* in the organized church, has such a quality. Only that use makes man-made ecclesiastical law binding, not on the basis of its own authority as an autocratically binding will, but only on the basis of the spiritually mandated care for fellow Christians. Strictly speaking, ecclesiastical law deserves its name only when it actively implements Christ's law for fellow Christians. If one uses one of Luther's phrases, one may say that ecclesiastical law is 'doing' law. Outside of this spiritual use, ecclesiastical law deserves no place in the system of law, neither in the *politia* (for it does not have to serve the tasks of the *politia*), nor in the church (for in the church is no law outside of Christ, that is, outside of that spiritual use of the law). The difference between this understanding of ecclesiastical law and that of Canon law, and also of secular law, is obvious.

VI

The contrast between Luther's position and that of medieval law thoroughly influenced his position on *marriage,* the second area of law in which a Christian exists. As mentioned, for Luther marriage was something secular; it was an institution grounded in the order of the kingdom of the world and, therefore, subordinated to the legal authority of

Appendix VII

the secular governmental authority. The marriage of Christians was no exception. This, however, does not cover all the problems of marriage law. Depending on the spiritual or carnal use of marriage *(usus spiritualis, usus carnalis matrimonii)*, the reformer differentiated between a Christian marriage (a marriage of believers) and a marriage of non-Christians. He called the former a spiritual estate; that is, he viewed such a marriage in a personalistic connection with Christ's kingdom. He assigned the latter to the kingdom of Satan; it is a heathen marriage without any connection with the church, even when the married non-Christians are baptized. These ideas are partially reminiscent of the canonistic distinction between *matrimonium (ratum) inter fideles* and *matrimonium (legitimum) inter infideles*.[3] But in Canon law the quality *fidelis* was connected with membership in the ‹external› community of the baptized, for Luther it was connected with the ‹spiritual› community of believers.

Luther's differentiation between a Christian and a heathen marriage of baptized persons is still significant today, not only for Protestant ecclesiastical law but especially for Roman Catholic marriage courts. A civil wedding of Protestants cannot have a sacramental meaning, as it is determined in Canon law, because the persons to be married do not consciously assign a spiritual meaning to the ceremony, that is, they do not intend to create a relationship with Christ and his church[4] through the ceremony. Hence the rejection of the Protestant church wedding. Protestants are not subject to the authority of Canon law regarding the form of a wedding ceremony. Therefore they could have a wedding ceremony with sacramental quality, even though the proper form ‹established in Canon law› would be missing. Yet the sacramental quality would not exist because of the lack of any spiritual intention on the part of the persons to be married. Therefore such a marriage is not valid in terms of Canon law.

VII

If one applies the criteria of the doctrine of the kingdoms to marriage, then the legal situation of a Christian in the estate of marriage has to be evaluated differently than has been done. This is true also for a Christian's position in the *politia*, the third area of law in which a Christian exists on earth. On the basis of misunderstood statements by Luther,

Announcement of Lex Charitatis

one has become accustomed to calling a Christian a citizen of two kingdoms, the kingdom of God at the right and the kingdom of God at the left. This makes it impossible to understand the reformer's position. The dependence of both kingdoms on God's sovereignty may not obscure the irreconcilable difference which exists between both kingdoms. A Christian has no citizenship in the kingdom of the world, he will always be a foreigner. As mentioned above, he is pulled out from under the law of this kingdom, yet because of his love for the neighbor he is still responsible for it. This situation results in two questions. First, where is the limit of a Christian's duty to intervene? Second, may a Christian assume the office of governmental authority[5] and participate in caring for the secular order without getting into a conflict with his faith? The first question leads to the problem of the resistance to a non-Christian governmental authority, the second to the problems connected with a 'Christian' governmental authority. Both questions have to be answered spiritually, that is, from the viewpoint of Christ's kingdom. In doing so, Luther developed a doctrine of the tyrant (which at many points differed from the medieval doctrine) and a *Fürstenspiegel*;[6] in it, the *cura religionis*[7] as a specifically Christian duty of a ruler has the first place.

VIII

The reformer's theological doctrine of law did not have a positive future. Melanchthon accepted Luther's doctrine, but at the turn of the sixteenth to the seventeenth century jurists and theologians replaced it with a philosophical idea of law, and this is the situation down to our days. Luther scholars, therefore, found themselves in a dilemma of sorts — they have to project their modern concept 'law' into Luther's concept. This explains, to mention one example which has been discussed frequently, why to this day the controversy about Luther's position regarding the so-called Christian body *(corpus christianum)*, as we find it especially in his *To the Christian Nobility*, has not ended.

IX

The same lack of clarity burdens a burning problem of our days, that is,

Appendix VII

the duty and the right of a Christian to resist governmental authority. This is the subject of the second title listed above, a lecture at the Bayerische Akademie der Wissenschaften. The lecture summarizes relevant passages in *Lex charitatis,* compares them with the medieval doctrine of the tyrant, and places them into the context of the doctrine of the two kingdoms. Luther knew three types of tyrants: In Christ's kingdom on earth, that is, in the church, the *spiritual tyrant* strives for lordship *(dominatio)* over souls. This is the most dangerous kind of tyranny because, claiming the authority of the ecclesiastical office, the tyrant establishes a governance which is prohibited in the church and which violates the spiritual basic right of Christian freedom. The second type is the *political tyrant* in secular lordships; breaking the secular natural law, he strives to enforce a corporeal despotism. More terrible than those two types is the third, the *world tyrant* who from time to time appears in history. The first two types of tyrant appear only in their respective kingdoms. The world tyrant places himself above both kingdoms in order to enslave mankind corporeally and spiritually. Each of the three types demands its own kind of ‹reaction› so that a Christian's resistance is also different. It ranges from the separation from the spiritual tyrant, to public disobedience, and even to an individual's ‹action› with force against the secular tyrant. In the fight against the world tyrant, resistance rises to revolution for God's sake. These different kinds of resistance faithfully reflect Luther's doctrine of law.

Notes

Notes to the Preface

1. ⟨*Rechtstheologische Positionen.*⟩
2. ⟨See below, 458 n. 10 (4).⟩

Notes to Martin Heckel's Preface to the Second German Edition

1. ⟨See Appendix VI.⟩

Notes to the Introduction

1. For abbreviations, see above, xxiii. — For Heckel, see *NDB* 8, s.v. "Heckel, Johannes." — Having finished his studies of law, Heckel served in the consistories of the evangelical church, first in Munich and then in Berlin. In 1931, when he was teaching at the University of Bonn, he played a decisive role in the treaty negotiations between the state of Prussia and the evangelical churches of its territory, and in the thirties and forties he dealt with some of the legal problems which confronted the evangelical churches in Germany.

2. For the bibliography, see *Johannes Heckel Festschrift,* 351ff.

3. See, e.g., above, Appendix III. See also Heinrich Scholler, "Martin Luther on Jurisprudence — Freedom, Conscience, Law," *Valparaiso University Law Review* 15 (1981): 265ff.; Siegfried Grundmann, "Das evangelische Kirchenrecht von Rudolph Sohm bis zur Gegegenwart," *ÖAKR* 16 (1965): 276ff., and id., "Verfassungsrecht in der Kirche des Evangeliums," *ZEvKR* 11 (1964/65): 9ff.; Karl Schwarz, "Anmerkungen und Aperçu zu innerprotestantischen Kontroversen hinsichtlich Begründung und Entfaltung eines evangelischen Kirchenrechts," *ZEvKR* 28 (1983): 172ff. — Martin Heckel was kind to send

some titles which reflect the scholarly echo to the book: Christoph Link, "Luther und das deutsche Staatsverständnis," *Juristenzeitung* 38 (1983): 869ff., and id., "Rechtstheologische Grundlagen des evangelischen Kirchenrechts," *ZEvKR* 45 (2000): 73ff.; Klaus Schlaich, "Kirchenrecht und Kirche. Grundfragen einer Verhältnisbestimmung heute," *ZEvKR* 28 (1983): 337ff.; the obituaries of Johannes Heckel in *ZSRG*.K 50 (1964): xvff., *ZEvKR* 11 (1964/65): 1ff., *JBAW* 1964:173ff., and *AÖR* 89 (1954): 113ff. — In some significant publications, Martin Heckel picked up Johannes Heckel's positions and expanded them: "Summum ius — Summa Iniuria," and "Rechtstheologie Luthers," in Martin Heckel, *Gesammelte Schriften. Staat, Kirche, Recht, Geschichte,* 1 (Tübingen, 1989): 83ff., 324ff.; id., "Luther und das Recht. Zur Rechtstheologie Martin Luthers und ihren Auswirkungen auf Kirche und Reich," *Neue Juristische Wochenschrift* 45 (1983): 2521ff.

4. See, e.g., Friedrich Lohmann, "Ein Gott — zwei Regimente. Überlegungen zur Zwei-Reiche-Lehre Martin Luthers im Anschluss an die Debatte zwischen Paul Althaus und Johannes Heckel," *Luther* 74 (2003): 112ff. <See also above, Appendix III.>

5. Franz Lau, "Leges charitatis. Drei Fragen an Johannes Heckel," *KuD* 2 (1956): 76.

6. For an orientation to the book, see above, Appendix VII.

7. See, e.g., the ongoing discussion on the understanding of ministry and of the call, or of supervision in the church, or of Ordination and Apostolic Succession.

8. We were conscious of this as we shaped the text and notes, and also as we organized the Index of Subjects. We presented the entries pertaining to law and related subjects separately as a sort of law index. Were it not for nontheological subjects, the remaining entries would be a sort of theology index.

9. E.g., *naturrechtlich* (natural-law), *rechtstheologisch* (juristic-theological), *staatsrechtlich* (public-law), *verfahrensrechtlich* (procedural-law). Most of the time we were able to paraphrase such composites.

10. For *Gesetz, Recht/lex, ius* and their derivatives, and for 'inconsistency', see, e.g., below, 247 n. 53, 285 n. 46, Index of Subjects: *Law,* s.v. "law, terminology of." For Canon law terminology, see *Dictionary of Ecclesiastical Latin,* ed. by Leo F. Stelten (Peabody, MA, 1995).

11. E.g., *Gerechtigkeit Gottes/iustitia dei;* see below, 236 n. 1.

12. E.g.: *Amt/officium/office* can designate an office as such; it can also designate — and does so for the most part — task, authority, duty, responsibility connected with, or derived from, an office. *Beruf/vocatio/vocation/call* can designate occupation, job, task, call into an occupation (appointment), inner calling to a specific occupation. *Gewalt/Macht/potestas/potentia* can designate the power through which something happens, or should or can happen; in most cases it designates the authority and responsibility to make something happen. (*Der Eltern Gewalt,* e.g., can designate the authority and responsibility parents have, or the force with which parents do something, e.g., prevent a daughter from marrying someone whom they do not approve.) Both meanings (power, authority) can be united, as, e.g., in *potestas clavium/Schlüsselgewalt/Power of the Keys.* The term designates the church's authority to use the Keys (granted by Christ) *and* the power innate to the word of absolving and binding. *Ordnen/to order* can designate commanding or setting up something (instituting, establishing). *Orden/Ordnung/ordo/order* can designate the command with which something is set up, or the document in which something is set up; it can also designate any situation of order, or an institution, or a way of living (e.g., monastic order). By Luther's times, *Oberkeit/Obrigkeit* encompassed

everything that was connected with government, from institutions to personnel. Sometimes the word was used with a technical meaning (day-by-day governing, bureaucracy), but more often it was used with a principle meaning, designating the *authority,* duty, and responsibility for, or involved in, governing. Therefore we use "governmental authority" and not "governing authority." (In *LW* 45 the title of Luther's famous book of 1523, *Von weltlicher Oberkeit, wie weit man ihr Gehorsam schuldig sei,* reads: "Temporal Authority: To what Extent It Should be Obeyed." The issue of the book, however, is not temporal vs. eternal, but spiritual vs. secular; therefore we use 'secular', and we try to do justice to Luther's "von"; hence *On Secular Authority.*) Luther sometimes spoke of the office or institution when he dealt with the incumbent, or he spoke of the incumbent when he dealt with the office or institution.

13. See, e.g., below, 236 n. 1.

14. E.g., free translations, additions to the author's text or to that of his citations, explanations, additional cross-references.

15. For the somewhat unorthodox Index of Subjects, see above, 234 n. 8. Also, in what is now the bibliography and in the Index of Subjects we sometimes used the adjective for alphabetizing; we did this esp. in the *Law* section (e.g., "natural law," not "law, natural") in order to avoid the overwhelming number of necessary subentries for "law".

16. For below, 482 n. 151, we did not translate a long citation from *Panormitani Proemium.*

17. WA, WA.B (Briefwechsel), WA.DB (Deutsche Bibel), WA.TR (Tischreden). WA 6:251.5, 258.5.9.11 = volume 6: page 251.line 5, and page 258.lines 5.9.11; WA 10.I.2:251.5 = volume 10.part(volume) I.section(volume) 2: page 251.line 5. In WA 57 the three Roman numerals designate parts within this volume, each part beginning with a new pagination.

18. 3d ed. rev. and expanded, Witten, 1970.

19. With the help of these numbers and *Vogel's Cross Reference and Index to the Contents of Luther's Works,* ed. by Heinrich Vogel (Milwaukee, 1983), one will be able to locate Luther's writings in different editions.

Notes to "Which Concept 'Law' Did Martin Luther Affirm?"

1. In 1951 Heinz H. Schrey presented to the study commission of the Ecumenical Council of Churches a summarizing report on the most recent German and foreign literature on our subject, entitled "Gerechtigkeit in biblischer Sicht." The aftermath of WW II made it difficult for me to consult foreign literature extensively. For kind help in this matter I am indebted to Professor Kjöllerström in Lund.

2. So according to Siegfried Lommatzsch, *Luthers Lehre vom ethisch-religiösen Standpunkt aus und mit besonderer Berücksichtigung seiner Theorie vom Gesetz dargestellt* (Berlin, 1879), 71, in connection with the evaluation of "the greatest difficulties in which Luther found himself in the struggle for law."

3. *Das Problem des geistigen Seins* (2d ed. Berlin, 1949), 2.

Notes to Chapter 1

1. ⟨For Luther the phrase *iustitia dei* (literally: "justice of God") had a specific content which he had shaped during the early years of his academic career, and for which the English equivalent is 'righteousness of God'. (For that content, see the excellent materials presented in Gordon Rupp, *The Righteousness of God. Luther Studies* [London, 1953], 81ff.) When *Gerechtigkeit/iustitia* has a social or juridical content, we use 'justice'; sometimes the difference in content may not be as precise as one wishes; see also, e.g. below, 327 n. 219, 396 n. 72.⟩

2. Instead of other authors, see Erik Wolf, *Große Rechtsdenker der deutschen Geistesgeschichte* (3d ed. Tübingen, 1951), 377ff.

3. Rudolph Sohm, *Kirchenrecht*, 1 (Leipzig, 1892; repr. Munich, Leipzig, 1923), 2 (Munich, Leipzig, 1923), 1:463ff., 468.

4. For the epochal significance of this transition for the public law concerning the church *(Staatskirchenrecht)*, see Johannes Heckel, "Melanchthon und das heutige Staatskirchenrecht," in *Um Recht und Gerechtigkeit. Festgabe für Erich Kaufmann zu seinem 70. Geburtstag — 21. September 1950 — überreicht von Freunden, Verehrern und Schülern* (Stuttgart, 1950), 88ff.

5. In the Lutheran confessional writings both qualities of the church are emphasized, the church as congregation of saints *(congregatio sanctorum)* and as kingdom of Christ *(regnum Christi)*; see *Augsburg Confession* 7.1; *Apology* 7.16. See also Edmund Schlink, *Theologie der lutherischen Bekenntnisschriften* (Munich, 1940), 300ff.

6. Groundbreaking was Georg F. Puchta, *Einleitung in das Recht der Kirche* (Leipzig, 1840).

7. Instead of other authors, see Wilhelm Kahl, *Lehrsystem des Kirchenrechts und der Kirchenpolitik*, 1 (Freiburg/Breisgau, 1894), 67ff.

8. See Siegfried Reicke, "Kirchenrecht," in *Einführung in die Rechtswissenschaft*, ed. by Rudolf Reinhard (Marburg, 1950), 362: "There was no justification for understanding this separation as being in agreement with the ideas of the reformers."

9. One is tempted to look especially in the system of Friedrich J. Stahl for the use of the concept 'kingdom of God' as a foundational principle of ecclesiastical law. Yet even he mentioned the significance of the church as kingdom of God only as a justification for the idea that the church is not only a congregation of saints but also an "institution"; see his *Kirchenverfassung nach Lehre und Recht der Protestanten* (2d ed. Erlangen, 1862), 46. For the justified critique of Stahl, see Sohm, *Kirchenrecht*, 1:466 n. 17.

10. See Carl Schmitt, *Die Lage der europäischen Rechtswissenschaft* (Tübingen, 1949), 14: "One hundred years ago the crisis of European jurisprudence begins with the victory of legal Positivism"; ibid., 27: "With Schelling's lectures, delivered in Berlin in the winter of 1841 to 1842, . . . begins the spiritual catastrophe of a generation, even more, of a whole era of German idealistic philosophy and theology."

11. See, e.g., Hans von Soden, "Die Verfassung der deutschen evangelischen Landeskirchen 1919-1933," *ThR*.NF 5 (1933): 370ff.

12. Ernst Kohlmeyer was correct when, in connection with the difference between Luther and the scholars mentioned above, he argued: ". . . the point of orientation ⟨in Luther's ecclesiology⟩ . . . is not man, the 'saints', but God. . . ." See his "Die Bedeutung der Kirche für Luther," *ZKG* 47 (1928): 479.

13. In general one was not aware of this inconsistency. Rather, following Holstein's differentiation between the church of the spirit and the church of the law, one felt confronted with a polarity, which one even considered to be *the* mark of Protestant ecclesiology. See Günther Holstein, *Die Grundlagen des evangelischen Kirchenrechts* (Tübingen, 1928), 227ff.; Otto Koellreutter, *Deutsches Staatsrecht* (Stuttgart, 1953), 83: "In contrast to Roman Catholic ecclesiastical law, evangelical ecclesiastical law does not have the close connection between faith, which determines the concept 'church', and the concept 'church' which determines ecclesiastical law." For a critique, see Hermann Diem, *Theologie als kirchliche Wissenschaft* (Munich, 1951), 168.

14. Sohm shortchanged the significance of the church as congregation of saints. In the second volume of his *Kirchenrecht* he tried to remedy this situation but was no longer able to master the problem.

15. See his *Die Reich-Gottes-Begriffe des neueren europäischen Denkens* (Göttingen, 1921), 7.

16. See Holstein, *Grundlagen*, 5ff. Herbert Wehrhahn ("Die Grundlagenproblematik des deutschen evangelischen Kirchenrechts 1933-1945," *ThR*.NF 18 [1950]: 71 n. 2) was correct when he remarked that Holstein's "broad presentation of God's kingdom" remains irrelevant for his concepts 'church' and 'law'.

17. *Kirchenrecht*, 1:1, 464ff.

18. ⟨In the sense of Canon law, or of any law dealing with spiritual matters.⟩

19. See Friedrich K. Schumann, "Bemerkungen zur Lehre vom Gesetz," *ZSTh* 16 (1939): 601 n. 2: "It is amazing to see how thoroughly the topic 'law' has been ignored in ⟨the textbooks of⟩ dogmatics of the nineteenth and also of the early twentieth century"; ibid., 602: "Only in the last two decades, for practical as well as principle reasons, it became impossible any longer to ignore the task of creating a theology of the church's law."

20. ⟨In a narrow sense, the (medieval) technical term for the two kinds of law, Roman law and Canon law; in a wider sense the phrase can designate secular and ecclesiastical law. See also above, 100f.⟩

21. See Sohm, *Kirchenrecht*, 2:135ff., 166ff. On this point there was no difference between Sohm and his opponents, and the next generations of scholars thought likewise. — For the present situation, see Herbert Wehrhahn, "Der Stand des Methodenproblems in der evangelischen Kirchenrechtslehre," *ZEvKR* 1 (1951): 72: law belongs to the specific way in which the secular governance acts; since during its pilgrimage on earth the church "stands" ⟨within the competency of that governance, it is also subordinated to law, i.e.,⟩ law according to its secular essence and not according to some kind of special sacred essence; ibid., 76: the total of the theoretical and practical possibilities available in secular law has to be available for the creation of order in the evangelical church. — Erdmann Schott ("Ist das Kirchenrecht eine Funktion des Kirchenbegriffs?" *ThLZ* 79 [1954]: 461ff.) criticized Sohm "for not having asked how throughout the changes of time this spiritual order, this ecclesiastical law of love, is to be coordinated with the secular order of law." This is the totally wrong question, because the "ecclesiastical law of love" is coordinated with the church and not with "secular authority" ⟨which creates the secular order of law, mentioned by Schott. For Schott's "this spiritual order" and "ecclesiastical law of love," see also above, 7: Sohm's theses concerning the kingdom of God as a kingdom of freedom and love.⟩

22. ⟨Cf. Luther's translation of Ps. 99:4, cited above, with the Vulgate text, cited by Heckel ("Honor regis iudicium diligit") and the NRSV text.⟩

23. The verse is inscribed in the banderol of the David plate of the German Imperial crown; see Eduard Eichmann, *Die Kaiserkrönung im Abendland*, 2 (Würzburg, 1942), 78, and the plate *King David*.

24. See Wilhelm Kahl, "Der Rechtsinhalt des Konkordienbuchs," p. 47 of a special offprint of *Festgabe der Berliner juristischen Fakultät für Otto Gierke zum Doktor-Jubiläum am 21. August 1910*, 1 (Breslau, 1910): 305ff. Sohm, *Kirchenrecht*, 2:145, agreed with Kahl. For the present situation in research, see Wehrhahn, "Grundlagenproblematik," ThR.NF 19 (1951): 230.

25. See Wilhelm O. Münter, *Kirche und Amt II. Die Gestalt der Kirche "nach göttlichem Recht"* (Munich, 1941); Schlink, *Theologie der Bekenntnisschriften*, 339 n. 32, 341 n. 34. See also above, 98.

26. So also Walther Schönfeld, *Über die Gerechtigkeit* (Göttingen, 1952), 10ff.

27. *Matthew, Chapters 18-24 Explained in Sermons*, 1537-40: WA 47:330.10.

28. ⟨In addition to divine law and kingdom of God; see above, 5, 7.⟩

29. ⟨I.e., the divine law for the kingdom of God.⟩

30. See Georg Wünsch, *Evangelische Ethik des Politischen* (Tübingen, 1936), 126.

31. Groundbreaking was Eugène Ehrhardt, "La notion du droit naturel chez Luther," in *Études de théologie et d'histoire, publiées par mm. professeurs de la Faculté de théologie protestante de Paris en hommage à la Faculté de théologie de Montauban* (Paris, 1901), 287ff. See also Franz Lau, *"Äußerliche Ordnung" und "Weltlich Ding" in Luthers Theologie* (Göttingen, 1933), 33 n. 1.

32. ⟨See n. 31.⟩

33. *Gesammelte Aufsätze zur Religionssoziologie*, 1 (Tübingen, 1920), 69f.

34. *Die Soziallehren der christlichen Kirchen und Gruppen* (3d ed. Tübingen, 1923), 486 n. 223 (on p. 488).

35. See his *Grundlagen*, 86.

36. Karl Holl, "Der Neubau der Sittlichkeit," in id., *Gesammelte Aufsätze zur Kirchengeschichte, 1. Luther* (6th ed. Tübingen, 1932), 243ff. Albrecht Oepke (*Das neue Gottesvolk in Schrifttum, Schauspiel, bildender Kunst und Weltgestaltung* [Gütersloh, 1950], 429) agreed with Holl, with the modification that Luther considered the Golden Rule "generally binding." "Natural law is identical with Christian law or is its forerunner, ⟨i.e.,⟩ reason as determined by Christian faith." (So also Holl, *Luther*, 247, whom Oepke cited.) For a critique of Holl, see Walther Köhler, "Sozialwissenschaftliche Bemerkungen zur Lutherforschung," ZGStW 85 (1928): 343ff.

37. ⟨Holl, *Luther*, 248.⟩

38. ⟨See above, 8.⟩

39. Ernst Kinder, "Gottes Gebote und Gottes Gnade im Wort vom Kreuz," *Kirchlich-Theologische Hefte* 7 (Munich, 1949), 62. Helmut Gollwitzer (*Die christliche Gemeinde in der politischen Welt* [Tübingen, 1954], 34) radically opposed natural law: "⟨Christians⟩ should not let themselves be seduced to walk into the swamp and murkiness of natural law; its precarious quality certainly is obvious, though man's longing for such a law can be well explained as the result of the most recent blunders of legal Positivism"; see, however, also ibid., 35: "⟨Christians⟩ do not deny that 'natural man' has some knowledge of humanity,

law, and justice; ⟨to the contrary,⟩ they have good reasons to search for such knowledge and learn from it."

40. ⟨Heckel often used the phrase "göttlicher Rechtswille." I.e., God's *will* for law and order, for a cosmos, as opposed to chaos or anarchy.⟩

41. So also Jacques Ellul, *Die theologische Begründung des Rechts* (Munich, 1948), 11. Ellul investigated "the meaning of law . . . in the sovereignty of Christ," and he continued: "Law belongs in the secular realm — after all, law itself is something secular — and therefore in a realm in which Christ is king." But for Luther, Christ's kingdom is a spiritual kingdom ⟨and not something secular⟩. On the basis of this theological starting point, Luther arrived at a question and answer which were totally different from Ellul's; therefore the debate with Ellul has to be excluded from the present discussion.

42. Walther Schönfeld, *Grundlegung der Rechtswissenschaft* (Stuttgart, 1951), 303, where we also find justified polemics against Stahl and Sohm. See also Edmund Schlink, "Das theologische Problem des Naturrechts," in *Viva Vox Evangelii. Eine Festschrift für Landesbischof D. Hans Meiser zum siebzigsten Geburtstag am 16. Februar 1951,* ed. by Lutherisches Kirchenamt in Hannover (Munich, 1951), 246ff.

43. Hans Liermann, "Zur Geschichte des Naturrechts in der evangelischen Kirche," in *Festschrift Alfred Bertholet zum 80. Geburtstag gewidmet,* ed. by Walter Baumgartner et al. (Tübingen, 1950), 296. See also Georges de Lagarde, *Recherches sur l'esprit politique de la Réforme* (Paris, 1926), 134: "The reformers frequently talked about law. However, nothing is more confusing than their ideas about it. There is no general definition. From scattered sources the reader has to glean fragmentary and mostly contradictory statements which confuse him from the start. Contradictions are especially frequent with Luther"; ibid., 292: "Luther has a discursive mind which, strictly speaking, is opposed to logic, indeed even to the most elementary coherence"; see further, ibid., 139ff., 145f.

44. See Hermann F. W. Hinrichs, *Geschichte des Natur- und Völkerrechts,* 1 (Leipzig, 1848), 10: "The lack of a clear sense of law was a medieval product of which one became increasingly aware at the time of the Reformation. Through the insight in the development of moral philosophy during the Middle Ages, this lack gradually came to the forefront. But even the reformers did not settle the matter. Luther, of course, had various thoughts about law, but only thoughts which were never treated in a scholarly way."

45. See esp. Lau, *"Äußerliche Ordnung,"* 30ff., 62ff.; id., *Luthers Lehre von den beiden Reichen* (Berlin, 1953), 40ff.; Hermann W. Beyer, "Glaube und Recht im Denken Luthers," *LuJ* 17 (1935): 56ff.

46. Wilhelm R. Beyer, *Rechtsphilosophische Besinnung* (Karlsruhe, 1947), 26: "Luther and Melanchthon do not deal with law in a scholarly serious way. For them law is, almost as a result of its natural origin, part of the religious world view, a part of the order set up by God." Alfred Grobmann's dissertation "Das Naturrecht bei Luther und Calvin" (Hamburg, 1935), is unproductive.

47. See August Lang, "Die Reformation und das Naturrecht," *BFChTh* 13.IV (1909): 13: "⟨In Luther's thought⟩ the . . . at all times vague idea of natural law was in danger of falling apart into the most diverse meanings"; ibid., 41: "For the Reformation, natural law was a part of the tradition, namely, a legacy of medieval Catholicism. One is tempted simply to assume the former when one considers how without any reflection, even naively, Luther here and there refers to natural law and accepts it in all its ambiguities without,

however, granting it any basic value"; ibid., 46: "The Reformation treated natural law with cool indifference without totally rejecting it."

48. For a modification of this view, see Ernst Wolf, "Zur Frage des Naturrechts bei Thomas von Aquin und Martin Luther," p. 9 of a special offprint of *JGGPÖ* 67 (1951): 186ff.: "Luther 'naively' speaks of a 'natural law' . . . , but he does *not only* 'naively' speak of it. In any case, it was impossible for him to evade the idea 'natural law'."

49. See also Georg Wehrung, *Kirche nach evangelischem Verständnis* (Gütersloh, 1945), 215: the Reformation was a renewal not only of the faith but also of the law of the church. For the opposite view, see Kahl, *Lehrsystem des Kirchenrechts und der Kirchenpolitik*, 1:11: the Reformation was not a basic renewal of the church in the area of law.

50. See Thomas Würtenberger, "Wege zum Naturrecht in Deutschland 1946-1948," *ARSP* 38 (1949): 105: "In contrast to Catholicism, Lutheranism for a long time did not develop a religious foundation for law."

51. *CR.Melanchthonis opera*, 18:14.

52. ⟨See above, 2.⟩

53. See also Gustaf Wingren, *Die Predigt* (Göttingen, 1955), 29: "The challenge issued by the Word of God also includes the demand that the Word determines the basic questions. The Word loses something of its content if it has to answer questions other than those which originate in the Word itself."

54. So also Ehrhardt, "La notion du droit naturel chez Luther," in *Études de théologie et d'histoire*, 304: "This concept is theological to a high degree."

55. *Against the Spiritual Estate of the Pope and the Bishops, Falsely So Called*, 1522: WA 10.II:105.2: "⟨Martin Luther,⟩ preacher ⟨or: 'man of the church'; or: 'theologian'⟩ by God's grace."

56. *On Secular Authority*, 1523: WA 11:273.2: ". . . I am unable to proscribe a law for a prince. I intend to instruct only his heart, how it should be disposed ⟨so that he may⟩ be well qualified to act in all matters of laws, counsels, judgments, and actions. If he acts accordingly, God certainly will enable him to execute all laws, counsels, and actions successfully and in a God-pleasing way." See also *On Keeping Children in School*, 1530: WA 30.II:537.4. — For 'instruction of the conscience ⟨or heart⟩ of Christians', see Harald Diem, *Luthers Lehre von den beiden Reichen* (Beiheft 5 of Evangelische Theologie. Munich, 1938), 36ff.

57. In this respect Liermann ("Zur Geschichte des Naturrechts," in *Bertholet Festschrift;* see above, 11.) was correct when he argued that Luther did not produce a system of legal philosophy. But this does not mean that Luther lacked an *"inner* relationship with law" ⟨italics by this ed.⟩, as Adalbert Erler (*Kirchenrecht* [Frankfurt, 1949], 46ff.) argued.

58. *Sermons on Matthew, Chapters 5-7*, 1530-32: WA 32:388.34: "Christ preaches only to his Christians." See also Franz Lau, "Bemerkungen zu Luthers Lehre von den beiden Reichen," *ELKZ* 6 (1952): 236.

59. *The Seven Penitential Psalms*, 1517: WA 1:219.21: "Someone might say to me: 'Can't you do anything else than talk about man's righteousness, wisdom, and strength? Can't you do anything else than always interpret Holy Scripture ⟨and draw from it⟩ God's righteousness and grace, and thus play only on one string and sing only one song?' I answer: 'Let everyone take care of himself, ⟨but⟩ insofar as I am concerned I confess . . . that this is the truth as I see it: God the Holy Spirit doesn't know anything else and doesn't

want to know anything else but Jesus Christ.... Christ is God's ... righteousness....'" See also Wilhelm Maurer, *Von der Freiheit eines Christenmenschen* (Göttingen, 1949), 154: "Luther knows that divine Revelation exists only in Christ."

60. Luther suggested this already in *First Lectures on the Psalms,* 1513-15: WA 4:134.29: "... the law turns our attention to the gospel, ... the gospel turns our attention to the law"; ibid., WA 4:324.6: "The gospel gives understanding through which the meaning of the old law is revealed and scrutinized."

61. See *Warning of His Dear German People,* 1531: WA 30.III:319.26.30; *Third Disputation against the Antinomians,* 1538: WA 39.I:489.5; *Defense against the Charge of Inciting Rebellion,* 1533: WA 38:113.23.

62. See also Rudolf Hermann, *Zu Luthers Lehre von Sünde und Rechtfertigung* (Tübingen, 1952), 5: "If we expect any answers and help from Luther for dealing with the most pressing problems of our day, ⟨then we have to go back⟩ to the article ... of faith and justification."

63. See Walther von Loewenich, *Luthers theologia crucis* (3d ed. Munich, 1939).

64. *Second Lectures on the Psalms,* 1518-21: WA 5:217.2; ibid., WA 5:176.32: "The cross alone is our theology."

65. ⟨'Spiritual', i.e., in contrast to secular law. Heckel's phrase "geistliches Recht" (spiritual law) can also designate Canon law. See also above, 237 n. 18.⟩

66. *Eine Schweizer Stimme 1938/45* (Zollikon, 1945), 13ff.

67. Erhardt ("La notion du droit naturel chez Luther," in *Études de théologie et d'histoire,* 317) already asked the question: "What is the relationship between justice according to natural law, a justice which is available even to non-Christians, and God's justice?"

68. See Johannes Heckel, *Initia iuris ecclesiastici Protestantium* (Munich, 1950), 15, 38ff.

69. ⟨Here and throughout the remainder of this paragraph in the narrow sense, i.e., Canon law, or in the wider sense of law dealing with spiritual matters, or of spiritual law in contrast to secular law.⟩

70. Sermons of ca. 1514-21: WA 4:695.3. ⟨For the addition "natural law," see n. 71.⟩

71. See the sermon cited in n. 70: WA 4:697.30: "Those who do not believe in Christ and do not hang on to him remain in the world." ⟨They return nothing to God, they withdraw from God, their hearts remain in the world. Therefore⟩ "it is impossible that such a person returns to his fellowman all that he should.... Because he does not hang on to Christ in faith he is thus far necessarily unclean.... And as a person with an unclean heart he can do nothing other than love himself more than his neighbor and be more concerned with his own affairs than with those of his neighbor. Therefore he does not give to the neighbor what he should, and he acts contrary to ⟨the saying in⟩ natural law ⟨literally: "the law of nature."⟩: 'What you do not wish that one does to you, you should not do to someone else.'"

72. The situation is, then, the opposite of Georg Müller's description (*Luthers Stellung zum Recht* [Leipzig, 1906], 12): "Luther ... felt that the spiritual element was incompatible with Canon law, was something that reaches into the area of legal arrangements and clouds the purity of law. Therefore he reached the point of ... rejecting the whole Canon law."

73. For the contrast between the spiritual understanding of the First Command-

ment and the wrong understanding of divine law in the legal praxis of the church of his day, see Luther's *Second Lectures on the Psalms,* 1518-21: WA 5:227.33ff.

74. See Wilhelm Link, *Das Ringen Luthers um die Freiheit der Theologie von der Philosophie,* ed. by Ernst Wolf and Manfred Mezger (Munich, 1940), 51.

Notes to Chapter 2

1. Instead of other authors, see Otto Scheel, *Martin Luther,* 1 (3d ed. Tübingen, 1921), 2 (3d and 4th ed. Tübingen, 1930), 2:422ff.; Karl A. Meissinger, *Der katholische Luther* (Munich, 1952), 109f. See also the proud statement in Luther's *Answer to the Theological Faculty of the University of Louvain and of Cologne,* 1520: WA 6:188.16: "You should firmly . . . believe that Luther knows your philosophy and theology. For more than twelve years he has studied them — not with a weak brain or laziness — and has been well-known among your compatriots."

2. See Hans Freiherr von Campenhausen, "Reformatorisches Selbstbewußtsein und reformatorisches Geschichtsbewußtsein bei Luther 1517-1522," *ARG* 37 (1940): 142ff.; Hans Preuß, *Martin Luther der Prophet* (Gütersloh, 1933), 207f.

3. *D. Martin Luther's Offer and Protest,* 1520: WA 6:477.31: "My spirit which God has given to me . . ."; sermon of March 9, 1522: WA 10.III:8.8: "I was . . . the one to whom God has revealed it first. . . ." See also Johannes Kühn, *Toleranz und Offenbarung* (Leipzig, 1923), 112; Ernst Wolf, *Peregrinatio,* 1 (Munich, 1954), 12, where other materials are cited.

4. For the consequences which result from Luther's obedience to the divine Revelation for research, see Link, *Das Ringen Luthers,* 3ff.

5. *First Lectures on the Psalms,* 1513-15: WA 4:323.11 ⟨*LW* 11:439 f.⟩: "What, what kind, and how great the law of God is can only be known by experience of the works. . . . The works produce more understanding, if I may say so, than the words. Otherwise he very quickly misuses the Scriptures who does not first put them to the test in life and morals, and he falls into error in understanding and measuring its words on the basis of himself and his own resources, and not as it is profitable"; see also ibid., WA 4:326.29. — For Luther's position on faith and experience, see Regin Prenter, *Spiritus creator. Studien zu Luthers Theologie* (Munich, 1954), 67, 320 n. 140 (literature); Bengt Hägglund, *Theologie und Philosophie bei Luther und in der occamistischen Tradition* (Lund, 1955), 68ff.

6. See Heinrich Bornkamm, "Iustitia dei in der Scholastik und bei Luther," *ARG* 39 (1942): 1ff.; Prenter, *Spiritus creator,* 45.

7. *Lectures on Hebrews,* 1517-18: WA 57.III:233.22 ⟨*LW* 29:236⟩: "The words of Holy Scripture should not be treated carelessly. For since they are the words of the Spirit, they are necessarily full of weight and majesty." See also Gabriel Biel, *Sacri canonis missae expositio* (Basel, 1510), lectio 67.C: "The Christian who daily asks that God's judgment bypass him has to have a pure conscience."

8. See Lennart Pinomaa, *Der Zorn Gottes in der Theologie Luthers* (Helsinki, 1938), 153 n. 1 (literature).

9. For materials from *First Lectures on the Psalms,* 1513-15, see Erich Vogelsang, *Die Anfänge von Luthers Christologie* (Berlin, 1929), 104 n. 1, and ibid., 89 n. 1, for materials from *Second Lectures on Galatians,* 1531.

Notes to Page 17

10. *First Lectures on the Psalms,* 1513-15: WA 4:305.28: "Whoever pays attention to God who gives a commandment, how could this person not be frightened by such great majesty?"

11. *Lectures on Psalm 51,* 1532: WA 40.II:351.5: "We are unable to erase the natural... feeling and this ⟨statement⟩: 'You are a sinner and God is righteous; therefore he hates you.'" See further, Luther to Eberhard Brisger: Nov. 29(?), 1527: WA.B 4:288.6 ff. — For *Anfechtung* ⟨see below, 248 n. 55⟩ as the experience of God's wrath, see Prenter, *Spiritus creator,* 30ff. (literature). For *Anfechtung* in Luther's life and thought in general, see Horst Beintker, *Die Überwindung der Anfechtung bei Luther* (Berlin, 1954).

12. *Second Lectures on Galatians,* 1531: WA 40.I:569.1. See also *Lectures on Isaiah,* 1527-30: WA 31.II:69.7, where Luther speaks of the three great tyrants, law, sin, and death; *The Book of Deuteronomy with Notes,* 1525: WA 14:581.10: "Law is an unjust tyrant." For more details, see Theodosius Harnack, *Luthers Theologie,* 1 (new edition: Munich, 1927), 368ff. See further, *Lectures on Romans,* 1515-16: WA 56:368.26: "God acts in a tyrannical way"; *First Lectures on the Psalms,* 1513-15: WA 4:207.23, with reference to Peter Lombard. — For Plato, see *Nomoi* 4.722E: "A tyrannical command," and Erich Gerner, "Historisch-soziologische Entwicklungstendenzen im attischen Recht," ZSRG.R 67 (1950): 37 n. 143.

13. See Gal. 3:10b; see also Ragnar Bring, *Dualismen hos Luther* (Lund, 1929), 103ff.

14. *First Lectures on the Psalms,* 1513-15: WA 4:308.10 ⟨LW 11:418⟩: ⟨Ps. 119:10. "Hence it follows that⟩ 'the whole heart' is spoken of in a twofold way. First, that there is nothing of one's own will present...."

15. Luther saw one expression of this strictness in the negative phrasing of the commandments of the Decalogue (except for the Fourth Commandment). See *Sermons on the Ten Commandments,* 1518: WA 1:398.21: "He commands in a final and negative way, because the negative phrasing is more strict than the affirmative phrasing"; ibid., WA 1:430.18, 470.6.16, 471.12.28, 504.9; sermons of ca. 1514-17: WA 1:70.5; appendix to Luther's letter to George Spalatin: Febr. 12, 1519: WA.B 1:329.66: "⟨This conforms to the tropus⟩ of Scripture which makes the most vehement affirmations through negative phrasing...." See also Helmut Thielicke, *Theologische Ethik,* 1 (Tübingen, 1951), Nos. 2163ff.

16. *First Disputation against the Antinomians,* 1537: WA 39.I:366.7: "The law demanded... perfect obedience."

17. *Lectures on Romans,* 1515-16: WA 56:249.20 ⟨LW 25:236⟩: "... faith is indivisible. Therefore it is either a whole faith and believes all that is to be believed, or it is no faith if it does not believe one part.... 'Christ is not divided' (cf. 1 Cor. 1:13), therefore He is either completely denied in one unit, or else He is completely affirmed."

18. *First Lectures on the Psalms,* 1513-15: WA 4:307.4 ⟨LW 11:416⟩: "... whatever work we do without relation to obedience is defiled."

19. *First Lectures on the Psalms,* 1513-15: WA 4:354.26 ⟨LW 11:483⟩: "... he who offends in one thing is guilty of all (James 2:10)"; *The Book of Deuteronomy with Notes,* 1525: WA 14:723.30; *Decretum Gratiani* c.1. D.V. de poen. ⟨Friedberg 1:1238⟩.

20. ⟨See below, 358 n. 10.⟩ The situation was different when man's nature had not yet been corrupted by the Fall; then the divine law was a law which man could obey and in which he delighted. See *First Disputation against the Antinomians,* 1537: WA 39.I:364.10; *Third Disputation against the Antinomians,* 1538: WA 39.I:515.16; *Disputation of Henry*

Schmedenstede, 1542: WA 39.II:196.11: "In the status of the incorrupt nature Adam fulfilled all of God's commandments without a mediator."

21. *Lectures on Romans*, 1515-16: WA 56:76.28: "It is impossible that concupiscence obeys God"; Luther to the Franciscans at Jüterbog: May 15, 1519: WA.B 1: 390.44; *On Christian Freedom* ⟨Latin text⟩, 1520: WA 7:52.36: "All ⟨of God's commandments⟩ are impossibilities for us"; *The Book of Deuteronomy with Notes*, 1525: WA 14:577.4; sermon of Dec. 7, 1516: WA 1:105.15, 106.1; sermons of ca. 1514-21: WA 4:689.11.33f.; Luther to George Spalatin: Febr. 15, 1518: WA.B 1:145.28: "Oh, for how long has the definition of righteousness been unknown! What is righteousness? It is self-accusation" ⟨of being a sinner⟩. — For *lex impossibilis*, see also Jerome *Against the Pelagians*, PL 23:546f. ⟨see also ibid., 571⟩, and WA 39.I:420. 3, 39.II:195.26ff., 428 to 39.I:420 n. 1; according to Luther (WA 39.I:420.4), the Jerome passage was cited in *Decretum Gratiani* ⟨at a place which apparently cannot be established; see WA 39.II:428 to 39.I:420.4⟩.

22. *Lectures on Romans*, 1515-16: WA 56:158.9: "Outside of ourselves and in Christ"; for this concept, see Hans J. Iwand, *Rechtfertigungslehre und Christusglaube* (Leipzig, 1930), 28, 40ff., 52. See also *Second Lectures on the Psalms*, 1518-21: WA 5:167.13: "You are not attacked with despair of conscience ... so that you trust in works but, to the contrary, that you turn away from works. For this is a totally spiritual, albeit most severe battle which must take place between you alone and God alone; in this battle you will be sustained only by hope, ⟨which⟩ expects ⟨victory to be granted by God, to whom you⟩ commend the whole matter, ⟨and when you⟩ overcome God with God, as is written about Jacob, Gen. 32⟨:24⟩." ⟨In the last clause Luther meant to say that God's law-word has to be overcome with God's gospel-word.⟩ See further, *Disputation against Scholastic Theology*, 1517, thesis 34: WA 1:225.37 ⟨*LW* 31:11⟩: "... man by nature has neither correct precept nor good will."

23. See the phrase "in God's ban" in *Against the Robbing and Murdering Hordes of Peasants*, 1525: WA 18:358.7.

24. See Lennart Pinomaa, "Die Heiligung bei Luther," *ThZ* 10 (1954): 31.

25. *First Lectures on the Psalms*, 1513-15: WA 4:309.17: "The law ... curses those who do not fulfill it"; *Lectures on Psalm 45*, 1532: WA 40.II:493.10: "The law is a doctrine of malediction."

26. And this in contrast to man's laws of punishment. *First Disputation against the Antinomians*, 1537: WA 39.I:396.6: "In worldly matters the situation is such that the punishment expiates the crime, but before God it is not so."

27. Sermon of Feb. 2, 1517: WA 1:516.6: "⟨In the Ninth and the Tenth Commandment⟩ is prohibited the evil of the tinder and, if I may say so, the essential or causative impurity in us"; ibid., WA 1:515.11: "the very root of evil thoughts."

28. Luther did not consider this condition *(status)* of the sinner to be a *habitus* ⟨disposition⟩ but, according to Rudolf Hermann (*Luthers These "Gerecht und Sünder zugleich"* [Gütersloh, 1930], 57), "a continuous being-in-action" against God.

29. *Lectures on Psalm 51*, 1532: WA 40.II:339.7.

30. Luther used the terms 'mortal sins' and 'venial sins' with a different meaning than did the theologians of his day. See, e.g., *Lectures on Romans*, 1515-16: WA 56:289.14, and Hermann, *Luthers These "Gerecht und Sünder zugleich,"* 162f. See further, *Second Lectures on the Psalms*, 1518-21: WA 5:111.27: "I know that there is no more dangerous foolhardiness than the wish to differentiate between venial and mortal sins, esp. in the hour

of agitation and temptation"; ibid., WA 5:112.4: "In every action one has to fear God's strictest judgment"; *On Confession*, 1520: WA 6:162.15.

31. For Luther's polemics against the idea that Baptism *eradicates* Original Sin, see *Lectures on Romans*, 1515-16: WA 56:273.3f. ⟨LW 25:260f.⟩, the notes to this passage, and 310.1 ⟨LW 25:297⟩; *Against Latomus*, 1521: WA 8:96.28; sermons of ca. 1514-21: WA 4:691.30.

32. *Lectures on Romans*, 1515-16: WA 56:271.6 ⟨LW 25:259⟩: ". . . act of sin . . . is more correctly sin in the sense of the work and fruit of sin, but sin itself is the passion, the tinder, and the concupiscence, or the inclination, toward evil and the difficulty of doing good. . . ."

33. Therefore the scholastic distinction between 'performing the works demanded by a commandment according to the substance of the action' and 'performing the works demanded by a commandment according to the intentions of the giver of the commandment' was for Luther a monstrosity; for details, see *Lectures on Romans*, 1515-16: WA 56:274, n. to line 12 ⟨LW 25:261, n. 12⟩. See also *Disputation of Henry Schmedenstede*, 1542: WA 39.II:189.8, 197.11.

34. *Disputation on Justification*, 1536: WA 39.I:112.20 ⟨LW 34:182⟩: "Original sin is not a quiescent thing, but a kind of continuous motion or entelechy, producing its own effects. It is not a quiescent quality, but a restless evil which labors day and night, even in those who sleep. . . . It is a restless animal, a beast which cannot stand still, yes, which must have its motions." See also ibid., WA 39.I:125.10, and the still traditional definition in the sermons of ca. 1514-21: WA 4:690.4: "According to the agreement of all doctors, Original Sin . . . is the lack of original righteousness, with which we have been punished on account of Adam's first sin in Paradise."

35. *First Lectures on the Psalms*, 1513-15: WA 4:51.30: "'Our hiddenness,' i.e., the secret sins which the law is unable to cleanse; only grace" ⟨can do this⟩.

36. *Second Lectures on the Psalms*, 1518-21: WA 5:171.15: "Under the maximum penalty" ⟨possible⟩.

37. *Lectures on Genesis*, 1535-45: WA 42:169.27 ⟨LW 1:226f.⟩: ". . . the tree of the knowledge of good and evil did not kill because its fruits were poisonous and destructive, but because a word, or a kind of label, had been attached to it with the warning written on it: 'On whatever day you eat from this tree, you will surely die.' . . . therefore, there hangs on the tree of death the spiritual death, namely, disobedience." Here "spiritual death" is understood as *poena latae sententiae* ⟨a punishment pronounced in an all-encompassing verdict⟩ which occurs simultaneously with the deed. — For the publication of Luther's *Lectures on Genesis*, see Peter Meinhold, *Die Genesisvorlesung Luthers und ihre Herausgabe* (Stuttgart, 1936).

38. *The Bondage of the Will*, 1525: WA 18:782.38 ⟨LW 33:287f.⟩: "The knowledge and confession of these two kingdoms ⟨i.e., of Christ and of Satan⟩ perpetually warring against each other with such might and main would alone be sufficient to confute the dogma of free choice, seeing that we are bound to serve in the kingdom of Satan unless we are delivered by the power of God." See also above, 33f.

39. *The Bondage of the Will*, 1525: WA 18:768.17 ⟨LW 33:264⟩: "For with God there is nothing intermediate between righteousness and sin, no neutral ground, so to speak, which is neither righteousness nor sin." See also Luther's polemics against 'neutral' works in *Second Lectures on the Psalms*, 1518-21: WA 5:394.3, 414.25.

40. *First Lectures on the Psalms,* 1513-15: WA 4:128.27: "Everyone who sins withdraws himself from obedience to God."

41. *Lectures on Romans,* 1515-16: WA 56:246.27: "God's ⟨court works with⟩ unlimited exactness. Nothing is so minute that it may not turn out to be gigantic before God."

42. *First Lectures on the Psalms,* 1513-15: WA 3:17.31 ⟨*LW* 10:14⟩: ". . . the first root of all good is to have delight in the law of the Lord."

43. For the battle of the 'rule of reason' with God, see *Second Lectures on Galatians,* 1531: WA 40.I:295.1.3: "In my thoughts . . . I want to fight with ⟨God⟩"; ibid., WA 40.I:306.3: "The law is beyond man's reason." Therefore it is impossible to agree with Georg Wünsch's argument (*Gotteserfahrung und sittliche Tat bei Luther* [Gotha, 1924], 19) that in the final analysis God can be comprehended as a judging and holy power also through reason; he understood reason as "the rational skill of thinking about the essence of God."

44. *The Bondage of the Will,* 1525: WA 18:707.32 ⟨*LW* 33:173⟩: ". . . it remains absurd (as Reason judges) that a God who is just and good should demand of free choice impossible things; that although free choice cannot will good but is in bondage to sin, he should hold this against it; and that when he does not impart the Spirit, he acts no more mildly or mercifully than if he hardened or permitted to be hardened. These things, Reason will repeat, are not the marks of a good and merciful God. They are too far beyond her comprehension. . . ." For the opposite view, see *Decretum Gratiani* c.2. D.IV ⟨Friedberg 1:5⟩, with Johannes Teutonicus, *Glossa ordinaria:* "If someone transgresses a law because of the impossibility of fulfilling it, there is no reason for punishing him." ⟨For the *Glossa,* see Johann F. Schulte, *Die Geschichte der Quellen und Literatur zum Canonischen Recht,* 1 (Stuttgart, 1875), 172f.⟩

45. *Second Lectures on the Psalms,* 1518-21: WA 5:388.17: ⟨Luther commented on the Vulgate text of Ps. 12:4 (13:3 in NRSV): "Listen to me, Oh Lord, my God." According to Luther, this plea has to be connected with the phrase of verse 1, "How long will you hide your face from me," as if the psalmist wanted to say:⟩ "You had turned away from me and, like a cold and stern judge who has no intention other than to condemn me, you were unmoved by my pleading; you did not only not hear me, but you turned your face from me in order not to hear me."

46. *The Book of Deuteronomy with Notes,* 1525: WA 14:639.25: "It certainly is a strange legislator ⟨if⟩ he simultaneously prescribes works ⟨to be done⟩ and yet condemns them when they have been done"; *Second Lectures on Galatians,* 1531: WA 40.I:218.1: "If you have done the works prescribed in the law, if you have fulfilled the law, 'love, etc.,' you will nevertheless not have been justified by ⟨this⟩"; ibid., WA 40.II:15.7: "Whoever strives to be justified by means of the law is farther from righteousness than other sinners who abandon the trust in their own works"; *Disputation against Scholastic Theology,* 1517, thesis 63: WA 1:227.16: "⟨Man⟩ sins by not spiritually fulfilling the law." See also *Disputation on the Power and Will of Man without Grace,* 1516: WA 1:146.35, 147.1.

47. *Sermons of 1523:* WA 12:569.35: "⟨Man⟩ rather wishes that there were no God"; *Second Lectures on Galatians,* 1531: WA 40.I:362.4: "Reason rejects God, his wisdom and power, and ⟨thus⟩ kills God."

48. *Lectures on Romans,* 1515-16: WA 56:369.18 ⟨*LW* 25:359⟩: ". . . to wish that someone be turned into nothing is the worst curse, which all the damned and those who have the prudence of the flesh hope for God."

49. *Second Lectures on the Psalms*, 1518-21: WA 5:64.8: "For the flesh the commandment, or the Word of God, is intolerable, and ⟨the flesh⟩ does not understand it because inwardly and in all ways ⟨the commandment⟩ is the opposite ⟨of the flesh⟩"; ibid., WA 5:209.39: "Man searches . . . for an escape and does not find one. Soon he will have the most ardent hatred for God, first wishing for another God, and then that he himself would not live. Thus man blasphemes the supreme majesty and wishes with all his might . . . that this majesty would not exist and, were it possible, that he himself would not have been born"; ibid., WA 5:33.13: "Man's will fights the law ⟨of the Lord⟩, ⟨hates⟩ the law, ⟨flees from⟩ the law"; *Lectures on Genesis*, 1535-45: WA 42:128.28: "Man ⟨flees from⟩ God, and there is nothing more hated and intolerable for man than God"; *Third Disputation against the Antinomians*, 1538: WA 39.I:559.12: "The law commands us to love and highly esteem God and trust him; when man realizes that he is unable to do justice to this command, he begins to despair, and to hate and blaspheme God." See also Prenter, *Spiritus creator*, 31.

50. Sermon of Dec. 7, 1516: WA 1:105.17: "What should man do, where should man go when he is pressured by a law which he is unable to obey?" *Second Lectures on the Psalms*, 1518-21: WA 5:65.9: "The unbearable burdens of the law"; ibid., WA 5:557.10.

51. *Second Lectures on the Psalms*, 1518-21: WA 5:502.7: "Nowhere opens up an escape."

52. See Günter Jacob, *Der Gewissensbegriff in der Theologie Luthers* (Tübingen, 1920), 30ff.

53. See Paul Althaus, *Gebot und Gesetz* (Gütersloh, 1952), 19. ⟨See also above, 234 n. 10. Heckel wrote "Naturgesetz," i.e., literally: "nature law." Sometimes he qualified *Naturgesetz* with *göttlich* (divine); e.g., above, 133. Therefore we shall use 'divine natural law', and we shall not place 'divine' in pointed brackets when Heckel did not use it. Since this divine natural law is a spiritual law (e.g., above, 45), Heckel sometimes qualified *Naturgesetz* also with *geistlich* (spiritual) and used "spiritual natural law" (e.g., above, 127); in such cases we add 'divine' in pointed brackets in order to be consistent in the terminology. God's legislation resulted in 'Das göttliche Naturgesetz' (*divina lex naturalis*, divine natural law) and 'Das positive göttliche Recht' *(ius divinum positivum)*, literally: "divine positive right"; to use the noun 'right' for *ius* (or *Recht*) could create a wrong impression for the American reader, whose understanding of 'right' is shaped by the *Bill of Rights*. Therefore we use 'divine positive law'. If *Recht* does designate 'right' (in the sense of inalienable right, or of privilege), then we use 'right'; this will be the case with, e.g., 'the divine spiritual basic rights of a Christian'; see above, 31, 97f.⟩

54. *Second Lectures on the Psalms*, 1518-21: WA 5:388.24: "When God has turned his face away from us come at once turmoil, confusion, gloom of mind, and lack of knowing what to do, just as if we were groping around in darkness and searching everywhere for an escape"; sermon of Aug. 23, 1517(?): WA 4:654.22: "If someone ⟨deals with⟩ God by way of ⟨his own⟩ righteousness and ability, he will be terrified into despair." — For the dread and horror which man experiences in his conscience when he is confronted with God's judgment, see *Second Lectures on the Psalms*, 1518-21: WA 5:203.1; for the insurmountable and unavoidable distress, see ibid., WA 5:217.27; for the despair, spiritual dejection, and confusion of a disturbed conscience, and the reason for them, see ibid., WA 5:158.10, and 159.23: "No works, even those done ⟨to avoid⟩ a single sin, even a venial one, will help in this situation." For *Anfechtung* ⟨see n. 55⟩ which man experiences in this situation, see

Second Lectures on the Psalms, 1518-21: WA 5:204.20: "Does prayer help anything once I am certain that <God> himself does this?"

55. <Roland H. Bainton, *Here I Stand. A Life of Martin Luther* (Festival Book ed. Nashville, 1978), 31: "Toward God [Luther] was at once attracted and repelled. Only in harmony with the Ultimate could he find peace. But how could a pigmy stand before divine Majesty; how could a transgressor confront divine Holiness? Before God the high and God the holy Luther was stupefied. For such an experience he had a word which has as much right to be carried over into English as *Blitzkrieg*. The word he used was *Anfechtung,* for which there is no English equivalent. It may be a trial sent by God to test man, or an assault by the Devil to destroy man. It is all the doubt, turmoil, pang, tremor, panic, despair, desolation, and desperation which invade the spirit of man.">

56. *First Lectures on the Psalms,* 1513-15: WA 4:443.11. See also sermons of ca. 1514-21: WA 4:699.22.

57. See Karl Holl, *Gesammelte Aufsätze zur Kirchengeschichte,* 3. *Der Westen* (Tübingen, 1928), 172: "It was difficult for Luther to understand how it is possible that God's action in the justification of the sinner can be the result of God's righteousness, and how this righteousness by which the sinner is justified can be brought into agreement with the usual understanding of God's righteousness." See also Carl Stange, *Luther und das Evangelium* (Berlin, 1953), 13ff.

58. WA.TR 5:439.34; *Lectures on Psalm 51,* 1532: WA 40.II:411.14.

59. *Lectures on Romans,* 1515-16: WA 56:355.14; for this passage see also the sermon of Oct. 28, 1515(?): WA 4:667.3: Luther dealt with the heathen poets and their fables *(fabulantur)* about the love of the flesh; its altruism is <in reality> a cover for love of self.

60. The interpretation of the divine natural law is the subject already of one of Luther's earliest extant sermons, WA 4:590.4; for this sermon see also *Luthers Werke in Auswahl,* 5. *Der junge Luther,* ed. by Erich Vogelsang (Berlin, 1933), 19ff.; Reynold Weyenborg, "La charité dans la première théologie de Luther (1509-1515)," *RHE* 45 (1950): 641ff., 668. — The article by Heinz Bluhm, "The Significance of Luther's Earliest Sermons," *HThR* 37 (1944): 175ff., was not available to me.

61. See also Emil Brunner, *Gerechtigkeit. Eine Lehre von den Grundgesetzen der Gesellschaftsordnung* (Zürich, 1943), 104: "The reformers, who broke with a tradition of a thousand years when they introduced a new understanding of God's righteousness, without second thought unanimously used the term 'natural law' of patristic and scholastic thought as an integrating part of their social ethics." For a different view, see de Lagarde, *Recherches sur l'esprit politique de la Réforme,* 174, who spoke of "the inability <of the reformers> to create a precise and clear idea of natural law."

62. Hans Welzel, *Naturrecht und materiale Gerechtigkeit. Prolegomena zu einer Rechtsphilosophie* (Göttingen, 1951), 100. See also Reinhold Niebuhr, *The Nature and Destiny of Man,* 2 (New York, 1943), 197: The Lutheran Reformation "relegates the 'natural law' . . . to the . . . background, as an inadequate guide"; Georg Dahm, *Deutsches Recht* (Stuttgart, 1951), 131: "Luther deemphasized the idea of natural law. God is not understood as *ratio* but as will, <and> Creation is understood as the product of God's will, which man cannot comprehend. In the system of others — so in that of Melanchthon — natural-law ideas do appear."

63. *Second Lectures on Galatians,* 1531: WA 40.II:74.2: "All laws are instituted to teach

faith first and thereafter love. In words, theology is brief and easy, but in the subject and practice it is wider, longer, and profounder than the whole world."

64. Luther had difficulties even with the biblical usage of the term 'law' because it could be understood in many ways; *The Book of Deuteronomy with Notes*, 1525: WA 14:583.26: "Throughout Scripture this width ⟨in the meaning⟩ of the word ⟨i.e., the Hebrew word for 'law'⟩ produces obscurity and ambiguity; therefore close attention must be paid"; *Preface to Romans*, 1522: WA.DB 7:2.17: "First we have to know the language and know what St. Paul means when he uses the words law, ⟨sin, grace, faith, righteousness, flesh, spirit, and similar ones⟩, otherwise we will not profit from our reading." See also below, 297 n. 141.

65. *Psalm 117 Explained*, 1530: WA 31.I:227.23: "One will never have completed learning the Word of God."

66. Luther to Philip Melanchthon: Aug. 4, 1530, Appendix II: WA.B 5:529.1; sermon of Jan. 1, 1540: WA 49:1.14: "Throughout the world and in all the books much attention is paid to this law ⟨in the sense of Gal. 3:23⟩; all the doctors write much about it, but they ⟨only⟩ confuse themselves and others. In the papacy they distinguished between three laws: natural law, the law of Moses, and the law of the gospel or of Christ. But they did not correctly understand ⟨the matter⟩. They made fine words, but they did not interpret the matter correctly." For this passage, see Erdmann Schott, "Kirchliche Gesetzgebungsgewalt im Urteil Luthers," *WZ(H)* 4 (1954): 141ff.

67. See also the judgment of Erich Seeberg, *Luthers Theologie*, 2 (Stuttgart, 1937), 205: "The problem 'law' is perhaps the most difficult one in Luther's theology."

68. ⟨See above, 7.⟩

69. See Johannes Heckel, "Das Decretum Gratiani und das deutsche evangelische Kirchenrecht," *StGra* 3 (1955): 485ff.

70. In that sense, André Siegfried was correct when he stated about Luther: "... basically a mind which remained medieval..."; see André Latreille and André Siegfried, "Les forces religieuses et la vie politique: Le Catholicisme, Le Protestantisme," *Cahiers de la Fondation nationale des sciences politiques* 23 (1951): 172. Already Adolf von Harnack (*Lehrbuch der Dogmengeschichte*, 3 [5th ed. Tübingen, 1932]: 811) made the same judgment: "The periphery of ⟨Luther's⟩ existence and even some central parts of his essence were old-catholic, medieval phenomena."

71. Ernst Troeltsch's presentation of this development ("Die kulturgeschichtliche Methode in der Dogmengeschichte. Bedeutung der lex naturae für Katholizismus und Reformation," in id., *Gesammelte Schriften*, 4 [Tübingen, 1925], 750f.), is pure fantasy, esp. in the case of Melanchthon's role; through him supposedly "Luther's previous, magnificent yet also super-idealistic positions were levelled out."

72. See Johannes Heckel, *Initia iuris*, 39ff., 63f. This difference between Luther's ecclesiology and that of his time is not discussed in the available literature; see, e.g., Meissinger, *Der katholische Luther*.

73. See Carl Stange, "'Evangelisches Erwachen' in der katholischen Theologie," *ZSTh* 22 (1953): 314: "Luther's Reformation does not begin with his study of the Pauline epistles, but with his perception of the unbridgeable gap between the heathen wisdom of the world and the gospel. Modern Luther research tries in vain to find in his first lectures on the Psalms the Pauline formula 'justification by faith', while from the very beginning the Reformation principle is expressed in Luther's opposition to Aristotle. Aristotle says:

by acting righteously man becomes righteous. But Luther says: man is capable of acting righteously only if he is righteous. In this formula the anthropological presupposition of the evangelical doctrine of justification is already present." See further, id., *Der johanneische Typus der Heilslehre Luthers im Verhältnis zur paulinischen Rechtfertigungslehre* (Gütersloh, 1949).

74. *First Lectures on the Psalms*, 1513-15: WA 3:621.14 ⟨LW 11:111⟩: "... whoever will have been found to conform to ⟨the Son of God⟩ is added to Him, but whoever does not conform will be separated" ⟨from him⟩. For 'conformity to Christ', see Prenter, *Spiritus creator*, 26f.

75. *First Lectures on the Psalms*, 1513-15: WA 4:339.28 ⟨LW 11:462⟩: "... we have called that knowledge 'moral' and 'doctrine' which directs the spirit, that is, the spiritual will, as far as it applies to willing, acting, suffering, loving, hating."

76. Notes on the *Sentences* of Peter Lombard, 1510-11: WA 9:44.4: "⟨A deed of love⟩ unites us with God." For this passage see Paul Vignaux, "Luther commentateur des sentences," *EPhM* 21 (1935): 43 n. 4, 44 n. 2, and id., "Sur Luther et Ockham," *FS* 32 (1950): 28.

77. *First Lectures on the Psalms*, 1513-15: WA 3:65.8, 429.19.

78. See Luther's discussion of Ex. 11:2, 12:35, and Hos. 1:2, in *First Lectures on the Psalms*, 1513-15: WA 4:196.10.27, 3:155.3. See also Heinrich Bornkamm, *Luther und das Alte Testament* (Tübingen, 1948), 21 n. 1.

79. See Gerhard Ebeling, "Die Anfänge von Luthers Hermeneutik," *ZThK* 48 (1951): 175, 177.

80. See Johannes Heckel, *Initia iuris*, 18ff.

81. *Lectures on Romans*, 1515-16: WA 56:198.6. See also Johannes Heckel, "Recht und Gesetz, Kirche und Obrigkeit in Luthers Lehre vor dem Thesenanschlag von 1517. Eine juristische Untersuchung," *ZSRG.K* 26 (1937): 338. One can find a first trace of this identification in *First Lectures on the Psalms*, 1513-15: WA 4:134.20: "The spiritual law and the gospel are the same." See also the sermons of ca. 1514-21: WA 4:695.3.

82. See, e.g., the sermon of Dec. 4, 1517(?): WA 4:644.25; *Psalm 110 Explained*, 1518: WA 1:692.8, 701.27.

83. As early as in *First Lectures on the Psalms*, 1513-15, Luther made statements to this effect: WA 3:386.28: "The kingdom of Christ the king exists in love and in the delight of Christ's people in one another."

84. See Johannes Heckel, *Initia iuris*, 22ff.

85. For this term, see above, 51f. ⟨and 219f. and below, 362 n. 39⟩ Luther connected the Decalogue more with the secular natural law ⟨see above, 54ff.⟩ than with the divine positive law.

Notes to Chapter 3

1. According to Lau ("*Äußerliche Ordnung*," 11), "it is not possible to use the system of the two kingdoms as a starting point" for the "objective interpretation of the systematic problem of ⟨secular⟩ orders." However, the meaning of the secular orders and of the Christian's place in them cannot be fully treated without constantly considering the two kingdoms.

2. *On Secular Authority*, 1523: WA 11:249.24. For a critique, see Georg Wehrung, *Welt und Reich* (Stuttgart, 1952), 111: "Luther's differentiation between the two kingdoms was significant and will remain correct in a fundamental way; but perhaps it was only a beginning, a first statement which has to be augmented with materials from the New Testament."

3. See Harald Diem, *Luthers Lehre von den beiden Reichen*, 107ff.; Hermann Diem, *Luthers Predigt in den zwei Reichen* (Munich, 1947), 22ff.; Karl G. Steck, "Die beiden Reiche," *Stimme der Gemeinde* 3 (1951), No. 6:8ff., No. 8:13ff., No. 9:4, No. 10:13ff.; Anders Nygren, "Luthers Lehre von den zwei Reichen," *ThLZ* 74 (1949): 1ff.; Heinz-Dietrich Wendland, "Die Weltherrschaft Christi und die zwei Reiche," in *Kosmos und Ekklesia. Festschrift für Wilhelm Stählin zu seinem siebzigsten Geburtstag, 24. September 1953*, ed. by Heinz-Dietrich Wendland (Kassel, 1953), 23ff.; id., "Zur kritischen Bedeutung der neutestamentlichen Lehre von den beiden Reichen," *ThLZ* 79 (1954): 321ff.

4. *De civitate Dei* 14.13: "This is the great difference between the two cities of which we speak: one city is the community *(societas)* of godly people, the other of ungodly people..., among one the love for God, among the other the love for self dominates." See also Johannes Spörl, "Augustinus — Schöpfer einer Staatslehre?" *HJ* 74 (1955): 62ff.; id., "Die 'Civitas Dei' im Geschichtsdenken Ottos von Freising," in *La Ciudad de Dios*, 2 (El Escorial, 1956), 577ff.

5. *Second Lectures on the Psalms*, 1518-21: WA 5:139.29: "... hatred and love ⟨are⟩ the most important of all affects and works."

6. See Oepke, *Das Neue Gottesvolk*, 460: there is an absolute contrast between a coercive order on one side, and an order of freedom derived from faith on the other side.

7. Anders Nygren discussed the connection and the difference that exist between Luther's theology and that of Augustine on this point; see his *Agape and Eros*, Part II.2 (London, 1939), 343, 495ff. See also Ernst Kohlmeyer, *Von Augsburg nach Wittenberg* (Halle, 1930), 9: "One may not separate Luther's 'faith' from the convictions on which it is based, even if he might often have gone far beyond this basis. Luther's own religious experience occurred on the basis and in the form of a theology; more precisely: it occurred in the contest between two theologies, the late scholastic theology and the New Testament-Pauline theology." See further, Prenter, *Spiritus creator*, 33ff., 101; Heinrich Bornkamm, *Luthers Lehre von den zwei Reichen im Zusammenhang seiner Theologie* (Gütersloh, 1958), 16ff.; Ernst Kinder, "Gottesreich und Weltreich bei Augustin und bei Luther," in *Gedenkschrift für D. Werner Elert. Beiträge zur historischen und systematischen Theologie*, ed. by Friedrich Hübner et al. (Berlin, 1955), 24ff.

8. See, e.g., Biel, *Expositio missae*, lectio 67.D.

9. See Ernst Wolf, "Naturrecht und Gerechtigkeit," *EvTh* 7 (1947/48): 247: "In the controversy on problems of anthropology, the ⟨representatives of the⟩ two great Christian confessions of the West penetrate to fundamental matters."

10. Thielicke (*Theologische Ethik*, 1:No. 1903) correctly pointed out the significance of the doctrine of Original Sin for the concept 'natural law'.

11. *Lectures on Romans*, 1515-16: WA 56:312.7 ⟨*LW* 25:299⟩: "⟨Original Sin⟩ is not only a lack of a certain quality in the will, nor even only a lack of light in the mind or of power in the memory, but particularly it is a total lack of uprightness *(rectitudo)* and of the power of all the faculties both of body and soul and of the whole inner and outer man"; *Lectures on Psalm 51*, 1532: WA 40.II:324.8; *Second Lectures on Galatians*, 1531: WA 40.I:293.4.

12. *Lectures on Romans*, 1515-16: WA 56:13.7 ⟨LW 25:11 n. 34⟩: "The nature of the human mind is so changeable that when it turns away from one thing, it of necessity turns to another. Therefore a person who turns away from the Creator of necessity turns to the creature."

13. See Scheel, *Martin Luther*, 1:210.

14. *Lectures on Romans*, 1515-16: WA 56:205.4 ⟨LW 25:189⟩: "... the more noble, more important, and more God-pleasing parts of man (that is, heart and will)..."; *German Exposition of the Lord's Prayer for Simple Laymen*, 1519: WA 2:105.23: "... the will is the head and top of all members."

15. *Lectures on Romans*, 1515-16: WA 56:11.3.

16. *Lectures on Romans*, 1515-16: WA 56:355.15 ⟨LW 25:344⟩: "It is certainly true that the law of nature is known to all men and that our reason does speak for the best things, but what best things? It speaks for the best not according to God but according to us, that is, for things that are good in an evil way. For it seeks itself and its own in all things, but not God. This only faith does in love"; see also ibid., WA 56:178.15 ⟨LW 25:158f.⟩.

17. *Lectures on Romans*, 1515-16: WA 56:177.15, 275.20. See also Loewenich, *Luthers Theologia crucis*, 56ff. In the present context it is impossible to deal with the gradual change in Luther's understanding of *synteresis*. For details, see Emanuel Hirsch, *Lutherstudien*, 1 (Gütersloh, 1954), 109ff.; Wolf, *Peregrinatio*, 1:14ff., 86 n. 12 (literature).

18. *The Bondage of the Will*, 1525: WA 18:670.6 ⟨LW 33:115⟩: "... if God is in us, Satan is absent, and only a good will is present; if God is absent, Satan is present, and only an evil will is in us."

19. For the lack of free will in man's relationship with God, see, e.g., *Lectures on Romans*, 1515-16: WA 56:355.3; for the presence of free will in man's relationship with the Creation, see ibid., WA 56:385.19, 403.10, and *Second Lectures on Galatians*, 1531: WA 40.I:293.7: "I concede that the natural things are sound." See also Erich Kaufmann, "Die anthropologischen Grundlagen der Staatstheorien. Bemerkungen zu Rousseau, Luther und Kant," in *Rechtsprobleme in Staat und Kirche. Festschrift für Rudolf Smend zum 70. Geburtstag, 15. Januar 1952, dargebracht von Freunden, Schülern und Kollegen* (Göttingen, 1952), 182.

20. *Second Lectures on Galatians*, 1531: WA 40.I:526.3: "... the ⟨existence of a⟩ Christian is divided in two time periods: to the extent that he is flesh he is ⟨in⟩ the law ⟨period⟩, to the extent that he is spirit he is ⟨in⟩ the gospel ⟨period⟩." See also Erdmann Schott, *Fleisch und Geist nach Luthers Lehre* (Leipzig, 1928).

Notes to Chapter 4

1. For the many meanings of this term, see Heinrich Bornkamm, "Äußerer und innerer Mensch bei Luther und den Spiritualisten," in *Imago Dei. Beiträge zur theologischen Anthropologie. Gustav Krüger zum siebzigsten Geburtstag am 29. Juni 1932 dargebracht*, ed. by Heinrich Bornkamm (Giessen, 1932), 85ff.

2. For Luther, atheism was a "matter of the mouth" ⟨a person's conscience can never be free from God⟩. See *Commentary on Jonah*, 1526: WA 19:206.1. See also Herbert Olsson, *Grundproblemet i Luthers Socialetik*, 1 (Lund, 1934): 36.

3. For the knowledge of God's divinity, eternity, and power, knowledge which can be

derived from the works of the Creation, and for God's attributes (wise, just, merciful to those who call on him, good, invisible, and immortal), see *Lectures on Romans,* 1515-16: WA 56:11.12, 176.28, 177.3.13, 198.23: "God or the supreme being." See further, *Commentary on Jonah,* 1526: WA 19:205.27 ⟨LW 19:53⟩: "Here you find St. Paul's statement in Rom. 1:19 concerning the universal knowledge of God among all the heathen, that is, that the whole world talks about the Godhead and natural reason is aware that this Godhead is something superior to all other things. This is here shown by the fact that the people in our text called upon a god, heathen though they were"; ibid., WA 19:206.12 ⟨LW 19:54⟩: "That is as far as the natural light of reason sheds its rays — it regards God as kind, gracious, merciful, and benevolent. And that is indeed a bright light. However, it manifests two big defects: first, reason does admittedly believe that God is able and competent to help and to bestow; but reason does not know whether He is willing to do this also for us. That renders the position of reason unstable. Reason believes in God's might and is aware of it, but it is uncertain whether God is willing to employ this on our behalf, because in adversity it so often experiences the opposite to be true"; ibid., WA 19:206.31ff. ⟨LW 19:54f.⟩: "The second defect is this: Reason is unable to identify God properly; it cannot ascribe the Godhead to the One who is entitled to it exclusively. . . . reason . . . plays blindman's buff with God; it consistently gropes in the dark and misses the mark. It calls that God which is not God and fails to call Him God who really is God. . . . So there is a vast difference between knowing that there is a God and knowing who or what God is. Nature knows the former — it is inscribed in everybody's heart; the latter is taught only by the Holy Spirit." For similar statements, see *Lectures on Isaiah,* 1527-30: WA 31.II:235.15, and Bornkamm, *Luther und das Alte Testament,* 47 n. 1; *First Lectures on the Psalms,* 1513-15: WA 4:45.9; *Second Lectures on the Psalms,* 1518-21: WA 5:392.35.

4. See Olsson, *Grundproblemet,* 1:37ff.

5. For critical observations on this term, see Rudolf Hermann, *Fragen um den Begriff der natürlichen Theologie* (Gütersloh, 1950), 29. In the context of the present study, the term is sufficiently clear. ⟨See also below, 358 n. 10.⟩

6. For the true knowledge of God, which is present in God's kingdom at the right hand of God, and for the inadequate knowledge of God, which is present in God's kingdom at the left hand of God, see *Sermons on John, Chapters 1 and 2,* 1537-38: WA 46:669.7ff. ⟨LW 22:152f.⟩: "This is the true and thorough knowledge and way of thinking about God; it is called the knowledge of grace and truth, the 'evangelical knowledge' of God. But this knowledge does not grow up in our garden, and nature knows nothing at all about it. Reason has only a left-handed and a partial knowledge of God, based on the law of nature and of Moses; for the Law is inscribed in our hearts. But the depth of divine wisdom and of the divine purpose, the profundity of God's grace and mercy, and what eternal life is like — of these matters reason is totally ignorant. This is hidden from reason's view. It speaks of these with the same authority with which a blind man discusses color. . . . The proper way to acquire a knowledge of God is the right-handed one, to know for sure what the thoughts and the will of God are. No human being can enlighten you on this. As a matter of fact, the human race stands in need of grace through the Son. Reason is confined to the first type of knowledge of God, which proceeds from the Law; and it speaks a vague language. . . . But the fact and the knowledge that all men are born in sin and are damned, that Christ, the Son of God, is the only source of grace, and that man is saved solely through Jesus Christ, who is the grace and truth — this is not Mosaic or legal knowledge

but evangelical and Christian knowledge." For similar statements, see *The Bondage of the Will*, 1525, WA 18:719.22. — See further, Heinz-Horst Schrey, "Die Wiedergeburt des Naturrechts," *ThR*.NF 19 (1951): 39; Emanuel Hirsch, *Lutherstudien*, 1:123.

7. *First Lectures on the Psalms*, 1513-15: WA 3:151.11: "God cannot be sought except through the intellect and affect which are turned toward him."

8. Gottlieb Söhngen, *Die Einheit in der Theologie* (Munich, 1952), 120. For 'participation' in Lutheran thought, see Prenter, *Spiritus creator*, 173f.

9. *Lectures on Romans*, 1515-16: WA 56:185.27 ⟨LW 25:167⟩: "... now very many people think in an unworthy way about God and claim in bold and impudent treatises that God is this way or that way. Not one of them is willing to give to God so much honor that he puts His exceedingly great majesty above his own judgment and understanding. Instead they so raise their own opinion to the skies that they judge God with no more trouble or fear than a poor cobbler judges his leather."

10. In such a view the motivating force of man's actions is egotism — Luther called it concupiscence. For details, see Walther von Loewenich, *Luthers evangelische Botschaft* (Munich, 1946), 8; *Second Lectures on the Psalms*, 1518-21: WA 5:70.16: "The whole Creation has been given ⟨to man⟩ for the purpose of raising him up and enlightening him; but man uses it to blind himself and concentrate on himself ⟨literally: 'be curved in upon himself'⟩."

11. For the knowledge of God in the frame of law, see Werner Elert, *Morphologie des Luthertums*, 1 (Munich, 1931), 2 (Munich, 1932), 1:44; Philip S. Watson, *Um Gottes Gottheit* (Berlin, 1952), 91ff.; Wolf, *Peregrinatio*, 1:13ff.

12. *Sermons on the Ten Commandments*, 1518 (sermon of Feb. 8, 1517): WA 1:518.14; *Disputation against Scholastic Theology*, 1517, thesis 17: WA 1:225.1 ⟨LW 31:10⟩; *Second Lectures on the Psalms*, 1518-21: WA 5:73.18, 103.25, 139.12, 446.17. For the consequences of man creating God in his image for the doctrine of natural law, see Thielicke, *Theologische Ethik*, 1:No. 1928.

13. See Loewenich, *Luthers evangelische Botschaft*, 30, with a reference to Feuerbach's view of the essence of religion. When God has become the image of man, then (to use an image of Bernard of Clairvaux) man is *homo incurvatus* ⟨"man curved in upon himself"; see n. 10⟩. See also Wolf, *Peregrinatio*, 1:20.

14. *Lectures on Romans*, 1515-16: WA 56:357.2 ⟨LW 25:346⟩: "... nature ... sets itself in the place of all other things, even in the place of God, and seeks only those things which are its own and not the things of God. Therefore it is its own first and greatest idol"; see also ibid., WA 56:177.8, 178.10; *Second Lectures on the Psalms*, 1518-21: WA 5:38.18 ⟨LW 14:300⟩: "... this ungodly passion not only gives no one his own, ... but snatches everything for itself, looks for its own in everything, even in God himself..."; ibid., WA 5:296.5: "'The ungodly' ... is ... the one who has no faith yet sparkles in a brilliant appearance and pretends to be anything else but an ungodly person"; ibid., WA 5:73.18 ⟨LW 14:348⟩: "Therefore such adoration is the greatest iniquity and a denial of the most high God, since the soul ascribes to itself what belongs to God and thus sets itself up as a Baal idol and worships itself. Furthermore, it makes itself the author of its own good...." — Paul Althaus, *Um die Wahrheit des Evangeliums* (Stuttgart, 1962), 39, argued that faith has no option but to be the mortal enemy of natural theology, esp. when that theology seems to be close to Christianity.

15. *Lectures on Romans*, 1515-16: WA 56:12.7.

16. *Lectures on Romans,* 1515-16: WA 56:238.8 ⟨*LW* 25:223⟩: "... these men ⟨of Rom. 3:11⟩ are too righteous, too understanding, too much given to seeking, so that they are incorrigible in their minds."

17. *Admonition to Peace,* 1525: WA 18:319.3.

18. *Lectures on Genesis,* 1535-45: WA 42:106.34: "Our will ⟨turns⟩ God into the devil."

19. *First Lectures on the Psalms,* 1513-15: WA 3:273.31: "From the beginning of the world to its end there are two families of man ⟨literally: 'generations'⟩, one consisting of ⟨godly⟩ people, the other of ungodly people"; ibid., WA 3:131.31; *Sermons on Genesis,* 1523-24: WA 14:167.10; *Second Lectures on the Psalms,* 1518-21: WA 5:126.22: "⟨There are⟩ two families of man, that oppose each other: in the one, people depend on their own strength, in the other, they depend on God's grace ..."; ibid., WA 5:445.16.

20. Sermons of ca. 1514-21: WA 4:706.32ff.: the two kingdoms, that of Christ and that of the world; *Sermons on the First Epistle of St. Peter,* 1523: WA 12:321.33: "The devil is the prince of the world and rules it; his citizens are the people of the world." See also Lau, "*Äußerliche Ordnung,*" 94; Wünsch, *Ethik des Politischen,* 149.

21. In the following, the problem of the 'pious' heathen will not be discussed. For some materials on this topic, see Erich Seeberg, *Grundzüge der Theologie Luthers* (Stuttgart, 1940), 109; Watson, *Um Gottes Gottheit,* 116.

22. *Second Lectures on Galatians,* 1531: WA 40.I:46.7; *First Lectures on the Psalms,* 1513-15: WA 4:447.3: "earthlings."

23. *First Lectures on the Psalms,* 1513-15: WA 3:429.26 ("mundus intellectualis" in the sense of spiritual world), 505.31, 511.14, 515.8, 524.18, 533.2, 590.4.17.27; ibid., WA 4:444.30; *Lectures on Hebrews,* 1517-18: WA 57.III:197.21.

24. For Luther's personalistic thinking about law, see Johannes Heckel, "Recht und Gesetz," *ZSRG*.K 26 (1937): 305ff. Gustaf Wingren, *Luthers Lehre vom Beruf* (Munich, 1952), 29, argued that "the understanding of the secular governance as a governance over a group of people (the evil ones), and of the spiritual governance as a governance over another group of people (the Christians) ... shortchanges ⟨the situation⟩. ... In reality, a Christian is simultaneously *peccator* and *iustus* ⟨sinner and righteous⟩, and as *peccator* he is subject to the law." Yet the formula 'simul peccator et iustus' designates indeed a "group of people," that is, the justified people of Christ's kingdom (see Elert, *Morphologie,* 1:436), in contrast to another "group of people," that is, the non-Christians in the kingdom of the world. See also, above, 92f. Wingren was nevertheless correct when he warned us ("Geistliches und weltliches Regiment bei Luther," *ThZ* 3 [1947]: 263ff.) not to understand the two governances as "human collective entities," such as church and state. The governances are modes of ruling two groups of people but not two institutions. For the argument that one may not destroy the *communicatio idiomatum* ⟨sharing of specific qualities; for this term, explained however in a different context, see Edmund Schlink, *Theology of the Lutheran Confessions* (Philadelphia, 1961), 187ff., esp. 190⟩ manifested in the formula 'simultaneously sinner and justified', see Olsson, *Grundproblemet,* 1:142f., esp. 143: "Faith really means a total inner sovereignty or freedom, which manifests itself also outwardly (love)." See also Bring, *Dualismen hos Luther,* 19: "According to Luther, a human being is 'spirit' to the degree that he or she is ruled by God, and 'flesh' to the degree that he or she is ruled by the devil. The dualism between flesh and spirit is therefore based on the dualism between God and the devil. The boundary line between the two hostile kingdoms runs through man, but not in such a way that one part of man belongs to one king-

dom, and another part belongs to the other kingdom. Man is wholly and entirely spirit or flesh. In fact, one can say that, according to Luther, man is entirely both spirit and flesh, *simul iustus et peccator.*" (See also ibid., 48.) Bring's position raises the question whether God and the devil rule jointly ⟨Heckel wrote "Kondominium"⟩. ⟨In any case,⟩ Bring's statement, ibid., 23, to the effect that justification means the collapse of the devil's power, does not fit together with the text quoted. — Bornkamm, *Luthers Lehre von den zwei Reichen,* 17, agrees with our view.

25. Such an institution would have fixed areas of competencies, which would belong to one or the other kingdom. Ragnar Bring was correct when he argued ("Lutherische Theologie angesichts der ökumenischen Arbeit," *Luthertum* 1 [1951]: 24): "These kingdoms are not to be understood as quantitative entities" in the sense of "a division between something which always belongs to one area and something which ⟨always⟩ belongs to another area." — According to Holstein (*Grundlagen,* 76), the two kingdoms are "two conditions of the soul."

26. *Psalm 127 Explained,* 1524: WA 15:370.8.

27. *Psalm 110 Explained,* 1518: WA 1:701.27: ". . . his ⟨i.e., Christ's⟩ kingdom is spiritual, a spiritual people, a spiritual power . . ."; see also ibid., WA 1:702.27.

28. See Gustaf Törnvall, *Geistliches und weltliches Regiment bei Luther* (Munich, 1947).

29. *Psalm 110 Explained,* 1518: WA 1:703.31: "Christ is the king and the head of righteousness; from that head righteousness must flow into all his members. . . ."

30. Sermon of Apr. 8, 1537: WA 45:70.3: "When I speak of the kingdom of heaven, I mean God and Christ with the angels and the saints dead and alive. 'World' is the devil with his angels and all the evil people on earth."

31. See above, 25.

32. E.g., Biel, *Expositio missae,* lectio 67.D.

33. Instead of other authors, see Friedrich A. Freiherr von der Heydte, *Die Geburtsstunde des souveränen Staates* (Regensburg, 1952), 19: "The basis of a kingdom is . . . a people. The idea 'people' as the nucleus of political order cannot be separated from the idea 'kingdom.'"

34. Heinz Brunotte was correct when he criticized a spatial understanding of the Lutheran concept 'kingdom of God'; see his article "Obrigkeit," in *Biblisch-theologisches Handwörterbuch zur Lutherbibel,* ed. by Edo Osterloh and Hans Engelland (Göttingen, 1952), 414.

35. Kurt Matthes was totally wrong when he argued (*Das Corpus Christianum bei Luther im Lichte seiner Erforschung* [Berlin, 1929], 14) that the *Christian quality* ⟨emphasis by this ed.⟩ of the Christian body *(corpus christianum)* "belongs to that institution ⟨i.e., the Christian body⟩ as such. That quality may not always be present in the members of that institution, and even if it were, this presence would be purely accidental and would have nothing to do with the institution itself. . . . The institution by itself is Christian. At this point it seems that Christian sacramental thinking penetrated from the idea 'church' into the institutional sphere."

36. This is esp. the case in the kingdom of the world. See *Psalm 117 Explained,* 1530: WA 31.I:233.36: "When we read in Scripture about kings, then we may not only think of the person and his crown; we have to think of his whole governance with laws, rights, customs, usages, and practices, ⟨things which⟩ make up his kingdom. . . ." For the office of the Word as the only office in the church which exists by the divine law, see above, 85.

Notes to Page 28

37. See above, 124f. and 256 n. 29. For 'head', see also sermons of ca. 1514-21: WA 4:715.19: "⟨Christ⟩ is called the head because it pours the force of life and the power of feeling and moving into the whole body, transfers them to all the members, and all life depends on it, ⟨or⟩ as the grammarians like to say, all meaning is derived from ⟨the 'head' word in the sense of first word⟩."

38. *Psalm 117 Explained,* 1530: WA 30.I:235.36; *The First 25 Psalms Explained at the Coburg,* 1530: WA 31.I:307.28: "The whole human race says in its heart that there is no God"; for this passage, see Rudolf Hermann, *Von der Klarheit der Heiligen Schrift* (Berlin, 1958), 60ff. For Satan as the prince of the world, see *The Bondage of the Will,* 1525: WA 18:750.33, 782.31 ⟨LW 33:238, 287⟩, and Harmannus Obendiek, *Der Teufel bei Martin Luther* (Berlin, 1931), 203.

39. *On Secular Authority,* 1523: WA 11:251.1: "All who are not Christians belong in the kingdom of the world or under the law."

40. *First Lectures on the Psalms,* 1513-15: WA 3:532.22; *Psalm 110 Explained,* 1518: WA 1:706.15: "... ⟨the devil's⟩ body is the world." See also *Decretum Gratiani* c.9. C.XII. q.2 ⟨Friedberg 1:689⟩: "The devil's members, vile children."

41. *The Babylonian Captivity of the Church,* 1520: WA 6:560.7: "... believers in name, unbelievers in substance..."; *On Secular Authority,* 1523: WA 11:251.35: "... the world and the crowd ⟨of people⟩ are and remain unchristian, even if all of them are baptized and are called Christians"; *First Lectures on the Psalms,* 1513-15: WA 3:584.32, 598.32.

42. *Second Lectures on the Psalms,* 1518-21: WA 5:350.33. "⟨To Ps. 10:16; Luther text:⟩ 'Heathen ⟨literally: "nations"⟩ in God's land' has to be understood as the Christians who confess Christ according to outward appearance but in reality are heathen since they deny Christ through their actions; ⟨therefore⟩ they are unworthy occupants of ⟨God's⟩ land"; ibid., WA 5:479.33: "... domestic enemies..."

43. *The Bondage of the Will,* 1525: WA 18:659.6 ⟨LW 33:98⟩: "For what is the whole human race without the Spirit but... the kingdom of the devil, a confused chaos of darkness [Gen. 1:2]?"

44. *Sermons on the Ten Commandments,* 1518 (sermon of Dec. 21, 1516): WA 1:491.19: "Great God, when will we open our eyes so that we might recognize what the world is? Is it not the worst perversion of all?" See also Luther to John Heß: March 12, 1524: WA.B 3:253.4f.

45. Luther to Michael Stifel: ca. May 4, 1527: WA.B 4:199.10f.; to some citizens exiled from Oschatz because of their faith: Jan. 20, 1533: WA.B 6:422.8ff. ⟨the devil is the host in the world, and the world is his house⟩.

46. See, e.g., n. 36: "whole governance"; "his kingdom."

47. *Second Lectures on Galatians,* 1531: WA 40.I:97.7: "The kingdom of the world is sinning and blaspheming all things which pertain to God"; ibid., WA 40.I:94.4; *Sermons on Matthew, Chapters 5-7,* 1530-32: WA 32:410.27 ⟨LW 21:134⟩: "It is really disgraceful, the way the world carries on: it may be pious or it may be wicked, but either way it is worthless. Either it tries openly to be a devil with its wicked works, or it tries to be God Himself with its good works. And both of these are intolerable. Therefore no one can do a truly good work unless he is a Christian. If he does it as a man, then he is not doing it for the glory of God, but for his own glory and advantage. On the other hand, if he claims that it is for the glory of God, that is a lie that smells to high heaven"; ibid., WA 32:448.22 ⟨LW 21:180⟩: "The world is one big whorehouse, completely submerged in greed."

48. See above, 25; *Second Lectures on the Psalms,* 1518-21: WA 5:38.14: "No creature lives for itself or serves itself except man and the devil"; *Sermons on John, Chapters 14 and 15,* 1537: WA 45:609.29: "This is the governance of the world: nothing is of value and practiced but lust, greed, and haughtiness"; *First Lectures on the Psalms,* 1513-15: WA 3:407.32, 4:363.37.

49. *Magnificat,* 1521: WA 7:590.5: "As long as the world exists, there has to be authority, governance, power . . ."; ibid., WA 7:592.13: "In this life such . . . differences among persons and estates have to remain on earth . . ."; *The Book of Deuteronomy with Notes,* 1525: WA 14:655.30: ". . . the world ⟨cannot exist without . . .⟩ inequalities among persons . . ."; ibid., WA 14:701.13. For the inequalities among people under the secular governance and the lack of such inequalities among people under the spiritual governance, see sermons of 1527: WA 23:735.14; *Sermons on John, Chapters 14 and 15,* 1537: WA 45:602.36: "In secular governance there have to be . . . differences among persons and estates, . . . but I ⟨Christ is speaking⟩ shall create a governance in which all people are equal before me." See also *Second Lectures on Galatians,* 1531: WA 40.I:178.9; *Admonition to Peace,* 1525: WA 18:327. 6; sermon of Feb. 1, 1534: WA 37:275.25; Olsson, *Grundproblemet,* 1:23f.

50. *Psalm 101 Explained,* 1534-35: WA 51:242.1: "God has subjected and entrusted secular governance to reason because that governance is to rule not Salvation of souls and eternal goods but only corporeal and temporal goods, which God subjects to man"; *Lectures on Psalms 120–134,* 1532-33: WA 40.III:237.3: "Reason and human wisdom want to be the cause, ruler, and lord of public affairs."

51. *On Secular Authority,* 1523: WA 11:250.10 ⟨LW 45:89⟩: ". . . the righteous man of his own accord does all and more than the law demands. But the unrighteous do nothing that the law demands; therefore, they need the law to instruct, constrain, and compel them to do good"; sermon of Oct. 27, 1537: WA 45:190.29: "I ⟨Christ is speaking⟩ do not want it to be the way things are in the world where one king or prince is lord above the other. But in my kingdom the lowest is the highest, he who serves the most and is the first servant ⟨of all⟩ is the greatest."

52. *Whether Soldiers, Too, Can Be Saved,* 1526: WA 19:640.4 ⟨LW 46:112⟩: ". . . the sword shows the nature of the children under it: people who, if they dared, would be desperate scoundrels"; sermons of 1523: WA 12:675.15: ". . . whoever is under secular governance is still far from the kingdom of heaven for all of this ⟨i.e., the secular kingdom and its governance⟩ belongs in hell."

53. *Open Letter on the Harsh Book against the Peasants,* 1525: WA 18:389.22 ⟨LW 46:69f.⟩: ". . . the kingdom of the world is a kingdom of wrath and severity. In it there are only punishment, repression, judgment, and condemnation to restrain the wicked and protect the good. For this reason it has the sword. . . ." For the pessimistic view of man, esp. 'Mr. Omnes' ⟨the masses⟩, see Olsson, *Grundproblemet,* 1:27. See also *Decretum Gratiani* c.1. D.IV ⟨Friedberg 1:5⟩: ". . . laws have been made so that through man's fear ⟨of them⟩ impudence is checked and integrity is ⟨kept⟩ safe among the wicked, and in those who are wicked the capability to do ⟨evil⟩ is checked ⟨because they⟩ fear the punishment."

54. *On Secular Authority,* 1523: WA 11:262.7 ⟨LW 45:105⟩: "The temporal government ⟨literally: 'governance'⟩ has laws which extend no further than to life and property and external affairs on earth . . ."; ibid., WA 11:263.26 ⟨LW 45:107⟩: ". . . we cannot conceive how an authority could or should act in a situation except where it can see, know, judge, con-

demn, change, and modify"; ibid., WA 11:266.9 ⟨LW 45:111⟩: "A human ordinance cannot possibly extend its authority into heaven and over souls; it is limited to the earth, to external dealings men have with one another, where they can see, know, judge, evaluate, punish, and acquit"; Luther to the City Council of Danzig (additional note): May 5(7?), 1525: WA.B 3:484.10.

55. *First Lectures on the Psalms,* 1513-15: WA 3:17.7 ⟨LW 10:13⟩: ". . . although the law could restrain the hand through fear of punishment and provoke to works through the hope of good things, it could nevertheless neither loose nor bind the will inwardly; it could not, I say, loose toward freedom, nor bind its desires. For this happens only by the bonds of love, which not the Law but Christ has given in His own spirit." Therefore in comparison with Christ, the only just king, the kings of the world as judges are only "picture kings"; see *Second Lectures on the Psalms,* 1518-21: WA 5:294.16. See also sermon of Nov. 4, 1537: WA 45:253.12; below, 322 n. 168, 384 n. 6.

Notes to Chapter 5

1. *On Secular Authority,* 1523: WA 11:250.26: "By nature no man is a Christian or godly, but totally a sinner and evil . . ."; *First Lectures on the Psalms,* 1513-15: WA 3:136.25: ". . . people come forth into the world from the womb of the mother and are thrown into the wrath and the power ⟨literally: 'hand'⟩ of the devil; therefore they are children of wrath."

2. *The Bondage of the Will,* 1525: WA 18:750.32 ⟨LW 33:238⟩: Scripture passages, that are neither ambiguous nor obscure, establish "that Satan is by far the most cunning and powerful ruler of this world . . . , and as long as he reigns the human will is not free nor under its own control, but is a slave of sin and Satan, and can only will what its master wills." See also Luther's negative judgments about the kingdom of the world in Lau, *Luthers Lehre von den beiden Reichen,* 33 n. 67.

3. *The Bondage of the Will,* 1525: WA 18:658.13 ⟨LW 33:97f.⟩: "As if we did not know that the world is the kingdom of Satan, where besides the blindness we are born with from our carnal nature, we are under the dominion of the most mischievous spirits, so that we are hardened in that very blindness and imprisoned in a darkness no longer human but demonic." See also above, 257 n. 38.

4. *Second Lectures on Galatians,* 1531: WA 40.I:97.2: "Through his Son, God pulls us out of the world"; sermon of March 24, 1537: WA 45:50.26: "When I am baptized and believe in Christ, I am transferred out of the devil's kingdom into Christ's kingdom."

5. *Open Letter on the Harsh Book against the Peasants,* 1525: WA 18:389.19: ". . . God's kingdom is a kingdom of grace and mercy. . . ."

6. Luther tried to make this clear by presenting different characteristics of the two kingdoms to his audience: The spiritual kingdom is a kingdom of listening, the kingdom of the world is a kingdom of seeing; sermon of Aug. 6, 1545: WA 51:11.29. Or, the spiritual kingdom "stands in the sense ⟨or: 'ability'⟩ of listening," the kingdom of the world "stands in doing and pressuring"; ibid., WA 51:13.31. Important for Luther was not the use of a different sense or the difference between the active and the passive posture, but whether or not these activities occur in faith; ibid., WA 51:13.32: Christ's kingdom stands only in the sense of listening, i.e., "that I hear the Word, accept it, and believe it." For 'in-

ternal listening', see Luther's notes on the *Sentences* of Peter Lombard, 1510-11: WA 9:92.30. See also *Lectures on Psalm 45,* 1532: WA 40.II:481.6: "⟨In the spiritual kingdom⟩ all things happen in a way that is contrary to that of the kingdom of the world"; see also ibid., WA 40.II:523.7. — For the spiritual "conformity between the interpreter and Holy Scripture," see Peter Meinhold, *Luthers Sprachphilosophie* (Berlin, 1958), 13, 15.

7. *First Lectures on the Psalms,* 1513-15: WA 3:480.35: ". . . the world is always and in all things in opposition to Christ"; *Second Commentary on Galatians,* 1535: WA 40.I:293.16: "The kingdom of the human reason has to be separated from the spiritual kingdom the farthest distance"; sermon of Nov. 1, 1537: WA 45:212.6: "I am the king of truth ⟨Christ is speaking⟩. The world is full of deceit, and it is obsessed by infidelity. In its core, the external kingdom is lying to God. I have a kingdom, ⟨and⟩ that is truth."

8. Even if they are only beginners in the faith.

9. *On Secular Authority,* 1523: WA 11:249.26: "All who truly believe in Christ and ⟨belong to⟩ Christ belong to God's kingdom"; ibid., WA 11:271.21; sermon of Dec. 15, 1532: WA 36:383.31: ". . . his kingdom is called the kingdom of the blind, of the poor, of sinners, etc.; all that have nothing belong in this kingdom"; *Postilla for the Home,* 1544: WA 52:24.26.

10. *On Secular Authority,* 1523: WA 11:259.19.

11. *First Lectures on the Psalms,* 1513-15: WA 3:532.25: ". . . the body of Christ, ⟨i.e.,⟩ those who hang on to the Lord until the future glory . . ."; sermon of Nov. 22, 1537: WA 45:303.4: "The Christian church ⟨is⟩ an assembled crowd of many people who hang together in their head."

12. *The Sacrament of the Body and Blood of Christ, against the Fanatics,* 1526: WA 19:512.1.9; *Psalm 117 Explained,* 1530: WA 31.I:241.13.

13. This term is shaped according to the Canon law concept 'Geistlicher Stand' or 'status ecclesiasticus' ⟨spiritual estate, ecclesiastical estate⟩: *Decretum Gratiani* c.1. D.23 ⟨§ 1; Friedberg 1:77⟩. For Luther, see *To the Christian Nobility,* 1520: WA 6:404.13.21 ("christlicher Stand" or "Christian estate"), and above, 119f.

14. *The Babylonian Captivity of the Church,* 1520: WA 6:566.16: "A Christian is a person who has been anointed with the oil of the Holy Spirit and sanctified in body and soul" ⟨hence he is a 'spiritual' person or a member of the 'spiritual estate'⟩; *To the Christian Nobility,* 1520: WA 6:407.13: "All Christians are truly members of the spiritual estate." In addition to this *general meaning,* Luther used 'spiritual estate' in the *narrowest possible sense,* designating the ministry of the Word, instituted by divine law; see, e.g., *On Keeping Children in School,* 1530: WA 30.II:527.1ff. ⟨One of the German words for pastor is *Geistlicher.*⟩ He also used it in *a less narrow sense,* designating the ecclesiastical, professional estate in contrast to secular estates. See, e.g., *The Large Catechism,* 1529: WA 30.I:162.8 ⟨BC 393.209⟩; *On Keeping Children in School,* 1530: WA 30.II:519.20; *On the Ban,* 1520: WA 6:70.12: "It is not right for a Christian ⟨i.e., a member of the spiritual estate in the general meaning⟩, much less for a member of the spiritual estate ⟨i.e., the clergy⟩, to harm someone"; *On Good Works,* 1520: WA 6:228.21, 240.28 ⟨'spiritual estate' for clergy⟩, 256.16 ⟨contrast of spiritual estate, i.e., clergy, to secular estate⟩. Luther used 'spiritual estate' even in a *wide sense,* designating a secular estate that lives in faith, such as marriage; see below, 400 nn. 4 and 6; *Commentary on 1 Corinthians, Chapter 7,* 1523: WA 12:105.27: ". . . nothing should be called spiritual unless in the heart, where the Spirit rules, the inner life of faith is present. But since one calls spiritual also what externally, corporeally, hap-

pens through the Spirit of faith, we can now ... understand that the estate of marriage should justly be called spiritual and, ⟨conversely,⟩ the monastic orders be called secular estates" ⟨because, according to Luther, the members of these orders lack that inner life of faith⟩. And finally, Luther used 'spiritual estate' to designate the *attitude of a Christian* as a person in contrast to the attitude which that Christian has when he holds a secular office; see, e.g., *Sermons on Matthew, Chapters 5–7*, 1530-32: WA 32:387.8: "⟨The difference between⟩ the secular and the spiritual estate, or between Christ and the kingdom of the world."

15. See above, 255 n. 23.

16. *First Lectures on the Psalms*, 1513-15: WA 4:123.23: "... Christ ... sits as king and judge ... over spiritual people ..."; *Sermons on Genesis*, 1527: WA 24:50.15: "... all heavenly people, that is, the believers"; see also ibid., WA 24:50.33.

17. Not in a local community! *Second Lectures on Galatians*, 1531: WA 40.I:662.7: "'Our law and city are in heaven' ⟨see Phil. 3:20⟩, not local, but as much as each Christian believes, so much he is in heaven" ⟨follows Eph. 1:3⟩.

18. *On Secular Authority*, 1523: WA 11:252.17: "... at all times Christians are a minority living among non-Christians."

19. *Against the Bull of Antichrist* ⟨Latin text⟩, 1520: WA 6:607.2: "... the church spread throughout the world ..."; *On Secular Authority*, 1523: WA 11:251.37: "The Christians live far from one another (as one says) ..."; *On the War against the Turks*, 1529: WA 30.II:117.7.

20. *On Secular Authority*, 1523: WA 11:263.3: "No one but God alone ... should and may command souls."

21. *On Christian Freedom* ⟨Latin text⟩, 1520: WA 7:56.22: "He himself rules ... in heavenly and spiritual matters"; *On Secular Authority*, 1523: WA 11:252.35: "... he is king over the Christians and rules without law, solely through his Holy Spirit"; Luther to the City Council of Danzig (additional note): May 5(7?), 1525: WA.B 3:484.10: "... the spiritual governance of the gospel ..."; *A Sermon against the Turk*, 1529: WA 30.II:179.1: "⟨Christ's⟩ kingdom is not corporeally on earth"; *Against the Roman Papacy*, 1545: WA 54:261.32: "Christ's kingdom is a spiritual and heavenly kingdom; even though it is on earth and has to exist corporeally, it does not rule corporeally."

22. *First Lectures on the Psalms*, 1513-15: WA 4:259.28: "... Christ does not rule over a corporeal kingdom but a spiritual and heavenly one ..."; sermon of March 25, 1537: WA 45:55.17: "⟨Christ's⟩ kingdom ⟨is⟩ in the height, it is not corporeal and low, but a kingdom ⟨of the⟩ height, i.e., spiritual, heavenly. Therefore it is called the kingdom of the heavens, i.e., not worldly, transitory, but heavenly."

23. *On Secular Authority*, 1523: WA 11:258.22: "Those who belong to ⟨Christ⟩ are being ruled inwardly ... ⟨with⟩ God's Word and Spirit."

24. *Psalm 110 Explained*, 1518: WA 1:692.8: "... the kingdom of the Lord Christ ⟨is⟩ a spiritual, hidden kingdom ..."; sermons of ca. 1514-21: WA 4:716.5.

25. *Magnificat*, 1521: WA 7:565.19: "... God does not look at works but at the heart and faith."

26. *On Secular Authority*, 1523: WA 11:262.9 ⟨LW 45:105⟩: "... God cannot and will not permit anyone but himself to rule over the soul."

27. *Sermons on John, Chapters 14 and 15*, 1537: WA 45:669.30 ⟨LW 24:228⟩: "Christ is speaking exclusively of His spiritual kingdom and government ⟨literally: 'governance'⟩, in which God Himself dwells, reigns, and works through His Word and Spirit toward a spiri-

tual, eternal life. For this is God's own realm ⟨literally: "governance"⟩: to baptize, to preach the Gospel, to administer the Sacrament ⟨i.e., the Lord's Supper⟩, to console and strengthen timid and grieving consciences, to terrify and punish the wicked with excommunication, to perform works of love and mercy, and to endure the cross."

28. *On Secular Authority,* 1523: WA 11:271.3: "Among Christians there is no superior other than only Christ himself."

29. ⟨In the sense of ecclesiastical.⟩

30. *On Secular Authority,* 1523: WA 11:266.18: "... the soul is not under the authority of the emperor..."; ibid., WA 11:263.14: "... the soul is taken out of the hand of all people and is subordinated to God's authority alone"; above, 258 n. 54.

31. See Johannes Heckel, *Initia iuris,* 114. For the difference between the authority and power which is Christ's alone in the spiritual governance and the authority and power which is granted to secular potentates in the secular governance, see Törnvall, *Geistliches und weltliches Regiment bei Luther,* 85.

32. *Psalm 117 Explained,* 1530: WA 31.I:233.19 ⟨*LW* 14:14⟩: "... the kingdom of Christ is not a temporal, transitory, earthly kingdom, ruled with laws and regulations, but a spiritual, heavenly, and eternal kingdom that must be ruled without and above all laws, regulations, and outward means"; ibid., WA 31.I:241.27 ⟨*LW* 14:23⟩: "Our reason always wants to mix the two, making out of the Christian estate a worldly or ecclesiastical structure ⟨literally: 'a worldly or spiritual (in the sense of ecclesiastical) governance'⟩ framed and governed by laws and works"; sermons of 1523: WA 12:675.4: "... the gospel, or the kingdom of God, is nothing other than an estate or governance in which there is only forgiveness of sin. Wherever there is not such a governance in which sins are forgiven, there the gospel and God's kingdom are not present. Therefore one has to separate the two kingdoms from each other: ⟨one⟩ in which sin is punished, ⟨the other⟩ in which sin is forgiven, ⟨one⟩ in which law is enforced, ⟨the other⟩ in which law is given up. In God's kingdom... law is not enforced, one does not even get involved in law; there are present only forgiveness, giving up ⟨the law⟩, giving, ⟨and⟩ no wrath or punishment ⟨can be found there⟩, only brotherly service and doing good."

33. *On Secular Authority,* 1523: WA 11:259.1: "⟨God's kingdom⟩ exists only through God's Word and Spirit"; *The Small Catechism,* 1529: WA 30.I:296.27 ⟨*BC* 345.6⟩: "... the Holy Spirit has called me through the Gospel, enlightened me with his gifts, and sanctified and preserved me in true faith, just as he calls, gathers, enlightens, and sanctifies the whole Christian church on earth and preserves it in union with Jesus Christ in the one true faith." — See also Kurt D. Schmidt, "Luthers Lehre vom Heiligen Geist," in *Schrift und Bekenntnis. Zeugnisse lutherischer Theologie. Festschrift für Simon Schöffel,* ed. by Volkmar Herntrich and Theodor Knolle (Hamburg, Berlin, 1950), 154ff.

34. Luther to the City Council of Danzig (additional note): May 5(7?), 1525: WA.B 3:484.5. See also below, 358 n. 13.

35. *Psalm 110 Explained,* 1518: WA 1:694.22; *On Secular Authority,* 1523: WA 11:258.26; sermon of Sept. 30, 1537: WA 45:145.7: "We hear often that these two ⟨types of⟩ sermons are ⟨preached⟩ in the church: 1. the doctrine about the law, 2. the doctrine about grace. The one of these two that disappears takes the other one along; whenever one is preached truly, it brings the other with itself."

36. *First Lectures on the Psalms,* 1513-15: WA 3:17.36 ⟨*LW* 10:14f.⟩: "... Christ does not want His rule ⟨literally: 'kingdom,' in the sense of governance⟩ to rest on force and vio-

lence, because then it would not stand firm, but He wants to be served willingly and with the heart and the affections. In this way His kingdom is eternal and will not be destroyed, since it does not rest on force."

37. *First Lectures on the Psalms*, 1513-15: WA 3:262.38, 263.3.14.18, 4:234.31; *Postilla for the Home*, 1544: WA 52:26.6.

38. Lau, *Luthers Lehre von den beiden Reichen*, 58.

39. Luther to Michael Dressel: June 23, 1516: WA.B 1:47.41: ". . . who willingly endures the cross . . . , experiences ⟨true⟩ peace."

40. *First Lectures on the Psalms*, 1513-15: WA 3:17.32.36 ⟨see n. 36⟩; sermon of Dec. 4, 1517(?): WA 4:644.25.

41. *First Lectures on the Psalms*, 1513-15: WA 3:379.39, 380.4.5 ⟨*LW* 10:319⟩; ⟨Heckel's text and the translation are selected from these lines in Luther's text⟩. See also *Second Lectures on the Psalms*, 1518-21: WA 5:257.2: ". . . the power of Christ and of the church is not derived from the world, ⟨Christ⟩ does not call on the help of secular power, does not turn toward fire and death, does not put trust in the weapons of kings and princes."

42. *First Lectures on the Psalms*, 1513-15: WA 3:259.26: ". . . Christ's kingdom begins, stands, and continues to stand in love and not in violence." See also Hermann Jordan, *Luthers Staatsauffassung* (Munich, 1917), 36; Julius Binder, *Luthers Staatsauffassung* (Erfurt, 1924), 12 n. 25.

43. Therefore 'Christian freedom' (see the following discussion) may not be played against 'Christian brotherly love'. See *Second Lectures on the Psalms*, 1518-21: WA 5:403.24ff.

44. See above, 97f.

45. *Sermons on the First Epistle of St. Peter*, 1523: WA 12:331.32: ". . . among the Christian people there should not and may not be coercion. If one begins to bind consciences with external laws, then soon faith and Christian life disappear."

46. Wilhelm Maurer has demonstrated (*Freiheit eines Christenmenschen*, 29) the significance of the dialectic of freedom and servitude for the difference between the two kingdoms. It is important to remember that for Luther the concept 'freedom' was governed by the concept 'law'; see *On Christian Freedom* ⟨Latin text⟩, 1520: WA 7:50.14 ⟨*LW* 31:344f.⟩, where Luther mentioned first the "righteous" and then the "free" man.

47. *On Monastic Vows*, 1521: WA 8:613.9: ". . . ⟨evangelical⟩ freedom is by divine law . . ."; ibid., WA 8:614.1; *Theses on Monastic Vows*, 1521: WA 8:330.3: "Evangelical freedom is by divine law and gift."

48. These three basic rights exist only on the foundation of faith. If one of them jeopardizes faith, then "let love perish so that faith may stand"; *Second Lectures on Galatians*, 1531: WA 40.I:201.1. For the connection of truth with love, see Luther to Wolfgang Capito: Jan. 17, 1522: WA.B 2:431.24; for the connection of faith with love, see ibid., WA.B 2:433.126 ⟨*LW* 48:No. 113⟩. See further, sermon of July 7, 1545: WA 49:786.12: "Love puts up with all things, faith with nothing."

49. Sermon of May 1, 1540: WA 49:165.11.

50. *The Babylonian Captivity of the Church*, 1520: WA 6:559.2. See also below, 398 n. 82.

51. For natural reason this light of faith is darkness and an enigma. See *Second Lectures on Galatians*, 1531: WA 40.I:204.5f.; sermon of Aug. 15, 1520: WA 4:646.13: from Christ's sufferings and wounds "flows the light of a right reason . . ."; for the date of this

sermon, see *Luthers Werke in Auswahl*, 5, ed. by Erich Vogelsang (Berlin, 1933), 428, n. to line 16. ⟨For the date of this sermon, see now Martin Elze, "Das Verständnis der Passion Jesu im ausgehenden Mittelalter und bei Luther," in *Geist und Geschichte der Reformation. Festgabe Hanns Rückert zum 65. Geburtstag dargebracht von Freunden, Kollegen und Schülern*, ed. by Heinz Liebing et al. (Berlin, 1966), 145 n. 87.⟩

52. For a critique of the assumption that the kingdom of the world is autonomous, see Loewenich, *Luthers evangelische Botschaft*, 49f.

53. *On Secular Authority*, 1523: WA 11:251.4: "... in addition to the Christian estate and the kingdom of God, God has instituted another governance and has subjected ⟨the unbelievers⟩ to the sword"; sermon of Nov. 21, 1537: WA 45:291.1: "According to his divinity, Christ is lord over caesar, kings, and whoever is the greatest on earth.... Not only is he the head over the church, but he also rules over kings and emperors..."; sermon of Nov. 22. 1537: WA 45:299.2: "According to his humanity he is our head..." ⟨Heckel quoted from the notes taken by someone in the audience; see also the edited version of this sermon, WA 45:298.41ff.: "'Christ is the head of [his] congregation and the savior of his body' [see Eph.5:23]. Also, 'we are members of his body...' [Eph. 5:30]. He became man, born of a woman, so that he would become our head and we his body and the members of his body. There was no other means for us to come to God. If we were to come to God, God's Son had to become man and our head so that we might cling to him as our head and through him come to God."⟩

54. See Hermann, *Fragen um den Begriff der natürlichen Theologie*, 24.

55. *Psalm 110 Explained*, 1518: WA 1:692.5, 707.8. Luther followed the biblical usage of 'head'. E.g., the Vulgate text of Am. 6:1 has the phrase "heads of the people" ⟨NRSV: "the notables of the first of the nations"⟩; see *First Lectures on the Psalms*, 1513-15: WA 3:388.12, 403.14. Or, in the Vulgate text of Isa. 9:14f. "head" (in the sense of elders and dignitaries) is connected with the people of Israel; see WA 3:403.16. But Luther transferred 'head' from the secular area to the Jewish religious community (see WA 3:388.12.32) and the church. Holl's argument (*Luther*, 340 n. 3) to the effect that Luther always used 'head' connected with Christ only when he dealt with Christ's church, "as the Scholastics did," is incorrect; it is also incorrect regarding the Scholastics.

56. *The Bondage of the Will*, 1525: WA 18:752.12 ⟨LW 33:240⟩: "... our contention is that man apart from the grace of God remains nonetheless under the general omnipotence of God, who does, moves, and carries along all things in a necessary and infallible course, but that what man does as he is thus carried along is nothing, in the sense that it is worth nothing in the sight of God, and is not reckoned as anything but sin. So in the realm of grace, anyone who is without love is nothing"; see also ibid., WA 18:709.18, 710.3 ⟨LW 33:175f., 176f.⟩.

57. *Open Letter on the Harsh Book against the Peasants*, 1525: WA 18:389.31: "The secular kingdom is nothing other than the servant of divine wrath over the evil ones and a true prelude to hell and eternal death; its office and work is not to be merciful, but severe, serious, and wrathful." See also above, 28f., and below, 326 n. 210.

58. Ps. 18:26 ⟨NRSV text; Heckel quoted the Vulgate text⟩; see also 2 Sam. 22:27. For Luther's comments on the Psalm verse, see *First Lectures on the Psalms*, 1513-15: WA 3:127.19 ⟨LW 10:123f.⟩, and *Second Lectures on the Psalms*, 1518-21: WA 5:27.16 ⟨LW 14:287⟩.

59. *Second Lectures on the Psalms*, 1518-21: WA 5:521.9 ⟨520.35ff.⟩: "... those who...

are holy, i.e., truly humble and consider themselves to be ⟨sinners⟩, ⟨and⟩ consider all that God says and does to be holy and the best . . . ⟨confess Pss. 119:137 and 145.17⟩. For they have mortified their will, and they delight in nothing other than God's will, through which they praise, bless, and honor all that happens to them. In contrast, the perverse and ungodly one, whose will is active in all things, condemns everything that God says and does. He wants everything to turn out according to his own idea, which he considers to be the most holy thing that is. Since this cannot happen, he perverts what truly is holy . . . and condemns it as most unholy and accursed. . . . In this way, for such a perverted person necessarily God is perverted and instead of being considered holy is considered to be accursed. How a person thinks about God, so God works in that person. Therefore all things of a perverted person are perverted, even whatever he has from God. You see, therefore, that God is not ⟨suddenly⟩ turned into someone holy, elect, innocent, ⟨or⟩ perverse as to his nature and being *(substantia, natura)*, but as to his Word and work. He does his work in good and evil ones ⟨literally: 'spirits'⟩, and each of them receives in himself whatever he ascribes to God."

60. ⟨For 'heart' and 'will', see above, 17, 252 n. 14, 259 nn. 2 and 5.⟩

61. Luther liked the image of the sun and its effect on mud (which it hardens) or on wax (which it melts); see, e.g., *First Lectures on the Psalms*, 1513-15: WA 3:266.35 ⟨and ibid., n. 1⟩, and Axel Gyllenkrok, *Rechtfertigung und Heiligung in der frühen evangelischen Theologie Luthers* (Uppsala, Wiesbaden, 1952), 28.

62. ⟨See also above, 259 nn. 2 and 3.⟩

63. In some passages of *First Lectures on the Psalms*, 1513-15, a different interpretation of God's wrath is suggested. WA 3:35.13ff.⟨*LW* 10:40⟩: "Not that the wrath is His because it is in Him, but because the creature, in whom the wrath is, is His, and by the creature's nod and command He afflicts the ungodly, though He Himself remains most quiet and calm, yes, is supremely good and not disturbed. . . . But in the case of the ungodly, while He withdraws Himself and remains in the highest goodness, He uses creatures and afflicts one of them with the other, as it happens when fire burns up wood. . . . God does not afflict directly by coming near, but He afflicts by withdrawing and leaving it to creatures"; ibid., WA 3:591.35ff.⟨*LW* 11:81⟩: "The effects of the punishing God are His wrath. Not He in Himself. This wrath of indignation, I say, or the effects of God's wrath I name and call wrath and indignation and trouble, which is in them and in their souls. It is as if he ⟨i.e, the psalmist; see Ps. 78:40-51⟩ were saying that this wrath is twofold. In one way it is God's wrath as if brought in, by which He causes them to be angry and indignant. Understood in a second way, they themselves are angered by it. Thus their wrath and jealousy with which they are inflamed, or that of the demons working on them, is God's wrath, that is, the effect of God's wrath sent to them, as the apostle says (Rom. 11:8)." — See also Erich Seeberg, *Luthers Theologie*, 2:32 n. 95, and his *Grundzüge der Theologie Luthers*, 97; for a critique of Seeberg, see Gyllenkrok, *Rechtfertigung und Heiligung*, 27f.

Notes to Chapter 6

1. See Törnvall, *Geistliches und weltliches Regiment bei Luther*, 10.

2. Ibid., 9. For a similar statement, though connected with the two kingdoms, see

Gollwitzer, *Christliche Gemeinde*, 6: "⟨God⟩ is connected with his Creation in two different ways of ruling."

3. For the two ways of the divine rule over the world, the internal and the external one, see *Against the Heavenly Prophets*, 1525: WA 18:136.9; sermon of May 10, 1535: WA 41:123.22; sermon of Nov. 15, 1528: WA 27:417.24: "There are . . . two kingdoms. . . . ⟨In one kingdom⟩ rules the Word of Salvation, life, grace, and mercy so that ⟨God⟩ consoles and encourages all the afflicted and terrified, and sustains those who struggle with sin, Satan, and the flesh. Its king and governor is Christ. ⟨In the other kingdom live⟩ all the ungodly, those who disobey their parents, the murderers, thiefs, adulterers, cheaters; they despise and make light of the Word, and they are so bad that they cannot be ⟨under⟩ the king's Word; they have to be controlled with the sword, cross, and these kinds of fetters. The princes and magistrates govern this kingdom. Their task is to govern and coerce those evil ones with the sword since they cannot be governed with God's Word. For that purpose God has entrusted the sword to the princes and magistrates and given them power. . . . Therefore ⟨in order to function as emperor⟩ it is not necessary to be a Christian"; ibid., WA 27:418.1 ⟨to be caesar, one does not have to be a saint; it suffices to have a sound mind⟩; ibid., WA 27:418.25.

4. Törnvall, *Geistliches und weltliches Regiment bei Luther*, 73: "When Luther separated the two governances, he established . . . two radically different positions, which man has to take within the one and same world of Creation"; see also ibid., 80f., 119. For the justified critique, see Wehrung, *Welt und Reich*, 216: "It does not at all suffice formalistically to subsume the kingdom of the world and the kingdom of Christ under the aspect of Creation so that the objective difference in God's will itself disappears. ⟨If one does this anyhow, then,⟩ consequently, in the discussion of ethics one denies a substantive doubleness, and the two different positions which man has to take within the one and same Creation are unimportant."

5. See Johannes Heckel, *Initia iuris*, 82f.; Lau, *Luthers Lehre von den beiden Reichen*, 15.

6. Only the spiritual man is conscious of this rule. For the non-spiritual man it is an external process without any spiritual significance so that in spite of the corporeal manifestation of ⟨God's⟩ rule it remains 'hidden'. See below, 333 n. 287.

7. For the governance of the angels, see below, 270 n. 29, and the sermon of Sept. 29, 1530: WA 32:111.10ff.

8. ⟨According to Lutheran theology, society is organized in three estates (or hierarchies) and their activities: *ecclesia* (church, faith, *Kirchenregiment* [ecclesiastical governance]), *politia* (state, socio-political life, *Obrigkeitsregiment* [governance of the secular governmental authority]), *oeconomia* (housefather, family, economics, *Hausregiment* [domestic governance]. See also below, 270 n. 29.⟩

9. ⟨*Geistliches Strafgericht*.⟩

10. Törnvall, *Geistliches und weltliches Regiment bei Luther*, 78.

11. Luther to some Swiss cities: Dec. 1, 1537: WA.B 8:151.47: "The Holy Spirit has to work internally, in the hearts of the listeners; the external⟨ly heard⟩ Word alone accomplishes nothing"; *Second Lectures on the Psalms*, 1518-21: WA 5:536.30: ". . . the Word of God has such a nature that you cannot grasp it unless you close all the senses except that ⟨of hearing because⟩ exclusively through hearing you take possession of the Word and believe it . . ."; *Sermons on John, Chapters 14 and 15*, 1537: WA 45:490.33ff.⟨*LW* 24:33f.⟩:

"... there are two kinds of sight and of hearing. The one is performed with physical eyes and ears, entirely without the Spirit.... This is a purely natural and physical sight.... The second is a spiritual sight, which only Christians have and which takes place by means of faith in the heart. With this — if we are Christians — we must also view and recognize one another. For I do not recognize a Christian by his external appearance and mien, by how he acts and lives, but by the fact that he is baptized and has God's Word. This makes him a child of God, a citizen of the kingdom of heaven, and an heir of eternal life, etc.... I see ... ⟨this⟩ with the spiritual vision of the heart." See also Hans J. Iwand, *Glaubensgerechtigkeit nach Luthers Lehre* (2d ed. Munich, 1951), 19f., and above, 259 n. 6.

12. For a different view on this point in Luther's doctrine of the kingdoms, see Thielicke, *Theologische Ethik*, 1:No. 1846: "⟨In Luther's thought there are⟩ *not two periods of time, but rather two areas of reality. This is the consequence of an obvious de-eschatologizing of the Sermon on the Mount.*" ⟨Italics by Thielicke.⟩ But see *Second Lectures on Galatians*, 1531: WA 40.I:527.7 (to Gal. 3:23): "'Under the law' is a period of time; 'in faith' is a second period of time — these two are most distinct time periods, and yet sin and grace, law and gospel have to be most tightly held together." In light of Luther's differentiation of these two time periods, the value of Thielicke's concern (*Theologische Ethik*, 1:No. 1820) regarding Luther's view of the divine governance may be considered nullified. Wehrung (*Welt und Reich*, 212) argued that God's activity in both governances is not eschatologically determined and directed toward a specific goal; rather, this activity describes a presence which is so strong that it does not point beyond itself. ⟨In light of the following materials Wehrung's view is invalid:⟩ *First Lectures on the Psalms*, 1513-15: WA 3:310.26.28, 311.1; ibid., WA 4:52.16: differentiation between the days of nature, the days of the law, and the days of grace; *Psalm 110 Explained*, 1518: WA 1:699.2.17. For the eschatological dualism in Luther's thought, see Thomas F. Torrance, "Die Eschatologie der Reformation," *EvTh* 14 (1954): 334ff. Bornkamm, *Luthers Lehre von den zwei Reichen*, 17, argued that the spiritual kingdom in Luther's thought can be defined only eschatologically.

13. Törnvall *(Geistliches und weltliches Regiment bei Luther)* did not ignore the contrast between the two kingdoms, but he did not make that contrast the constitutional-law basis of the two governances doctrine. This, so it seems to me, resulted in an occasional uncertainty in his presentation of the kingdoms doctrine: "There are instances when Luther, in addition to the kingdom of the world and the kingdom of Christ, thinks in terms of an additional kingdom, i.e., that of the devil." (Ibid., 187.) For a critique, see Wendland, "Weltherrschaft Christi," in *Stählin Festschrift*, 24 n. 3 (on p. 25). — Lau (*Luthers Lehre von den beiden Reichen*, 33 n. 67, 34, 54) also did not use the eschatological battle between the two kingdoms as the basis of his presentation, though, of course, he knew of it. Therefore he did not define the two kingdoms as two mystical bodies, and he ignored the problem of the external order of the church; Luther, supposedly, did not concern himself with that order because in the "Christian commonwealth" of his time "the representative of the secular governance also took care of the external order of the church." "Luther himself hardly will help us" to find an answer to the question "what is secular order in the church." (Ibid., 93 n. 195.) "Time and again one is surprised to see how far removed Luther was from the problem connected with an order of the church created and implemented by the church" ⟨in contrast to an order created and implemented by the state for the church⟩. "Apparently Luther did not even see this problem. He had an almost childlike trust that the secular princes can reform the church. For this, there are good reasons

in history, and one may not consider this trust the result of naiveté on Luther's part." (Ibid., 67.) It is correct that the external order of the church did not present difficulties for Luther's theology, but this was based on theology and not on historical circumstances. See further, above, 98. — Bornkamm, *Luthers Lehre von den zwei Reichen,* 26 n. 61, agreed with Lau.

14. *The Bondage of the Will,* 1525: WA 18:743.29 ⟨*LW* 33:227⟩: "But when Christ distinguishes the Spirit from the flesh by saying: 'That which is born of the flesh is flesh,' and adds that what is born of the flesh cannot see the Kingdom of God [John 3:6, 3], it plainly follows that whatever is flesh is ungodly and under the wrath of God and a stranger to the Kingdom of God. And if it is a stranger to the Kingdom and Spirit of God, it necessarily follows that it is under the kingdom and spirit of Satan, since there is no middle kingdom between the Kingdom of God and the kingdom of Satan, which are mutually and perpetually in conflict with each other"; ibid., WA 18:782.30 ⟨*LW* 33:287⟩: ". . . Christians know there are two kingdoms in the world, which are bitterly opposed to each other. In one of them Satan reigns, who is therefore called by Christ 'the ruler of this world' [John 12:31], and by Paul 'the god of this world' [II Cor. 4:4]. He holds captive to his will all who are not snatched away from him by the Spirit of Christ, . . . nor does he allow them to be snatched away by any powers other than the Spirit of God. . . . In the other Kingdom, Christ reigns, and his Kingdom ceaselessly resists and makes war on the kingdom of Satan. Into this kingdom we are transferred, not by our own power but by the grace of God, by which we are set free from the present evil age and delivered from the dominion of darkness." For these passages, see Hans H. Pflanz, *Geschichte und Eschatologie bei Martin Luther* (Stuttgart, 1939), 17ff. See also *The Papacy at Rome,* 1520: WA 6:314.35: ". . . from its beginning to the Day of Judgment and into eternity the world is and will be evil, even though God himself, together with all holy angels and people, preaches, writes, and works against it ceaselessly."

15. See Horst Stephan, *Luther in den Wandlungen seiner Kirche* (2d ed. Berlin, 1951), 85. ⟨Heckel quoted from Stephan the word "Vergutmütigung"; i.e., making someone kindhearted or meek, or taking out the sharp edges of something.⟩

16. See above, 93, and below, 381 n. 190.

17. *Psalm 110 Explained,* 1518: WA 1:692.8: "We understand God's right ⟨hand⟩ to mean that the kingdom of the Lord Christ is a spiritual, hidden kingdom, while the visible, corporeal kingdoms and goods are called God's left hand"; sermon of Dec. 15, 1532: WA 36:385.6: ". . . secular governance . . . is also our Lord God's kingdom, but it is ⟨one of⟩ temporal laws and governance; nevertheless, he wants it to be preserved, and it is the kingdom ⟨which God rules⟩ with the left hand. His kingdom at the right, however, is the place where he himself rules; there he does not need parents, magistrates, officials ⟨for⟩ he himself is present and preaches the gospel to the poor"; ibid., WA 36:387.3: ". . . the strict governance is his left kingdom, which is to come to an end, but the eternal kingdom is the one at the right"; *Postilla for the Home,* 1544: WA 52:26.20. — See also Lau, *Luthers Lehre von den beiden Reichen,* 46 n. 104. Paul Althaus, "Die beiden Regimente bei Luther. Bemerkungen zu Johannes Heckels 'Lex charitatis,'" *ThLZ* 81 (1956): 133, rejected my position. Oepke, *Das Neue Gottesvolk,* 460, had developed a position which agreed with my presentation.

18. *First Lectures on the Psalms,* 1513-15: WA 4:85.5: "Having assumed the governance ⟨*regnum;* see also above, 28⟩ over the church, the Lord Christ has become its king according to his humanity"; ibid., WA 4:104.7; *Psalm 110 Explained,* 1518: WA 1:693.1: ". . . this

way Christ . . . rules according to his humanity until the Day of Judgment. . . . But then Christ will turn his governance over to the Father, and God himself will rule eternally . . ."; ibid., WA 1:691.13; *First Commentary on Galatians*, 1519: WA 2:457.22 ⟨*LW* 27:171⟩: "The kingdom of grace is a kingdom of faith, in which Christ reigns as a man placed over all things by God the Father in accordance with Ps. 8:6-7. In this kingdom He receives gifts from God for men, as Ps. 68:18 states; and this holds true until the Last Judgment. For then, as the apostle teaches us in 1 Cor.15:24-28, He will turn the kingdom over to God His Father, and God will be all in all when He will have destroyed every authority and power. This is the kingdom of glory, in which God Himself will reign through Himself, no longer through his humanity for the purpose of stirring up faith. It is not that the two kingdoms are different from each other, but they are ruled over in different ways — now in faith and 'dimly' (1 Cor. 13:12) through the humanity of Christ, then visibly and in the revelation of Christ's divine nature. For this reason the apostles usually call Christ the Lord; but they call the Father God, even though Christ and the Father are the same God. As I have said, however, they do this because of the difference in the kingdom, which consists of us, who are cleansed in faith but whose salvation will be in plain view." — For the governance of Christ's humanity, see also Wilhelm Maurer, "Kirche und Geschichte nach Luthers Dictata super Psalterium," in *Lutherforschung heute. Referate und Berichte des 1. Internationalen Lutherforschungs-kongresses, Aarhus, 18.–23. August, 1956*, ed. by Vilmos Vajta (Berlin, 1958), 87ff.

19. *Preface to John Lichtenberger's Prophecies*, 1527: WA 23:9.24: "Through himself and his angels God rules the ungodly in the realm of the secular governmental authority . . . primarily for the sake of his Word, so that it can be preached; this can take place only if there is peace in the land"; *Commentary on Zechariah*, 1527: WA 23:514.19. See also Peter Brunner, "Der Christ in den zwei Reichen," *ELKZ* 3 (1949): 324. Lau (*Luthers Lehre von den beiden Reichen*, 53f., 54 n. 127) was correct when he warned us not to overemphasize "the dependence . . . of the preaching of the Christian message on a peaceful order in this world." With the preaching of the gospel Christ breaks into the kingdom of the world in order to liberate mankind from its servitude to Satan; this battle, therefore, takes place in the midst of the kingdom of the world. As a result, following Ps.110:2 ("Rule in the midst of your foes"), Luther called this kingdom a "middle kingdom"; sermon of Aug. 4, 1531: WA 34.II:78.36; Luther to Konrad Cordatus: Sept. 1(Dec. 3?), 1544: WA.B 10:645. 26; *Psalm 110 Explained*, 1518: WA 1:696.29, 704.10. Yet, ⟨following Barth,⟩ Gollwitzer argued (*Christliche Gemeinde*, 33) that "the realm of preservation depends on the realm of Redemption."

20. See Pinomaa, *Zorn Gottes in der Theologie Luthers*, 73ff., and esp. 42 n. 3.

21. *Commentary on Zechariah*, 1527: WA 23:517.2; for this passage, see Watson, *Um Gottes Gottheit*, 179f.

22. At this point I shall not deal with the domestic governance. As far as it is important for Luther's doctrine of law, I shall deal with it later; see above, 72f., 77f., and Törnvall, *Geistliches und weltliches Regiment bei Luther*, 38, 40.

23. *Second Lectures on Galatians*, 1531: WA 40.I:176.13: "In the *politia* . . . ⟨God⟩ wants ⟨the magistrates⟩ to be honored as his masks and instruments through which he oversees and rules the world."

24. See above, Appendix II.

25. *Psalm 82 Explained*, 1530: WA 31.I:204.18.27.

26. For the connection of Luther's understanding of the state with that of the Germanic Middle Ages, see instead of other authors, Elert, *Morphologie*, 2:318ff.

27. *Psalm 101 Explained*, 1534-35: WA 51:207.2: "The final purpose of all punishment is the terror for, and improvement of, the ⟨evil ones⟩ . . . and peace and security for the righteous ones"; sermon of Nov. 18, 1526: WA 20:558.11: "Stay away from evil and do good. For these are the two parts of righteousness. And since there are no other parts than these two, Scripture uses these two words, 'judgment' and 'righteousness'. Through judgment or law God punishes, i.e., he removes what is evil; through righteousness he accomplishes that people become righteous, and he preserves and protects innocence"; sermons of 1523: WA 12:675.22: "⟨Secular governance⟩ is only a protection against, and an obstacle to, evil."

28. Sermon of Oct. 28, 1526: WA 20:531.2: "The ⟨earthly⟩ kingdom belongs to God, . . . it is not our task to preserve that ⟨earthly⟩ kingdom; if we were to preserve it through our efforts, the world would have perished long ago. . . . God wants there to be peace ⟨on earth⟩. . . ."

29. In his *Commentary on Zechariah* (1527) Luther described in detail how the devil works against God. He differentiated (WA 23:513.36) between God's "own divine governance" and the "three external governances and three external ways and means": the "secular governance of the sword and fist," the "spiritual governance of the Word and mouth," the "angelic governance of the intellect and reason" (to which belongs "everything that the dear angels use to move and keep us from evil or help us to do good"). He continued (514.32 ⟨*LW* 20:173⟩): "Against this rule of God, however, Satan rages; for his sole purpose ⟨literally: 'office'⟩ is to crush and destroy everything that God creates and does through this rule ⟨literally: 'these governances'⟩. First he opposes the rule ⟨literally: 'governance'⟩ of God and, as far as God permits him, throttles and destroys and spoils everything that God creates, preserves, and improves. For he is the prince of this world (John 16:11; 2 Cor. 4:4), yes, even a god; in opposition to the rule ⟨literally: 'governance'⟩ of the angels he has his own angels, who inspire, counsel, and incite the princes, lords, and all men to nothing but evil and promote all hindrances to good and all furtherance to evil, incite the people against one another, set things aflame wherever they can, and fill the world with grief and heartache. Opposed to the spiritual rule ⟨literally: 'governance'⟩ he has the heretics, false teachers, hypocrites, false brethren; and he does not rest until he has destroyed this rule. Opposed to the secular rule ⟨literally: 'governance'⟩ he has the rebellious, lawless scoundrels, evil, venomous counselors at the courts of the princes, flatterers, traitors, spies, tyrants, madmen, and everything that promotes war, discord, and destruction of lands and people." See also *Second Lectures on the Psalms*, 1518-21: WA 5:275.20: "God takes care of our total well-being ⟨or: 'Salvation'⟩ through the service of the angels" ⟨follows Ps. 91:11f.⟩; *Sermons on John, Chapters 14 and 15*, 1537: WA 45:534.13 ⟨*LW* 24:81⟩: "They ⟨i.e., 'vile knaves and rascals . . . at court'⟩ take money from him and would gladly betray him ⟨i.e., a prince⟩ if it were not for God, who upholds his ⟨i.e., either God's or the prince's⟩ rule ⟨literally: 'order'⟩, and for the Christians in his realm, who pray. Hence these men ⟨i.e., princes and burgomasters⟩ receive a hidden help, a help that is unseen by them and unknown to them, namely, God's Word and order and the prayers of Christians. But just as they do not know that their reign is God's order and work and does not rest in the hands of man, so they do not know that God tolerates and preserves their rule solely for the sake of the godly Christians and their prayers"; ibid., WA 45:535.3 ⟨*LW*

24:81): "But we, as Christians, must know that the whole system of earthly government ⟨literally: 'corporeal governance'⟩ stands and remains for its allotted time solely through God's order or command and the prayers of Christians. These are the two pillars that support the entire world."

30. *On the War Against the Turks,* 1529: WA 30.II:121.11: "How can one interfere with Christ more powerfully than by using these two things, force and cunning? With force one fights the preaching and the Word, with cunning one daily presents evil, dangerous examples, and incites people to follow them"; *Psalm 101 Explained,* 1534-35: WA 51:226.3.

31. Anders Nygren, "Staat und Kirche," in *Ein Buch von der Kirche,* ed. by Gustaf Aulén et al. (Göttingen, 1951), 438: "Sin caused the establishment of the secular kingdom. Luther can also formulate it this way: secular governance has been founded to oppose the devil."

32. See above, 30f.

33. Therefore this governance of God can be seen only with the eye of faith, otherwise it is "invisible"; *On Christian Freedom* ⟨German text⟩, 1520: WA 7:27.5.9.

34. *The Papacy at Rome,* 1520: WA 6:318.26: "... no power ⟨in the sense of 'ruling in a secular way'; ibid., line 25⟩ can rise up without God's secret order ⟨in the sense of arrangement⟩ ..."; ibid., WA 6:318.27: "⟨In⟩ 1 Pet.2:13 secular governmental authorities are called man-made ⟨literally: 'human'⟩ orders ⟨in the sense of arrangements⟩ because they rule without God's Word, yet not without God's counsel; therefore it is not necessary that they are righteous" ⟨in the spiritual sense⟩; sermon of Apr. 14, 1540: WA 49:137.13.

35. *Psalm 101 Explained,* 1534-35: WA 51:238.16 ⟨LW 13:193⟩: "Thank God, it is now manifest enough to all the world how the two areas of authority ⟨literally: 'governances'⟩ need to be distinguished.... We see very well that God distributes secular dominions or kingdoms among the godless in the grandest and most wonderful way, just as He also lets the good sun and rain minister to the godless, without establishing the Word or worship of God among them or teaching or directing them through prophets as He did at Jerusalem among His people. Still He calls this secular government ⟨literally: 'governance'⟩ of the godless His ordinance and creation, though they may abuse it as badly as they can.... From this it certainly is to be concluded that the secular kingdom is a different one and can have its own existence without God's kingdom." For this passage see, however, Oepke's position in *Das neue Gottesvolk,* 465: "Luther was far removed from advocating the autonomy of the secular governance, or from separating state and church, God's people and empire, in an abstract and absolute way. Now finally the true meaning of the two kingdoms doctrine is totally clear. It is nothing other than a critical reservation, a protest against the efforts to make the Holy concrete in a tangible institution, be it spiritual ⟨in the sense of ecclesiastical⟩ or secular; it is a protest against papal caesarism or caesaropapism, but it is not a rigid theory. In all things and at all times the duty to obey God is the decisive factor. In different situations, this duty can demand passive suffering or couragous resistance, humble gentleness or 'strict' mercy, and in each situation a Christian has to make a decision guided by his conscience. For such a decision the sharp demarcations drawn by Luther in his doctrine of the two kingdoms still can be an excellent, even necessary help, even though one might not be able simply to adopt them in each case."

36. *First Lectures on the Psalms,* 1513-15: WA 3:151.26: "'Land of the living' ⟨Ps. 27:13⟩ is the church, but the world is the land of the dead ..."; ibid., WA 4:390.4ff. ⟨LW 11:531, to

Ps.119:168 ("I keep your precepts and decrees, for all my ways are before you"): "... he does not live for men in the reality, but for God in hope. And all his ways are in God's sight. But they who live in the sight of men necessarily keep the things that are of men, namely, perishable goods. And therefore in the sight of God they go astray and are dead, while in the sight of men they walk and live uprightly. On the contrary, the righteous go astray in the sight of men and ... are dead, but in the sight of God are all their ways, and they are right ways. For 'our commonwealth is in heaven' (Phil. 3:20). But why does he say, 'all my ways,' as if he had none in the sight of men? Answer: because although he is in the flesh, he does not walk or fight according to the flesh, but according to the Spirit"; *Notes on Some Chapters of Matthew,* 1538: WA 38:471.2.

37. *First Lectures on the Psalms,* 1513-15: WA 4:265.11; for carnal people who in God's eyes are dead, see ibid., WA 4:390.7, as above, n. 36.

38. See above, 260 n. 7. See also *Sermons on the Ten Commandments,* 1518: WA 1:418.16. Luther discussed (line 13) "the new opinion" of those who argue that in the same way in which the saints of the church, while living on earth, had "various gifts of the Spirit," so now, when they are in heaven, have "different graces," with which they can help the faithful (by interceding for them in different circumstances). He continued: "I do not see how these people could prove this, unless they do it by drawing a conclusion from likeness <or: 'comparison'> *(arguendo a simili).* <I.e., as the lives of the saints on earth demonstrate, they have various gifts of the Spirit; saints are saints, regardless whether they are on earth or in heaven; therefore those in heaven also have gifts, just as those had who were on earth.> But in matters of faith <i.e. in the present argumentation, the 'new opinion' that the saints in heaven have 'different graces' with which they can intercede with God on behalf of the faithful on earth> this argumentation is extremely harmful. For what else does the devil do when he transforms himself into an angel of light than prove something from likeness? <I.e., by appearing in the likeness of an angel of light, the devil tries to prove that he is not the devil.> How many errors have flooded the church ... while appearing in the likeness of holiness *(sub specie sanctitatis),* ... and under the zeal for the catholic faith, i.e., because of likeness *(a simili)!*" See also Gollwitzer, *Christliche Gemeinde,* 8: "The two kingdoms ... are not commensurate at all. There is no basis whatever for proposing that the kingdom of grace heightens or surpasses the kingdom at the left, as it does in Thomism. The relationship between the two kingdoms is by no means comparative; at best, it is teleological, but only if it is perceived through the gospel, so that there is an irreversible movement from the law preserving <Creation> toward Redemption."

Notes to Chapter 7

1. If I am correct, then among jurists Schönfeld is the only exception. He stated (*Grundlegung der Rechtswissenschaft,* 296) that "the fundamental distinction between the two kingdoms" is "the A and O of Luther's doctrine."

2. Lau, *Luthers Lehre von den beiden Reichen,* 13, was correct when he mentioned his astonishment at the fact that "the controversy about the two kingdoms in Luther's thought has not been more thoroughly introduced into the discussion of natural law."

3. See Heinz-Horst Schrey, *Die Bedeutung der biblischen Botschaft für die Welt des Rechts* (Tübingen, 1952), 16.

4. See Johannes Heckel, "Recht und Gesetz," *ZSRG*.K 26 (1937): 323; Werner Elert, *Zwischen Gnade und Ungnade* (Munich, 1948), 138ff.

5. ⟨In the sense of constitution.⟩

6. *The Bondage of the Will*, 1525: WA 18:771.36 ⟨*LW* 33:270⟩: ". . . what does the Scripture say? 'Abraham believed God, and it was reckoned to him as righteousness.' Please notice here too the distinction Paul makes by referring ⟨Rom. 4:1ff.⟩ to a twofold righteousness of Abraham. First, there is the righteousness of works, or moral and civil righteousness; but he denies that Abraham is justified in God's sight by this, even if he is righteous in the sight of men because of it"; ibid., WA 18:772.11 ⟨*LW* 33:270f.⟩: "The other kind of righteousness is the righteousness of faith, which does not depend on any works, but on God's favorable regard and his 'reckoning' on the basis of grace"; *Second Disputation against the Antinomians*, 1538: WA 39.I:460.21: ". . . the law is twofold and is understood in two ways . . ."; *On Psalms 23-25*, 1513-16, WA 31.I:465.36 ⟨to Ps. 23:3; note l of NRSV text⟩: "Righteousness . . . is not that of which Aristotle, *Nicomachean Ethics* 5, or the legal experts speak, but the justifying faith or grace of Christ . . . ."

7. See Peter Brunner, "Der Christ in den zwei Reichen," *ELKZ* 3 (1949): 326; Gustaf Törnvall, "Der Christ in den zwei Reichen," *EvTh* 10 (1950/51): 69.

8. See Franz X. Arnold, *Zur Frage des Naturrechts bei Martin Luther* (Munich, 1937), 128.

9. Heinrich Rommen, *Die ewige Wiederkehr des Naturrechts* (2d ed. Munich, 1937), 62, correctly stated that the doctrine of the destroyed nature, developed by the reformers, "made it intellectually impossible to affirm traditional natural law." He did not go beyond this negative statement.

10. Helmut Coing, "Die Naturrechtsdebatte im Raume des Protestantismus," *Der Juristenrundbrief der Evangelischen Akademie* 2 (1950): 4: "There is something of a hidden and potential contradiction between the following two positions: The doctrine of the undestroyed natural moral ability of man (outside of the Christian Revelation), the basis of the doctrine of natural law, . . . and the understanding of man as a radical evil being, destroyed down to the roots, which some Protestant theologians affirm. This contradiction emerged in connection with the discussion of natural law and, in my opinion, is the real issue of the present discussion." See also Franz Wieacker, *Privatrechtsgeschichte der Neuzeit* (Göttingen, 1952), 145; de Lagarde, *Recherches sur l'esprit politique de la Réforme*, 178: "The idea of natural law in Reformation thought is a nearly useless, even dangerous category. . . ."

11. Hans M. Müller, "Das christliche Liebesgebot und die lex naturae," *ZThK*.NF 9 (1928): 165: "The not yet clarified concept 'natural law' is a totally non-transparent combination of different things."

12. Johann Sauter (*Die rechtsphilosophischen Grundlagen des Naturrechts. Untersuchungen zur Geschichte der Rechts- und Staatslehre* [Vienna, 1932]) and Georg Stadtmüller (*Das Naturrecht im Lichte der geschichtlichen Erfahrung* [Recklinghausen, 1948]) did not mention Luther. On the other hand, Johannes Messner, *Das Naturrecht* (Innsbruck, 1950), 96f., dealt with Luther in detail, although in a negative way. Experts correctly have called this book the "standard work"; see Leopold Wenger, "Zur christlichen Begründung des Naturrechts," *ZSRG*.R 69 (1952): 14 n. 21. The significance of the book and the author's efforts to support his judgment with Protestant historical and theological scholarship recommend that we quote in detail from this most recent contribution to our sub-

ject: "In the evaluation of man's nature, the realism of ⟨the Roman Catholic⟩ doctrine of natural law is as equally far removed from the pessimism of Manichaeism, Lutheranism, and Jansenism as it is from the optimism of Pelagianism and Rationalism. Especially Luther sees in the Fall an all-encompassing slippage of human nature into sin and evil; man has become totally incapable of implementing the moral order in his personal existence, and in that of society, by his own ability and must totally depend on grace. The externals of man's existence, especially the political and social realms, in short, 'the world', are set by God as a result of sin. These externals cannot be a part of the morality which is based on faith; in fact, according to Luther it would be impossible that these externals would be a part of such a morality, as Paul Joachimsen, who affirms Lutheranism, has recently again demonstrated in his *Sozialethik des Luthertums* (1927). According to Luther, it is the task of society's authorities to bring order into these external realms; man is required to subordinate himself to this order, because these authorities act by order of the divine promise. Connected with this position is the promotion of tyranny through Luther's 'peculiarly perverse' social ethics and 'negativism in the area of social ethics,' as the American Protestant theologian Reinhold Niebuhr pointed out (*The Nature and Destiny of Man*, 2:195ff.). In the optimism of Enlightenment, on the other hand, an unlimited ability to reach truth and accomplish good by means of its own strength is ascribed to reason. This results in the belief of unlimited progress in spiritual and material matters, which is characteristic of the humanitarian world view of the nineteenth century. The effects of both errors — the wrong pessimistic and the wrong optimistic doctrine of man — are identical; both impede the moral efforts of man: Lutheran pessimism because it robs man's moral effort of meaning, rational optimism because it negates the necessity of any such effort. But without a doubt, Lutheran pessimism and Enlightenment optimism have released energies in all areas of culture by divorcing them from any moral obligations. Connected with this was the separation of culture and morality, of religion and life. After a period of remarkable external progress, this separation had to lead to a crisis in culture as a result of the abandonment of natural law, the fundamental law of culture. This development was accelerated because a religious movement and a secular movement — Protestantism and Rationalism — were united in neutralizing the moral and religious forces in culture. With this began the age of modern secularism; its twilight of the gods we experience today in the catastrophes of a world torn apart." See further, below, 305 n. 29, 308 n. 51, 424 n. 148.

13. Emil Brunner, *Das Gebot und die Ordnungen* (repr. by Amerikanische Hilfskommission des ökumenischen Rates. New York, s.a.), 649: "The reformers do not have a Christian philosophy of state in the same way in which they do not know of a divine natural law"; Hans Steubing, *Naturrecht und natürliche Theologie im Protestantismus* (Göttingen, 1932), 30, 74, did not deal with Luther but stated: "In Protestantism, God can never be used as cause and source of natural law"; Törnvall, *Geistliches und weltliches Regiment bei Luther*, 104: "In Luther's thought the idea of a divine law which is placed above the secular governance is missing"; Arnold Köttgen, "Glaube und Recht," *LuJ* 17 (1935): 51: "Luther decisively opposed natural law because for him God's sovereignty was despised in it"; Thielicke, *Theologische Ethik*, 1:No. 1886: "I am able to speak of natural law . . . only if I assume that sin means only a limited disturbance, but under no circumstances a total perversion. . . ."

14. *On Secular Authority*, 1523: WA 11:262.3 ⟨LW 45:105⟩; for the historical circum-

stances which caused Luther to write this book, see Bornkamm, *Luthers Lehre von den zwei Reichen*, 7f. Luther made similar statements already in *The Estate of Marriage*, 1522: WA 10.II:288.10ff.: "In the law of Moses, God established two kinds of governances and commandments: some spiritual ones which taught what righteousness is before God, such as love and obedience. . . . But also some secular ones for the sake of those who did not obey the spiritual ones so that they, too, have a rule; they were to be restricted so that they would not act according to their wantonness and do worse things"; *Sermons on the First Epistle of St. Peter*, 1523: WA 12:330.30 ‹LW 30:76›: "Thus there are two kinds of governments in the world, just as there are two kinds of people, namely, believers and unbelievers. Christians let the Word of God rule them; for themselves they have no need whatever for the secular government. But non-Christians need another rule, namely, the secular sword, because they refuse to be guided by the Word of God. Otherwise, if we were all Christians and followed the Gospel, it would not be necessary or profitable at all to wield the secular sword and power. For if there were no transgressors, there could be no punishment either. But since we cannot all be pious, Christ has entrusted the wicked to the government to be ruled as they must be ruled. But the pious He keeps for Himself and rules them Himself with His Word alone"; *Second Lectures on the Psalms*, 1518-21: WA 5:126.21: "I would not be opposed — in fact, I would strongly agree with it — if someone would understand 'inheritances' ‹Ps. 5:1; Vulgate› to signify the two families of man, which are opposed to each other; one relies on its own strength, the other relies on God's grace . . ."; ibid., WA 5:127.21f. — Ferdinand Kattenbusch ("Die Doppelschichtigkeit in Luthers Kirchenbegriff," ThStKr 100 [1928]: 325 n. 1) called *On Secular Authority* "one of Luther's poorest writings"; in a "totally abstract" and "stereotyped way" "Luther says that 'Adam's children' have to be divided into two parts. . . ." Yet already in his first lectures on the Psalms (1513-15) Luther differentiated between "the righteous and unrighteous in the congregation," that is, the church; see Johannes Heckel, *Initia iuris*, 14. Essentially, the differentiation between the righteous, who live according to God's law, and man, who lives according to his own laws, can be found already in those first lectures on the Psalms; WA 4:372.33 ‹LW 11:507f. to Ps. 119:143›. See also *Psalm 110 Explained*, 1518: WA 1:698.28.30 (Adam's children and Christ's children), and ibid., WA 1:701.42.

15. *Lectures on Genesis*, 1535-45: WA 42:136.32 ‹LW 1:183›: ". . . after sin no Law was put upon Adam, although the perfect nature had its Law. But this happened because God sees that nature, which is now corrupt, not only can receive no support from a Law but has gone through such a complete convulsion and disturbance that it cannot bear even a syllable of the Law. Therefore He does not further burden sin-burdened nature with the Law."

16. *First Lectures on the Psalms*, 1513-15: WA 4:354.35: ". . . love ‹is› the best of all laws . . ."; *First Lectures on Galatians*, 1516-17: WA 57.II:100.8: "The sum of all laws is this: 'Love your neighbor, etc.'"; *Sermons on the Ten Commandments*, 1518: WA 1:508.20 (sermon of Jan. 4, 1517): ". . . the goal, life, and strength of all laws are peace, love, unanimity; whoever does not want these, does not use the law but abuses it" (in this sermon Luther also criticized the different understanding of law held by litigious jurists, and he criticized the study of law, which for him was full of dangers); ibid., WA 1:513.3 (sermon of Jan. 25, 1517): law of nature *(lex naturae)*; *Postilla for Lent*, 1525: WA 17.II:91.13: love is the primary law, rule, and standard of all laws; ibid., WA 17.II:100.6.

17. For 'love' in *City of God*, see above, 251 n. 4.

18. Notes on the *Sentences* of Peter Lombard, 1510-11: WA 9:52.25: "... to love is the same as to be..."; *Second Lectures on the Psalms*, 1518-21: WA 5:38.16: "... each creature serves the law of love, and its total substance is in the Lord's law...." — For ontology in Luther's thought, see Schönfeld, *Grundlegung der Rechtswissenschaft*, 299. For the reshaping of Aristotelian ontology by Luther, see Edmund Schlink, "Weisheit und Torheit," *KuD* 1 (1955): 5ff., 15.

19. With this idea Luther's legal doctrine makes an important contribution to Anders Nygren's thesis: "Luther's reforming work is not confined to the doctrine of justification by faith; he is also the great reformer of the idea of Christian love"; see *Agape and Eros*, Part I (London, 1941), 39f.

20. *Second Lectures on the Psalms*, 1518-21: WA 5:559.26: "... the law works ⟨sin⟩ in all human beings as long as it is outside of their will. Yet the law is not in their will, nor is their will in the law until such time that the law is being cherished, and what it prescribes is being loved"; *First Lectures on the Psalms*, 1513-15: WA 3:23.29: "... the will... ⟨of the ungodly⟩ is not in the Lord's law."

21. *Lectures on Romans*, 1515-16: WA 56:263.26 ⟨*LW* 25:251⟩: "... the Law is upheld both in itself and in us. In itself, when it is promulgated; in us, when we fulfill it with our will and our works."

22. *The Seven Penitential Psalms*, 1517: WA 1:192.4: "What is maintained through force does not last. But what is maintained through the will has durability"; *Second Lectures on the Psalms*, 1518-21: WA 5:560.32: "... when the law is not loved or fulfilled ⟨through love⟩, it is a temporary matter, and it is often forgotten..."; *First Lectures on the Psalms*, 1513-15: WA 3:17.32: "Nothing... that has been accomplished by force is permanent, and what is maintained without love and will is not maintained for long."

23. Notes on the *Sentences* of Peter Lombard, 1510-11: WA 9:44.3: "... ⟨an act of love⟩ unites us with God..."; for this passage, see Vignaux, "Luther commentateur," *EPhM* 21 (1935): 43 n. 4, 44 n. 2, 94, and id., "Sur Luther et Ockham," *FS* 32 (1950): 28. — At the meeting of the Luther Akademie in Goslar in August of 1952, Louis Saint-Blancat of Badevel (Doubs) delivered a paper with the title "L'Augustinisme de Luther en 1510"; he dealt with the theological connection between Luther and Gregory of Rimini, and he promised a detailed study. For the connection between Luther and Gregory of Rimini, see also Carl Stange, "Luther über Gregor von Rimini," in id., *Theologische Aufsätze* (Leipzig, 1905), 109ff.; id., *Studien zur Theologie Luthers*, 1 (Gütersloh, 1928), 10, 13ff. — For Luther's connection with Bernard of Clairvaux, see Carl Stange, *Bernhard von Clairvaux* (Berlin, 1954), 5ff. — For Luther's connection with Peter Lombard, see Louis Saint-Blancat, "Luthers Verhältnis zu Petrus Lombardus," *ZSTh* 22 (1953): 300ff. — For Luther's connection with Occam in the early period of his life, see Louis Saint-Blancat, "Recherches sur les sources de la théologie Luthérienne primitive (1509-1510)," *VC* 8.29/30 (1954): 81ff. — For Luther, see also sermons of ca. 1514-21: WA 4: 684.7: "... in the long run the law with all its commandments wants to accomplish nothing else than that people are kind, loving, of one heart, of good will with each other, etc."

24. *Decretum Gratiani* c.30. D.II. de poen. ⟨Friedberg 1:1199⟩, quotes Augustine: "Tolle charitatem, odium tenet" (take away love, ⟨and⟩ hatred rules), and "Omnis, qui non diligit, odit" (everyone who does not love, hates)." ⟨Friedberg 1199, n. 306, lists Augustine's *Homilies on 1 John*, tractatus V. § 10, as source for the quotations. The first quotation can be found in tractatus VII. § 1: "Tolle charitatem de corde; odium tenet..." (*PL*

35:2029.) Throughout the *Homilies* I found passages which only come close to the second quotation; e.g., *PL* 35:2017.>

25. *First Lectures on the Psalms*, 1513-15: WA 4:233.22 <*LW* 11:367>: "... <this> is the real difference between the new and the old people. The latter were forced to do everything from fear of punishment <literally: 'do almost everything'>, but the former do everything with love of righteousness in the spirit of freedom"; *On Trade and Usury*, 1524: WA 15:306.28: "I have often taught that one should not and cannot rule the world with the gospel and Christian love. The world has to be ruled with strict laws, and the sword, and force, because it is evil and accepts neither the gospel nor love; if the world is not forced <to behave otherwise>, it acts and lives according to its wantonness." See also Lau, *Luthers Lehre von den beiden Reichen*, 50 n. 115.

26. *Lectures on Hebrews*, 1517-18: WA 57.III:112.14 <*LW* 29:122>: "Scripture has an idiom of its own when it says that the Law or the message is 'valid' or 'invalid.' For to be 'valid' means to be fulfilled; but to be 'invalid' means not to be fulfilled, as Rom. 8:3 says: ... that is, <the Law> was not fulfilled but was rather neglected. In the same way the Law is said to be established and ratified, and, on the other hand, to be destroyed and to become invalid, as below in [Heb.] 10:28, where 'a man making void the Law of Moses' is mentioned."

27. *First Lectures on the Psalms*, 1513-15: WA 3:400.16 <*LW* 10:336f.>: "... Scripture describes two generations, and the same nouns apply to either one with an opposite meaning, as, for example, the wisdom of the world and of the church; the cross of the world and of the church; the strength of the world and of the church"; ibid., WA 4:314.34 <*LW* 11:427>: "Third: they are wonders <Ps. 119:18> of the law of Christ, that the Gospel judges good evil and evil good, light darkness and darkness light, bitter sweet and sweet bitter; that is to say, what is good according to the flesh is evil according to the spirit, and vice versa"; notes on the *Sentences* of Peter Lombard, 1510-11: WA 9:58.11: "... all nouns about God are spoken <in> the discourse of the creatures and, therefore, are not able to do justice to God." — For the "antithetical structure of spiritual understanding," see Gerhard Ebeling, "Luthers Auslegung des 44. (45.) Psalms," in *Lutherforschung heute*, 43.

28. *Second Lectures on the Psalms*, 1518-21: WA 5:32.20 <*LW* 14:294>: "See that you always separate most widely and distantly the Law of the Lord <Ps. 1:2> from the laws of any men, and watch with all diligence that the two, confused in one chaos (as is done by the doctors of destruction) <literally: 'doctors of the pestilence'; Ps. 1:1; Vulgate; NRSV: 'those ... who sit in the seat of scoffers'>, do not miserably destroy you. They either turn the Law of God into human tradition <literally: 'a tradition of men'> or human tradition into the Law of God"; ibid., WA 5:518.2: "... there is no comparison <or: 'connection'> between the righteousness of the flesh (which is the operation of the law) and the righteousness of the spirit (which is faith in Christ)." — See also Gerhard Ebeling, *Evangelische Evangelienauslegung* (Munich, 1942), 266ff.

29. This is, e.g., the case regarding the question whether one and the same action is accepted or not accepted by God *(actus acceptatus et deacceptatus)*, a question which has to be decided on the basis of divine law. <See *Heidelberg Disputation*, 1518: *LW* 31:64: "... away with arguments which are like so much smoke: 'One and the same action cannot be accepted and unaccepted by God. For it follows that it would be good and not good at the same time.'"> *Explanations of Luther's Theses Debated in Leipzig*, 1519: WA 2:420.10: Luther cited this argument, calling it "nonsense," and then continued: "... I mention this

argument of Scotist sophistry *(subtilitatis Scoticae)* in order to demonstrate how far removed they ⟨i.e., the Scotists⟩ are from the truth while they start to measure these divine matters with petty syllogisms *(ratiunculis)*. For if they would know the truth of Scripture ⟨one could consider this the "divine law" mentioned by Heckel at the beginning of this note⟩, they would not say this. If they would correctly understand the substance *(materia)* of grace, sin, and free will, they would not bring forth such empty sophistical stuff as sound reasons *(cavillationes pro bonis rationibus)*." Then Luther presented his position (lines 17ff.): One and the same action is accepted and not accepted by God. That it is accepted is not the result of the action's quality, its goodness, but of God's forgiveness and mercy. Without that forgiveness and mercy (having made an action acceptable), all actions are not accepted. "Therefore it is sufficiently clear that the Scotists do not know of divine mercy . . . because ⟨they argue⟩ that there is a good action which is worthy of being accepted by God without the forgiving mercy ⟨having made it so⟩; for *acceptatio*, see *Dictionary of Latin and Greek Theological Terms Drawn Principally from Protestant Scholastic Theology*, ed. by Richard A. Muller (Grand Rapids, 1985), 18⟩. — See Hägglund, *Theologie und Philosophie bei Luther*, 54: "The disaster of ⟨nominalistic⟩ theology is the mixing of rational considerations with the revealed truth." ⟨See also above, 249 n. 73.⟩

30. *Second Lectures on Galatians*, 1531: WA 40.I:306.3: "The law has been given above the reason of man . . ."; *The Bondage of the Will*, 1525: WA 18:784.9 ⟨LW 33:290⟩: "For if ⟨God's⟩ righteousness were such that it could be judged to be righteous by human standards, it would clearly not be divine and would in no way differ from human righteousness. But since he is the one true God, and is wholly incomprehensible and inaccessible to human reason, it is proper and indeed necessary that his righteousness also should be incomprehensible. . . ."

31. *First Lectures on the Psalms*, 1513-15: WA 4:17.8 ⟨LW 11:170⟩: ". . . our righteousness is from above and not on earth. Hypocrites or work-righteous people say, 'Righteousness looks up from earth to heaven,' for they think that their own righteousness reaches upward and is worthy of being acknowledged by God."

32. See *Lectures on Hebrews*, 1517-18: WA 57.III:30.9ff.: the contrast of the understanding of Scripture which 'children' have to that which the 'perfect ones' have.

33. See *Lecture on Hebrews*, 1517-18: WA 57.III:30.11.20, 179.7, and notes ⟨LW 29:179, and ibid., nn. 19-20⟩.

34. See Luther's critical statements on the 'easy doctrine' in which the way to heaven is made easy; *First Lectures on the Psalms*, 1513-15: WA 3:416.17 ⟨LW 10:351f.⟩; sermon of Aug. 15, 1520: WA 4:647.19: "Each ascent to the knowledge of God is dangerous except the one that leads through Christ's humility ⟨so the WA text⟩, because that is the Jacob's ladder ⟨Gen. 28:12⟩, on which one has to ascend." For this sermon, see also above, 263 n. 51; the text presented by Vogelsang reads: "per humanitatem Christi" (through Christ's humanity). See also *Postilla for Christmas*, 1522: WA 10.I.1:472.1ff.

35. *First Lectures on the Psalms*, 1513-15: WA 3:373.30: ". . . the old law is not understood unless one first has the new law"; see also Otto Ritschl, *Dogmengeschichte des Protestantismus*, 2.I (Leipzig, 1912), 66. See further, *Postilla for Christmas*, 1522: WA 10.I.1:471.23: "If we were without sin, as Adam was prior to the Fall, we would not need Christ and could come before God by ourselves. But in the difficult time after the Fall we . . . must have ⟨Jesus⟩, who has to be without sin yet would accept us sinners and people in need who come to him and desire him"; Luther to George Spalatin (additional material):

Feb. 12, 1519: WA.B 1:329.50: "Whoever ⟨wishes⟩ to think and speculate about God in a salutary way by all means should ignore everything except Christ's humanity."

36. *Second Lectures on Galatians*, 1531: WA 40.I.48.19: "If this doctrine ⟨about Christian righteousness⟩ has been lost . . . we have lost everything"; ⟨see also *LW* 26:8f.⟩.

37. See also Elert, *Morphologie*, 1:59.

Notes to Chapter 8

1. We use an approach which is different from that which Lau used in his *"Äußerliche Ordnung"*; he began (32) with an analysis of the concept 'natural law' according to its "natural aspect." Olson (*Grundproblemet*, 1:21, 51) proceeded in a similar way. Therefore he did not find a natural-law dualism in Luther's system. He found only (93ff.) *one* natural law which, as external law, obligates the Christian and the non-Christian in the same way, with one difference: for the Christian this natural law as "divine law" has a "new perspective"; it is commanded by God in the Revelation and, therefore, it is obeyed in faith; for natural man this natural law is dictated by reason: "The demands established in natural law are the same as those established in divine law" (97).

2. See also Heinrich Lammers, *Luthers Anschauung vom Willen* (Berlin, 1935).

3. For the following, see Ferdinand Kattenbusch, "Deus absconditus bei Luther," in *Festgabe für D. Dr. Julius Kaftan zu seinem 70. Geburtstag, 30. September 1918, dargebracht von Schülern und Kollegen* (Tübingen, 1920), 195ff.

4. "Regierendes Weltprinzip"; for this phrase I am indebted to Ernst Kohlmeyer.

5. *First Lectures on the Psalms*, 1513-15: WA 4:38.4.22: "'Lord, you are powerful' ⟨Vulgate text of NRSV Ps. 89:8⟩, and you alone are power. . . . For no created power is absolute power; in relationship to another power it is either a weaker or a stronger power. All things are power but not pure power because they are not infinite; on the basis of their nature they all can become weak."

6. *The Book of Deuteronmy with Notes*, 1524: WA 14:618.22: ". . . ⟨the divinity is⟩ free, uncircumscribed, and undefinable"; *The Bondage of the Will*, 1525: WA 18:636.27 ⟨*LW* 33:68⟩: "It follows now that free choice is plainly a divine term, and can be properly applied to none but the Divine Majesty alone. . . ."

7. *Lectures on Romans*, 1515-16: WA 56:91.19: "There is no law for God's will, and he is not at all indebted to anyone"; ibid., WA 56:116.1: "There is no judgment ⟨literally: 'reason'⟩ . . . over those things which we see done by ⟨God⟩."

8. *First Lectures on the Psalms*, 1513-15: WA 4:262.34: ". . . ⟨God⟩ has no law except his will. This shows that he truly is God"; *Lectures on Romans*, 1515-16: WA 56:396.14: "Truly, there is no other cause of God's righteousness than his will, nor can there be"; ibid., WA 56:212.22: "In himself God cannot be justified by anything because he is righteousness itself; he cannot be judged because he himself is the eternal law, judgment, and truth"; *The Bondage of the Will*, 1525: WA 18:712.32 ⟨*LW* 33:181⟩: "He is God, and for his will there is no cause or reason that can be laid down as a rule or measure for it, since there is nothing equal or superior to it, but it is itself the rule of all things. For if there were any rule or standard for it, either as cause or reason, it could no longer be the will of God. For it is not because he is or was obliged so to will that what he wills is right, but on the contrary, because he himself so wills, therefore what happens must be right. Cause and reason can be as-

signed for a creature's will, but not for the will of the Creator, unless you place over him another creator." See also Karl Zickendraht, *Der Streit zwischen Erasmus und Luther über die Willensfreiheit* (Leipzig, 1909), 126: "In the case of God, the reason for declaring his action to be good does not rest in a norm to which that action corresponds, but it rests in the person who acts."

9. *The Seven Penitential Psalms,* 1517: WA 1:187.19: "... who sits in judgment over God? It is obvious that no one judges or justifies God himself, or his nature, because God himself is the eternally identical... and never changing righteousness and the supreme judge over all things."

10. *Lectures on Romans,* 1515-16: WA 56:91.21 ⟨*LW* 25:82 n. 13⟩: "The free will which is subject to no one cannot be unrighteous, since it would be impossible that it be unrighteous unless it should do something against the Law."

11. *The Bondage of the Will,* 1525: WA 18:632.22 ⟨*LW* 33:61⟩: "I answer:... we must not ask the reason *(ratio)* for the divine will, but simply adore it, giving God glory that, since he alone is just and wise, he does no wrong to anyone..."; *That These Words of Christ, "This is My Body," Still Stand Firm against the Fanatics,* 1527: WA 23:265.23: "... who asks why God has to speak and act ⟨in a particular way⟩ wants to be superior to God, and wiser and better than God."

12. *Lectures on Genesis,* 1535-45: WA 42:108.36, 109.9 ⟨*LW* 1:144⟩: "... who can supply the reason *(ratio)* for the things that he sees the Divine Majesty has permitted to happen? Why do we not rather learn with Job that God cannot be called to account and cannot be compelled to give us the reason for everything He does or permits to happen?... these are all things under the divine power and will. To know this is enough. Besides, it is wicked curiosity to investigate these problems in greater detail"; for this passage, see Johannes von Walter, *Die Theologie Luthers* (Gütersloh, 1940), 109. For the warning not to speculate about predestination, see Luther's letter to Count Albrecht of Mansfeld: Febr. 23, 1542: WA.B 9:627.33, 628.61.

13. *The Bondage of the Will,* 1525: WA 18:685.32. See also below, 282 n. 29.

14. ⟨Literally: "the nude God."⟩

15. *Lectures on Genesis,* 1535-45: WA 42:9.32 ⟨*LW* 1:11⟩: "God... does not manifest Himself except through His works and the Word because the meaning of these is understood in some measure. Whatever else belongs essentially to the Divinity cannot be grasped and understood, such as being outside time, before the world, etc. Perhaps God appeared to Adam without a covering *(nudus),* but after the fall into sin He appeared in a gentle breeze as though enveloped in a covering.... This nature of ours has become so misshapen through sin, so depraved and utterly corrupted, that it cannot recognize God or comprehend His nature without a covering. It is for this reason that those coverings are necessary. It is folly to argue much about God outside and before time, because this is an effort to understand the God-head without a covering, or the uncovered divine essence. Because this is impossible, God envelops Himself in His works in certain forms, as today He wraps himself in Baptism, in absolution, etc. If you should depart from these, you will get into an area where there is no measure, no space, no time, and into the merest nothing, concerning which, according to the philosopher, there can be no knowledge"; ibid., WA 42:11.22, 293.32. — For the fact that the substance and nature of God cannot be defined, see ibid., WA 42:294.1.18; for the fact that "God's nude majesty" cannot be grasped, see ibid., WA 42:294.23; for the danger involved in debating God's absolute power

(potentia absoluta), see ibid., WA 42:295.21. Luther made identical statements already in one of his earliest sermons, 1519? (WA 4:704.22), and then again in *The Bondage of the Will*, 1525 (WA 18:719.12 ⟨LW 33:190⟩).

16. Instead of other authors, see Fritz Blanke, *Der verborgene Gott bei Luther* (Berlin, 1928), 7ff.

17. Wünsch misunderstood Luther's position when he argued (*Ethik des Politischen*, 136): "Within Protestantism God has absolute power *(potestas absoluta)* but not *potestas ordinata* ⟨ordained, or restricted, or defined power⟩." Luther, of course, used both terms, well-known in his day, but he emphatically warned of the danger involved in speculating about them. For him such speculations documented the kind of thinking about God which he rejected; see n. 15. For both terms, see also *Lectures on Genesis*, 1535-45: WA 43:71.8.13.

18. *Lectures on Psalm 51*, 1532: WA 40.II:329.7: "The hypocrites . . . ascend into heaven through their speculations"; *First Lectures on the Psalms*, 1513-15: WA 4:79.2: ". . . ⟨God's⟩ wonderful power, wisdom, and goodness . . . are the true objects of the joy of the irrational nature. . . ." See also Erich Seeberg, *Grundzüge der Theologie Luthers*, 54: "The religious line from below to above is missing in Luther's thinking."

19. For the idea of participation through contact, see Söhngen, *Einheit in der Theologie*, 107ff.

20. *The Bondage of the Will*, 1525: WA 18:633.7 ⟨LW 33:62⟩: ". . . faith has to do with things not seen [Hebr.11:1]. Hence in order that there may be room for faith, it is necessary that everything which is believed should be hidden. It cannot, however, be more deeply hidden than under an object, perception, or experience which is contrary to it. Thus when God makes alive he does it by killing, when he justifies he does it by making men guilty, when he exalts to heaven he does it by bringing down to hell . . . (I Sam. 2[:6])."

21. For the dissolving of such paradoxes, see *The Bondage of the Will*, 1525: WA 18:785.26 ⟨LW 33:292⟩: "Let us take it that there are three lights — the light of nature, the light of grace, and the light of glory, to use the common and valid distinction. By the light of nature it is an insoluble problem how it can be just that a good man should suffer and a bad man prosper; but this problem is solved by the light of grace. By the light of grace it is an insoluble problem how God can damn one who is unable by any power of his own to do anything but sin and be guilty. Here both the light of nature and the light of grace tell us that it is not the fault of the unhappy man, but of an unjust God; for they cannot judge otherwise of a God who crowns one ungodly man freely and apart from merits, yet damns another who may well be less, or at least not more, ungodly. But the light of glory tells us differently, and it will show us hereafter that the God whose judgment here is one of incomprehensible righteousness is a God of most perfect and manifest righteousness. In the meantime, we can only *believe* this, being admonished and confirmed by the example of the light of grace, which performs a similar miracle in relation to the light of nature."

22. *Confession concerning Christ's Supper*, 1528: WA 26:339.34.

23. See, e.g., *Second Lectures on the Psalms*, 1518-21: WA 5:170.2: ". . . truly, God is all things in all, equal and the same, and yet at the same time most unequal and diverse. For he is the one who in complexity is simple and in simplicity is complex, in inequality equal and in equality unequal, in sublimity weak, in height low, in the innermost the external, and vice versa. Thus he is powerful in the weak and weak in the powerful, foolish in the wise, and, in short, all things in all." Luther made similar statements already in *First Lec-*

tures on the Psalms, 1513-15: WA 3: 407.25 ⟨LW 10:347⟩. See also *That These Words of Christ, "This is My Body," Still Stand Firm against the Fanatics*, 1527: WA 23:135.3, 137.25; Ebeling, *Evangelische Evangelienauslegung*, 276f.

24. *The Bondage of the Will*, 1525: WA 18:633.14ff. ⟨LW 33:62f.⟩: ". . . God hides his eternal goodness and mercy under eternal wrath, his righteousness under iniquity. This is the highest degree of faith, to believe him merciful when he saves so few and damns so many, and to believe him righteous when by his own will he makes us necessarily damnable. . . . If, then, I could by any means comprehend how this God can be merciful and just who displays so much wrath and iniquity, there would be no need of faith."

25. See above, 17f. ⟨For 'natural man', see below, 358 n. 10.⟩

26. *First Lectures on the Psalms*, 1513-15: WA 4:323.21: "God's law is unchangeable."

27. *First Lectures on the Psalms*, 1513-15: WA 4:286.14: ". . . the law of grace is eternal"; ibid., WA 4:323.27: "The spiritual law . . . lasts for ever"; *Lectures on Romans*, 1515-16: WA 56:212.23: "God himself is eternal law, judgment, and truth"; *The Bondage of the Will*, 1525: WA 18:615.13 ⟨LW 33:37⟩: ". . . God . . . foresees and purposes and does all things by his immutable, eternal, and infallible will"; *Lectures on Genesis*, 1535-45: WA 42:293.25: ". . . from eternity God stands firm and is consistent in his plan"; Luther to Duke Frederick, elector of Saxony: Nov. 21(?), 1518: WA.B 1:239.120. For Luther's criticism of the scholastic distinction between the eternal will of God's good pleasure ⟨see, e.g., Eph. 1:9⟩ and 'the mutable will of the sign', see *Lectures on Genesis*, 1535-45: WA 42:293.1ff., 294.36 ⟨LW 2:43f., 44 n. 57, 46f.; for this distinction, see also Richard A. Muller, *Dictionary*, 331⟩. These materials document Luther's knowledge of the concept 'eternal law' (Arnold, *Naturrecht bei Luther*, 101, was correct on this point). For Luther, however, this concept had a different meaning than for Thomas Aquinas. See further, Theobald Suss, "La loi éternelle," *Positions luthériennes* 10 (1962): 108ff.

28. *Lectures on Romans*, 1515-16: WA 56:234.1 ⟨LW 25:219⟩: "God is as changeable as possible. . . . For as each person is in himself, so God is to him as an object. If he is righteous, God is righteous; if he is pure, so is God; if he is wicked, God is wicked, etc. Hence to the damned He will forever seem evil, but to the righteous, righteous and as He actually is in Himself. But this changeableness is external. . . ." ⟨See also above, 32.⟩ For the interpretation, see the justified critique of Erich Seeberg (*Grundzüge der Theologie Luthers*, 50; *Luthers Theologie*, 2:152) by Gyllenkrok (*Rechtfertigung und Heiligung*, 27).

29. Sermon of Febr. 24, 1517: WA 1:139.17: Cicero says that people are wise because they follow reason as the best guiding principle. "This correct reason, this prescription ⟨of reason⟩, this natural intelligence, which now is being taught . . . and praised, is that wisdom and intelligence from which the Father hides what belongs to him in order to make that reason foolish and guilty, and compel man to seek grace as the guiding principle"; *The Bondage of the Will*, 1525: WA 18:685.3.25.31 ⟨LW 33:139f.⟩: ". . . we have to argue in one way about God or the will of God as preached, revealed, offered, and worshiped, and in another way about God as he is not preached, not revealed, not offered, not worshiped. To the extent, therefore, that God hides himself and wills to be unknown to us, it is no business of ours. . . . God must therefore be left to himself in his own majesty, for in this regard we have nothing to do with him, nor has he willed that we should have anything to do with him. . . . Diatribe ⟨i.e., the title of the book by Erasmus⟩, however, deceives herself in her ignorance by not making any distinction between God preached and God hidden, that is, between the Word of God and God himself. God does many things

that he does not disclose to us in his word; he also wills many things which he does not disclose himself as willing in his word. . . . we must be guided by the word and not by that inscrutable will. After all, who can direct himself by a will completely inscrutable and unknowable? It is enough to know simply that there is a certain inscrutable will in God, and as to what, why, and how far it wills, that is something we have no right whatever to inquire into . . . but only to fear and adore."

30. *The Book of Deuteronomy with Notes*, 1525: WA 14:640.30: "All these ⟨i.e., whatever conclusions the prophets drew from the First Commandment⟩ flow from that great sea of the First Commandment and flow again back into it. ⟨Therefore⟩ there is no richer consolation, and there is no stronger voice that has been heard or ever should be heard, ⟨but⟩ also no voice that is harder or stricter than that voice of the First Commandment: 'I am the Lord your God.'"

31. *First Lectures on the Psalms*, 1513-15: WA 4:318.40; see also ibid., WA 3:22.4: "An experienced person knows that whoever meditates on the Lord's law will be taught very many things in a short time, and as if a deluge of understanding invades him 'through the ⟨thunder of God's⟩ cataracts' ⟨Ps. 42:7⟩."

32. Instead of other authors, see Welzel, *Naturrecht und materiale Gerechtigkeit*, 67ff.; for the most recent materials, see Günter Stratenwerth, *Die Naturrechtslehre des Johannes Duns Scotus* (Göttingen, 1951), 73ff.

33. For Gabriel Biel, see Georg Ott, "Recht und Gesetz bei Gabriel Biel," *ZSRG*.K 38 (1952): 251ff.

34. See, e.g., Biel, *Expositio missae*, lectio 68.G: "Out of itself the divine will is right and its own norm because it is supreme and eternal, and has no higher or prior norm to which it conforms itself in order to be right. It is the norm both of its own and of all rectitude and justice ⟨or: 'righteousness'⟩; therefore it cannot be ambiguous, and it cannot be not right ⟨at all times⟩."

35. See Lammers, *Luthers Anschauung vom Willen*, 18f., 55ff.; Hägglund, *Theologie und Philosophie bei Luther*, 9: "Luther's relationship to Occamism is . . . not unequivocal."

36. *The Book of Deuteronomy with Notes*, 1525: WA 14:583.30 ⟨*LW* 9:49f.⟩: ". . . if we consider carefully, only two or three words ⟨of the Old Testament⟩ will properly signify law, namely, *huqqa* and *mishpat*, statute and law, . . . *huqqa* means that by which we are set in order toward God; . . . *mishpat* means that by which we are set in order toward man. These two are enough, and this contrast seems to me to be valid and consistent. For so also Moses begins in this chapter ⟨Deut. chapt. 4⟩: 'Hear the statutes and laws which I teach,' as though he were gathering together everything in these two words, as if he said: 'I shall teach you how to live properly before God and men.'" See also *First Lectures on the Psalms*, 1513-15: WA 4:370.25.

37. The differentiation between the divine positive law and the divine natural law according to the procedure of their promulgations is a longstanding doctrine; see, e.g., Thomas Aquinas, *Summa theologiae* II.2. q.57. art.2 ad 3. But prior to the voluntaristic doctrine of law, promulgation does not have the quality of a statute.

38. *That These Words of Christ, "This is My Body," Still Stand Firm against the Fanatics*, 1527: WA 23:261.12: "God . . . does not give a word or commandment to us without setting it in a corporeal, external thing and presenting it to us"; ibid., WA 23:261.16: ". . . in all of Scripture you will not find a word of God in which is not enclosed a corporeal, external thing and presented."

39. *Lectures on Romans*, 1515-16: WA 56:23.8, 74.9. Prenter (*Spiritus creator,* 21) considered the phrase 'the law written in the hearts' the "basic formula" for Luther's understanding of the work of the Holy Spirit.

40. For the beginnings of this legal doctrine in Luther's thinking, see Johannes Heckel, *Initia iuris,* 18. For Luther's "realistic pneumatism" or "pneumatic realism," see Karl G. Steck, *Luther und die Schwärmer* (Zürich, 1955), 12f.

41. *First Disputation against the Antinomians,* 1537: WA 39.I:387.8: "In Matt. 5⟨:20⟩ . . . ⟨Christ⟩ defines ⟨law⟩ as a doctrine to which one does not do justice with any kind of external conduct, but which requires a clean heart and demands perfect obedience, perfect fear ⟨in the sense of respect or awe⟩, and perfect love for God"; ⟨Matt. 5:20 does not deal with 'law' but with 'righteousness' which has to be 'better' than the righteousness of the scribes and Pharisees; on that basis, Luther discussed what he considered to be Christ's definition of the kind of law which demands this 'better' righteousness;⟩ see also ibid., WA 39.I:404.24. Luther made similar statements already in *On Christian Freedom* ⟨Latin text⟩, 1520: WA 7:50.15. Of course, Luther also knew of 'external' laws which God gave to the people of Israel and to Christians; *The Book of Deuteronomy with Notes,* 1525: WA 14:601.25. Yet this does not mean that God himself acts as legislator of external norms; rather, such laws are man-made law, and yet at the same time they are *God's external order* in the sense which is discussed above, 69f.

42. *Magnificat,* 1521: WA 7:546.24: "No one is able to understand God or God's Word correctly unless he has received such an understanding from the Holy Spirit without any means. But no one can receive this understanding of God's Word from the Holy Spirit unless he experiences, tries, and feels God's Word. Through such an experience the Holy Spirit teaches us as if we were in his own school, and outside of this school nothing but phony words and balderdash are being taught."

43. *First Commentary on Galatians,* 1519: WA 2:468.33 ⟨LW 27:188⟩: "The Law — not only the Ceremonial Law but also the Moral Law, indeed, even the most sacred Decalog, which contains God's eternal commandments — is the letter and a tradition of the letter *(litera, literalis traditio),* which, as St Augustine amply demonstrates in his book *On the Spirit and the Letter,* neither gives life nor justifies but kills and causes sin to abound." In this sense Luther differentiated between divine laws and divine righteousness; *Second Commentary on Galatians,* 1535: WA 40.I:241.17 ⟨LW 26:138⟩: "Thus we must learn to distinguish all laws, even those of God, and all works from faith and from Christ, if we are to define Christ accurately"; *Second Lectures on Galatians,* 1531: WA 40.I:360.5: "Faith is the creator of the divinity, not in the *persona* ⟨of God⟩ but in us. Outside of faith, God loses his righteousness, glory, works, etc., and there is nothing of ⟨his⟩ majesty and divinity where there is no faith"; ibid., WA 40.I:612.8 ("⟨Outside of grace,⟩ law . . . is . . . hell"), 241.5; *First Lectures on the Psalms,* 1513-15: WA 3:28.32: "The gospel is not Christ's law unless it is grasped in faith. For the Lord's law is alive and efficacious; therefore it is not letters or words"; ibid., WA 4:306.11: "The law of Moses contains two things: the letter which signifies something and the Spirit which is signified by the letter"; ibid., WA 3:457.8, 4:314.21; *Postilla for Christmas,* 1522: WA 10.I.1:628.18: ". . . it is impossible to perceive Christ and his gospel through reason — faith alone is the perception."

44. See Gabriel Biel, *Collectorium in IV libros Sententiarum* (Basel, 1512), lib. III. dist. 37.q.un.D: "The divine law is acquired through Revelation, the natural law from the natural light of the intellect. Yet whatever is acquired from the natural light of the intellect,

God can reveal directly. This is obvious in the giving of the commandments, with which the ⟨section⟩ about the two laws deals, the old one and the new one."

45. According to our present terminology. In the later Middle Ages 'positive law' was still often restricted to man-made law, and the positive divine law was simply called divine law, i.e., revealed law. See Biel, *Collectorium*, lib. III. dist. 37.q. un.C: "The preceptive law . . . is divine law, natural ⟨law⟩, man-made or positive law." But our present usage, which starts with that of Thomas Aquinas (see above, 283 n. 37), can also be found at that time; see e.g., John of Turrecremata ⟨Juan de Torquemada⟩, *Summa de ecclesia domini* (Lyons, 1496), lib. III. c.57.

46. Yet Luther used *lex divina* or *ius divinum* also with the traditional meaning. In light of the reformer's known lack of concern for precision in terminology, it is necessary to determine in each case the meaning of a term he used. ⟨When one does this, then it becomes clear that Luther used both terms sometimes in a rather general sense, sometimes in the specific sense outlined thus far (divine natural law, divine positive law), and sometimes interchanged both terms. In any case, the context has to supply the meaning of *lex* and *ius*, or *Gesetz* and *Recht* (literally: "law" and "right"); this is especially the case if one considers the specific meaning which 'right' has for the American reader.⟩ *Lex divina* (divine law) could have the following meanings for Luther: (1) *The divine natural law* and the *divine spiritual basic rights* of a believer derived from this law ⟨see above, 247 n. 53⟩. E.g.: *Theses on Monastic Vows*, 1521: WA 8:330.3: evangelical freedom is a gift *divini iuris* (of divine law), *ius* designating the divine natural law; *Second Lectures on the Psalms*, 1518-21: WA 5:646.15. (2) *The substantive secular natural law* (see above, 54ff.), esp. in the form of the Decalogue. E.g.: *On Trade and Usury*, 1524: WA 15:321.27.32; *Disputation on Matt. 19:21*, 1539, thesis 24: WA 39.II:40.25: the Second Table, "i.e., by divine and natural law" *(iure divino et naturali)*; *The Papacy at Rome*, 1520: WA 6:307.30: something is contrary to God, law, reason, and nature; *Second Lectures on the Psalms*, 1518-21: WA 5:337.22: greed, deceit, and usury are crimes according to the divine law *(iuris divini)*. (3) *The divine positive law of the hidden church* (see Johannes Heckel, *Initia iuris*, 24). E.g.: *Against Eck's Judgment*, 1519: WA 2:642.16: in matters of the Power of the Keys exists equality of all "bishops" ⟨in the sense of priests, or pastors, and bishops⟩ by divine law *(iure divino)*; *Explanations of the Ninety-five Theses*, 1518: WA 1:531.36, 533.15: evangelical penance, or Christ's doctrine about penance, is *lex divina* or *ius divinum*; ibid., WA 1:536.19: in matters of penance the pope is not authorized to interfere with the divine judgment, which is *ius divinum*; *Against Eck's Judgment*, 1519: WA 2:645.21: public penance (Matt. 18:15ff.) is a matter of the divine law *(iuris divini)*; *On the New Testament, That Is, the Mass*, 1520: WA 6:354.21, and *The Babylonian Captivity of the Church*, 1520: WA 6:503.13: Christ's law *(Gesetz, lex)*. (4) *The institutional secular natural law* (see above, 70ff.). E.g.: *The Babylonian Captivity of the Church*, 1520: WA 6:555.4, 556.8, and *The Estate of Marriage*, 1522: WA 10.II:280.22, 281.13: marriage is a matter of the divine law *(ius divinum)*, or God himself has prohibited something; *The Book of Deuteronomy with Notes*, 1525: WA 14:552.34: the qualifications demanded in divine law *(iure divino)* of those who hold offices of governmental authority. (5) *The law of the Jewish nation* issued by God, or upon God's command issued by Moses and other rulers (see above, 81f.). E.g.: *The Babylonian Captivity of the Church*, 1520: WA 6:557.30, *Second Lectures on the Psalms*, 1518-21: WA 5:226.36, *Second Lectures on Galatians*, 1531: WA 40.I: 543.11f.: *lex divina*. (6) *The natural law* as used in natural science. E.g.: *Sermons on the Ten Commandments*, 1518: WA 1:416.8: some people make out of a miracle that God has

enacted once "a natural law *(ius naturale)* and an infallible consequence ⟨in the sense that it has to happen again if the saints, who are connected with such a miracle, are entreated and intercede with God on behalf of the petitioner⟩, something, so it seems to me, that certainly is not far removed from tempting God." — For a list of the possible meanings of *ius divinum,* see *Admonition to Peace,* 1525: WA 18:291ff. — See also Irmgard Schmidt, "Das göttliche Recht und seine Bedeutung im deutschen Bauernkrieg" (phil. diss. Jena, 1939), 23ff., and below, 302 n. 5.

47. ⟨See also above, 42: *figura* and *res* of the law.⟩

48. *Lectures on Romans,* 1515-16: WA 56:199.21 ⟨*LW* 25:182f.⟩: ". . . the law that is inborn and present in creation, not given; found at hand, not handed down to them ⟨i.e., the Gentiles⟩; alive, not contained in letters."

49. ⟨See also above, 44f.⟩

50. See Horst Quiring, "Luther und die Mystik," *ZSTh* 13 (1936): 150ff., 179ff. For the connections and the differences between Luther and Mysticism, see Prenter, *Spiritus creator,* 26; for secondary literature, see ibid., 305f., nn. 23-24.

51. See Althaus, *Gebot und Gesetz,* 12: "It is the Creator's action that God's will confronts us as commandment."

52. *Disputation on Faith and Law,* 1535: WA 39.I:48.1 ⟨*LW* 34:113⟩: ". . . we are not all apostles, who by a sure decree of God were sent to us as infallible teachers"; *First Lectures on the Psalms,* 1513-15: WA 4:370.25 ⟨*LW* 11:504f. to Ps. 119:37⟩: "⟨The Psalmist says:⟩ '. . . those Pharisees malign You as unjust in setting up Your spiritual law *(in constitutione legis tuae spiritualis),* which is the law of faith and the Gospel. . . .'"

53. *Against Eck's Judgment,* 1519: WA 2:642.12: "The divine law . . . rules among us in Holy Scripture"; *On the Councils and the Church,* 1539: WA 50:616.3: Holy Scripture is the kingdom's law *(Recht),* which is the law of the holy church; *That These Words of Christ, "This is My Body," Still Stand Firm against the Fanatics,* 1527: WA 23:153.1: "my ⟨i.e., God's⟩ Word."

54. *Admonition to Peace,* 1525: WA 18:304.9: "If you ⟨i.e., the revolting peasants⟩ and your undertakings are to last, even though both the law *(Recht)* of God and the Christian law in the New and the Old Testament, and also natural law *(das natürliche Recht)* are against you, you have to produce a new and specific command of God, . . . a command which is confirmed through signs and miracles . . ."; ibid., WA 18:321.2. For details, see *The Book of Deuteronomy with Notes,* 1525: WA 14:684.19.31 ⟨*LW* 9:188ff.⟩. For a situation in which miracles are tested, see Luther to George Spalatin: April 12, 1522: WA.B 2:493.24.

55. For the right and duty of examining such revelations and signs, see *The Book of Deuteronomy with Notes,* 1525: WA 14:647.14.21 ⟨*LW* 9:129f.⟩. See further, *Sermons on John, Chapters 14 and 15,* 1537: WA 45:529.20: "Therefore all miracles and miraculous events have to be judged in light of God's Word, whether they are in accord with it and agree with it"; *Sermons on Matthew, Chapters 5-7,* 1530-32: WA 32:531.9.36: "One should not accept miracles or signs which are contrary to the confirmed doctrine." — For 'Word-bound Spirit', see Heinrich Bornkamm, *Das Wort Gottes bei Luther* (Munich, 1933), 10. See further, Kurt D. Schmidt, "Luthers Lehre vom heiligen Geist," in *Schöffel Festschrift,* 154ff.

56. *Against the Heavenly Prophets,* 1525: WA 18:136.17: "God does not want to give the Spirit and faith to anyone without the external Word and sign which he has instituted for this purpose . . ."; *The Bondage of the Will,* 1525: WA 18:654.33 ⟨*LW* 33:92⟩: "The psalmist celebrates ⟨Scripture's⟩ clarity thus: 'A Lamp to my feet and a light to my path' [Ps.

119:105]. He does not say: 'A lamp to my feet is thy Spirit alone,' though he speaks of the work of the Spirit too: 'Thy good Spirit shall lead me on the level ground' [Ps. 143:10]. In this way it is called both a 'way' and a 'path', no doubt because of its entire certainty." See also Hermann, *Klarheit der Heiligen Schrift*, 35f. — For 'Word' as a 'tool' of the Holy Spirit, see Prenter, *Spiritus creator*, 107ff.; Meinhold, *Luthers Sprachphilosophie*, 21ff., 38, 56ff.

57. *The Book of Deuteronomy with Notes*, 1525: WA 14:684.17: "⟨The Spirit does not speak⟩ without the Scripture"; *Against the Heavenly Prophets*, 1525: WA 18:185.19; Luther to Philip Melanchthon: Jan. 13, 1522: WA.B 2:424.16 ⟨*LW* 48:366⟩: ". . . God has never sent anyone, not even the Son himself, unless he was called through men or attested by signs." See also Wilhelm Maurer, "Luther und die Schwärmer," *SThKAB* 6 (1952): 7ff.; Prenter, *Spiritus creator*, 247ff.; Steck, *Luther und die Schwärmer*, 13.

58. ⟨In the sense of dead or killing letter; see 2 Cor. 3:5f.⟩

59. For 'law of personification' in Luther's theology, see Jacob, *Gewissensbegriff in der Theologie Luthers*, 8. See also Kohlmeyer, *Von Augsburg nach Wittenberg*, 6: "For Luther grace . . . is realistically present in the Word — but only in a definite personalistic form as the divine Spirit"; Gerhard Ebeling, "Zur Lehre vom triplex usus legis in der reformatorischen Theologie," *ThLZ* 75 (1950): 235ff.; below, 446 n. 7.

60. *Lectures on Genesis*, 1535-45: WA 42:318.5ff. ⟨*LW* 2:78f.⟩: "The general rule ⟨of the jurists⟩ is that one must consider, not who is saying something but what someone is saying; for the blunders of teachers are often manifest. But when we are dealing with God's commands and true obedience, this statement must be inverted. In this instance one must consider, not what is being said or commanded but who is speaking. If, in the instance of the divine commands, you should consider what is being said and not who is saying it, you would easily stumble. . . . If, then, we consider Him who gives the command, it will readily become clear that even though God's commands appear ordinary and trivial, they are nevertheless of the highest order. . . . Therefore we must diligently adhere to this rule: We should consider, not what is commanded, but who gives the command." Luther made similar statements in *First Lectures on the Psalms*, 1513-15: WA 4:305.27. For the opposite view, see *Glossa ordinaria* ⟨see above, 246 n. 44⟩ ad verbum 'Quantalibet' in *Decretum Gratiani* c.5. D.IX ⟨Friedberg 1:17⟩: "One may not consider who speaks but what is being spoken"; see also *Decretum Gratiani* c.8. D.XIX ⟨Friedberg 1:63⟩: ". . . it may not be questioned who or what sort of a person proclaims something, but what he proclaims."

61. ⟨In the sense of speaking into man's ears, and through them into man's heart.⟩

62. *First Lectures on the Psalms*, 1513-15: WA 4:323.3: "The words ⟨of the Lord⟩ are life and spirit . . ."; ibid., WA 4:341.35: "⟨The Lord⟩ speaks a living and spiritual word . . ."; ibid., WA 4:380.18: "Blessed are they who hear God's Word, a word of such a great majesty which by a nod ⟨i.e., as the nod of the head of the majesty⟩ holds, makes, and accomplishes all things"; *On Psalms 23-25*, 1513-16: WA 31.I:480.23: "When God . . . himself teaches, he does not speak letters and syllables but inspires living love *(charitas)*." See also Ragnar Bring, *Luthers Anschauung von der Bibel* (Berlin, 1951), 13: "The Word ⟨of God⟩ is understood as a creating word which transforms all that is being said into action"; Prenter, *Spiritus creator*, 118.

63. See 1 Cor. 4:20, and Emil Brunner, *Das Mißverständnis der Kirche* (Stuttgart, 1951), 47.

64. *Lectures on Psalm 51*, 1532: WA 40.II:421.16: "Having given us his gifts, God does not disappear and leave us alone. He did not act and disappear . . . ⟨for⟩ to create is to pre-

serve continuously and to strengthen. Hence the Holy Spirit is present as a helper and works his gift in us, a gift which the Holy Spirit himself works in us"; ibid., WA 40.II:422.14: "the Holy Spirit does not rest quietly."

65. *Confession concerning Christ's Supper*, 1528: WA 26:282.19, 283.4: ". . . a doing word . . . . ⟨God's Word is⟩ a word of power which creates what it says." See also Wingren, *Die Predigt*, 45; Meinhold, *Luthers Sprachphilosophie*, 11.

66. See Schott, *Fleisch und Geist nach Luthers Lehre*, 23.

67. With this judgment on man-made laws Luther under no circumstances intended to promote an external legal formalism ⟨see at the end of this note⟩ of obedience to the law; see sermon of Nov. 24, 1532: WA 36:362.13: ". . . in the eyes of people it means nothing to do something without the heart being involved, simply from hypocrisy. . . . The emperor and the people, too, ⟨demand that⟩ the heart ⟨be involved⟩, even though they are unable to see it." See also Erik Wolf, *Rechtsgedanke und biblische Weisung* (Tübingen, 1948), 36: ". . . we have to free ourselves from the unbiblical prejudice that law and justice are matters only of the external order of life. . . ." For Luther's position on man-made commandments and external legal formalism, see also *First Lectures on the Psalms*, 1513-15: WA 4:323.33, 324.8, 407.9. ⟨Heckel wrote "äußerliche Legalität," which we translated with "external legal formalism"; for this interpretation, see *Meyers enzyklopädisches Lexikon*, 9th ed., s.v. "Legalität."⟩

68. Therefore Luther rejected the scholastic differentiation between the fulfillment of the law in terms of the substance of the action and the fulfillment of the law in terms of the intention of the legislator. He accepted as valid only the latter position; *Sermons on the Ten Commandments*, 1518: WA 1:462.31, 469.27, 500.3.

69. Instead of other authors, see Biel, *Collectorium*, lib. II. dist. 42.q.un. art. 1. C; lib. III. dist. 37.q.un. art. 3. dub.1.P, and Ott, "Recht und Gesetz bei Biel," *ZSRG*.K 38 (1952): 274f.

70. *First Lectures on the Psalms*, 1513-15: WA 3:621.13: ". . . the Father judges through the Son. . . . whoever will have been found to be in conformity to him, will be added to him. However, whoever is not in conformity to him, will be separated ⟨from him⟩"; *Sermons on the Ten Commandments*, 1518: WA 1:436.36 (see also Johannes Heckel, *Initia iuris*, 47 n. 194): ". . . the truly righteous is God-formed . . ."; *Magnificat*, 1521: WA 7:597.16: ". . . through faith man does what God wants and, conversely, God does what man wants; therefore Israel is a God-formed and God-possessing man, who in God, with God, and through God is a lord who can do and is able to do all things"; *On Christian Freedom* ⟨Latin text⟩, 1520: WA 7:60.6: "The internal man conforms to God, and through faith he is created in God's image . . . , his only task is to serve God with joy and gratitude in freely given love." — See also Biel, *Expositio missae*, lectio 68.H: "All justice ⟨or: 'righteousness'⟩ and uprightness of the rational creature consists of his conformity to God's will. In fact, crookedness and injustice ⟨or: 'unrighteousness'⟩ of the rational creature arise from the lack of conformity of his will to the divine will." For 'conformity', see also Prenter, *Spiritus creator*, 25ff.

71. *Sermons on the Ten Commandments*, 1518: WA 1:462.5: "Spiritual is only what is or signifies a will alive to do or to omit"; *The Book of Deuteronomy with Notes*, 1525: WA 14:729.31 ⟨*LW* 9:278⟩: "The Law demands an inner nature which loves it and has pleasure in it; thus it is satisfied and fulfilled if it is loved."

72. After the Fall, love will again be given by God only through faith in Christ; see

above, 89f. See also *Second Lectures on the Psalms*, 1518-21: WA 5:37.25: "... by nature the will to do the Lord's law is in no one; that will is bestowed upon us from heaven by the heavenly Father, the farmer and planter who transplants us from Adam into Christ."

73. *Sermons on the Ten Commandments*, 1518: WA 1:437.27 (see also Johannes Heckel, *Initia iuris*, 47 n. 194): "... all commandments (as I said) require love; if they are fulfilled without love, that is, without an eager, prompt, joyful, and willing will, they are not fulfilled."

74. *First Lectures on the Psalms*, 1513-15: WA 4:100.21; *Second Disputation against the Antinomians*, 1538: WA 39.I:460.17: "<The law> says: 'I am spiritual, i.e., I require a pure and spiritual heart; my demands are met only through a joyful heart and spirit which have been renewed by the Holy Spirit'"; *Second Lectures on the Psalms*, 1518-21: WA 5:630.15.

75. *Summer Postilla*, 1526: WA 10.I.2:405.32: "... in this law God demands of us ... to surrender our will to his will so that we abandon our intellect, will, power, and abilities, and are able to declare from our heart: 'Your will be done'"; *Reply to the Dialogue of Silvester Prierias on the Power of the Pope*, 1518: WA 1:649.28: "In each good work the children of God are rather acted upon than that they act; <follows Rom. 8:14>. And those works ... are the best which Christ does in us, without us ..."; *Psalm 110 Explained*, 1518: WA 1:709.6.15.

76. *First Lectures on the Psalms*, 1513-15: WA 4:407.10: "... God does not demand a work but the subordination and obedience of the will and mind"; ibid., WA 3:280.27: "<God> does not demand our things but us"; ibid., WA 3:323.26; *Sermons on Genesis*, 1523-24: WA 14:160.11: "God looks first at the person before he looks at the work, etc."; ibid., WA 14:161.5.

77. A moral will does not suffice to fulfill God's law; only a theological will, which is faith, fulfills God's law; *Second Lectures* and *Second Commentary on Galatians*, 1531/1535: WA 40.I:457.5.22. For similar materials, see *First Lectures on Galatians*, 1516-17: WA 57.II:79.16.

78. Following 1 Thess. 5:23, Luther had a trichotomous psychology: spirit, soul, and body; see Maurer, *Freiheit eines Christenmenschen*, 93. The spirit is "the highest, deepest, noblest part of man ... capable of grasping eternal, invisible things which are beyond understanding." The soul is "according to its nature identical with the spirit, but has another task"; i.e., "it makes the body alive and works through the body"; it is capable of grasping only those things "which reason can recognize and judge." Finally, the body has the "task" of "developing and using the things which the soul recognizes and the spirit believes." See *Magnificat*, 1521: WA 7:550.20.28.35, 551.4.12. This structure of man is either oriented toward God — and then the whole man is spiritual man (see Schott, *Fleisch und Geist nach Luthers Lehre*, 56ff.; Hermann, *Luthers Lehre von Sünde und Rechtfertigung*, 11) — or it is turned away from God, and then the whole man is carnal man. For the difference between seeking God "with the whole mind" and "the whole heart," developed in the context of Ps. 119:10, see *First Lectures on the Psalms*, 1513-15: WA 4:307.34 <LW 11:417f.>. — For 'spiritual understanding of law', see sermon of Dec 7, 1516: WA 1:105.10, and the notes on the sermons of Tauler, 1516: WA 9:103.39.

79. *Sermons on the Ten Commandments*, 1518: WA 1:447.23: "... the Lord's law is spiritual ... and organizes internal man. Therefore it binds and claims the heart first"; sermon of Oct. 31, 1516: WA 1:96.9: "... God wants man's internal <life> and his heart; if someone would do or give everything except the heart, he would do nothing"; *Second Lectures on the*

Psalms, 1518-21: WA 5:553.36: "... the law is not fulfilled through works but through love, and it does not want to be loved with works fictitiously done, but it wants to be loved ⟨with the heart⟩"; *Sermons on the First Epistle of St. Peter*, 1523: WA 12:353.23: "If you want to do the best good works and live in the best estate, you will find nothing else than faith and love, the highest estate"; *First Lectures on the Psalms*, 1513-15: WA 4:308.14.

80. *Lectures on Genesis*, 1535-45: WA 42:349.4: "... God did not create an evil man, but a perfect, wholesome, holy, and God-acknowledging man, endowed with the right reason and good will toward God." See also sermons of 1514-21: WA 4:690.6.

81. *Magnificat*, 1521: WA 7:571.24 ⟨LW 21:325⟩: "The ... words of the Spirit are so great and profound that no one can comprehend them without having, at least in part, the same Spirit."

82. *Disputation against Scholastic Theology*, 1517, thesis 63: WA 1:227.16: "⟨Man outside of God's grace⟩ sins by not fulfilling the law spiritually."

83. *Summer Postilla*, 1526: WA 10.I.2:406.36: "If you love God with all your heart, with all your soul, and with all your emotions, then it is impossible that you do not experience ⟨this also⟩ in your external life; i.e., when all that you do, whether you sleep or be awake, work or rest, eat or drink, is directed toward that ⟨one point, namely,⟩ that it is done out of love for God and from the heart"; *First Lectures on the Psalms*, 1513-15: WA 3:17.31: "... the primary root of all good is the grounding of the will in the law of the Lord"; ibid., WA 3:26.3 ⟨LW 10:26⟩: "... where there is an abundance of opportunity for doing, the will is not enough; yes, it never is a will, unless it proceeds to words and deeds and becomes incarnate in them (i.e., makes its appearance in the physical word and deed)"; ibid., WA 3:248.27 ⟨LW 10:206⟩: "... it is not enough for any virtue to be internal, unless it also proceeds into the open to a work of the senses"; ibid., WA 3:25.20; *Second Lectures on the Psalms*, 1518-21: WA 5:35.15.

84. *First Lectures on the Psalms*, 1513-15: WA 4:19.24.28 ⟨LW 11:174⟩: "He must be righteous in the will and thus go on to the deed. ... Just as original sin is there before our every evil work, so original righteousness would have been there before our every good work"; ibid., WA 3:593.37: "This is the fire of love which occupies all things that are in man and subdues them to itself"; *Sermons on the Ten Commandments*, 1518: WA 1:430.22: "Who does not sin with the heart, sins neither with word nor deed"; ibid., WA 1:500.22: "... whatever the will does before God is called an action, even if the work does not follow"; *The Seven Penitential Psalms*, 1517: WA 1:163.20: "... the will in someone is the most important thing in all external action and life ..."; *Second Lectures on the Psalms*, 1518-21: WA 5:28.14: "... who has the right faith in God ⟨literally: 'who is orthodox toward God'⟩ cannot but do good works and maintain good morals"; ibid., WA 5:35.13; *The Book of Deuteronomy with Notes*, 1525: WA 14:619.25: "... ⟨Moses⟩ has set the heart straight, the source of ⟨all⟩ works ..."; *First Commentary on Galatians*, 1519: WA 2:576.29.

85. *Sermons on the Ten Commandments*, 1518: WA 1:461.28: "... ⟨the law⟩ is called spiritual because it can be fulfilled only through the spirit, and it demands the spirit, i.e., it is not fulfilled unless it is fulfilled with the heart and a cheerful will. Such a spirit is not in us, but it is given to us through the grace of the Holy Spirit, and that grace ⟨creates⟩ people who voluntarily are in the Lord's law."

86. *Lectures on Romans*, 1515-16: WA 56:239.10 ⟨LW 25:225⟩: "... the desire for God or the search for Him is the very love of God which makes us will or love what our under-

standing causes us to know"; sermon of June 10, 1537: WA 45:100.13: "... God in his divine essence ⟨is⟩ love itself." See also *First Commentary on Galatians*, 1519: WA 2:499.22f.

87. *Sermons on the Ten Commandments*, 1518: WA 1:502.23: "... only through love are the law and the prophets fulfilled. Therefore if it is the law of nature, it is the law of the healthy and incorrupt nature, which is identical with love."

88. *Lectures on Romans*, 1515-16: WA 56:86.16 ⟨*LW* 25:78 n. 42⟩: "... we ourselves do not love Him, but He has first loved us and still loves us. He does not love because we love, but because He loves, we love (cf. 1 John 4:10)." For Luther's and Augustine's understanding of God's love, see Prenter, *Spiritus creator*, 29, 32, 34.

89. *To the Christian Nobility*, 1520: WA 6:444.30: "It is impossible that God is pleased with any work, or that any work accomplishes something with God, which is not done in voluntarily given love"; *Second Lectures on the Psalms*, 1518-21: WA 5:52.2: "⟨The law of Christ is a law⟩ of freedom and agreeableness..."; *First Lectures on the Psalms*, 1513-15: WA 4:320.3 ⟨*LW* 11:434f.⟩: "Not that it is necessary for us to understand and do everything in this life, but that the mind should be prepared never to want to stop doing and understanding more fully..., to know no boundary, no end, no restriction. This is what it means to be in the spirit of freedom for which no law and statute has been set, because ⟨if one lives in this spirit one⟩ does more than is commanded so that if one could live eternally, one would strive eternally to know and do, and never move backward."

90. *Sermons on the Ten Commandments*, 1518: WA 1:512.35: "You say: 'It is a counsel and not a commandment.' I answer: how can it be a counsel and not a commandment since Christ at once adds ⟨Matt. 7:12⟩: 'For this is the law and the prophets'?" See also *Lectures on Genesis*, 1535-45: WA 42:82.10, 83.9; *On Monastic Vows*, 1521: WA 8:581.35, 582.26.

91. *First Commentary on Galatians*, 1519: WA 2:500.24: "... no good work is good unless it is being done with a cheerful, willing, and rejoicing heart, i.e., in the spirit of freedom."

92. In thesis 19 of the disputation of Palladius and Tilemann (1537) Luther argued (WA 39.I:203.20) that in the life to come there is no law, because then the substance of the law itself ⟨i.e., love; see thesis 18⟩ exists, which in the present life the law demands. For this thesis, see also Hermann, *Luthers Lehre von Sünde und Rechtfertigung*, 46ff. For 'lex vacua', see *Second Disputation against the Antinomians*, 1538: WA 39.I:433.5.

93. ⟨I.e., an 'empty law' *(lex vacua)*, in the sense of a law which is not experienced as oppression or as a threat of punishment.⟩

94. *Lectures on Romans*, 1515-16: WA 56:481.23 ⟨*LW* 25:474⟩: "... though ⟨Paul⟩ was free, yet he made himself the servant of all. This kind of servitude is the highest freedom, for it lacks nothing and receives nothing, but rather gives and bestows. Thus it is truly the best freedom and one which is the peculiar property of Christians"; *Second Lectures on the Psalms*, 1518-21: WA 5:38.27: "... the freedom of Christian righteousness.... This 'blessed man' ⟨Ps. 1:1; Vulgate⟩ is free at all times, in each work, for each situation, toward each person"; ibid., WA 5:39.4: "... he serves all people, everywhere, through all things...." Instead of other authors, see Wingren, *Luthers Lehre vom Beruf*, 40.

95. *The Babylonian Captivity of the Church*, 1520: WA 6:537.15: "... the conscience of freedom..."; *note:* Luther did not say "the freedom of conscience"! See also below, 375 n. 150, 387 n. 32.

96. Therefore Luther occasionally spoke of *pactum legis* ⟨in the sense of legal contract or legal covenant⟩; see e.g., *First Lectures on the Psalms*, 1513-15: WA 4:41.2.21.

97. ⟨For 'external legal formalism', see above, 288 n. 67.⟩ *Lectures on Romans*, 1515-16: WA 56:22.7: "... those who do the works of the law, but without the will ⟨motivating them⟩, do not do them."

98. *Lectures on Romans*, 1515-16: WA 56:341.27 ⟨LW 25:330⟩: "... we must not think that the apostle wants to be understood as saying ⟨Rom. 7:14-20⟩ that he does the evil which he hates, and does not do the good which he wants to, in a moral or metaphysical sense, as if he did nothing good but only evil; for in common parlance this might seem to be the meaning of his words. But he is trying to say that he does not do the good as often and as much and with as much ease as he would like. For he wants to act in a completely pure, free, and joyful manner, without being troubled by his rebellious flesh, and this he cannot accomplish."

99. In *A Model for Consecrating a True Bishop*, 1542, Luther spoke of "spiritual, eternal matters," i.e., matters which are related to God; WA 53:246.8.15.

100. In *Lectures on Romans*, 1515-16: WA 56:172.10ff. ⟨LW 25:152⟩, Luther argued that righteousness precedes works so that the righteous works of a man who is not yet righteous through faith "are to be compared with the antics of hucksters in the marketplace," just as no one can perform the works of a priest or bishop "who has not been consecrated and made holy for this" ⟨i.e., lacks the specific spiritual quality of a consecrated priest. *Note:* Luther made this comparison at a time when he had not yet questioned the assumed *special spiritual quality* of priests.⟩ — See also above, 289 n. 78.

101. *Lectures on Romans*, 1515-16: WA 56:356.22.27 ⟨LW 25:346⟩: "... grace has set before itself no other object than God toward which it is carried and toward which it is moving; it sees only Him, it seeks only Him, and it always moves toward Him, and all other things which it sees between itself and God it passes by as if it had not seen them and directs itself only toward God. This is the 'upright heart' (Ps.7:10) and the 'right spirit' (Ps. 51:10). But nature set for itself no object but itself toward which it is borne and toward which it is directed; it ... seeks ... only itself in all matters, and it passes by all other things and even God Himself in the midst, as if it did not see them, and is directed only toward itself. This is the 'perverse heart' (Ps. 101:4) and the 'wicked heart' (Prov. 26:23)."

102. *First Commentary on Galatians*, 1519: WA 2:500.33: "They all ⟨i.e., works⟩ are carnal works or matters of the letter when they are being done under the force of the letter while the law of the Spirit is absent. They are spiritual works when they are being done under the presence of the law of the Spirit ..."; *Second Lectures on Galatians*, 1531: WA 40.I:347.10: "Whatever in man is most outstanding is called 'flesh' if it is outside of the Spirit, even his religion"; for a similar satement, see *The Bondage of the Will*, 1525: WA 18:740.19. See further, *Preface to Romans*, 1522: WA.DB 7:12.5.18: "⟨This is the way one has to understand 'flesh' and 'spirit':⟩ 'Flesh' is a human being which internally and externally lives and does those things which benefit the flesh and serve temporal life. 'Spirit' is a human being which internally and externally lives and works in such a way that he serves the Spirit and the life to come. Without this understanding of these words you will not ever be able to understand ... a single book of Holy Scripture"; *First Lectures on the Psalms*, 1513-15: WA 3:37.34: "... 'letter' are all those things which pertain only to the body and the senses and not to the spirit"; ibid., WA 4:390.17: "⟨'Letter'⟩ is the carnal sense in Scripture...."

103. See Schott, *Fleisch und Geist nach Luthers Lehre*, 35, 50.

104. Therefore Luther rejected 'spiritual things' *(res spirituales)* as defined in Canon

law. He especially was offended by the fact that 'temporal goods' *(temporalia),* which were the property of the church, or of which the church was the beneficiary, were called 'spiritual things' *(spiritualia),* ⟨i.e., things belonging to the spiritual world, the church, and therefore being beyond the control of the non-spiritual world, secular society⟩. See Johannes Heckel, "Recht und Gesetz," *ZSRG*.K 26 (1937): 366. Important for him was the connection of something with its actual use in the service of the hidden church, i.e., Christ's kingdom. See sermon of Nov. 24, 1532: WA 36:354.32: "⟨In God's kingdom⟩ all things, dates, persons, places, and churches are consecrated and used in a special way"; sermon of Aug. 3, 1544: WA 49:532.8: "It is a scandal how they ⟨i.e., the papists⟩ abuse the word 'spiritual'. . . . ⟨But⟩ 'spiritual' designates whatever is not carnal because it is sanctified through the Word and the Holy Spirit"; *Second Lectures on the Psalms,* 1518-21: WA 5:58.28: ". . . it is holy because it has been separated from secular use and dedicated to sacred and divine use only. In terms of ceremony and writing, this dedication happens through the popes as human beings, but in truth and in spirit it happens through the Holy Spirit poured into our hearts"; ibid., WA 5:447.22: "Above we have said that holy is what is removed ⟨i.e., from the world and sin⟩ and hidden and only in God's presence; this is not that profane ⟨understanding of⟩ 'holy' with which today the popes call only houses, vestments, and the clergy holy in order to mislead the souls of men, but ⟨that understanding⟩ in which the Holy Spirit sanctifies by his anointing. Thus saints are not the Jews, the clergy, or a human being which has a specific name ⟨i.e., the name of a saint of the church⟩, unless they hold on to God through faith and through this faith become a participant in God's nature, whose 'life is hidden with Christ in God' < Col. 3:3⟩"; ibid., WA 5:570.12: ". . . we have often enough said that 'holy' designates something which is removed, hidden, and invisible, where the senses do not reach and where reason does not comprehend anything. . . . Through this ⟨the psalmist⟩ nicely indicates the nature of faith"; ibid., WA 5:359.19; sermons of 1527: WA 23:734.20: "When God orders something external, in whatever way it may be external, it is nevertheless spiritual in those cases which are connected with him. . . . My Christ is something external, and yet in my faith I grasp him; therefore he is something spiritual. Parents are flesh and blood, but with the presence of God's commandment ⟨they are⟩ spiritual"; *The Papacy at Rome,* 1520: WA 6:297.24: only through faith are things truly spiritual.

105. *Lectures on Romans,* 1515-16: WA 56:448.1 ⟨*LW* 25:440⟩: ". . . God rules the world with universal righteousness, by which He acomplishes what ought to be done in all, by all, and through all. . . ." — For 'law as genus', see below, 353 n. 2.

106. See above, 17.

107. *Lectures on Romans,* 1515-16: WA 56:234.15: "⟨Universal righteousness⟩ is infinite, eternal, and totally divine. . . ."

108. *Lectures on Hebrews,* 1517-18: WA 57.III:162.2 ⟨*LW* 29:165⟩: ". . . since the Word of God is above all things, outside all things, within all things, before all things, behind all things, and therefore everywhere, it is impossible to escape to any place. But since it is 'living' and therefore eternal, it is impossible for the punishment or the cutting ⟨see Heb. 4:12⟩ ever to cease. But since it is 'powerful' and potent, it is impossible to resist it."

109. *First Lectures on Galatians,* 1516-17: WA 57.II:102.1: "Universal love"; *Postilla for Lent,* 1525: WA 17.II:95.17: "This commandment of love is a short and a long commandment, one single commandment and many commandments. It is no commandment and it is all commandments. In itself it is a brief and single commandment, and intelligence

can soon grasp its meaning. But it is a long and many commandments when it is practiced, for it contains all commandments and governs them all. If one considers the works ⟨by which this commandment is fulfilled, then⟩ it is no commandment at all, for there is no specially designated work ⟨by which this commandment is fulfilled⟩. Yet it is all the commandments, because all the works which fulfill all the commandments are and ought to be its work. Therefore the commandment of love nullifies all commandments and yet affirms all commandments."

110. *First Lectures on the Psalms,* 1513-15: WA 3:157.5: ". . . God's Word is efficacious, strong and strengthening, and makes strong people."

111. *The Book of Deuteronomy with Notes,* 1525: WA 14:584.34: "In one short sentence this passage ⟨Deut. 4:2⟩ condemns all man-made laws, and it decrees that in a matter of conscience nothing be valid except God's law and Word."

112. See also Suss, "La loi éternelle," *Positions luthériennes* 10 (1962): 130ff.

113. *Lectures on Genesis,* 1535-45: WA 42:128.6 ⟨LW 1:171⟩: "Moreover, this detriment ⟨i.e., the immensity of Original Sin⟩ also helps us to gain an insight into original righteousness on the basis of what we have lost, or by way of contrast"; ibid., WA 42:86.11 ⟨LW 1:113⟩.

114. ⟨See above, 41f.⟩

115. ⟨See above, 25f.⟩

116. *First Lectures on Galatians,* 1516-17: WA 57.II:73.21: "It is the law of the letter that is written in letters, or pronounced in words, or thought through in the mind without the will delighting in it." We find a part of this passage almost verbatim also in *First Commentary on Galatians,* 1519 (WA 2:499.34), with the addition: "This is the law of works, the old law, the law of Moses, the law of the flesh, the law of sin, the law of wrath, the law of death. . . ."

117. *First Lectures on Galatians,* 1516-17: WA 57.II:73.15: ". . . it is the law of the Spirit that is not at all written with letters, is not promulgated in words, is not conceived in the mind. But it is the living will and the living experience, 'written with God's finger' ⟨Deut. 9:10⟩, i.e., through the Holy Spirit, 'in our hearts'; Rom. 5⟨:5⟩. I.e., it is total righteousness, simultaneously internal and external, namely, the 'good tree' with its fruits ⟨Matt. 7:17⟩." In *First Commentary on Galatians,* 1519, Luther added to this description of the spiritual law (WA 2:499.20) that this spiritual law is "the intellectual light of the mind and a fire ⟨in⟩ the heart"; as "law of faith ⟨the spiritual law is⟩ the new law, Christ's law, law of grace which justifies and fulfills all ⟨commandments⟩ and crucifies the lusts of the flesh"; *The Misuse of the Mass,* 1521: WA 8:539.17: "⟨Christ's⟩ law is faith, i.e., a living, spiritual fire with which hearts are enflamed by the Holy Spirit ⟨and⟩ newly born and converted so that they desire, will, do, and are nothing other than what the law of Moses demands and commands with words." — See also Ernst Wolf, "'Natürliches Gesetz' und 'Gesetz Christi' bei Luther," *EvTh* 2 (1935): 315f.

118. *First Lectures on the Psalms,* 1513-15: WA 3:348.11: ". . . God does not speak to ears, as man does, but only to the heart. . . . the voice of a man cannot speak to the heart, it can speak only to ears. . . ." According to Luther, law is instruction *(doctrina);* therefore the difference between God's legislation and man's legislation can be determined just as the difference in the pronouncement of doctrines can be determined; sermon of January 6, 1517: WA 1:124.10: "This is the difference between a doctrine pronounced by man and God's doctrine pronounced by God himself: the preacher can speak, and the sound of his

words can reach ears but not farther; but God reaches the heart and teaches there, indeed, God accomplishes that his Word at once ⟨becomes effective⟩, both inwardly and outwardly." For this passage, see also *First Lectures on the Psalms*, 1513-15: WA 4:308.4 ⟨*LW* 11:418⟩: "'The heart,' however, is the very power of desiring, namely, the will, in which love is, as knowing is in the mind, there, affection, here, understanding."

119. *Lectures on Romans*, 1515-16: WA 56:74.9: "'... the law of the Spirit' ⟨Rom. 8:2⟩, 'written with the finger of God' ⟨Deut. 9:10⟩, i.e., '⟨God's⟩ love ... poured out in ⟨our⟩ hearts through the Holy Spirit' ⟨Rom. 5:5⟩"; ibid., WA 56:203.8: "I think that 'the law has been written in ⟨our⟩ hearts' ⟨Rom. 2:15, though that passage speaks of the Gentiles⟩ is the same as 'love being poured out in ⟨our⟩ hearts through the Holy Spirit' ⟨Rom. 5:5⟩. Actually, this love is Christ's law and the fulness of the law of Moses; indeed, it is a law without law, measure, terminal point, limitations; it is a law which extends, however, far beyond all that ⟨any⟩ law commands or can command."

120. See above, 290 n. 84. ⟨See also above, 252 n. 14.⟩

121. And this in contrast to man-made law "which has been perceived from the outside, or has been made known through man"; *Lectures on Romans*, 1515-16: WA 56:22.18 ⟨*LW* 25:18 n. 11⟩.

122. *First Lectures on the Psalms*, 1513-15: WA 3:281.2 ⟨*LW* 10:230⟩: "... His Word *(verbum)* always comes into being and is done.... For then God speaks *(dicit)* without intermediary through the internal Word *(verbum)*, and that is omnipotent and efficacious. But quite often He also spoke *(locutus est)* many things that were not done and heard and received by men. Therefore God's speaking *(locutio)* and God's Word *(verbum)* differ greatly"; ibid., WA 3:262.15.18, 280.17.19. See also Erich Seeberg, *Luthers Theologie*, 1 (Göttingen, 1929), 197f., 2:28f.

123. In contrast to this, human speech is mediated ⟨through word and sound⟩; see *First Lectures on Galatians*, 1516-17: WA 57.II:94.23.

124. *First Lectures on the Psalms*, 1513-15: WA 4:355.11: "God, you teach internally through the Spirit; it pours out that love which is your law." See also above, 294 n. 118.

125. For the believing members of Christ's kingdom this process is being described as "enduring, rapture, impulse *(passio, raptus, motus)*, through which the soul is captured ..., and seized by the Word ..., which captures and miraculously leads the soul"; see *Second Lectures on the Psalms*, 1518-21: WA 5:176.13ff., and Loewenich, *Luthers theologia crucis*, 119 n. 3. But this "supreme ecstasy" *(extasis suprema; Second Lectures on the Psalms*, 1518-21: WA 5:202.25) is at the same time the most terrible *Anfechtung* ⟨see above, 248 n. 55⟩ by the devil (see Maurer, *Freiheit eines Christenmenschen*, 120), it is an ecstasy of enduring or suffering *(extasis passionis; Second Lectures on the Psalms*, 1518-21: WA 5:107.17). For *Anfechtung*, see instead of other authors, Prenter, *Spiritus creator*, 30ff., 308 n. 44 (where literature is cited); Ernst Wolf, *Peregrinatio*, 1:75ff. See also *Second Lectures on the Psalms*, 1518-21: WA 5:144.34: ⟨Luther commented on Ps. 5:8: "Lead me ... in your righteousness ... ; make *your way* straight before me." To say⟩ "'My way' ⟨would not be wrong, because⟩ on the basis of God working in us it is correct for us to say that we act, even though this acting is rather being raptured and led, and enduring God who acts ⟨in us⟩, as is pointed out in this verse when it is stated: 'Lead me' and 'make your way straight'; this means that man does not act by himself but that he is being led and moved by God."

126. *On Good Works,* 1520: WA 6:245.17, and Maurer, *Freiheit eines Christenmenschen,* 100, 102.

127. ⟨A true, or pure, suffering of (or in) the will, or enduring in the will.⟩ See *Second Lectures on the Psalms,* 1518-21: WA 5:177.11.26; *Magnificat,* 1521: WA 7:550.10; Maurer, *Freiheit eines Christenmenschen,* 101. Similar statements can be found already in the sermon of Oct. 12, 1516 (*Sermons on the Ten Commandments,* 1518): WA 1:437.21: "... we are good not through doing but through enduring, because when we endure the divine actions we are at rest" (see also Johannes Heckel, *Initia iuris,* 47 n. 194). See also *First Lectures on Galatians,* 1516-17: WA 57.II:31.19: "God's action is our enduring ⟨or: 'suffering'⟩"; *The Seven Penitential Psalms,* 1517: WA 1:210.11: "... the total life, activity, and conduct of the internal man ⟨is⟩ ... nothing other than trusting in God and total surrender to God's will."

128. *Explanations of Luther's Theses Debated in Leipzig,* 1519: WA 2:421.7: "From this ... follows that free will is purely passive in all its actions.... ⟨It follows further⟩ that the distinction of the sophists, to the effect that a good action as a whole comes from God but not totally, is empty chattering. Such an action comes from God as a whole and totally, because the will is seized, pulled, and moved ⟨toward such a good action⟩ by grace. This pulling, which flows over into the members and forces both of the soul and the body, is the activity of grace and nothing other. ⟨The following illustrates the situation:⟩ The moving of a saw which cuts wood is something totally passive, done by the woodcutter to the saw, which contributes nothing to its being moved. Yet because the saw is being moved, it acts nevertheless upon the wood, being driven to do so rather than driving itself. This sawing is called the work of the saw with the woodcutter, even though the saw is only passive; more about this later on."

129. ⟨See above, 46.⟩

130. *Psalm 110 Explained,* 1518: WA 1:698.9. See also Luther's notes on the sermons of Tauler, 1516: WA 9:102.34: "... Salvation in its totality is resignation of the will in all things ... both in spiritual and temporal things, and only faith ⟨literally: 'nude faith'⟩ in God"; ibid., WA 9:103.6: "... it is necessary ... that one has an indifferent and empty ⟨literally: 'nude'⟩ will"; ibid., WA 9:103.35: "... it is necessary that ⟨man's spiritual condition⟩ be empty ⟨literally: 'nude'⟩ and stripped bare of all of our wisdom and righteousness, and ⟨that man⟩ rely only on God and think nothing of himself."

131. ⟨See Gen. 12:1, 4.⟩ *Psalm 110 Explained,* 1518: WA 1:700.6.

132. *Decretum Gratiani* post c.3. D.IV ⟨Friedberg 1:6: "Gratianus"⟩.

133. ⟨Rechtsgenossen.⟩ *Lectures on Romans,* 1515-16: WA 56:262.29 ⟨LW 25:250⟩, and Johannes Heckel, "Recht und Gesetz," ZSRG.K 26 (1937): 308f.

134. ⟨See above, 41f., 45, 46f.⟩

135. *First Lectures on the Psalms,* 1513-15: WA 4:309.14 ⟨LW 11:419⟩: "... You are such a lawgiver who gives blessing. You command and grant the grace of fulfilling what You command. You give the Law and at the same time also its fulfillment. Not so Moses: Such a lawgiver did not bestow blessing but curse. For the Law works wrath (Rom. 4:15) and curses those who do not fulfill it"; ibid., WA 3:541.39: "They are ... not the works of God ... unless God does them in us." See also *The Bondage of the Will,* 1525: WA 18:753.35.

136. *Lectures on Genesis,* 1535-45: WA 42.17.16 ⟨LW 1:21⟩: "... God calls into existence the things which do not exist (Rom. 4:17). He does not speak grammatical words; He speaks true and existent realities. Accordingly, that which among us has the sound of a

word is a reality with God." — See also Meinhold, *Genesisvorlesung Luthers*, 148, and id., *Luthers Sprachphilosophie*, 11.

137. ⟨For "substantive content," see *BLD*, s.v. "Substantive Law."⟩ Luther called this "forma legis, quid debeamus"; *The Bondage of the Will*, 1525: WA 18:681.27 ⟨*LW* 33:134: "the essential meaning of the law and what we ought to do"⟩.

138. *The Book of Deuteronomy with Notes*, 1525: WA 14:609.2: ". . . ⟨man knows⟩ that God demands his works, his own work"; ibid., WA 14:609.26: ". . . I want to do all things which God wants . . ."; *First Lectures on the Psalms*, 1513-15: WA 3:154.5: "The works of God are what he wants us to do and what is in agreement with God [Gal. 5⟨:22⟩: 'the works and fruit of the Spirit'] . . ."; ibid., WA 3:320.2: to do heavenly works; *On Good Works*, 1520: WA 6:204.31: "In this ⟨divine good⟩ work ⟨of faith in Christ; see line 25f.⟩ all works have to be done, and their goodness has to be received ⟨from faith⟩ the way one receives a fief"; *Second Lectures on the Psalms*, 1518-21: WA 5:394.29: ". . . the work of the Lord (i.e., faith) . . ."; ibid., WA 5:395.9, 396.24.32; *The Babylonian Captivity of the Church*, 1520: WA 6:530.14: ". . . ⟨faith⟩ is the most outstanding and lofty work of all works. . . . For it is God's and not man's work, as Paul teaches ⟨see Eph. 2:8f.⟩. All other works are done with us and through us, this one alone is done in us and without us"; sermon of March 10, 1523: WA 11:57.30: "The works which we do through the Holy Spirit in faith, we do not do, but God does them . . ."; *Second Lectures on Galatians*, 1531: WA 40.I:411.8: "In theology, 'to do' ⟨Gal. 3:10⟩ means something other than . . . in law"; ibid., WA 40.I:412.2: ". . . 'to do' requires faith."

139. *Second Lectures on the Psalms*, 1518-21: WA 5:553.36: "The law is not being fulfilled through works but through love, and the law does not want to be cherished with phony works but wants to be cherished with affection." — See also Nygren, *Agape and Eros*, Part II.2:463ff.

140. See above, 46f.

141. *Preface to Romans*, 1522: WA.DB 7:2.19: "Here you may not understand the little word 'law' in human terms, as if it were teaching you what to do and what not, as man-made laws do, so that one fulfills the law with works, regardless whether the heart is involved. God judges according to what is at the bottom of the heart. His law, therefore, demands the bottom of the heart and is not content with works; rather, his law punishes those works which are not done from the bottom of the heart as hypocrisy and lies"; ibid., WA.DB 7:4.29: ". . . the law is spiritual — what is this? Were the law corporeal, then one could fulfill it with works. But since it is spiritual, no one can fulfill it unless whatever you do comes from the bottom of the heart. But such a heart no one gives to you except God's Spirit; that Spirit makes man conform to the law so that man from the heart delights in the law and henceforth does all things motivated not by fear or coercion but by a free heart. The law is, then, a spiritual law; it wants to be loved and fulfilled with such a spiritual heart, and it requires such a spirit. . . ." For a similar statement, see the sermon of Nov. 24, 1532: WA 36:360.11: "⟨Love⟩ should be a gushing love flowing from the heart outwardly, just as a little brook or a swiftly running water which flows on and on and cannot be stopped, nor will it dry up."

142. See Otto Hof, "Luthers Lehre von Gesetz und Evangelium," *ELKZ* 3 (1949): 133; Althaus, *Gebot und Gesetz*, 29; Hermann, *Luthers Lehre von Sünde und Rechtfertigung*, 46f.

143. *Lectures on Genesis*, 1535-45: WA 42:124.6: ". . . Adam's nature was to love God . . ."; *Disputation of Henry Schmedenstede*, 1542: WA 39.II:196.11: "In his incorrupt na-

ture Adam fulfilled all of God's commandments without a mediator." See also *Second Lectures on the Psalms*, 1518-21: WA 5:37.18.

144. ⟨Law coexisting with nature.⟩ In *Lectures on Genesis*, 1535-45: WA 42:123.38, Luther opposed the Scholastics who understood man's original righteousness to have been an '*additional* gift' given to man in the status of the incorrupt nature.

145. See above, 260 n. 14.

146. *Second Lectures on Galatians*, 1531: WA 40.II:155.11: "The spiritual people say: 'This I do, this I know because of the divine call'"; sermon of Sept. 30, 1537: WA 45:147.1: "The law indicates what you have been, what you should be, and what you should become."

147. Throughout Luther's doctrine of natural and of Christian ethics, as well as throughout his legal doctrine, we find the admonition to use the gifts and works of the Creation in a correct, i.e., God-pleasing way; see, e.g., *Whether Soldiers, Too, Can Be Saved*, 1526: WA 19:624.19, and many passages, esp. in his writings which deal with sociopolitical issues. See also Lau, *"Äußerliche Ordnung,"* 65ff.; Törnvall, "Der Christ in den zwei Reichen," *EvTh* 10 (1950/51): 76; Ebeling, "Triplex usus legis," *ThLZ* 75 (1950): 235ff.

148. Richard Nürnberger ("Die lex naturae als Problem der vita christiana bei Luther," *ARG* 37 [1940]: 12) maintained the opposite position when he argued: "For the evangelical Christian natural law cannot provide a solid foundation for the order of human life."

149. In his sermon of Oct. 8, 1531 (WA 34.II:313.6ff., 314.2ff.), Luther dealt with the "best and highest status" of the spiritual man ⟨i.e., to love God and the neighbor⟩ and the relationship of that status to the estates in the secular law and in the man-made ecclesiastical law. He saw in this status the "highest order" ⟨i.e., in contrast to monastic orders⟩; but since for him this status was *common* to all Christians, he saw in it also a "low order." — See also Wingren, *Luthers Lehre vom Beruf*, 53 n. 167. Emil Brunner was to the point (*Gerechtigkeit*, 104) when he stated that the natural law was the nucleus of Luther's doctrine of the estates. Wünsch also affirmed this position; but in terms of the history of law, he was only partially correct when he stated: "Luther adopted the concept 'natural law' from the scholarly tradition; he modified it by replacing it with the concept 'vocation', and he understood the concept 'natural law' in this sense"; see Wünsch, *Ethik des Politischen*, 137.

150. *First Lectures on Galatians*, 1516-17: WA 57.II:78.12ff.; sermon of March 17, 1518: WA 1:271.26: ". . . I will freely follow Christ by surrendering my will."

151. See, e.g., *Instruction for the Confession of Sinners*, 1518: WA 1:259.13: "⟨This⟩ is the compendium of the Ten Commandments: Whatever you want people to do to you, you also do to them. For this is the law and the prophets. Matt. 7 ⟨:12⟩"; *Sermons on the Ten Commandments*, 1518: WA 1:502.17.20.23, 512.31, 513.3: Christ's law and natural law.

152. *Decretum Gratiani* preface to D.I ⟨Friedberg 1:1⟩.

153. *Lectures on Romans*, 1515-16: WA 56:136.4.

154. ⟨Literally: "divine positive right" *(Recht, ius).*⟩ For the history of the term 'positive law', see Stephan Kuttner, "Sur les origines du terme 'droit positif,'" *Revue historique du droit français et étranger*, 15 (1936): 728ff. — If I see correctly, Luther used the term 'positive law' *(ius positivum)* only for human positive law, just as Gabriel Biel had done (see above, 285 n. 45). See, e.g., Luther's brief in the matter of the divorce of Henry VIII, dated Sept. 3, 1531: WA.B 6:181.132 ⟨for this brief, see also *LW* 50:No. 245⟩: Henry VIII

may not divorce his wife because "First, neither according to natural nor divine law *(ius)* is it prohibited to marry the wife of one's ‹deceased› brother, but only according to positive law *(ius)*"; ibid., WA.B 6:181.139: human and civil law *(lex)*; ibid., WA.B 6:186.132: positive laws *(leges)*, natural law *(lex)*, God's law *(lex)*; *First Lectures on the Psalms*, 1513-15: WA 4: 294.11ff.: contrast between positive law *(lex)* and spiritual law; *Lectures on Genesis*, 1535-45: WA 42:268.20: ". . . they had no respect for God ‹i.e., the divine positive law regarding marriage›, the natural and the positive law *(ius)*." ‹These passages also show (see above, 285 n. 46) Luther's lack of concern for precision in terminology; *ius* and *lex* could have the same content.›

155. *Lectures on Genesis*, 1535-45: WA 42:83.17: ". . . the law has been given to the righteous Adam . . ."; see also ibid., WA 42:83.33.

156. *That These Words of Christ, "This is my Body," Still Stand Firm against the Fanatics*, 1527: WA 23:263.4.

157. See Meinhold, *Genesisvorlesung Luthers*, 408.

158. Münter (*Kirche und Amt II*, 24ff.) pointed out that in the confessional writings of the Evangelical Lutheran church the term 'divine law' *(ius divinum)*, if it is used for the order of the church, is understood as Christ's spiritual law for the spiritual church. If the term 'divine law' is used in connection with the secular order, then, according to Münter, one has to assign to it "a broader and more general meaning, which is close to the use of the term in the scholastic natural-law tradition." Münter was unable to explain these quite different meanings in the use of the same term.

159. *Second Lectures on the Psalms*, 1518-21: WA 5:142.16: "Just as God's Word was never absent from the world, so the worship of God was never absent. Therefore we have to accept that in all ages there were places where this worship was conducted ‹literally: 'divine things were done'› . . ."; ibid., WA 5:142.33, 504.13ff. See esp. *Lectures on Genesis*, 1535-45: WA 42:79.3: "‹In Gen. 2:16f.› the church is established before there was an *oeconomia* and a *politia*"; for this passage, see also ibid., WA 42:71.33, 72.10, 73.23, 80.19, 82.41, 105.37. See further, Bornkamm, *Luther und das Alte Testament*, 178; Gottfried Forck, *Die Königsherrschaft Jesu Christi bei Luther* (Berlin, 1959), 53f.

160. For the chronological sequence of the establishment of church and of marriage, which is also the sequence of the important before the less important, see *Lectures on Genesis*, 1535-45: WA 42:79.20 ‹LW 1:104›: ". . . after the establishment of the church the government of the home *(oeconomia)* is also assigned to Adam in Paradise. But the church was established first because God wants to show by this sign, as it were, that man was created for another purpose than the rest of the living beings. Because the church is established by the Word of God, it is certain that man was created for an immortal and spiritual life . . ."; sermon of Oct. 7, 1537: WA 45:163.7: "Adam stood upright before God, . . . his body was chaste and pure, . . . ‹therefore his› marriage would have been pure. He was created in the image of God for being in relationship with God, as the angels are to this moment."

161. *Lectures on Genesis*, 1535-45: WA 42:100.25: "The legitimate joining of male and female is a divine ordinance and institution." For marriage as an institution set up in the divine positive law, see Luther's brief in the matter of the divorce of Henry VIII, dated Sept. 3, 1531: WA.B 6:182.2 (*lex divina* which says Matt. 19:6). See also *Second Lectures on the Psalms*, 1518-21: WA 5:550.13: "Consent . . . makes marriage." — For a different view, see Gunnar Hillerdal, *Gehorsam gegen Gott und Menschen. Luthers Lehre von der Obrigkeit*

und die moderne evangelische Staatsethik (Göttingen, 1955), 53 n. 6 (on p. 54). He argued that "even though one would be on shaky ground, it is possible to differentiate in Luther's thinking between a kind of 'creation order' and an order which emerged after the Fall. *Yet theologically seen, this distinction is irrelevant for Luther.* This fact is obvious on the basis of the way in which the doctrine of the governances is structured; here is emphasized God's ongoing creating 'anew' in the face of all the perversion in the world. Granted, for Luther the *oeconomia* was the 'source of the state' (see *Lectures on Psalms 120–134*, 1532-33: WA 40.III:220.13), and granted that in one single passage Luther also stated about secular governance that 'such governance ⟨can be⟩ proposed by an evil man, who had no mandate from God to do this' (see *Sermons on Exodus*, 1524-27: WA 16:353.21ff.), *yet the principal separation has been eliminated:* the *oeconomia* functions in the world of sin, and in the *politia* God fights against the devil. Therefore one may not consider the *oeconomia* to be a special legal institution the way in which recently Johannes Heckel in *Lex charitatis* (1953) has done; in the section 'the divine law in the status of the incorrupt nature' he dealt with 'church and marriage as institutions of the divine positive law.'" Hillerdal followed Lau, *Luthers Lehre von den beiden Reichen*, 36f.

162. *The Book of Deuteronomy with Notes*, 1524: WA 14:603.37 ⟨LW 9:63f.⟩: "'I am the Lord your God' ⟨Deut. 5:6⟩. This Commandment seems to establish for a simple and childish people mere ceremonies concerning images. Nevertheless it is indeed a spiritual Law, which demands the inner worship of the Spirit even in regard to those external images."

163. *Against the Heavenly Prophets*, 1525: WA 18:168.27: ". . . the perverted way of ⟨Karlstadt's⟩ spirit makes all of God's external and corporeal orders into something spiritual and internal, and conversely, what God wants to be internal and spiritual, into something external and corporeal . . ."; see also ibid., WA 18:181.23.30ff.

164. *The Large Catechism*, 1529: WA 30.I:134.35 ⟨BC 366.17⟩.

165. *The Estate of Marriage*, 1522: WA 10.II:276.21.25.31.

166. *Lectures on Genesis*, 1535-45: WA 42:XXII.25 ⟨preliminary sketches for the lecture to be delivered⟩: without the Fall of Adam and Eve "there would have been only the church and *oeconomia*."

167. *Lectures on Genesis*, 1535-45: WA 42:105.38: "⟨In the Garden of Eden⟩ the external worship ⟨of God in⟩ the future church is established by divine authority."

168. According to Luther, the married life of believing Christians again shows a trace of the "spiritual, internal desire," which was characteristic of marriage in Paradise; see *The Estate of Marriage*, 1522: WA 10.II:298.23, and Reinhold Seeberg, "Luthers Anschauung von dem Geschlechtsleben und der Ehe und ihre geschichtliche Stellung," *LuJ* 7 (1925): 113.

169. For the most sacred and to be revered work of procreation as a common good and gift of blessing bestowed upon Adam and Eve, see *Lectures on Genesis*, 1535-45: WA 42:87.33, 88.2, 89.2 ⟨LW 1:115ff.⟩.

170. *Lectures on Genesis*, 1535-45: WA 42:XXII.20 ⟨preliminary sketches⟩: "Thus far there is no *politia*. It begins in the following chapter on Cain. There would not have been any need for the *politia*, just as there would not have been any need for medicine or the arts; all things would have been healthy, all things would have been upright under the dominion of man"; ibid., WA 42:87.11; *Sermons on Genesis*, 1523-24: WA 14:172.9: ". . . Cain . . . has become a worldly man, and thereafter he created the worldly kingdom, from

which originate all things which the world uses." See also Meinhold, *Genesisvorlesung Luthers*, 194. For Augustin, see Spörl, "Augustinus — Schöpfer einer Staatslehre?" *HJ* 74 (1955): 75.

171. As the relationship of a husband with his wife would have been understood in a purely spiritual way, so the relationship of children with parents, "God's vicars," would have been understood in a purely spiritual way; the spiritual interpretation of the Fourth Commandment proves this; *Sermons on the Ten Commandments*, 1518: WA 1:447.27: "The spiritual honor of parents is a manifestation of the heart and the respect <for> a manifest will" <i.e., the will of the parents, or God's will expressed in the Fourth Commandment; another possible translation of the last section would be: "the respect of a will ready (to obey)">.

172. One cannot eliminate one section of the divine law without destroying the whole of the divine law. See Luther's statement regarding withholding the cup of the Lord's Supper from the laity in *The Babylonian Captivity of the Church*, 1520: WA 6:503.13: ". . . if we permit that one institution of Christ be changed, we have already made all his laws void, and everyone may dare to say that he is not bound by any law or institution of Christ. For especially in Scripture one thing sets up the whole."

173. See Luther on natural law in *Second Lectures on Galatians*, 1531: WA 40.II:72.2: "You have the best of all law books in your heart; <therefore> pay attention only to yourself and you need not open <any other law> books." The divine positive law also is exhaustive because only God himself can grant an exception to the obligation of obeying its institutions; *The Estate of Marriage*, 1522: WA 10.II:276.21ff., 277.1ff.

174. *Second Lectures on the Psalms*, 1518-21: WA 5:167.39: ". . . each man who does not put his hope only in God is a liar. For man is man until such time that he becomes God, who alone is truthful; through participating in God, man, too, will become truthful while he adheres to God through true faith and hope . . . ." For 'participation in God' in Luther's thought, see Söhngen, *Einheit in der Theologie*, 60, 63ff.

175. For Troeltsch's interpretation, see his *Die Sozialehren der christlichen Kirchen und Gruppen*, 533; he argued that Luther had a "deeply rooted feeling for the contrast between the order of love and the order of law." Yet Luther always spoke of the law of love! *(Lex charitatis, ius charitatis, der Liebe Recht.)*

176. *Second Lectures on Galatians*, 1531: WA 40.I:676.11: "If you want to be a Christian and proclaim this article <of the righteousness of Christ>, then know that you will put the whole world upsidedown."

177. *Second Lectures on Galatians*, 1531: WA 40.I:418.5ff. <see also the edited version of these lectures, WA 40.I:418.12ff., or *LW* 26:267f.>; *Disputation of Palladius and Tilemann*, 1537: WA 39.I:231.18: "All words which are transferred from philosophy to theology are made new." See also thesis 20 of *Disputation on Christ's Divinity and Humanity*, 1540: WA 39.II:94.17, together with Hägglund, *Theologie und Philosophie bei Luther*, 100. <See also below, Index of Subjects: *Law*, s.v. "law, needs/has new grammar, rules, vocabulary.">

178. <Literally: "political.">

179. *Second Lectures on Galatians*, 1531: WA 40.I:393.5: "Few people pay attention <to the distinction between the two kinds of righteousness>, and it is easy to mix the heavenly and the <earthly; see n. 178> righteousness"; *Disputation of Palladius and Tilemann*, 1537: WA 39.I:233.11: "There are two different kinds of righteousness; one is of the law and is accomplished through our efforts and works, the other is the divine mercy imputed to us

from God through faith ⟨or: 'the other is through the divine mercy imputed to us from God through faith'⟩." See also Hägglund, *Theologie und Philosophie bei Luther*, 96.

180. *Second Lectures on Galatians*, 1531: WA 40.I:569.10: ". . . man is unable to judge the law because the law rules in man; therefore it judges man. No jurist is able to judge the law — only Christ can do this — because the law is above man; no one can judge the law unless he is a Christian"; see also ibid., WA 40.I:572.7f.

Notes to Chapter 9

1. ⟨"Human law" and "natural law" would literally read "human right" and "natural right." The following materials make clear, however, that in light of our common understanding of 'right' (see also above, 247 n. 53) law is the appropriate translation in both cases. — For "substantive law," see *BLD*, s.v. "Substantive Law."⟩

2. See *First Lectures on the Psalms*, 1513-15: WA 4:51.12.

3. *First Lectures on Galatians*, 1516-17: WA 57.II:98.12: "Righteousness is two-fold, i.e., of the flesh and of the spirit, figuratively and in reality, shadow and truth, external and internal, old and new, of works and of faith. . . . "

4. *The Seven Penitential Psalms*, 1517: WA 1:187.24: ". . between ⟨God⟩ and ⟨the people who justify themselves and think highly of their abilities⟩ is a constant legal battle going on about God's words and works."

5. The first traces of this idea can be found as early as in *Lectures on Romans*, 1515-16: WA 56:507.25 ⟨*LW* 25:501⟩. Here Luther said about Rom. 14:4 ("Who are you to pass judgment on a servant who does not belong to you?"): ". . . it is contrary to the law of nature *(ius naturae)* and ⟨offensive to⟩ all men to pass judgment on ⟨another man's⟩ servant, and thus it is not only against God but also against every human judgment . . . that people of this kind act." "Law of nature" designates the divine natural law, and "every human judgment" designates the secular natural law. From Luther's early period I cite, e.g., *To the Christian Nobility*, 1520: WA 6:418.7.9; here Luther spoke of "God's commandments and Christian law *(Recht)*" and of "natural or secular law *(Recht)* and reason." The difference between the divine natural law, which for Luther was identical with the spiritually understood Decalogue and the law of Christ, and the secular natural law is most clearly expressed in *Admonition to Peace*, 1525: WA 18:304.7: "⟨To usurp the role of judge in one's own case and to avenge oneself⟩ is not only contrary to the Christian law and the gospel but also contrary to natural law ⟨in the sense of secular natural law⟩ and equity"; ibid., WA 18:304.9: ". . . both the divine and the Christian law in the New and in the Old Testament, and also natural law ⟨in the sense of secular natural law⟩ oppose you ⟨i.e., the rebelling peasants⟩"; ibid., WA 18:328.5: "⟨The peasants should act as people⟩ who want ⟨to live by⟩ human and natural law, and not as people who want Christian law"; ibid., WA 18:310.16: "A Christian is a rare bird. Would God grant that the majority of us would ⟨at least⟩ be good, pious heathen who observe the natural law, I won't even mention the Christian law."

6. When Luther used the term 'natural law' *(Naturrecht)*, he did so in a rather loose way. ⟨And he could exchange the content of *ius* and *lex* (*Recht* and *Gesetz*); see also above, 285 n. 46, 298 n. 154.⟩ The term could designate: (1) The spiritual ⟨divine⟩ natural law; e.g., *Whether Soldiers, Too, Can Be Saved*, 1526: WA 19:638.30: "the natural law *(Recht)*

taught by Christ in Matt. 7<:12>." (2) The secular natural law; e.g., *Admonition to Peace,* 1525: WA 18:307.5.17: "the universal divine and natural law" *(Recht),* which also the heathen have to obey; *On Keeping Children in School,* as below, 313 n. 88. Luther could use the term 'natural law' *(Gesetz)* with the meaning 'spiritual <divine> natural law', and with the meaning 'secular natural law'; e.g., *Against the Heavenly Prophets,* 1525: WA 18:80.30: "In Matt. 7<:12> Christ himself summarizes all the prophets and laws in this natural law *(Gesetz,* i.e., the divine natural law): 'What you want people to do to you, do also to them,' for this is the law and the prophets. And in Rom. 13<:9> Paul does the same when he summarizes all the commandments of Moses <in the commandment of> love, which the natural law *(Gesetz,* i.e., the secular natural law) also teaches: 'Love your neighbor as yourself.'" See also Luther's *Answer to the Theological Faculty of the University of Louvain and of Cologne,* 1520: WA 6:185.30. — Gerhard Pfeiffer *(Totaler Staat — und Luther?* [Neuendettelsau, 1951], 15ff.) did not recognize the difference between the divine natural law and the secular natural law.

7. <Even when Heckel occasionally used "human natural law," we shall use "secular natural law" in order to be consistent.>

8. The use of 'law' *(ius)* in the term 'natural law' can be justified with Luther's usage. See, e.g., *The Book of Deuteronomy with Notes,* 1525: WA 14:582.8: "That law *(lex)* is called *ius,* which pertains to the governing of people and does not especially pertain to God"; ibid., WA 14:583.22: "<*Mishpat*> . . . designates, strictly speaking, that which in Latin is called *iura,* i.e., the laws *(leges)* through which in secular matters order is established among people in a civilized way; therefore the word is also often used for some convention and custom, as, e.g., for the law of nations or <secular> natural law *(ius)* . . . ."

9. *Lectures on Genesis,* 1535-45: WA 42:106.12: ". . . through <the Fall> we have lost a most beautifully illuminated reason and will which conformed to God's Word and will."

10. *Lectures on Romans,* 1515-16: WA 56:356.18 <LW 25:345f.>: "In vain do some people magnify the light of nature and compare it with the light of grace, since it is actually more a shadow and something contrary to grace"; *Second Lectures on the Psalms,* 1518-21: WA 5:153.26: "Reason's ideas about God and the divine works and words" are "the advice of the wicked" <Ps. 1:1>; *On Monastic Vows,* 1521: WA 8:629.23: "<We will place monastic vows in the context of> natural reason, i.e., that dim light of nature; through itself <natural reason> does not understand God's light and work so that in affirmative statements (as one says) its judgment is deceptive, yet in negative statements it is reliable. For reason does not grasp what God is, yet it grasps most certainly what God is not. Therefore reason does not see what is right and good before God (i.e., faith), yet it clearly knows that infidelity, murder, and disobedience are evil." See also below, 331 n. 266; Luther to George Spalatin: May 18, 1518: WA.B 1:173.38.

11. *Lectures on Romans,* 1515-16: WA 56:356.27 <LW 25:346>, as above, 292 n. 101: "But nature set for itself no object. . . . "

12. *Second Lectures on the Psalms,* 1518-21: WA 5:327.26: ". . blindness is the first perdition of the godless"; *Sermons on the First Epistle of St. Peter,* 1523: WA 12:319.11: "<In matters of faith the vision of reason> is obstructed by cataracts."

13. *Second Lectures on Galatians,* 1531: WA 40.I:607.5: "There is natural knowledge of God; nevertheless, people do not know what God in his innermost self thinks about us, what he wants to give and do so that we may be saved"; *Lectures on Genesis,* 1535-45: WA 42:106.18: ". . . we do not know what God is, what grace is, what righteousness is . . .";

ibid., WA 42:291.30, 292.28; *Second Lectures on the Psalms*, 1518-21: WA 5:392.26: "The first evil, undoubtedly the source of all evil, is the ignorance of God. . . . "

14. *The Bondage of the Will*, 1525: WA 18:762.1 ⟨*LW* 33:254⟩: "For what does it mean to be wicked but that the will — which is one of the most excellent things — is wicked?" See also above, 252 n. 14.

15. *The Bondage of the Will*, 1525: WA 18:709.12 ⟨*LW* 33:175f.⟩: "Now, Satan and man, having fallen from God and been deserted by God, cannot will good, that is, things which please God or which God wills; but instead they are continually turned in the direction of their own desires, so that they are unable not to seek the things of self."

16. *Second Lectures on Galatians*, 1531: WA 40.I:523.8: "I am an enemy of the law."

17. *Disputation against Scholastic Theology*, 1517, thesis 13: WA 1:224.28 ⟨*LW* 31:10⟩: "It is absurd to conclude that erring man can love the creature above all things, therefore also God"; thesis 17: ibid., WA 1:225.1 ⟨*LW* 31:10⟩: "Man is by nature unable to want God to be God. Indeed, he himself wants to be God, and does not want God to be God"; *Second Lectures on Galatians*, 1531: WA 40.II:80.11, 81. 4: "If there were no sin in me, and I were entirely pure and perfectly burning in love, then I would be holy and righteous through this love. But in this life this is not the case. Here the gift of the Spirit and the first fruit begin indeed ⟨to be with me⟩ so that I begin to love someone, but ⟨only in a small way⟩. . . . We are totally submerged in sins, ⟨and⟩ we do not think anything that is good before God"; see also ibid., WA 40.I:226.7.

18. *The Large Catechism*, 1529: WA 30.I:133.2 ⟨explanation of the First Commandment; *BC* 365.1f.⟩. See also Holl, *Luther*, 84 n. 4; Vilmos Vajta, *Die Theologie des Gottesdienstes bei Luther* (Göttingen, 1952), 5.

19. *Heidelberg Disputation*, 1518, thesis 13: WA 1:354.5 ⟨*LW* 31:40⟩: "Free will, after the fall, exists in name only, and as long as it does what it is able to do, it commits a mortal sin." In *The Bondage of the Will*, 1525 (WA 18:600ff. ⟨*LW* 33⟩), Luther developed the theme of the bound will in great detail.

20. Luther's basis was the scholastic doctrine of *synteresis* ⟨see *ODCC*, 1957 ed., s.v. "Synteresis"⟩. He modified it to the effect that after the Fall ⟨man no longer has a *synteresis theologica* (see above, 25), but⟩ man's inborn inclination toward what is good and right is directed only toward what is good and right in a corporeal sense. To use Paul's statement in Rom. 2:14 ⟨". . . Gentiles, who do not possess the law, do *instinctively* what the law requires . . ." (NRSV); ". . . the Gentiles, who do not have the law, *naturally* do the [works] of the law . . ." (Vulgate); ". . . the Gentiles, who do not have the law, yet *by nature* do the content of the law . . . " (Luther, September Testament); italics by this ed.⟩, *synteresis* is now directed toward the works of the law but not toward the love of the law itself; therefore it is not directed toward the universal or divine righteousness ⟨see above, 17, 48⟩, but it is directed toward the particular or human righteousness. It is impossible to pursue this problem in detail. For Luther, see *Lectures on Romans*, 1515-16: WA 56:203.6, 234.15, 244.18; notes on the *Sentences* of Peter Lombard, 1510-11: WA 9:79.16; notes on the sermons of Tauler, 1516: WA 9:103.25. For the Scholastics, see Biel, *Expositio missae*, oratio initialis: a.ij. — See also Johannes Heckel, "Recht und Gesetz," *ZSRG*.K 26 (1937): 335; Loewenich, *Luthers Theologia crucis*, 56ff.; Emanuel Hirsch, *Lutherstudien*, 1:113 n. 2, 122f.

21. In this sense, Emil Brunner's judgment (*Gerechtigkeit*, 106) about the reformers was correct insofar as Luther is concerned: "The reformers emphasized the corruptness

of the human nature through sin more than the scholastic theologians did; nevertheless, the reformers did not hesitate to use the term 'natural law' because they thought that sin did not destroy the *Schöpfungskonstanten* ⟨i.e., those elements which continuously are present in Creation⟩." But Luther would not affirm Brunner's opinion that "sin did not alienate those continuously present elements from their original meaning." On this point, Ernst Kohlmeyer, review of Heinrich Bornkamm, *Luther und das Alte Testament* (1948), *ARG* 43 (1952): 269, was correct.

22. See Walther Köhler, review of Alfred Farner, *Die Lehre von Staat und Kirche bei Zwingli* (1930), *ZSRG*.K 20 (1931): 679 n. 4. For the following, see esp. Ernst Kohlmeyer, "Die Geschichtsbetrachtung Luthers," *ARG* 37 (1940): 155ff.

23. *First Disputation against the Antinomians*, 1537: WA 39.I:361.19: "All people have a certain knowledge of the law naturally, yet it is quite weak and obscure"; *First Lectures on the Psalms*, 1513-15: WA 4:255.23: "No one lacks some illumination by the divine light, regardless how many evil people there may be"; above, 81.

24. See Friedrich Gogarten, "Die Lehre von den zwei Reichen und das 'natürliche Gesetz,'" *DTh* 2 (1935): 336: "Regardless how distorted and marred this knowledge of law might be, in it is an original knowledge of God" — or more precisely formulated, not of God, but of the deity. See also above, 25f.; Günther Dehn, Ernst Wolf, *Gottesrecht und Menschenrecht* (Munich, 1954), 21.

25. See Hans M. Müller, *Erfahrung und Glaube bei Luther* (Leipzig, 1929), 16. In light of Müller's arguments one has to correct Hans H. Walz, "Die biblische Botschaft von der Gerechtigkeit Gottes und unser Recht," in *Gerechte Ordnung. Gedanken zu einer Rechts- und Staatslehre in evangelischer Sicht*, preface by Hans H. Walz (Tübingen, 1948), 7ff.; see also Johannes Heckel, "Naturrecht und christliche Verantwortung," in *Zur Politischen Predigt*, 47 n. 1.

26. *Lectures on Romans*, 1515-16: WA 56:23.8 ⟨*LW* 25:19f.; Paul's text of Rom. 2:15 in italics⟩: "By nature and indelibly the law of nature ⟨*sic*⟩ is imprinted on their minds, *while their conscience bears witness to them*, a good witness about the good works and an evil witness about the evil works. How? Supply 'they show it,' through their conscience now to themselves and in the Last Judgment before God . . ."; *Against the Heavenly Prophets*, 1525: WA 18:80.35: "If the ⟨divine natural law⟩ would not be naturally written in man's heart, one would have to teach and preach many laws before the conscience would be bothered. No one would be bothered in his conscience unless conscience finds and feels law in itself. . . ." In natural man, conscience is a bad conscience, "an evil beast, which makes man stand against himself"; *Lectures on Genesis*, 1535-45: WA 44:545.16. — See also Ernst Wolf, *Peregrinatio*, 1:90, 132f.: the order of the divine will for law, with which man is confronted in his conscience, is the law of wrath.

27. See Welzel, *Naturrrecht und materiale Gerechtigkeit*, 94 n. 16.

28. WA.TR 2:No. 2243; see also Emanuel Hirsch, *Lutherstudien*, 1:124f.

29. Schrey ("Wiedergeburt des Naturrechts," *ThR*.NF 19 [1951]: 42) was correct in pointing this out. See also above, 273 n. 12. For Luther, see *Sermons on Matthew, Chapters 5-7*, 1530-32: WA 32:516.14ff.; *On Good Works*, 1520: WA 6:245.15.

30. *First Lectures on the Psalms*, 1513-15: WA 4:233.28 ⟨*LW* 11:367⟩: ". . . in a human day and before men who do not see except according to the light of this world . . ."; *Psalm 118 Explained*, 1530: WA 31.I:175.34: ". . . the light of reason . . . ⟨is⟩ also a sun . . . , which points out and teaches external works and ⟨what is right in the judgment of⟩ the world."

— This situation was not seen by Nürnberger ("Lex naturae," *ARG* 37 [1940]: 6). In his critique of Holl (*Luther*, 247) he argued that "Luther did not know a specially Christian commandment of love." ⟨Therefore:⟩ "The fundamental difference between natural and Christian ethics is not based on a difference in the moral commandment; the basic difference is the power of doing: only a Christian — but this is decisive! — as a person acting in faith is different from the erring, despairing, or obstinate person who is outside of grace." Nürnberger's statements are applicable to a Christian's spiritual use of the secular natural law in the kingdom of the world, but he ignored Christ's kingdom and its legal order, the divine natural law.

31. *Second Lectures on the Psalms*, 1518-21: WA 5:26.30: "How to be blessed is a question common to all mortals. There is no one who does not wish that things go well for himself and hates it if things go bad for himself. Yet all people, regardless how many there are, strayed from the knowledge of true blessedness. Those who have thoroughly investigated this problem strayed the most, namely, the philosophers. The more excellent among them argued that this blessedness is based on virtue or the works of virtue. By means of this argument they became more miserable than the rest of the people and deprived themselves of the goods of this and the future life. Of course, the mass of people fooled itself, desiring blessedness through the lusts of the flesh, but at least it acquired the goods of this life. But this one ⟨Ps. 1:1⟩ speaks from heaven and, having detested the efforts of all, he presents a unique definition of blessedness unknown to all: 'Blessed is he who loves God's law'"; notes on the Sermons of Tauler, 1516: WA 9:101.16: "⟨God⟩ gives the natural goods to all people; the ungodly ones enjoy them, and, having abandoned God, they see in his gifts the end of all things and rely on them, while the godly people are drawn through these gifts to God and use them for God."

32. *First Lectures on the Psalms*, 1513-15: WA 3:176.24 ⟨*LW* 10:148; "character" in the sense of personalistic quality, i.e., spirit or flesh⟩. See also Iwand, *Rechtfertigungslehre und Christusglaube*, 43 n. 2.

33. *Lectures on Romans*, 1515-16: WA 56:171.27 ⟨*LW* 25:151⟩: "In human teachings the righteousness of man is revealed and taught, that is, who is and becomes righteous before himself and before other people and how this takes place."

34. The jurists claimed that their arguments were based on what supposedly was divine law. See *Lectures on Romans*, 1515-16: WA 56:448.4ff. ⟨*LW* 25:440⟩; *Second Lectures on the Psalms*, 1518-21: WA 5:227.39; *Lectures on Psalms 120-134*, 1531-33: WA 40.III:241.6, 246.7: a diabolic addition (in the sense of claiming) of the divinity to oneself occurred in the Fall; Wehrung, *Welt und Reich*, 75.

35. *Magnificat*, 1521: WA 7:551.6: ". . if, as with a higher light, the Spirit does not enlighten ⟨and⟩ rule this light of reason through faith, it is impossible that reason does not err"; *First Lectures on the Psalms*, 1513-15: WA 4:308.36 ⟨*LW* 11:419⟩: ". . . in the commandments of God straying is easy, and in endless ways our mind and our will try to mix themselves in through the most secret pride. . . ."

36. *Lectures on Psalms 23-25*, 1513-15: WA 31.I:475.25: ". . . they strongly believe that they are seeking the Lord, but they do not know ⟨that they do not do this,⟩ because ⟨in reality⟩ they are seeking themselves and their own things even before God ⟨in the sense of when they are confronted with God⟩, and this is a horrible perversion."

37. See Ecclus. 10:13; *Sermons on the Ten Commandments*, 1517: WA 1:518.14:

"... pride is the beginning of sin, or, and this would be the same, the beginning of sin is to fall away from God ..."; Augustine, *The City of God* 14.13.

38. See Hans Preuß, *Martin Luther der Christenmensch* (Gütersloh, 1942), 21.

39. *Disputation on Man*, 1536, theses 4, 5: WA 39.I:175.9 ⟨LW 34:137⟩: "And it is certainly true that reason *(ratio)* is the most important and the highest in rank among all things and, in comparison with other things of this life, the best and something divine. It is the inventor and mentor of all the arts, medicines, laws, and of whatever wisdom, power, virtue, and glory men possess in this life."

40. *The Estate of Marriage*, 1522: WA 10.II:295.16. For similar harsh judgments, see *Second Lectures on Galatians*, 1531: WA 40.I:362.6, 365.5; sermon of Jan. 17, 1546: WA 51:129.2. These passages show that Luther's harsh judgments are applicable to reason only when it places itself above the divine natural or positive law rather than subordinate itself to the divine law. Luther condemns reason *only* when in the relationship to the Creator it is perverted. See also Schönfeld, *Grundlegung der Rechtswissenschaft*, 296; Watson, *Um Gottes Gottheit*, 109f.

41. *First Lectures on the Psalms*, 1513-15: WA 3:149.30: "When we turn the mind ... to the creatures, we turn the face away from God and turn the back to God." See also *The Seven Penitential Psalms*, 1517: WA 1:189.2; *Second Lectures on the Psalms*, 1518-21: WA 5:145.12.

42. *Psalm 101 Explained*, 1534-35: WA 51:212.26, 214.30, 215.1. See also Lau, "Äußerliche Ordnung," 51f.

43. *Lectures on Genesis*, 1535-45: WA 42:343.13 ⟨LW 2:114⟩.

44. See Cicero *De natura deorum* 2.66. In *Psalm 101 Explained* (1534-35) Luther explicitly referred to Cicero; WA 51:244.24.

45. *Psalm 101 Explained*, 1534-35: WA 51:222.5.

46. As is known, Luther did not ascribe identical mental abilities for recognizing the secular natural law to all people; *Psalm 101 Explained*, 1534-35: WA 51.212. 14: "If the secular natural law and reason would be in all heads, and all heads would be equal, then fools, children, and women could rule and fight wars as well as David, Augustus, Hannibal. ... In fact, all people would have to be equal and no one would have to rule over another one. What sort of an uprising and chaos would come out of this?" Such a negative judgment about the average people can already be found in *Second Lectures on the Psalms*, 1518-21: WA 5:628.8: "... the mass and the multitude of people are hard-headed, without understanding, judgment, and discipline." See also sermon of Nov. 18, 1526: WA 20:556.3.21.

47. *Psalm 101 Explained*, 1534-35: WA 51:214.36.

48. *The Bondage of the Will*, 1525: WA 18:763.41 ⟨LW 33:257⟩: "... it was only the best and noblest that were zealous for the law and its works, and that only with the best and noblest parts of themselves, namely, their reason and will."

49. Emil Brunner (*Gerechtigkeit*, 316 n. 19) critically pointed out that "one of the unclarities of the Reformation doctrine of natural law, which had the most severe consequences, was the lack of precision in the relationship of justice to love, of secular natural law to divine natural law." In Luther's thinking this lack of precision did not exist. This also answers the question of Hermann Weinkauff ("Das Naturrecht in evangelischer Sicht," *Zeitwende* 23 [1951/52]: 94ff.) whether "the primeval legal order, i.e., the basic natural-law statements," can be derived from "one word in Scripture (or from individual

words), or from the synopsis of all that God has ordained for man as the meaning and aim of his earthly existence."

50. *Second Lectures on Galatians*, 1531: WA 40.I:665.12: "The whole human race is unable to lift itself higher ⟨than to the works of the law⟩, ⟨and⟩ the wisdom in all the world pertains to law." "Law" *(lex)* designates also the secular natural law; see the next sentence in the edited version of these lectures (ibid., 666.12f.): ". . . ⟨in⟩ the term 'law' *(lex)* I include all laws *(leges)*, the human and the divine ones."

51. See Carl Stange, "Die Schmalkaldischen Artikel Luthers," *ZSTh* 14 (1937): 452: "From Holy Scripture Luther did not learn to reject the seriousness of man's moral efforts. Rather, the moral ideas which, influenced by Holy Scripture, he developed for the shaping of human life can hold their own over against the most sublime ideas which ever have been developed in philosophical ethics. His doctrine of hereditary sin does not mark a descent below moral idealism; rather, it begins only when moral idealism has reached its absolute end. That doctrine does not assign man to a lower level of morality, but it opens man's view for that perfection which is far beyond all human ability and being." See also above, 273 n. 12.

52. *Psalm 101 Explained*, 1534-35: WA 51:212.24: ". . . the precious jewel called ⟨secular⟩ natural law and reason is a rare thing among the children of men."

53. This results also in the duty to be ready for sharing common burdens and enduring common dangers; *The Book of Deuteronomy with Notes*, 1525: WA 14:686.34 ⟨*LW* 9:194⟩: "Whoever, therefore, wants to live in a community and to enjoy its peace, security, protection, and all its laws, advantages, and benefits, must also endure dangers, damage, disadvantages, and the whole range of fortune, whatever it may bring."

54. See Luther's description of the various "works and offices" in the kingdom of the world. According to God's will they are to "benefit and serve the neighbors," ". . . just as each member of a body serves the other one"; *To the Christian Nobility*, 1520: WA 6:409.7. This nullifies the value of Wünsch's supposition (*Ethik des Politischen*, 127) that "as far as I see, nowhere does Luther base the public order on human needs, on the necessities of living together while dividing the work, or on the social disposition of man." See also Olsson, *Grundproblemet*, 1:21: "In Luther's thinking natural law achieves its concrete application within a viewpoint of natural rights, a viewpoint which firmly distinguishes itself from every rational-egalitarian understanding of natural rights. . . . Natural law demands that every one . . . ought to receive what is due him in his individual situation"; see also ibid., 26: "The antiegalitarian application of natural law."

55. *Second Commentary on Galatians*, 1535: WA 40.I:410.27 ⟨*LW* 26:262⟩: ". . . we say in theology that moral philosophy does not have God as its object and final cause, since Aristotle or a Sadducee or a man who is good in a civic sense calls it right reason and good will if he seeks the common welfare of the state and tranquillity and honesty"; *Postilla for Lent*, 1525: WA 17.II:96.26. — One has to question Olsson's argument (*Grundproblemet*, 1:29, 42) that Luther's understanding of the state was not based on the general welfare, a common good.

56. *Sermons on the Ten Commandments*, 1517: WA 1:439.18; for this sermon, see also Johannes Heckel, *Initia iuris*, 47 n. 194.

57. *Against the Heavenly Prophets*, 1525: WA 18:93.1f.; sermon of Nov. 8, 1545: WA 51:84.7. — Thielicke (*Theologische Ethik*, 1:Nos. 2088, 2092) raised doubts regarding the assumption that Luther had a "consistent" image of man. Yet these doubts are not appli-

Notes to Page 56

cable to Luther's "Weltschau des Glaubens" (world view formed by faith), a phrase coined by Törnvall, *Geistliches und weltliches Regiment bei Luther*, 117.

58. *First Lectures on the Psalms*, 1513-15: WA 3:91.10f., and many other passages; sermons of 1523: WA 12:685.1: "This is the secular law as established by reason: 'To each his own.'" See also Arnold, *Naturrecht bei Luther*, 104. For the connection of the imperative 'to each his own' with all doctrines of natural law, see Emil Brunner, *Gerechtigkeit*, 102. For the fact that this imperative is unable to provide a basis for a system of substantive legal values but presupposes such a system, see Erik Wolf, *Rechtsgedanke und biblische Weisung*, 23; Thielicke, *Theologische Ethik*, 1:Nos. 2093ff.

59. Emil Brunner (*Gerechtigkeit*, 59, 147ff.) argued that love and justice are essentially opposed to each other, even though a connection exists between both. According to Brunner, justice is a part of the world of orders, not a part of the world of persons, as love is; therefore the imperative 'love the neighbor' cannot be the foundation of justice, for the commandment of love, being what it is, does not recognize claims and rights, or clearly defined areas of action. Brunner's position does not agree with Luther's position on ⟨secular⟩ natural-law love. This kind of love indeed recognizes clearly defined areas of action, and therefore it differs from the Christian love of the neighbor. For arguments against Brunner's position, see also Schrey, *Die Bedeutung der biblischen Botschaft für die Welt des Rechts*, 20f. See further, Theodor Heckel, "Liebe und Gerechtigkeit," in *Dienst unter dem Wort. Festgabe Helmuth Schreiner*, ed. by Karl Janssen et al. (Gütersloh, 1953), 78f.

60. *On Secular Authority*, 1523: WA 11:279.19: "... nature teaches us what love does, namely, that I should do what I want to be done to me"; ibid., WA 11:279.24: "Therefore ... love and the ⟨secular⟩ natural law should always be on top. For if you judge according to love, it will be easy for you to decide and judge all things without any law books. But if you lose sight of love and the ⟨secular⟩ natural law, you will never make a decision that is pleasing to God, even if you have swallowed all the law books and jurists"; ibid., WA 11:279.30: "It is not possible to pronounce a right and good judgment on the basis of books; this is possible only on the basis of a mind which is free from the wisdom of law books. Love and the ⟨secular⟩ natural law, with which reason is filled, give such a free judgment ⟨in the sense of being unencumbered by book learning⟩"; ibid., WA 11:280.12: "... such a judgment ... has jumped from free reason over all the books of law so well that everyone has to approve it ⟨because⟩ he finds written in his heart that it is right"; *Sermons on Matthew, Chapters 5-7*, 1530-32: WA 32:353.32: "... the common works, which everyone should do to the other because of love, of which ⟨Matt. 25:35ff.⟩ speaks." See also Olsson, *Grundproblemet*, 1:19: "The law of love."

61. *German Exposition of the Lord's Prayer for Simple Laymen*, 1519: WA 2:120. 22: "Nature and its law ⟨sic⟩ say: 'What you want to be done to you, do also to the neighbor'"; *Postilla for Lent*, 1525: WA 17.II:102.8: "There is no one who does not feel and has to confess that it is right and true what the ⟨secular⟩ natural law says: 'What you want to be done and granted to you, do and grant also to the neighbor.' This light exists and shines in the reason of all people; if they would pay attention to it, why would they need books, teachers, or any law? At the bottom of their hearts they carry with themselves a living book, which would tell them abundantly what to do and not to do, to grant, judge, accept, and reject"; ibid., WA 17.II:96.32; *Sermons on Matthew, Chapters 5-7*, 1530-32: WA 32:494ff.,

495.5: a true summary of all sermons on the Second Table; Luther to George Spalatin: Feb. 12, 1544: WA.B 10:532.10.

62. Therefore it is incorrect to suggest that Luther had no room for social ethics, as Paul Joachimsen did (*Sozialethik des Luthertums* [Munich, 1927], 4). He argued: "The essence of religion is not to create social ethics. The motto of religion is: 'Upwards.' The way of religion leads upwards, and if it is true religion then it is marked by the longing of the individual soul"; ibid., 26: Luther does not know "of an ethics of vocations, which could come from the vocations themselves"; ibid., 28: for Luther, "morality . . . comes only from faith." See also above, 273 n. 12.

63. In *On Secular Authority*, 1523, Luther developed a good illustration of the difference between the spiritual and the corporeal understanding and use of the Golden Rule; WA 11:278.33ff.: (1) Both a debtor and a creditor are Christians; in this situation there is no room for legal action of one against the other. (2) One is a Christian, the other not. Again, there is no room for legal action of one against the other; according to the spiritual ⟨divine⟩ natural law, a Christian as a debtor voluntarily pays his debts, and as a creditor does not press the debtor to pay up. (3) The creditor is not a Christian, but he agrees with the debtor that their case should be settled according to the corporeally understood commandment of love; in this situation the judge has to grant to the debtor the minimum of what is needed to exist. (4) The creditor does not agree that the case be judged according to "the law of love"; i.e., he rejects the secular natural law and demands "the strict enforcement of the law." In this situation the church can only use its spiritual office of censuring the despisers of the natural law by pronouncing that such despisers "act contrary to God's law and the natural law, even though according to man-made law they receive the strict enforcement of the law." See also *Long Sermon on Usury*, 1520: WA 6: 40.12. — For the minimum always to be granted to a debtor so that he would be able to exist, see *The Book of Deuteronomy with Notes*, 1525: WA 14:716.9 ⟨*LW* 9:243⟩: ". . . above all debts and obligations ⟨literally: 'rights' in the sense of the right to collect the debt⟩ stands this law that a poor man must have the necessary food and clothing; he should not have to give them up to pay a creditor, but the creditor should yield and give that the poor man lives."

64. ⟨See above, 55.⟩

65. See Helmut Coing, *Die obersten Grundsätze des Rechts* (Heidelberg, 1947), 12.

66. *Lectures on Romans*, 1515-16: WA 56:175.2 ⟨*LW* 25:155⟩: "Therefore we must interpret this passage ⟨Rom. 3:9⟩ to mean that the apostle, as he writes, sees before his eyes the whole world as one body."

67. ⟨For Luther's ideas about 'body', 'head', and 'member', and the individual's membership in an ecclesiastical or a political body,⟩ see *Lectures on Romans*, 1515-16: WA 56:514.20; *To the Christian Nobility*, 1520: WA 6:407.15, 408.33f., 409.18, 410.4ff., 413.28; *Open Letter on the Harsh Book against the Peasants*, 1525: WA 18:397.32; *Disputation on Matt. 19:21*, 1539, thesis 32: WA 39.II:41.1; sermon of Oct. 28, 1515: WA 4:669.10; WA.TR 4:No. 4342; Luther to Lazarus Spengler: Mar. 18, 1531: WA.B 6:56.10ff.; to his friends in Augsburg: Sept. 1530: WA.B 5:615.70; to Duke John, elector of Saxony: May 15, 1525: WA.B 3:496.8f., 497.30; to Duke John Frederick of Saxony: May 15, 1525: WA.B 3:498.5.

68. ⟨Literally: "a membered concept"; i.e., law creates or reflects membership.⟩

69. It produces "the righteousness of nature"; *First Lectures on the Psalms*, 1513-15: WA 3:369.5. — For "the purpose of *Lebensordnungen* to ⟨create⟩ communions of love," see Hermann W. Beyer, "Der Christ und die Bergpredigt nach Luthers Deutung," *LuJ* 14

(1932): 55. ⟨*Lebensordnung* is the technical term designating the structures in which a Christian lives and the ways in which he is to live.⟩

70. *Against the Sabbatarians,* 1538: WA 50:330.33: ". . . not only prior to Moses, but also prior to Abraham and all the patriarchs . . . were the Ten Commandments spread across the whole world"; *First Commentary on Galatians,* 1519: WA 2:580.18: "The law goes through all the ages." — For the significance of the Ten Commandments for the kingdom of Christ, see above, 89f.

71. In this process one has to be extremely careful not to become the victim of paralogisms. For an example of such a paralogism ⟨'on the basis of natural law all people are equal'⟩, see *Psalm 101 Explained,* 1534-35: WA 51:212.14ff., as above, 307 n. 46.

72. *Against the Heavenly Prophets,* 1525: WA 18:81.11: ". . . in contrast to the special laws and orders ⟨of a territory⟩, such as the *Sachsenspiegel* ⟨i.e., the law of the Saxons; see below, 353 n. 6⟩ . . . the universal natural laws, such as to honor the parents, not to murder, not to commit adultery, to serve God, etc., are spread throughout all regions and remain forever."

73. *Admonition to Peace,* 1525: WA 18:307.6. See also *Against the Sabbatarians,* 1538: WA 50:331.13: "As the universal God of all heathen, God himself ⟨gives⟩ these universal Ten Commandments also orally to this special people ⟨i.e., the Jews⟩, which before had been planted into the hearts of all human beings with the Creation . . ."; sermon of Jan. 1, 1540: WA 49:2.13.

74. There is no Christian secular natural law, only a Christian doctrine of the secular natural law. With this doctrine the secular natural law is sometimes intermingled; therefore a spiritual quality is ascribed to the secular natural law, which it does not have. Ernst Wolf, "Frage des Naturrechts bei Thomas und bei Luther," 10, was correct on this point.

75. For the contrast between a "Christianity of attitude and action" and a "Christianity of the Word and faith," ⟨e.g.,⟩ in Goethe's thought, see Eckermann's conversation with Goethe on March 11, 1832 ⟨Flodoard von Biedermann, gen. ed., *Goethes Gespräche*. Gesamtausgabe, 4 (2d ed. Leipzig, 1910), 440ff.; *Conversations of Goethe with Eckermann and Soret,* transl. by John Oxenford (rev. ed. London, 1883), 566ff.⟩, and Friedrich Gogarten, *Die Kirche in der Welt* (Heidelberg, 1948), 95.

76. *Against the Heavenly Prophets,* 1525: WA 18:81.19: ". . . the natural laws are nowhere as beautifully and orderly expressed as in ⟨the writings of⟩ Moses"; *Second Lectures on Galatians,* 1531: WA 40.II:18.1. See also esp. Olsson, *Grundproblemet,* 1:32ff.; he found in the Decalogue a "formal greatness which can be made clear only in a concrete, historical context." But this "formal greatness" is in reality the universality of the Decalogue in terms of substantive law.

77. Sermon of Jan. 1, 1540: WA 49:2.1: "⟨The secular natural law⟩ has been clearly and beautifully expressed on Mount Sinai, more beautifully than by the philosophers."

78. Luther considered the secular natural law also in terms of procedural law. Such procedural law is the result of a judge's implementation of his official duties in agreement with the Golden Rule; i.e., it is the result of the interaction of the substantive and of the institutional secular natural law (see above, 70). In this connection Luther listed, e.g., the following items: (1) Before sentencing, the accused has the right to be heard by the court; *Warning of His Dear German People,* 1531: WA 30.III:284.14: "It is divine, Imperial, and secular natural law . . . , not to condemn anyone unless one has first listened to what ⟨the accused⟩ has to say. God, too, did not wish to condemn Adam, he demanded that

Adam answer first"; Luther to George Spalatin: ca. Feb. 16, 1520: WA.B 2:44.42, and July 9, 1520: WA.B 2: 135.34; to an unknown noble lady: Dec. 14, 1523: WA.B 3:204.9; to Gregory Brück, chancellor of Electoral Saxony: Jan. 14, 1524: WA.B 3:233.13, and March 28, 1528: WA.B 4:432.23. (2) It is prohibited to be the judge in one's own case; *Admonition to Peace*, 1525: WA 18:303.17: "According to secular natural law and the laws of the whole world, no one should nor may be his own judge or avenge himself"; *Whether Soldiers, Too, Can Be Saved*, 1526: WA 19:636.15; *A Model for Consecrating a True Bishop*, 1542: WA 53:245.10; Luther to Duke John Frederick, elector of Saxony, and Duke Maurice of Saxony: Apr. 7, 1542: WA.B 10:33.48. (3) For deciding a case one needs two witnesses; *The Private Mass and the Consecration of Priests*, 1533: WA 38:211.3: "God has commanded . . . not to pass judgment on the basis of one man's word. . . ."

79. Therefore the secular natural law may not be played off against the Second Table of the Decalogue; *Disputation on Matt. 19:21*, thesis 47: WA 39.II:41.34: "We do not have another Second Table which would permit us to act contrary to that first Second Table."

80. For those pious heathen who do not progress beyond a natural knowledge of the divinity and do not create from that knowledge a god for themselves, see Erich Seeberg, *Luthers Theologie*, 2:121ff.

81. This is esp. the case for the First Commandment, which is also part of the secular natural law; *Against the Heavenly Prophets*, 1525: WA 18:80.18: ". . . to have a god is not only a law of Moses ⟨in the sense of the law of the Jewish nation⟩ but also a natural law. . . ."

82. Only the members of Christ's kingdom, who live according to the divine natural law, are able to obey the commandments of the First Table. But even the children of the world, who live according to the secular natural law, obey the commandments of the Second Table, though only in a certain way. Therefore Luther occasionally equated the First Table with the divine natural law and the Second Table with the secular natural law, and he described their relationship with each other in terms of superior and inferior law. See also below, 410 n. 54.

83. This includes the Third Commandment, even though its phrasing is connected with the Sabbath ⟨in the sense of the *Jewish* day of rest and worship⟩; see *How Christians Should Regard Moses*, 1527: WA 24:7.22. Nevertheless, it is a universal commandment (*Against the Sabbatarians*, 1538: WA 50:332.22), but only Christians are able to obey it; only they know what the true worship of God is; *Second Disputation against the Antinomians*, 1538: WA 39.I:481.13: "⟨God⟩ wants to be worshipped . . . in that way which he himself has set up. . . ." See also Vajta, *Theologie des Gottesdienstes bei Luther*, 18.

84. *The Book of Deuteronomy with Notes*, 1525: WA 14:608.9: "When Ahab ⟨see 1 Kings 16:31ff.⟩ put up Moloch, also Baal, etc., they worshiped the living God under that image. This was rejected, however, because nothing is decreed in Scripture about this, nor is the mercy of God present in it, etc., only the name of God is present. . . . that worship was for ⟨the worshipers of Baal and Moloch⟩ a matter of the ⟨heart⟩, . . . therefore they worshiped only pure shadows, etc."

85. ⟨Heckel wrote "Rechtsweistum." *Weistum* is the term for German law (derived from sources of the Middle Ages and the early modern period) which was established in the decision-making process by those who were versed in common law. See *HDRG*, s.v. "Weistümer"; *BLD*, s.v. "Common Law."⟩

86. *Second Disputation against the Antinomians*, 1538: WA 39.I:454.4: ". . . from the beginning of the world the Decalogue has been inscribed in the minds of all people. . . ."

87. Ibid., WA 39.I:454.14: "Moses was only so to speak an interpreter and illustrator of the laws written in the minds of all people, wherever on earth they may be under the sun"; *Against the Sabbatarians*, 1538: WA 50:330.35: "Even if Moses never had lived nor Abraham never had been born, the Ten Commandments would have had to rule among all people from the beginning, as they did and still do."

88. See, e.g., *The Babylonian Captivity of the Church*, 1520: WA 6:559.9: "Certainly, according to every law, deceit must afflict the deceiver, and he who damaged ⟨someone or something⟩ is held responsible for making good the damage"; *On Keeping Children in School*, 1530: WA 30.II:544.13: "Natural law *(natürlich Recht)* . . . states: 'Who could prevent damage and does not is just as guilty of the damage as someone who certainly would like and be willing to do such damage, and would do it had he a reason or opportunity' "; *Whether Soldiers, Too, Can Be Saved*, 1526: WA 19:647.9: "All laws approve that self-defense is not to be punished"; *Admonition to Peace*, 1525: WA 18:316.2: ". . . it is natural that one does not want to endure injustice and evil"; *A Model for Consecrating a True Bishop*, 1542: WA 53:252.19: ". . . according to natural law, one is not to maintain an oath which has been sworn in opposition to God and law, but one is to break such an oath: 'In evil promises, break the promise' "; for this passage, see *De regulis iuris*, reg. 69 in VI⁰ ⟨*Liber Sextus*⟩. V.12 ⟨Friedberg 2:1124; see also *DMA*, s.v. "Maxims, Legal"⟩.

89. See *First Lectures on the Psalms*, 1513-15: WA 3:249.13; *Against the Heavenly Prophets*, 1525: WA 18:66.7; *Sermons on Matthew, Chapters 5-7*, 1530-32: WA 32:350.18.

90. *Lectures on Hebrews*, 1517-18: WA 57.III:113.21 ⟨*LW* 29:123⟩: "The Law and the Gospel also differ for this reason, that in the Law there are very many works — they are all external — but in the Gospel there is only one work — it is internal — which is faith." See also Hof, "Luthers Lehre von Gesetz und Evangelium," *ELKZ* 2 (1949): 134; Althaus, *Gebot und Gesetz*, 16: "Law has no longer the personalistic simplicity of the commandment, but it is divided into the multiplicity of material prohibitions made necessary by our transgressions."

91. See *Third Disputation against the Antinomians*, 1538: WA 39.I:570.5.

92. See Erik Wolf, *Rechtsgedanke und biblische Weisung*, 44.

93. *Second Lectures on the Psalms*, 1518-21: WA 5:227:33: "No one should hope to obey or defend any one of God's commandments the right way if he violates the first of all the commandments (which is to worship God in fear and humility). For this commandment governs all the others, and without it they are indeed not God's commandments."

94. For the following, see instead of other authors, Welzel, *Naturrecht und materiale Gerechtigkeit*, 62, 77, 84ff.

95. *Summa Theologiae* II.1. q.100. art. 2 and 3.

96. *Opus Oxoniense* III. dist. 37.q.un. n. 6; so also Biel, *Collectorium*, lib. III. dist. 37.q.un.Q. For Scotus, see also Stratenwerth, *Naturrechtslehre des Duns Scotus*, 74.

97. *Commentary on the Sentences of Petrus Lombardus*, lib. IV. q.14.D (rejection of Scotus's position on the First Commandment). We shall not deal with the question whether later Occam changed his position; see Erich Hochstetter, "Viator mundi. Einige Bemerkungen zur Situation des Menschen bei Wilhelm von Ockham," *FS* 32 (1950):14ff.

98. WA.TR 4:No. 3911 ⟨*LW* 54:No. 3911⟩: "Natural law *(ius naturale)* is a practical first principle *(principium practicum)* in the sphere of morality; it forbids evil and commands good." As the context makes clear, with this medieval school definition of secular natural law Luther intended to emphasize the position of natural law above positive law. See also

Otto Scheel, *Evangelium, Kirche und Volk* (Leipzig, 1934), 54ff. Scheel was wrong, however, when he assumed that Luther did not at all think in terms of "rational law," "which would create universally binding legal maxims, which were valid and usable at all times and in all places." ⟨For this critique,⟩ see *D. Martin Luther's Preface to Ecclesiastes, 1532:* WA 20:8.21: "This ⟨i.e, to make laws or regulate how to govern the state or the family⟩ the law of nature *(ius naturae)* or human reason very well accomplishes, to which earthly matters are subjected, Gen. 1⟨:28⟩, and which at all times was, is, and will have to be the source, the judge, and goal of all laws, both the political ones and those of the household."

99. In *Lectures on Romans* (1515-16) Luther quoted a saying of Terence *Heauton timorumenos* 796, but he changed it to suit his argumentation; WA 56:238.11. The saying states: "Supreme justice often is supreme malice." Luther said: "Supreme righteousness ⟨or: 'justice'⟩ often is supreme foolishness," ⟨and then he added (*LW* 25:223): "indeed, the highest unrighteousness, when one stubbornly holds to it and refuses to yield to the opposite opinion. Hence we have the popular saying . . . 'the wiser the man, the worse the madness'"⟩. See also *Psalm 101 Explained,* 1534-35: WA 51:204.7ff. ⟨*LW* 13:150f.: The citation of (paraphrased) Isa. 6:10 and 8:10 raises the questions: "'Should one not do what is right, what reason teaches, what God enjoins? Of what use are the laws to us? What is reason good for? . . . Is it all to be in vain?' Answer: This is not to condemn or reject law, sound reason, or Holy Scripture but rather the miserable admixture of the filth of our arrogance — the fact that we do not begin such a plan and proceeding with the fear of God and with a humble, earnest prayer, just as if it were enough to have a right and proper proposal and the intention to convert this plan into action speedily according to one's own ability. To do this is to despise God and to seek glory for yourself as the man who can do it. It is contrary to the First Commandment. Therefore such an admixture⟩ changes the best law into the greatest injustice (footnote: reference to Cicero *De officiis* I.10.33), the finest reason into the greatest folly, ⟨and the Holy Scripture into the greatest error. For if the First Commandment is missing and does not give light, then none of the others will give proper light, and the understanding will be entirely faulty"⟩.

100. See Lau, *"Äußerliche Ordnung,"* 50ff.

101. *Lectures on Genesis,* 1535-45: WA 43:218.3 ⟨*LW* 4:115⟩: "Here ⟨Gen. 22:11⟩ you see with what unconcern the Divine Majesty toys with ⟨literally: 'in'⟩ death and all the powers of death"; ibid., WA 43:219.11 ⟨*LW* 4:116⟩: "By this deed ⟨i.e., the order to sacrifice Isaac⟩, as though by some show, God wanted to point out that in his sight death is nothing but a sport and empty little bugaboo of the human race, yes, an annoyance and a trial, as, for example, if a father sports with his son, takes an apple away from him, and meanwhile is thinking of leaving him the entire inheritance."

102. Ibid., WA 43:71.20 ⟨*LW* 3:274⟩.

103. Ibid., WA 43:642.34: "Every one should remain in his place, ⟨which is designated for him⟩ in the moral law and in the common law, until such time that God would have called and compelled him to do something that is unique"; ibid., WA 43: 643.6: "God is the manager and ruler of all things ⟨or: 'people'⟩. If God would have inspired someone ⟨to do something⟩ that is contrary to the common norm, the norm must not be dissolved or set aside by this. One has to maintain it as ⟨literally: 'in'⟩ common law, and God has to be permitted to exempt those he wishes to exempt ⟨from this law⟩."

104. Sermon of Jan. 1, 1540: WA 49:3.22: ". . . ⟨secular⟩ natural law and the Ten Commandments . . . do not accept any condition or dispensation."

105. For the 'irrational' quality of secular natural law in Luther's thought, see Troeltsch, *Die Soziallehren der christlichen Kirchen und Gruppen,* 536 n. 246; Emil Brunner, *Das Gebot und die Ordnungen,* 608; Georg Wünsch, *Evangelische Wirtschaftsethik* (Tübingen, 1927), 107, and id., *Ethik des Politischen,* 127ff. For the simultaneity of reason and history in law according to Luther's theology, see esp. Schönfeld, *Grundlegung der Rechtswissenschaft,* 300ff. See further, Friedrich Gogarten, *Der Mensch zwischen Gott und Welt* (Heidelberg, 1952), 103; Hans-Walter Krumwiede, *Glaube und Geschichte in der Theologie Luthers* (Göttingen, 1952), 69ff. Wünsch (*Ethik des Politischen,* 132) is of the opinion that "the connection between the absolute validity of the divine natural law — and therefore of the Christian commandment of love — and the process of change in history is a modern problem, which Luther did not know." Wehrung, *Welt und Reich,* 63 n. 61, has to be corrected in part. He argued that the secular natural law is "a totally irrational entity," "something hardly to be found among mankind." "Luther's ideas presuppose the inequality of human beings. The secular natural law is not an abstract, tenuous, rational truth, which remains identical through all ages, but it embodies itself in concrete manifestations; they appear suddenly, driven by a higher force and . . . pointing into the future. There is a great discrepancy between Luther's position and that of medieval Scholasticism, and even more the thought of antiquity. — One could say that Luther did know of the secular natural law, but for him it was something connected with the First Article; it was a part of his faith affirmation of Creation, but it did not precede that affirmation."

106. See Kohlmeyer, "Die Geschichtsbetrachtung Luthers," *ARG* 37 (1940): 158ff.; Schönfeld, *Grundlegung der Rechtswissenschaft,* 404.

107. For details, see Lau, *"Äußerliche Ordnung,"* 53f.

108. In *Luther und das Alte Testament* — a book which is esp. informative if it is studied also from a legal viewpoint — Bornkamm differentiated (113) in Luther's thought between the divine and the secular natural law. According to Bornkamm, the divine natural law is identical with the commandments to worship God and to love the neighbor. The secular natural law is not a system of simple norms, as we find in antiquity; it is "the embodiment of the laws of growth and existence of a community and nation"; to understand these secular natural laws is the gift of the great statesmen, God's miracle people. Bornkamm was correct when he pointed out that Luther had a dualistic concept 'natural law'. But the principle of structuring this dualism was for Luther different than for Bornkamm. Luther's dualism is based on the spiritual and the corporeal interpretation of the Golden Rule. If the Golden Rule is understood corporeally, then it dominates "the laws of growth and existence" of mankind, if this biological term has to include also a legal component; the gift of God's miracle people is the ability to apply that normative principle to the concrete historical situation of mankind and its nations in such a way that the demands of the principle and of the historical situation are met. This is the meaning esp. of that passage in Luther's explanation of Psalm 101 (1534-35; WA 51:211.36-212.25 ‹*LW* 13:160: "At present people are beginning . . ." to 161: "The noble gem called natural law and reason is a rare thing among the children of men."›) used by Bornkamm as the basis of his argumentation. — Scheel (*Evangelium, Kirche und Volk,* 54) . . . based his view esp. on Luther's statement that "strictly speaking, jurists do not ‹work› with the natural law *(ius naturale)* but only with the law of nations *(ius gentium),* which comes from human reason"; WA.TR 1:No. 581, on p. 268.4. He concluded: "Thus for Luther natural law is dissolved into the laws of individual nations." But in this passage Luther attacked Ulpian's

concept 'natural law' spelled out in *Digest* I.1.3: "Natural law is that law which nature has taught to all animals." Luther argued ⟨see also WA.TR 1:268.12ff.⟩ that one may speak of law only if the obligation to obey is present; this is the situation only in the case of man, and not in the case of any other living thing; therefore the jurists work only with the law of the human community, which Ulpian called *ius gentium* ⟨see *BLD*, s.v. "Jus gentium"⟩ and defined as law "common only to human beings among themselves." Neither Ulpian, nor Luther in the passage quoted by Scheel, spoke of "law of nations" as Scheel understood this term. ⟨For the Ulpian passages, see *The Digest of Justinian*, English translation ed. by Alan Watson (Philadelphia, 1985).⟩ — For Luther's use of the term *ius gentium* in the sense of law of nations, see below, 344 n. 411. In *Lectures on Romans* (1515-16: WA 56:481.12, or *LW* 25:473) Luther used this term also for the law of the heathen in contrast to the law of the Christians.

109. *Lectures on Genesis*, 1535-45: WA 43:643.33.

110. ⟨Literally: "office."⟩

111. *Lectures on Genesis*, 1535-45: WA 43:643.28 ⟨*LW* 5:312⟩: "It is necessary for ⟨God's miracle worker⟩ to be so heroic in order that he may not break the customs *(moralia)*. Indeed, he should rather preserve, defend, and guide them. Even though he himself for his own person has been excepted in a special manner, yet he must descend ⟨in the sense of basing himself on, or risking working with⟩ to . . . the rule *(regula)*." See also Gerhard Ritter, *Die Weltwirkung der Reformation* (2d ed. Munich, 1959), 171 n. 10. — The opposite of God's miracle people are the "apes" of God's miracle people, the miracle people of the devil; *Psalm 101 Explained*, 1534-35: WA 51:212.26. — See also Paul Althaus, *Luther und die politische Welt* (Weimar, 1937), 14; Lau, *Luthers Lehre von den beiden Reichen*, 80. — For a different view, see Wehrung, *Welt und Reich*, 74: "The . . . weight of their ⟨i.e., God's true miracle workers⟩ actions is not at all contained in the universally accessible reason or secular natural law."

112. Luther saw a striking example of a natural-law "rule or rather error" (see also *Decretum Gratiani* c.7. D.I ⟨Friedberg 1:2⟩) in the saying: "One may fight force with force"; *Second Lectures on the Psalms*, 1518-21: WA 5:190.22. See also above, 134; *Disputation on Law and Faith*, 1519: WA 6:24;9, theses 6, 7, 8: "To fight force with force is fixed in human law. Divine law commands to turn also the cloak over to him who takes the shirt. The human law is unjust when it does not agree with the divine law"; *Long Sermon on Usury*, 1520: WA 6:36.17, 37.32; *First Commentary on Galatians*, 1519: WA 2:594.20; *Commentary on 1 Corinthians, Chapter 7*, 1523: WA 12:118.31: "In the Imperial law there are many sections for the worldly people, yet Christians are not permitted to use them; e.g., to fight force with force, to use the court, etc."

113. *First Lectures on the Psalms*, 1513-15: WA 4:58.15: ". . . the letter and every form *(figura)* of the law are like a fleeting word."

114. *Disputation on Justification*, 1536, thesis 16: WA 39.I:83.1 ⟨*LW* 34:152⟩: "For the righteousness of the law is very ill and so weak that it often not only does not fulfill its own highest law ⟨i.e., the Golden Rule as secular natural law⟩ but even loses sight of it entirely at the slightest movement." — For material from the philosophy of law, see Coing, *Die obersten Grundsätze des Rechts*, 115ff.

115. See the differentiation between concept and form of the natural law in Edmund Mezger, "Gerechtigkeit und soziale Ordnung in evangelischer Sicht," in *Zur politischen Predigt*, 22ff. For "a natural law which is flexible throughout history," see Eduard

Notes to Page 60

Spranger, "Zur Frage der Erneuerung des Naturrechts," *Universitas* 3 (1948): 409. Luther would see in such a natural law the form of the derived secular natural law ⟨see above, 57⟩ in a specific age of the history of mankind.

116. *Postilla for Lent*, 1525: WA 17.II:91.13. For law as instruction, document, and doctrine, see *First Lectures on the Psalms*, 1513-15: WA 4:322.33 ⟨*LW* 11:439⟩.

117. ⟨Literally: "... and the obedience-demanding convincing power (or: 'authority') of all positive law."⟩

118. *The Book of Deuteronomy with Notes*, 1525: WA 14:665.1 ⟨*LW* 9:161⟩: "... unless there are administrators and executors of the law who bear and use the sword, all legislation, however sacred, is futile; for the sword is the force, the efficacy, and the very life of the law; it restrains those who are evil and protects those who are good. . . . where a law is set up, there the sword must be set up at the same time. Thus the law teaches what things are to be done and not to be done; but the sword enforces it and punishes those who offend and those who fail, as it forcibly drives the ungodly to do the right and avoid what is wrong. For without the sword the law is useless and only a reason for multiplying crimes. On the other hand, the sword without law is tyranny and bestial violence. But law and the sword joined together are a beautiful and stable political order."

119. *Psalm 101 Explained*, 1534-35: WA 51:214.15.

120. Ibid., WA 51:214.18.

121. Ibid., WA 51:214.16f. See also *On Secular Authority*, 1523: WA 11:279.26: "When you judge according to love, it will be easy for you to analyze and settle all matters without any law books."

122. *To the Christian Nobility*, 1520: WA 6:459.30. See also *Sermons on John, Chapters 14 and 15*, 1537: WA 45:553.21: "... it has always been the case that if one rules (esp. consciences) with laws there is never an end or moderation in commanding and issuing laws; one law makes a hundred other laws, and a hundred laws will become a hundred thousand laws."

123. *On the New Testament, That Is, the Mass*, 1520: WA 6:353.5. See also *The Babylonian Captivity of the Church*, 1520: WA 6:554.24: "This I know: no state can be ruled well with laws. For if a magistrate would be skilled, he will administer all things better under the guidance of nature than of laws; if he would not be skilled, then he, using laws, will promote only evil since he does not know how to use the laws or adjust them to the circumstances of the time. Therefore in public matters one has to be more concerned that good and skilled men govern than that laws are issued; these men themselves will be the best laws since they will judge the variety of the cases by means of a lively feeling for fairness. If one is well versed in the divine law and is endowed with a natural skill, it is quite unnecessary and harmful to have written laws." This passage was quoted in the *Confutatio* of the *Augsburg Confession*, Artikel 16: responsio; Johannes Ficker, *Die Konfutation des Augsburgischen Bekenntnisses* (Leipzig, 1891), 57. See also the sermons of ca. 1514-21: WA 4:651.26.

124. For an illustration, see *Psalm 101 Explained*, 1534-35: WA 51.214.20.

125. *On the New Testament, That Is, the Mass*, 1520: WA 6:353.26.

126. In order to understand Luther's position one has to remember that for him the ruler was primarily judge. He still had a strong awareness of the medieval understanding of government as jurisdiction. See above, 35.

127. See *Babylonian Captivity of the Church*, as above, n. 123.

128. WA.TR 6:No. 6955, on p. 291.1.

129. *Second Lectures on the Psalms,* 1518-21: WA 5:27.31: "... no civilized conduct *(conversatio)* can exist among men if it is not shaped and preserved by fixed decrees and laws" ⟨to *conversatio* Heckel added Phil. 3:20; here the Vulgate translated Paul's *politeuma* with *conversatio;* NRSV reads "citizenship" and suggests "commonwealth" as a variant reading⟩; ibid., WA 5:628.8.12; *Disputation on Matt. 19:21,* 1539: WA 39.II:85.21.

130. *On Good Works,* 1520: WA 6:261.16: "Therefore lords would profit the most if from youth on they would read, or have read to them, the stories in both the sacred and heathen books; there they would find more examples of the art of ruling than in all law books.... For examples and stories always provide and teach more than laws and rights. In the former, certain experience is the teacher, in the latter, the unexperienced teach uncertain words."

131. Luther to Philipp of Hesse: Jan. 7, 1527: WA.B 4:157.13, 158.29. See also *To the Christian Nobility,* 1520: WA 6:459.33: "Certainly, rational rulers, in addition to Holy Scripture, would provide sufficient law." This means that the secular natural law is sufficient as source of law for secular life, and the divine positive and the divine natural law are sufficient as source of law for the church. Olsson, *Grundproblemet,* 1:103, misunderstood this passage.

132. Wenger, "Zur christlichen Begründung des Naturrechts," *ZSRG*.R 69 (1952): 16.

133. *On Secular Authority,* 1523: WA 11:280.16: "... one should subordinate written laws to reason, from which they flowed as from a fountain of law"; *Psalm 101 Explained,* 1534-35: WA 51:211.36: "Now one begins to praise the ⟨secular⟩ natural law and natural reason as ⟨the sources⟩ from which all written law has come and flown. This is true, and the praise is justified." — The description of the secular natural law as the fountain of law was soon used in the 16th century literature dealing with the reforming of society; see the quotation from Harthmut von Cronberg's *Christliche Schrift und Vermahnung an alle Stände,* 1523, in Hermann Krause, *Kaiserrecht und Rezeption* (Heidelberg 1952), 137 n. 709. For von Cronberg, see Wilhelm Bogler, *Harthmut von Cronberg* (Halle, 1897), 39.

134. *Summer Postilla,* 1526: WA 10.I.2:393.28: "... we conclude ... that all laws, be they divine or human, do not bind anyone ⟨if they contradict love⟩. Love is to interpret all laws; where it is not found, nothing goes"; ibid., WA 10.I.2:398.32: "This is the sum of the Gospel ⟨Luke 14:1-11⟩: love and need ⟨in the sense of want, or necessity, or emergency⟩ are the masters of all laws, and there should be no law unless it is adjusted to, and governed by, love; if it is not, it should be eliminated even if an angel from heaven had made it"; ibid., WA 10.I.2:393.37. See also Schönfeld, *Über die Gerechtigkeit,* 32. — See further, Luther to Robert Barnes: Sept. 3, 1531: WA.B 6:179.55: "This is the situation in divine law: a superior law nullifies an inferior law"; ibid., WA.B 6:185.117, 186.132 ⟨in this letter Luther illustrated that secular natural law and divine law as superior laws take precedence over positive laws when they contradict the law of love. For this brief on the divorce of Henry VIII, see also *LW* 50:No. 245⟩; sermon of January 1, 1540: WA 49:2.15: "Secular natural law is the master... over all laws. If a law contradicts this natural law, it is not law." — For 'need' as a limitation of laws, see Luther to Duke John Frederick, elector of Saxony: May 29, 1538: WA.B 8:235.47; to Philip Melanchthon: June 18, 1540: WA.B 9:145.36. According to Luther, a decision based on need may not be elevated to the status of a regular law, however; see Luther to John Feige(?): soon after July 16, 1540: WA.B 9:178.21ff. — For the medieval background, see *Dictum Gratiani* p. c.1. D.VIII ⟨Friedberg 1:13⟩: "Whatever

things . . . are contrary to natural law must be considered void and without effect"; *Dictum Gratiani* p. c.11. D.IX ⟨Friedberg 1:18⟩: "If ecclesiastical or secular laws are proven to be contrary to natural law, they have to be completely abolished."

135. *Summer Postilla*, 1526: WA 10.I.2:394.16.29: "All laws are to be directed toward love so that one maintains them, if they serve and benefit the neighbor, and abolishes them, if they harm him. . . . All laws are to be directed by love for the neighbor and adjusted to it"; ibid., WA 10.I.2:403.19: ". . . if a law opposes love, it ceases to be law and ⟨therefore⟩ should no longer be law. But whenever there is nothing that obstructs love, then obeying law manifests the love which is hidden in a heart. For one uses laws to demonstrate love for the neighbor. But if laws cannot be obeyed without hurting the neighbor, it is God's will that they be abolished"; ibid., WA 10.I.2:402.36, 403.2.

136. For Luther's doctrine of the tyrant, see above, 110ff.

137. *On Secular Authority*, 1523: WA 11:272.15: "At all times reason is to rule all laws and is to be the supreme law and master of all laws"; ⟨above, 313 n. 98, the passage from *Preface to Ecclesiastes*⟩. — See also Erik Wolf, *Rechtsgedanke und biblische Weisung*, 44ff.; Hans E. Weber, *Reformation, Orthodoxie und Rationalismus*, 2 (Gütersloh, 1951), 56 n. 3.

138. For the following, see esp. Olsson, *Grundproblemet*, 1:30ff.

139. *Whether Soldiers, Too, Can Be Saved*, 1526: WA 19:632.12.22: "Since the law must and should be phrased in simple, precise, and short words, it cannot deal with all details and circumstances. . . . ⟨We have to deal with⟩ various, countless, and unclear ⟨circumstances⟩ . . . which can arise, and no one can describe or deal with them in advance."

140. As an example Luther mentioned esp. *Not* ⟨i.e., need in the sense of want, or necessity, or emergency⟩; *On Secular Authority*, 1523: WA 11:272.11: "Regardless how good and fair laws are, they all have the one condition: they may not go against *Not*." See also *Dictum Gratiani* before c.40. C.I.q.1 ⟨Friedberg 1:374⟩: ". . . need *(necessitas)* has no law but makes law for itself. . . ."

141. For the connection of secular natural law with equity, see *Admonition to Peace*, 1525: WA 18:304.8; Luther to the City Council of Danzig: May 5 (or 7), 1525: WA.B 3:485.27.47; sermon of Oct. 1, 1533: WA 37:157.19.22: "In the kingdom of the world . . . things should be handled with *epieikeia*, not the strict law, but equity." — See also Aristotle *Nicomachean Ethics* 5.14 ⟨1137b⟩. — Wünsch, *Gotteserfahrung und sittliche Tat bei Luther*, 54, erred when he connected equity with Christ's law and not with the secular natural law. — See further, Eugen Wohlhaupter, "Aequitas canonica," *VGG*.R 56 (1931): 107f.; Carl J. Hering, "Die Aequitas bei Gratian," *StGra* 2 (1954): 101ff.

142. *Postilla for Lent*, 1525: WA 17.II:92.12.26 ⟨for "clearest" Luther wrote "allerstrengest," and "scherffist," i.e. literally, strictest and most severe⟩. — See also Johannes Stroux, "Summum ius summa iniuria. Ein Kapitel aus der interpretatio iuris," in *Festschrift Paul Speiser-Sarasin zum 80. Geburtstag am 16. Oktober 1926, überreicht von seinen Kindern* (Basel, 1926), 115ff.; Guido Kisch, "Summum ius summa iniuria. Basler Humanisten und Juristen über Aequitas und *Epieikeia*," in *Aequitas und bona fides. Festgabe zum 70. Geburtstag von August Simonius*, ed. by Juristische Fakultät der Universität Basel (Basel, 1955), 197; Guido Kisch, "Die Aequitaslehre des Marsilius von Padua," in "Festgabe Professor Hermann Rennefahrt zu seinem 80. Geburtstag," *Archiv des Historischen Vereins des Kantons Bern*, 44.II (1959): 413ff. See also below, 351 n. 462.

143. Regarding the essence of equity one has to agree with Lau's critique ("Äußer-

liche Ordnung," 42ff.) of Holl (*Luther,* 264f.). Equity is a part of the kingdom of reason, i.e., the kingdom of the world. Wingren's objections to this position (*Luthers Lehre vom Beruf,* 100) were the result of his not recognizing the personalistic quality of both kingdoms (see above, 255 n. 24). He quoted from Luther's *Postilla for Advent,* 1522: WA 10.I.2:174-180: Luther differentiated between the spiritual use (180.4: "Christian mildness") and the carnal use (179.21ff.) of equity. The first use, practiced by Christians, has other practical consequences than the second use, practiced by non-Christians; the first use is "plain and total," the second one is "uneven and piecemeal" (180.3). This differentiation corresponds to the different interpretation of the Golden Rule by a spiritual man and by a non-spiritual man. Yet equity itself belongs in the kingdom of reason, and therefore in the kingdom of the world, just as does man-made law, in the implementation of which equity is to be practiced. Hermann Diem, *Luthers Predigt in den zwei Reichen,* 33, also has to be corrected. He argued that the divine natural law interpreted as the Golden Rule is valid for both a Christian and a non-Christian, ⟨but that⟩ "equity is added on for a Christian." For the different attitude of a Christian and a non-Christian in the handling of man-made law, see below, 403 n. 11.

144. *On Confession,* 1520: WA 6:166.32: ". . . I know that the laws of man have to be subjected to *epieikeia* . . ."; *Whether Soldiers, Too, Can Be Saved,* 1526: WA 19:631.12.25: ". . . equity has to be the master of the law"; ibid., WA 19:633.8; *Postilla for Lent,* 1525: WA 17.II:91.20; Luther to the City Council of Danzig: May 5 (or 7), 1525: WA.B 3:485.24ff.; *Matthew, Chapters 18-24 Explained in Sermons,* 1537-40: WA 47:365.28: "*Epieikeia* means that one can be lenient ⟨Luther used the popular phrase "durch die Finger sehen"⟩ and does not act according to the strictness ⟨of the law but⟩ bears the burden and puts up with it"; *First Lectures on the Psalms,* 1513-15: WA 4:323.24: ". . . *epieikeia,* the moderater of laws according to the differences in times, places, and people. At one time a law could be most wholesome, at another time it would be most injurious. . . ." — See also Guido Kisch, *Erasmus und die Jurisprudenz seiner Zeit* (Basel, 1960).

145. Because equity breaks the rigid rule of the law; *Lectures on Genesis,* 1535-45: WA 43:62.27 ⟨LW 3:262⟩.

146. *The Book of Deuteronomy with Notes,* 1525: WA 14:554.38 ⟨LW 9:20⟩: ". . . before ⟨God⟩ gave laws He established judges, in order to impress equity upon us. For judges are living laws or the soul of the law. Therefore they are before and above laws, just as they are before and above the sword. They should judge according to the laws and carry out judgment through the sword; nevertheless, they should have both the law and the sword in their power, lest they use laws against laws, like those fools who fix their eyes on the law, neglect the circumstances of the case, and keep on mouthing only this: 'As it is written, so let it be done.'" For other passages from Luther's writings, see Wingren, *Luthers Lehre vom Beruf,* 102.

147. ⟨I.e., the jurists who follow the letter rather than the spirit of the law, the "fools" mentioned in n. 146.⟩

148. In *The Babylonian Captivity of the Church* (1520) Luther expressed this with the phrase *publica lex* (public law); WA 6:548.3. ⟨The context makes clear that this phrase designated not "that branch or department of law which is concerned with the state in its political or sovereign capacity, including constitutional and administrative law, and with the definition, regulation, and enforcement of rights in cases where the state is regarded as the subject of the right or object of the duty" (*BLD,* s.v. "Public Law"; *Staatsrecht* in Ger-

man), but law in a general sense.⟩ See also *The Bondage of the Will*, 1525: WA 18:654.6 ⟨*LW* 33:91*⟩*: "In all government of peoples, however, it is the rule that all matters of dispute should be settled by means of laws. But how could they be settled if the laws were not entirely certain and like shining lights among the people? For if laws are ambiguous and uncertain, not only would no disputes be decided, but neither would there be any certain norms of conduct; for laws are made in order that conduct may be regulated according to a certain pattern, and questions of dispute thus settled. That which is the standard and measure of other things, therefore, as the law is, ought to be the clearest and most certain of all."

149. *On Monastic Vows*, 1523: WA 8:630.18: "When it comes to external works, even the divine commandments, though they are immutable..., have an exception in case of impossibility"; see also ibid., WA 8:630.36f. See above, 318 n. 134, 319 n. 140, Wingren, *Luthers Lehre vom Beruf*, 97ff., esp. 100, and *First Commentary on Galatians*, 1519: WA 2:582.17: "...legislators... are debtors to love so that, once they see that their laws are a burden to the subjects or even injure them, they take care to serve with all means possible the advantage of others and abolish these laws. This is especially the case for ecclesiastical legislators."

150. *Whether Soldiers, Too, Can Be Saved*, 1526: WA 19:633.13: "In us humans is a vice, called deceit, i.e., trickery or knavery. When it hears that equity supersedes law, ... then it is totally hostile to law; day and night it tries and ruminates to find a way to become popular and sell itself by using the title and pretense of equity so that the law is being destroyed...."

151. *Psalm 101 Explained*, 1534-35: WA 51:242.20: "The Imperial law... is nothing other than the wisdom of the heathen, which the Romans... wrote down and put in order.... for this task they... had been endowed with... much intellect and understanding. Summa: Those who had such wisdom in matters of secular governance have lived and will not live again." See also *Second Lectures on the Psalms*, 1518-21: WA 5:293.26; sermon of Aug. 13, 1525: WA 16:354.8.

152. *To the Christian Nobility*, 1520: WA 6:460.2, 459.39.

153. *On Keeping Children in School*, 1530: WA 30.II:568.7: "Truly, laws are the good armour and weapon for the preservation and protection of land and people, indeed of a kingdom and secular governance." It is possible that this passage has to be seen in the light of Article 16 of the *Augsburg Confession*.

154. *Psalm 101 Explained*, 1534-35: WA 51:257.33: "...I do not want to have the Imperial laws tampered with or changed, even though lords and subjects, judges and jurists not only live contrary to them but also boldly abuse them. The heathen also say that a change of the governance and laws does not take place without great bloodshed...." ⟨For "Imperial laws," see n. 151. The term designates Roman law; it could also designate laws established by the emperor and the Imperial estates.⟩ See also *On Keeping Children in School*, 1530: WA 30.II:557.16.

155. *Psalm 101 Explained*, 1534-35: WA 51:242.20, as above, n. 151.

156. *On Keeping Children in School*, 1530: WA 30.II:558.3 ⟨*LW* 46:239⟩: "It is a fine thing, to be sure, if an emperor, prince, or lord is by nature so wise and able that he can instinctively hit upon what is ⟨the law⟩.... Such rulers are pretty rare birds. It would be dangerous to make an example of them because others may not have this power by nature. In ruling it is better to stick to the written law ⟨literally: 'universal book-law'⟩, which carries

157. *Second Lectures on the Psalms,* 1518-21: WA 5:140.31: "They do not fear you ⟨i.e., God⟩, they ignore your horrible judgments, securely they adore you"; ibid., WA 5:167.36: "One should not put one's trust in any of God's gifts ... but only in God himself, the giver; him we should believe, he should be our hope, to him we should cling"; *Second Lectures on Galatians,* 1531: WA 40.II:65.9: the Apostle Paul criticizes the 'philosophical' interpretation of the divine natural law.

158. See *Second Lectures on the Psalms,* 1518-21: WA 5:196.35, 256.17, 306.18, 198.39; *First Lectures on the Psalms,* 1513-15: WA 3:496.15: "... the earthly people or the saints according to the flesh."

159. For Luther's judgment on the justice worked out by the jurists, which for him was only a partial justice though they presented it as universal, i.e., divine justice, see *Lectures on Romans,* 1515-16: WA 56.448.2ff., and Johannes Heckel, "Recht und Gesetz," ZSRG.K 26 (1937): 313f. — For Luther's invectives against the jurists, see Hermann W. Beyer, *Luther und das Recht. Gottes Gebot, Naturrecht, Volksgesetz in Luthers Deutung* (Munich, 1935), 52f.

160. *Second Lectures on the Psalms,* 1518-21: WA 5:107.5: "There is nothing more pernicious that could be presented to a Christian than moral philosophy and the decrees of men when they are presented in such a way that he may believe that in abiding by them he is doing the right thing before God"; ibid., WA 5:101.2.

161. *Lectures on Hebrews,* 1517-18: WA 57.III:110.12: "... the virtues of all philosophers, indeed of all men or jurists or theologians, are virtues only in appearance, but in reality they are vices"; *Second Lectures on Galatians,* 1531: WA 40.I:477.7: Luther dealt with the belief in justification through works as Satan's supreme empire in the world. — For the "horrible misunderstanding of law," see Gogarten, *Kirche in der Welt,* 119.

162. *Lectures on Romans,* 1515-16: WA 56:327.27 ⟨LW 25:315⟩: "... God is eternal and a spirit, before whom nothing counts except what is spiritual and eternal; but the flesh and temporal things are nothing with Him."

163. See above, 313 nn. 90-91.

164. This is applicable even to Roman law; *Second Lectures on the Psalms,* 1518-21: WA 5:293.29: "In the eyes of men, the justice ⟨of Roman laws⟩ had a glorious appearance, but before God it is nothing in terms of substance."

165. *Second Lectures on the Psalms,* 1518-21: WA 5:411.39: "... they all search for their own things.... And this vice of the human heart is more subtle than that it could be recognized by man...."

166. Therefore the spiritual or the corporeal interpretation of the Golden Rule demands different ways of implementing the rule.

167. ⟨Literally: "a painted gulden."⟩

168. *The Seven Penitential Psalms,* 1517: WA 1:213.2: "... a play-penny or a counterfeit gulden is not a true gulden, but only a figure of a gulden; in fact, it is nothing other than a deception when it is given as a true gulden and considered as such. A true gulden, however, is truth without deception. Therefore, the life, works, and righteousness of all haughty saints are in comparison with the righteousness and work of God's grace a mere show and a deadly and pernicious guile when they are considered to be the true stuff; truth is not in them, truth belongs to God, who gives the true, fundamentally good righ-

teousness, which is faith in Christ." See also Luther's remarks about the "picture kings," above, 259 n. 55. — For the copper or lead *denarius*, which only appears to have value, see Aegidius Romanus ⟨Giles of Rome⟩, *De regimine principum* (Venice, 1498), lib. I. p.secunda. cap. VII. ⟨On Giles of Rome, see *NCE* 6 (2d. ed. 2003), 220f.⟩

169. See the controversy between Troeltsch (*Die Soziallehren der christlichen Kirchen und Gruppen*, 486 n. 223; "Das Christliche Naturrecht," in Troeltsch, *Gesammelte Schriften*, 4:156ff., esp. 161f.) and Holl (*Luther*, 481 n. 2); Lau, *"Äußerliche Ordnung,"* 62f. Emil Brunner (*Gerechtigkeit*, 324 n. 44) and Watson (*Um Gottes Gottheit*, 136) also rejected this differentiation between absolute and relative natural law. Schönfeld (*Grundlegung der Rechtswissenschaft*, 301) differentiated between the absolute natural law as the idea of law and the relative natural law which is connected with the positive law and gives durability to it. Since both concepts are on the level of human law, the considerations mentioned above do not apply to them.

170. For the carnal law of the external, carnal, temporal righteousness of the flesh, see *Lectures on Hebrews*, 1517-18: WA 57.III:40.5f., and *First Commentary on Galatians*, 1519: WA 2:533.35 ⟨*LW* 27:286⟩.

171. *First Lectures on Galatians*, 1516-17: WA 57.II:87.10: "'Elements of the world' ⟨Gal. 4:3; Vulgate; NRSV: 'elemental spirits of the world'⟩ are writings, doctrines, laws, etc., affirmed and passed on by humans. But the elements of God . . . are writings impressed by God's living finger upon hearts, such as . . . righteousness."

172. *First Lectures on the Psalms*, 1513-15: WA 4:325.26 ⟨*LW* 11:443⟩.

173. See above, 55.

174. *Second Lectures on the Psalms*, 1518-21: WA 5:161.38: ". . . do I condemn the governmental authority, peace, and life, things without which one cannot live and which are God's best creatures? ⟨Not at all,⟩ but I condemn that the heart hangs on them. Therefore sometimes things have to endure to be labelled with a shameful word, as when Ecclesiastes calls them vain ⟨1:2⟩ . . . not because of their own fault, but because of the vanity of someone else. . . . When these excellent works ⟨i.e., governmental authority, peace, life⟩ are handled by the godless — since they are God's gifts through which others sometimes are helped but the godless ruined — they are called sacrilege, iniquity, idolatry, disobedience, not because of their own fault, but because of the contamination by those godless people."

175. This limitation makes law into a *Notordnung* ⟨an order generated by need, or necessity, or emergency, a make-do order⟩ and not a matter of external legal formalism; see also above, 288 n. 67. — See further, *Sermons on John, Chapters 16*, 1538: WA 46:43.6 ⟨*LW* 24:345⟩: "In the world and according to all reason, righteousness means the governing and the conduct that conform to laws and commandments issued by Moses or the emperor, rulers or parents. Those who obey such commands are called righteous"; ibid., WA 46:43.24: this definition is valid for "external secular righteousness."

176. *First Commentary on Galatians*, 1519: WA 2:500.6: "There is a difference between the law of the letter and the law of the spirit, just as there is a difference between a sign and what is signified, or a word and a thing." — For 'letter', see Prenter, *Spiritus creator*, 69f.

177. Sermons of ca. 1514-21: WA 4:698.30: "At this point you will say: 'Are the laws not good? Is it not good to give back to someone what belongs to him?' I answer: 'The law is a good thing, but it is not used well unless it is handled with a heart which is . . . lifted up

to the heavens...'"; *Sermons on the Ten Commandments*, 1518: WA 1:416.28: "... God bestows external goods upon external righteousness..."; *Magnificat*, 1521: WA 7:581.33: "Law is something good and God's gift, who doubts it? God's Word itself says that law is good..."; *Psalm 101 Explained*, 1534-35: WA 51:204.7: "... law, good reason, ... are not condemned or rejected, but our self-confidence."

178. *Disputation on Justification*, 1536: WA 39.I:125.35 ⟨LW 34:196⟩: "A divine ordinance is not godless. ⟨Civic⟩ righteousness is a divine ordinance. Therefore, it is not godless. Response: With respect to God. For in us it is defiled, since we are godless and corrupt."

179. *First Lectures on Galatians*, 1516-17: WA 57.II:97.25: "An external work is neutral. But a totally different situation exists in the conscience, opinion, mind, determination, intention, etc. Therefore, if works of the law are done with a bound conscience they are sins against grace; if they are done because of dedication to love, however, they are meritorious works according to grace. They are done because of dedication to love when they are done according to the need or desire of the neighbor, for then they are no longer works of the law but works of love; they are done not because of the law but because of the brother."

180. *Disputation against Scholastic Theology*, 1517, thesis 70: WA 1:227.25: "By necessity, a good law turns out to be bad through the natural will"; *Second Lectures on the Psalms*, 1518-21: WA 5:560.21: "... law ... is not being loved, not because of its own fault but because of the fault of the will..."; *Lectures on Malachi*, 1526: WA 13:681.17: "All commandments are mindful of the person who obeys them, and the question is not raised how good a thing is, but whether the thing is being used in a good or evil way."

181. *Lectures on Hebrews*, 1517-18: WA 57.III:217.18: "... on the basis of its nature ... nothing that is external does any good to the soul at all."

182. For 'doing things spiritually', see below, 334 n. 294. The situation is identical regarding the relationship between an office and the implementation of its duties. See, e.g., *Whether Soldiers, Too, Can Be Saved*, 1526: WA 19:624.18: "First we have to consider the difference between the office and the person, or the work and the actor. For by itself an office or work certainly can be good and righteous, and yet it is evil and not righteous when the person or actor is not good or righteous, or does not do the work in a righteous way"; sermons of ca. 1514-21: WA 4:707.24: "All of God's creatures are good and blessed because of the goodness of the Creator. But ... man abuses them to destruction because of his wickedness"; see also ibid., WA 4:696.17.30. For one of the earliest passages, see *First Lectures on the Psalms*, 1513-15: WA 3:144.3: "⟨The Lord instructs sinners⟩ 'in the way' ⟨Ps. 25:8⟩, i.e., in the use of the law, because 'the way' is the law in the process of being implemented ⟨literally: 'in the act of the work'⟩."

183. *First Lectures on the Psalms*, 1513-15: WA 4:188.8 ⟨LW 11:338f.⟩: "... from the letter you have this fruit, that it teaches you to look at the creatures not absolutely, but in their order toward the Creator. For as with the finger at the same time as he shows you the creature, he leads you to its Creator.... No philosophy ... does this. It seeks only the quiddities, as the saying goes"; ibid., WA 4:306.11 ⟨LW 11:415⟩: "... the law of Moses has both, the signifying letter and the spirit signified by the letter"; ibid., WA 3:516.8, as below, 333 n. 283 (in this passage the 'use of the creature' is compared with a 'cup' which contains both spiritual and non-spiritual things); ibid., WA 3:456.29.

184. Sermons of ca. 1514-21: WA 4:708.1: "Whatever the godless and the nonbeliever are able to do must not be called divine and Christian."

185. See, e.g., the phrase "A Christian citizen or peasant," in *On the Councils and the Church,* 1539: WA 50:608.9.

186. ⟨See above, 35.⟩

187. ⟨For the second feature, "kingdom of the world" as "God's kingdom at the left," see above, 66-70.⟩

188. *Lectures on Romans,* 1515-16: WA 56:406.18: "... the flesh and the wisdom of the flesh are in no way capable of grasping God's righteousness and wisdom...." — Althaus (*Gebot und Gesetz,* 10f., 14) differentiated two forms of God's will, the supralapsarian form, i.e., the commandment *(Gebot),* and the infralapsarian form, i.e., the law *(Gesetz).* It has to remain open whether the terms of this differentiation can be based on the New Testament, but Luther did not know this differentiation. Althaus was correct when he described the form of the law (prohibitive rather than imperative statements, multiplicity of material commandments). According to Luther, this form is not of divine origin but was added by Moses, i.e., it originated with man. In the divine law it is impossible to separate the content from the form or appearance; see above, 49f.

189. *Lectures on Genesis,* 1535-45: WA 42:356.20 ⟨*LW* 2:134⟩: "... God's wrath is unbearable when He has begun to be incensed...." — For the destructive power of law in the words of preachers, see *Second Lectures on the Psalms,* 1518-21: WA 5:502.14.

190. *Second Commentary on Galatians,* 1535: WA 40.I:37.5: "... as if the law is or could be anything other than the revelation of wrath"; *Second Lectures on Galatians,* 1531: WA 40.I:257.13: "The law is nothing other than the kingdom of sin and wrath."

191. ⟨Heckel cited the Vulgate text of this psalm, we cite the NRSV text.⟩

192. *Second Lectures on the Psalms,* 1518-21: WA 5:27.15: "The way you are, that way God himself is to you, not to mention the creature. Since God is indeed the elect one to him who is elected, the crooked one to him who is crooked, the holy one to him who is holy, there is then nothing good for the evil one, nothing delightful for him who does not delight in the Lord's law"; see also ibid., WA 5:70.15.

193. *Second Lectures on the Psalms,* 1518-21: WA 5:521.9: "Therefore you see that in terms of his nature and being God does not become holy, ... crooked, but in terms of his Word and work which he does in good and evil spirits; both receive in themselves whatever they attribute to God"; ibid., WA 5:523.25: "For God does not become crooked in his being but in his Word and work, with which he rules in godly people."

194. See above, 282 n. 28.

195. See also Thielicke, *Theologische Ethik,* 1:Nos. 691ff. Thielicke, however, described law as "God's will *modified* through the fallen world," in the sense that "God in an exclusive way has to be understood as the subject of this modification." ⟨Nos. 694, 695.⟩ — For the correlation of God and man, see Axel Gyllenkrok, "Die Anfänge von Luthers Theologie und das Wesen der Reformation," offprint of *Für Arbeit und Besinnung,* 7.No. 3: March 1, 1954. Norddeutsche Beilage, 7.

196. See *First Lectures on the Psalms,* 1513-15: WA 3:116.31, 266.35, 310.23, and Gyllenkrok, *Rechtfertigung und Heiligung,* 28.

197. ⟨Heckel used the phrase "geistlicher Stand." In medieval society this phrase designated the *estate* of the spiritual ones (the people who have been made spiritual through the sacrament of Ordination, i.e., in a narrow sense, the clergy, in a wider sense,

all the religious ones) *and* their standing in society. Above, the phrase designates the *spiritual status* of people (a quality) in contrast to a corporeal status. See also above, 260 n. 14.>

198. *First Lectures on the Psalms,* 1513-15: WA 3:35.13, as above, 265 n. 63. See also Pinomaa, *Zorn Gottes in der Theologie Luthers,* 208.

199. *Second Lectures on the Psalms,* 1518-21: WA 5:269.37. See also stanzas 2 ("Fast bound in Satan's chains I lay") and 3 ("My own good works availed me naught") of Luther's hymn *Dear Christians, Let Us Now Rejoice:* WA 35:423 <LW 53:219>.

200. For the quality of the divine law as positive legal order *(Rechtsgesetz),* see above, 273 n. 4.

201. For 'law of wrath' as God's challenge of man, see Jacob, *Gewissensbegriff in der Theologie Luthers,* 31.

202. For "office" <in the sense of task> of the law, see *Second Lectures on the Psalms,* 1518-21: WA 5:560.42: ". . . on the basis of its office, the law of the Lord is called the Lord's judgment because it judges and condemns the flesh or the old man. . . ."

203. *Second Lectures on Galatians,* 1531: WA 40.I:531.18: "<The law> cannot offer anything other than killing, accusing, and condemning"; ibid., WA 40.I:553.5; Elert, *Zwischen Gnade und Ungnade,* 141.

204. This explains the negative titles (e.g., torturer, hangman, jailer, creator of servitude and oppressive labor) which Luther assigned to Moses. See *Second Lectures on Galatians,* 1531: WA 40.I:91.7; *Lectures on Psalm 45,* 1532: WA 40.II:482.10; sermons of ca. 1514-21: WA 4:629.27; Bornkamm, *Luther und das Alte Testament,* 122.

205. See above, 17.

206. *Second Lectures on Galatians,* 1531: WA 40.I:481.4, and *Second Commentary on Galatians,* 1535: WA 40.I:480.32. — On the origin of Luther's doctrine of the *usus legis,* see Ebeling, "Triplex usus legis," *ThLZ* 75 (1950): 242: "It seems to me that 'usus legis' was a theological term which Luther coined, probably around 1522."

207. <"Office" in the sense of task.> *Smalcald Articles,* 1537: WA 50:224.25 <BC 303.4: "The chief function or power of the law . . . ">.

208. *Second Lecture on Galatians,* 1531: WA 40.I:394.5.3: "The laws of the pope and of the emperor are cursed <because> they are under the law <i.e., the law of wrath>." — Erik Wolf (*Große Rechtsdenker* [2d ed. Tübingen, 1944], 141) pointed out Luther's "strong emphasis of the *Notstandscharakter* <i.e., the quality of emergency, or of a situation of need> also <see above, 46 with 288 n. 67; 323 n. 175 for the positive law> of the secular natural law." Wehrung (*Welt und Reich,* 202) agreed with this view.

209. *First Lectures on Galatians,* 1516-17: WA 57.II:90.1: "All our works are rather our enduring and God's works"; ibid., WA 57.II:90.6: "In the same way in which an artisan's tool is . . . acted upon by the artisan when he uses it, so, when it acts, the creature is . . . acted upon by the Creator."

210. *Open Letter on the Harsh Book against the Peasants,* 1525: WA 18:389.31: "The secular kingdom . . . is nothing other than the servant of divine wrath over the evil ones and a true prelude to hell and eternal death; its office and work is not to be merciful, but it is to be severe, serious, and angry"; ibid., WA 18:389.22, as above, 258 n. 53. Luther made similar statements already in *First Lectures on the Psalms,* 1513-15: WA 4:381.23, and in one of his early sermons (Dec. 27, 1514): WA 4: 660.28. — See also *Decretum Gratiani,* as above, 258 n. 53.

211. *Psalm 101 Explained,* 1534-35: WA 51:205.32. A balanced secular governance is

therefore possible only if law *and* mercy are practiced; ibid., WA 51:205.35ff. — For the difference between law and grace measured with the standard of earthly justice, see Wilhelm Grewe, *Gnade und Recht* (Hamburg, 1936), 11ff., 20; Gustav Radbruch, *Rechtsphilosophie* (5th ed. Stuttgart, 1956), 276ff. For the theological view of this problem, see Edmund Schlink, "Gerechtigkeit und Gnade," *KuD* 2 (1956): 256ff.

212. *On Secular Authority*, 1523: WA 11:251.1: "All who are not Christians belong to the kingdom of the world or under the law."

213. *Second Lectures on the Psalms*, 1518-21: WA 5:33.13: "... it follows that the will of man is opposed to the law, hates the law, flees the law. Even if sometimes, motivated by fear of punishment or eagerness for ⟨a reward⟩, man pretends to love the law, yet the hatred for the law always remains in him, and he is unable to love the law gratis; he loves the law not because it is good but because it is profitable for him." — See also *Decretum Gratiani* c.4. D.III ⟨Friedberg 1:5⟩: "Human life is regulated by the reward or punishment ⟨distributed by⟩ the law."

214. *On the New Testament, That Is, the Mass*, 1520: WA 6:353.15: "Even if the law pushes and forces man to do good works and abandon evil ones, yet it is not possible that he wants and likes to do this; he is always negatively inclined to the law and would rather be free from it"; *Second Lectures on the Psalms*, 1518-21: WA 5:574.19: "Man is unable to ⟨live with⟩ God's commandments ⟨literally: 'walk in God's commandments'⟩, unless he does and endures many things which he does not want to do, from which he ⟨rather⟩ flees, which he hates, and ⟨with which he would rather not deal⟩"; *Postilla for Christmas*, 1522: WA 10.I.1:451.10.

215. Since the law of wrath is written in man's heart, it is impossible for man to escape this law. On this point Georg Müller, *Luthers Stellung zum Recht*, 27, has to be corrected; according to Müller, for Luther law is "the moral law which confronts man from outside of himself, makes demands on him, and drives him to action."

216. *First Lectures on the Psalms*, 1513-15: WA 4:285.9: "... no human law can last forever"; Luther to George Spalatin: March 23, 1525: WA.B 3:457.11: "A new age certainly demands new laws and new practices *(mores)*; if those who ought to create them do not do this studiously, then those who ought not to create them will introduce them by force."

217. *First Commentary on Galatians*, 1519: WA 2:527.32: "They would prefer ... that the law does not exist. And this preference is identical with hate for the law." See also Hermann, *Luthers Lehre von Sünde und Rechtfertigung*, 15.

218. *Postilla for Christmas*, 1522: WA 10.I.1:451.12: "Everyone has to confess: if there were not hell and the punishment by the law, no one would do any good. Therefore since such ⟨good⟩ works are not the product of man's free spirit, they do not belong to him but to the coercing and driving law...."

219. *First Lectures on the Psalms*, 1513-15: WA 4:16.34: "There is peace in the world — though it is a very bad one — but it does not have righteousness. There is righteousness in the law, but that righteousness does not have peace." ⟨For "righteousness" Luther wrote *iustitia*. Here is a case where the meaning of *iustitia* is not absolutely clear (see above 236 n. 1); therefore one could also use "justice". The context (*LW* 11:169f.) seems to suggest that "righteousness" would be the more adequate reading.⟩

220. *Second Lectures on the Psalms*, 1518-21: WA 5:52.2: "They ⟨i.e., the 'crooked' ones of Ps. 18:26⟩ call Christ's law, which is a law of freedom and pleasantness, chains and yoke, and they consider it a matter of servitude and distress. On the other hand, they

believe that their law is a matter of freedom and ease, while in truth it is servitude and sickness."

221. For the insecurity of a security guaranteed by law, see *Lectures on Genesis,* 1535-45: WA 42:225.15, 226.30. ⟨For these passages, see *LW* 1:305f., 307.⟩

222. *Second Lectures on Galatians,* 1531: WA 40.I:391.15: "If God's law, handed down by Moses on the basis of a divine mandate, curses people who are under this law, what will those laws do which are invented by human reason?"; ibid., WA 40. I:202.4: "In this world ceremony and the law and its works are necessities, yet there is always the danger that they will develop into a denial of Christ; from laws grows at once trust in works . . ."; *On the Ban,* 1520: WA 6:74.35: "To make many laws means to put many ropes around poor souls." In this last passage Luther targeted ecclesiastical laws, but his statement is valid in general; see *First Commentary on Galatians,* 1519: WA 2:494.14 ⟨*LW* 27:226⟩: ". . . the misery of the church and of the Christians confronts me when I look at the forests, deserts, clouds, and oceans of Roman laws, the titles of which you would not be able to learn in your whole life"; ibid., WA 2:527.11 ⟨*LW* 27:276⟩.

223. For the ostensive and the effective function of the law, see Pinomaa, *Zorn Gottes in der Theologie Luthers,* 43f. See also *Postilla for Christmas,* 1522: WA 10.I.1:464.3.

224. *On Good Works,* 1520: WA 6:213.15: ". . . 'why do we have so many ecclesiastical and secular laws . . . ?' Answer: exactly because not all of us have or value faith; had everyone faith, we would never need any law at all. . . ."

225. ⟨See above, 60.⟩

226. *First Commentary on Galatians,* 1519: WA 2:577.10 ⟨*LW* 27:350⟩.

227. *Second Lectures on Galatians,* 1531: WA 40.I:554.5: "If I have the law, either the civic or the theological one, I remain in the world, I do not get into heaven or the next world."

228. *To the Christian Nobility,* 1520: WA 6:459.26: ". . . we have to confess that there is no governance more abominable than the one we have; this is the result of the ecclesiastical and the secular law so that no estate conducts itself according to natural reason, not to mention Holy Scripture."

229. *Second Lectures on Galatians,* 1531: WA 40.I:393.1. See also *First Commentary on Galatians,* 1519: WA 2:500.36, 527.11 ⟨*LW* 27:236, 276⟩; *Second Lectures on the Psalms,* 1518-21: WA 5:671.33: "The people ⟨of this world⟩ are shaped by laws, morals, and customs; but through these one can do nothing to get people to true righteousness; one only accomplishes a fictitious righteousness, a theatrical production."

230. ⟨See above, 35f.⟩

231. *Second Lectures on the Psalms,* 1518-21: WA 5:203.37: "⟨In Ps. 6:1f.⟩ the psalmist teaches God's two rods, one of mercy, one of wrath." See also above, 269 n. 20, and Maurer, *Freiheit eines Christenmenschen,* 113, 115.

232. *The Seven Penitential Psalms,* 1517: WA 1:160.27: ". . . all of God's punishments are very kindly ordained for our blessed consolation, . . . because God . . . holds and gives his goodness and kindness hidden under wrath and punishment."

233. *First Lectures on the Psalms,* 1513-15: WA 3:427.1 ⟨*LW* 10:365⟩: "Zeal is nothing else than hatred, ill will, or displeasure of evil or vice in what we love. Therefore no one can be zealous except one who loves. Zeal presupposes love and is directed to the same object as love. Love is that which loves and promotes the good in the object, while zeal is that which hates and removes the evil in it. Therefore Christ is called a zealous God in the

prophets (Ex. 20:5; 34:14), because He especially loves righteousness and hates wickedness in His believers."

234. *Lectures on Genesis*, 1535-45: WA 42:356.22 ⟨*LW* 2:134⟩: "Compassion . . . is a part of God's nature, since wrath is truly God's alien work, in which He engages contrary to His nature, ⟨and⟩ because He is forced into it by the wickedness of man."

235. See Jacob, *Gewissensbegriff in der Theologie Luthers*, 8ff.

236. ⟨See n. 234.⟩

237. Althaus, *Gebot und Gesetz*, 20: ⟨The law as God's alien Word makes his original own Word transparent.⟩

238. *Explanations of the Ninety-five Theses*, 1518: WA 1:540.23: "⟨In the perturbation of man⟩ God does his alien work so that he may do his own work"; ibid., WA 1:560.28: ". . . through punishments God seeks nothing other than that love be perfected."

239. Ernst Wolf, "Frage des Naturrechts bei Thomas und bei Luther," 11.

240. *The Bondage of the Will*, 1525: WA 18:677.9 ⟨*LW* 33:127⟩: "The whole meaning and purpose of the law is simply to furnish knowledge, and that of nothing but sin."

241. ⟨See above, 65f.⟩

242. For the sequence 'theological — civic use of the law', see Ebeling, "Triplex usus legis," ThLZ 75 (1950): 245: Just as Melanchthon does, so "Luther places the civic use of the law before the theological use when both uses are placed side by side. Calvin . . . from the very beginning puts the theological use of the law in the first place and the civic use in the second place." See *Calvini Opera*, Peter Barth edition, 1:61f. (*Institutes* 1536 ed.); ibid., 3:332ff. (*Institutes* 1559 ed.).

243. *Second Commentary on Galatians*, 1535: WA 40.I:528.9 ⟨*LW* 26:344⟩: "Those who are not to be justified are restrained by the civic use of the Law; for they should be bound with the chains of laws, as wild and untamed beasts are bound with ropes and chains. This use of the Law never ceases. . . . Those who are to be justified, on the other hand, are disciplined by the theological use of the Law for a time; for it does not last for ever, as the civic use does, but it looks forward to the coming of faith, and when Christ comes, it is finished."

244. *Against the Heavenly Prophets*, 1525: WA 18:194.31.

245. *Commentary on Habakkuk*, 1526: WA 19:361.14.

246. *Postilla for Christmas*, 1522: WA 10.I.1:454.10, 460.4. For the "threefold use of the law," see ibid., WA 10.I.1:456.8.

247. *Commentary on Habakkuk*, 1526: WA 19:361.17. ⟨Literally: "Where things are done rightly, there is no longer . . . "⟩

248. See *Second Lectures on Galatians*, 1531: WA 40.I:480.8, 552.13. ⟨For these passages, see also the edited version of these lectures, *LW* 26:308f., 361f.⟩

249. *On Marriage Matters*, 1530: WA 30.III:216.10.

250. *Second Lectures on Galatians*, 1531: WA 40.I:530.11: "One has to examine ⟨the paragraph about the law⟩ carefully — how does one have to think about the law so that the law is not being rejected the way the rebellious peasants did; they said that the freedom of the gospel absolves from all laws. They sin in the same way who want to be justified through the law as do those . . . who want to be totally freed from law. This is the true and best use of the law: to restrain the ignorant ones and those who have not yet been justified. This is the use: restrain in such a way that ⟨the law⟩ does not restrain only in a civic way, which is the lowest *(infimus)* use, but also in a theological way. As Paul said: 'We were

imprisoned and guarded' ⟨Gal. 3:23⟩. ⟨He speaks here⟩ not only of the civic use by which the godless are restrained through force but also that we were guarded and driven toward . . . Christ. . . . The law should be imposed only on the godless, of which there are two kinds: those who are to be justified and those who are not to be justified. ⟨Those who are not to be justified⟩ are restrained through the civic use of the law and are to be chained like wild beasts. Here Paul does not speak chiefly about this use, but about the true use of the law, which lasts until the arrival of Christ, ⟨and⟩ which drives the conscience toward . . . Christ."

251. Both kinds of the use of the law, therefore, make up the legitimate use of the law (1 Tim. 1:8); *Second Lectures on Galatians*, 1531: WA 40.I:620.10: Paul calls the law good (1 Tim. 1:8) "if it is legitimately used; then we use it in the *politia* for restraining the godless and in theology for terrifying ⟨proud sinners⟩. Paul says ⟨1. Tim. 1:9⟩ that 'the law is for the unjust' so that they are restrained in the civic realm and terrified in the theological realm."

252. *First Lectures on the Psalms*, 1513-15: WA 3:550.33: "The creation of corporeal things is the beginning, image, and shadow of the Redemption and of spiritual things. These are the goal of the former things, and without them the former things are empty. Therefore these former things have to be understood as parables of the spiritual things."

253. *On Keeping Children in School*, 1530: WA 30.II:527.8: "In this world the office ⟨of pastoral care⟩ not only promotes and helps maintain temporal life and all secular estates but also gives eternal life and redeems from death and sin — and this is its very own and chief work. Of course, the world is and remains always ⟨but⟩ only for the sake of this estate ⟨i.e., of the pastor⟩, otherwise it would have long ago collapsed." See also *Second Lectures on Galatians*, 1531: WA 40.I:480.4: "The magistrate protects the whole world, which is besieged by the devil and carried headlong into all ⟨sorts of⟩ crimes, and he holds in check hands and feet; . . . and ⟨God⟩ instituted that constraint because of the public peace, raising offsprings, and esp. because of the gospel"; above, 269 n. 19.

254. *Second Lectures on Galatians*, 1531: WA 40.I:552.13f.

255. See above, 329 n. 250.

256. *The Papacy at Rome*, 1520: WA 6:291.3; *Sermons on Matthew, Chapters 5-7*, 1530-32: WA 32:360.26.

257. *On Good Works*, 1520: WA 6:207.15. See also *First Lectures on the Psalms*, 1513-15: WA 3:249.13; *Sermons on Matthew, Chapters 5-7*, 1530-32: WA 32:494.20; *Second Lectures on the Psalms*, 1518-21: WA 5:379.31.

258. *Second Lectures on Galatians*, 1531: WA 40.I:309.8: ". . . the office of ruling has to have power ⟨literally here and throughout the quotation, 'wrath' in the sense of severity, rigour, strictness, maybe even passion⟩ because without power one cannot accomplish anything in matters of peace or war. A teacher, a magistrate, a ruler, a head of a household is of no value unless he uses power. Therefore for the office of magistrate power is as necessary as any other strength. But this power has to be used moderately, and not in a childish or womanish way seek revenge. A father, a teacher disciplines not for revenge, but he is concerned with the vice which he wishes to correct. So acts a mother, etc. These are ⟨manifestations of the⟩ good ⟨use⟩ of power, i.e., of zeal, when I wish to cleanse something in a brother or subordinate and do not seek his destruction but his advantage, education. . . . This is called a good power and necessity; where it is not, things are not well."

259. *First Lectures on Galatians*, 1516-17: WA 57.II:68.21: "No one is justified

⟨through works of the law⟩; they are necessary nevertheless, because righteousness cannot exist internally if works are not done externally"; ibid., WA 57.II:99.23; *First Commentary on Galatians,* 1519: WA 2:574.28, 575.14 ⟨*LW* 27:347, 348⟩; above, 273 n. 12; *Disputation on the Power and Will of Man without Grace,* 1516: WA 1:146.37: "⟨In God's court⟩ they will be punished in a more bearable way ⟨who⟩ naturally did . . . the things of the law, ⟨because⟩ they have inscribed in their hearts the ⟨book⟩ of the law, which tells them not to do to others what they themselves do not wish to endure. They sin nevertheless, because as people without faith they did not direct their works to that goal to which they should have directed them."

260. *The Bondage of the Will,* 1525: WA 18:638.5 ⟨*LW* 33:70⟩: ". . . free choice is allowed to man only with respect to what is beneath him and not what is above him. That is to say, a man should know that with regard to his faculties and possessions he has the right to use, to do, or to leave undone, according to his own free choice, though even this is controlled by the free choice of God alone, who acts in whatever way he pleases."

261. ⟨Wrath of severity.⟩ *First Lectures on the Psalms,* 1513-15: WA 3:488.35: ". . . the wrath of severity, without . . . mercy, without hope"; ibid., WA 3:488.27, 556.7; ibid., WA 4:6.24: ⟨Ps. 85:4; Vulgate. God's⟩ "'wrath of indignation' . . . is a spiritual wrath and not a simple, temporarily restricted wrath"; ibid., WA 4:1.14. — See also Pinomaa, *Zorn Gottes in der Theologie Luthers,* 73ff.

262. For man's reason it is "an astonishing problem that God rewards the righteousness which he considers to be iniquity and malice"; *Disputation on Justification,* 1536, part III, thesis 10: WA 39.I:82.23. See also ibid., WA 39.I:116.4: "Previously I said that our righteousness is dung before God. Now I add: if God wishes to adorn dung, he can do this; nothing harms the sun because it sends its rays into the cloaca"; ibid., WA 39.I:100.27 ⟨God's immense goodness and mercy⟩, and 123.1.

263. If one spiritually evaluates human law and its battle against evil, then human law is only the very end of God's law, an end which reaches into a different level than God's law itself, i.e., the corporeal level. Therefore, following Deut. 28:13, Luther called human law, including the Decalogue, the "tail" or "feet of the law," while Christ was for Luther the "head," "goal," or "summit" of the law; *Lectures on Hebrews,* 1517-18: WA 57.III:220.11ff. — For Luther's concept 'gradation', see Kühn, *Toleranz und Offenbarung,* 90ff., esp. 94.

264. For law as school for righteousness, see *Second Lectures on Galatians,* 1531: WA 40.I:511.11.

265. In this sense one can affirm Weinkauff's statement ("Naturrecht in evangelischer Sicht," *Zeitwende* 23 [1951/52]: 94): "Even though the earthly law certainly has religious value, nevertheless by no means is this an ultimate value but only a penultimate one."

266. *On Monastic Vows,* 1521: WA 8:629.23, as above, 303 n. 10, with the addition at the end: "Therefore what is clearly contrary to reason certainly is even more contrary to God. For how ⟨should⟩ what opposes earthly truth not oppose heavenly truth?"

267. *First Lectures on the Psalms,* 1513-15: WA 3:482.28: "What is done and said against truth and righteousness, is done and said against God." Luther thought here of God's righteousness. But his statement is valid also for human righteousness ⟨or: "justice"⟩ insofar as God's will for law is present in an earthly secular natural-law order of law.

268. *Sermons of 1523:* WA 12:674.14: In the parable of the wicked slave (Matt.

18:23ff.) "we are to see how before God things are quite different than before the world, and how what is unjust before God is just and fair before the world"; ibid., WA 12:676.5: ". . . no one who is under secular governance may boast that therefore he acts legally before God — before God all ⟨he does⟩ is still not right."

269. *Magnificat,* 1521: WA 7:585.33.

270. ⟨Literally: "strengths."⟩

271. *Magnificat,* 1521: WA 7:588.10f. — Helmut Thielicke was to the point when he stated in *Kirche und Öffentlichkeit* (Tübingen, 1947), 64: "It is impossible to recognize in the orders God's absolute will."

272. Therefore all the pomp that is used in the kingdom of the world when its courts decide legal matters is only "a fable or comedy." See *Second Lectures on the Psalms,* 1518-21: WA 5:294.1; sermon of Nov. 18, 1526: WA 20:555.6: "God ⟨says⟩ there ⟨is⟩ no righteousness on earth. I speak ⟨here⟩ not only of the righteousness before God, but also of worldly righteousness; it is a beggar's coat, because the world is nothing but a school of the devil's scoundrels. ⟨This worldly righteousness,⟩ God says, is nothing but unrighteousness on earth, even in the secular kingdom, and in the spiritual kingdom it is nothing but blasphemy."

273. ⟨Above, 67: "If one understands the law of wrath . . ." to 68: ". . . lesson for understanding divine righteousness." The issue is the civic use of the law as God's tool and a part of the "constitution" of God's kingdom at the left (above, 68).⟩

274. See Wingren's justified critique (*Luthers Lehre vom Beruf,* 58f.) of the argument that ⟨having a, or meeting the requirements of one's⟩ vocation *(Beruf)* is ⟨a sign of the⟩ forgiveness of sin. — *The Large Catechism,* 1529: WA 30.I:182.20 ⟨*BC* 411. 1f.⟩: "The Creed . . . teaches us to know ⟨God⟩ perfectly. It is given in order to help us do what the Ten Commandments require of us. For . . . they are set on so high a plane that all human ability is far too feeble and weak to keep them"; sermons of ca. 1514-1521: WA 4:698.5: ". . . human righteousness through which is restored to someone what belongs to him ⟨is⟩ hypocrisy, because although publicly people are forced to return the item, nevertheless they do not return it ⟨motivated by⟩ the heart. ⟨Their heart is not totally involved⟩ as long as they love themselves more than they love their neighbor. In this way they do not love their neighbor as they love themselves"; *To Pastors, That They Preach against Usury,* 1540: WA 51:374.3: "To obey the emperor's law is not enough to get into heaven."

275. *Magnificat,* 1521: WA 7:590.14: "If the world is to continue, one has to have reason, wisdom, and law"; *On Secular Authority,* 1523: WA 11:262.5: ". . . each kingdom has to have its laws . . . , and without law no kingdom can survive, as daily experience sufficiently . . . shows."

276. *The Bondage of the Will,* 1525: WA 18:752.3 ⟨*LW* 33:239f.⟩: "For it is strictly true that a man is nothing in the sight of God if he is without love."

277. ⟨Literally: "a begging work."⟩ *Second Lectures on Galatians,* 1531: WA 40.I: 612.8ff., 557.4.

278. *Second Disputation against the Antinomians,* 1538: WA 39.I:461.7: "This is the solution of the argument that the law condemns itself: corporeal righteousness is condemned and judged through the spiritual law, because before God corporeal righteousness is impure, foul, hypocrisy, and a lie. In this way law nullifies law. Indeed, we have to say . . . that human presumption, esteem of one's own corporeal righteousness . . . are condemned through the spiritual law."

279. The relationship between the divine natural law and human law, and also the tension existing between them explain "⟨Luther's⟩ contradictory statements with which sometimes he praises law as a necessary means for order, sometimes outright condemns it"; so Wünsch, *Ethik des Politischen*, 541.

280. ⟨I.e., the secular natural law.⟩

281. *First Lectures on the Psalms*, 1513-15: WA 4:16.26: "⟨The law of the earthly city⟩ is barely a symbol *(figura)* of the righteousness and peace which exist in the city of God, the true righteousness and true peace . . ."; *Whether Soldiers, Too, Can Be Saved*, 1526: WA 19:629.25: "Even though ⟨God⟩ will not reward ⟨corporeal⟩ righteousness with eternal life, he nevertheless wants it to exist so that peace is preserved among mankind, and he rewards it with temporal goods." See esp. Luther's praise of peace in *Psalm 82 Explained*, 1530: WA 31.I:201.26, esp. 202.11; *Psalm 118 Explained*, 1530: WA 31.I:77.34. — See also Kurt Matthes, *Luther und die Obrigkeit* (Munich, 1937), 88 n. 36.

282. Erich Seeberg, *Luthers Theologie*, 2:321, emphasized that 'sign' is not an empty symbol but "signification that something is really present," a "token." See also Maurer, *Freiheit eines Christenmenschen*, 152; Meinhold, *Luthers Sprachphilosophie*, 13; Luther's *Second Lectures on the Psalms*, 1518-21: WA 5:65.25.

283. From the wealth of Luther's statements on this subject see, e.g., *First Lectures on the Psalms*, 1513-15: WA 3:129.20: ". . . all law and human righteousness are a shadow and symbol *(figura)* of that righteousness which exists in the spirit before God . . ."; ibid., WA 3:516.8 ⟨*LW* 10:460⟩: ". . . the true good things, which are spiritual, are contained in visible things as in their signs, shadows, and cups. For as the cup is the speech, the wine in the cup is the meaning in the speech, and the dregs are the carnal sense, so the use of any creature is like the cup. If it is received and used spiritually, it is a cup of pure wine and mixed. But if it is received only as what is seen, it is a cup of dregs." — For the difference between reality and sign, see also Luther to Michael Dressel: July 23, 1516: WA.B 1:47.29: "My best father, do you ignore that God is wonderful among his people because he places his peace in the midst of no peace, i.e., in the midst of all ⟨possible⟩ turmoil ⟨*tentationes*; see above, 248 n. 55, for *Anfechtung*⟩? . . . Therefore that person whom no one confounds does not have peace — or rather, he has the peace of the world — but that person has peace whom all people and things confound and who endures all this with joy and calmness. With Israel you say: 'Peace, peace,' and there is no peace ⟨Jer. 6:14; Ezek. 13:10⟩. Rather say with Christ: 'Cross, cross,' and there is no cross. For as quickly as you joyfully would say 'blessed cross, among wood there is none like you' ⟨see WA.B 1:48 n. 12⟩, so quickly the cross would cease being the cross."

284. After the Fall, divine righteousness can be attained only in Christ; therefore Luther called Moses a good Christian because the Decalogue pointed toward Christ; *The Last Words of David*, 1543: WA 54:77.24, 55.2, and Bornkamm, *Luther und das Alte Testament*, 127.

285. *Psalm 82 Explained*, 1530: WA 31.I:218.31: "Therefore we see the need that beyond worldly righteousness, wisdom, and power, though they, too, are divine works, has to be another kingdom, in which are another righteousness, wisdom, and power."

286. ⟨See above, 35, 68.⟩

287. Therefore a Christian sees in the secular law an example of "God's mummery"; *Psalm 127 Explained*, 1524: WA 15:373.14: "One can easily say that the events of the world

and especially the doings of God's saints are God's mummery, in which he hides himself, and rules and works so wonderfully in the world"; ibid., WA 15:373.8: "God's mummery."

288. The situation is identical in the case of the secular governance; *Whether Soldiers, Too, Can Be Saved*, 1526: WA 19:633.20: "... the heathen knew nothing of God, and also ... did not recognize that secular governance is God's order ⟨for they considered it to be something man does⟩"; *The Large Catechism*, 1529: WA 30.I:192.10 ⟨*BC* 419.66⟩: "All who are outside the Christian church, whether heathen, Turks, Jews, or false Christians and hypocrites, even though they believe in and worship only the one, true God, nevertheless do not know what his attitude is toward them. They cannot be confident of his love and blessing ⟨as, e.g., secular law or governance⟩. Therefore they remain in eternal wrath and damnation, for they do not have the Lord Christ, and, besides, they are not illuminated and blessed by the gifts of the Holy Spirit." — See also Kühn, *Toleranz und Offenbarung*, 53 n. 56; Lau, *Luthers Lehre von den beiden Reichen*, 42 n. 97.

289. WA 30.I:133ff. ⟨*BC* 365ff.⟩. See also below, 380 n. 182.

290. *Second Lectures on the Psalms*, 1518-21: WA 5:198.2: "... in the First Commandment of the Decalogue all the following commandments are ⟨contained⟩ so that ... the First Commandment is the ... standard of all the other commandments"; ibid., WA 5:227.40. — For the literal and the spiritual interpretation of the Fifth Commandment, see *Second Lectures on the Psalms*, 1518-21: WA 5:34.14.

291. *Second Lectures on Galatians*, 1531: WA 40.II:64.7: "What does it mean to serve ⟨the neighbor?⟩ ... The Decalogue ⟨provides the best answer⟩, ... " See also *On Good Works*, 1520: WA 6:204ff. ⟨*LW* 44:23ff.⟩.

292. *First Lectures on the Psalms*, 1513-15: WA 4:246.31 ⟨*LW* 11:383⟩: "... the purer and holier anyone is, of that much greater sensitivity he is in spirit. Such a person sees, hears, and feels God present everywhere, as Ps. 16:8 says."

293. *Whether Soldiers, Too, Can Be Saved*, 1526: WA 19:648.25: "Even if ⟨princes⟩ are not Christians, they nevertheless should do what is right and good according to God's external order — this is what God wants from them"; ibid., WA 19:630.1, 634.4; *Second Lectures on Galatians*, 1531: WA 40.I:555.10: "... laws ... are secular matters and God's ordinances in this world."

294. *That These Words of Christ, "This is My Body," Still Stand Firm against the Fanatics*, 1527: WA 23:185.6: "Something before us *(obiectum)* is not always spiritual, but the use of it has to be spiritual"; ibid., WA 23:189.8: "When God's Word is added to all that we do with our bodies externally and corporeally, and when we do it in faith, it is done spiritually and called spiritual. Nothing can be so corporeal, carnal, or external that it cannot become spiritual when we do it in the Word and faith. Spiritual is nothing other than what happens in and through us by means of the spirit and faith — may God grant this — regardless whether the thing with which we deal is corporeal or spiritual. That is to say, the spirit is in the use of something and not in the thing itself. ... For if someone serves his neighbor and does it corporeally, it does him no good, because the flesh is useless ⟨John 6:63⟩. But if he does it spiritually, i.e., if his heart does it motivated by faith ⟨literally: 'out of faith'⟩ in God's Word, it is life and Salvation. Therefore there is one corporeal neighbor with whom he deals, but there are two kinds of dealing with the neighbor"; *Second Lectures on Galatians*, 1531: WA 40.I:348.1: "... spirit is whatever ... happens in us through the spirit; flesh is whatever ⟨happens in us⟩ according to the flesh and outside of the spirit. Therefore all tasks *(officia)* and fruits of the Holy Spirit, such as feeding children,

loving the spouse, obeying the magistrate, are fruits of the spirit. Among the papists these tasks are corporeal matters, because they do not understand what a creature is." — See also Prenter, *Spirtus creator*, 234.

295. *Whether Soldiers, Too, Can Be Saved*, 1526: WA 19:629.30. See also *Sermons on Matthew, Chapters 5-7*, 1530-32: WA 32:318.29.35, 319.13ff.

296. ⟨A literal translation of the title would read: "The Institutional Human Natural Right." See also above, 302 n. 1, 303 n. 7.⟩

297. ⟨See above, 51f.⟩

298. *Second Lectures on the Psalms*, 1518-21: WA 5:143.24: "The world never has been without false religion and idolatry."

299. ⟨See above, 55f.⟩

300. For the following, see esp. Bornkamm, *Luther und das Alte Testament*, 176ff., 217f.; Maurer, "Kirche und Geschichte," in *Lutherforschung heute*, 85ff.; Jaroslav Pelikan, "Die Kirche nach Luthers Genesisvorlesung," in *Lutherforschung heute*, 102ff.

301. *Lectures on Genesis*, 1535-45: WA 42:187.18f.

302. For 'church of the devil', see *Against Jack Sausage*, 1541: WA 51:477.25, 512.19, 530.27, 531.23, 534.26; *Letter of D. Martin Luther concerning His Book on the Private Mass*, 1534: WA 38:268.28f.; *First Lectures on the Psalms*, 1513-15: WA 3:194.33, 226.2; *On the War against the Turks*, 1529: WA 30.II:128.17; *Defense against the Charge of Inciting Rebellion*, 1533: WA 38:99.32; sermon of May 21, 1531: WA 34.I:438.4.

303. *Lectures on Genesis*, 1535-45: WA 42:232.3 ⟨LW 1:315⟩: ". . . he ⟨i.e., Cain⟩ is the first to build a city, . . . to show that he not only despises the true church but also intends to suppress it. These were his thoughts: '. . . I shall build a city in which I can gather my own church.'"

304. Ibid., WA 42:187.13 ⟨LW 1:252⟩: "Moreover, here ⟨i.e., at the sacrifice made by Cain and by Abel⟩ the church begins to be divided into two churches: the one which is the church in name but in reality is nothing but a hypocritical and blood-thirsty church; and the other one ⟨i.e., the true church⟩. . . ." — For the two kinds of people who implore God, see *On Psalms 23-25*, 1513-16: WA 31.I:472.25ff.

305. *Lectures on Genesis*, 1535-45: WA 42:232.9 ⟨LW 1:315⟩: "Thus Cain did not build the city on account of fear and for his defense but because of his sure hope of success and his pride and lust for ruling."

306. Ibid., WA 42:232.8. See also *Matthew, Chapters 18-24 Explained in Sermons*, 1537-40: WA 47:253.2.

307. ⟨Literally: "corporeal".⟩

308. ⟨Literally: "under the title (in the sense of a legally fixed description, as e.g., the title of a property) 'church'."⟩ *Lectures on Genesis*, 1534-45: WA 42:192.23 ⟨LW 1:260⟩: "We observe . . . that up to the present time kings and princes are most intolerant of the church's censure. It is not enough for them to be kings and princes; but they also want to be righteous and saints before God, and they usurp the title 'church'. In the same way Cain, too, is filled with resentment when he sees that he is being deprived of the glory of righteousness and grace before God."

309. Ibid., WA 42:193.1 ⟨LW 1:260f.⟩: "Indeed, no wrath in the entire world is more cruel than that of this bloodthirsty and hypocritical church. Where the government shows its wrath, there is still something left of human emotion. No bandit, be he ever so brutal, is led to execution without people being touched by some compassion. But . . . the wrath

and pharisaical fury of the false church is clearly a devilish fury. It had its beginning in Cain and continues in all children of Cain."

310. Ibid., WA 42:289.5 ⟨LW 2:38⟩: "Noah, . . . together with his people, was condemned as a rebel, a heretic, and an enemy of the sovereignty of both the state and the church."

311. Ibid., WA 42:187.37 ⟨LW 1:253⟩: ". . . the true church is hidden; it is banned; it is regarded as heretical; it is slain."

312. ⟨See above, 248 n. 55.⟩

313. *Lectures on Genesis,* 1535-45: WA 42:288.17. See also *First Lectures on the Psalms,* 1513-15: WA 4:54.14 ⟨LW 11:196⟩: ". . . that people ⟨i.e., the Jews⟩, at one time exceedingly turned toward spiritual things, was at the time of Christ turned away altogether from its glory . . ."; ibid., WA 4:292.24: ". . . in the synagogue the ⟨presence of the⟩ spiritual people was reduced to almost nothing, . . . because of the dull and nebulous glosses of the scribes"; ibid., WA 4:298.25: ". . . ⟨in the days⟩ of the synagogue the corrupters of the law arose, and the spirit and the spiritual people disappeared, because the corrupters set forth the letter only and produced letter-oriented people, as is obvious in the gospels. Therefore then was the time that ⟨Christ⟩ should come. Hence one has to pray against the heretics and the false Christians in the last days."

314. WA.TR 5:No. 5242 (on p. 24.1).

315. See Bornkamm, *Luther und das Alte Testament,* 179ff.

316. Sermon of March 16, 1539: WA 47:678.19: "St. Paul wants to say that there are two kinds of people on earth: one people of the law, the other of freedom or grace. The people of the law want to be saved through works"; ibid., WA 47:683.8: "Paul ⟨using Sarah and Hagar as types⟩ says . . . what the true and the false Christian church is"; ibid., WA 47:683.16: "It is therefore a carnal church because it moves in carnal matters and chooses ⟨carnal⟩ righteousness."

317. *Psalm 90 Explained,* 1534-35: WA 40.III:505.2ff. For the different meanings of *absconditus* (hidden), see Ernst Kinder, "Die Verborgenheit der Kirche nach Luther," in *Festgabe Josef Lortz,* ed. by Erwin Iserloh and Peter Manns, 2 vols. (Baden-Baden, 1958), 1:173ff.

318. *Lectures on Amos,* 1524-25: WA 13:149.17: "⟨Amaziah, king of Judah,⟩ rejected the true worship and elevated his worship of deceit"; *Second Lectures on the Psalms,* 1518-21: WA 5:332.17.

319. See Bornkamm, *Luther und das Alte Testament,* 23ff.

320. *Lectures on Psalm 51,* 1532: WA 40.II:450.10: "To preach against familiar customs, the law of Moses, the religious observances of the people, ⟨and say⟩ 'you ⟨God⟩ do not want sacrifices' ⟨see Ps. 51:16⟩, that was a horrible heresy" ⟨in the sense that it was considered to be a heresy by the Jewish religious authorities⟩.

321. *Lectures on Amos,* 1524-25: WA 13:149.26; *Second Lectures on the Psalms,* 1518-21: WA 5:149.7. For the identical situation in which the preacher of the only truth finds himself in the corrupted Christian church, see ibid., WA 5:153.1ff.

322. For the persecution of the true church by a secular governmental authority as a meritorious work, see *Sermons on John, Chapter 16,* 1538: WA 46:14.17.

323. For Satan's synagogue of heretics, see *First Lectures on the Psalms,* 1513-15: WA 4:406.9ff. The heretics are not church because (ibid., WA 4:406.20) "Christ does not have two churches."

324. *Sermons on John, Chapters 14 and 15*, 1537: WA 45:615.1 ⟨*LW* 24:168⟩: "Christians need this comfort ⟨i.e., John 14:26 combined with the opening phrase of the Third Article of the Apostles' Creed⟩, lest they doubt that the Christian Church will remain in the world in the midst of all the unbelievers, Turks, heathen, Jews, heretics, and sects, as well as the devil and his angels."

325. *Sermon on the Estate of Marriage*, 1519: WA 2:167.16: ". . . woman has been created as man's companion and helper in all things, especially to bring forth children. And this has remained so, though after the Fall evil lust has been mixed into this. Now the desire of man and woman for each other is not pure; ⟨both⟩ seek not only companionship and children, for which alone ⟨marriage⟩ was instituted, but they very much seek also ⟨the gratification of⟩ evil lust."

326. *The Estate of Marriage*, 1522: WA 10.II:304.9: ". . . marital duty is not fulfilled without sin, but because of grace, God ⟨maintains⟩ marriage since the order of marriage ⟨i.e., a way of living just as a monastic order provides a way of living⟩ is his work. In spite of sin, marriage retains all the good which God had planted in it and blessed." See also Olsson, *Grundproblemet*, 1:46: "Luther's concept of marriage is constituted . . . of two elements, one of which can be designated libido, and the other the devotion ⟨of spouses to each other⟩ demanded by natural law."

327. *The Estate of Marriage*, 1522: WA 10.II:283.8: "Therefore know that marriage is an external corporeal thing, just like other secular doings"; *On Marriage Matters*, 1530: WA 30.III:205.12; *Sermons on Matthew, Chapters 5-7*, 1530-32: WA 32:376.38.

328. *A Marriage Booklet for Simple Pastors*, 1529: WA 30.III:74.3 ⟨*BC*.Kolb-Wengert ed., 367.1⟩.

329. Ibid., WA 30.III:75.16 ⟨*BC*.Kolb-Wengert ed., 368.3⟩.

330. At this point we shall not deal with the controversy whether the structural orders in the kingdom of the world may be divided into orders of Creation and orders resulting from sin; in this case marriage would be classified among the former and governmental authority among the latter. We also shall not deal with the controversy about Creation orders. For details, see Paul Althaus, *Theologie der Ordnungen* (2d ed. Gütersloh, 1935), 15, and now, Lau, *Luthers Lehre von den beiden Reichen*, 36.

331. *On Marriage Matters*, 1530. WA 30.III:207.15. Since for Luther marriage was a public estate, he vigorously opposed *secret engagements*. ⟨In Luther's days, engagement was understood to be a legally binding arrangement between a man and a woman; therefore, according to Luther, one had to enter into this arrangement in public. A secret engagement often could lead to the abandonment of one spouse by the other.⟩ See sermon of Jan. 7, 1532: WA 36:96.18. — For the way in which in Wittenberg the situation was handled when a man engaged to a woman had sexual relations with another woman, and Luther's efforts to arrive at a position on this matter, see Luther's brief of Jan. 1528: WA.B 4:333.26ff., 337.16ff., 338.55, and Luther to Duke John, elector of Saxony: Jan. 21, 1528: WA.B 4:354.5. — Early on, in marital matters the reformers administered what amounted to a spiritual, pastoral jurisdiction (which had legal consequences in the civic realm). By 1530 this changed. See Luther to Nicholas Hausmann: Apr. 24, 1531: WA.B 6:81.21, and Luther's brief of May 1531: WA.B 6:114.164ff.

332. *A Marriage Booklet for Simple Pastors*, 1529: WA 30.III:74.2 ⟨*BC*.Kolb-Wengert ed., 367.1⟩: "'So many lands, so many customs,' says the common proverb. For this reason, because weddings and the married estate are worldly affairs, it behooves those of us

who are 'spirituals' or ministers of the church in no way to order or direct anything regarding marriage, but instead allow every city and land to continue their own customs that are now in use"; WA.TR 3:No. 3267: marital matters belong before the magistrate; WA.TR 4:No. 3980: "I wish we would not be burdened with marital matters.... They belong before the magistrate"; Luther to Leonard Beyer: Nov. 2, 1535: WA.B 7:320.8. — For the possible conflict between a verdict rendered by a secular judge in a court and that rendered by a theologian in the spiritual court of the conscience ⟨Confession⟩, see Luther and Bugenhagen to the councilors of Electoral Saxony: March 26, 1528: WA.B 4:419.11.

333. Emil Friedberg, *Das Recht der Eheschließung in seiner geschichtlichen Bedeutung* (Leipzig, 1865), 157ff., is an example of the consequences which develop if one fails to recognize the difference between the two kingdoms and, therefore, also between a Christian marriage and a secular natural-law marriage. Friedberg argued (159) that in Luther's thinking about marriage there was a "conflict."

334. The example set by Christ proves this; *On Secular Authority,* 1523: WA 11: 258.38.

335. *Lectures on Psalms 120–134,* 1532-33: WA 40.III:223.1: "In the hearts of people are established ... the *politia,* the *oeconomia,* the written laws."

336. *Lectures on Genesis,* 1535-45: WA 42:114.4 ⟨LW 1:151⟩: "Just as in all the rest of nature the strength of the male surpasses that of the other sex, so also in the perfect nature the male somewhat excelled the female."

337. Ibid., WA 42:151.22: "... Eve has been subjected to the authority of the man, she who before was absolutely free and in no way inferior to the man, ⟨and⟩ shared in all of God's gift"; ibid., WA 42:103.32. — See also Ernst Wolf, "'Evangelisches' Eherecht," in *Smend Festschrift,* 413ff.

338. ⟨Domestic governance, or *oeconomia* in the narrow sense; see above, 266 n. 8.⟩

339. *Commentary on 1 Corinthians, Chapter 7,* 1523: WA 12:101.14 ⟨LW 28:13⟩: "... the state of matrimony is constituted in the law of love so that no one rules over his own body but must serve his partner, as is the way of love"; *Sermon on the Estate of Marriage,* 1519: WA 2:167.29: "Marital love transcends ... ⟨all kinds of natural love, such as, e.g., the love between father and child, or brother and sister⟩.... All other kinds of love seek something other than the beloved one. Alone marital love desires the beloved totally as ⟨his or her⟩ own. Had Adam not fallen, marital love would have been the most delightful thing — bride and groom. But now love also is not pure...." See also *Decretum Gratiani* c.un. C.35. q.1 ⟨Friedberg 1: 1262⟩: "Copulation ... of male and female, as much as it pertains to the human race, is a sort of nursery for love."

340. *The Babylonian Captivity of the Church,* 1520: WA 6:555.28: ⟨A marriage may not be dissolved in order to maintain human laws concerning the impediments of marriage because⟩ "as a divine institution marriage itself is incomparably superior to laws; therefore a marriage should not be dissolved because of laws, but laws deserve to be broken because of marriage."

341. *Sermons on John, Chapter 14 and 15,* 1538: WA 45:669.23 ⟨LW 24:228⟩: "For when He created the world, He commanded and empowered man to rule physically over beasts, birds, and fish, to maintain home life, to rear children, to cultivate fields, to rule over lands and people, etc. It was not necessary for Christ to give instruction about this, for it was implanted in nature and written in their hearts. Furthermore, all books, with the exception of Holy Writ, are derived from that source and spring."

342. *Lectures on Psalms 120–134,* 1532-33: WA 40.III:221.12: "In this psalm ⟨127⟩ Sol-

omon does not teach how commonwealths are to be organized and laws to be established for these things are already in nature." See also Wehrung, *Welt und Reich*, 39ff. Because Olsson ignored the divine foundation ⟨of marriage⟩, one has second thoughts when he argued (*Grundproblemet*, 1:51): "Luther concludes...that his... understanding of the state and marriage has its foundation in reason and, therefore, can be designated by him as natural law." For the difference between this way of thinking and the way in which the philosophers of the Enlightenmant thought about the rational natural law, esp. the social contract theory, see Gogarten, *Der Mensch zwischen Gott und Welt*, 124ff.

343. *The Babylonian Captivity of the Church*, 1520: WA 6:555.4: "The union of man and woman is ⟨a matter⟩ of divine law ⟨and⟩ stands firm, regardless of whatever way contrary to the laws of man it has come about. ⟨Therefore⟩ without any scruples the laws of man have to yield to the divine law"; Luther to Robert Barnes: Sept. 3, 1531: WA.B 6:181.131ff., esp. 182.144ff. ⟨*LW* 50:39f.⟩.

344. *The Estate of Marriage*, 1522: WA 10.II:276.18. See also *Lectures on Genesis*, 1535-45: WA 43:294.40 ⟨*LW* 4:222⟩: "Marriage... is the inseparable union of one man and one woman, not only according to the law of nature but also according to God's will and pleasure, if I may use this expression. For the will and approval and that favor of God cover the wretched depravity of lust and turn away God's wrath, which is in store for such lust and sins. In this way matrimony is treated with reverence."

345. *The Estate of Marriage*, 1522: WA 10.II:276.22.

346. *The Large Catechism*, 1529: WA 30.I:161.28 ⟨*BC* 393.207⟩. For Luther marriage was also a "necessary" estate; ibid., WA 30.I:162.12f. ⟨*BC* 393.211⟩. See also below, 400 n. 5.

347. ⟨"Order," just as a monastic order provides a certain way of life.⟩ *The Estate of Marriage*, 1522: WA 10.II:279.25.

348. Ibid., WA 10.II:279.29. ⟨Literally: "God's implanted work and nature" of being male and female.⟩ — For Luther's discussion of 1 Cor. 7, see Wehrung, *Welt und Reich*, 31f.

349. *The Estate of Marriage*, 1522: WA 10.II:300.3: "The estate of marriage is for the good not only of the body, property, honor, and soul of individuals but also of cities and territories as a whole, so that they remain free from God's plagues ⟨see Ex. 8:2⟩. For we certainly know that because of whoring the most horrible plagues have come over land and people." ⟨Was Luther thinking of the spread of syphilis in his days?⟩

350. Sermon of Jan. 14, 1532: WA 36:97.13: "In the secular governance there is nothing more glorious than the estate of marriage."

351. *The Estate of Marriage*, 1522: WA 10.II:276.31.

352. In *The Estate of Marriage*, 1522, Luther discussed some of these impediments ⟨predominantly degrees of relationship which make a marriage impossible⟩; see WA 10.II:280.22, 281.1.13, 282.25, etc. ⟨In other contexts Luther listed the following impediments:⟩ Impotency prior to marriage and perpetual as reason for divorce (Luther to John Heß: March 21, 1524: WA.B 3:257.1; brief of Luther and others: Feb. 20, 1525: WA.B 3:445.4). Lack of parental consent to a marriage (Luther to George Spalatin: Jan. 7, 1527: WA.B 4:153.5ff., together with Luther's brief of January 1528: WA.B 4:337.22). Family relationship in the third degree of a sideline (brief of Melanchthon of August 1543: WA.B 10:362.1ff.). Consanguinity as impediment ⟨incest⟩, derived from secular natural law (Luther to Robert Barnes: Sept. 3, 1531: WA.B 6:180.92ff.⟨*LW* 50:37⟩). — For Luther's controversy with the Wittenberg consistory and the electoral aulic court about secret engage-

ments ⟨see above, 334 n. 331⟩ and the settlement of that controversy, see Luther to Duke John Frederick, elector of Saxony: Jan. 18, 1545: WA.B 11:22.6; the impediment of marriage in case of a secret engagement is derived from the secular natural law and the Fourth Commandment; ibid., WA.B 11:23.58. — For the rejection of man-made ecclesiastical laws (inspired by an "evil spirit") about a spiritual relationship as impediment of marriage, see Luther to Jhan von Schleinitz: June 18, 1523: WA.B 3:92.81 ⟨Baptism establishes a spiritual relationship which does not prohibit marriage; hence a godfather may marry his goddaughter provided there is no other impediment⟩.

353. *The Estate of Marriage*, 1522: WA 10.II:277.5; Luther's *Smalcald Articles*, 1537: WA 50:248.26 ⟨BC 314.XI⟩.

354. ⟨See the materials listed in n. 352.⟩

355. *The Estate of Marriage*, 1522: WA 10.II:277.24. — Luther was ready to tolerate man-made laws which added to the degrees of consanguinity, established in the Mosaic law as impediments of marriage, other degrees according to which a marriage had to be divorced. He made the condition that such laws were understood as rules which were not binding consciences; in his opinion such laws were "sick law"; *On Marriage Matters*, 1530: WA 30.III:244.18. — Apparently Luther's position on the impediment of marriage between a man and the widow of his brother was similar; Luther to Robert Barnes: Sept. 3, 1531: WA.B 6:186.151. — For the marriage between an uncle and his niece, see Luther's brief of January 1528: WA.B 4:331.1; Luther to Margrave Albrecht of Brandenburg, grand master of the Teutonic Order: Dec. 1523: WA.B 3:213.171; to Marquard Schuldorp: Dec. 22, 1525 (WA.B 3:644.3) and Jan. 5, 1526 (WA.B 4:10.24). — God did not prohibit a marriage between relatives in the third degree; therefore, according to Luther, such a marriage did not need a dispensation issued by a bishop; Luther to Joseph Levin Metzsch: Apr. 9, 1528: WA.B 4:439.1.

356. ⟨See above, 57.⟩

357. Luther to Margrave Albrecht of Brandenburg, grand master of the Teutonic Order: Dec. 1523: WA.B 3:213.171; to George Spalatin: Feb. 26, 1530: WA.B 5:243.4; together with others to Leonard Beyer: Jan. 18, 1535: WA.B 7:152.11, 153.20.

358. Luther and others to Landgrave Philip of Hesse: Dec. 10, 1539: WA.B 8:640.36 (Melanchthon wrote this letter, but Luther and others also signed it).

359. *The Babylonian Captivity of the Church*, 1520: WA 6:555.3.

360. ⟨Deut. 21:15.⟩ Letter of Dec. 10, 1539 (as in n. 358): WA.B 8:640.43.

361. ⟨Deut. 24:1.⟩ *The Large Catechism*, 1529: WA 30.I:175.7 ⟨BC 404.295⟩.

362. *Lectures on Genesis*, 1535-45: WA 43:60.16 ⟨LW 3:259⟩: "So far as the Jewish divorce is concerened, Lyra is right when he cites those who maintain that Moses, as a lawgiver, allowed this by divine authority, not on his own authority; for God, he says, is able to join people in marriage and to dissolve marriages. Similarly, the Jews carried off the property of the Egyptians by divine authority. Yet they were not sinning (Ex. 12:36)."

363. Instead of other authors, see Thomas Aquinas, *Summa theologiae* 3 Suppl. q. 65: art. 1 and 2; q. 67: art. 2 and 3.

364. Thomas Aquinas, *Summa theologiae* 3 Suppl. q. 65: art. 2.

365. *The Book of Deuteronomy with Notes*, 1525: WA 14:696.4 ⟨LW 9:210f.⟩: "Polygamy, ... was characteristic of this people ⟨i.e., the Israelites⟩ on the basis of both the example of the patriarchs and of legal right." For this problem, see Werner Elert, *Das christliche Ethos* (Tübingen, 1949), 127.

Notes to Pages 74-75

366. *The Book of Deuteronomy with Notes,* 1525: WA 14:714.8 ⟨*LW* 9:241⟩: "That the law of divorce ⟨Deut. 24:1ff.⟩ is merely a civil one, allowed for the sake of the hardness of the people, Christ sufficiently proves in Matt. 19:8. Hence also we have no example of this law being invoked by holy men."

367. *Sermons on Matthew, Chapters 5-7,* 1530-32: WA 32:376.36.

368. *Decretum Gratiani* C.XXVIII. q.1 at the end ⟨Friedberg 1:1089⟩; c.7. X⟨*Liber Extra*⟩. de divortiis IV.19 ⟨Friedberg 2:722f.⟩. See also Peter Lombard, *Sententiae,* lib. IV. dist. 39. cap. 7. ⟨True (or valid) and legitimate marriage *(matrimonium ratum et legitimum):* a man and a woman have expressed their promise to marry each other. Through the sacrament of marriage the church has made valid, or ratified, or sanctified their action so that their marriage was a valid and true marriage. A true and valid marriage was a spiritual matter in the realm of the church and its law, and the marriage was valid even if had not been corporeally consummated *(ratum et non consummatum),* though that was debated. In any case, the corporeal consummation made the valid and true marriage legitimate in terms of the law of the church *and* the law of society. A marriage was *only legitimate* (but not valid or true) when the law of society had been fulfilled, but the marriage had not been sanctified through the sacrament of marriage.⟩

369. Luther to the Mayor, Council, and Pastor Michael Cramer of Dommitsch: Aug. 18, 1525: WA.B 3:557.5.

370. ⟨See above, 72.⟩

371. ⟨See above, 102-4.⟩

372. *On Marriage Matters,* 1530: WA 30.III:205.18: "Among Christians or believers it is easy to deal with such and all ⟨other⟩ matters. But with the non-Christians, of which the world is full, it is impossible to deal with such matters unless the secular sword uses its severity"; ibid., WA 30.III:205.24: "Therefore I absolutely do not wish to get mixed up with these matters"; *Sermons on Matthew, Chapters 5-7,* 1530-32: WA 32:377.9; *Matthew, Chapters 18-24 Explained in Sermons,* 1537-40: WA 47:321.22.

373. ⟨For Luther this authority was the result of three circumstances:⟩ The need to warn a governmental authority not to transgress its limits which God has set up for its legal power (see above, 74); the consciences of Christians have to be set free to enter a second marriage under certain circumstances (Luther to Nicholas von Amsdorf: Dec. 30, 1528: WA.B 4:627.3); the possible transgression of the natural law by a groom and bride or a marital court has to be prevented (see Luther's opposition to secret engagements, above, 339 n. 352). *Matthew, Chapters 18-24 Explained in Sermons,* 1537-40: WA 47:314.19: "If the law is not understood correctly, then it is the task of an evangelical preacher to interpret the law and inform the people so that they understand the law correctly"; ibid., WA 47:316.1: ". . . if there is any kind of false understanding or of misuse of the law, a preacher of the gospel teaches about ⟨such⟩ external things." — See also Luther's upbraiding of the Wittenberg jurists in his sermon of Jan. 20, 1544 (WA 49:323.8): "Why did you not consult me? Who do you think I am? . . . You should do what I faithfully teach you."

374. *The Estate of Marriage,* 1522: WA 10.II:288.20; *Commentary on 1 Corinthians, Chapter 7,* 1523: WA 12:119.6; *Sermons on Matthew, Chapters 5-7,* 1530-32: WA 32:377.32ff.

375. In his Jan. 7, 1527, letter to George Spalatin, Luther dealt with the difficulties faced by an evangelical theologian when he has to deal with someone who pretends to be a Christian but in reality is not; WA.B 4:No. 1069.

376. *Commentary on 1 Corinthians, Chapter 7,* 1523: WA 12:93.29.

377. Luther to Robert Barnes: Sept. 3, 1531: WA.B 6:179.44 ⟨*LW* 50:34⟩: "But that law of God and that statement of divine ⟨positive⟩ law according to which matrimony is established as something which ought to be maintained forever, until death, binds the King ⟨i.e., Henry VIII⟩. For the sake of this law, Christ abolished the letter of divorce handed down from Moses when he said: 'From the beginning it was not so' ⟨Matt. 19:8⟩"; ibid., WA.B 6:179.50 ⟨*LW* 50:35⟩: "If the law of God is in conflict with the law of man, then the law of man has to yield so that one does not sin against the law of God; the law of God does not have to yield to the law of man so that one does not sin against the law of man." According to Luther, a papal dispensation from a *matrimonium ratum et non consummatum* ⟨see above, 341 n. 368⟩ violated divine law (Matt. 19:6); Luther to Margrave Albrecht of Brandenburg, grand master of the Teutonic Order: Dec. 1523: WA.B 3:213.159: "⟨The pope may not⟩ divorce legitimately married spouses unless one of them has committed adultery, ⟨or⟩ grant a dispensation to either party, so that they can make a second marriage vow."

378. *Sermons on Genesis*, 1527: WA 24:304.33ff. See also Luther's brief of January 1528: WA.B 4:332.1. For Luther sexual infidelity of those who were engaged ⟨see above, 337 n. 331⟩ also was adultery; Luther to Leonhard Beyer: Sept. 6, 1525: WA.B 3:567.2, 568 n. 2.

379. *Commentary on 1 Corinthians, Chapter 7*, 1523: WA 12:101.22.

380. *The Babylonian Captivity of the Church*, 1520: WA 6:559.20ff., 560.3; *Sermons on Matthew, Chapters 5–7*, 1530-32: WA 32:380.7.

381. *Commentary on 1 Corinthians, Chapter 7*, 1523: WA 12:123.6ff.; sermon of May 8, 1524: WA 15:561.11ff.; Luther to the Mayor, Council, and Pastor Michael Cramer of Dommitsch: Aug. 18, 1525: WA.B 3:557.7.; to Wolfgang Fues: Nov. 14, 1526: WA.B 4:127.6ff.

382. *The Estate of Marriage*, 1522: WA 10.II:290.5: illegal refusal of the marital duty; sermon of May 8, 1524: WA 15:561.24: treachery; Luther to Duke John, elector of Saxony: Jan. 25, 1526: WA.B 4:No. 975: malevolent desertion.

383. *The Babylonian Captivity of the Church*, 1520: WA 6:559.20: ⟨Is divorce permitted?⟩ "I detest divorce so much that I would prefer bigamy to divorce, but I myself do not dare to decide whether it is permitted."

384. See Luther's brief of Jan. 1528: WA.B 4:332.4ff.

385. *On Marriage Matters*, 1530: WA 30.III:241.19: ". . . such a divorce is not to take place on one's own authority but has to be pronounced through the . . . judgment of the pastor or the governmental authority . . ."; Luther to Gregory Brück, chancellor of Electoral Saxony: Jan. 14, 1524: WA.B 3:232.4: the reason for a desired divorce has to be established through investigation or witnesses; brief of Luther and others: Feb. 20, 1525: WA.B 3:445.6: how to deal with a woman's charge that her husband is impotent and cannot fulfill the marital duty, and that, therefore, she wishes a divorce; Luther's brief of Jan. 1528: WA.B 4:332.7: divorce is a matter to be handled publicly; Luther to an unknown nobleman: March 10, 1528(?): WA.B 4:No. 1237: legal proceedings in the case of an engagement ⟨see above, 337 n. 331⟩ with subsequent wedding ceremony but without corporeal consummation; ibid., WA.B 4:407.2: ". . . a publicly enacted engagement and wedding have to be publicly dissolved; if ⟨they are not publicly dissolved,⟩ the virgin has the right to demand that the man enters the marriage"; Luther to Joachim I, elector of Brandenburg: Oct. 5, 1528: WA.B 4:580.114: in a divorce case both partners have to be present and deal

with each other; brief issued by Melanchthon, Luther, and others for the clergy of Nordhausen: Feb. 11, 1542: WA.B 9:No. 3711.

386. *On Marriage Matters*, 1530: WA 30.III:243.20.

387. Ibid., WA 30.III:241.24.

388. *Theses on the Remarriage of Widowed Pastors*, 1528: WA 26:527.18.

389. *Sermons on Genesis*, 1523-24: WA 14:252.19; *Lectures on Genesis*, 1535-45: WA 42:578.32.

390. *Sermons on Genesis*, 1527: WA 24:306.13.

391. Ibid., WA 24:303.14.

392. *Sermons on Genesis*, 1523-24: WA 14:252.26; *Sermons on Genesis*, 1527: WA 24:303.33ff.

393. *Sermons on Genesis*, 1527: WA 24:306.12.

394. Ibid., WA 24:306.22.

395. See Gal. 3:15ff., 4:22f.

396. *Sermons on Genesis*, 1523-24: WA 14:253.4; *Sermons on Genesis*, 1527: WA 24:305.9.

397. Luther to Joseph Levin Metzsch, lord of Mylau: Dec. 9, 1526: WA.B 4:141.4: "This is my answer to your first question, whether someone may be married to more than one woman: The unbelievers may do as they please, but Christian freedom has to be governed by love; all things are to be directed to the service of the neighbor, provided that there is no situation of need and that things can be done without harming faith or conscience"; ibid., WA.B 4:141.13: "Even if the people of old had many women, Christians may not follow that example because there is no situation of need, nor is anything improved by ⟨having many women⟩, nor is there a specific Word of God which commands it; if one were to follow that example, offense and turmoil would be the outcome. Therefore Christians should not consider themselves to be free to follow that example unless God has commanded such freedom first." See also Luther to Clemens Ursinus: March 21, 1527: WA.B 4:177.24.

398. Luther to Landgrave Philip of Hesse: Nov. 28, 1526: WA.B 4:140.16; to Clemens Ursinus: March 21, 1527: WA.B 4:177.26; to Nicholas von Amsdorf: Dec. 30, 1528: WA.B 4:627.1; Luther's brief of Jan. 1528: WA.B 4:336.4. — For the permission to enter bigamy when a woman is unable to fulfill her marital duty (rejected by Gratian), see *Decretum Gratiani* c.18. C.XXXII. q.7 ⟨Friedberg 1:1144f.⟩.

399. *Sermons on Genesis*, 1523-24: WA 14:253.5; *Sermons on Genesis*, 1527: WA 24:305.20ff. See also the addition to Luther's Table Talks: WA 48:670:No. 6915.

400. For the following, see William W. Rockwell, *Die Doppelehe des Landgrafen Philipp von Hessen* (Marburg, 1904), 6ff., 29ff., 137ff., 202ff., 236ff.; Wilhelm Maurer, "Luther und die Doppelehe Landgraf Philipps von Hessen," *Luther* 24 (1953): 97ff.

401. For details, see Rockwell, *Doppelehe des Landgrafen*, 247ff.

402. Luther to Robert Barnes: Sept. 3, 1531: WA.B 6:179.26 ⟨*LW* 50:33⟩: "Before I would approve of such a divorce I would rather permit the King ⟨Henry VIII⟩ to marry still another woman and to have, according to the examples of the patriarchs and kings, two women or queens at the same time." — See also Hans Thieme, "Die Ehescheidung Heinrichs VIII. als europäischer Rechtsfall," in *Syntagma Friburgense. Historische Studien Hermann Aubin dargebracht zum 70. Geburtstag am 23.12.1955* (Lindau, 1956), 272ff.

403. ⟨"Confessional," i.e., as in the privacy of the Confession of sins.⟩ For the praxis

of granting a dispensation, see Luther to John Heß: Dec. 10, 1543: WA.B 10: No. 3945. ⟨In this letter Luther also discussed the difference between a law and a *Beichtrat,* i.e., a counsel given in the context of Confession.⟩

404. ⟨I.e., what happens between the father confessor and the confessing person.⟩

405. Luther to Philip Melanchthon: June 18, 1540: WA.B 9:145.37: ". . . through Christ I beg you ⟨not to be troubled but⟩ have a quiet mind. Those whose affair this is ⟨i.e., the case of the bigamy of the Landgrave⟩ should also do something, carry their burden and not only burden us; they know that we are upright and faithful, and they are unable to charge us with any crime except the crime of compassion and of the most humane readiness ⟨to help⟩." — For Luther's understanding of the authority of a father confessor to grant a dispensation in matters of marriage, see *On Marriage Matters,* 1530: WA 30.III:246.32; Luther to Leonard Beyer: Nov. 2, 1535: WA.B 7:320.1ff.; Rockwell, *Doppelehe des Landgrafen,* 138ff.

406. ⟨I.e., after the Landgrave's bigamy had become a scandal.⟩ See Meinhold, *Genesisvorlesung Luthers,* 136f.

407. *Lectures on Genesis,* 1535-45: WA 43:640.32.40; ibid., WA 43:643.2: "We should remain within the limits of the laws unless a special call or heroic inspiration calls us away"; for this position, see above, 56.

408. Therefore Luther could occasionally call the authority of a husband "God's glory" ⟨in the sense of God's image and reflection; see the Greek text of 1 Cor. 11:7, and the variant reading in NRSV⟩; Luther and Bugenhagen to Stephen Roth: April 12, 1528: WA.B 4:442.9.

409. *The Large Catechism,* 1529: WA 30.I:161.27 ⟨*BC* 393.207⟩: ". . . ⟨God⟩ wishes us to honor, maintain, and cherish ⟨the estate of marriage⟩ as a divine and blessed estate. Significantly he established it as the first of all institutions . . ."; ibid., WA 30.I:152.20 ⟨*BC* 384.141⟩: "Out of the authority of parents all other authority is derived and developed. Where a father is unable by himself to bring up his child, he calls upon a schoolmaster to teach him; . . . if he passes away, he confers and delegates his authority and responsibility to others appointed for the purpose. Likewise he must have domestics (man-servants and maid-servants) under him to manage the household. Thus all who are called masters stand in the place of parents and derive from them their power and authority to govern"; ibid., WA 30.I:162.6 ⟨*BC* 393.209⟩: "⟨The marital estate⟩ is not an estate to be placed on a level with the others; it precedes and surpasses them all, whether those of the emperor, princes, bishops, or anyone else. Important as the spiritual ⟨in the sense of ecclesiastical⟩ and civil estates are, these must humble themselves and allow all people to enter the estate of marriage. . . . It is not an exceptional estate, but the most universal and the noblest, pervading all Christendom and even extending throughout the whole world." — See also Schönfeld, *Über die Gerechtigkeit,* 34, 93.

410. *Lectures on Genesis,* 1535-45: WA 42:354.23: ". . . marriage is the fountain of the *oeconomia* and *politia,* and a nursery of the church."

411. Ibid., WA 42:360.23ff. ⟨*LW* 2:140⟩: "Here ⟨Gen. 9:6⟩ . . . God shares his power with man and grants him power over life and death among men, provided that the person is guilty of shedding blood. . . . Here we have the source from which stem all civil law and the law of nations ⟨*ius gentium;* see above, 315 n. 108⟩"; *Lectures on Psalms 120-134,* 1532-33: WA 40.III:220.4, 221.1: "The home is the fountain of all commonwealths. . . . From the home grows the city, from the city the duchy ⟨and⟩ the king. The city is the joining of many

households *(oeconomia)* and families, the kingdom the joining of many cities; therefore the *oeconomia* is the fountain ⟨of all of them⟩"; sermon of Aug. 4, 1545: WA 49:797.32: "Much has to be preached about this sacred estate and divine order of marriage because it is the oldest estate among all estates of the world; in fact, all other estates stem from it. . . ."

412. Luther to George Spalatin: Sept. 8, 1528: WA.B 4:552.13ff.

413. See Luther's preliminary sketches for his lectures on Genesis, 1535-45: WA 42:XXII.20: "Thus far there is no *politia*. It begins in the following chapter on Cain. There would not have been any need for the *politia*, just as there would not have been any need for medicine or the arts; all things would have been healthy, all things would have been upright under the dominion of man. *Politia* is the branding mark ⟨literally: 'iron'⟩ of the fallen nature. *Oeconomia* is a leftover of nature ⟨before the Fall⟩. The church is the Redemption and reparation of ⟨fallen⟩ nature. Otherwise there would have been only church and *oeconomia*." See also *Sermons on Genesis,* 1523-24: WA 14:171.30 (in Gen. 4:15f. "started the law of the sword because of the ungodly, and the civil laws"), 202.11 (in Gen. 9:6 the secular sword is established), 202.15 (the new commandment, i.e., the law and the sword); *Sermons on the First Epistle of St. Peter,* 1523 (1. version): WA 12:329.8: ". . . if there were no evil people, one would not need governmental authority."

414. Thielicke (*Theologische Ethik*, 1:No. 2085) was correct when he argued that it is impossible to find the idea and reality of the state in the Original Status. Thielicke's position cannot be contradicted with Luther's argument that the *form* of sovereignty was already present in the Original Status because "in Paradise Adam received power over all that had been created"; *Matthew, Chapters 18–24 Explained in Sermons,* 1537-40: WA 47:368.20. However, between sovereignty in the Original Status and that of the infralapsarian secular governance exists a decisive legal difference: Adam's power in the Original Status extended only over the animal world, but the power of the secular governmental authority extends over humans. — See also Wehrung, *Welt und Reich,* 41 n. 28: "In Paradise the order of governmental authority . . . is both set up and not set up: not set up is the form as it is conditioned by sin." (In reality, however, the concept 'governmental authority' is not at all present in Paradise.) Ibid., 196: the beginning ⟨of sovereignties⟩ logically precedes sin. — According to Oepke, *Das Neue Gottesvolk,* 460, "one has to think of the state as being grounded already in the order of Creation prior to the Fall"; Oepke's basis was Lau, *"Äußerliche Ordnung,"* 23ff., and Elert, *Morphologie,* 2:56ff. See further, Oepke, *Das Neue Gottesvolk,* 460 n. 5: "Adam's Fall significantly altered the *politia* and *oeconomia,* just as it altered the church ⟨see above, 70-72.⟩ but it did not create them. They belong to the status of man set up in Creation"; see, however, also ibid., 460: "In its present form the state exists because of sin."

415. *Commentary on Zechariah,* 1527: WA 23:514.1: ". . . Sword . . . I understand to mean all things which belong to secular governance, such as secular . . . laws, morals and customs, habits, estates, differences in offices, persons, and dress, etc." See also Lau, *Luthers Lehre von den beiden Reichen,* 32.

416. *On Good Works,* 1520: WA 6:213.38: "As St. Paul says in Rom. 13⟨:3ff.⟩, secular power has the sword and serves God with it, not to frighten the godly but the evil ones."

417. ⟨See above, 35.⟩

418. See esp. Hellmuth Mayer, "Die Strafrechtstheorie bei Luther und Melanch-

Notes to Page 78

thon," in *Rechtsidee und Staatsgedanke. Festgabe für Julius Binder,* ed. by Karl Larenz et al. (Berlin, 1930), 77ff.

419. Therefore one may not simply state that ⟨supposedly⟩ Luther did not in principle differentiate between the secular and the spiritual governance ⟨because⟩ God instituted both; both originate with God and are his orders; see Georg Lenz, "Luthers und Calvins Verhältnis zum Staat," *ELKZ* 5 (1951): 268. For Luther, see *Against the Roman Papacy,* 1545: WA 54:282.9: "God the Father, Son, and Holy Spirit testify that to feed the sheep is the work most precious to God"; ibid., WA 54:284.38: "The office of preaching, or the office of bishop ⟨in the sense of pastor⟩, is the highest office; God's Son himself has administered it, and so did all the Apostles, prophets, and patriarchs. For God's Word and faith are more important than all things, more important than gifts and persons"; *On Good Works,* 1520: WA 6:259.33: "... before God secular power is of little importance...."

420. Sermon of May 4, 1522: WA 10.III:122.6: "Secular authority is not very important to God; it does not help anyone's soul, even if someone rules in the best way, be he prince or whoever."

421. *On Keeping Children in School,* 1530: WA 30.II:554.2 ⟨LW 46:237⟩: "In the first place, it is true that the office of temporal authority cannot at all be compared with the spiritual office of preaching, as St. Paul calls it [Col. 1:25].... For all the works of this estate belong only to this temporal, transient life.... As far, then, as eternal life surpasses this temporal life, so far does the preaching office exceed the temporal office — even as the substance surpasses the shadow.... The office of preaching — where it exists as God ordained it — brings and bestows eternal righteousness, eternal peace, and eternal life.... Worldly government, on the other hand, preserves peace, justice, and life, which is temporal and transient. Nevertheless, worldly government is a glorious ordinance and splendid gift of God, who has instituted and established it and will have it maintained as something men cannot do without"; sermon on Psalm 110, 1535: WA 41:186.14: "It is the highest honor to be a priest, higher than being a king or prince...."

422. *Commentary on Zechariah,* 1527: WA 23:514.15: "Secular governance ⟨is⟩ the lowest and least significant of God's governances because it makes no one godly, only punishes the evil and obstructs those who reject order."

423. Sermon of Jan. 16, 1529: WA 28:281.3. See also *Whether Soldiers, Too, Can Be Saved,* 1526: WA 19:640.4.

424. *On Secular Authority,* 1523: WA 11:268.4. — See also de Lagarde, *Recherches sur l'esprit politique de la Réforme,* 222: "The simplistic idea of a police state, of which all activity is situated between the court room and the gallows, dominates the whole philosophy of the Reformation."

425. The worst case of such a transgression is the usurpation of the spiritual governance by a ruler; i.e., when a ruler is determined to extend his competency from matters pertaining to the Second Table of the Decalogue to those of the First Table. See *On Secular Authority,* 1523: WA 11:265.18, 267.5; Luther to John Heß: March 12, 1524: WA.B 3:253.1: "One should not be amazed when the princes seek their own good in the ⟨preaching of the⟩ gospel, and new robbers ambush the old robbers. The light of the world has risen through which we see what the world is, namely, Satan's kingdom." See also above, 108.

426. See below, 431 n. 201.

427. *Psalm 82 Explained,* 1530: WA 31.I:198.23 ⟨LW 13:51⟩: "⟨In Ps. 82:2-5 the princes⟩ find what lofty, princely, noble virtues their estate can practice so that temporal

government, next to the preaching office, is the highest service of God and the most useful office on earth." Luther was aware that he praised governmental authority more highly than all his predecessors; *Defense against the Charge of Inciting Rebellion,* 1533: WA 38:102.30, 114.4.

428. By maintaining peace, a governmental authority indirectly serves the spreading of the gospel because it makes the functioning of the preaching office easier; sermon of Aug. 13, 1525: WA 16:352.10: ". . . the sword . . . has been established so that peace might be on earth. Otherwise, who could preach if there were no peace?"; above, 269 n. 19, 330 n. 253.

429. *Psalm 82 Explained,* 1530: WA 31.I:201.26. See also above, 69 n. 281.

430. *Psalm 82 Explained,* 1530: WA 31.I:200.31, 201.16 ⟨*LW* 13:53f., 54, 55⟩: "If the law were not kept, no one could keep anything from another, and all would have to become beggars together and be ruined and destroyed. . . . In a word, after the Gospel or the ministry, there is on earth no better jewel, no greater treasure, nor richer alms, no fairer endowment, no finer possession than a ruler who makes and preserves just laws. . . . ⟨The princes should⟩ administer law and peace. Law is wisdom and should be the first of the two; for government by force without wisdom does not last."

431. *Open Letter on the Harsh Book against the Peasants,* 1525: WA 18:392.4, 394.2.

432. *Psalm 82 Explained,* 1530: WA 31.I:214.3 ⟨*LW* 13:68⟩.

433. *On Keeping Children in School,* 1530: WA 30.II:555.5 ⟨*LW* 46:237⟩.

434. Ibid., WA 30.II:556.6.9 ⟨*LW* 46:238⟩.

435. *Confession concerning Christ's Supper,* 1528: WA 26:504.30: "These are the three holy orders and true religious institutions established by God: the office of priest, the estate of marriage, the governmental authority"; ibid., WA 26:505.7: "These three institutions or orders ⟨are⟩ constituted in God's Word and commandment. Whatever is constituted in God's Word has to be holy, for God's Word is holy and sanctifies all which is connected with it and is in it." — For the office of preaching as a "sign of revelation," see Prenter, *Spiritus creator,* 261. — See further, Kattenbusch, "Doppelschichtigkeit in Luthers Kirchenbegriff," *ThStKr* 100 (1928): 335; Wehrung, *Welt und Reich,* 42ff.

436. ⟨See above, 266 n. 8.⟩ For the 'three visible governances' (of which the higher in rank always is to protect the lower in rank), and for the invisible hierarchy of the angels which stands above all of them, see sermon of Sept. 29, 1539: WA 47:854.2. Luther used various terms for these three governances: *status* (estate), *das Christlich Reich* (the Christian kingdom), *ordines* (orders), *hierarchiae* (hierarchies), *Reich* or *Regiment* (kingdom or governance), *geistliches Regiment, weltliches Regiment, Hausregiment* (spiritual governance, secular governance, domestic governance). See sermon of Feb. 15, 1540: WA 49:30.16.17.28, 31.3.4.

437. See Philip S. Watson, *The State as a Servant of God* (London, 1946).

438. *Against the Robbing and Murdering Hordes of Peasants,* 1525: WA 18:360.1: "God's officer and servant of God's wrath."

439. *Psalm 82 Explained,* 1530: WA 31.I:192.25 ⟨*LW* 13:45⟩: "God will not have the world desolate and empty but has made it for men to live in, to till the land and fill it. . . . Because this cannot happen where there is no peace, He is compelled, as a Creator, preserving His own creatures, works, and ordinances, to institute and preserve government and to commit to it the sword and the laws. Thus He may slay and punish all those who do not obey it ⟨literally: '. . . sword and the laws, that it (i.e., the government) should kill and

punish all, who do not obey it'>, as men who also strive against God and His ordinance, and are not worthy to live."

440. ⟨Heckel wrote "Abbild," i.e., copy or likeness.⟩ *Psalm 101 Explained*, 1534-35: WA 51:241.39: "God wants the governance of the world to be a model of true Salvation and of his heavenly kingdom, just as a diversion or mask *(larva)*; *On Keeping Children in School*, 1530: WA 30.II:554.11: "Secular sovereignty is an image, shadow, or metaphor of Christ's sovereignty"; *Sermons on Exodus*, 1524-27: WA 16:548.21: "Princes, judges, etc., are God's masks *(larvae)*...."

441. *Instruction for the Confession of Sinners*, 1518: WA 1:258.21: "The Lord placed parents and superiors in his place and commanded to have them as his vicars"; *Sermons on Matthew, Chapters 5-7*, 1530-32: WA 32:529.35: "The law, judgment, and all their *ex officio* actions are my ⟨i.e., God's⟩ law and judgment if they rule in the right way.... If they remain within ⟨the limitations of⟩ their office and do as the law demands, then all that they do is God's business."

442. *Magnificat*, 1521: WA 7:603.7 ⟨LW 21:358⟩: "In this spirit ⟨for details, see LW 21:3567ff.⟩, then, let things ⟨i.e., actions of a ruler⟩ go as they will, in God's name."

443. *On Secular Authority*, 1523: WA 11:257.20.

444. *Whether Soldiers, Too, Can Be Saved*, 1526: WA 19:629.14 ⟨LW 46:99⟩: "That is the sum and substance of it. The office of the sword is in itself right and is a divine and useful ordinance...."

445. *Psalm 82 Explained*, 1530: WA 31.I:217.11 ⟨LW 13:71⟩: "... those estates that are appointed in God's Word are all holy, divine estates, even though the persons in them are not holy." — On the basis of an office being divinely constituted there exists, then, a charisma of office; theses for *Disputation of Jerome Nopp and Frederick Bachofen*, 1543: WA 39.II:236.8; *Disputation of Henry Schmedenstede*, 1542: WA 39.II:198.22: "... the ministry which they have is not their own but God's. Therefore it is effective through the power of the Holy Spirit, although ⟨it is administered by⟩ ungodly persons." See also Paul Althaus, "'... und hätten allen Glauben....' 1. Kor. 13,2 in der Auslegung Martin Luthers,' in *Elert Gedenkschrift*, 135ff. — Paul Althaus, *Die Todesstrafe als Problem der christlichen Ethik*. SBAW. PH 1955. Heft 2 (Munich, 1955), 5, argued that "Luther's affirmation of capital punishment is based on biblical principles and not those of natural law or sociology. Therefore for Luther capital punishment is simply a part of the office of governmental authority. That authority has the sword, it is the 'secular sword' ⟨in contrast to the sword of the Spirit; Eph. 6:17⟩. Luther proves this with the biblical passages which are the basis for the state, Rom. 13: esp. 4, Gen. 9:6, Ex. 21, and others." (See also *On Secular Authority*, 1523: WA 11:247ff.; *Lectures on Genesis*, 1535-45: WA 42:360f.) — Yet that 'biblical' basis of capital punishment has the quality of natural law insofar as it is based on the institutional secular natural law.

446. *Psalm 82 Explained*, 1530: WA 31.I:192.8 ⟨LW 13:44⟩: "... we see how high and how glorious God will have rulers held, and that men ought to obey them as His officers and be subject to them with all fear and reverence, as to God Himself. Whoever resists them or is disobedient to them or despises them, whom God names with His own name and calls 'gods,' and to whom He attaches His own honor — whoever, I say, despises, disobeys, or resists them is thereby despising, disobeying, and resisting the true Supreme God, who is in them, who speaks and judges through them, and calls their judgment His judgment."

447. Therefore Luther said in *Second Lectures on Galatians*, 1531: WA 40.I:106.6: "Grace ‹Gal. 1:6› brings ‹sound› judgment of all things, strengthens the magistrate, the *oeconomia*, and all orders *(ordines)"*; ibid., WA 40.II:59.8: "So that it does not look as if our doctrine ‹in the sense of the doctrine St. Paul presented in Galatians, which 'we' affirm› destroys good morals and public institutions *(ordinationes)* ‹the Apostle Paul› teaches good conduct better than any philosopher of the Gentiles. Therefore they ‹i.e., Paul's and 'our' enemies› are unable to accuse us that we are against good morals and public institutions."

448. *Lectures on Psalm 2*, 1532: WA 40.II:238.14, 240.2.9. — According to Luther, there are two kinds of holiness, general holiness and holiness of grace. General holiness belongs to the institutional secular natural law; because of the connection between that law and the law of Moses, that holiness is also called legal holiness. One partakes in the holiness of grace through the gospel. The political order has general holiness. See Törnvall, *Geistliches und weltliches Regiment bei Luther*, 57 n. 62; Wehrung, *Welt und Reich*, 197: "Through ‹marriage, family, social structures› God sanctifies ‹people› by the power of his creating which bestows a secret blessing on these forms that tie people together."

449. This statement is valid regardless whether a governmental authority is Christian or not, because even prior to Christ's appearance there existed legitimate governmental authority; *The Babylonian Captivity of the Church*, 1520: WA 6:551.2. See also *Sermons on Matthew, Chapters 5-7*, 1530-32: WA 32:529.38, as above, 348 n. 441.

450. *Second Lectures on the Psalms*, 1518-21: WA 5:65.26: ". . all law, all activity outside of Christ's law ‹is› a shadow and sign of the hidden righteousness . . ."; *Whether Soldiers, Too, Can Be Saved*, 1526: WA 19:660.19: God "‹gives› us the great grace ‹by placing before us› the governmental authority as an external monument and sign of his will. . . ." — For a critical view, see de Lagarde, *Recherches sur l'esprit politique de la Réforme*, 376: "With the disappearance of natural law, whose objectivity had been taught during the Middle Ages, the state had lost the axis of its life."

451. *Admonition to Peace*, 1525: WA 18:305.7: ". . . you ‹i.e., the rebellious peasants› . . . deprive governmental authority of its power and law."

452. As a contrast to this authority of the secular office, see the authority of ruling in the spiritual office in *Lectures on Romans*, 1515-16: WA 56:160.22 ‹LW 25:138f.›.

453. *Admonition to Peace*, 1525: WA 18:313.9: ". . . as much as I was able I have defended the power and honor ‹of governmental authority›."

454. *Whether Soldiers, Too, Can Be Saved*, 1526: WA 19:625.15: ". . . I almost want to praise myself, because since the days of the Apostles the secular sword and governmental authority have never been so clearly described and gloriously extolled . . . as through me"; *On the War against the Turks*, 1529: WA 30.II:110.1.

455. *On Good Works*, 1520: WA 6:260ff. ‹LW 44:93ff.›. ‹*Fürstenspiegel*, or mirror of princes, were texts written in an effort to present an ideal image of a ruler, or educate an heir of the throne in that sense. See *DMA*, s.v. "Mirror of Princes." In addition to the passage in *On Good Works*, Luther's *Psalm 82 Explained* (1530: WA 31.I:189ff. ‹LW 13:42ff.›) and *Psalm 101 Explained* (1534-35: WA 51:200ff. ‹LW 13:146ff.›) are *Fürstenspiegel*.› — Wehrung, *Welt und Reich*, 225, argued critically that "Luther did not deal with matters of state and politics. In the world of the petty principalities in which he lived, he was not expected to give counsel for mastering such matters; he, who understood a prince to be only the father of the territory *(Landesvater)* and not a statesman, did not concentrate on such

Notes to Page 79

matters. Among all the reformers Luther was probably the last one to think about politics. Questions concerning power, the assertion, increase, and value of power, not to mention questions concerning the power of a nation, were alien issues for him." — But was Luther, a theologian, called to give counsel on such matters?

456. *On Keeping Children in School,* 1530: WA 30.II:537.5, 538.4; *On the War against the Turks,* 1529: WA 30.II:129.24; *Lectures on Genesis,* 1535-45: WA 44:610.5; sermon of March 17, 1538: WA 46:211.23: "When the pulpit is down, then the *politia* and *oeconomia* are also down."

457. *On Keeping Children in School,* 1530: WA 30.II:538.4. ⟨Literally: "fruit of the *rechte* preaching office." Luther's word can mean 'right' in the sense that the preaching office is the right, legitimate one in contrast to a preaching office which for whatever reason is not right or legitimate. Or it can mean 'right' in the sense of true; i.e., the (incumbent of the) preaching office does the right and true thing (i.e., preach law and gospel). In the first meaning the emphasis is on the legal form of the preaching office, in the second meaning it is on what the incumbent of the office does. In any case, the thrust of Luther's sentence is the affirmation that true peace on earth is the product of the work of the office of preaching, with the secular office 'only' being the helper.⟩

458. *On Good Works,* 1520: WA 6:264.17f. See also Luther to Duke John Frederick of Saxony: May 20, 1525: WA.B 3:501.16.

459. Esp. of orphans, widows, and the poor, people who need legal protection and material assistance in a special way; *Psalm 82 Explained,* 1530: WA 31.I:200.5 ⟨LW 13:53⟩. See also *Admonition to Peace,* 1525: WA 18:299.4: "Governmental authority is not instituted for the purpose of seeking its own advantage or practicing wantonness on the subjects, but to create the good and best for the subjects"; *Second Lectures on the Psalms,* 1518-21: WA 5:569.22: "'In the day of trouble.' ⟨Ps. 20:1.⟩ Here, too, the princes are reminded of their office; they are to know that they are placed in their high position for the welfare of the people, that for the sake of that welfare they are to endure and suffer much, and that their position of prince in reality is their day of trouble. For those idle and pleasure-seeking princes, who are princes only for their own ⟨good⟩, are not worthy that one pray in their behalf for these mighty works of God, in fact, they are not even princes but swine in their slough. But he who seeks the welfare of the people with his heart will never be without trouble, for Satan and the whole world will be against him"; sermon of July 2, 1529: WA 29:457.17: ". . . whoever is in power should be called healer, one to help." — See also Oepke, *Das Neue Gottesvolk,* 430.

460. *On Secular Authority,* 1523: WA 11:270.25; *Whether Soldiers, Too, Can Be Saved,* 1526: WA 19:640.25 ⟨LW 46:113⟩: "It is right and proper for rulers to govern according to laws and administer them and not to rule arbitrarily. I add, however, that a king does not only promise to keep the law of his land or the articles of his election, but God himself commands him to be righteous, and he promises to do so."

461. This is important esp. for criminal law; *The Book of Deuteronomy with Notes,* 1525: WA 14:686.19 ⟨LW 9:193⟩: ". . . God demands *epieikeia* or justice ⟨literally: 'equity'⟩ in laws; He wants judgment to be based not only on facts but also on intention. This principle is to be applied to all laws in general. Whatever the offense has been, the heart rather than the hand of the offender is to be considered. Thus Moses expressly states here ⟨Deut. 19:4ff.⟩ that anyone who kills another without hate, but unwillingly and acciden-

tally, is not guilty of murder. But such innocence should be proved by sure signs and circumstances so that not everyone can say after something happens: 'It was an accident.'"

462. Luther developed the difference between 'appropriate severity' and 'tyrannical severity' first in connection with the functioning of the office of an ecclesiastical superior; *Lectures on Romans*, 1515-16: WA 56:160.25 ⟨LW 25:139⟩. See also *Psalm 101 Explained*, 1534-35: WA 51:206.1: "This also the heathen say, i.e., daily experience: supreme law, severe law, is supreme injustice. In the same way one may say about grace: trivial grace is supreme nongrace *(Ungnade)*"; ibid., WA 51:206.7: "In all things moderation is good. To find it, one needs skill, in fact, God's grace. Yet in such a case in which it is difficult to hit the center ⟨i.e., moderation⟩ the next best shot is to have grace take precedence over law"; sermon of Nov. 13, 1530: WA 32:160.2. — For the legal saying 'supreme law, supreme injustice', see also *Whether Soldiers, Too, Can Be Saved*, 1526: WA 19:630.13; *To Pastors, That They Preach against Usury*, 1540: WA 51:352.9; sermons of 1533: WA 37:157.18. ⟨For this saying, see Cicero *De officiis* 1.10.33, and Kisch, *Erasmus und die Jurisprudenz*, 1ff., 55ff.⟩

463. *Against the Robbing and Murdering Hordes of Peasants*, 1525: WA 18:361.16; sermon of Jan. 1, 1545: WA 49:653.6.

464. *The Book of Deuteronomy with Notes*, 1525: WA 14:686.9 ⟨LW 9:193⟩: "... love demands that provision be made for public peace; but unless evil men are held in check, peace cannot abide. Therefore it is the part of love to administer laws severely and without mercy, to punish evil men, that the good and pious may be preserved. On the other hand, it is the part of love also that strictness of the laws be tempered with equity, to show mercy to one who perhaps seems like an evil and harmful person and yet is neither evil nor harmful, since he acted unintentionally and unwillingly"; *Lectures on Genesis*, 1535-45: WA 42:505.21: "Learn, therefore, that peace and love are the moderator and steward of all virtues and laws"; ibid., WA 42:504.37.

465. *On Secular Authority*, 1523: WA 11:272.3.

466. Luther to Cardinal Albrecht, archbishop of Mainz: July 21, 1525: WA.B 3: 548.25.

467. *Psalm 82 Explained*, 1530: WA 31.I:193.27 ⟨LW 13:46⟩: "Observe that ⟨the psalmist⟩ calls ⟨Ps. 82:1; Vulgate⟩ all communities or organized assemblies 'the congregation of God,' because they are God's own, and He accepts them as His work.... For He has made, and makes, all communities. He still brings them together, feeds them, lets them grow, blesses and preserves them.... But even though experience ought to teach us this, He has to say it in plain words, and openly confess and boast that the communities are His. For mad reason, in its shrewdness, and all the worldly-wise do not know at all that a community is God's creature and His ordinance. They have no other thought about it than that it has come into being by accident, through people holding together and living side by side in the same way murderers and robbers and other wicked bands gather to disturb the peace and the ordinance of God; these are the devil's congregations"; ibid., WA 31.I:194.23 ⟨LW 13:47⟩: "For this word 'congregation of God' is a precious word; and anyone who is in it ought to be ten times happier than if he were enrolled as a Roman citizen, which was once a great honor on earth. But reason does not consider this"; *Against Jack Sausage*, 1541: WA 51:555.22: "... it is called the Holy Roman Empire (as it should be) for God's sake, who is holy and who has ordained it; and all the princes praise their estate as existing by God's grace, that is, ⟨they are⟩ holy."

468. *Admonition to Peace*, 1525: WA 18:303.13: "The fact that a governmental authority is evil and unjust does not excuse mob-actions or rebellion"; *Whether Soldiers, Too, Can*

Be Saved, 1526: WA 19:638.30, 639.2: God has possibilities for punishing an evil governmental authority. "⟨Secular⟩ natural law agrees with this, . . . ⟨that⟩ it is to be unjust for any subject to act against his tyrant." Luther developed this position first for the constitution of the church (*First Lectures on the Psalms*, 1513-15: WA 4:405.1ff. ⟨LW 11:546f.⟩), and then later applied it to the *politia*.

469. ⟨Literally: "disturb" or "upset."⟩

470. *Psalm 82 Explained*, 1530: WA 31.I:196.16. See also *Whether Soldiers, Too, Can Be Saved*, 1526: WA 19:627.21; see above, 107, 108f., and the notes to these pages.

471. *Open Letter on the Harsh Book against the Peasants*, 1525: WA 18:398.26: ". . . no evil deed on earth equals ⟨rebellion⟩. Others are individual actions, but rebellion is a flood of evil." — See also Gustaf Wingren, *Schöpfung und Gesetz* (Göttingen, 1960), 164.

472. *Open Letter on the Harsh Book against the Peasants*, 1525: WA 18:397.21: "You have to make a big, big difference between a rebel and a murderer or robber, or any other evildoer. For a murderer or other evildoer does not attack the head and governmental authority but attacks only its members or goods; in fact, he is afraid of the governmental authority." ⟨Since the head remains, it can punish the evildoer.⟩ "But a rebel attacks the head itself and interferes with its sword and office so that his crime is not equal to that of the murderer. . . ." See also *Admonition to Peace*, 1525: WA 18:305.13.

473. *Admonition to Peace*, 1525: WA 18:319.14: "⟨Rebellion against the governmental authority⟩ violates the law of the land and natural justice."

474. Luther to Nicholas von Amsdorf: May 30, 1525: WA.B 3:517.26ff. ⟨LW 49: 114⟩.

475. *Open Letter on the Harsh Book against the Peasants*, 1525: WA 18:398.29ff.

476. Ibid., WA 18:397.31.

477. Ibid., WA 18:398.6.

478. *Against the Robbing and Murdering Hordes of Peasants*, 1525: WA 18:361.7ff.; *Open Letter on the Harsh Book against the Peasants*, 1525: WA 18:394.28.33ff.; Luther to John Rühel: May 30, 1525: WA.B 3:515.16.

479. The divine natural law proceeds against such a governmental authority in a spiritual *and* a corporeal way; *Second Lectures on Galatians*, 1531: WA 40.II:121.6.ff.

480. *Psalm 82 Explained*, 1530: WA 31.I:192.37 ⟨LW 13:45⟩: ". . . it is not ⟨God's⟩ will to allow the rabble to raise their fist against the rulers or to seize the sword, as if to punish and judge the rulers. No, they must leave that alone! It is not God's will, and He has not committed this to them. They are not to be judges and avenge themselves, or resort to outrage and violence; but God Himself will punish wicked rulers and impose statutes and laws upon them. He will be Judge and Master over them."

481. Ibid., WA 31.I:193.24, 214.7 ⟨LW 13:46, 68⟩.

482. Therefore Otto Gierke, *Johannes Althusius* (4th ed. Breslau 1929), 308, went too far and has to be corrected; he argued that Luther and the other reformers assigned to the individual subject only a duty of obedience which was conditioned by the legitimacy of the ruler's action.

483. *Disputation of Henry Schmedenstede*, 1542: WA 39.II:195.1: ". . . it is not Christian and godly but carnal to argue and affirm that whatever the emperor does is justice and law" ⟨that is to be obeyed⟩.

484. ⟨See above, 108f.; Appendix I.⟩

Notes to Chapter 10

1. *Sermons on Exodus,* 1524-27: WA 16:447.12: ". . . ⟨the natural law⟩ has been ⟨inscribed⟩ in the heart, but because of Satan's work of blinding us we do not see it . . ."; *Postilla for Lent,* 1525: WA 17.II:102.15ff., esp. 19.

2. For the relationship of the divine natural law with the law of Moses, see *Third Disputation against the Antinomians,* 1538: WA 39.I:539.7: "Law as genus *(lex in genere dicta)* has not been given to . . . a particular people but to the whole human race; indeed, this is so because together with the Decalogue very many laws useful for this life have been written down and were engraved upon the minds of all people from the time of birth itself, . . . unless people would have been absolutely monsters. But man has fallen into sin; gradually people have more and more forsaken God, turned away from God, ⟨despised⟩ God in ⟨very evil ways⟩ until the law ⟨so according to Heckel's reading of the text⟩ was almost completely obliterated and obscured. That we would not totally forget his law, God was forced again to set before us a turning point so that we at least would ⟨think about⟩ who we once were and who we are now. Therefore the law has been renewed and even written down, and it was given to a particular people, but only in its written form, . . . because ⟨the knowledge of these legal ideas was⟩ common to all people, as experience itself demonstrates"; ibid., WA 39.I:541.1: "They are, therefore, natural laws, not political or Mosaic laws. . . ."

3. For the following, see esp. Bornkamm, *Luther und das Alte Testament,* 104ff.

4. *Against the Heavenly Prophets,* 1525: WA 18:76.24: ". . . from the Ten Commandments flow . . . all the other commandments and ⟨all the laws of⟩ Moses."

5. ⟨See above, Chapter 8.⟩

6. *Against the Heavenly Prophets,* 1525: WA 18:81.9ff., 82.15ff., 76.4. ⟨*Sachsenspiegel* (i.e., mirror of the Saxons), "a compilation of German customary law dating from the early thirteenth century"; see *DMA,* s.v. "Sachsenspiegel"; see also above, 311 n. 72.⟩

7. *How Christians Should Regard Moses,* 1526: WA 16:375.10ff., 378.1.11; Luther to Robert Barnes (second version): Sept. 3, 1531: WA.B 6:186.144; to the City Council of Danzig: May 5 (or 7), 1525: WA.B 3:484.2; to George Spalatin: March 14, 1524: WA.B 3:254.21; to Duke John Frederick of Saxony: June 18, 1524: WA.B 3:306.4.

8. *The Last Words of David,* 1543: WA 54:78.27: ". . . the called prophet and head of the people of Israel, to whom ⟨God⟩ gives the law."

9. *The Babylonian Captivity of the Church,* 1520: WA 6:557.30: ". . . the people of Israel, having been endowed with the best and divine laws . . ."; *Second Lectures on Galatians,* 1531: WA 40.I:543.11: "⟨The Jews⟩ had divine laws and a divinely set up *politia,* and they were the first to have these"; *Psalm 118 Explained,* 1530: WA 31.I:81.33: ". . . the most beautiful laws and customs set up by God himself through Moses"; *The Book of Deuteronomy with Notes,* 1525: WA 14:656.1; sermon of June 9, 1538: WA 46:402.23. — See also Wünsch, *Ethik des Politischen,* 132.

10. Sermon of June 23, 1539: WA 47:806.21: "All heathen law is kid's play ⟨in comparison with Moses' legislation which contains⟩ the most beautiful laws for manners and ceremonies."

11. E.g.: The Jewish criminal law concerning theft, which was less severe than the brutal German law (Luther to George Spalatin: May 2, 1524: WA.B 3:283.5; sermon of Dec. 28, 1516: WA 1:501.3); the law concerning divorce, which was to be used for non-

Christians (*The Estate of Marriage*, 1522: WA 10.II:288.20; ⟨see also above, 341 n. 374⟩); the law concerning the tithe (Luther to Wolfgang Capito: June 15, 1524: WA.B 3:303.3; to Duke John Frederick of Saxony: June 18, 1524: WA.B 3:307.33; *How Christians Should Regard Moses*, 1526: WA 16:376.16), the Jubilee Year (*How Christians Should Regard Moses*, 1525: WA 16:377.14), the Sabbatical Year (*Against the Heavenly Prophets*, 1525: WA 18:81.22), and asylum (*The Book of Deuteronomy with Notes*, 1525: WA 14:600.28, 688.6). — See also Bornkamm, *Luther und das Alte Testament*, 106.

12. *Psalm 117 Explained*, 1530: WA 31.I:238.26 ⟨*LW* 14:20⟩: "It is certainly true that in the Mosaic Law secular government and outward custom are more finely framed than in all the laws and customs of heathendom, and it would be well if the whole world had more of such laws. But since this is not necessary, and since such a change could not be effected without unbearable dangers and damage ⟨addition by Heckel: "Allusion to the enthusiasts!"⟩, then let it be our one wish that each country keep its own laws, habits, and customs, as the saying goes: 'Many lands, many customs.'" See also *Second Lectures on Galatians* (1531) and *Second Commentary on Galatians* (1535): WA 40.I:673.3.15 ⟨*LW* 26:448⟩; Luther to the City Council of Danzig: May 5 (or 7), 1525: WA.B 3:484.2: "Moses' law is dead . . . ; it was given only to the Jews; we Gentiles should obey the laws of the territory in which we live. . . ."

13. Yet Mosaic law remains very important as an 'example' in cases of the dispensation from the marital law; see above, 76.

14. ⟨For "secular natural law," see above, 57f.⟩ Occasionally Luther contrasted the law of Moses (as the law of the Jewish nation) and the Decalogue as two different laws; *Second Disputation against the Antinomians*, 1538: WA 39.I:478.12.16: the law of Moses belongs to the Jewish people, "but the Decalogue belongs to the whole world, having been inscribed in, and engraved upon, the minds of all people from the beginning of the world."

15. *Against the Heavenly Prophets*, 1525: WA 18:81.4: "Whenever the law of Moses and natural laws are one, the law ⟨of Moses⟩ remains valid. It is externally abolished only spiritually in faith; this is nothing other than to fulfill the law, Rom. 3⟨:31⟩"; *The Book of Deuteronomy with Notes*, 1525: WA 14:622.10; *Second Disputation against the Antinomians*, 1538: WA 39.I:479.22.

16. See above, 313 n. 87.

17. ⟨See above, 48f.⟩

18. *Second Lectures on Galatians*, 1531: WA 40.I:174.2: "With a naked face we cannot deal with God"; *Lectures on Psalm 51*, 1532: WA 40.II:329.9: "Whoever wants to be saved has to leave God in his majesty, because God and the human creature are enemies."

19. See Gal. 3:19.

20. ⟨For "force," see above, 49.⟩ *Against Latomus*, 1521: WA 8:70.24: "Without the protection by grace no one is able to endure the force of the law. Therefore Moses was compelled to veil his face."

21. *First Lectures on the Psalms*, 1513-15: WA 4:30.10 ⟨*LW* 11:183⟩: ". . . at the time of Christ Moses, the slave, will stop speaking, and then not the letter, not the word of the slave in fear, but the Word of the Lord in spirit and in freedom will be told everywhere. . . ."

22. *Second Commentary on Galatians*, 1535: WA 40.I:502.21 ⟨*LW* 26:324⟩: ". . . Moses is

the sort of intermediary who merely changes the sound of the Law and makes it tolerable to hear, not one who provides the strength *(vis)* to keep the Law."

23. ⟨I.e., the law of Moses.⟩

24. *First Lectures on the Psalms,* 1513-15: WA 3:451.22: "Each law which is not directly given by God is burdensome, difficult, irritating, and weak because it does not give also the grace of fulfilling it."

25. *Against Latomus,* 1521: WA 8:70.20: "The clarity of the law is the discovery of sin."

26. *Second Lectures on Galatians,* 1531: WA 40.I:498.10. See also below, n. 34.

27. *Second Lectures on Galatians,* 1531: WA 40.I:501.5: "The people cannot endure the theological use of the law ⟨see above, 65, 66f.⟩; a new face of the law has to be made, and the law has to change its voice. That voice, the living . . . theological law, has to put on a mask and become bearable, ⟨and it does this⟩ through the human voice of Moses. Thus the law speaks no longer through its own authority but through the mouth of Moses."

28. ⟨In the sense of the divine natural and the divine positive law.⟩

29. *First Lectures on the Psalms,* 1513-15: WA 3:258.29: ". . . Moses, or any human legislator, . . . commands only temporal things. . . ."

30. Thielicke *(Kirche und Öffentlichkeit,* 92ff.) emphasized the negative phrasing of the commandments in the Decalogue and ⟨therefore⟩ concluded that they are a "protest against the way man is ('das SoSein des Menschen')"; the ⟨secular⟩ natural law and the Decalogue are grounded in different worlds (ibid., 97). See also Thielicke, *Theologische Ethik,* 1:No. 2163, n. 1, and Nos. 2178, 2188. According to Thielicke, the Decalogue contains no statements about the natural law, only about the *"Natur-Un recht ⟨sic⟩",* and "this Natur-Unrecht ⟨sic⟩ consists in killing, stealing, adultery, etc." No. 2178; italics by Thielicke. ⟨*Unrecht* designates something which is not law, right, or just. Literally, *Natur-Unrecht* would be "nature non-law," or "nature non-justice"; i.e., law which in terms of nature is not law (or right, or justice), or nature has another law than the law of killing, etc. The issue is not the absence of law from nature but the presence of a law which for nature is not law. Therefore "natural law-*lessness,*" as in Helmut Thielicke, *Theological Ethics,* 1. *Foundations,* ed. by William Lazareth (Philadelphia, 1966): 444 (italics by the present ed.), does not do justice to Thielicke's *Unrecht.*⟩ Luther would only partially agree with this argumentation; see our text!

31. *First Lectures on the Psalms,* 1513-15: WA 4:9.36: ". . . through his word ⟨Moses announces⟩ God's Word. . . ." ⟨For Luther's text and the context, see *LW* 11:160f.⟩

32. See Luther's statements about Christ's law in relationship with Moses' law in *First Lectures on the Psalms,* 1513-15: WA 4:439.20: ". . . in Christ all words are one word ⟨in the sense of Christ speaking one word, i.e., the gospel⟩, outside of Christ they are very many and empty ⟨words⟩. . . ."

33. *Sermons on John, Chapters 6-8,* 1530-32: WA 33:48.12 ⟨*LW* 23:35⟩: "Therefore if any law, doctrine, or counsel of man could help, it would surely be that of Moses rather than that of all other men on earth." — According to Erik Wolf *(Rechtsgedanke und biblische Weisung,* 44), the Ten Commandments are "God's categorical imperative and, therefore, also simultaneously the categorical imperative of the God-created human reason." For the degree to which this is correct according to the qualifications to be derived from our text above, see above, 55, and 305 n. 28.

34. *First Lectures on the Psalms,* 1513-15: WA 3:347.29 ⟨*LW* 10:293f.⟩: ". . . when God spoke through an intermediary, as through Moses and the prophets, His Word soon be-

came veiled, and an intermediary was placed between God and the people, between God speaking and the people hearing. Just so it still happens, although in a different way. For then there was an intermediary even as far as understanding was concerned. What was clear to the prophets was hidden to the people under the type of earthly goods or evils."

35. *Sermons on the Ten Commandments,* 1518: WA 1:461.31: ". . . when one hears any law ordering us to do this or that, one always has to think and supply the idea ⟨that⟩ the law orders us to do this voluntarily, i.e., freely, without fear of punishment and with cheerfulness. But such qualities are not in us; therefore we at once understand that for its fulfillment the law drives us to grace."

36. *Second Lectures on the Psalms,* 1518-21: WA 5:65.26 ⟨LW 14:337⟩: "The Law of Moses was carried in an ark, with the tablets obscured by a dark veil (Ex. 40:20), because every Law and every deed without the Law of Christ is a shadow and the sign of a hidden righteousness, but not the genuine thing, which is revealed through the Law of Christ"; *First Lectures on the Psalms,* 1513-15: WA 4:305.19 ⟨LW 11: 414⟩: ". . . the prophet looks with spiritual eyes at the law of Moses and sees hidden and enclosed in it the law of faith, the Gospel of grace, and the invisible things promised, like the kernel under the shell or the treasure under the ground. . . ."

37. See Prenter, *Spiritus creator,* 220: "If one understands the spiritual use of the law in the strictest sense, then that use does not at all belong in the kingdom of the law but in the kingdom of the gospel."

38. ⟨Another possible reading of Heckel's text would be: "All other people don't quite know what to do with law."⟩ *The Book of Deuteronomy with Notes,* 1525: WA 14:642.6 ⟨LW 9:114⟩: ". . . the Law does not reach the people, because it is not understood by a fleshly people."

39. *The Book of Deuteronomy with Notes,* 1525: WA 14:638.9 ⟨LW 9:108⟩: ". . . the doctrine of works, which is a perversion of the words and the Law of Scripture, a distortion carried out through the ministry and artifice of priests, who ought to lead the people instead of doing this."

40. For the inability of the Jews to comprehend the theological use of the law, see *Second Lectures on Galatians,* 1531: WA 40.I:499.5.

41. *On Secular Authority,* 1523: WA 11:259.31: ". . . I tell you, Moses gave this law ⟨Matt. 5:38⟩ because of the evil ones, who do not belong to God's kingdom, so that they do not take the law in their hands, or do worse things; through this external law they are forced not to do evil because they are placed with such an external law and governance under the power" ⟨of the governmental authority⟩.

42. *First Lectures on the Psalms,* 1513-15: WA 3:492.7 ⟨LW 10:431⟩: ". . . the ungodly Jewish interpreters corrupt Scripture and, with the spiritual understanding of the Law destroyed, build up their own carnal sense ⟨of the Law⟩."

43. *Sermons on the Ten Commandments,* 1518: WA 1:462.30: "⟨The scribes and Pharisees⟩ accepted the law according to the words and the meaning of syllables, i.e., not according to the intention of the legislator"; sermons of ca. 1514-21: WA 4:695.23. ⟨See also above, 56.⟩

44. *Magnificat,* 1521: WA 7:600.15. See also Bornkamm, *Luther und das Alte Testament,* 64.

45. This intention is esp. promoted by the form of the Decalogue: a promise is con-

nected with the Old Testament, but the fulfillment of this promise depends on doing the "works of the law"; *The Book of Deuteronomy with Notes*, 1525: WA 14: 602.37ff. ⟨*LW* 9:63⟩.

46. ⟨I.e., the Ten Commandments.⟩ *Second Lectures on the Psalms*, 1518-21: WA 5:358.6: ". . . we force God's holy words to serve our desires and opinions."

47. Ibid., WA 5:557.3: ". . . those who presume to fulfill ⟨the law⟩ by means of their own efforts have not yet recognized how spiritual the law is. Therefore they ⟨brag⟩ about their righteousness; in their blindness they think that they have fulfilled the law and become good, converted, and without blemish, while ⟨in reality⟩ through this ungodliness they were doubly defiled and perverted. . . ."

48. ⟨See above, 55f.⟩

49. For Moses as a creator of hypocrites, see *Second Lectures on the Psalms*, 1518-21: WA 5:544.4, 671.35.

50. For the two kinds of people, see *First Lectures on the Psalms*, 1513-15: WA 4:210.20 ⟨*LW* 11:347⟩: ". . . there are two kinds of men ⟨literally: 'human beings'⟩ who do not give thanks to the Lord because He is good. The first kind is that of the despairing, who certainly believe that He can and knows how to save, but they do not believe that He also is willing to do it, measuring the divine will according to their own will. The second kind is that of the presumptuous, who regard themselves as good and self-sufficient, as if they did not need divine goodness"; ibid., WA 4:238.25, 279.9; *Second Lectures on the Psalms*, 1518-21: WA 5:556.40, 557.1.37; sermons of ca. 1514-21: WA 4:695.23.

51. *The Book of Deuteronomy with Notes*, 1525: WA 14:633.31 ⟨*LW* 9:97⟩: "Unbelief makes a judge and enemy out of God and the Father. . . ." — See also Erich Seeberg, *Luthers Theologie*, 2:129.

52. ⟨See above, 54f.⟩

53. For the abuse of the law by the Jews through a wrong interpretation of the law, see *First Lectures on the Psalms*, 1513-15: WA 3:345.8 ⟨*LW* 10:290⟩.

54. *Third Disputation against the Antinomians*, 1538: WA 39.I:500.5: "We do not concede the power of Salvation to the law, not even to the divine law ⟨i.e., the Decalogue⟩, not to mention the human law, because the Lamb of God has been sent to bring" ⟨that power of Salvation; for "power of Salvation," see Rom. 1:16⟩.

55. ⟨See above, 16-18.⟩

56. ⟨Literally: ". . . of the legal people," i.e., the people who "misuse" the Decalogue in a legalistic way.⟩

57. ⟨In the sense of present.⟩

58. ⟨Or: ". . . preserve only written letters."⟩

59. *The Book of Deuteronomy with Notes*, 1525: WA 14:638.1.5; ⟨see also *LW* 9:108⟩.

Notes to Chapter 11

1. ⟨See above, 82f.⟩

2. *To the Christian Nobility*, 1520: WA 6:446.22. — Luther spoke also of a "change" in the law, or of "two" legislators, Moses and Christ; *Second Lectures on Galatians*, 1531: WA 40.I:456.9ff.; *Second Lectures on the Psalms*, 1518-21: WA 5:61.13.

3. Therefore Luther could say that Christ undertook not to "destroy the law" but to "establish" it; *First Lectures on the Psalms*, 1513-15: WA 4:340.7.

4. A misunderstood law does not deserve to be called law; *Second Lectures on the Psalms*, 1518-21: WA 5:561.4.

5. Sermons of ca. 1514-21: WA 4:688.35.38.

6. *Lectures on Hebrews*, 1517-18: WA 57.III:99.3: "... ⟨Christ's⟩ humanity is our sacred ladder on which we ascend to recognize God." ⟨See Gen. 28:12.⟩

7. *First Disputation against the Antinomians*, 1537: WA 39.I:391.5; *On Psalms 23-25*, 1513-16: WA 31.I:474.33.

8. *The Book of Deuteronomy with Notes*, 1525: WA 14:676.36 ⟨LW 9:178⟩: "... it is necessary that He ⟨i.e., the prophet of Deut. 18:15 as Christ⟩ be a teacher of life, grace, and righteousness, just as Moses is a teacher of sin, wrath, and death." But Christ is not a legislator in the sense of being a new Moses; *Sermons on John, Chapters 6-8*, 1530-32: WA 33:86.32; *Second Lectures on Galatians*, 1531: WA 40.I:532.5.

9. *Second Disputation against the Antinomians*, 1538: WA 39.I:446.2: "... the law has to be interpreted through the gospel and led back ... to a salutary use, ⟨i.e.,⟩ to Christ ..."; ibid., WA 39.I:452.12: "⟨Christ⟩ interprets the law perfectly and spiritually."

10. ⟨I.e., a person who has not been redeemed by Christ through faith.⟩

11. Even though God deals with man first externally ⟨ "confront"⟩, and then internally; *Against the Heavenly Prophets*, 1525: WA 18:136.9, 137.14, 139.20; *Second Lectures on Galatians*, 1531: WA 40.I:142.1.

12. *First Lectures on the Psalms*, 1513-15: WA 4:2.11: "⟨The Lord⟩ speaks in me, but those others ⟨i.e., Moses and all other legislators⟩ speak only at me or against me ..."; *The Book of Deuteronomy with Notes*, 1525: WA 14:603.16: "When the law does not speak spiritually from God in man's heart, then its words remain human words."

13. *First Lectures on the Psalms*, 1513-15: WA 4:134.20: "... the spiritual law and the gospel are identical."

14. Ibid., WA 4:134.38: "... the gospel cannot be known without understanding *(intellectus)* and faith"; ibid., WA 4:324.6, and ibid., WA 3:479.35; *Lectures on Romans*, 1515-16: WA 56:336.10: "The spirit ... alone understands the Scriptures correctly and according to God's intention."

15. See the last text cited in n. 12.

16. ⟨See above, 54f.⟩ *First Lectures on the Psalms*, 1513-15: WA 3:451.24: "Even the gospel preached and written down is a law impossible to fulfill unless God himself teaches it internally." — For the change in the meaning of God's commandments through the fact that in *Kulturprotestantismus* ⟨i.e., a Protestantism in which the difference and the tension between gospel and secular culture are ignored⟩ God, the author of the law, has been removed from man's intellectual horizon, see Thielicke, *Kirche und Öffentlichkeit*, 44.

17. *Lectures on Hebrews*, 1517-18: WA 57.III:142.18: "This is the one and most important thing which God requires of ... all people, that they hear his voice"; ibid., WA 57.III:143.7 ⟨LW 29:148⟩: "... human nature violently recoils from this hearing. ..."

18. *Second Lectures on the Psalms*, 1518-21: WA 5:328.14: "... ⟨man⟩ has to despair of his natural strength."

19. *Lectures on Hebrews*, 1517-18: WA 57.III:192.23 ⟨LW 29:194⟩: "Properly speaking, ... it is not the office of the new priest to teach the Law but to point out the grace of Jesus Christ ..."; *Second Lectures on Galatians*, 1531: WA 40.I:91.7: "Even though ⟨Christ⟩ inter-

prets the law, nevertheless that is not his proper office . . ." ⟨in the sense of task⟩; ibid., WA 40.I:568.9.

20. *First Disputation against the Antinomians,* 1537: WA 39.I:375.4: ". . . Christ's office is to restore mankind even in this life to that lost innocence and cheerful obedience to the law which was a given in Paradise. . . ."

21. *Lectures on Genesis,* 1535-45: WA 42:48.11.27 ⟨*LW* 1:64f.⟩: "But now the Gospel has brought about the restoration of that image. . . . In this manner this image of the new creature begins to be restored by the Gospel in this life, but it will not be finished in this life." See also Wingren, *Die Predigt,* 96ff. — For the difference between Luther's understanding of the new man and the understanding of the new man developed in Pietism, see Ragnar Bring, "Gesetz und Evangelium und der dritte Gebrauch des Gesetzes in der lutherischen Theologie," *Aus der Arbeit der Luther-Agricola Gesellschaft in Finnland* 1 (Helsinki, 1943): 49ff.; Prenter, *Spiritus creator,* 77f.

22. *Second Lectures on Galatians,* 1531: WA 40.I:503.1, 501.8.

23. ⟨I.e., the interpretation of the divine natural law and the rebirth of man.⟩

24. *First Lectures on the Psalms,* 1513-15: WA 4:81.3: ". . . the new creation is the church in Jesus Christ"; ibid., WA 4:81.12; ibid., WA 4:245.16 ⟨*LW* 11:381⟩: "⟨The works of Christ's hands are⟩ the construction and building of the church, which is to be built in truth, because it is not in the figure and the letter, but, as was promised, in the spirit, so now it is done and set forth as truth"; *Lectures on Hebrews,* 1517-18: WA 57.III:16.18: "Christ . . . ⟨is the church's⟩ head, . . . lord, and founder. . . ." — For the outpouring of the Holy Spirit at Pentecost as the "external sign" of the church's beginning, see sermon of May 28, 1531: WA 34.I:460.4.6. For the public call of the Apostles from heaven, see sermon of May 29, 1531: WA 34.I:478.2. See also *Matthew, Chapters 18-24 Explained in Sermons,* 1537-40: WA 47:410.8: "God's Word constitutes the church."

25. According to Emil Brunner (*Das Mißverständnis der Kirche,* 96), Luther wanted "basically to nullify the institutionalization of the church." This could not have been the reformer's goal if one considers his understanding of the connection of the spiritual church with the universal church (see Johannes Heckel, *Initia iuris,* 39f., and above, 120f.); rather, Luther's goal was only the ordering of the corporeal ⟨institutional⟩ church according to the principles which govern the spiritual church.

26. For the connection of the spiritual with the corporeal church, see Johannes Heckel, *Initia iuris,* 39ff. If one considers the spiritual connection between the spiritual and the corporeal church, and Luther's understanding of the man-made ecclesiastical law as a product of the brotherly love of Christians, then one has to abandon the idea that Luther was a religious individualist. Luther's high regard for the communal prayer in the church strongly supports this argument. See *German Exposition of the Lord's Prayer for Simple Laymen,* 1519: WA 2:114.28 ⟨*LW* 42:60⟩: "He ⟨i.e., Christ⟩ wants to hear the throngs and not me or you alone, or a single isolated Pharisee. Therefore sing with the congregation and you will sing well. Even if your singing is not melodious, it will be swallowed up by the crowd. But if you sing alone you will have your critics"; *On Good Works,* 1520: WA 6:238.10: "This communal prayer is precious and the most powerful prayer, and the reason for our coming together, and for calling the church a house of prayer. . . ." — Gerhard Ritter was to the point when he rejected (*Die Neugestaltung Europas im 16. Jahrhundert* [Berlin, 1950], 86) the assumption that Luther represented "a new religious individualism." For a different view, see Siegfried, "Le Protestantisme," 173: "It is the question of an

almost integral religious subjectivism, the heart of the matter being the communion of the soul with God, the individual's religious life, which is fundamentally independent from the visible church." How can one square this position with the materials presented above, 249 n. 70?

27. *The Large Catechism,* 1529: WA 30.I:191.18 ⟨*BC* 419.61f.⟩: "Creation is past and redemption is accomplished, but the Holy Spirit carries on his work unceasingly until the last day. For this purpose he has appointed a community on earth, through which he speaks and does all his work. For he has not yet gathered together all his Christian people, nor has he completed the granting of forgiveness." — See also Ernst Sommerlath, "Kirche und Reich Gottes," *ZSTh* 16 (1939): 573.

28. *First Lectures on the Psalms,* 1513-15: WA 3:268.37: "... outside of the church there is no true knowledge of God"; *The Book of Deuteronomy with Notes,* 1525: WA 14:588.14: "... where God's Word is not, there is no true knowledge of God ..."; *Postilla for Christmas,* 1522, WA 10.I.1:140.8.14: "... whoever wants to find Christ has to find the church first.... The church is not wood and stone, but the crowd of the people who believe in Christ. To that church one has to hang on and see how these people believe, live, and teach; certainly, these people have Christ, for outside of the Christian church there is no truth, no Christ, no Salvation."

29. *The Large Catechism,* 1529: WA 30.I:188.20 ⟨*BC* 416.40⟩: "... 'I believe that the Holy Spirit makes me holy, as his name implies.' How does he do this? By what means? Answer: 'Through the Christian church, the forgiveness of sins, the resurrection of the body, and the life everlasting.' In the first place, he has a unique community in the world. It is the mother that begets and bears every Christian through the Word of God. The Holy Spirit reveals and preaches that Word, and by it he illumines and kindles hearts so that they grasp and accept it, cling to it, and persevere in it."

30. Luther to Count Albrecht of Mansfeld: June 3, 1523(?): WA.B 3:80.36: "... ⟨Christ⟩ instituted that ⟨Christians⟩ come together and celebrate two ceremonies, Baptism and the sacrament of his body and blood...."

31. Sermon of Oct. 5, 1544: WA 49:615.26: "You are called into a special estate, which the world does not know and which it does not seek.... This is your vocation to which you are called through the gospel and Baptism"; sermon of March 3, 1538: WA 46:197.3: "Through Baptism I enter the kingdom ... of Christ, which he has by his humanity"; ibid., WA 46:198.24: "We know ... that Baptism is an eternal covenant through which we are given the right of citizenship under Christ's rule"; sermon of Febr. 10, 1538: WA 46:171.19: "Baptism is an eternal covenant made ⟨with me⟩ once. If I am baptized before I believe, ... Baptism is nevertheless true, though not beneficial for me.... If sometime after Baptism I sin, I remain baptized except that I do not derive any benefit from Baptism. When I fall ⟨into sin⟩, I have lost the use of Baptism, but I remain baptized. But if I say: 'God is merciful, and I am absolved,' I am returning to the benefit of Baptism"; sermon of Oct. 14, 1537: WA 45:177.20: "I have been baptized ⟨and⟩ called into the church"; *The Babylonian Captivity of the Church,* 1520: WA 6:534.31: "... you see that ... in terms of the ⟨external⟩ sign the sacrament of Baptism is a matter not of one moment but of perpetuity. Granted, the enactment ⟨literally: 'use'⟩ of the sacrament is over quickly, yet the matter itself *(res),* signified ⟨by the action⟩, lasts until death, even more, the Resurrection on the Last Day"; sermon of Jan. 14, 1532: WA 36:101.2: "The holy spiritual estate" ⟨see also above, 260 n. 14⟩; *Sermons on John, Chapters 14 and 15,* 1537: WA 45:616.28 ⟨*LW* 24:170⟩:

"'And what does the Holy Spirit have to do with me?' Answer: 'He baptized me; He proclaimed the Gospel of Christ to me; and He awakened my heart to believe. Baptism is not of my making; nor is the Gospel; nor is faith. He gave these to me. For the fingers that baptized me are not those of a man; they are the fingers of the Holy Spirit. And the preacher's mouth and the words that I heard are not his; they are the words and message of the Holy Spirit. By these outward means He works faith within me and thus He makes me holy.'" For Luther's refutation of the rejection of Infant Baptism (because children are unable to have faith), see *Matthew, Chapters 18-24 Explained in Sermons, 1537-40*: WA 47:328.17. For Infant Baptism as a universal, divine, and public order, see *Concerning Rebaptism, 1528*: WA 26:151.15.

32. See Vajta, *Theologie des Gottsdienstes by Luther*, 87ff.; Prenter, *Spiritus creator*, 150, 254ff. See also *The Blessed Sacrament of the Body of Christ and the Brotherhoods, 1519*: WA 2:743.20 ⟨LW 35:51⟩: "To receive this sacrament in bread and wine, then, is nothing else than to receive a sure sign of this fellowship and incorporation with Christ and all saints. It is as if a citizen were given a sign, a document, or some other token to assure him that he is a citizen of the city, a member of that particular community. St. Paul says this very thing in I Corinthians 10[:17]: 'We are all one bread and one body, for we all partake of one bread and one cup'"; sermons of ca. 1514-21: WA 4:706.9: "⟨The sacrament of the altar⟩ is the communion and symbol of love."

33. Luther's *Smalcald Articles, 1537*: WA 50:243.13 ⟨BC 311.VII.1⟩: "The keys are a function and power given to the church by Christ . . . "; *Against the Roman Papacy, 1545*: WA 54:249.17. — Erdmann Schott ("Anfänge evangelischen Kirchenrechts in Luthers 95 Theses?" *ZEvKR* 2 [1953]: 131ff.) raised objections regarding my position (Johannes Heckel, *Initia iuris*, 71ff.) that the Power of the Keys has been transferred to the church. These objections become irrelevant if one carefully considers the relationship of the two churches (the spiritual and the universal church; see also above, 120f.) with each other, and if one takes excommunication seriously. I.e., if one understands excommunication as the punitive consequence of *the already lost membership in the spiritual church*, a consequence pronounced by the universal church in the realm for which its law is valid ⟨italics by this ed.⟩; *On the Power of Excommunication, 1518*: WA 1:640.2: "Excommunication, if it is just, signifies . . . that the soul has been turned over to the devil and deprived of the church's spiritual communion . . ."; ibid., WA 1:640.10: "Excommunication . . . is instituted . . . for the internal communion . . . to be restored . . . if excommunication has been enacted justly. . . ." In order to be able to make such a pronouncement, the universal church has to establish first that the loss of membership in the spiritual church has already occurred; ⟨only then can⟩ the universal church draw the consequence and deprive a person of the active membership in the universal church. Schott failed to recognize the connection of the corporeal ecclesiastical punishment ⟨i.e., excommunication enacted by the church⟩ with the spiritual punishment of an all-encompassing verdict *(poena latae sententiae)*.

34. *Concerning the Ministry, 1523*: WA 12:173.2. — For the meaning of "public" as it is being used here, see *Sermons on Matthew, Chapters 5-7, 1530-32*: WA 32:351.3, and Vajta, *Theologie des Gottsdienstes bei Luther*, 216. — For the public nature of the preaching office, see *The Private Mass and the Consecration of Priests, 1533*: WA 38:231.13. — For shepherding *(pascere)* as the only task of the preaching office, and for the meaning of this word, see *Against the Roman Papacy, 1545*: WA 54:280.1. — For the personal qualities of

the shepherd, see ibid., WA 54:279.10. — For the connection of the sermon with the sacraments, see *The Private Mass and the Consecration of Priests*, 1533: WA 38:231.8, 253.30. — For the vocal quality of the sermon and its superiority over writing books, see *Postilla for Christmas*, 1522: WA 10.I.1:625.20.ff.

35. Therefore Luther called the estate of pastor an estate instituted by God; *To the Christian Nobility*, 1520: WA 6:441.24. See further, *On Keeping Children in School*, 1530: WA 30.II:527.1; *On the Councils and the Church*, 1539: WA 50:632.35, and below, 386 n. 27.

36. For the tasks *(officia)* of the office, see *Concerning the Ministry*, 1523: WA 12:180.1; *Sermons on the First Epistle of St. Peter*, 1523: WA 12:309.24: "The true priesthood . . . does three things . . . : sacrificing spiritually, praying for the congregation, and preaching."

37. In *The Babylonian Captivity of the Church* (WA 6:503.13ff.) Luther differentiated explicitly between 'law' and 'institution' *(lex, institutio)* but based both on Christ's authority to make laws. ⟨Luther dealt with the withholding of the cup from the laity in the Lord's Supper, a situation which in his opinion was no longer in agreement with "the first institution" (i.e., Christ's legislative act in which he instituted the sacrament of the altar) and, therefore, has to be changed. Then he continued⟩: "Otherwise, if we permit that one of Christ's institutions is changed, then we soon have destabilized all his laws, and everyone may say that he is not bound by any law or institution of Christ." — Emil Brunner (*Das Mißverständnis der Kirche*, 66ff.) criticized the understanding of the sacraments as "institutions"; in the New Testament they are that "form of the Word through which the individual in a real way is incorporated in the congregation." But Christ has determined this "form of the Word" in a specific way, and in so doing he issued a positive order. See Heinrich Vogel, *Gott in Christo* (Berlin, 1951), 834. — Walter Geppert, *Ist kirchliches Lehrchaos protestantisches Schicksal?* (Neuffen/Württemberg, 1953), 28ff., tried to develop a theological rationale for ecclesiastical law; at important points his position is different from the one presented above. The book appeared while my manuscript was being printed; therefore I am unable to deal with it.

38. Therefore the often mentioned thesis that Christ was not a legislator has to be qualified. (See *On the New Testament, That Is, the Mass*, 1520: WA 6:354.21: ". . . ⟨Christ did⟩ not institute for his . . . people more than one custom or law, i.e., the holy Mass . . ."; ibid., WA 6:378.1: ". . . Christ burdened his holy church with very few laws and works. . . .") But Christ's work as legislator did not result in "legal prescriptions for external ceremonies" (as Vajta, *Theologie des Gottesdienstes bei Luther*, 45, correctly stated); the essence of the divine positive law makes this quite clear. See above, 51f.; Luther to Duke Charles III of Savoy: Sept. 7, 1523: WA.B 3:153.117: "⟨For giving bread and wine to the communicants we have⟩ the authority and testimony of the divine majesty, even more, ⟨his⟩ institution and commandment."

39. If I see correctly, Luther, following the tradition, used the term *ius divinum* ⟨divine positive law⟩ for the first time in *Explanations of the Ninety-five Theses*, 1518: WA 1:533.15: "Without a doubt, Christ is a divine legislator and his doctrine is *ius divinum*"; ibid., WA 1:536.18: ". . . it is most ungodly to think that the pope has the power to change *ius divinum* . . . ." See also Johannes Heckel, *Initia iuris*, 23. Luther also used other terms for this divine positive law of the New Testament: "heavenly and divine traditions" (*The Babylonian Captivity of the Church*, 1520: WA 6:563.8), or "ceremonies divinely instituted" (*Second Lectures on the Psalms*, 1518-21: WA 5:401.9). In connection with the law for the preaching office Luther spoke of "Christian law"; *The Right and Power of a Christian Con-*

gregation, 1523: WA 11:415.23. See further, sermon of Jan. 20, 1538: WA 46.146.20: "Our doctrine does not originate in our designs but in God's old institutions, i.e., the ministry of the gospel, Baptism, the Eucharist, absolution; these things we have cleaned up . . ."; Werner Elert, *Der christliche Glaube* (Berlin, 1940), 509: "Being constituted in Word and sacrament is the absolutely binding permanent organization of the church. This constitution of the church is *jus divinum* in the strict sense of the word"; Paul Althaus, *Die christliche Wahrheit,* 2 (Gütersloh, 1948), 294: "Divine law in the church is only the proclaiming and hearing of the Word, and the enactment and receiving of the sacraments in the vis-à-vis of office and congregation."

40. All this has nothing in common with the secular natural law. — One has to question Reinhold Seeberg, *Lehrbuch der Dogmengeschichte,* 4.I (4th ed. Leipzig, 1933), 321, who argued: "The tendency inherent in the secular natural law for social activity, through which people are mutually supported, is the precondition for the existence of the Spirit-created community of love, in which Christians live with one another." For a justified critique, see Ernst Wolf, "'Natürliches Gesetz' und 'Gesetz Christi' bei Luther," *EvTh* 2 (1935): 325. — For the significance of the divine natural law for the church as institution, see above, 98.

41. *Matthew, Chapters 18-24 Explained in Sermons,* 1537-40: WA 47:535:15: "The only mark of the Christian church . . . is to follow the divine Word and be obedient"; *Psalm 117 Explained,* 1530: WA 31.I:232.34: "Wherever are the gospel, Baptism, and Lord's Supper, there is ⟨Christ's⟩ church, and in it certainly are living saints . . . even if they are only young people and children . . ."; *The Private Mass and the Consecration of Priests,* 1533: WA 38:203.1.

42. *On the New Testament, That Is, the Mass,* 1520: WA 6:359.6: "We poor people, because we live in our five senses, have to have at least an external sign, in addition to the words, to which we can cling and under which we can come together. That sign has to be a sacrament, i.e., it has to be something external but have and signify something spiritual so that we are drawn through the external into the spiritual, grasp the external with the eyes of the body, the spiritual, internal with the eyes of the heart." — For the significance of the sacramental sign, see Prenter, *Spiritus creator,* 146ff., 258ff. — For the relationship of the divine natural law with the divine positive law, see *Receiving Bread and Wine in the Sacrament,* 1522: WA 10.II:30.17 ⟨LW 36:255f.⟩: "Now therefore, since Satan has so terribly confused the matter through the ordinance of the pope that one cannot use the sacrament in both kinds ⟨i.e., receiving bread and wine⟩ without violating the law of love towards weaker consciences, and since one cannot exercise love without violating the institution of both kinds, one must give preference to the exercise of love and for a time overlook the institution. But this does not mean that one denies or condemns the use of the sacrament in both kinds; it simply means that love is something that lays us under obligation and compulsion whereas the reception of the sacramental elements is not a matter of compulsion. One can forego them and simply cling to the words. For Christ has not commanded us to partake of the sacrament, but has left it free for anyone to partake who wishes to do so, and to do this in both kinds if he can. But in our situation it is not possible to do so on account of the consciences which love is in duty bound to serve."

43. Following Alfred von Quervain, *Kirche, Volk, Staat, Ethik,* 2.I (Zollikon-Zürich, 1945), 158, one may say about the spiritual use of the divine positive law ⟨as ecclesiastical

law⟩ that a church ordinance is a "sign of Christ's sovereignty." But that use being enacted in the church is also a sign of the spiritual unity of all Christians.

44. *The Babylonian Captivity of the Church,* 1520: WA 6:533.12: "The ⟨significance of the⟩ sacraments is not accomplished when they are enacted but when they are believed."

45. For the effect of a sacrament which is received in unbelief, see Luther's *Smalcald Articles,* 1537: WA 50:242.7 ⟨BC 311.VI.1⟩; *The Large Catechism,* 1529: WA 30.I:219.1 ⟨BC 443.54⟩; *The Private Mass and the Consecration of Priests,* 1533: WA 38:235.9ff.; *Matthew, Chapters 18-24 Explained in Sermons,* 1537-40: WA 47:334.19; Vajta, Theologie des Gottesdienstes bei Luther, 262 n. 100.

46. ⟨See above, 84f.⟩

47. *The Bondage of the Will,* 1525: WA 18:697.26.

48. *On Christian Freedom* ⟨Latin text⟩, 1520: WA 7:54.31: "The . . . grace of faith . . . unites *(copulat)* the soul with Christ as a bride with a groom." — See also Prenter, *Spiritus creator,* 43ff.

49. *First Lectures on the Psalms,* 1513-15: WA 3:434.13: "Christ . . . changes us into himself. . . ." — For 'incorporation in Christ', see *Second Lectures on the Psalms,* 1518-21: WA 5:311.8, and ibid., 608.7: ". . . through a wonderful trade *(commertio)* our sins are now not our sins but Christ's sins, and Christ's righteousness is not Christ's but our righteousness."

50. *First Lectures on the Psalms,* 1513-15: WA 4:16.20: ". . . now Christ is our righteousness and our peace, which God has given us"; ibid., WA 4:19.37 ⟨LW 11: 174⟩: ". . . Christ is not called our Righteousness, Peace, Mercy, and Salvation in His Person except in an effectual sense. But it is faith in Christ by which we are justified and granted peace, and by that faith Christ reigns in us."

51. *The Babylonian Captivity of the Church,* 1520: WA 6:519.5: ". . . you will reach . . . the very source of life, that is to say, faith in the Word, ⟨and from this faith⟩ flows all good."

52. *Second Lectures on Galatians,* 1531: WA 40.I:360.5 ⟨and the edited version of these lectures, WA 40.I:360.24f., or LW 26:227⟩.

53. In our disquisition it is not possible to deal with Luther's polemics against the medieval doctrine of grace of the Roman Catholic Church. See, e.g., *Second Lectures on Galatians,* 1531: WA 40.I:229.7; *Second Lectures on the Psalms,* 1518-21: WA 5:479.12.

54. *The Babylonian Captivity of the Church,* 1520: WA 6:514.21: "By no other way is man able to meet God and deal with him than by faith. . . ."

55. *First Lectures on the Psalms,* 1513-15: WA 3:567.14.

56. For the gospel's *via compendii* (short way) in contrast to the *ambages* (roundabout, rambling, dark, or ambiguous ways, detours) of the law, see *Second Lectures on the Psalms,* 1518-21: WA 5:65.21 ⟨LW 14:337⟩; *On the New Testament, That Is, the Mass,* 1520: WA 6:378.8: "Faith is to the point ⟨literally: 'faith is a short thing'⟩." — The way of faith is also the way of the cross; *Second Lectures on the Psalms,* 1518-21: WA 5:145.17.

57. *On the New Testament, That Is, the Mass,* 1520: WA 6:370.24: ". . . faith has to do all things."

58. *Second Lectures on the Psalms,* 1518-21: WA 5:559.15: "The will . . . having been changed . . . pays attention to the Lord's law . . ."; *First Lectures on the Psalms,* 1513-15: WA 4:356.12 ⟨LW 11:485⟩: ". . . the Word does not enlighten the eyes. . . . Yet it is a lamp, because it guides the feet and the heart, and faith does not require understanding. Not un-

derstanding, but willing, not knowing but doing...";ibid., WA 3:98.32, 99.9, 297.2. — For the connection of this doctrine about the soul with Nominalism, see Holl, *Luther,* 34 n. 2.

59. It is not only a "change which occurred in our consciousness," as Erich Seeberg (*Luthers Theologie,* 2:205) stated. In contrast, Iwand (*Rechtfertigungslehre und Christusglaube,* 36) was correct when he wrote: "Through faith in Christ one gains a new being, not a new idea."

60. For speaking in theological categories, to the effect that in spite of sin remaining in man, man is changed, in contrast to speaking in moral or metaphysical categories, to the effect that man remains the same but sin is being taken away from him, see *Lectures on Romans,* 1515-16: WA 56:334.14, 337.18 ⟨LW 25:322f., 325f.⟩, and Link, *Das Ringen Luthers,* 98.

61. Therefore in *On Christian Freedom* ⟨Latin text⟩, 1520: WA 7:61.12, Luther described the justified person this way: "Through his faith he has been placed again into Paradise and created anew"; see also the German text, WA 7:31.29.

62. ⟨The issue is man's being (status, *Da-Sein*) and his daily existence *(So-Sein)* which is, or should be, a manifestation of his being.⟩

63. ⟨"Christian being" would be the closest translation of *Christentum,* a word which is to designate something other than Christianity or Christendom. See below, 381 n. 190, 423 n. 147, 432 n. 213, 451 n. 30.⟩ Luther used *Christentum* seldom. According to information kindly provided by Professor Gustav Bebermeyer (Tübingen), *Christentum* could mean for Luther "estate and dignity of a Christian, the Christian faith, the Christian life." See, e.g., *The German Mass,* 1526: WA 19:75.1: "⟨The German Mass⟩ is a public enticement to faith and *Christentum*"; Luther to Caspar Müller, chancellor of Mansfeld: May 26, 1526: WA.B 4:80.10: through Baptism a child is to be born to *Christentum; Psalm 118 Explained,* 1530: WA 31.I:95.33; *Matthew, Chapters 5-7 Explained in Sermons,* 1530-32: WA 32:440.11; *Sermons on the Ten Commandments,* 1518: WA 1:491.1.

64. ⟨See also above, 64f.⟩

65. Gollwitzer (*Christliche Gemeinde,* 8) erred when he argued that the reborn Christian *(renatus)* is subordinated to the law and placed in the kingdom at the left in two ways: since he is still a sinner, he is, of course, still subordinated to the kingdom ⟨at the left⟩; but precisely as a reborn Christian he is subordinated to the kingdom at the left — even though he has been totally liberated from it — because he subordinates himself again to it, ⟨now⟩ in freedom.

66. See above, 84.

67. See Luther's polemics against Thomas Aquinas in *Second Lectures on Galatians,* 1531: WA 40.I:671.13.

68. *Second Lectures on Galatians,* 1531: WA 40.I:268.9: ⟨Commenting on Gal. 2:19, Luther developed the idea that the believer has died to the law, and that the law has been abolished. According to Luther, Paul did speak not only about the ceremonial law (because he did keep it when necessary, e.g., he circumcised Timothy), but he spoke about law in a universal sense; "the entire law" has been abolished, be it the ceremonial law or the Decalogue, because the Christian has died to the law.⟩ Continuing this line of thinking, Luther could say that Christ was a legislator, not in order to prescribe laws but in order to abolish the law of Moses; ibid., WA 40.I: 470.2, 535.14, 561.1.7; sermon of Aug. 23, 1532: WA 36:276.18: "Christ is our Lord so that he makes out of us such people as he himself is. As he does not tolerate being bound by laws but is lord over all laws and things, so also a

Christian's conscience is not to tolerate being bound ⟨by laws⟩. Through Christ and ⟨our⟩ Baptism ⟨literally: 'his Baptism' in the sense of the Baptism which he gives to us⟩ we are to be . . . liberated so that our consciences do not know of any law but simply remain . . . free from being dominated and judged by the law. Therefore on the basis of this internal condition of our consciences, we are to think nothing other than that at no time has any law come down to earth, neither ten commandments nor one commandment, neither from God, nor the pope, nor the emperor, but that we are at all times free to say: 'I know of no law, and I do not want to know of any law'"; ibid., WA 36:276.34: "This is . . . our treasure ⟨through⟩ which we are Christians and live and survive before God; how we are to live externally in flesh and blood before the world is of no concern in this connection."

69. 1 Tim. 1:9; Vulgate. *Second Commentary on Galatians*, 1535: WA 40.I:528.6 ⟨*LW* 26:343f.*⟩: "What I have stated earlier so often about both uses of the Law, the political or Gentile use and the theological use, indicates clearly that the Law was not laid down for the righteous but, as Paul teaches elsewhere (1 Tim. 1:9), for the unrighteous. But there are two kinds of unrighteous men: those who are to be justified and those who are not to be justified. Those who are not to be justified are restrained by the civic use of the Law; for they should be bound with the chains of laws, as wild and untamed beasts are bound with ropes and chains. This use of the Law never ceases. . . . Those who are to be justified, on the other hand, are disciplined by the theological use of the Law for a time; for it does not last forever, as the civic use does, but it looks forward to the coming of faith, and when Christ comes, it is finished. From this it is abundantly clear that all the passages in which Paul treats the spiritual use of the Law must be understood about those who are to be justified, not about those who have already been justified. For, as has been said often enough, these latter are far above and beyond any Law. Therefore the Law should be imposed upon those who are to be justified, so that they may be kept in custody under it until the righteousness of faith comes. This is not because they obtain righteousness through the Law — for that would be to abuse the Law, not to use it correctly — but so that when they have been terrified and humbled by the Law they may take refuge in Christ, who 'is the end of the Law, that everyone who has faith may be justified' (Rom.10:4)."

70. Theses 48 and 49 of *Third Disputation against the Antinomians*, 1538: WA 39. I:356.31: "*Relative* . . . , not *formaliter* or *substantialiter* has sin been taken away, the law abolished, death destroyed. And all this happens in this life because of Christ until such time that we reach the perfect man in the fulness of Christ." ⟨Eph. 4:13; Vulgate.⟩

71. *Lectures on Hebrews*, 1517-18: WA 57.III:193.8: ". . . in this time ⟨here⟩, the righteous man, on whom the law has not been placed, makes only a beginning"; *Lectures on Genesis*, 1535-45: WA 42:83.22 ⟨*LW* 1:110⟩: ". . . 'righteous' does not have the same meaning after sin and before sin."

72. *Disputation on Justification*, 1536: WA 39.I:95.10.16, 96.19 ⟨*LW* 34:164f.⟩: "Original sin which is inborn and evil continually cleaves to us, making us guilty of eternal death. It lasts as long as we live and can be called an inborn disposition *(habitus)*. . . . But at this point we say that original sin, although ⟨in Baptism⟩ forgiveness has been imputed and thus sin is removed so that it is not imputed, nevertheless, is not substantially or essentially destroyed except in the conflagration of fire by which the whole world and our bodies will be completely purified on the last day. When we have been reduced to dust, then at last sins will be entirely extinguished. In the meantime, while we live, original sin also lives, as we see even in the saints up till the last breath. . . . original sin is a root and in-

born evil, which only comes to an end when this body has been entirely mortified, purged by fire, and reformed. Meanwhile, however, it is not imputed to the godly"; ibid., WA 39.I:111.9, 117.5. — See also Luther's polemics against understanding Original Sin as mere tinder *(fomes)* in *First Disputation against the Antinomians*, 1537: WA 39.I:395.11.

73. *Lectures on Romans*, 1515-16: WA 56:350.27: "The flesh is man's weakness or wound . . . ; insofar that he lusts, it is ⟨the result of this⟩ weakness of the spirit and wound of sin, which begins to be healed." See also *Disputation on Justification*, 1536: WA 39.I:113.16; Iwand, *Rechtfertigungslehre und Christusglaube*, 59, and id., *Glaubensgerechtigkeit nach Luthers Lehre*, 41f.

74. *Against the Bull of Antichrist* ⟨German text⟩, 1520: WA 6:623.3; sermon of Oct. 21, 1537: WA 45:184.30.

75. *Second Disputation against the Antinomians*, 1538: WA 39.I:436.12: ". . . ⟨we have⟩ sin, but it does not have dominion over us." — For the difference between *dominating* sin and *dominated* sin, see Prenter, *Spiritus creator*, 82f. — For law as "good friend and companion" of believing Christians, see *Postilla for Christmas*, 1522: WA 10.I.1:467.14.

76. *The Babylonian Captivity of the Church*, 1520: WA 6:534.12. — For the significance of the contrast between flesh and spirit and the battle between both for anthropology and ethics, see esp. Stange, *Studien zur Theologie Luthers*, 1:172.

77. Therefore the righteousness of a justified believer is never a *habitus* (quality, disposition). For Luther's polemics against the understanding of justification creating a *habitus*, see *Second Lectures on the Psalms*, 1518-21: WA 5:33.7; *Second Lectures on Galatians*, 1531: WA 40.I:225.10, 228.12, 370.9; ibid., WA 40.II:65.5; Törnvall, *Geistliches und weltliches Regiment bei Luther*, 177ff. — For the question whether Original Sin may be called a *habitus*, see *Disputation on Justification*, 1536: WA 39.I:95.12, as above, 366 n. 72, and Althaus, *Christliche Wahrheit*, 2:122ff.

78. For the significance of prayer for the certainty of salvation, see Hermann, *Luthers These "Gerecht und Sünder zugleich,"* 291ff., esp. 295.

79. *First Disputation against the Antinomians*, 1537: WA 39.I:394.14: "The whole life of the believers is an effort against, and some sort of hatred for, the remains of sin in the flesh, which rebels against the spirit and faith."

80. For this continuous battle of the believer, see *First Lectures on the Psalms*, 1513-15: WA 4:205.4; *Second Disputation against the Antinomians*, 1538: WA 39.I: 438.13. — For the Christian as ideal and reality, see Gyllenkrok, *Rechtfertigung und Heiligung*, 83ff.

81. Thesis 1 of *Ninety-five Theses*, 1517: WA 1:233.10 ⟨LW 31:25⟩; *Explanations of the Ninety-five Theses*, 1518: WA 1:530.16ff. ⟨LW 31:83ff.⟩.

82. *Sermons on the Ten Commandments*, 1518 ⟨sermon of June 29(?), 1516⟩: WA 1:398.10: ". . . each of God's commandments is given rather to show a sin already committed in the past or present than to prohibit a sin about to be committed in the future . . ."; sermon of Dec. 14, 1516: WA 1:108.13: ". . . the spiritual understanding of the law, which is the gospel, educates people to have the most perfect cognition of sin and self . . ."; *First Disputation against the Antinomians*, 1537: WA 39.I:375. 9: "The crowd is stiff-necked and without remorse; ⟨even⟩ the saints in this life do not ⟨take off⟩ the old man internally, and they feel that the law holds them captive ⟨and⟩ rebels in their members against the law of their mind; ⟨therefore⟩ the law is not to be removed from the church but retained and faithfully taught"; ibid., WA 39.I:399.4: "The law's office ⟨in the sense of task⟩ is always necessary and useful both for the stiff-necked ones to be terrified and for the godly ones

to be admonished to persevere to the end of life in the repentance which they have begun." — See also Gollwitzer, *Christliche Gemeinde*, 7f.: "Since only when connected with the gospel does the law destroy man's self-reliance, and since only the gospel enables man to recognize the meaning of this preserving, divine action, one may not simply assign law and gospel to one or the other kingdom — law and gospel are relevant for both kingdoms. But the kingdom at the left, i.e., God's way of ruling to accomplish the external preservation of his Creation, is characterized by the significance of the law in its . . . form not yet radicalized in the Word through the Holy Spirit. On the other hand, the kingdom at the right is connected with law because only when this kingdom passes through the killing activity of the law (its proper function) does it become the kingdom of our life." — Hermann Diem *(Luthers Predigt in den zwei Reichen)* was correct when he pointed out the weighty consequences which emerged when in later Lutheranism the two contrasts, law and gospel, kingdom at the left and kingdom at the right, were leveled, a process which had to lead to a separation of the two kingdoms, and that this leveling was made possible since even in Luther's thinking there was a special affinity between law and kingdom at the left, and gospel and kingdom at the right.

83. ⟨Mirror of penance.⟩ *Sermons on the Ten Commandments*, 1518: WA 1:438.2: ". . . the Decalogue of the commandments is a sort of mirror, in which man sees himself and finds out where and to what degree he fails or makes progress"; *On the Councils and the Church*, 1539: WA 50:643.19ff.; *On Good Works*, 1520: WA 6:236.21.

84. Sermon of Nov. 24, 1532: WA 36:368.9: "The law presses on you and accuses you in your conscience, which testifies against you and simply demands the verdict against you. Then you have to despair, and you will have no help or counsel unless you know to flee from the throne of judgment to the throne of mercy"; sermons of 1523: WA 12:677.24: "God . . . has his law preached, through which we find out what we owe."

85. ⟨See also above, 65.⟩ *Second Disputation against the Antinomians*, 1538: WA 39.I:435.7: "The law is powerful, it demands, accuses, condemns ⟨because⟩ those who are subject to the law do not fulfill it. This is the way the law acts upon man. But Christ once paid all debts for which we are liable to the law, he has released ⟨us⟩, and he has made satisfaction for us so that the law, although in some way it is powerful among us, nevertheless is empty *(lex vacua)* and also has ceased to exist for us. . . ."

86. There is, then, a difference in the office ⟨in the sense of task⟩ of the law for a Christian (who is simultaneously sinner and righteous) on the one side, and for a non-Christian (who is only sinner) on the other side. We may ignore the question whether in order to emphasize this difference one should speak of a third use of the law *(tertius usus legis)*. For a positive answer, see esp. Friedrich Brunstäd, *Theologie der lutherischen Bekenntnisschriften* (Gütersloh, 1951), 99ff.; for a negative answer, see Bring, "Gesetz und Evangelium," *Aus der Arbeit der Luther-Agricola Gesellschaft in Finnland* 1 (Helsinki,1943): 48ff., and Elert, *Zwischen Gnade und Ungnade*, 161ff. See also Wilfried Joest, *Gesetz und Freiheit* (Göttingen, 1951), 71ff.; Wehrung, *Welt und Reich*, 72 n. 68; Ebeling, "Triplex usus legis," *ThLZ* 75 (1950): 235ff.; Walter Geppert, "Zur gegenwärtigen Diskussion über Problem und Bedeutung des tertius usus legis," *ELKZ* 9 (1955): 387ff.

87. *Lectures on Hebrews*, 1517-18: WA 57.III:39.17: "There is the saying: 'A new king, a new law.' But this is Christ's law, i.e., love, not written in books but 'poured into hearts by the Holy Spirit'" ⟨Rom. 5:5; see also Heb. 8:10.⟩; Luther's letter of recommendation for

Notes to Pages 87-88

Theobald Diedelhuber: May 15, 1535: WA.B 7:186.6: "... to put into operation love or Christ's law"; *First Commentary on Galatians*, 1519: WA 2:580.7.18 ⟨LW 27:354f.⟩.

88. Sermon of Jan. 25, 1517: WA 1:126.7: "The gospel is nothing other than the revelation and interpretation of the old law."

89. *Second Lectures on Galatians*, 1531: WA 40.I:50.4: "If I consider Christ to be a legislator, then I am lost"; ibid., WA 40.I:568.2: "⟨Christ⟩ did not come to make laws, but he came to abolish them. He did not become the teacher of the law, but he became its executioner and jailer"; ibid., WA 40.I:568.7: "⟨Christ⟩ is not a legislator but our Redeemer from the law..."; *First Disputation against the Antinomians*, 1537: WA 39.I:387.5.16: "...⟨Christ⟩ interprets the law, not as legislator or some kind of a Moses, but ⟨in such a way⟩ that we understand the work or the fulfillment of the law, which the law demands from us...."

90. *Matthew, Chapters 18–24 Explained in Sermons*, 1537-40: WA 47:451.21: "Christ is the chief preacher, ⟨the other preachers⟩ are his instruments and tongues"; *John, Chapters 3 and 4 Explained in Sermons*, 1538-40: WA 47:60.17: "... in comparison with all the other Apostles, Christ was the best preacher." — See further, Volkmar Herntrich, "Luther und das Alte Testament," *LuJ* 20 (1938): 105 (Herntrich did not use the dualism in Luther's natural law concept).

91. ⟨See also above, 66f., 82f.⟩ Keeping this hidden spiritual law *(lex spiritualis latens)* in mind, Luther said in *First Disputation against the Antinomians*, 1537: WA 39.I:413.14: "The Decalogue... is engraved on the hearts and minds of all people, and it will remain with us even in the future life"; ibid., WA 39.I:413.17: "... alone the Decalogue is eternal, not as law but in terms of substance *(res)*, because in the future life there will exist the very thing which the Decalogue demanded ⟨now and⟩ here." See also *Second Disputation against the Antinomians*, 1538: WA 39.I:454.4, 478.16; *Third Disputation against the Antinomians*, 1538: WA 39.I:539.7, as above, 353 n. 2.

92. See above, 50f.

93. See above, 46f.

94. See Althaus, *Gebot und Gesetz*, 22.

95. *Second Lectures on Galatians*, 1531: WA 40.I:291.5, 294.6.

96. *Third Disputation against the Antinomians*, 1538: WA 39.I:563.13, 564.4; *The Private Mass and the Consecration of Priests*, 1533: WA 38:205.26: "... against the devil ⟨you⟩ are able... to boast: 'If I am a sinner, then I am not a sinner; I am a sinner in myself, outside of Christ; outside of myself and in Christ I am not a sinner for Christ has destroyed my sin through his holy blood...'"; *Lectures on Psalms 120–134*, 1532-33: WA 40.III:411.6. — For the difference in the understanding of the new man in Luther's thought and in Pietism, see Pinomaa, "Heiligung bei Luther," *ThZ* 10 (1954): 43ff., where further references are listed. ⟨See also above, 359 n. 21.⟩

97. See Hermann, *Luthers These "Gerecht und Sünder zugleich,"* passim. For this formula, see Alfred Adam, "Bericht über die Theologische Woche in Bethel 1952," *DtPfrBl* 53 (1953): 10. — See also Luther to George Spenlein: Apr. 8, 1516: WA.B 1:35.29: "Christ... dwells only in sinners"; to George Spalatin: Feb. 15, 1518: WA.B 1:145.38: "... all saints are sinners." — For the mingling of good and evil in a Christian, see *First Lectures on the Psalms*, 1513-15: WA 4:364.15: "... we who are righteous always need to be justified"; ibid., WA 4:336.14; sermon of May 28, 1531: WA 34.I:467.4: "... the holy Christian church is holy through the article concerning the forgiveness of sinners, otherwise it is a sinner."

98. *Second Lectures on Galatians*, 1531: WA 40.I:370.10; *Disputation on Justification*,

1536, thesis 27 of the third set of theses on Rom. 3:28: WA 39.I:83.24 ⟨*LW* 34:153⟩. — For the difference in the understanding of "foreign righteousness" *(iustitia aliena)* by Luther and in Lutheran Orthodoxy, see Prenter, *Spiritus creator,* 61: "For Luther our foreign righteousness is the living Christ as person, not a material accomplishment abstracted from him."

99. ⟨ "Passive" in the sense that this righteousness is something which is given to man, and that man 'endures' receiving this gift.⟩ *Second Lectures on Galatians,* 1531: WA 40.I:41.3, 44.9; *Second Commentary on Galatians,* 1535: WA 40.I:45.24. — See also Friedrich Loofs, "Der articulus stantis et cadentis ecclesiae," *ThStKr* 90 (1917): 353ff.; Emanuel Hirsch, "Initium theologiae Lutheri," in *Kaftan Festgabe,* 155ff.; Gyllenkrok, *Rechtfertigung und Heiligung,* 54ff.

100. *First Lectures on the Psalms,* 1513-15: WA 4:19.30 ⟨*LW* 11:174⟩: "In its place ⟨i.e., in the place of original righteousness⟩ the righteousness of Christ is now given us prior to every meritorious work."

101. *Second Lectures on Galatians,* 1531: WA 40.I:364.9. See also *Second Lectures on the Psalms,* 1518-21: WA 5:144.17: "⟨Scripture's⟩ way of speaking about God's righteousness tropologically . . . is different from the usual human way of speaking ⟨and⟩ has created many difficulties for many people. . . ."

102. *First Commentary on Galatians,* 1519: WA 2:498.25: ". . . through faith, love for the law is infused ⟨in man⟩ . . ."; *Disputation on Justification,* 1536: WA 39.I: 115.7: ". . . insofar as the *causa efficiens* is concerned, faith is greater than love"; *The Babylonian Captivity of the Church,* 1520: WA 6:514.19: "God's Word has the first place before all other things; faith follows, and love follows faith. Then love does every good work because it does no evil, in fact, it is the fullness of the law" ⟨in the sense of fulfilling the law; see Rom. 13:10⟩; *First Lectures on the Psalms,* 1513-15: WA 3:454.19: ". . . ⟨faith in Christ⟩ is the true law and the true light"; ibid., WA 4:379.30. — See also Hermann, *Luthers Lehre von Sünde und Rechtfertigung,* 45.

103. ⟨Rom. 3:27.⟩

104. For this development, see Prenter, *Spiritus creator,* 91, 328 n. 223.

105. Therefore Luther rejected the concept *fides charitate formata* ⟨faith formed by love; see Richard A. Muller, *Dictionary,* s.v. "fides caritate formata"⟩; *The Private Mass and the Consecration of Priests,* 1533: WA 38:226.29; *Disputation on Matt. 22:1-14,* 1537: WA 39.I:318.7; *Disputation of John Marbach,* 1543: WA 39.II:207.38, 213.34; Paul Althaus, "Liebe und Heilsgewißheit bei Martin Luther," in *Lortz Festgabe,* 1:71.

106. *The Book of Deuteronomy with Notes,* 1525: WA 14:714.12 ⟨*LW* 9:241⟩: ". . . one must distinguish among laws; there are some which command what is good, others which permit what is evil. Among those which command what is good the first is the law of faith, which also takes precedence over charity. If faith toward God demands it, charity is to be denied to one's neighbor, because God, who is worshiped by faith, must be held higher than man, who is served by charity. After faith comes charity, which sets limits to all laws, the ceremonial as well as the secular, faith alone excepted"; ibid., WA 14:590.32, 609.19.

107. *Postilla for Lent,* 1525: WA 17.II:98.25 (for this passage see also Ernst Wolf, "Frage des Naturrechts bei Thomas und bei Luther," 14); *The Book of Deuteronomy with Notes,* 1525: WA 14:638.29: ". . . the power of the First Commandment . . . is faith . . ."; *The Gospel of the Ten Lepers Explained,* 1521: WA 8:355.20: "Faith and love are the total essence

of a Christian, as I have often said. Faith receives, love gives. Faith brings man to God, love brings man to his fellowmen. Through faith, man lets God do good to him, through love man does good to his fellowmen. He who believes has all things from God, and he is saved ⟨or: 'blessed'⟩ and rich. Therefore from now on he needs nothing further. But he directs his whole life and actions to the good and benefit of his neighbor; through love he does to the neighbor as God has done to him through faith; through faith he draws good from above, through love he does good to below"; *Second Lectures on the Psalms,* 1518-21: WA 5:408.4: "The gate to Christ ⟨John 10:9⟩ is faith. . . . But the exit ⟨see John 10:3b⟩ is love . . ."; *The Private Mass and the Consecration of Priests,* 1533: WA 38:227.6: ". . . the whole Christian life . . . ⟨is to be⟩ faith and love: toward God, faith, which grasps Christ and receives the forgiveness of sin without any works; then follows love toward the neighbor; as the fruit of faith it demonstrates that faith is true and not lazy ⟨or: 'putrid'⟩ or false, but active and living"; *On Good Works,* 1520: WA 6:275.22: faith has to be the *Werckmeyster* ⟨master of works, not only in the sense of overseer but also in the sense of the one who is always working⟩; sermon of May 19, 1522: WA 36:178.15. — See also Prenter, *Spiritus creator,* 97.

108. See Nygren, *Agape and Eros,* Part II.2:500ff.

109. See, however, Walter von Loewenich, *Luther und das Johanneische Evangelium* (Munich, 1935), 13f.

110. ⟨Or: "estate"; see also above, 86.⟩

111. See Luther's statement about the relationship of faith with love with respect to the law of love in *Postilla for Lent,* 1525: WA 17.II:96.28, and Johannes Gottschick, *Luthers Theologie. ZThK* 24 (1914), Ergänzungsheft 1:53: "When Luther designates love alongside of faith as the fulfillment of the First Commandment, then he clarifies what are only different facets of faith." But the reason for this designation of love alongside of faith as the fulfillment of the First Commandment is Luther's understanding of law. See also Althaus, "Liebe und Heilsgewißheit bei Luther," in *Lortz Festgabe,* 1:72: "Love with its manifestations is the mark of true faith." Luther presented a slightly different reason for the connection of faith and love in his letter to John Sylvius Egranus: Feb. 2, 1519: WA.B 1:313.28: ". . . I do not separate justifying faith from love; indeed, ⟨this is the reason for⟩ believing: he in whom one believes pleases ⟨me?⟩ and is being loved. Grace accomplishes that the Word pleases and is being believed; this, however, is to love."

112. *Postilla for Lent,* 1525: WA 17.II:98.19f. See also *Second Lectures on the Psalms,* 1518-21: WA 5:176.8: "One sees that the activity and being of faith, hope, and love are identical"; sermon of Jan. 29, 1531: WA 34.I:140.6.

113. For the different functions and places of law in the history of Salvation, see Thielicke, *Theologische Ethik,* 1:No. 696.

114. ⟨See also above, 86.⟩

115. *Second Lectures on the Psalms,* 1518-21: WA 5:33.25: "But this will ⟨delighting in the Lord's law; Ps. 1:2⟩ comes from faith in God through Jesus Christ." — See also Georg Wehrung, "Theologie, Kirche, Kirchenleitung," *ZSTh* 22 (1953): 155: "Perceiving takes place through receiving in faith, it does not precede this receiving."

116. *Postilla for Christmas,* 1522: WA 10.I.1:233.18: "⟨He who is reborn⟩ becomes a totally new and different human being; he looks at all things differently than before, he judges, evaluates, thinks, wills, speaks, loves, desires, works, and acts differently than before; then he is able to recognize whether all estates and actions of all people are right or

wrong, as St. Paul says in 1 Cor. 2<:15>: 'A spiritual man judges all others, <but> he is judged by no one.'" <See also the Vulgate text: "A spiritual man judges all things, <but> he is judged by no one.">

117. This is identical with being illuminated by Christ; sermon of Nov. 11, 1516: WA 1:100.8: "<Christ is> the true light"; *First Lectures on the Psalms*, 1513-15: WA 4:53.4: "The light of knowing God . . . is faith in Christ"; Luther to George Spalatin: May 18, 1518: WA.B 1:173.39: ". . . we do not preach another light than Jesus Christ, the true and only light." — For the relationship of God's grace *(favor dei)* with faith (God's gift; *donum dei)*, see Prenter, *Spiritus creator,* 46.

118. *Two Sermons on Christ's Passion,* 1518: WA 1:341.37: ". . . Christ's Incarnation and suffering are recommended to us to be viewed for . . . <generating> compassion and educating understanding; yet throughout Scripture they are presented to us much more for <our> contemplation so that we may see and recognize God's love toward us."

119. <Literally: "When he views . . . , the spiritual meaning of Christ's law reveals itself to the intellect . . ."> *First Lectures on the Psalms,* 1513-15: WA 3:172.19: ". . . only the spiritual and believing people have . . . understanding *(intellectus).*"

120. *Lectures on Hebrews,* 1517-18: WA 57.III:200.16: ". . . God's law and wisdom cannot be understood unless they are understood in Christ. . . ."

121. In the sermon of Sept. 16(?), 1516: WA 1:470.16, Luther emphasized the affirmative content of God's law over against the efforts by some Scholastics to weaken God's law by interpreting it negatively; in such an interpretation, e.g., the commandment to love God would only prohibit the hatred for God.

122. *Heidelberg Disputation,* 1518: WA 1:368.26: ". . . whatever is done with less than perfect love <is> sin." <For Luther's text and its context, see *LW* 31:61f.>

123. *First Lectures on Galatians,* 1516-17: WA 57.II:41.17: "There is nothing more deeply rooted in man than that disposition of the mind to love himself"; *Second Lectures on the Psalms,* 1518-21: WA 5:437.15.

124. *Sermons on Matthew, Chapters 5-7,* 1530-32: WA 32:406.29: "<This is> a total, . . . undivided love . . . , that one shows love and does good to the enemy in the same way in which one does good to a friend." The opposite would be a "divided" or "half" love; see also above, 319 n. 143: "piecemeal" vs. "total" equity. — Hans M. Müller ("Das christliche Liebesgebot und die lex naturalae," *ZThK.*N.F. 9 [1928]: 163) argued that "the commandment to love, which we call a Christian commandment, is not a specifically Christian commandment." In this argument the difference between the divine natural-law commandment to love the neighbor and the secular natural-law commandment to love the neighbor has been ignored.

125. *First Lectures on Galatians,* 1516-17: WA 57.II:101.9. For true and false love of the neighbor, see ibid., WA 57.II:101.21. In his *First Commentary on Galatians,* 1519, Luther presented these materials in greater detail; WA 2:577.15ff. <*LW* 27:350ff.>.

126. Therefore one may not wait with helping a brother until he has fallen into "extreme need"; *Disputation on the Power and Will of Man without Grace,* 1516: WA 1:149.20; Luther to John Lang: Oct. 1516: WA.B 1:66.36. In his 1518 *Asterisci* against John Eck's *Obelisci* Luther criticized the efforts to weaken this position; WA 1:304.31. See also *Sermon on the Pope's Indulgence and Grace,* 1518: WA 1:387.19ff., 388.11; Lau, *Luthers Lehre von den beiden Reichen,* 22.

127. With this position Luther stood in sharp opposition to the Scholastics, for

whom the love for the neighbor as *charitas ordinata* (structured love) began with love for self; see the materials presented by Johannes Ficker in *Lectures on Romans*, 1515-16: WA 56:390, note to line 26, 517, note to line 5 ⟨*LW* 25:380f., 512⟩. See also *First Lectures on Galatians*, 1516-17: WA 57.II:100.25; Theodor Heckel, "Regula aurea," in *Zur politischen Predigt*, 57ff.; Wehrung, *Welt und Reich*, 282: "love which does not know that it is love." ⟨Following Augustine, some of the Scholastics argued that immediately after his love for God man loves himself; this love for self manifests itself in man's desire to gain Salvation for his soul. *Charitas ordinata* means love is active in a certain structure: man loves God first, then man loves his soul, then man loves his neighbor and his neighbor's soul, and finally man loves his body. This structure extends to the degrees in which a neighbor is connected with me; the closer the connection, the greater is my duty to love him. See also Holl, *Luther*, 165, 210.⟩

128. Theses 52-54 of *Disputation on Faith and Law*, 1535: WA 39.I:47.25ff. ⟨Heckel adjusted the opening phrase to read: "having the law," i.e., the law of Christ.⟩

129. *First Lectures on the Psalms*, 1513-15: WA 4:286.22.36: ". . . the works of Christ's law are lofty and heavenly. . . . In the gospel are commanded both, to do good and to endure evil, both ⟨to be done⟩ in a heroic way and with the . . . highest degree of ability and will, as in the case of the martyrs." — In *German Exposition of the Lord's Prayer for Simple Laymen*, 1519: WA 2:88.10 ⟨*LW* 42:28⟩, Luther described the qualities and actions of a child of God.

130. ⟨This becoming more fervent of the faith, and the becoming more divine and all-encompassing of the Christian commandment of love⟩ go hand in hand, so to speak. Therefore it seems that Paul Althaus, *Paulus und Luther über den Menschen* (Gütersloh, 1938), 70, has to be expanded, when he stated: "The reformers maintain the concept 'perfection of the Christian'. . . . Yet not love and obedience but repentance and faith will be perfected. Christian perfection is the maturity of repentance and faith."

131. *On Secular Authority*, 1523: WA 11:249.18: "Perfection and imperfection are not matters of works and do not create a special external status among Christians ⟨as, e.g., the clerical or monastic estate over against the laity⟩, but are matters of the heart, faith, and love; he who believes and loves more is perfect." In God's judgment, therefore, there is no difference in works as such; *On Monastic Vows*, 1521: WA 8:638.16.

132. *First Lectures on the Psalms*, 1513-15: WA 3:512.24: "⟨On the way⟩ from the beginning of holiness to perfection are infinite steps"; ibid., WA 4:217.30; *Sermons on the Ten Commandments*, 1518: WA 1:466.8, 467.20; sermon of Nov. 30, 1516 (WA 1:102.13), and of Dec. 27, 1517 (WA 1:115.12); *Second Lectures on the Psalms*, 1518-21: WA 5:224.20. — Since the goodness of an action permitted according to the secular natural law depends on the faith of the actor, the ⟨medieval⟩ concept 'the *perfect estate* of the clergy and religious' is the absolute opposite of Luther's position. *Not the estate is perfect; perfect is only its correct use in faith.* ⟨Italics by this ed.⟩ Therefore the medieval differentiation between a perfect person and a perfect estate is also nullified. See *On Monastic Vows*, 1521: WA 8:584.23; *On Secular Authority*, 1523: WA 11:249.9.18; *Postilla for Christmas*, 1522: WA 10. I.1:496.8. (For the discussion of Luther's position, see, on the one side, Prenter, *Spiritus creator*, 85, 103f., and Pinomaa, "Heiligung bei Luther," *ThZ* 10 [1954]: 39f., and on the other side, Gyllenkrok, *Rechtfertigung und Heiligung*, 111.) — For the medieval materials, see, e.g., Aegidius Romanus ⟨Giles of Rome⟩, *De ecclesiastica potestate*, ed. by Richard Scholz (Weimar, 1929), book I, chapt. 2 (p. 7: "There are two kinds of perfection, two kinds of ho-

liness, two kinds of spirituality: one according to the person, the other according to the estate ⟨or: 'status'⟩, so that the clerical estate is more perfect than the estate of the laity and lords as of subjects"); *Decretum Gratiani* p. c.14. D.II. de poen., and ibid., c.15 ⟨Friedberg 1: 1194-96⟩.

133. *First Lectures on the Psalms*, 1513-15: WA 4:319.8 ⟨*LW* 11:433⟩: ⟨2 Cor. 3:18.⟩ "So it happens also in the active life: It is always a progressing from act to act, from virtue to virtue, as here ⟨i.e., in the understanding of Scripture⟩ it is from understanding to understanding, from faith to faith, from glory to glory, from knowledge to knowledge. This is the true contemplative life. And thus the first step is always the spirit, and the later step is the letter. Therefore, as the end is not to be obtained speculatively, so it is not actively either."

134. ⟨See Eph. 4:13.⟩ Wingren, *Die Predigt*, 100ff. — Man's fundamental attitude in the process of such growth is humility; *Second Lectures on the Psalms*, 1518-21: WA 5:141.30: "Nothing can please God unless it is done in humility."

135. *On Christian Freedom* ⟨Latin text⟩, 1520: WA 7:69.12: "Therefore we conclude that a Christian does not live in himself but in Christ and in his neighbor, otherwise he is not a Christian. Through faith he lives in Christ, through love he lives in the neighbor. Through faith he is lifted up above himself to God, through love he is moved again down, below himself, to his neighbor, and yet he always remains in God and God's love." ⟨See also above, 370 n. 107.⟩ — See Wingren's critical remarks (*Luthers Lehre vom Beruf*, 46) regarding "a general shortcoming in modern Luther research"; "one always deals with faith, but one does not at the same time deal with love, one deals with man's relationship with God without at the same time dealing with man's relationship with his fellowman."

136. See above, 50f.

137. *On Christian Freedom* ⟨Latin text⟩, 1520: WA 7:65.26.32 ⟨*LW* 31:366⟩: "So a Christian, like Christ his head, is filled and made rich by faith and should be content with this form of God which he has obtained by faith; only, as I have said, he should increase this faith until it is made perfect.... Although the Christian is thus free from all works, he ought to empty himself again..., take upon himself the form of a servant, be made in the likeness of men, be found in human form, and to serve, help, and in every way deal with his neighbor as he sees that God through Christ has dealt and still deals with him." ⟨See also Phil. 2:6-8.⟩

138. In the relationship with fellow Christians, this help takes the form of brotherly friendship *(fraterna amicitia); Lectures on Hebrews*, 1517-18: WA 57.III:85.23: to Hebr. 13:1: "... for Christians not only friendship is proper, but ⟨only⟩ brotherly friendship...." ⟨The Vulgate text of Hebr. 13:1 reads literally: "love *(charitas)* of the brotherhood"; NRSV: "mutual love."⟩

139. *First Lectures on the Psalms*, 1513-15: WA 3:427.10 ⟨*LW* 10:365⟩: "... it is characteristic of divine love to love and desire the good for someone, not any kind of good nor for any kind of purpose, but eternal good and for spiritual welfare."

140. For Luther 'Christian law' or 'law of Christians' designated the following: (1) The legal order among Christians, which is the result of obedience to the divine natural law ⟨in Christ's interpretation⟩, i.e., Christ's law; *To the Christian Nobility*, 1520: WA 6:418.7, as above, 302 n. 5; see also above, 117. (2) The right, i.e., the privilege, to bear the cross in following Christ. When Luther had this second meaning in mind, he used 'Christian law' or 'law of Christians' sometimes with the meaning 'objective' law ⟨in the sense of law pertaining to things or situations⟩, sometimes with the meaning 'subjective' law

⟨in the sense of law pertaining to persons⟩. See *Admonition to Peace,* 1525: WA 18:309.15ff.: Rom. 12:19, 1 Cor. 6:1f., 2 Cor. 11:20, Matt. 5:44, "these are our Christian laws..."; ibid., WA 18:310.6 ⟨*LW* 46:29⟩: "On the basis of these passages even a child can understand that the Christian law tells us not to strive against injustice, not to grasp the sword, not to protect ourselves, not to avenge ourselves, but to give up life and property, and let whoever takes it have it. We have all we need in our Lord, who will not leave us, as he has promised [Heb. 13:5]. Suffering! suffering! Cross! cross! This and nothing else is the Christian law!" See also ibid., WA 18:311.1, 312.8 ⟨*LW* 46:29f.⟩. — For the cross as the treasure and mark *(nota)* of the believers, see Luther to Anthony Lauterbach: May 5, 1542: WA.B 10:59.10. For 'Christian law' as divine positive law, see above, 362 n. 39. — Wehrung (*Welt und Reich,* 77) was critical of Luther's position: "When Luther tells the peasants that suffering and the cross are the true law of Christians, does he really answer the question what one has to tell to a totally oppressed estate on the basis of the gospel?" But this was not Luther's intention at all; he opposed the mingling of the spiritual with the political freedom!

141. *Second Lectures on the Psalms,* 1518-21: WA 5:432.9; *Second Disputation against the Antinomians,* 1538: WA 39.I:452.13, 453.1.

142. *First Commentary on Galatians,* 1519: WA 2:579.12 ⟨*LW* 27:353⟩: "... the cross is the means of testing and, as they say, the Lydian touchstone of love...." See also Lau, *Luthers Lehre von den beiden Reichen,* 58.

143. *On Christian Freedom* ⟨Latin text⟩, 1520: WA 7:66.3: "I shall give myself as Christ to my neighbor..."; ibid., WA 7:66.35: "... one to another we are Christ, and we do to the neighbor as Christ has done to us."

144. See above, 302 n. 5 (the last text).

145. *That These Words of Christ, "This is My Body," Still Stand Firm against the Fanatics,* 1527: WA 23.189.15: "... who serves his neighbor and does it ⟨only⟩ corporeally will not derive any good from it.... But if he does it spiritually, i.e., if his heart does it, motivated by faith in God's Word, then it is life and Salvation. There is one kind of corporeal neighbor with whom he deals, but two kinds of dealing with this neighbor. The body does not know what it does and lets itself be driven like an animal. But the heart certainly knows what the body does. From what source? Not from the neighbor but from God's Word, which says: 'Love your neighbor.'"

146. Sermon of Dec. 7, 1516: WA 1:105.25. — See also Olavi Tarvainen, "Der Gedanke der Conformitas Christi in Luthers Theologie," *ZSTh* 22 (1953): 22ff.; Prenter, *Spiritus creator,* 26ff.

147. *The Babylonian Captivity of the Church,* 1520: WA 6:529.19: "... vanity of vanities and torture of the spirit are the things with which one is being vexed ⟨if one is⟩ outside of faith in God's truth."

148. *Sixteen Theses on Faith and Ceremonies,* 1520: WA 6:380.26: "Everything which does not originate in faith is sin"; ibid., WA 6:380.23; *Second Lectures on the Psalms,* 1518-21: WA 5:396.14; sermons of ca. 1514-21: WA 4:696.9.24.

149. *The Babylonian Captivity of the Church,* 1520: WA 6:539.9: "God evaluates ⟨righteousness and holiness⟩ alone on the basis of faith; with God there is no difference in works, except that there is a difference in the degree of faith."

150. *On Monastic Vows,* 1521: WA 8:606.31: "This... is Christian freedom or evangelical freedom of the conscience, ⟨that⟩ the conscience is set free from works, not that works

should not be done, but that the conscience does not trust in works." For 'freedom of conscience', see Ernst Wolf, *Peregrinatio*, 1:92ff.

151. *The New Testament in German*, 1522: WA.DB 7:10.9: "Speaking of faith, oh, how lively, busy, active, and powerful a thing it is, so that it is impossible that faith does not do good incessantly. Also, faith does not ask whether good works should be done, but before one ⟨even⟩ asks, faith has done good works and is always doing them"; *Second Lectures on the Psalms*, 1518-21: WA 5:460.13: "... faith ... is never idle, in fact, it is always extremely busy"; Luther to Duke Charles III of Savoy: Sept. 7, 1523: WA.B 3:151.56: "... through active *(efficax)* love we demonstrate faith ..."; *First Lectures on the Psalms*, 1513-15: WA 4:326.28.

152. *Second Lectures on the Psalms*, 1518-21: WA 5:176.4. See also *First Lectures on the Psalms*, 1513-15: WA 4:356.32 ⟨*LW* 11:486⟩: "But when you have begun to walk and to do what you believe, then the way is recognized more clearly than your feet recognize it, so that you have the light more brightly as a result of doing than as a result of believing with the heart alone. For while you believe, you have the light shut up in the heart, but when you act, then you will be led correctly on the way by the light that has now, as it were, been brought out. The doers are much more enlightened in faith than the speculative, as even the philosopher ⟨i.e., Aristotle⟩ says in his *Metaphysics* ⟨1.1⟩, that an experienced person acts more surely"; *Second Lectures on Galatians*, 1531: WA 40.I:415.3; sermon of June 10, 1537: WA 45:99.22.

153. *On Good Works*, 1520: WA 6:206.15.

154. Ibid., WA 6:213.14. See also *The Babylonian Captivity of the Church*, 1520: WA 6:520.26: "Faith is not a work but the teacher and life of works."

155. *Second Lectures on the Psalms*, 1518-21: WA 5:177.21: "The will which has been incarnate or poured out in an external work can correctly be called to cooperate ⟨with the Creator⟩ ..."; ibid., WA 5:408.4: "The gate to Christ ⟨John 10:9⟩ is faith; it brings us into the richness of God's righteousness through which we have already satisfied God, are righteous, and not in need of works in order to procure righteousness. But the exit ⟨see John 10:3b⟩ is love; it distributes us, who have been covered with God's righteousness, ⟨in⟩ the service of our neighbor and the exercise of our body, with the goal of coming to the aid of the poverty of others so that they, too, drawn through us, will enter Christ together with us"; ibid., WA 5:230.13: "⟨David⟩ descends from the love for God to the love for the neighbor in order to serve people on the basis of the same commandment of God"; ibid., WA 5:169.8: good works are done by those who do them "as if they were God's tools"; ibid., WA 5:169.12: "Good works ⟨are done⟩ when God himself alone and totally does them in us so that no part of the work belongs to us"; *On Justification*, 1530: WA 30.II:659.32: "One does not believe because of works, but works are done because of faith. Faith does not require works in order to be justified by them, but works require faith so that they become righteous through it. Faith is, then, the active righteousness of the works, and the works are the passive righteousness of faith." ⟨See also above, 370 n. 107.⟩ — For 'cooperation of God and man', see *The Bondage of the Will*, 1525: WA 18:753.25 ⟨*LW* 33:241f.⟩. — See also Ritschl, *Dogmengeschichte*, 2.I:151.

156. For the fact and the reason that God does not need man's good works yet wants them to be done, see *The Babylonian Captivity of the Church*, 1520: WA 6:516.32; *Second Lectures on Galatians*, 1531: WA 40.II:66.9: "It is equally necessary ⟨now⟩ to promote the doctrine of good works, as it was previously necessary to promote the doctrine of

faith. . . ." — See also Robert Stupperich, "Die guten Werke in der Theologie Martin Luthers," in *Schreiner Festgabe,* 289ff.

157. *Second Lectures on Galatians,* 1531: WA 40.II:78.6: "It is dangerous and difficult to teach at the same time that we are justified without works and yet demand works. If we teach works, faith is being lost. If the opposite, etc." — For the correct intention for doing works, see Luther to George Spalatin: Feb. 15, 1518: WA.B 1:145.12ff.

158. *Second Lectures on Galatians,* 1531: WA 40.I:287.3: "⟨Good works are⟩ to be done as fruit of righteousness, but they are not to be done as means of producing righteousness. We who have been made righteous must do them, not the other way around. The ⟨good⟩ tree must bear fruit."

159. *On Christian Freedom* ⟨Latin text⟩, 1520: WA 7:63.15: ". . . we do not . . . reject good works, in fact, we especially embrace and teach them"; ibid., WA 7:64.15.20: "Man does not live for himself and by himself alone in this mortal body for the purpose of functioning in it; rather, he lives also for all people on earth, in fact, he lives only for others and not for himself. . . . Therefore it is impossible that he be idle in this life and without ⟨doing⟩ works directed toward his neighbors"; ibid., WA 7:61.2: comparison of the works of a believer with those of Adam and Eve in Paradise; *Disputation on Justification,* 1536: WA 39.I:96.6 ⟨LW 34:165⟩: "Works are necessary to salvation, but they do not cause salvation, because faith alone gives life. On account of the hypocrites we must say that good works are necessary to salvation. It is necessary to work. Nevertheless, it does not follow that works save on that account, unless we understand necessity very clearly as the necessity that there must be an inward and outward salvation or righteousness. Works save outwardly, that is, they show evidence that we are righteous and that there is faith in a man which saves inwardly . . ."; ibid., WA 39.I:114.28: "True faith is not idle." See also above, 273 n. 12.

160. For the following, see also Gyllenkrok, *Rechtfertigung und Heiligung,* 81ff.

161. *Sermons on Matthew, Chapters 5-7,* 1530-32: WA 32:488.20: ". . . next to the office of preaching, prayer is the noblest work of a Christian. . . ."

162. See Eduard Ellwein, *Vom neuen Leben* (Munich, 1932), 98ff.; Joest, *Gesetz und Freiheit,* 110.

163. *Assertion of All Articles,* 1520: WA 7:107.3: ⟨The parable of the good Samaritan⟩ "shows that no one will suddenly be healed from all his sins, but having been received in the body of Christ through the covenant of faith he is increasingly healed from day to day." — For Christ as physician and medicine, see *Second Lectures on the Psalms,* 1518-21: WA 5:311.1.

164. *On Christian Freedom* ⟨German text⟩, 1520: WA 7:30.15. — For fasting with a proper Christian attitude, see *Sermons on Matthew, Chapters 5-7,* 1530-32: WA 32:432.1, 433.10.

165. See Hermann, *Luthers These "Gerecht und Sünder zugleich,"* 207ff.; Gyllenkrok, *Rechtfertigung und Heiligung,* 85ff.; Joest, *Gesetz und Freiheit,* 124ff.

166. For Augustine's and Luther's position on partial justification, see Pinomaa, "Heiligung bei Luther," *ThZ* 10 (1954): 31; Prenter, *Spiritus creator,* 46f., and id., "Luthers Lehre von der Heiligung," in *Lutherforschung heute,* 69; Philip Watson, "Luther und die Heiligung," in *Lutherforschung heute,* 82.

167. *First Disputation against the Antinomians,* 1537: WA 39.I:394.14: ". . . the whole

life of the believers is an effort against, and some sort of hatred for, the remains of sin in the flesh which rebels against the spirit and faith."

168. For the following, see the brief by Luther and others: Jan. 25, 1544: WA.B 10:512.14.19, 513.43, and esp. Hermann, *Luthers These "Gerecht und Sünder zugleich,"* 164ff.

169. *Against Latomus*, 1521: WA 8:120.35: ⟨Luther dealt with Rom. 7:16.⟩ ". . . who agrees with a good law, ⟨but⟩ does what he does not will to do, i.e., does what is contrary to the good law which he wills to ⟨obey⟩ . . . ⟨follows Rom. 7:17⟩."

170. *Lectures on Romans*, 1515-16: WA 56:351.11 ⟨*LW* 25:340⟩: ". . . concupiscence is that weakness in us toward the good. In itself the concupiscence is guilty, to be sure, but yet it does not render us guilty unless we yield to it and commit sin. From this comes the remarkable fact that we are guilty and not guilty. For we ourselves are this weakness, therefore it is guilty and we are guilty until this weakness ceases and is cleansed. But we are not guilty as long as we do not act in accord with this weakness, since God in His mercy does not impute the guilt of the weakness but only the guilt of the will which consents to the weakness"; *Second Lectures on the Psalms*, 1518-21: WA 5:280.11: "If you sin and fall, do not despair of Christ, for you do not fall out of Christ's realm *(imperium)* unless you have ceased to be God's handiwork. If you acknowledge Christ's rule, and together with that man in The Wisdom of Solomon 15⟨:2⟩ say to Christ, 'Even if we have sinned, we are yours, knowing of your power, etc.,' he cannot send you away, and you will not be sent away by him unless you do not trust in his mercy. He will acknowledge you to be his own if you have acknowledged him to be your lord"; sermon of Nov. 1, 1523: WA 12:676.18: "⟨Christ⟩ has . . . established such a kingdom in which only never-ending grace is present; in this kingdom you are to be forgiven for all things, regardless how often you sin, because Christ has let the gospel be proclaimed, which announces that there is no punishment but only grace. Because now this governance is present, you may always get up again ⟨after you have fallen into sin⟩, regardless how deep and often you are falling from this governance. Even if you fall, this gospel and throne of mercy will always be present. Therefore as soon as you approach it again . . . , you have grace again"; sermons of ca. 1514-21: WA 4:692.3.

171. Instead of other scholastic authors, see Biel, *Collectorium*, lib. II. dist. 22. q. un.dub.2.J.

172. For an overview of this problem, see Hans Welzel, *Vom irrenden Gewissen* (Tübingen, 1949), in which Luther's position is not discussed, however; id., "Gesetz und Gewissen," in *Hundert Jahre deutschen Rechtslebens. Festschrift zum hundertjährigen Bestehen des Deutschen Juristentages 1860-1960*, ed. by Ernst von Caemmerer et al., 1 (Karlsruhe, 1960), 383ff.

173. ⟨ "Error" in the sense of ignorance which causes error in man's judgment.⟩ Thesis 35 of *Disputation against Scholastic Theology*, 1517: WA 1:225.38 ⟨*LW* 31:11⟩: "It is not true that an invincible ignorance excuses one completely (all scholastics notwithstanding)"; Luther to George Spalatin: Nov. 11, 1517: WA.B 1:124.17: "Certainly, for us all ignorance is invincible, but for God's grace no ignorance is invincible." ⟨In this letter Luther elaborated on thesis 35. He rejected the differentiation the Scholastics had made between vincible and invincible ignorance (error) in the judgment of a man's conscience regarding a specific moral issue. (For material from Gabriel Biel's *Commentary on the Sentences of Peter Lombard*, see n. 2 of WA.B 1:124; for additional scholastic materials, see

Martin Luther. Studienausgabe, 1, ed. by Hans-Ulrich Delius [Berlin, 1979], 168, nn. 38, 40; for Thomas Aquinas, see *TRE. Studienausgabe*, 13:221.27ff.) For the Scholastics an error in the judgment of a man's conscience was invincible (Luther's invincible ignorance), i.e., could not have been avoided or defeated, if it was the result of an (unintended) lack of knowledge ('I tried my best, but I didn't know better'), and therefore the erring conscience was excused. Conversely, an error was vincible, i.e., could have been avoided or defeated, if it was the result of a man's stubborn refusal to develop (or accept) knowledge ('you could have known better, but you didn't want to') — in the letter Luther called it *crassa ignorantia*, so did Biel — and therefore the erring conscience not only was not excused but it "enlarged the sin" (so Luther, and also Biel). Luther concluded: "... it is not true that invincible ignorance excuses from guilt for committing sin; were it otherwise there would be no sin in the world."⟩

174. See above, 17, 87f. In contrast, according to the Scholastics, for a heathen or a Christian an invincible error is no sin at all.

175. For a concrete situation which shows the possibility that a conscience could err, see Luther to Lazarus Spengler(?): March 18, 1531: WA.B 6:57.33. ⟨This was the issue: May a Christian with a good conscience enter an alliance against Emperor Charles V who unjustly deals with the subscribers of the *Augsburg Confession?*⟩: "... when one starts something and truly trusts God, it will end well, even if it would be an error and sin. . . ."

176. *Lectures on Psalm 51*, 1532: WA 40.II:409.12: "When the conscience is confounded, only listening to ⟨the word of the forgiveness of sins⟩ accomplishes something, yet nothing but running around happens. The conscience is as smart as a goose. The goose wants to escape the hawk by flying, yet it should be running; when the wolf threatens the goose, it wants to run in order to escape, though it should fly. So when we are oppressed by ⟨God's⟩ wrath and the pangs of conscience, we run hither and yon.... We want to calm the conscience *active* ⟨i.e., by doing something⟩, we do not want the *passivum* ⟨in the sense of receiving the Word, or enduring or suffering⟩." ⟨Heckel cited the notes of the lecture delivered in class; for the translation it was necessary to use also the edited version of the lecture, which is translated in *LW* 12:368.⟩ — See also Hans M. Müller, *Erfahrung und Glaube bei Luther*, 22.

177. For the difference in the standards, and in the actions determined by them, in Christ's kingdom on the one side, the kingdom of the world on the other side, see *Second Lectures on the Psalms*, 1518-21: WA 5:671.33.36: "... the people of other kings are shaped by laws, morals, and customs. But through these you cannot bring them to true righteousness; ⟨you accomplish⟩ only a fable of righteousness and a theatrical production.... The people of this king ⟨i.e., Christ⟩ are not shaped by laws for the sake of appearance, but they are totally ⟨re⟩born through the Spirit and water to the new creature of truth ⟨John 3:5⟩." This statement agrees with the fact that the divine natural law is no law in the sense of an earthly law ⟨it is "empty law" *(lex vacua)* law; see above, 47, 368 n. 85⟩; therefore Christians live without laws.

178. *The Babylonian Captivity of the Church*, 1520: WA 6:540.3: "A Christian is bound to no law except the divine law."

179. *The Bondage of the Will*, 1525: WA 18:654.10 ⟨*LW* 33:91f.⟩: "... for laws are made in order that conduct may be regulated according to a certain pattern, and questions of dispute thus settled. That which is the standard and measure of other things, therefore, as the law is, ought to be the clearest and most certain of all. And if this light and certainty

in laws is necessary, and is granted freely to the whole world by the bounty of God, in profane societies which have to do with temporal things, how is it conceivable that he should not give his Christians, his elect, laws and rules of much greater light and certainty by which they might direct themselves and settle all their disputes, seeing that he wishes temporal things to be despised by those who are his?"

180. *Second Lectures on Galatians,* 1531: WA 40.I:569.12: ". . . the law is above man; no one judges the law except a Christian"; ibid., WA 40.II:71.1: ". . . the whole world does not comprehend ⟨the word, 'love your neighbor as yourself'; Gal. 5:14⟩; nevertheless, the world says that it knows this word and has it written in the heart — yet it does not understand it. . . ."

181. *On Secular Authority,* 1523: WA 11:252.16: "Christ's governance does not extend to all people; at all times the Christians are the minority and live among non-Christians."

182. In the Decalogue this Christian natural law is expressed in the First Commandment; therefore Luther understood it as the standard for all the other commandments. See, e.g., *The Book of Deuteronomy with Notes,* 1525: WA 14:611.31 ⟨*LW* 9:70⟩: ". . . the First Commandment ⟨is⟩ the measure and yardstick of all others . . ."; *The Large Catechism,* 1529: WA 30.I:137.2 ⟨*BC* 369. 31⟩. — For Luther's various interpretations of the First Commandment, see Bornkamm, *Luther und das Alte Testament,* 151. — See also Olsson, *Grundproblemet,* 1:55: "A Christian fulfills the natural law ⟨in the sense of divine natural law⟩, the natural person ⟨see above, 358 n. 10⟩ by contrast does not"; ibid., 59: "The faith that expresses a Christian's relationship with God . . . is the organizing principle for Christian action"; ibid., 64: "Reason is the organizing principle for a ⟨natural⟩ person's action."

183. Since in God's presence only a believer can have a good conscience, Luther occasionally equated faith and conscience; e.g., *Lectures on 1 John,* 1527: WA 20:718.19: "Faith is nothing other than a good conscience." — See also Ernst Wolf, "Vom Problem des Gewissens in reformatorischer Sicht," in id., *Peregrinatio,* 1:93 n. 27.

184. Holl (*Luther,* 251) erred when he argued that Luther considered "the idea of the invisible congregation of God's kingdom" to be the standard for the construction of a correct social order. This argument results in a confusion of the divine natural law with the secular natural law.

185. ⟨See also above, 27f., 149, 357 n. 50.⟩

186. Faith marks the spiritual boundaries *(termini spirituales)* between both kinds of people; *Second Lectures on the Psalms,* 1518-21: WA 5:455.34: ⟨Deut. 32:8f.⟩ ". . . fixed are . . . the spiritual boundaries of the people according to the number of the spiritual children so that wherever in the whole world my ⟨i.e., God's⟩ believers cease to be, there begin the unbelievers. The two do not intermingle ⟨according⟩ to the spirit, though they might intermingle according to the body. Faith, however, is the border or measuring cord, that distributor of the inheritance ⟨i.e., of God's children⟩. . . ."

187. *Second Lectures on Galatians,* 1531: WA 40.I:235.3: "⟨Man⟩ to the extent that he is a Christian is above all law, because he has . . . Christ, the lord of the law"; ibid., WA 40.I:235.8: "A Christian, to the extent that he is a Christian, is free from all laws and not subject to law, neither internally nor externally." A Christian is a person (ibid., WA 40.I:235.10) whose "conscience ⟨and⟩ heart are filled, . . . with faith," or a person (ibid., WA 40.I:236.4) who is "set up as lord over all laws"; *Admonition to Peace,* 1525: WA 18:308.16: the Christian law does not obligate the heathen to obey, as do the divine and

the ⟨secular⟩ natural law; ibid., WA 18:319.9: "... you ⟨i.e., the rebelling peasants⟩ have forgotten the Christian law"; Luther to Gerard Wiskamp: Jan. 1, 1528: WA.B 4:319.14.

188. See above, 86-89.⟩.

189. *Admonition to Peace,* 1525: WA 18:329.4: "Heathen or worldly law." This phrase does not simply designate something "universal-human in contrast to Christian, a word which always is connected with something specific" (Lau, *"Äußerliche Ordnung,"* 56f.), but through the connection with the kingdom of the world and its members the phrase has a fixed, law-creating meaning.

190. ⟨No one is a citizen of both kingdoms.⟩ This applies also to those who are Christians in name only; *First Lectures on the Psalms,* 1513-15: WA 3:631.31 ⟨LW 11:124⟩: "... we are fellow citizens of the saints and of the household of God (Eph. 2:19). But they are citizens of the world and members of the devil's household. We are foreigners and strangers of the world, while they are foreigners and strangers of God"; ibid., WA 3:632.11 ⟨LW 11:125⟩: "They are strangers and visitors, and they have a share in the same city, but they are not citizens"; ibid., WA 4:454.2: "The Lord watches over the foreigners ⟨Ps. 146: 9⟩, i.e., all who are pilgrims in the world, the citizens of heaven." (For the legal status of the foreigner according to German law, see Hans Thieme, "Die Rechtsstellung des Fremden in Deutschland vom 11. bis zum 18. Jahrhundert," *Recueils de la Société Jean Bodin* 10 [Brussels, 1958]: 201ff.) — See also *First Lectures on the Psalms,* 1513-15: WA 4:250.30 ⟨LW 11:385⟩: "... it has rightly been said that for a righteous man there is no law (1 Tim. 1:9), because he goes beyond the law, and therefore is exceedingly willing in it"; *Sermons on the First Epistle of St. Peter,* 1523: WA 12:291.3: "In prior days you have been citizens in the world and lived under ⟨the authority of⟩ the devil. Now God has pulled you out of this way of living and placed you into another estate so that you are citizens in heaven but foreigners and guests on earth"; ibid., WA 12:394.24: "Here we are in the devil's kingdom, we are like a pilgrim who enters a hostel, of which he knows that all people in the house are robbers..."; ibid., WA 12: 321.28.32: "You are to follow ⟨Christ⟩ and conduct yourselves as if you were no longer citizens in the world.... The devil is ⟨the⟩ prince of the world and rules it, and his ⟨citizens⟩ are the people of the world. Therefore, because you are not of the world, conduct yourselves as if you were a foreigner in a hostel"; ibid., WA 12:322.6: "In heaven we are citizens, on earth we are pilgrims and guests"; sermon of Aug. 11, 1532: WA 36:495.20: "The world and what belongs to it has to have the devil as its lord; with all his might he attaches himself to us, and he is far superior to us, for we are his guests as if we were in a strange hostel"; *John, Chapters 3 and 4 Explained in Sermons,* 1538-40: WA 47:19.24: "This is the way a Christian thinks: 'Today here on earth as a guest..., but tomorrow... life eternal where we are citizens and have our citizenship in the kingdom of heaven,'..."; Luther and other theologians to John Weinlöben and James Stradner: Oct. 12, 1540: WA.B 9:244.4: "... the church in the world is in exile..."; sermon of May 4, 1544: WA 49:392.6: "... ⟨I⟩ am baptized into another citizenship" ⟨than the citizenship in the kingdom of the world⟩; ibid., WA 49:392.15: "God ⟨calls us to be⟩ heavenly citizens ⟨but⟩ guests, pilgrims, and foreigners in the world"; sermon of April 26, 1545: WA 49:722.36: "In the world you are to be obedient, not for the sake of the ⟨secular⟩ lord but for the sake of being a Christian ⟨literally: 'for the sake of your *Christentum*'; see above, 365 n. 63⟩. We obey the emperor not because he is the emperor but in order to please and serve our Lord God so that we are called a servant of God, a maid of God." Forck, *Königsherrschaft Jesu Christi,* 132, agreed with Luther at this point. — See also *First Lectures on the Psalms,* 1513-

15: WA 3:121.31, 484.36, 597.19; sermon of Nov. 1, 1537: WA 45:214.2, and Andrew Poach's edited version of this sermon (1572), WA 45:214.33; sermon of Apr. 27, 1539: WA 47:737.24.34, 738.27, 739.21, 741.23.

Wendland ("Weltherrschaft Christi," in *Stählin Festschrift*, 24ff.) agreed with the position developed in the text above ⟨93⟩, Hans Köhler ("Das Problem der politischen Ethik in der systematischen Theologie unserer Zeit," *ELKZ* 9 [1955]: 122ff., esp. 125) opposed it when he argued: "We are citizens of two worlds." Prenter, *Spiritus creator*, 225, was correct when he argued: "Everyone is always either in one or the other of the two kingdoms."

According to Arnold, *Naturrecht bei Luther*, 39, a Christian is a citizen of two kingdoms. In support of this argument one could cite Luther's *Disputation on Matt. 19:21*, 1539: WA 39.II:81.16: "As a Christian, a Christian lives in the First Table, only outside of the heavenly kingdom is he a citizen of this world. Therefore he has two *politeuma* ⟨Phil. 3:20 (Greek text); *conversatio* (Vulgate); "citizenship" (NRSV)⟩, being subject to Christ through faith, being subject to the emperor through the body." The context supplies the true meaning of this passage. Luther replied to the argument that a Christian is not to concern himself with the world because his *politeuma* is in heaven. He argued that a Christian may not withdraw from the responsibility for the well-being of his fellowmen in the world but has to conduct himself according to the emperor's laws. "Citizen of this world" does not designate a person who has citizenship in the kingdom of the world ⟨the way Luther understood this term⟩, but it designates a subject of a secular governmental authority. See thesis 30 of this disputation, WA 39.II:40.36: "Outside of an issue in which a stand has to be taken for the sake of the faith *(causa confessionis)*, a Christian is a citizen of this world and must do and endure the things of his citizenship according to the Second Table"; see also *Sermons on Matthew, Chapters 5-7*, 1530-32: WA 32:391.9f.

One also has to correct the following: *Das Evangelium und die Ordnungen des öffentlichen Lebens*, ed. by Eberhard Klügel (Göttingen, 1952), 19: ". . . an individual Christian has his estate in both kingdoms as a citizen of two kingdoms"; ⟨but see also⟩ ibid., 20: "In the world ⟨a Christian⟩ lives simultaneously as . . . a foreigner and pilgrim in faith." Ernst Kinder, "Politische Verantwortung des Christen," *ELKZ* 8 (1954): 34: "A Christian as a citizen of two kingdoms . . . , ⟨is⟩ a citizen of two worlds, which both are God's worlds; yet for the sake of their different final purposes different legal principles are valid in them. Therefore we cannot unite them in one kingdom, but we have to see the fundamental and always present double aspect of God's world policy and clearly differentiate between both kingdoms"; ibid., 35, the phrase "eschatologische Fremdlingschaft" (eschatological status of the foreigner in this world). See also above, 105. Gollwitzer, *Christliche Gemeinde*, 8: "A Christian . . . ⟨is⟩ a citizen of both kingdoms." Althaus ("Die beiden Regimente bei Luther," *ThLZ* 81 [1956]: 134f.) defended the old formula ⟨that a Christian is a citizen in both kingdoms⟩ by arguing that "a Christian is a 'citizen' in the political world"; see also id., "Luther und die Bergpredigt," *Luther* 1956:7: "A Christian lives in two spaces or dimensions" — but in a kingdom one is either a citizen or a foreigner! Lau (*Luthers Lehre von den beiden Reichen*, 34) also used the phrase 'citizen of two worlds' in connection with a Christian, but he did it in a way which lacks juristic precision. (See also Lau's review of Hans R. Gerstenkorn, *Weltlich Regiment zwischen Gottesreich und Teufelsmacht. Die staatstheoretischen Auffassungen Martin Luthers und ihre politische Bedeutung*, in *LuJ* 26 [1959]: 143.) Kurt Klein, *Kirche und Staat* (Berlin,

1953), 12, argued in a similar way: "The doctrine of the two governances . . . demonstrates that we are citizens in both kingdoms."

191. *First Lectures on the Psalms*, 1513-15: WA 3:484.36 ⟨*LW* 10:426⟩: ". . . the saints, though they are in the days of the wicked, yet . . . they do not share with them in anything of this world. . . . the wicked share in nothing of the spirit . . ."; *Lectures on Romans*, 1515-16: WA 56:476.20 ⟨*LW* 25:468⟩: ". . . the spirit of the believers cannot be or become subject to anyone but is exalted with Christ in God . . ."; *Psalm 117 Explained*, 1530: WA 31.I:233.19 ⟨*LW* 14:14⟩: ". . . the kingdom of Christ is not a temporal, transitory, earthly kingdom, ruled with laws and regulations, but a spiritual, heavenly, and eternal kingdom that must be ruled without and above all laws, regulations, and outward means. He tells the heathen to remain heathen ⟨Ps. 117:1; Vulgate⟩; He does not ask them . . . to run away from their countries or cities to go to Jerusalem. He does not demand that they give up or abandon their secular laws, customs, and habits to become Jews, just as he does not demand of the Jews that they abandon their laws. What He demands is something different from, and higher than, external, worldly laws or ceremonies. Every country and city can observe or change its laws. He does not concern Himself about this. Where laws are retained, they do not hinder His kingdom . . ."; *That These Words of Christ, "This is My Body," Still Stand Firm against the Fanatics*, 1527: WA 23:193.25: "In summary: The whole life of Christians is called spiritual. . . ."

192. Therefore a Christian living in the human community has to pay attention to "both laws" (*Sermons on Matthew, Chapters 5-7*, 1530-32: WA 32:393.14): the law governing the Christ-person, and the law governing the world-person. The former is the law of his citizenship, the latter is the law of a commonwealth in which he lives as a foreigner; *First Lectures on the Psalms*, 1513-15: WA 3:650.31 ⟨*LW* 11:148⟩: ". . . one who disposes his ways and ascents to God, how can he fail to cross over the world and to regard it as a place of exile?"

193. Therefore the secular law obligates the Christian to obedience not by itself, but God assigns the duty to obey the secular law to the Christian; *First Lectures on the Psalms*, 1513-15: WA 4:281.12: ". . . you ⟨i.e., God⟩ alone are the legislator whom one has to obey, ⟨i.e., your commandments,⟩ not the commandments which those set up ⟨line 8:⟩ who think they ⟨know and⟩ own righteousness." — See also Bring, "Gesetz und Evangelium," *Aus der Arbeit der Luther-Agricola Gesellschaft in Finnland* 1 (Helsinki, 1943), 67: "In one sense the new man is totally without law, yet at the same time in another sense he is the only person who fulfills God's law acording to its deepest meaning"; Gollwitzer, *Christliche Gemeinde*, 11 n. 1.

Notes to Chapter 12

1. ⟨For this chapter, see below, 471 n. 7.⟩

2. *Matthew, Chapters 18-24 Explained in Sermons*, 1537-40: WA 47:452.41: "Thus speaks Christ: '. . . see to it that you serve only me, that I alone am your lord. If this does not happen, nothing will last, all things will perish, the spiritual governance, the secular governance, the domestic governance'"; ibid., WA 47:453.7: "The difference between all estates remains ⟨in the *politia;* in the church⟩ all of them are, however, pulled into a unity so that there is only one teacher, father, and lord."

3. See above, 118ff.

4. The reason of Christians is governed by faith and does not affirm the autonomy of reason directed against God; therefore their living with one another is not governed by the kingdom of reason; *Second Lectures on Galatians*, 1531: WA 40.I:457. 7: "A right reason through faith"; sermons of 1523: WA 12:675.9: "In God's kingdom, where he rules through the gospel, there is no demand for law ⟨or: 'one does not demand one's right'⟩, one does not handle law, there is only forgiveness, remitting ⟨of claims⟩, giving, no wrath or punishment, but only brotherly service and doing good."

5. *On the Power of Excommunication*, 1518: WA 1:639.2: "... the communion of believers is twofold: one is internal and spiritual, the other external and corporeal. The spiritual communion is unity in faith, hope, and love for God. The corporeal communion is the participation in the sacraments, i.e., participation in the signs of faith, hope, and love; this participation extends, however, further to the communion of things, of custom, assembly, living together, and other corporeal undertakings." This passage is shaped according to Biel, *Collectorium*, lib. IV. dist. 18. qu.2.art.1. For this passage and for Luther's new formulation, see Johannes Heckel, *Initia iuris*, 13.

6. *On the New Testament, That Is, the Mass*, 1520: WA 6:354.18: "... Christ created for himself a pleasing, dear people, which is harmoniously bound together through love..."; *On Secular Authority*, 1523: WA 11:254.12: "Christ ... teaches that among themselves Christians should have neither the secular sword nor law"; ibid., WA 11:250.6: "... it is impossible that among Christians the secular sword and law would find anything to do because Christians voluntarily do more than all laws and doctrine could demand..."; *Sermons on the First Epistle of St. Peter*, 1523: WA 12:334.9: "... the apostles differentiate between universal love and brotherly love. We are obligated to love also our enemies; this is the universal Christian love. This is the brotherly love: we Christians love one another as brothers, one takes care of the other, because we all have the same goods from God." See also as early as in *The Babylonian Captivity of the Church*, 1520: WA 6:554.32: "... love does not need any laws at all." For "universal order of Christian love," see *Confession concerning Christ's Supper*, 1528: WA 26:505.11. See also Luther to the Congregation in Esslingen, 1523: WA 12:157.5ff.; sermon of Febr. 2, 1546: WA 51:170.13ff.; *Sermons on the Ten Commandments*, 1518: WA 1:436.15.

7. See Emil Brunner, *Gerechtigkeit*, 144; *Second Lectures on the Psalms*, 1518-21: WA 5:115.22: "... there is no need for rights and laws."

8. *To the Christian Nobility*, 1520: WA 6:409.9. See also *Against the Bull of Antichrist* ⟨German text⟩, 1520: WA 6:616.18. — For the participation of Christians in Christ and with one another, see *First Lectures on the Psalms*, 1513-15: WA 4:398.16f., 29f., 400.31ff. ⟨*LW* 11:540⟩; only Christians form a true commonwealth; the world is dominated by separation and war. — Kohlmeyer, *Von Augsburg nach Wittenberg*, 13: "From the sum of Luther's totally religious ethics we gain an exceptionally strong impression of community. Community is an event in the realm of the natural, yet it is the outgrowth of the supernatural; even if it takes place among sinful people, it is nevertheless a communion of saints."

9. *On Christian Freedom* ⟨German text⟩, 1520: WA 7:21.3. See also *Second Lectures on the Psalms*, 1518-21: WA 5:407.42ff.

10. Therefore Christian freedom may not lead to the withdrawal from the duties of brotherly love. In such a case it means "put one's freedom aside"; *Second Lectures on the Psalms*, 1518-21: WA 5:403.29; *The German Mass*, 1526: WA 19:72.23: "... freedom is and

has to be the servant of love and the neighbor"; Luther to Catherine Zell: Jan. 24, 1531: WA.B 6:27.9. Conversely, Christian brotherly love may not be used to justify accepting the suppression of Christian freedom by a tyrant; Luther to John Agricola: Aug. 31, 1527: WA.B 4:241.4.19: "... thus far we have taught that a Christian is responsible to affirm ⟨the freedom of conscience⟩, and he has to defend it bravely if tyrants want to enforce the opposite.... Therefore one may not use love to violate freedom, for if love would be permitted to violate freedom, then it would also be free to violate the whole gospel, something which the tyrants also would want"; Luther's 1535 statements about the Council of Constance: WA 39.I:23.11: "Faith has to be the lord of love, and love has to yield to faith and not faith to love."

11. See above, 31; appendix of Luther's letter to George Spalatin: May 16, 1519: WA.B 1:397.44: "... each law has to yield to love, even the law of praying and sacrificing" ⟨in the sense of celebrating Mass⟩.

12. Therefore Luther justified the 1528 visitation of the congregations in Electoral Saxony with the elector's "office of love" (Holl, *Luther,* 366), or he used the "duty of love" when, on Oct. 5, 1528, he issued a letter of warning to Elector Joachim of Brandenburg; WA.B 4:579.99.

13. Sermon of March 17, 1518: WA 1:269.6: "We all ⟨Luther addressed 'friends of Christ'⟩ are to be equal"; *Concerning the Ministry,* 1523: WA 12:189.9: "Name and communion of the brotherhood do not permit that one is superior to the other, or receive more, or have more rights, esp. in spiritual matters..."; *Second Lectures on the Psalms,* 1518-21: WA 5:169.22: "Before God we all are, have been, and always shall remain equals..."; *Sermons on Matthew, Chapters 5-7,* 1530-32: WA 32:536.31: ⟨We are are called Christians; therefore⟩ "there is no inequality nor preference among persons, but one is like the other..."; ibid., WA 32:537.19: "... there is only one Christian estate, just as all humans have one natural essence"; *On Secular Authority,* 1523: WA 11:271.3.

14. Among themselves Christians do not have a secular governmental authority because "their governance is a spiritual governance, and according to the spirit they are subordinated to no one but Christ"; *Whether Soldiers, Too, Can Be Saved,* 1526: WA 19:629.3. See also *Magnificat,* 1521: WA 7:578.22: "... in Scripture we find neither a spiritual ⟨in the sense of ecclesiastical⟩ governmental authority nor power, but only service and subordination."

15. For Luther's polemics against the differentiation between perfect and imperfect estates, see above, 373 n. 132.

16. *First Lectures on Galatians,* 1516-17: WA 57.II:28.16: "'God does not regard the person' ⟨see Gal.2:6⟩. Therefore there is neither priest nor layman ... , nor the status, rank, or order of one of them, or of anyone else. All these things are of such a nature that they do not make a believer when they are present, or an unbeliever when they are missing"; ibid., WA 57.II:85.12; see also the edited version of these lectures, 1519, WA 2:530.25 ⟨LW 27:281⟩; *Psalm 118 Explained,* 1530: WA 31.I:168.26. The passages cited by Holl, *Luther,* 305 n. 4, from *First Lectures on the Psalms,* 1513-15, do not deal with this basic right of spiritual equality.

17. *Lectures on Genesis,* 1535-45: WA 42:342.28 ⟨LW 2:113⟩: "Attention must ... be directed, not to the works of an individual but to his faith. One faith is common to all the saints, although their works differ very much."

18. For the opposite, see the ⟨social⟩ differences among persons in the *politia; Second Lectures on Galatians,* 1531: WA 40.I:178.9, and above, 258 n. 49.

19. *Concerning the Ministry,* 1523: WA 12:189.8 ⟨*LW* 40:33⟩: ". . . we have this word: 'For you have one Master, Christ. You are all brethren' [Matt. 23:8, 10]. We have then altogether the same right ⟨or: 'law'⟩."

20. Sermon of March 17, 1518: WA 1:269.7; *On Secular Authority,* 1523: WA 11:271.8: ". . . the . . . nature ⟨of Christians⟩ does not permit to have superiors because no one wishes nor is able to be a superior."

21. *Concerning the Ministry,* 1523, WA 12:189.17.21: ". . . this ⟨see n. 19⟩ we have said about the common law of Christians . . . the *communio* of law. . . ." ⟨See also above, 193, and below, 489 n. 205.⟩

22. As early as in *First Lectures on the Psalms,* 1513-15, Luther attacked exemptions and privileges as some of the fundamental wrongs in the church because they violated the universal commandment of obedience; WA 3:155.8ff. ⟨*LW* 10:130⟩.

23. ⟨In the sense of ecclesiastical estate, or in the sense of spiritual over against secular.⟩

24. *To the Christian Nobility,* 1520: WA 6:407.13. See also *The Babylonian Captivity of the Church,* 1520, WA 6:566.16, as above, 260 n. 14.

25. If one understands the phrase in a universal sense, describing *all members* of this estate, then it can also mean *das (ein) christlich(es) Wesen* ⟨the Christian essence or being, or what it means to be a Christian; see also below, 387 n. 32, and 399 n. 91⟩, i.e., the universal church ⟨as embodiment of *das christliche Wesen*⟩; see *To the Christian Nobility,* 1520; WA 6:404.2, together with below, 435 n. 242; *Psalm 117 Explained,* 1530: WA 31.I:241.12, 242.12. "Christian estate" is also used in polemics, and then it is directed against the papal clergy and hierarchy.

26. This explains the difference between the Christian estate and the estates set up in man-made law; *Psalm 117 Explained,* 1530: WA 31.I:241.25: "It is very difficult for reason . . . . to comprehend that the spiritual ⟨in the sense of ecclesiastical⟩ estate and the secular estate⟨s⟩ are nothing when compared with the Christian estate. Reason always wants to mix the two, making out of the Christian estate a worldly or ecclesiastical governance, which is framed and governed by laws and works. And in this process reason forgets and no longer knows who Christ is, or what the estate of Christians is. . . ."

27. This is not contradicted by Luther's statement that God himself set up the estate of pastor; see above, 362 n. 35. The *estate* of pastor as such does not exist by divine law. By divine law exists the ministry of the Word, with which the servant of the church, ⟨the incumbent of the estate,⟩ is charged.

28. Luther to George Spalatin: Dec. 18, 1519: WA.B 1:595.29; *On Christian Freedom* ⟨German text⟩, 1520: WA 7:27.17ff. — For the difference between the priesthood of all believers and the ministry of the ecclesiastical priesthood, see *Answer to the Book of Goat Emser,* 1521: WA 7:630.8; sermon of June 9, 1535: WA 41:207. 9; *The Private Mass and the Consecration of Priests,* 1533: WA 38:230.14. — For the rejection of the ⟨medieval⟩ idea that the consecration of a priest bestows an indelible quality *(character indelibilis)* on the priest, see *The Private Mass and the Consecration of Priests,* 1533: WA 38:227.32; *Sermons on the First Epistle of St. Peter,* 1523: WA 12:317.10.: ". . . it is all one thing, priests, baptized persons, Christians." — See also Hans Storck, *Das allgemeine Priestertum bei Luther* (Munich, 1953), 19.

29. *Decretum Gratiani* c.12. D.XL ⟨Friedberg 1:148⟩: "... each holy person is a priest."

30. Maurer, *Freiheit eines Christenmenschen,* 60 n. 4, and Ernst Kinder, *Der evangelische Glaube und die Kirche* (2d ed. Berlin, 1960), 162ff., agree with the following argument.

31. According to Luther, the authority to make laws in the church and govern the church externally is not based on the priesthood, and especially not on the Power of the Keys! See *The Babylonian Captivity of the Church,* 1520: WA 6:536.35. See also the correct description of the power of the priesthood ⟨of believers⟩, based on Luther's *Concerning the Ministry* (1523; WA 12:180ff. ⟨*LW* 40:21ff.⟩), in Paul Althaus, *Communio sanctorum* (Munich, 1929), 69 ⟨esp. n. 71⟩.

32. *On Christian Freedom* ⟨German text⟩, 1520: WA 7:20.1. Luther called it also "theological freedom" (*First Lectures on Galatians,* 1516-17: WA 57.II:99.13), or "freedom of consciences" (Luther to John Agricola: Aug. 31, 1527: WA.B 4:241.3). *Sermons on the First Epistle of St. Peter,* 1523: WA 12:331.32 ⟨*LW* 30:77⟩: "... in a Christian people there should and can be no compulsion, and if one begins to bind consciences with external laws, faith and the Christian way of life ("das christlich Wesen"; see above, 386 n. 25) soon perish. For Christians must be guided and governed only in the Spirit, so that they know that through faith they already have everything by which they are saved, that they need nothing else for this, that they are not obligated to do anything more than serve and help their neighbor with all they have, just as Christ helped them. All their works are performed without compulsion and for nothing; they flow from a happy and cheerful heart, which thanks, praises, and lauds God for all the good things it has received from Him. Thus St. Paul writes in 1 Tim. 1:9 that 'the law is not laid down for the just'; for of their own accord they do without recompense and unbidden everything God wants."

33. *The Babylonian Captivity of the Church,* 1520: WA 6:537.12: "For this ... freedom and conscience I raise my voice, and I shout with confidence that there is no law by which either men or angels may impose any law upon Christians unless they consent, for we are free from all laws." (This passage dealt directly only with the freedom from ecclesiastical laws, but it also expressed a general principle. The passage was cited in article 16 of *Confutatio*. Responsio ⟨1530⟩; see Ficker, *Konfutation,* 56f.) For passages from Luther's early period, see *First Lectures on Galatians,* 1516-17: WA 57.II:105.23: "... the righteous does not have the law because he, having love and grace required by the law, owes nothing to the law"; *Lectures on Hebrews,* 1517-18: WA 57.III:192.22 ⟨*LW* 29:193f.⟩: "... a righteous man has all that the Law requires, he is now outside the Law. For he owes the Law nothing; but he keeps the Law, and his life is the Law itself, living and fulfilled."

34. On the hiatus between the 'majesty of the theological freedom' and all other kinds of freedom, see *Second Lectures on Galatians,* 1531: WA 40.II:3.9 ⟨and the edited version of these lectures, *LW* 27:4f.⟩. This freedom has limits, however; Luther to George Spalatin: beginning of June 1522: WA.B 2:553.44: "The fear of the Lord rules the heart so that he who is strong ⟨in the faith⟩ is not haughty toward him who is weak and does not turn freedom either into an opportunity of the flesh or an offense of the brother but, fearing the Lord, uses freedom in a temperate and salutary way."

35. Sermon of Aug. 23, 1532: WA 36:280.32: "⟨Christ does⟩ much more ... than the law commanded. With this example he teaches you to do likewise. He is so ⟨confident of victory⟩ that he does not want to be subject to the law, and yet he does much more than the law can demand." This is valid notwithstanding that a Christian remains a sinner in

Notes to Page 98

spite of his justification by faith alone; ibid., WA 36:282.24: "Where the Spirit is, who brings Christ to us, there a person is above all laws, as Paul says: 'To the just no law is given.' ⟨1 Tim. 1:9.⟩ Nevertheless, that person does much more than he would be able to do according to the flesh. According to the flesh we are sinners, and as such we certainly would have to remain under the law. But for the sake of Christ and Baptism we are elevated high above all laws." If the baptized one ignores Christ's example to the degree that he acts contrary to the secular natural law and the man-made positive law derived from it, he is subject to the coercive force of the law just as is the non-Christian; ibid., WA 36:282.30: "Outside of Christ, Moses has to do his tough job so that he ... makes godly ... those who are not Christians"; ibid., WA 36:283.11: "Over those who are not Christians one has to let Moses reign. ..." — This legal situation may not be used as proof for the thesis that a Christian is a citizen of two kingdoms ⟨see above, 93 and 381 n. 190⟩ because as old ⟨sinful⟩ man he is subject to the secular laws. — See also Bornkamm, *Luthers Lehre von den zwei Reichen*, 28.

36. *On Christian Freedom* ⟨German text⟩, 1520: WA 7:21.1; *Lectures on Romans*, 1515-16: WA 56:476.6. — Rudolf Laun (*Die Menschenrechte* [Hamburg, 1948], 10) pointed out that as an idea the first human right, freedom of religion, emerged when Luther rejected any kind of jurisdiction in matters of conscience.

37. *Third Disputation against the Antinomians*, 1538: WA 39.I:491.18. For other passages from Luther's writings, see Wehrung, *Kirche nach evangelischem Verständnis*, 31. — See also Prenter, *Spiritus creator*, 243: "... church and Luther's testimony of the Holy Spirit belong organically together. Life in the reality of the Spirit is an *ecclesiastical existence* ⟨italics by Prenter⟩. ..."

38. ⟨Heckel wrote "das irdische Kirchenwesen."⟩ For the phrase 'ein christlich Wesen', see above, 386 n. 25; see also *Sermons on Matthew, Chapters 5-7*, 1530-32: WA 32:389.13: "Der Christen Wesen." — The phrase is the translation of *respublica christiana* (Christian commonwealth), or as sometimes Luther also said, *respublica ecclesiastica* (churchly commonwealth); see below, 389 n. 45, the first passage from *First Commentary on Galatians*. The phrase has the same meaning as "Christian church"; see *Psalm 117 Explained*, 1530: WA 31.I:242.12. — Holl's observations (*Luther*, 341 n. 2) on the use of *respublica christiana* in the later Middle Ages need to be corrected. It is not correct that in the Middle Ages this phrase was used only in public law. To cite only one source against Holl's position, I refer to John of Turrecremata's *Summa de ecclesia domini* ⟨see above, 285 n. 45⟩. Here the phrase is always used to designate the spiritual-secular commonwealth of Christendom, the totality of believers (*universitas fidelium;* book I. chapt. 87). That commonwealth is governed by two authorities, the spiritual ⟨i.e., ecclesiastical⟩ and the secular, in such a way that the secular is subordinated to the spiritual so that a plurality of principalities does not exist (book I. chapts. 89 and 93). Therefore the pope is the chief of the whole Christian commonwealth (*princeps totius reipublicae christianae;* book III. chapt. 18). He rules the whole church (!), not only in spiritual but also in temporal matters; therefore he is head and ruler *(caput, rector)* of the whole Christian *politia* (book II. chapt. 116). For Luther, on the other hand, a *politia christiana* did not exist, and *respublica ecclesiastica* can only describe the external existence of the church, the universal church *(ecclesia universalis)*. According to the sources, Holl erred when he argued (*Luther*, 342 n. 1) that Luther opposed the term *ecclesia universalis*. ⟨For Holl, see further, below, 436 n. 256.⟩

39. See below, 436 n. 256. For *tota ecclesia*, see *The Private Mass and the Consecration*

of Priests, 1533 (preliminary sketches): WA 38:187.16; *First Lectures on the Psalms*, 1513-15: WA 3:216.10, 394.13, 397.31, 452.34, 466.28, 601.36, 640.26, 646.2, 647.28, 650.5, 651.3; ibid., WA 4:26.13, 41.9.27, 49.36, 68.31, 84.23, 166.30, 173.26, 234.5.37, 240.29, 242.14; *Second Lectures on the Psalms*, 1518-21: WA 5:456.18. Sometimes Luther used *tota ecclesia* for "church made up of old and new people" (in the sense of Jews and Gentiles; WA 3:604.26, 607.12), sometimes he connected it with the earliest church (WA 4:67.12), and sometimes he suggested that it is the same as "Christian world"; Luther to Gerard Listrius: July 28, 1520: WA.B 2:149.10; to George Spalatin: Aug. 5, 1520: WA.B 2:164.15; to Duke Charles III of Savoy: Sept. 7, 1523: WA.B 3:152.114; to Duke Frederick, elector of Saxony: Aug. 18, 1519: WA.B 1:471.231f.; *Reply to Ambrosius Catharinus*, 1521: WA 7:761.26; *Second Lectures on the Psalms*, 1518-21: WA 5:550.8; *Reply to the Bishop of Meissen*, 1520: WA 6:144.26f.

40. ⟨Literally: "collections."⟩ *On the New Testament, That Is, the Mass*, 1520: WA 6:368.14, 373.2; *First Lectures on the Psalms*, 1513-15: WA 3:489.34; ibid., WA 4:181.28, 456.26, 23.26: *ecclesiae singulares, ecclesiae particulares per totum mundum*; *Second Lectures on the Psalms*, 1518-21: WA 5:456.20 (*singulae ecclesiae*), 530.21 (*ecclesiae partiales*). (See also *Decretum Gratiani* c.8. D.I. de cons. ⟨Friedberg 1: 1296⟩: "Church, that is, the assembly *[collectio]* of the catholics....") All the particular churches are on the same legal level, and none is the head of the others, esp. not the church of Rome; *Against the Roman Papacy*, 1545: WA 54: 245.30. This legal equality of all particular churches is by divine positive law; *Assertion of All Articles*, 1520: WA 7:136.6.

41. *On the Councils and the Church*, 1539: WA 50:625.21: "Church should be called the holy Christian people..."; *First Lectures on the Psalms*, 1513-15: WA 4:413.26, 414.1. — See also Oepke, *Das Neue Gottesvolk*, 406ff.

42. *First Lectures on the Psalms*, 1513-15: WA 3:299.2, 406.4, 599.8; ibid., WA 4:410.3.

43. *First Lectures on the Psalms*, 1513-15: WA 3:295.29. See also above, 310 n. 68.

44. Luther also used *respublica christiana*, or *Christenstand*, or *ecclesiasticus status; D. Martin Luther's Offer and Protest* ⟨Latin text⟩, 1520: WA 6:483.9; *Concerning the Ministry*, 1523: WA 12:173.5; above, 386 n. 25. In *First Lectures on the Psalms*, 1513-15: WA 4:181.28, Luther sometimes used *ecclesiastica civitas*. Sometimes Luther called the papal church *papistica respublica* (papal commonwealth); Luther to John Lang: July 29, 1520: WA.B 2: 151.13f.

45. *First Commentary on Galatians*, 1519: WA 2:617.1; ⟨for the text of Heckel's citation, see also *LW* 27:409⟩. See also Luther to Nicholas Hausmann: March 17, 1522: WA.B 2:474.28 ⟨*LW* 48:402⟩: "...love will rule with regard to...external works and regulations"; to George Spalatin: Jan. 22(?), 1522: WA.B 2:446.61 ⟨*LW* 48:385⟩: "Love reproves faults but does not desert [him who falls]"; *First Commentary on Galatians*, 1519: WA 2:475.10 ⟨*LW* 27:198⟩: "Therefore the fact remained that the churches of Judea kept the provisions of the Law, not because they were compelled to do so for the sake of salvation but out of unrestrained love, by rendering service to the weakness of others. Would that in the church today our laws were taught and observed with similar understanding!" — Luther turned this wish into criticism of the papal church; here people "instead of practicing love, ⟨waste⟩ their ⟨money⟩... to decorate stones... and wood ⟨of temples⟩ while in the meantime they ignore the needs of the neighbor"; *Second Lectures on the Psalms*, 1518-21: WA 5: 652.1. — For disciplining love, see Luther to Wolfgang Capito: Jan. 17, 1522: WA.B 2:431.24ff. ⟨*LW* 48:374f.⟩. — See also above, 263 n. 48.

46. ⟨For love and the divine natural law, see above, 47, 50, 88.⟩ For the divine positive law of the church, see above, 362 n. 39. — In light of these materials, Hubert Jedin's presentation of Luther's doctrine of the church and of ecclesiastical law (*Geschichte des Konzils von Trient*, 1 [2d ed. Freiburg, 1951], 137), has to be corrected; he wrote: "For Luther the church is no longer Christ's institution of grace and Salvation but the community of the predestined. Visible of that community are congregations of which the order is not based on divine law but only on positive ⟨secular⟩ law."

47. See Erik Wolf, "Zur Rechtsgestalt der Kirche," in *Bekennende Kirche. Martin Niemöller gewidmet*, ed. by Joachim Beckmann and Herbert Mochalski (Munich, 1952), 259, the phrase "Christokratische Bruderschaft" ⟨brotherhood ruled by Christ⟩; *Sermons on John, Chapters 14 and 15*, 1538: WA 45:702.20: "⟨Mutual love is⟩ the mark by which one recognizes true believers and Christians"; Luther to Anthony Lauterbach: Oct. 19, 1545: WA.B 11:200.17: ". . . for the sake of the need or weakness of the brothers" ⟨we are to do certain things⟩; sermon of Apr. 18, 1538: WA 46:282.10.

48. Erik Wolf presented (*Rechtsgedanke und biblische Weisung*, 35) a different position when he wrote: Luther "always understood 'law' only as a governmental statute; he never understood it as an order of an autonomous congregation, which for Calvin manifested the essence of law."

49. At the Leipzig Disputation (1519) Luther was still willing to accept the jurisdictional primacy of the pope ⟨but only as *human* ecclesiastical law; see also below, 392 n. 50⟩; *Explanations of Luther's Theses Debated in Leipzig*, 1519: WA 2:397.3: "The contention concerning the primacy of the Roman church was more passionate ⟨than the debate about indulgences⟩. I did not deny that the Roman church has primacy of honor; I did not grant that it has primacy of jurisdiction, at least not by divine law. I did not want to oppose that jurisdiction but rather affirm and defend it firmly, provided that the Roman church has this jurisdiction as a result of circumstances or by man-made law." See also *The Private Mass and the Consecration of Priests*, 1533: WA 38:195.19: "⟨We offered to the pope and bishops⟩ that we do not want to destroy their ecclesiastical laws and authority but . . . help in implementing their law and authority." — According to Wilhelm Maurer (*Pfarrerrecht und Bekenntnis* [Berlin, 1957], 130), Luther used the term *ius ecclesiasticum* ⟨ecclesiastical law, i.e., law of the legally constituted (corporation called) church, a law which essentially is different from secular law⟩ for the first time in his July 21, 1530, letter to Philip Melanchthon: WA.B 5:493.63 ⟨LW 49:386⟩.

⟨There are three important contributions to our topic:⟩ Theodosius Harnack, *Die Kirche, ihr Amt, ihr Regiment. Grundlegende Sätze* (Nürnberg, 1862; italics by Harnack), 60: ". . . the church has to organize itself according to *the norm of the Salvation order* while *paying attention to the Creation order*"; ibid., 61: ". . . man-made traditions ⟨or rules in the church⟩ *(traditiones humanae)* may claim to be valid only if it can be substantiated that they agree with the above mentioned norms and principles with which the church organizes itself; under no circumstances may they be enforced as something which is necessary for Salvation. . . . At this point we have to remind the reader of the actual significance which the differentiation between man-made and divine law has for our topic. Human traditions may claim, of course, only the status of man-made law; as such, they have no normative and directly binding authority for the faith. But what exists in the church by man-made law is, therefore, not by itself arbitrary, or unevangelical, or irrelevant for faith, just because it does not exist on the basis of the gospel. For man-made law . . . participates in the moral nature and validity of law only because, and to the degree that, it also has its source and norm in the *divine* will, i.e., in that will which has manifested itself in the natural and the moral law of the world (*jus naturale, creatio, ordinatio divina*; see *Apology* XXIII.9; *BC* 240.9). When man uses and develops this law, he can make mistakes. By necessity the results of his labor will be different according to changing external circumstances; therefore these results may never be presented as divine law. This does not mean, however, that one may be indifferent toward ⟨these⟩ human traditions and in the name of some arbitrarily selected faith principle declare them to be purely secular. Such an attitude would be contrary to the moral nature of the evangelical faith, and it would be antinomian because it would include a rejection or disregard of the divine Creation order. To reject reason, history, the existing order are not acts of faith; such actions would be without logic, and they would also be immoral; therefore they would be contrary to the faith. In contrast to man-made law as interpreted thus far, divine law belongs to the topic 'Redemption'. In a very real sense this law is to be understood as divine, as evangelical law of grace, ⟨or⟩ evangelical order of grace. *This* divine law has the special quality that it is divine law only for the faith and church. Both the order of Creation and that of Redemption include divine law, which is understood in the light of the normative principle of the church, ⟨i.e.,⟩ the contrast between law and gospel. In both orders that ⟨divine⟩ law is present in different ways, has a different content, and has a different authority for the faith and Salvation of the soul. In this way the authors of our confessional writings contrasted the natural law — even though for them it was based on the Creation or divine ordinance — to the divine law (*Apology* XXIII.60; *BC* 247.60); they understood the latter as being in a very real sense identical with 'existing by the gospel' or 'according to the gospel'; see, e.g., *Augsburg Confession* XXVIII.21, Latin text: '. . . *according to the gospel,* or as they say, *by divine law*.'" ⟨See also *BC* 84.21.⟩

Dietrich Oehler, "Evangelisches Kirchenrecht als bekennende Ordnung," in *Festschrift Friedrich Giese zum 70. Geburtstag, 17. August 1952, dargebracht von Freunden, Schülern und Fachkollegen* (Frankfurt/Main, 1953), 202: "⟨The church⟩ receives the charge ⟨to create law⟩ from Christ. He commands that the Word be proclaimed and the sacraments be administered in an orderly way . . ."; ibid., 203: "Norms are needed in the church, which serve the implementation of this charge"; ibid., 206 n. 15, Oehler's comments on Johannes Heckel, *Initia iuris,* 53 and 51: "It seems to me that . . . one has to differentiate more precisely between a law of the church which deals only with the necessary external order, and a law of the church which, going beyond that external order, deals with the spiritual life of people. Christ's liberation from law may be connected only with this second kind of law. . . . Whether a law issued by an ecclesiastical governance binds consciences is not decided by the fact that this law is administered by a governmental authority (essentially this was Luther's position) or by the church itself. This law, regardless whether it is issued by a governmental authority or the church, is a part of the ecclesiastical law, which as law is unique. *Ecclesiastical law* and *law* issued by a governmental authority *dealing with secular matters* are in contrast, *not ecclesiastical law* and *law issued by a governmental authority*. This is especially important for the past." ⟨Italics by this ed. Heckel's comment:⟩ Therefore Luther's battle against the obedience regulated by Canon law was a mistake."

Hans Liermann, *Grundlagen des kirchlichen Verfassungsrechts nach lutherischer Auffassung* (Berlin, 1954; italics by Liermann), 14: "In the Lutheran church the congregation . . . is not rooted in the divine law through the office of the presbyter, as it is in the Reformed church. The Lutheran ecclesiastical law of the Reformation generally ignores the congregation. By no means does it draw from the doctrine of the *universal priesthood <of believers>*, which endowed the congregation with a *spiritual role,* the consequence that in the external order of the church a *legal role* would have to correspond to that spiritual role"; ibid., 21: "According to the divine law, the pastoral office primarily is the central base of the organized church's order. For the sake of this order the priesthood of all believers will have to be eclipsed again and again."

50. A governmental authority with power to command, as in secular law, does not exist in the church; *The Babylonian Captivity of the Church,* 1520: WA 6:536.7: ". . . neither the pope, nor a bishop, nor any human being has the right to impose one syllable on a Christian unless it is done with his consent. Whatever is done in another way is done in a tryrannical spirit"; *On Secular Authority,* 1523: WA 11:271.11: "What are priests and bishops? Answer: 'Their governance is not a governmental authority or power but a service and an office' <in the sense of task or duty>"; ibid., WA 11:262.31, together with 263.3, 270.32, 271.3; Luther to Philip Melanchthon: July 21, 1530: WA.B 5:492.27 <LW 49:384f.>: ". . . as bishop, a bishop has no authority to impose on his congregations any statute or ceremony, except with the expressed or silent agreement of the church. For the church is free and is the lord of all, and the bishops ought not to dominate the faith of the congregations, nor . . . oppress the congregations against their will. The bishops are, . . . only servants and stewards, and not the lords of the church. If the congregations, as one body, have agreed with the bishop, however, then the bishop may impose upon the faithful whatever the bishop wishes, as long as [the principles of] faith remain unviolated, and he can also abolish [such rules] according to [his] judgment"; to Nicholas Hausmann: March 17, 1522: WA.B 2:474.20 <LW 48:401>: "No one should be forced to faith and to what belongs to faith, but he should be drawn by the Word so that, willingly believing, he may come of his own accord." See also *Propositions against the School of Satan,* 1530: WA 30.II:421.23.26; *Order of the Mass,* 1523: WA 12:214.14; sermon of Oct. 5, 1544 (WA 49:591.23), and of March 6, 1523 (WA 11:53.28); Luther to Nicholas Hausmann: Nov. 17, 1524: WA.B 3:373.16 <LW 49:90>.

51. See Johannes Heckel, *Initia iuris,* 42 n. 172; Hans E. Weber, "Von den Kirchenrechtstheorien im alten Luthertum," *EvTh* 6 (1946/47): 195.

52. See Schönfeld, *Über die Gerechtigkeit,* 37f.

53. This would be the case already when the holder of an ecclesiastical office *neglects* the duties of his office, a situation which would result in the duty of ecclesiastical resistance; *On Good Works,* 1520: WA 6:259.23, 260.1. (*Note:* In fulfilling the duty to resist there is a difference when the situation involves holders of ecclesiastical *or* of secular offices. There exists no right to resist, <and, therefore, no duty,> when the holder of a secular office neglects the duties of his office.) — For resistance in the case of heresy <or> misuse of ecclesiastical authority, see *On Good Works,* 1520: WA 6:228.3, 256.31: ecclesiastical laws which are contrary to the first three commandments of the Decalogue are invalid; to obey them would be sin.

54. *The Private Mass and the Consecration of Priests,* 1533: WA 38:231.3ff.

55. <In the sense of congregation, or of the sum of congregations in a specific geographic area.>

56. *Against the Roman Papacy,* 1545: WA 54:245.25 <LW 41:311>: "<The Roman

church〉 separates itself from 〈universal〉 Christendom and the spiritual edifice built upon this stone 〈see Eph. 2:20〉, and instead invents for itself a fleshly, worldly, worthless, lying, blasphemous, idolatrous authority over all of Christendom. One of these two things must be true: if the Roman church is not built on this rock along with the other churches, then it is the devil's church; but if it is built, along with all the other churches, on this rock, then it cannot be lord or head over the other churches. For Christ the cornerstone knows nothing of two unequal churches, but only of one church alone, just as the Children's Faith, that is, the faith of all of Christendom, says, 'I believe in one holy, Christian church,' and does not say, 'I believe in one holy Roman church.' The Roman church is and should be one portion or member of the holy Christian church, not the head, which befits solely Christ the cornerstone. If not, it is not a Christian but an un-Christian and anti-Christian church, that is, a papal school of scoundrels"; ibid., WA 54:276.28: "In Christ all churches are equal"; ibid., WA 54:291.9: "All bishops and churches 〈are〉 equal"; ibid., WA 54:284.10. — For the demand of the pope and his supporters to obey man-made laws in the church, see *Postilla for Christmas*, 1522: WA 10.I.1:481.11.

57. *Addition to Goat Emser's Book*, 1519: WA 2:678.4: ". . . there are no superiors 〈in the church〉 because Christ prohibited it . . ."; *Reply to Ambrosius Catharinus*, 1521: WA 7:721.30: "The gospel and the church do not know of any jurisdictions, which are nothing other than tyrannical inventions of people. 〈The gospel〉 knows only love and service, not power and tyranny." — Theodosius Harnack (*Die Kirche*, 80; italics by Harnack) was not correct when he argued: "It is not at all at the church's discretion to create a constitution and governance for the sake of order, or not to do so. Likewise, it is not at the discretion of congregations and the holders of the office 〈of the public ministry〉 to obey the existing ecclesiastical governance, or not to do so, nor do they only obey themselves by obeying that governance. But they freely subordinate themselves to the *objective authority of order*, which has been set up by the creative will of God and legitimated and sanctified in the *Fourth Commandment* of the Decalogue. Regarding the moral nature of the relationship 〈of congregation and office holder to the ecclesiastical governance〉 there is no difference when, in the process of creating its constitution, the church has incorporated the highest secular holders of the governmental office in its constitution and placed them ahead of all other members of the church, or has not so done; in both cases, by constitution the church has a legitimate *ecclesiastical governmental authority*, to which for the sake of God it owes obedience to the degree and as long as that authority rules according to God's will."

58. Here is the reason for Luther to recognize the Roman church, a particular church, as a holy church, in spite of the shortcomings which he found in it; *Second Lectures on Galatians*, 1531: WA 40.I:68.9: ". . . today we call the Roman church and all its episcopal sees holy, even if they are turned upside down and are ungodly. God rules nevertheless in the midst of 〈his〉 enemies 〈see Ps. 110:2〉. . . . in the city of Rome, even though it is worse than Sodom, there remain Baptism, the voice of the gospel, its text, Holy Scripture, the ministries, the name of Christ and of God. Those who have these, have with them the substance (i.e., the treasure of the church: *Second Commentary on Galatians*, 1535; WA 40.I:69.27), those who do not, etc. Therefore the Roman church is holy, because it has God's holy name, Baptism, the Word. If these things are among the people, the people are called holy . . ."; *Concerning Rebaptism*, 1528: WA 26:147.33 〈LW 40:232〉: "And since he 〈i.e., the pope as the Antichrist〉 is to sit and reign there 〈i.e., "in the temple of God";

2 Thess. 2:4⟩ it is necessary that there be Christians under him. God's temple is not the description for a pile of stones, but for the holy Christendom (I Cor. 3[:17]), in which he is to reign. The Christendom that now is under the papacy is truly the body of Christ and a member of it. If it is his body, then it has the true spirit, gospel, faith, baptism, sacrament ⟨of the Lord's Supper⟩, keys, the office of the ministry, prayer, holy Scripture, and everything that pertains to Christendom. So we are still under the papacy and therefrom have received our Christian treasures"; *Against Jack Sausage,* 1541: WA 51:506.3, together with Ernst Wolf, *Peregrinatio,* 1:162. — For similar statements, see *The Private Mass and the Consecration of Priests,* 1533: WA 38:221.18; *On the Councils and the Church,* 1539: WA 50:563.19 (however, see also ibid., 626.1ff.); Luther to Gottschalk Crusius: Oct. 27., 1525: WA.B 3:590.12; *Sermons on John, Chapters 1 and 2,* 1537-38: WA 46:624.23. — See also Gustaf Aulén, "Die Einheit der Kirche," in *Ein Buch von der Kirche,* 472ff.; Paul Althaus, "Martin Luther über die Autorität der Kirche," in *Stat crux dum volvitur orbis. Eine Festschrift für Landesbischof D. Hanns Lilje, Abt zu Loccum, zum sechzigsten Geburtstag am 20. August 1959,* ed. by Georg Hoffmann and Karl Heinrich Rengstorf (Berlin, 1959), 98ff.; Kinder, *Der evangelische Glaube und die Kirche,* 76 (where further Luther materials are listed).

59. *A Model for Consecrating a True Bishop,* 1542: WA 53:235.6: "⟨The sheep have⟩ the authority and right . . . , not to obey ⟨the wolf-bishop⟩, even more . . . by God's commandment they are forced to resist him, not to mention not to obey him"; ibid., WA 53:233.27, 241.25, 242.24; *The Private Mass and the Consecration of Priests,* 1533: WA 38:251.33.

60. For the medieval background, see *Decretum Gratiani* p. c.4. C.XXIV. q.1; ibid., c.19 ⟨Friedberg 1:967f., 972f.⟩. For Luther, see *The Private Mass and the Consecration of Priests,* 1533: WA 38:251.27: "Until Judgment Day it is impossible . . . that we or holy church corporeally separate ourselves . . . from the abominable papacy or Antichrist"; *Concerning Rebaptism,* 1528: WA 26:148.27: the goal of the reformers is only "to reject the abuse and the additions" to the Word of God; ibid., WA 26:149.1; *First Commentary on Galatians,* 1519: WA 2:605.25. — Secession from the church would have contradicted Luther's respect for God's activity in history; *Concerning Rebaptism,* 1528: WA 26:168.5 ⟨LW 40:256⟩: ". . . where we see God's work we should yield and believe in the same way as when we hear his Word, unless the plain Scripture tells us otherwise. I indeed am ready to let the papacy be considered as a work of God. But since Scripture is against it, I consider it as a work of God but not as a work of grace. It is a work of wrath from which to flee, as other plagues also are works of God, but works of wrath and displeasure." For this "positivism of God's twofold work," see Steck, *Luther und die Schwärmer,* 46ff. — According to Luther, the hypocritical church excludes itself from the true church; *On the Councils and the Church,* 1539: WA 50:512.25, 514.8 ⟨LW 41:12, 13⟩. ⟨For *sanior pars,* see above, 202.⟩

61. *On the Councils and the Church,* 1539: WA 50:512.17: ". . . before all else, one must turn to our Lord Christ and . . . ask him for a reformation."

62. *The Right and Power of a Christian Congregation,* 1523: WA 11:411.13 ⟨LW 39:308f.⟩: "Thus we conclude that wherever there is a Christian congregation in possession of the gospel, it not only has the right and power but also the duty — on pain of losing the salvation of its souls and in accordance with the promise made to Christ in baptism — to avoid, to flee, to depose, and to withdraw from the authority that our bishops, . . . and the like are now exercising. For it is clearly evident that they teach and rule contrary to God and his word. This first point is established certainly and firmly enough, and one

should depend upon it, that it is a divine right and a necessity for the salvation of souls to depose or to avoid such bishops, abbots, monasteries, and whatever is of their government." — A specially striking example of the ecclesiastical right of resistance is Luther's Dec. 1, 1520, letter to Cardinal Albrecht, archbishop of Mainz, in which Luther dealt with 'the idol at Halle'; WA.B 2:No. 442 ⟨LW 48:No. 106⟩. See also Luther to Nicholas Hausmann: March 17, 1522: WA.B 2.474.15 ⟨LW 48:401⟩: resistance is to be implemented only with the Word and not with violence; to Philip Melanchthon: July 21, 1530: WA.B 5:493.71 ⟨LW 49:387⟩; Johannes Heckel, *Initia iuris,* 72f.

63. *On the Ban,* 1520: WA 6:72.21ff. ⟨LW 39:18f.⟩.

64. *The German Mass,* 1526: WA 19:72.1, and Vajta, *Theologie des Gottesdienstes bei Luther,* 316ff.; Luther to William Pravest: March 14, 1528: WA.B 4:411.7. — Not the church but secular governmental authority has the legal competency for issuing laws concerning fasting; sermon of Feb. 17, 1538 (WA 46:177.1) and of March 10, 1538 (WA 46:203.19f.).

65. *First Commentary on Galatians,* 1519: WA 2:483.23: "You see that the other apostolical work ⟨i.e., in addition to preaching the gospel⟩ is the concern for the poor"; *Ordinance of a Common Chest,* 1523: WA 12:13.20 ⟨LW 45:172f.⟩: "The third way ⟨of using ecclesiastical properties, or the income derived from them, which are no longer used, such as monasteries or endowments of Mass celebrations⟩ is the best, however, to devote all the remaining property to the common fund of a common chest, out of which gifts and loans could be made in Christian love to all the needy in the land, be they nobles or commoners. In this way, too, the will and testament of the founders would be carried out. For although they erred and were misled when they gave this property to monasteries, their intention certainly was to give it for the glory and service of God; but their purpose was not realized. Now there is no greater service of God than Christian love which helps and serves the needy, as Christ himself will judge and testify at the Last Day, Matthew 25[:31-46]. This is why the possessions of the church were formerly called *bona ecclesiae,* that is, common property, a common chest, as it were, for all who were needy among the Christians."

66. *On the Councils and the Church,* 1539: WA 50:552.25; sermon of Oct. 5, 1544: WA 49:600.11: "It is not my word or doing that I preach when we come together as a congregation, but it happens for the sake of all of you and on behalf of the whole church. Yet there has to be one who speaks ... as a result of the command and consent of the others. By listening to the sermon they all affirm the Word and in this way teach others." See also *Against the Roman Papacy,* 1545: WA 54:280.19: Christians have the duty to support preachers economically; *The Private Mass and the Consecration of Priests,* 1533: WA 38:228.19, 236.5: the consecration of a priest as call into the ministry. See further, Storck, *Das allgemeine Priestertum bei Luther,* 31ff., 53ff.

67. Sermon of Feb. 13, 1539: WA 47:669.28: "I would send two of the elders who would entreat the person to stop" ⟨doing what he is doing⟩. ⟨If this does not accomplish anything,⟩ "then I would proceed" ⟨and appear before the congregation⟩. "There I would pronounce him excommunicated because according to Christ's commandment ⟨Matt. 18:15-18⟩ he has been admonished, as you can see from ⟨that⟩ order."

68. For the legal position of bishops, see *To the Christian Nobility,* 1520: WA 6: 440.28: "Scripture does not know of bishops as we have them now. Nevertheless, bishops are appointed through the order of a Christian congregation so that one ⟨pastor⟩ rules many pastors"; *Second Lectures on the Psalms,* 1518-21: WA 5:57.13: "⟨I do not say this⟩ to condemn the lordship *(monarchia)* of the Roman church but because I detest that this lord-

ship is obtained by power and manipulation, and that one pretends that this lordship is commanded by God. This lordship should be built on the mutual consent of the believers and the bond of love so that it would be a lordship not of dominating power but of serving love."

69. ⟨Esp. the church's properties.⟩ *On the Councils and the Church,* 1539: WA 50: 552.22: the external, temporal governance of churches ⟨i.e., governance of the church's *secular* matters; see above, 197f.⟩.

70. Christians do not have an external, 'half spiritual, half secular' ecclesiastical order existing by divine law, as the Jews had; *How Christians Should Regard Moses,* 1527: WA 24:5.28, 6.4ff. See also Georg Merz, "Gesetz Gottes und Volksnomos bei Martin Luther," *LuJ* 16 (1934): 57. — For the significance of order for the church, see Hans Freiherr von Campenhausen and Heinrich Bornkamm, *Bindung und Freiheit in der Ordnung der Kirche* (Tübingen, 1959).

71. Luther emphasized this esp. for the order of worship; *The German Mass,* 1526: WA 19:73.14: "One has to have such an order for the sake of those who still are to become Christians or are to become stronger ... ⟨so that⟩ they are daily exercised and educated in Scripture and God's Word...." — From this educational significance of an order of worship for the beginners in the faith one may, of course, not conclude that worship itself has only this educational meaning. Already the foundation of the church in Paradise for the purpose of the communal worship of God (see above, 299 n. 159) opposes such a meaning. Vajta (*Theologie des Gottesdienstes bei Luther,* 33ff.) was correct at this point. — See also *On the Councils and the Church,* 1539: WA 50:614.8ff.

72. *Second Lectures on Galatians,* 1531: WA 40.I:40.4: "... righteousness ⟨or: 'justice'; see above, 236 n. 1⟩ is manifold. There is political righteousness, with which the emperor and princes, the philosophers, and the wise men deal. Another righteousness is the ceremonial one. It is practiced ⟨in⟩ the man-made traditions of the pope — or rather, housefathers and teachers practice it better; they ⟨observe⟩ man-made traditions ⟨literally: 'ceremonies'⟩ not as means for gaining righteousness but as something that is necessary for the building up of morality. Above these kinds of righteousness there are those derived from the Decalogue, the legal ones; Moses teaches them, and we also teach them whenever we correctly expound the fundamentals ⟨of the faith⟩." See also *Second Lectures on the Psalms,* 1518-21: WA 5:402.33, 403.10.

73. See Walter Künneth, "Das Selbstverständnis der lutherischen Kirche und ihre Sendung," *ELKZ* 2 (1948): 194.

74. But not all ecclesiastical laws have the same purpose. Some legal actions are to draw the legal consequences which an event in the spiritual church has for the communal life of the universal church. In such cases the universal church only serves the divine ecclesiastical law and does not have the authority to act according to its own judgment. Therefore the legitimacy of such legal actions is not connected with the divine natural law but with the divine positive law. An example would be the ecclesiastical ban, a legal action of ecclesiastical discipline. See *Against the Perverters and Forgers of the Imperial Mandate,* 1523: WA 12:65.37: "... because the pure gospel has to be preached, punishment according to the ecclesiastical law has to be governed by the gospel. In it, Matt. 18⟨:17⟩, Christ teaches ... that one should ban and separate from the congregation the person who does not obey the congregation." See also Johannes Heckel, *Initia iuris,* 108ff. — Schott ("Anfänge evangelischen Kirchenrechts?" *ZEvKR* 2 [1953]: 136f.) doubted that Luther held

the position which we developed. He argued: The sentence of excommunication is a matter of human judgment; therefore it is fallible, but God's judgment is infallible; excommunication is only the cancellation of the external fellowship; once it has taken place, it is the task of the punished person to search his conscience in an effort to find out whether he has not already excluded himself from the fellowship with God and the spiritual church. One appreciates the thoroughness of Schott's argumentation, but it shows how far a presently widespread understanding of ecclesiastical discipline has moved away from Luther's position. Now ecclesiastical discipline is understood as if it were the discipline of a club, the church club. In this understanding the spiritual quality of ecclesiastical discipline is shortchanged. Excommunication, the small ban, may only be imposed on a person who <already> has forfeited the right of citizenship in Christ's kingdom; if this is not the case, one may not deny that person the right to partake in the sacraments <"external fellowship">. The judgment whether this condition for excommunication exists is up to the church, i.e., the spiritual church which acts within the universal church; the statement, "the spiritual man judges all things" <1 Cor. 2:15>, qualifies the spiritual church as a whole as well as its individual members to make this judgment. Because of this spiritual legal authority the judgment of the spiritual church is infallible. Schott was afraid of a divergence between God's judgment and that of the church. But that divergence does not at all occur when the spiritual church, called to execute God's judgment, acts within the institutional church; only then is excommunication valid, otherwise it is totally invalid. This is the way Luther saw the legal situation; had he not, he would not have been able to continue considering himself a member of the "ancient church" in spite of having been excommunicated. See also below, 434 n. 230.

75. *Second Lectures on Galatians*, 1531: WA 40.I:166.6 <see also the edited version of these lectures, *LW* 26:89f.>; *Matthew, Chapters 18–24 Explained in Sermons*, 1537-40: WA 47:584.38: "Differentiate between temporal and eternal matters.... In temporal matters one may yield, compromise, and give in, but not in eternal matters; there such actions are worthless, or <if one considers them to have value,> one is lost." <Some illustrations for this situation:> Receiving bread and wine in the Lord's Supper, or only the bread: Luther to Duke John Frederick of Saxony: March 18, 1522: WA.B 2:477.8; to John Heß: March 25, 1522: WA.B 2:482.10; to Nicholas Hausmann: March 26, 1522: WA.B 2:483.21 (for this letter see also WA.B 4:328f.); to John Rühel: March 2, 1528: WA.B 4:400.2; to the Christians in Halle: Apr. 26, 1528: WA.B 4:445.13. — The veneration of saints: Luther to John Lang: May 29, 1522: WA.B 2:548.15; *Instruction about Saints*, 1522: WA 10.II:159. — Patience with those who are weak in the faith and the limit of such patience: Luther to the members of the All Saints Chapter in Wittenberg: Aug. 19, 1523: WA.B 3:131.24: "... it is one thing to tolerate those who are weak in neutral matters; but it is ungodly to be tolerant in matters which are openly ungodly..."; to Count George of Wertheim: June 17, 1523: WA.B 3:88.10; to the members of the All Saints Chapter in Wittenberg: July 11, 1523: WA.B 3:112.19; to Michael von der Straßen: Oct. 16, 1523: WA.B 3:171.8; to Nicholas Hausmann: Oct. 1523: WA.B 3:183.14. — Eating meat during periods of fasting: Luther to Philip Glüenspieß: end of 1526: WA.B 4:145.5.

76. *The German Mass*, 1526: WA 19:72.6. See also Luther to Duke Charles III of Savoy: Sept. 7, 1523: WA.B 3:151.66: "... none of the traditions or decrees of the Fathers or statutes of the councils are necessary...." Therefore excommunication for the violation of ecclesiastical laws is not permissible. It is permissible only (ibid., WA.B 3:152.83) "if some-

one sins against faith or love." — See also *First Commentary on Galatians,* 1519: WA 2:582.17ff. ⟨LW 27:358⟩.

77. ⟨See above, 5of., 84, 87f., 92f.⟩

78. *On Monastic Vows,* 1521: WA 8:579.5.8: ". . . he who said, 'I am the way,' ⟨John 14:6⟩ . . . condemned with this word whatever is law and tradition which is outside of Christ. . . ." According to Luther, the universal church transgressed its legal authority when it introduced a vocational estate ⟨such as the monastic estate⟩ which did not serve the office of preaching; such an estate would be "sinful"; *Postilla for Christmas,* 1522: WA 10.I.1:317.16ff. See also *Second Lectures on Galatians,* 1531: WA 40.I:245.6: Satan's estates, i.e., estates of which the incumbents trust in the meritorious quality of works; Holl, *Luther,* 237 n. 1; Wingren, *Luthers Lehre vom Beruf,* 16.

79. *Against the Bull of Antichrist* ⟨Latin text⟩, 1520: WA 6:599.6.

80. *On the Councils and the Church,* 1539: WA 50:553.16, 552.21: the God-given reason suffices to create order in matters of the external, temporal governance of the church.

81. *Second Lectures on Galatians,* 1531: WA 40.I:418.7: "Before it works ⟨in the sense of work correctly⟩, reason has to be illuminated by faith"; sermon of May 16, 1529: WA 29:355.12: "To rule the church and boys in school . . . is a matter of reason alone" ("rule" refers to the management of the external affairs of the church and not to the spiritual governance of the church). — See also Ernst Wolf's review of Johannes Heckel, *Initia iuris,* in *ZEvKR* 1 (1951): 107; Theodosius Harnack, *Die Kirche,* 66: ". . . order ⟨in the church⟩ is a work of the church's faith, even though that order is a . . . human creation"; Oehler, "Evangelisches Kirchenrecht," in *Giese Festschrift,* 207: "Ecclesiastical law is spiritualized order"; ibid., 208: "As order of the church, ecclesiastical law is ⟨identical with proclaiming⟩ God." (According to a note in Lilje's *Sonntagsblatt* of Febr. 28, 1954 [No. 9, p. 23], Rudolf Hermann criticized this last thesis of Oehler.)

82. *The Babylonian Captivity of the Church,* 1520: WA 6:559.2. See also *The Papacy at Rome,* 1520: WA 6:291.8ff.; *Concerning the Ministry,* 1523: WA 12:191.16; *The Right and Power of a Christian Congregation,* 1523: WA 11:415.23.

83. *Second Commentary on Galatians,* 1535: WA 40.I:293.16: ". . . the kingdom of the human reason has to be very far separated from the spiritual kingdom"; this sentence was directed against the attempt (ibid., 293.3) "to project political maxims into the church," but it is valid in general terms.

84. Matthes (*Luther und die Obrigkeit,* 27) was wrong when he argued that the external church "is a part of the worldly kingdom"; see also ibid., 48.

85. See Helmuth Schreiner, *Vom Recht der Kirche* (Gütersloh, 1947), 104.

86. ⟨I.e., Christ's kingdom.⟩ Therefore the man-made ecclesiastical law is not a product of the Holy Spirit; just as all other works which a true Christian does in his earthly existence, so this law is a product of man; *On the Councils and the Church,* 1539: WA 50:553.18: ". . . the Holy Spirit has to explain Christ and not deal with those things which are subjected to reason."

87. Luther to George Spalatin: Feb. 24(?), 1519: WA.B 1:354.69: "I count ⟨the⟩ papal authority among those things which are neutral, such as wealth, health, and other temporal matters"; *First Commentary on Galatians,* 1519: WA 2:533.27.32.35; *The Private Mass and the Consecration of Priests,* 1533: WA 38:187.1 (preliminary sketches): "Orders ⟨e.g., deacon, priest, bishop, etc.⟩ in the church have been civic ranks, ⟨but the papists⟩ made spiritual orders out of them."

Notes to Page 101

88. For a different position, see Wünsch, *Ethik des Politischen,* 149. He argued that the church "does not have an independent ecclesiastical law" but only its "own orders, which are not law"; "governmental authority, on the other hand, operates with power and law."

89. ⟨Or: "congregation."⟩ *To the Christian Noblility,* 1520: WA 6:440.29, 442.4. See also *Against the Roman Papacy,* 1545: WA 54:239.16.

90. ⟨See above, 31, 86, 97f., 247 n. 53, 285 n. 46⟩ — Binder was not correct when he wrote (*Luthers Staatsauffassung,* 22; italics by Binder): "In the *kingdom of God* only the gospel and love rule, but this is not applicable to the *church*. In this sense Luther was correct when he argued that to rule the church is a matter of reason alone ⟨see also above, 100 n. 81⟩. In practical terms it is impossible that in the *church* only the principles of the gospel rule. This argument provides the basis for the need and justification of the *landesherrliche Kirchenregiment*." On the other hand, Coing was correct when he argued (*Die obersten Grundsätze des Rechts,* 100) that the churches "through the revelation of the Divine, which is their basis, are given their constitutional law *(Grundgesetz);* all other elements for their organization are not pertinent to this task." ⟨*Landesherrliches Kirchenregiment,* i.e., the governance of the church by a territorial prince. For cities, the phrase would have to be modified to read: "Städtisches Kirchenregiment."⟩

91. *Psalm 117 Explained,* 1530: WA 31.I:241.12 ⟨LW 14:22⟩: ". . . the substance of Christianity ("ein christlich Wesen"; see above, 386 n. 25) is a much nobler thing and altogether different from all secular and spiritual laws ⟨in the sense of ecclesiastical laws or Canon law⟩, outward holiness, government, and whatever other such things there may be among the Jews or heathen"; *Against the Roman Papacy,* 1545: WA 54:244.17 ⟨LW 41:309f.⟩: "In John 6[:63] the Lord says, 'The words that I have spoken to you are spirit and life.' Accordingly, the words in Matthew 16 must also be spirit and life, namely, when he says, 'On this rock I will build my church.' 'Build' must here mean a spiritual, living building. 'Rock' must be a living, spiritual rock. 'Church' must be a spiritual, living assembly, indeed, so alive that all of it lives eternally. For 'the flesh is of no avail,' etc. [John 6:63]; it dies and does not live eternally. Now this rock is solely the Son of God, Jesus Christ, of whom the Scripture is full, and no one else. . . . To build or to be built on this rock is something that cannot be done with laws or good works, for Christ is not grasped by hands or works, but must come through faith and word. Thus the church cannot, through itself or its own works, make itself spiritual or living; instead, it is built on this rock, through faith, and thus is spiritual and living as long as it remains built on the rock, that is, until eternity. . . . And in summary, this text, Matthew 16, speaks of faith: he who has faith is built on this rock, as one says, 'He who trusts God has built well.' Note this well (I say), that in Matthew 16 Christ speaks of faith and not of our works, for thereby it will become evident what a little pious prancer the pope is"; ibid., WA 54:249.3 ⟨LW 41:315⟩: ". . . the Lord in Matthew 16 does not speak of laws, Ten Commandments, or the works we should or could do, but of the Christian faith or the work of the Father, which he, with the Son and the Holy Spirit, performs in us, namely, that he spiritually builds us on the rock, his Son, and teaches us to believe in Christ, that we might become his house and dwelling, as is proven in I Peter 2[:4-7] and Ephesians 2[:19-22]."

92. ⟨See above, 237 n. 20.⟩

93. See Alfred D. Müller, *Grundriß der praktischen Theologie* (Gütersloh, 1950), 86ff.

94. *The Book of Deuteronomy with Notes*, 1525: WA 14:593.28: "Our mind, having been instructed by God's wisdom or God's law, can judge all rites and ceremonies."

95. ⟨I.e., the true believers.⟩ *The Right and Power of a Christian Congregation*, 1523: WA 11:410.21: ⟨According to 1 Thess. 5:21, the Apostle Paul⟩ "does not want any doctrine or statement to be affirmed unless the congregation, which hears them, has examined them and found them to be good"; this statement should be placed in the context of ibid., WA 11:408.8: ". . . the Christian congregation certainly is to be found ⟨literally: 'recognized'⟩ wherever the pure gospel is preached." See also *Postilla for Christmas*, 1522: WA 10.I.1:141.1.

96. ⟨"Blind" in the sense of useless, not saying something precise.⟩ *Against Jack Sausage*, 1541: WA 51:545.23: "⟨The papists⟩ want to defend all their abominations with that blind, empty ⟨literally: 'nude'⟩ word 'church'." ⟨See also *On the Councils and the Church*, 1539: WA 50:625.5.32.⟩

Notes to Chapter 13

1. See above, 72.

2. *The Babylonian Captivity of the Church*, 1520: WA 6:550.22 ⟨LW 36:92⟩. In *Sermon on the Estate of Marriage*, 1519, Luther still affirmed the sacramental quality of marriage; WA 2:168.13 ⟨LW 44:10⟩.

3. This is applicable also to the relationship of parents with their children and vice versa; Luther to George Spalatin: Jan. 7, 1527: WA.B 4:153.19.

4. *A Marriage Booklet for Simple Pastors*, 1529: WA 30.III:75.18 ⟨BC.Kolb-Wengert ed., 368.3⟩.

5. *Sermon on the Estate of Marriage*, 1519: WA 2:170.35 ⟨LW 44:13⟩; *The Large Catechism*, 1529: WA 30.I:161.28 ⟨BC 393.207⟩.

6. *Commentary on 1 Corinthians, Chapter 7*, 1523: WA 12:105.19 ⟨LW 28:17: "the most religious [estate]" in contrast to other religious estates, such as the monastic estate⟩.

7. ⟨Because God has richly blessed it.⟩ *The Large Catechism*, 1529: WA 30.I:161.32 ⟨BC 393.208⟩.

8. *Sermon on the Estate of Marriage*, 1519: WA 2:167.34 ⟨LW 44:9⟩.

9. *On Monastic Vows*, 1521: WA 8:654.19 ⟨LW 44:376f.⟩: "In no sense does God attribute sin to the conjugal rights of married people, which is due solely to his mercy, although Psalm 51[:5] refers to it as sin and iniquity in no way differing from adultery and whoredom, because it springs from passion and impure lust. It is impossible to avoid this emotion, since we are restrained from foregoing it." For a partially different explanation, see *Sermon on the Estate of Marriage*, 1519: WA 2:168.34, 169.3 ⟨LW 44:10f.⟩.

10. ⟨Or: "as worship of himself."⟩

11. ⟨See above, 248 n. 55.⟩

12. One case would be the use of the parental authority in connection with the wedding or engagement of a child. ⟨The girl wants to marry the man whom she loves. The parents want her to marry the man to whom they have promised her.⟩ The strict use of the law ⟨of parental authority would permit the parents to force the daughter to comply with their wish. As true Christians, who live by the power of Christ's law, they cannot insist on this strict use of the law *and* have a good conscience,⟩ because among Christians "laws have to

make room for love." Therefore "for the good of the daughter" the parents consent ⟨to the daughter's wish to marry the man whom she loves⟩. See Luther to Nicholas Hausmann: Jan. 27, 1528: WA.B 4:No. 1216. Another case would be divorce; *Sermons on Matthew, Chapters 5–7*, 1530-32: WA 32:378.4: "... those who want to be Christians should not divorce" their marriages ...; see also ibid., WA 32:379.25ff.

13. ⟨I.e., the person who lives by "the power of Christ's law."⟩

14. ⟨See above, 75f.⟩

15. *Sermon on the Estate of Marriage*, 1519: WA 2:169.33 ⟨*LW* 44:12⟩. Luther dealt with this topic quite often; see, e.g., *On Keeping Children in School*, 1530: WA 30.II:531.3 ⟨*LW* 46:222⟩.

16. ⟨See above, 344 n. 410.⟩

17. For "divine law" and "public estate," see *On Marriage Matters*, 1530: WA 30.III:207.15 ⟨*LW* 46:268⟩. ⟨For "secular natural law," see above, 72f., 339 n. 344.⟩ For Luther's battle against secret engagements, which are contrary to the 'public' nature of engagements ⟨see above, 337 n. 331⟩, for his affirmation of the public nature of engagements and weddings, and for his sometimes abusive remarks about jurists and their position on this topic, see sermon of Aug. 4, 1545 (WA 49:802.26), of Jan. 6, 1544 (WA 49:297.14, 298.25), of Jan. 13, 1544 (WA 49:316.17), of Jan. 20, 1544 (WA 49:318.10), and of May 28, 1531 (WA 34.I:460.4ff.). See also brief on marriage matters of Jan. 1528: WA.B 4:336.151.

18. *A Marriage Booklet for Simple Pastors*, 1529: WA 30.III:74.4 ⟨*BC*.Kolb-Wengert ed., 367.1⟩.

19. *The Babylonian Captivity of the Church*, 1520: WA 6:556.9 ⟨*LW* 36:100⟩; *Commentary on 1 Corinthians, Chapter 7*, 1523: WA 12:130.35 ⟨*LW* 28:44⟩. ⟨For "impediment," see above, 73.⟩

20. Instead of other authors, see Hans Liermann, *Deutsches Evangelisches Kirchenrecht* (Stuttgart, 1933), 322.

21. See Johannes Heckel, *Initia iuris*, 44. ⟨See also above, 186.⟩

22. *A Marriage Booklet for Simple Pastors*, 1529: WA 30.III:74.7 ⟨*BC*.Kolb-Wengert ed., 367.1⟩.

23. See Johannes Heckel, *Initia iuris*, 43. ⟨See also above, 187.⟩

24. ⟨Literally: "the small ban," i.e., excommunication from the community of believers in contrast to the large ban or the outlawing from the secular community.⟩ *Exhortation to All Clergy Assembled at Augsburg*, 1530: WA 30.II:309.16, 310.5 ⟨*LW* 34:33⟩; *On the Keys*, 1530: WA 30.II:501.11, 502.5 ⟨*LW* 40:369ff.⟩; Luther's *Smalcald Articles*, 1537: WA 50:247.9 ⟨*BC* 314.IX⟩.

25. ⟨See above, 75.⟩

26. *Commentary on 1 Corinthians, Chapter 7*, 1523: WA 12:119.6 ⟨*LW* 28:32⟩.

Notes to Chapter 14

1. In contrast to *religio*, *politia* is the organized world without faith and, therefore, without grace, in short, without Christian righteousness; *Second Lectures on Galatians*, 1531: WA 40.I:51.12, 208.3 ⟨and the edited version of these lectures, *LW* 26:116⟩; *Commentary on Zechariah*, 1527: WA 23:514.1 ⟨*LW* 20:172⟩. — Törnvall went too far when he argued (*Geistliches und weltliches Regiment bei Luther*, 124): "*Politia* designates only the created

world, to which man belongs and over which he is placed to rule . . . , the kingdom in which . . . reason is to rule." In this understanding of *politia* there is no room for the universal church, the external form of *religio;* for the argument *e contrario,* see *Second Lectures on Galatians,* 1531: WA 40.I:178.6. — In addition to the understanding of *politia* as institution, Luther understood *politia* also to designate the secular governance, the *Polizei,* which rules in the *politia; Disputation on Matt. 19:21,* 1539: WA 39.II:44.10. ⟨I.e., *politia* designated the administrative structure of society, be it on the local or the national level. In Luther's days *Polizeiordnung* (police ordinance) covered some of what we would consider civil and administrative (sometimes even criminal) law, but also much more; e.g., regulations about dress, or about the amount of wine or beer that could be made available at a wedding. In modern scholarship *Polizei* and *Polizeiordnung* are treated under the topic 'social discipline'.⟩ — Watson, *Um Gottes Gottheit,* 232 n. 87, erred when he argued that Luther used only this second understanding of *politia.*

2. See above, 379 n. 179: "in profane societies" *(in prophanis politiis). Politia* can be used in a universal and a particular sense, just as *ecclesia.* This was the case already in the Middle Ages; see above, 388 n. 38.

3. *Psalm 101 Explained,* 1534-35: WA 51:242.6 ⟨*LW* 13:198⟩: ". . . the heathen can speak and teach about this ⟨i.e., secular governance⟩ very well, as they have done"; ibid., WA 51:243.14 ⟨*LW* 13:199⟩: "Because God willed to give temporal dominion to the heathen or to reason, He also had to provide people who had wisdom and courage, who had the necessary inclination and skill, and who would preserve it"; ibid., WA 51:243.2 ⟨*LW* 13:199⟩.

4. *The Babylonian Captivity of the Church,* 1520: WA 6:555.12: ". . . to the Christians Christ gave freedom from all laws of men, esp. when a divine law opposes them"; ibid., WA 6:563.7: ". . . it is an infamous and unjust slavery that a Christian, a free person, is subjected to traditions ⟨in the sense of regulations, laws⟩ other than the heavenly and divine ones"; *On Christian Freedom* ⟨Latin text⟩, 1520, WA 7:57. 3.8.14.24 ⟨*LW* 31:354f.⟩: ". . . every Christian is by faith so exalted above all things that, by virtue of a spiritual power, he is lord of all things . . . . This is not to say that every Christian is placed over all things to have and control them by physical power . . . . The power of which we speak is spiritual. . . . ⟨It is⟩ a truly omnipotent power, a spiritual dominion . . . . ⟨We are⟩ the freest of kings . . ."; *Second Lectures on Galatians,* 1531: WA 40.I:235.3: ". . . a Christian . . . as far as he is a ⟨true⟩ Christian, is above all law, . . . is free from all laws and not subjected to any law, neither internally nor externally"; *Sermons on the First Epistle of St. Peter,* 1523 (first version): WA 12:328.27: "We are not obligated to obey governmental authority for its own sake . . . , but for God's sake, whose children we are"; ibid., WA 12:329.22: "Though we do not benefit ⟨from being subordinated to secular governmental authority and paying taxes⟩, we nevertheless should do it voluntarily in order to please God, and for the reason that God's enemies, who rebuke us, are put in their place so that they . . . have to say we are good and obedient people"; ibid., WA 12:333.2: "We are free from all laws, but we have to be concerned for the weak and simple Christians, which is a work of love"; ibid., WA 12:332.21; Luther to Philip Melanchthon: July 13, 1521: WA.B 2:357.35 ⟨*LW* 48:258⟩: ". . . the gospel is a law for those who are willing and free, those who have nothing to do with the sword or the law of the sword"; to Duke John Frederick of Saxony: June 18, 1524: WA.B 3:306. 9: "Because secular laws are external matters, like eating and drinking, clothes and house, Christians have nothing to do with them; they are ruled by God's Spirit according to the

gospel"; to Duke Charles III of Savoy: Sept. 7, 1523: WA.B 3:152.103: "... what kind of insanity is it to coerce those who are voluntarily good with laws issued for the evil ones, or for those who do not want to be good? Of course, as Christians are doing all things voluntarily, so they also submit to the sword and laws because of the evil ones. Even more, Christians also handle the sword, not for their own benefit (since they need nothing for being righteous and saved except faith), but as an example for others, for preserving the common peace, and for strengthening the law of the sword. Therefore they are free and should freely use whatever traditions and ceremonies ⟨they encounter⟩"; *Whether Soldiers, Too, Can Be Saved,* 1526: WA 19:648.7: "... we Christians have nothing to do with your governance. But we serve you and tell you what before God has to be done in your governance"; *First Lectures on the Psalms,* 1513-15: WA 4:390.11; above, 114f. ⟨where Luther argued that as a foreigner in the kingdom of the world a true Christian is not subjected to law and governmental authority and its power, but for God's sake he subjects himself voluntarily; as God's tool he works in the kingdom at the left, promoting the secular natural law, serving in the office of governmental authority, and thus assisting in maintaining peace in the world⟩.

5. ⟨I.e., the righteousness or justice valid in the *politia,* secular righteousness in contrast to spiritual righteousness.⟩ Luther to Nicholas von Amsdorf: July 20, 1528: WA.B 4:501.2.

6. *First Lectures on the Psalms,* 1513-15: WA 4:89.6: "... each righteous person is a citizen of heaven and a foreigner on earth"; *Notes on Some Chapters of Matthew,* 1538: WA 38:666.39, as above, 166f. (Luther's comments on Matt. 17:27). See also above, 35, 41, 381 n. 190. — Karl Barth presented a different position when he argued (*Christengemeinde und Bürgergemeinde* [Munich, 1946], 31): "The *Polis* is in Christ's kingdom even if the representatives of the *Polis* are not aware of this situation or do not want to be aware of it." Gollwitzer (*Christliche Gemeinde,* 38) agreed with Barth. See also above, 114f.

7. *On Secular Authority,* 1523: WA 11:260.4 ⟨LW 45:102⟩: "There you see that Christ does not interpret his words ⟨Matt. 5:38f.⟩ to mean that he is abrogating the law of Moses or prohibiting temporal authority. He is rather making an exception ⟨for⟩ his own people. They are not to use the secular authority for themselves but leave it to the unbelievers."

8. ⟨We use "legal associate" for Heckel's *Rechtsgenosse.*⟩

9. *Second Lectures on Galatians,* 1531: WA 40.I:573.6: "On the outside there is no big difference between those who live honorably in society and a Christian, because in the eyes of the world ⟨a Christian's⟩ works do not stand out but are most ordinary: he takes care of his office.... When push comes to shove, however, and when it comes to the article of the cross, ⟨i.e.,⟩ when in matters of the confession of faith ⟨life⟩ is to be forsaken, then he is in his own work and in a most important office...."

10. See *On Christian Freedom* ⟨Latin text⟩, 1520: WA 7:64.15.

11. *On Secular Authority,* 1523: WA 11:250.18 ⟨LW 45:89⟩: "Just so, by the Spirit and by faith all Christians are so thoroughly disposed and conditioned in their very nature that they do right and keep the law better than one can teach them with all manner of statutes; so far as they themselves are concerned, no statutes or laws are needed"; *The Book of Deuteronomy with Notes,* 1525: WA 14:655.12: "⟨Christians⟩ are above every law and do more than laws order to do..."; sermon of Feb. 2, 1546: WA 51:168.42: "... we have such a law which orders us to do not only those things which one is obligated to do according to these secular laws but also to do more than one has to do" ⟨according to these secular

laws>. See also *First Lectures on the Psalms*, 1513-15: WA 4:387.9; sermon of August 15, 1520: WA 4:647.6; for the date of this sermon, see Vogelsang in *Luthers Werke in Auswahl*, 5:428, n. to line 16 <and above, 263 n. 51>.

12. *Sermons on the Ten Commandments*, 1518: WA 1:513.38 (sermon of Jan. 25, 1517): "Finally, it has to be noted that, as the Apostle Peter says <1 Pet.4:15; see also below, 198 n. 252, no one should suffer the charge of being a thief or evildoer <if he is innocent;> if he is innocent he should not say that he is being treated justly <when he is accused of such crimes>, but he should denounce the person who steals something from him as being guilty and leave a thorn in that person's conscience"; sermon on John 18:19-24 (Jan. 16, 1529): WA 28:283.6: "... if in a forest a robber would strip me and tell me, 'I am doing the right thing, because the coat belongs to me,' I may not agree with him nor condone his action; otherwise I would take his guilt upon me and become the thief of my own coat. In this situation one has to separate the mouth from the hand. I am not to be silent <literally: 'I am not to give up the mouth'> so that <the action> is condoned, <but> the hand should let go <the coat>"; *Long Sermon on Usury*, 1520: WA 6:37.14 <*LW* 45:274f.>: "That is Christian and brotherly fidelity, to terrify him who does you wrong by holding up before him his wrongdoing and God's judgment. It is your duty to say to him: 'Very well; you are taking my coat and this and that; ... you will have to answer for it.' You must do this, not primarily because of your own loss, nor to threaten him, but to warn him and to remind him of his impending ruin. If this fails to change his purpose, let go what will, and do not demand its return." — See also Hellmuth Mayer, "Darf der Christ sein eigenes Recht suchen?" *Zeitwende* 12.II (1936): 354ff., and id., *Strafrecht. Allgemeiner Teil* (Stuttgart, 1953), 177.

13. See above, 374 n. 140.

14. Thesis 1 of *Disputation on Revenge*, 1520: WA 6:575.3: "<A Christian> ought not only not avenge the injury inflicted upon him but also do good to the evildoers"; *Admonition to Peace*, 1525: WA 18:309.2, 310.7. — Governmental authority has the duty to repel injustice, however; *On the New Bulls and Lies of Eck*, 1520: WA 6:583.1: "... everyone has to endure violence and injustice, but governmental authority has to be on guard that injustice is not done to anyone; even if no one complains, it is to repel injustice wherever it is in the position to do so, or sees it and knows about it ..."; *On Secular Authority*, 1523: WA 11:259.13 <*LW* 45:101>: "... the governing authority should, on its own initiative or through the instigation of others, help and protect him <i.e., the Christian> too, without any complaint, application, or instigation on his own part"; *Psalm 110 Explained*, 1518: WA 1:692.15.

15. *First Lectures on the Psalms*, 1513-15: WA 3:633.9 <*LW* 11:126>: "... God's true people are a rational people who swallow spiritual things and lick earthly things, for they have a taste for spiritual things but only lick things of the flesh and, as it were, on the surface only from necessity for this life use them as if they did not use them (1 Cor. 7:31)." In *Exposition of the Lord's Prayer for Simple Laymen*, 1519 (WA 2:92.27), Luther dealt with the problem whether it is permissible for Christians to be involved in judicial proceedings for the sake of the imperfect people and for preventing evil. And in one of his earliest sermons (delivered sometime between 1514 and 1520; WA 4:698.20) he dealt with the fact that the exigencies of this life, or the concern for other people and the amendment of their lives, justify that Christians — reluctantly! — call upon courts to act.

16. *Second Lectures on Galatians*, 1531: WA 40.II:46.5: "We differentiate between liv-

ing and doctrine; doctrine pertains to God, living pertains to us. Doctrine does not belong to us, life does.... I am unable to give up anything pertaining to doctrine, in matters pertaining to life ⟨I can give up⟩ all things. Love ⟨can endure⟩ all things, but doctrine nevertheless always has to be unharmed."

17. ⟨To settle such a conflict in matters of faith. Only the members of the church have that competency.⟩

18. *Sermons on Matthew, Chapters 5-7*, 1530-32: WA 32:391.35, together with 392.7.

19. See below, 452 n. 44; *Long Sermon on Usury*, 1520: WA 6:39.26 ⟨LW 45:278⟩: "This ⟨i.e., 'punish the wicked and rescue the oppressed'⟩ should be done in such a way, however, that no one would be the complainant in his own case, but that others, in brotherly fidelity and care for one another, would inform the rulers that this man is right and that one wrong. Thus, the authorities would proceed to punish in a just and orderly way, on proof furnished by others. Indeed, the aggrieved party ought to request and insist that his case not be brought to trial; the others, in their turn, ought not to desist until the offense is punished. In this way affairs would be conducted in a friendly, Christian, and brotherly spirit, with more regard to the sin than to the injury"; *Second Lectures on the Psalms*, 1518-21: WA 5:189.13.33, 190. 6; *On Good Works*, 1520: WA 6:226.20 ⟨LW 44:50⟩: the duty to help poor and lowly people who suffer injustice.

20. *Sermons on Matthew, Chapters 5-7*, 1530-32: WA 32:392.11; *On Two Kinds of Righteousness*, 1519: WA 2:151.11 ⟨LW 31:305⟩. — See also Bornkamm, *Luthers Lehre von den zwei Reichen*, 22ff.

21. *First Lectures on the Psalms*, 1513-15: WA 4:320.6: "... this is being in the spirit of freedom, for which no law or statute has been set up, because he ⟨who is in the spirit of freedom⟩ does more than is commanded to him...."

22. See above, 78f.

23. *Sermons on Matthew, Chapters 5-7*, 1530-32: WA 32:529.35: "⟨Prov. 8:15.⟩ ... the law and judgment ⟨of kings⟩ are my ⟨i.e., God's⟩ law and judgment, together with all that they are doing *ex officio*, provided that they rule justly."

24. *Whether Soldiers, Too, Can Be Saved*, 1526: WA 19:629.4: "According to the spirit, ⟨Christians⟩ are subject to no one except Christ. Nevertheless, with their body and property they are subject to secular governmental authority, and they are obligated to be obedient."

25. ⟨See above, 105.⟩

26. *Sermons on the First Epistle of St. Peter*, 1523: WA 12:332.21 ⟨LW 30:78⟩: "St. Peter ... wants to say: Even though you — if you are Christians — are free in all external matters and should not be compelled by law to be subject to the secular government, since, as we have said, no law is laid down for the just (1 Tim. 1:9), yet of your own accord you should be willing and unconstrained. It is not that you must obey the law out of necessity, but you must do so to please God and to serve your neighbor"; *Theses on Monastic Vows*, 1521: WA 8:331.23.25: "According to Paul, law is not law if you obey it voluntarily.... For you obey law not because it is law, but because without law those things which belong to the law are pleasing." See also above, 105; Matthes, *Luther und die Obrigkeit*, 37ff.

27. ⟨See above, 88.⟩

28. Using different images, Luther repeatedly tried to impress this duty upon his followers. One such image is that of a Christian's soul being subject only to Christ, but his body being subject to the secular ruler (brief on matters of marriage: Jan. 1528: WA.B 4:337.36). The juristic dimension of such images is often misjudged. *Second Lectures on*

the Psalms, 1518-21: WA 5:402.36: "... on the basis of love ⟨a believer⟩ is a debtor" ⟨of people with whom he has to deal day-by-day; for the context of Heckel's citation, see WA 5:401.22-403.9⟩. — Wehrung, *Welt und Reich*, 76, presented a critical position: "The separation of an un-free body ⟨i.e., a body subject to law⟩ from a free soul ⟨i.e., a soul freed by Christ⟩ is dangerous and unnatural, and absolutely not based on the New Testament." See also Olsson, *Grundproblemet*, 1:120ff.

29. *On Christian Freedom* ⟨Latin text⟩, 1520: WA 7:67.29: "Paul ... prescribes ... that ... the righteous ... in the freedom of the spirit ... serve others and the governmental authorities, and obey their will freely, motivated by ... love"; *On Secular Authority*, 1523: WA 11:253.17 ⟨*LW* 45:93f.⟩: "... you say: if Christians then do not need the temporal sword or law, why does Paul say to all Christians in Romans 13[:1], 'Let all souls be subject to the governing authority' ... ? Answer: I have just said that Christians, among themselves and by and for themselves, need no law or sword, since it is neither necessary nor useful for them. Since a true Christian lives and labors on earth not for himself alone but for his neighbor, he does by the very nature of his spirit even what he himself has no need of, but is needful and useful to his neighbor. Because the sword is most beneficial and necessary for the whole world ... , the Christian submits most willingly to the rule of the sword, ... and does all he can to assist the governing authority, that it may continue to function and be held in honor and fear. Although he has no need for these things for himself — to him they are not essential — nevertheless, he concerns himself about what is serviceable and of benefit to others ..."; *On Good Works*, 1520: WA 6:250.24: "... disobedience is a bigger sin than murder, unchastity, stealing, cheating. ..."

30. *On Secular Authority*, 1523. ⟨Summary of the continuation of the text cited above, n. 29: A Christian visits the sick, feeds the hungry, and respects, supports, and serves governmental authority; he does these things not because he needs them for himself, but because others benefit from his actions, which also help that the wicked do not become worse.⟩ WA 11:254.3: "If he did not do this, he would be acting not as a Christian, and in addition he would act contrary to love ⟨i.e., the secular natural law⟩ and give an evil example to others, who also would not want to endure governmental authority even though they are not Christians."

31. See above, 126f.

32. For the thesis of the decretalists, "outside of the church there is no empire," see Sergio Mochi Onory, *Fonti canonistiche dell'idea moderna dello stato* (Milan, 1951), 198, 225; Francesco Calasso, *Gli ordinamenti giuridici del rinascimento medievale* (2ª ed. Milan, 1949), 242; id., *I glossatori e la teoria della sovranità* (2ª ed. Milan, 1951), 77. See also Heinrich Mitteis, "Zur Lage der rechtsgeschichtlichen Forschung in Italien," *ZSRG*.G 69 (1952): 231; Mitteis erred when he ascribed the thesis to Pope Innocent IV. — For Luther's polemics against this thesis, see *The Babylonian Captivity of the Church*, 1520: WA 6:551.3 ⟨*LW* 36:93⟩; *Second Lectures on the Psalms*, 1518-21: WA 5:650.3: "One sings ⟨to the 'simple German people'⟩, 'There is no empire outside of the church.' ... Obviously, it is appropriate that one calls this empire holy, not because it was created by God, but by God's most holy vicar — whatever he wants to be holy, is holy." ⟨Luther probably wrote this biting statement shortly after the Diet of Worms; see WA 5:10.⟩ Apparently Luther focused on *De ecclesiastica potestate* (book I, chapt. 4) of his fellow Augustinian, Aegidius Romanus ⟨see above, 322 n. 168, 373 n. 132⟩; for Aegidius Romanus, see Alois Dempf, *Sacrum imperium* (Munich, 1929), 448ff., esp. 454f.

33. ⟨In the sense of secular natural law; see the following sentences, and above, 57f., 309 n. 60, 313 n. 98. God's commandment limits the Christian's duty of obedience to the secular law. God gives this commandment through the institutional secular natural law, which protects the church and marriage (see above, 108f.), and through the substantive secular natural law, which secures the position of the Ten Commandments (see above, 109).⟩

34. *On Monastic Vows*, 1521: WA 8:609.38: "A Christian . . . can observe all laws, rites, and customs and accommodate himself to them, as long as they are not contrary to the divine mandates, and he does not put the trust of his conscience in them"; sermons of ca. 1514-20: WA 4:607.17.

35. Luther to Philip Melanchthon: Aug. 4, 1530: WA.B 5:528.23; *First Lectures on the Psalms*, 1513-15: WA 4:380.20 ⟨LW 11:518⟩.

36. *Psalm 101 Explained*, 1534-35: WA 51:241.22 ⟨LW 13:197⟩; *On Good Works*, 1520: WA 6:265.16 ⟨LW 44:100⟩.

37. *First Lectures on the Psalms*, 1513-15: WA 3:482.28: "Whatever is being done and said against truth and righteousness, is said and done against God"; ibid., WA 3:625.2; *On Good Works*, 1520: WA 6:226.19 ⟨LW 44:50⟩.

38. *On Good Works*, 1520: WA 6:259.14.17: ". . . to commit an unjust act toward God or man destroys the soul, even if it would benefit the whole world." This nullifies Gollwitzer's concerns (*Christliche Gemeinde*, 19ff., 29) that in Luther's thinking is a danger that both kingdoms would "stand side-by-side," and that 'love' does not cause a "critical evaluation of present laws." Thielicke's statements in *Theologische Ethik*, 1:No. 1841, also are not to the point.

39. Therefore it is a mistake to see in Luther a champion of legal positivism, as Otto Veit did when he wrote ("Die geistesgeschichtliche Situation des Naturrechts," *Merkur* 1 [1947]: 396f.): "In principle, the positivist is . . . a Lutheran. To him the moral demand of the secular natural law is arrogance before God." One also has to correct Joseph Klein's statement (*Kanonistische und moraltheologische Normierung in der katholischen Theologie* [Tübingen, 1949], 39): "Protestants . . . will reject the secular and the divine natural law and commit themselves to legal positivism." Walter Künneth (*Das Widerstandsrecht als theologisch-ethisches Problem* [Munich, 1954], 5) expressed doubts ⟨about my position⟩: "Certainly, it would be a question, with which one would still have to deal thoroughly, whether Johannes Heckel's significant theses, in which he attempts to affirm a right of resistance based on secular natural law in Luther's thought, can nullify the more restrained interpretation of Luther's statements on legal philosophy presented by Hans Liermann." Edmund Schlink ("Gerechtigkeit und Gnade," *KuD* 2 [1956]: 274) opposed the "assertion, . . . that Luther was guilty of the rise of positivism and the splintering of the Christian existence in autonomous realms."

40. ⟨Literally: ". . . each individual controls those limits . . . ." I.e., on the basis of the secular natural law the individual sets the limits of his obedience to secular governmental authority, or determines what is right or wrong positive law.⟩ Barth (*Christengemeinde und Bürgergemeinde*, 12) criticized in Luther's translation of Rom. 13:1a the phrase 'Untertansein' ⟨literally: "the being subject," either in the sense of being a subject or of the being subjected to⟩; Luther should have used the more appropriate phrase 'Untergeordnet sein' ⟨to be subordinated to⟩: "For ⟨what Paul meant to say⟩ is not at all that the Christian congregation and individual Christians relate to the civic congregation

or its functionaries with hopefully totally blind obedience of subjects who say 'Yes Sir.'" ⟨Paul spoke of⟩ "the implementation of *joint responsibility* ⟨italics by Barth⟩, in which Christians together with non-Christians tackle the same tasks" (i.e, "the foundation, preservation, and defense of the civic congregation"). For Luther obedience to governmental authority was obedience controlled by secular natural law; therefore he could have taken Barth's interpretation of Rom. 13:1a for granted. See, e.g., the sharp reproach of princes ⟨and the criticism of subjects⟩ in *On Secular Authority*, 1523: WA 11:246.23 ⟨*LW* 45:83⟩: "... God the Almighty has made our rulers mad; they actually think they can do — and order their subjects to do — whatever they please. And the subjects make the mistake of believing that they, in turn, are bound to obey their rulers in everything." See also the warning of princes who were most eager to go to war; Luther to Duke John Frederick, elector of Saxony, and Duke Maurice of Saxony: Apr. 7, 1542: WA.B 10:33.20. — It is another question whether Luther's translation of Rom. 13:1 still expressed his intentions when within Lutheranism secular natural law was no longer affirmed.

41. *On Secular Authority*, 1523: WA 11:264.16 ⟨*LW* 45:108⟩: "How he believes or disbelieves is a matter for the conscience of each individual ..."; for this passage, see, e.g., *Decretum Gratiani* c.92-98. C.XI.q.3 ⟨Friedberg 1:669-671⟩. See also *The Private Mass and the Consecration of Priests*, 1533: WA 38:189.14: "If a magistrate ... calls me to do something ungodly, I am not obligated to obey him; if I obey, then my vocation does not excuse me, but I share with the magistrate the same guilt" ⟨of committing a sin against the Second Table. "My vocation" could mean my vocation in the sense of my job, or it could mean my having been called by the magistrate to obey. In light of the following clause, this meaning seems to be more appropriate: if I obey, I cannot excuse my sin against the Second Table with the command (or call) of the magistrate; to the contrary, my obedience makes me just as guilty as the magistrate is in the first place⟩; Luther to Duke Frederick, elector of Saxony: May 8, 1522: WA.B 2:521.27: "No seal, law, custom, or governmental authority can stand up to God"; sermon of Aug. 2, 1523: WA 12: 649.17ff. — Among the secondary literature are esp. important Hermann Dörries, "Menschengehorsam und Gottesgehorsam bei Luther," *ARG* 39 (1942): 47ff., and Hermann Steinlein, "Luthers scharfe Abgrenzung des Gehorsams gegen die Obrigkeit," *JMLB* 3 (1948): 14ff.

42. *Against Jack Sausage*, 1541: WA 51:534.30 ⟨*LW* 41:226⟩: "God has committed enough to the emperor, more indeed than he can manage, namely, the earthly kingdom, that is, men's bodies and goods. There his office ends. If he reaches beyond that into God's kingdom, then he robs God of what is his, and that is called *sacrilegium*, 'stealing from God,' or as St. Paul calls it in Philippians 2[:6], 'grasping equality with God'"; ibid., WA 51:558.22 ⟨*LW* 41:248⟩: "... he ⟨i.e., the emperor⟩ has no business in the first table (no more than any angel or creature has). He can do nothing but fear and tremble before God, his name and his word — let alone change anything — for here God alone rules. And although he has no power to change the commandments in the second table, he can nevertheless govern both the life and property (which are subject to him) so that they are used in accordance with, not contrary to, these commandments, just as father and mother have authority in the home." See also sermon of Aug. 2, 1523: WA 12:649.20; *On the War Against the Turks*, 1529: WA 30.II:131.8; *Sermons on the First Epistle of St. Peter*, 1523: WA 12:334.32, 335.20.

43. *On Secular Authority*, 1523: WA 11:268.8 ⟨*LW* 45:113⟩: "It pleases his divine will that we call his hangmen gracious lords, fall at their feet, and be subject to them in all hu-

mility, so long as they do not ply their trade too far and try to become shepherds instead of hangmen"; sermon of Nov. 15, 1528: WA 27:419.4: "⟨Princes⟩ always want to rule where God rules"; *Sermons on Matthew, Chapters 5-7*, 1530-32: WA 32:336.27ff.; *On Good Works*, 1520: WA 6:274.16.26 ⟨*LW* 44:111f.⟩: "Satan has never been able to endure ⟨the gospel and the truth of faith⟩. He is always contriving to turn the leaders of the people against it, and compels them to persecute it. These [leaders] are the very hardest to resist.... ⟨This is especially the case⟩ if the gospel should be revived and heard once again, no doubt the whole world would arise and bestir itself." — A governmental authority may not obstruct the spiritual resistance to an unfaithful shepherd by arguing that such resistance "could disturb the public peace"; Luther to George Spalatin: Nov. 11, 1521: WA.B 2:402.6 ⟨*LW* 48:326⟩. — For the separation of the secular from the spiritual authority in the office of an Imperial ecclesiastical prince, see Luther to Philip Melanchthon: July 21, 1530: WA.B 5:492.10 ⟨*LW* 49:383f.⟩.

44. This could be the case only if a ruler is a heathen or a bad Christian. See thesis 36 of *Disputation on Matt. 19:21*, 1539: WA 39.II:41.11, and Rudolf Hermann, "Luthers Zirkulardisputation über Matth. 19,21," *LuJ* 23 (1941): 66 n. 2.

45. *On Secular Authority*, 1523: WA 11:262.9 ⟨*LW* 45:105⟩: "... God cannot and will not permit anyone but himself to rule over the soul."

46. Ibid., WA 11:246.27, 262.10 ⟨*LW* 45:83f., 105⟩.

47. The tasks of the ecclesiastical governance by the office of the public ministry also includes battling heretics; see below, 457 n. 10.

48. Luther to Daniel Greiser: Oct. 22, 1543: WA.B 10:436 n. 1, the last text quoted. ⟨See also below, 483 n. 162.⟩

49. *On Good Works*, 1520: WA 6:265.15 ⟨*LW* 44:100⟩: "But if, as often happens, the temporal power and authorities, or whatever they call themselves, would compel a subject to do something contrary to the commandment of God, or hinder him from doing what God commands, obedience ends and the obligation ceases"; *The Book of Deuteronomy with Notes*, 1525: WA 14:612.23: "No ⟨laws bind a Christian⟩ unless they serve faith and love; if they serve faith and love, all ⟨laws bind a Christian⟩"; *Warning of His Dear German People*, 1531: WA 30.III:283.24: suppression of true doctrine through military actions is "contrary to all divine and secular laws"; ibid., WA 30.III:291.20.26: therefore there exists no duty to obey the emperor's call for mobilization against the evangelicals; ibid., WA 30.III:291.28: "⟨For⟩ in this case the emperor acts not only against God and the divine law but also against his own Imperial law, oath, duty, seal, and written document"; *Defense Against the Charge of Inciting Rebellion*, 1533: WA 38:100.22, 111.15: no one has the competency for investigating what is in a person's heart and conscience, and for ruling over it. See also Luther to Christopher Jörger: Dec. 31, 1543(?): WA.B 10:485.26ff.

50. E.g., the order of a governmental authority to turn over evangelical books ⟨e.g., Luther's New Testament in German⟩; *On Secular Authority*, 1523: WA 11:267.2.11 ⟨*LW* 45:111f.⟩. — See also Friedrich Loy, "Das Widerstandsrecht und seine Grenzen bei Luther und heute," in *Zur politischen Predigt*, 69.

51. *Magnificat*, 1521: WA 7:580.20: "... for the sake of truth and what is right we are to suffer all things ..."; ibid., WA 7:584.9: no one may give up faith and the gospel, the highest goods; *Sermons on the First Epistle of St. Peter*, 1523: WA 12:334.32 ⟨*LW* 30:80⟩: "But if they ⟨i.e., lords and kings⟩ want to encroach on the spiritual rule and want to take our conscience captive where God alone must sit and rule, one should by no means obey them

and should sooner let them have one's life ⟨literally: 'give up one's neck'⟩. Secular domain and rule do not extend beyond external and physical matters"; ibid., WA 12:335.26 ⟨LW 30:81⟩: "St. Peter calls the secular government merely a human institution. Therefore they have no power to interfere in God's arrangement and to give commands concerning faith." ⟨In the following letters, some signed also by John Bugenhagen, Luther applied this principle to specific circumstances.⟩ Luther to the City Council of Crossen/Oder: Apr. 13, 1527: WA.B 4:No. 1095; to the brothers Einsiedel: Dec. 28, 1527: WA.B 4:No. 1187; to George Spalatin: Jan. 5, 1528: WA.B 4:No. 1201; to Henry von Einsiedel: Jan. 24, 1528: WA.B 4:No. 1213.

52. Luther to Daniel Greiser: Oct. 22, 1543: WA.B 10:436.3.

53. One may not use Christ's cleansing of the Temple ⟨Matt. 21:12, John 2:13-17⟩ to justify such a change because Christ had both governances in his hand, and because "at that time ⟨i.e., when he acted against the merchants and bankers⟩ he lived between the Old and the New Testament"; *Sermons on John, Chapters 1 and 2*, 1537-38: WA 46:732.8, 733.1, 734.13.

54. *The Book of Deuteronomy with Notes*, 1525: WA 14:611.29ff.; *Lectures on Genesis*, 1535-45: WA 43:507.6, 507.27: "The First Table must be carried before the Second Table"; *Lectures on Psalm 45*, 1532: WA 40.II:578.6. See also Bornkamm, *Luther und das Alte Testament*, 20, 114. — In *Disputation on Matt. 19:21* (1539) Luther expressed this relationship of the Two Tables with each other in juristic formulas; WA 39.II:70.31. His statements were criticized by Hermann, "Luthers Zirkulardisputation über Matth. 19,21" *LuJ* 23 (1941): 58. Luther's statements can be understood only on the basis of his dualistic natural law doctrine. Luther called (WA 39.II.64.2) the First Table of the Decalogue *lex superior* over against the Second Table, because for him the First Table contained the divine natural law, the Second Table the secular natural law. With this understanding in mind, one may express the relationship of the Two Tables with each other in the following formula: The superior law checks the inferior law (*lex superior refutat inferiorem;* ibid., WA 39.II:70.31); the issue is the priority of the divine law over the transpositive human law. Theses 8, 9, 30, and 48 of this disputation ⟨ibid., WA 39.II:39.16-19, 40.36f., 41.36f.⟩ clearly show that Luther understood the Second Table as fixing the secular natural-law order of the kingdom of the world, because the Second Table is connected with the secular commonwealth; ibid., WA 39.II:40.36, 41.36. Luther qualified his derogation of the Second Table over against the First Table by arguing (ibid., WA 39.II:70.19) that not the commandment itself may be passed over but the subject matter *(non . . . negligatur praeceptum, sed res).* 'Res sacramenti' (content, thing, subject matter of a sacrament) seems to have been the model for 'res praecepti'. This phrase designates the totality of things legally secured by the Second Table ("what we have *virtute* [because, or by means of, the strength, or power, maybe authority or prestige] of the Second Table may not be let go *[omittere]* because of the First Table"; ibid., WA 39.II:70.16). ⟨Derogating the Second Table,⟩ Luther intended to say that the secular natural-law order of the kingdom of the world ⟨expressed in the Second Table⟩ remains in force, *but* in *casu confessionis* ⟨i.e., when the First Table creates a situation in which one has to confess the faith at the risk of one's life⟩ a Christian has to give up the rights ⟨and laws⟩ which are the product of this order. See also *Postilla for Lent*, 1525: WA 17.II:54.1: "The First Commandment is the standard for all the other commandments; therefore, if according to the First Commandment it is God's honor and will, I can, contrary to the commandments of the other Table, kill, rob, abduct women and children, as

the people of Israel did with their enemies, the heathen"; sermons of ca. 1514-20: WA 4:608.5.

55. Luther to Duke Frederick, elector of Saxony: March 7(8?), 1522: WA.B 2:460.17 ⟨*LW* 48:395⟩: "Human ⟨governmental⟩ authority is not always to be obeyed, namely, when it undertakes something against the commandments of God; yet it should never be despised but always honored"; *On Good Works,* 1520: WA 6:259.6.13 ⟨*LW* 44:92⟩: ". . . even when the government commits an injustice, . . . God wants the government obeyed, without treachery or deception . . . unless, of course, it should try openly to compel us to do wrong against God or men . . ."; ibid., WA 6:259.33 ⟨*LW* 44:93⟩. — In connection with such passages one has to think also of Luther's loathing of the dangers created by the anarchy of mob-rule; Olsson, *Grundproblemet,* 1:27; sermon on John 18:10f. (Dec. 5, 1528): WA 28:250.6: "God is willing to endure a magistrate who is delinquent of the duties of his office rather than an unjust people"; *Whether Soldiers, Too, Can Be Saved,* 1526: WA 19:635.11: "If one has to suffer injustice, one has to prefer suffering it from a governmental authority than that a governmental authority suffers it from the subjects; for the mob . . . knows no moderation, and among the members of a mob are more than five tyrants. It is better, then, to suffer injustice from one tyrant, i.e., from a governmental authority, than from innumerable tyrants, i.e., from a mob." — For the following, see *Decretum Gratiani* c.9.§3. C.XIV.q.5 ⟨Friedberg 1:740⟩, and above, Appendix I.

56. *Second Lectures on the Psalms,* 1518-21: WA 5:436.1: "⟨One has to differentiate between⟩ authority and misuse of authority. For those who have authority are to be respected ⟨literally: 'the names (in the sense of title) of authorities are to'⟩, but their vices are to be despised, nor are the vices to be covered or approved because someone has authority. One may not . . . despise authority because of its vice, because there is no authority except from God, Rom. 13⟨:1b⟩; therefore authority belongs not to man but to God, but the vices do not belong to God but to man"; Luther to Duke John, elector of Saxony: March 6, 1530: WA.B 5:258.31 ⟨*LW* 49:276⟩: ". . . since the emperor remains emperor, [or] a sovereign remains sovereign, even if he trespasses all of God's commandments, or even if he were a heathen, so he is to be [governmental authority for his subjects] even if he does not fulfill his oath and duty, until he has been removed from office, or is no longer emperor." Luther developed this doctrine of resistance first in connection with resistance to ecclesiastical superiors; *First Lectures on the Psalms,* 1513-15: WA 3:259.1 ⟨*LW* 10:216⟩.

57. Luther to Duke John, elector of Saxony: March 6, 1530: WA.B 5:258.13 ⟨*LW* 49:275⟩.

58. *Against Jack Sausage,* 1541: WA 51:554.24: "We say in German that the law is always an honest man, but the judge is often a scoundrel"; ibid., WA 51:555.29: ". . . there is a difference between the thing *(res)* and the person, that is to say, 'the thing', the law, is always an honest man, but 'the person', the judge, is often a scoundrel." Luther made similar statements as early as 1530; Luther to Gregory Brück, chancellor of Electoral Saxony: Aug. 5, 1530: WA.B 5:532.56.61 ⟨*LW* 49: 397f.⟩, and Theodor Pauls, *Luthers Anschauung von Staat und Volk* (Bonn, 1925), 67. Luther developed the differentiation between the person and the office first in connection with the office of preaching and its incumbent; *First Lectures on the Psalms,* 1513-15: WA 3:259.1.

59. Sermon of March 13, 1529: WA 28:361.6: "There is a big difference between suffering the violence of injustice and being silent. Evil has to be endured, but not being silent, because I must give a witness to the truth. If I must die for the sake of truth, it be-

hooves me to speak up and punish the lie with the mouth. It behooves us to die for the sake of truth and ⟨what is⟩ right."

60. See *First Lectures on the Psalms*, 1513-15: WA 4:446.25.

61. It is esp. the task of the incumbent of the preaching office to censure the sin of a governmental authority; *Psalm 82 Explained*, 1530 ⟨in the following we use 'censure' for what literally would be 'punish'⟩: WA 31.I:196.6: "⟨In his congregation⟩ God has ordained his priests and preachers, whom he has charged with the office to teach, admonish, censure, comfort, in summary, proclaim God's Word. Wherever it is commanded to proclaim God's Word, there is God's office of censuring"; ibid., WA 31.I:197.29: ". . . it is not seditious to censure governmental authority if it is done . . . by the office with which God has charged someone, and with God's Word, in broad daylight, and candidly. ⟨Then⟩ such censuring is . . . a specially important service to God . . . . It would be more seditious if a preacher would not censure the vices of a governmental authority; ⟨then⟩ he would make the mob indignant and angry, strengthen the wickedness of tyrants, and participate in all their wickedness and be guilty of it." — For the 'salt' office of Christians ⟨Matt. 5:13⟩, esp. of preachers, to be implemented in the world, see *Sermons on Matthew, Chapters 5-7*, 1530-32: WA 32:344.9ff. ⟨LW 21:55⟩; see also ibid., WA 32:349.4 ⟨LW 21:60⟩. — For the affirmation that the implementation of the office of censuring is not an act of rebellion against governmental authority, see Luther to Simon Wolferinus: Sept. 19, 1544: WA.B 10:659.13; to Count Albrecht of Mansfeld: Feb. 23, 1542: WA.B 9:No. 3716. — See also Lau, *Luthers Lehre von den beiden Reichen*, 74ff.; Eivind Berggrav, "Staat und Kirche in lutherischer Sicht," in *Das lebendige Wort in einer verantwortlichen Kirche. Offizieller Bericht der zweiten Vollversammlung des Lutherischen Weltbundes* (Hannover, 1952), 79.

62. *On Secular Authority*, 1523: WA 11:277.2: "Governmental authority is not to be resisted with force, but only with the confession of the truth"; *Sermons on the First Epistle of St. Peter*, 1523: WA 12:335.17 ⟨LW 30:81⟩: ". . . if an emperor or a prince were to ask me now what my faith is, I would have to tell him, not because of his command, but because it is my duty to confess my faith publicly before everybody"; *First Lectures on the Psalms*, 1513-15: WA 4:309.23 ⟨LW 11:420⟩: "It is not enough to believe with the heart unto righteousness, unless confession unto salvation is also made with the mouth (Rom. 10:10)"; *Second Lectures on Galatians*, 1531: WA 40.I:586.15.

63. *On the Ban*, 1520: WA 6:72.31 ⟨LW 39:18f.⟩: ". . . God neither likes nor tolerates blasphemous and wanton resistance to authority, as long as it does not drive us to act against God or against his commandment — although it [authority] itself may act as much against God as it wants to, or hurt us as much as it wants to. He himself intends to judge and to condemn those who are great and powerful tyrants, as well as to help those who are oppressed sufferers. That is why we should yield to his will and let the tyrants fall under his sword and judgment. On the other hand, we should let ourselves be helped by him. . . ."

64. If necessary, one may emigrate; *Admonition to Peace*, 1525: WA 18:323.3; *Whether Soldiers, Too, Can Be Saved*, 1526: WA 19:634.15; Luther to George Rauth: March 1, 1524: WA.B 3:250.5.

65. *Open Letter on the Harsh Book against the Peasants*, 1525: WA 18:395.9: "You should fear and respect God's commandment more than the people, even if you must therefore risk danger and death"; *Second Lectures on the Psalms*, 1518-21: WA 5:189.15:

"For the sake of righteousness we must ⟨be ready⟩ to suffer death and whatever evil, ⟨though we⟩ are innocent."

66. *Second Lectures on Galatians,* 1531: WA 40.I:188.1: "In matters of faith one must be inflexible, invincible, ⟨hard⟩ like a diamond."

67. *The Estate of Marriage,* 1522: WA 10.II:285.23: "You should rather give up life ... than act contrary to love." A wedding into which parents forced their child is not valid; *On Marriage Matters,* 1530: WA 30.III:236.8. ⟨See also above, 400 n. 12.⟩

68. *On Good Works,* 1520: WA 6:259.6 ⟨LW 44:92⟩: "... even when the government commits an injustice, ... God wants the government obeyed, without treachery or deception."

69. *Against Jack Sausage,* 1541: WA 51:557.21 ⟨LW 41:247⟩: "... God's Ten Commandments, which demand obedience not only of kings and emperors, but also of prophets, apostles, and all creatures, stand against this and compel them to do what is right according to their office, not what they want to do as persons"; ibid., WA 51:558.30 ⟨LW 41:248⟩: "Now when ... ⟨they⟩ cry, 'The pope and emperor, to whom one ought to be obedient, have commanded it,' then the answer is, 'With the exception of the Ten Commandments and the gospel, which the pope and emperor, like us, are bound to obey and be subject to.'" — In the sense of these statements one has to qualify Ernst Wolf, "Frage des Naturrechts bei Thomas und bei Luther," 16: "Refusal to obey occurs only when in its dealing with us a secular authority, or an ecclesiastical authority, idolizing itself and thus becoming secular, wants to act contrary to the first three commandments." — See also Luther to Duke Frederick, elector of Saxony: March 5, 1522: WA.B 2:456.102 ⟨LW 48:392⟩: "... no one should overthrow or resist authority save him who ordained it; otherwise it is rebellion and an action against God." — In later years Luther made more precise statements: resistance to a secular governmental authority which, contrary to divine and secular law, oppresses the evangelical faith with force, is not rebellion, though it is a violation of law; *Warning of His Dear German People,* 1531: WA 30.III:283.13: "It is not rebellion if someone acts contrary to law; otherwise all violations of law would have to be called rebellion. But he is a rebel who does not want to endure governmental authority and law but attacks and fights them, wants to suppress them and himself be lord and make laws, as Müntzer did (there is a difference between a usurper and a transgressor)." ⟨For usurper, see below, 416 nn. 84-85.⟩ — It is permissible for an evangelical vassal to appeal to the Imperial court for help against a tyrannical overlord, who deprives him of his fief because of his faith; Luther and Bugenhagen to Henry von Einsiedel: Jan. 24, 1528: WA.B 4:359.93.

70. See above, 331 n. 266.

71. *The Babylonian Captivity of the Church,* 1520: WA 6:557.22: "⟨God's⟩ command is to be given preference if it contradicts the commands of men."

72. Emil Brunner, *Gerechtigkeit,* 322 n. 38, presented an opposite position and added: "Here is the point where the Reformation doctrine of natural law departs from the medieval-Catholic one in the most definite way." One has to differentiate, however, between two cases: When a governmental authority commits an unjust act against me, then, being a Christian, I have to endure it. But when a governmental authority demands that I act against my neighbor in a way which violates secular natural law, I have to reject this; were I not to do this, I would have to be responsible for an action which opposes God, and no command of a governmental authority can absolve me from this responsibility. ⟨See also above, 107f.⟩

73. The situation is different, of course, when positive law permits the right of active

resistance. Secular natural law does not prohibit such a limitation of the power of governmental authority. See above, Appendix I.

74. *Whether Soldiers, Too, Can Be Saved*, 1526: WA 19:634.12: "... even if lords act unjustly, it would therefore not be just and right also to act unjustly, i.e., be disobedient and destroy God's order, which does not belong to us; rather, one should endure the injustice of the lords."

75. ⟨See above, 108f.⟩

76. See Erich Seeberg, *Grundzüge der Theologie Luthers*, 200ff. For additional materials, see Matthes, *Luther und die Obrigkeit*, 96 n. 48. In the present context we cannot deal with details; instead of other authors, see Heinz Zahrnt, *Luther deutet Geschichte* (Munich, 1952), 88ff. — Gollwitzer (*Christliche Gemeinde*, 18f.) was critical of Luther's position on war. Luther was "too quick to accept the fact that there are wars within Christendom. With this readiness he stood within a European tradition, originating in Antiquity, which Christianity had been unable to change. In his teachings Luther did not appeal to Christians to be ashamed of that situation." Against Gollwitzer's argumentation, see *Second Lectures on the Psalms*, 1518-21: WA 5:409.23: "... do people not praise as the highest of all things that which is the worst? For who does not ⟨see in⟩ the glory derived from wars (i.e., the shedding of human blood) the highest virtue among men? What else are Homer, Virgil, and the other authors of heroic poems than the most bloodstained and cruel inciters, inflamers, and braggarts of murderers, tyrants, and the most ferocious enemies of the human blood and race? Therefore if a Christian reads these books there is a danger that he would develop a disposition for such bloody glory; or, titillated by the honey-sweet eloquence, or rather corrupted by the innate thirst for human blood, he might be delighted by such great slaughter of the human race"; ibid., WA 5:409.34: "Isn't it great ⟨mental blindness⟩ that one can even rejoice and sing about the slaughter, defeat, blood, murder, and the large amount of evil which war causes, and praise all this? ⟨In reality⟩ it would be appropriate to mourn all this with tears of blood, esp. if one wages war not by God's command, but driven by insane lust for power and property, as the people ⟨of the world⟩ did and still do. And today, oh, what grief! Christians, the people of peace, the children of God, wage war even more cruelly than all the heathen"; ibid., WA 5:569.17, 577.13; *Sermons on Matthew, Chapters 5-7*, 1530-32: WA 32:330.10 ⟨LW 21:39⟩; *On Good Works*, 1520: WA 6:261.1 ⟨LW 44:94⟩.

77. *On Good Works*, 1520: WA 6:265.21: "When a prince wants to wage war over a clearly unjust issue, one should not at all obey or help him because God has commanded not to kill our neighbor or act unjustly toward him"; *On Secular Authority*, 1523: WA 11:277.28: "What if a prince's action is unjust? Are then his people also obligated to obey him? Answer: 'No'"; *Whether Soldiers, Too, Can Be Saved*, 1526: WA 19:653.23ff.: subjects are obligated to assist their lord with body and property, and obey when they are called upon to go to war; ibid., WA 19:656.22: "Another question is: What is to happen if my lord would be unjust in waging war? Answer: If you know for certain that he is unjust, then you have to fear God and obey him rather than man, Acts ⟨5:29⟩, and you are not to go to war or serve; otherwise you could not have a good conscience before God."

78. ⟨Heckel wrote "Notkrieg"; see below, n. 79.⟩

79. Luther differentiated between a war which was 'made' and a 'necessary' war; *Whether Soldiers, Too, Can Be Saved*, 1526: WA 19:647.28 ⟨LW 46:121⟩: "No war is just, ... unless one has such a good reason for fighting and such a good conscience that one can

say, 'My neighbor compels and forces me to fight, though I would rather avoid it.' In that case, it can be called not only war, but lawful self-defense *(Notwehr)*, for we must distinguish between wars that someone begins because that is what he wants to do, and he does so before anyone else attacks him, and those wars that are provoked, when an attack is made by someone else. The first kind can be called wars of desire; the second, wars of necessity *(Notkrieg)*. The first kind are of the devil; ⟨may God not give it good fortune⟩. The second kind ⟨is⟩ a human ⟨disaster⟩; ⟨may God help in it⟩. Take my advice, dear lords. Stay out of war unless you have to defend and protect yourself, and your office compels you to fight"; *Matthew, Chapters 18-24 Explained in Sermons*, 1537-40: WA 47:558.10. — Only if a war is just may one hope for God's help; *Second Lectures on the Psalms*, 1518-21: WA 5:569.11: Luther cited Ps. 33:16f.: "A king is not saved by his great army; a warrior is not delivered by his great strength"; he continued: "The strength of the horse contributes little to victory ⟨literally: 'the horse is fallacious for well-being,' or: 'safety'⟩, . . . but ⟨a king⟩ should expect help to come from heaven, should know that victory comes from heaven, place his hope on . . . the Lord only, and do battle through prayer, as did Moses ⟨Ex. 17:11⟩." Luther saw the opposite of this attitude of waging war in the attitude with which in his day war was waged against the Turks; see ibid., WA 5:577.15. ⟨See also Luther to George Spalatin: Dec. 21, 1518: WA.B 1:282.15: ". . . in the Old or the New Testament no war has been waged by means of human strength, which did not always result in misery and shame; if, however, something turned out well, then war had been waged from heaven." In this letter Luther answered the question whether on the basis of Scripture he could approve the pending war against the Turks. He doubted that, even if such a war were waged for the sake of true zeal for piety (religious war against the infidels?), and he argued that a "carnal war" in "foreign" lands will accomplish nothing as long as "at home we are defeated in spiritual wars." Then he made the statement cited. He continued that in view of the sinful ways of the papacy and clergy, there is no hope for a "good war" and "victory" because "God fights against us"; he has to be "overcome first through tears, pure prayers, holy living, and pure faith." "War waged from heaven" could mean that as a result of a good outcome a war was waged with heaven's blessing. But it could also mean the "spiritual wars" in which "we" are now involved as a result of God's actions "from heaven" (attack of Germany by the Turks? attack of the gospel by the papacy?), and in which we will be defeated unless God, through prayer, etc., is overcome, i.e., drawn to our side and gives us the victory by which things will turn out well. If one understands the sentence in this way, then it would seem that Luther wanted to say the following: Let's first fight the spiritual war at home and gain God's blessing; otherwise, when we fight the Turks, we fight a carnal war, fight in human strength, and this will result only in misery and shame.⟩ — Gollwitzer *(Christliche Gemeinde,* 48) was correct when he pointed out that participation in war and the preparation for war "again and again need the concrete proof, justification, and evaluation ⟨of the situation⟩ in light of the main task *(opus proprium)* of love." Yet this principle does not only apply specifically to war, but it applies to each action in the kingdom of the world.

80. *Whether Soldiers, Too, Can Be Saved*, 1526: WA 19:645.9. See also *On the War Against the Turks,* 1529: WA 30.II:111.7; Luther's brief dated end of April(?), 1528: WA.B 4:432.45.

81. *On Secular Authority,* 1523: WA 11:277.31 ⟨*LW* 45:125f.⟩.

82. Luther and Melanchthon to Duke John, elector of Saxony: May 1 or 2, 1528: WA.B

4:449.50 ⟨*LW* 49:194⟩. See also Luther's warning not to start a war prior to law having been violated; Luther to Duke John Frederick, elector of Saxony, and Duke Maurice of Saxony: Apr. 7, 1542: WA.B 10:33.35.

83. *Lectures on Genesis*, 1535-45: WA 43:62.35: "... in order to demonstrate his power and wisdom, God does many things which are contrary to the norm, and he does them through heroic human beings, whom he himself calls individually . . . ."

84. ⟨Tyrant in terms of the administration of the office.⟩ For the terminology, see Friedrich Schoenstedt, *Der Tyrannenmord im Spätmittelalter* (Berlin, 1938), 40, 50ff., on the basis of Bartolus de Sassoferrato (1314-57) *De tyrannia:* Tyrant on the basis of action ⟨a legitimate ruler misuses his office⟩ — tyrant on the basis of a wrong title ⟨the person uses the title, though he has no right to do so, he is a usurper or *invasor,* who holds the office illegitimately and uses it as he pleases⟩. ⟨For Bartolus de Sassoferrato (or Saxoferrato), see Martin Heckel, *Staat und Kirche nach den Lehren der evangelischen Juristen Deutschlands in der ersten Hälfte des 17. Jahrhunderts* (Munich, 1968), 178f.⟩

85. Most of the time, the *tyrannus quoad executionem* was for Luther *the* tyrant. Sometimes he also called the usurper tyrant, and sometimes he differentiated between tyrant and *invasor*. *Warning of His Dear German People*, 1531: WA 30.III:283.17, as above, 413 n. 69; *Disputation on Matt. 19:21*, 1539: WA 39.II:75.6f.; *Lectures on Genesis*, 1535-45: WA 42:401.13.15 ⟨comments on Gen. 10:8f.⟩: "... ⟨Nimrod,⟩ not content with the land he had, invaded the land of his neighbors. . . . he wanted to have power not only in the *politia*, but he also wanted to have power over religion; he invaded religion and tyrannized it, as the pope does today"; *Sermons on Genesis*, 1523-24: WA 14:210.3: "⟨Nimrod⟩ oppressed the people and became lord through force. This is the nature of all princes to this day."

86. *Psalm 110 Explained*, 1518: WA 1:692.37: "All of Christ's enemies are tyrants, all who present themselves as governmental authority, though God did not call them. . . ."

87. ⟨See above, 78f., 107.⟩

88. *Summer Postilla*, 1526: WA 10:I.2:426.18: "... ⟨you may⟩ not ask whether they possess and administer the governance and governmental authority legally or illegally." — It is another problem whether it is permissible to depose an *insane ruler*. According to the secular natural law such deposing is not prohibited; *Whether Soldiers, Too, Can Be Saved*, 1526: WA 19:634.18 ⟨*LW* 46:105⟩.

89. See Fritz Kern, *Gottesgnadentum und Widerstandsrecht im früheren Mittelalter* (Leipzig, 1915), esp. 396ff.; Heydte, *Geburtsstunde des souveränen Staates*, 362ff.

90. For the Middle Ages, see Kern, *Gottesgnadentum*, 220.

91. ⟨To each his own.⟩

92. ⟨One may fight force with force. See also above, 134, 316 n. 112; *Digest* (Watson ed.) XLIII.16.27.⟩

93. ⟨I.e., citizen against citizen.⟩

94. ⟨See above, 108f.⟩ *On Good Works*, 1520: WA 6:259.12 ⟨*LW* 44:92⟩: "... the power of the temporal authority, whether it does right or wrong, cannot harm the soul, but only our body and our property — unless, of course, it should try openly to compel us to do wrong against God or men. . . . For to suffer wrong destroys no man's soul, in fact, it improves the soul, though it does inflict hurt to our body and our possessions. But to do wrong destroys the soul, even though all the world's wealth be gained."

95. ⟨See above, 109.⟩

96. For the Middle Ages, see the decretal *Venerabilem* (1202): c.34. X⟨*Liber extra*⟩. I.6. ⟨Friedberg 2:79ff.⟩.

97. ⟨As the church had claimed in the Middle Ages.⟩ See Luther's polemics in *A Model for Consecrating a True Bishop,* 1542: WA 53:236.26: "⟨The pope⟩ interferes in the secular and the domestic governance, which is neither for a bishop nor the church proper to do...."

98. ⟨In comparison with the Middle Ages; see, e.g., above, 388 n. 38.⟩

99. ⟨See above, 108f.⟩

100. See esp. Wingren, *Luthers Lehre vom Beruf,* 80, 120ff.

101. *Admonition to Peace,* 1525: WA 18:317.10 ⟨*LW* 46:33⟩: "Therefore I beg you ⟨i.e., the rebelling peasants⟩ not to despise my prayer and the prayer of those who pray along with me, for it will be too mighty for you and will arouse God against you, as St. James says, 'The prayer of the righteous man who prays persistently has great effects, just as Elijah's prayer did' [Jas. 5:16-17]." ⟨Throughout his life Luther emphasized the proper attitude for praying, and the power and effectiveness of prayer in spiritual battles and in secular matters. His sermons and books, and esp. his letters often reflect the concrete circumstances for his rich prayer life, or for his understanding of prayer as a powerful weapon against his enemies or worldly injustice. See, e.g.,⟩ *Second Lectures on the Psalms,* 1518-21: WA 5:234.38: "... we fight ... by means of prayer, the Word, and patience"; ibid., WA 5:239.26: "... what else is God's sword than the word of the eternal judgment?"; sermon of June 23, 1539 (WA 47:804.15) and of Aug. 2, 1523 (WA 12:650.24); *On the War Against the Turks,* 1529: WA 30.II:119.27; *Sermons on Matthew, Chapters 5-7,* 1530-32: WA 32:400.15: "Since you do not wish to tolerate ⟨God's Word⟩, I shall pray ... that God will crush you to the earth"; *On Good Works,* 1520: WA 6:239.3.11.18; Luther to Justus Jonas: March 13, 1542: WA.B 10:6.9; to the Mayor and the Judge of Frauenstein: March 17, 1531: WA.B 6:54.36; to the Christians in Frauenstein: June 27, 1531: WA.B 6:131.5; to Valentine Hausmann: June 24, 1532: WA.B 6:323.35; to Philip Melanchthon: Apr. 24, 1530 (WA.B 5:285.10 ⟨*LW* 49:289⟩) and Apr. 8, 1540 (WA.B 9:89.12); to the Canons of the All Saints Chapter in Wittenberg: July 11, 1523: WA.B 3:112.37; to the City Council of Ölsnitz: Dec. 4, 1523: WA.B 3:201.17; to Nicholas Hausmann: Apr. 26, 1524 (WA.B 3:279.7) and Oct. 26, 1529 (WA.B 5:167.15); to Duke George of Saxony: Dec. 21, 1525: WA.B 3:643.68.76; to Wenceslas Link: ca. Dec. 21, 1528: WA.B 4:626.14; to Nicholas von Amsdorf: Dec. 30, 1528: WA.B 4:628.13; to Margrave Joachim I, elector of Brandenburg: Aug. 8, 1528 (WA.B 4:513.33) and Oct. 5, 1528 (WA.B 4:580.122); to Gregory Brück, chancellor of Electoral Saxony: Dec. 23, 1534: WA.B 7:144.21; to Christopher Froschauer: Aug. 31, 1543: WA.B 10:387.13; to Mrs. Martin Luther: July 10, 1540: WA.B 9:172.26 ⟨*LW* 50:215⟩.

102. *Second Lectures on the Psalms,* 1518-21: WA 5:243.15: "It suffices to know that we handle God's cause ..."; ibid., WA 5:50.9: God takes care of our cause.

103. ⟨See below, Index of Subjects: *Law,* s.v. "law, of wrath."⟩

104. *Second Lectures on the Psalms,* 1518-21: WA 5:233.27, as below, 418 n. 108.

105. Luther to Count Albrecht of Mansfeld: beginning(?) of 1525: WA.B 3:416.53. For the spiritual victory of a Christian in such a war, see sermon of Jan. 11, 1540: WA 49:24.2: "On one day the tyrants ⟨of the world⟩ were defeated on the cross through ⟨Christ's⟩ blood; Christ still defeats them without letting up because he preaches that all who believe in him are to be free from the law, sin, and death. Today the battle still continues through the Word and the sacraments."

106. *Second Lectures on the Psalms,* 1518-21: WA 5:235.15: ⟨The danger to which the service of God *(dei ministerium)* and the Salvation of the people are exposed will not end unless the evil of the godless has ended and⟩ "the case of the innocence of the just has been judged and firmly established, and this by God the judge and avenger."

107. *Sermons on Matthew, Chapters 5-7,* 1530-32: WA 32:402.19 ⟨*LW* 21:124⟩: "As He himself says (Deut. 32:35): 'Vengance is mine, I will repay.' On the basis of this, St. Paul admonishes the Christians (Rom. 12:19): 'Never avenge yourselves, but leave it to the wrath of God.' These words are not only instruction but also consolation, as if He were to say: 'Do not take it upon yourselves to avenge yourselves on one another, or to speak curses and maledictions. The person that does you harm or injury is interfering with an office that is not his. He is presuming to inflict punishment or injury upon you without the command of God, indeed, contrary to it. Now, if you do the same, then you, too, are interfering with the office of God and sinning against God as gravely as this man has sinned against you. Therefore keep your fist to yourself."

108. *Seond Lectures on the Psalms,* 1518-21: WA 5:50.10 ⟨*LW* 14:316; to Ps. 2:2⟩: "But ⟨the psalmist⟩ also arranges the words in this manner that we may learn for our consolation and exhortation that we never suffer injustice without God suffering it first and more than we and that God the Father's solicitude for us is so great that He feels our suffering before we do and bears it with greater resentment than we ourselves. Therefore we should refrain from a feeling of revenge but should rather have compassion on those whom we see dashing themselves to their destruction against a majesty so great; for not only are they unable to do any harm, but they destroy themselves horribly"; ibid., WA 5:100.18: "As often as I suffer injustice, I call on the God of my righteousness ⟨or: 'justice'⟩, and I am ready to accept as righteousness ⟨or: 'justice'⟩ whatever his judgment establishes"; ibid., WA 5:233.27: "So we see that, if someone suffers because of a just cause or for the sake of truth, it is not enough that one commends the matter to God and is ready to give in and have oneself and one's honor reduced to dust; rather, one has to pray earnestly that God judge and vindicate the cause of truth not for one's own benefit but for the benefit of serving God and of the Salvation of the people, whose Salvation is always endangered. You are not free from guilt if, ⟨because of⟩ foolish humility, you do not most earnestly pray for the preservation and restoration of the truth and of justice for you.... Lies and injustices have to be endured. But it has to be done in such a way that you do not give up love for other people. That love should not be concerned about how you rise ⟨i.e., rise in the opinion of the people because of your humility which endures evil and injustices⟩, but it should be concerned about how it can be accomplished that the people are not offended and perish"; ibid., WA 5:235.9: the right attitude for the prayer against the injustice of the godless is the zeal for the love of God and man; ibid., WA 5:308.24: "... in one's own cause every one has to be patient, free from eagerness for revenge, and turn to God through ... prayer"; ibid., WA 5:116.20: commend our cause to God and confidentially wait for his mercy; see also ibid., WA 5:112.32, 115.14, 221.25.

109. See, e.g., the most recent account ⟨*note:* the first ed. of *Lex charitatis* was published in 1953⟩ in Lau, *Luthers Lehre von den beiden Reichen,* 86: "In Luther's doctrine of the two kingdoms there is no room for active disobedience and ... rebellion against any kind of state, regardless how tyrannical or hostile to the gospel such a governance might be." See, however, Hans-Joachim Iwand and Ernst Wolf, "Entwurf eines Gutachtens zur Frage des Widerstandsrechts nach evangelischer Lehre," *Junge Kirche* 13 (1952): 192ff.;

Berggrav, "Staat und Kirche in lutherischer Sicht," in *Das lebendige Wort,* 79. Berggrav started from the argument that according to Lutheran doctrine the state is *Rechtsstaat* ⟨state of law, or state based on, and operating according to, law⟩. Kurt Klein (*Kirche und Staat,* 20) was correct when he pointed out that for this term the meaning of law needs to be clarified, and he raised the question of Luther's concept 'secular natural law'. If one uses this concept, then indeed parts of Berggrav's theses would juristically become more precise.

110. ⟨For Luther this was the pope.⟩ For disobedience to a tyrannically ruling ecclesiastical authority, see above, 99f.

111. ⟨See above, 105.⟩

112. ⟨See above, 108f.⟩

113. For the change in Luther's position on the Turks, see instead of other authors, Zahrnt, *Luther deutet Geschichte,* 119ff.

114. ⟨Hence the references to the pope in the following materials.⟩

115. ⟨Literally: "hunter."⟩

116. *Lectures on Genesis,* 1535-45: WA 42:400.32, 401.6.12.14.30, 402.1 ⟨LW 2:196, 197, 198⟩: ". . . Nimrod was the first after the Flood to strive for the sovereignty of the world. . . . he was the first Turk or pope on earth after the Flood. . . . Not satisfied with his own territory, however, he encroaches on his neighbors. And, what is worse, he wants to be a mighty hunter, not only on earth but also before the Lord. That is, he not only wanted to be mighty in government *(politia),* but also wanted to rule in religion; he invades it and exercises tyranny over it, just as the pope does today. . . . Not satisfied with his tyranny in the state *(respublica),* he also wants to be lord in the church. He sets up new forms of worship, and he oppresses those who stand before God. . . . Thus Scripture depicts a tyrant who makes inroads not only on other kingdoms but also on religion." — In the polemics of Orthodox Lutheran theologians against the *monarcha universalis* one can sometimes still find the image of the grand tyrant. See, e.g., Balthasar Meisner ⟨1587-1626; *RE* (3d ed.), 12:511f.⟩, *Discursus theologicus de Regimine ecclesiastico* (Tübingen, 1610), page 10.LVI: "I distinguish between 'universal monarchy in the absolute sense' and 'monarchy which in a certain way is particular' *(monarchia absolute univeralis, monarchia quodammodo particularis).* I use these terms until someone suggests more appropriate ones. I call it universal monarchy — which includes the totality of subjects, goods, jurisdiction, and authority — when one person is, or wants to be, the lord of all people totally and at the same time appropriates to himself all authority, both the secular one pertaining to matters of ⟨position⟩ and external goods, and the spiritual one pertaining to matters of the soul or internal goods of all people, all who live in the whole world. But I call it particular monarchy, when one person is king and ruler *(rex et monarcha),* yet has not all authority but only partial secular or ecclesiastical authority, not over all people but only over some people — regardless whether or not they are the ⟨outstanding⟩ people of the world — and not over all goods but only over parts of the political or ecclesiastical goods." ⟨See also Martin Heckel, *Staat und Kirche,* 179, and ibid., n. 946.⟩

117. *Disputation on Matt. 19:21,* 1539: WA 39.II:60.2: ". . . to a large degree a tyrant is subject to laws"; ibid., WA 39.II:85.22: "A tyrant remains within the commonwealth constituted by laws, ⟨but⟩ he misuses those forms of the commonwealth."

118. ⟨Literally: "Power goes before law."⟩

119. *Disputation on Matt. 19:21,* 1539: WA 39.II:85.10; see also ibid., 82.13: "This is

the pope's word: 'As I want it, so I command,' . . ."; ibid., WA 39.II:82.37: "Not only is ⟨the pope⟩ without law ⟨*sine lege;* i.e., he is the lawless one, mentioned below⟩, but he also breaks all laws and rights. He is the devil incarnate. Therefore he has to be resisted"; ibid., WA 39.II:60.38; WA.TR 1:295.7 (1533): the pope has been established neither by natural law, nor by divine or man-made law ⟨see, however, also above, 390 n. 49, at the beginning⟩; he established himself by means of power; his will rules in his kingdom, he simply says, "This I want."

120. Notwithstanding occasional statements in which Luther modified his position somewhat, the Turk was for him *the* example of a secular grand tyrant of his day. See *On the War against the Turks,* 1529: WA 30.II:120.26, 122.16, 123.19, 126.21, 127.12 ⟨LW 46:174, 177, 178f., 181, 182; in some of the following *LW* texts we have eliminated some of the ellipsis marks which the quotation would require, and we have adjusted the punctuation accordingly⟩: "The Turk . . . is the servant of the devil. . . . Mohammed is a destroyer of our Lord Christ and his kingdom. . . . The Turk's Koran or creed teaches him to destroy not only the Christian faith but also the whole temporal government. His Mohammed . . . commands that ruling is to be done by the sword, and in his Koran the sword is the commonest and noblest work. Thus the Turk is really nothing but a murderer and highwayman, as his deeds show before men's eyes. St. Augustine calls other kingdoms, too, a great robbery; Psalm 76[:4] also calls them 'the mountains of prey' because an empire seldom has come into being except by robbery, force, and wrong; or, at the very least, it is often seized and possessed by wicked people without any justice, so that the Scriptures, in Genesis 10[:9], call the first prince upon earth, Nimrod, a mighty hunter. But never has any kingdom come into being and become so mighty through murder and robbery as that of the Turk; and he murders and robs every day, for robbing and murdering, devouring and destroying more and more of those that are around them, is commanded in their law as a good and divine work; and they do this and think they are doing God a service. Their government, therefore, is not a godly, regular rulership, like others, for the maintenance of peace, the protection of the good, and the punishment of the wicked, but a rod of anger and a punishment of God upon the unbelieving world, as has been said. The work of murdering and robbing pleases the flesh in any case because it enables men to gain high place and to subject everyone's life and goods to themselves. How much more must the flesh be pleased when this is a commandment, as though God would have it so and is well pleased by it! So it is among the Turks that the most highly regarded are those who are diligent to increase the Turkish kingdom and constantly murder and rob those around them. . . . The third point is that Mohammed's Koran has no regard for marriage, but permits everyone to take wives as he will. . . . What would be a more horrible, dangerous, terrible imprisonment than life under such a government? As I said, lies destroy the spiritual estate; murder, the temporal; disregard of marriage, the estate of matrimony. Now if you take out of the world *veram religionem, veram politiam, veram oeconomiam,* that is, true spiritual life, true temporal government, and true home life, what is left in the world but flesh, world, and devil?"

For the Turk as Gog, see *On Gog according to Ezekiel, Chapters 38 and 39,* 1530: WA 30.II:223.8. — For the parallelism between Turk and pope, see *Admonition to Prayer against the Turk,* 1541: WA 51:620.10ff.; *A Sermon against the Turk,* 1529: WA 30.II:162.1ff.; *On the War against the Turks,* 1529: WA 30.II:143.1ff. (and also Luther to John Bugenhagen and others: Jan. 22, 1544: WA.B 10:505.42). — For the pope as the head and body in opposition to Christ the head, see sermon of Nov. 22, 1537: WA 45:313.11. — For the papacy as "something fictitious in the world," see *Assertion of All Articles*, 1520: WA 7:136.3.

121. *Disputation on Matt. 19:21*, 1539: WA 39.II:52.22: "And so the devil always made a new *politia*, church, and *oeconomia* outside of Holy Scripture"; *A Sermon against the Turk*, 1529: WA 30.II:168.15: "⟨The⟩ law with which ... ⟨the Turk⟩ rules, ... is ... nothing other than human reason without God's Word and Spirit. For his law teaches nothing other than what human sense and reason can very well accept."

122. *Disputation on Matt. 19:21*, 1539: WA 39.II:62.21.

123. Ibid., WA 39.II:88.9: "This is the substance of the pope: The pope is outside, above, and in opposition to the natural, the divine, and the human law, and he does all things according to his will." — Matthias Stephan ⟨one of the leading evangelical scholars of ecclesiastical law and a professor at the University of Greifswald (1624-1646); see Martin Heckel, *Staat und Kirche*, s.v. "Stephani, Matthias"⟩, *Discursus academici*, 2 (Rostock, 1625), 242, attacked the thesis of Philip Decius ⟨a leading Italian jurist at the turn of the sixteenth to the seventeenth century, with whom many German jurists studied⟩ that the pope can do all things in opposition to law, above law, and outside of law. — For the pope as a "mixture of god and man," see *Second Lectures on the Psalms*, 1518-21: WA 5:344.6; *On the War against the Turks*, 1529: WA 30.II:109.20: "At that time the pope and the clergy were all in all things, above all things, and through all things, just as a god in the world." For the pope as "earthly god," see *The Private Mass and the Consecration of Priests*, 1533: WA 38:233.17. — For the Turk as a type of the Antichrist, who claims that only he has the authority to interpret Scripture and who persecutes the believers, see *Second Lectures on the Psalms*, 1518-21: WA 5:339.15, 344.1; a similar idea can be found already in *First Lectures on the Psalms*, 1513-15: WA 3:610.4.19 ⟨LW 11:100⟩. — See also *A Sermon against the Turk*, 1529: WA 30.II:161.26: "... through his efforts the devil attempts to enable the Turk not only ⟨to destroy⟩ secular sovereignty but also the kingdom of Christ, and to force Christ's saints and members to abandon the faith, as Daniel says in chapter seven." — For Nimrod, see ⟨above, 112 and⟩ *Sermons on Genesis*, 1527: WA 24:222.4.

124. *Disputation on Matt. 19:21*, 1539: WA 39.II:85.9: "⟨The pope⟩ is such a great monster ⟨i.e., a grand tyrant⟩ which will not be restrained by any law but will have the kingdom, i.e., his will"; ibid., WA 39.II:83.1.

125. Hence he is a monster. See thesis 56 of *Disputation on Matt. 19:21*, 1539: WA 39.II:42.11: the pope is the *monstrum* of which Dan. 11:36 speaks; *Against the Roman Papacy*, 1545: WA 54:272.36 ⟨LW 41:344⟩: "The pope lies in his own filth, and thus one finds out that his rule and rank come neither from God nor man, but from all the devils in hell, sheer idolatry, blasphemy, lies, murder of souls, murder, robbery, disorder, and enmity against God, emperor, king, and all men, especially against Christendom — all far worse than the Turk"; ibid., WA 54:282.24: the pope claims to be "lord of all lords, king of all kings, Rev. 19⟨:16⟩."

126. *Disputation on Matt. 19:21*, 1539, thesis 53: WA 39.II:42.5: "It is obvious that the pope is not an ecclesiastical ⟨*magistratus*⟩ because he condemns the gospel and crushes it through his blasphemies in the Canon law." In thesis 51 (ibid., WA 39.II: 42.1) Luther argued that the pope is not *magistratus*, neither an ecclesiastical nor a political, nor a domestic one.

127. Ibid., thesis 54: WA 39.II:42.7.: "It is obvious that the pope is not a political *magistratus* because he subjects the civil laws to himself, just as the gospel."

128. Ibid., WA 39.II:82.10: "... the pope is the *anomos* one ⟨see also above, 420 n. 119: *sine lege*⟩ because, preferring his will, he places himself not only above all laws but also above Holy Scripture...." See also Hermann, "Luthers Zirkulardisputation über Matth. 19,21," *LuJ* 23 (1941): 86f.

129. *Against the Roman Papacy*, 1545: WA 54:290.4: "All things are widely known in terms of fact and law — the action of the pope is public knowledge, the mandate of our Lord Jesus Christ is public knowledge."

130. ⟨Criticizing *Lex charitatis*,⟩ Helmut Thielicke, *Theologische Ethik*, 2.II. *Ethik des Politischen* (Tübingen, 1958):Nos. 2540, 2556, emphasized that not "the" church but the "Christian citizen" is "the holder of secular, political responsibility" ⟨in the sense of resistance to governmental authority⟩.

131. In *Disputation on Matt. 19:21*, 1539, thesis 58: WA 39.II:42.15, Luther used "Beerwolf"; ⟨this is a form of 'Werwolf' or 'man-wolf'⟩. In *Against the Roman Papacy*, 1545, Luther used this word frequently; see, e.g., WA 54:291.37 ⟨LW 41:367⟩.

132. *Disputation on Matt. 19:21*, 1539, thesis 69: WA 39.II:42.39: "Who fights under ⟨the command of⟩ a robber (regardless who he is), may expect the danger connected with his military service together with eternal damnation."

133. Luther to John Lüdicke: Febr. 8, 1539: WA.B 8:367.52: ⟨If the emperor acts unconstitutionally⟩ "because of foreign causes and causes of the devil" ⟨armed resistance to the emperor is permitted; the prior text makes clear that "foreign causes and causes of the devil" are identical with the political manipulations of the papacy, a 'foreign and devilish' power, for the purpose of having the emperor make war against the evangelicals⟩.

134. ⟨Literally: "defense."⟩

135. *Disputation on Matt. 19:21*, 1539, thesis 61: WA 39.II:42.22: "One may not wait for the sentence of a judge or the ⟨decision⟩ of a council, but one has to consider the present disaster and necessity" ⟨and therefore fight the *Beerwolf*; see above, n. 131⟩; *Against the Roman Papacy*, 1545: WA 54:295.3: "... one should flee ⟨from the pope⟩, one should pray against him, and earnestly act against him and live in opposition to him ..., as against the devil himself."

136. *Disputation on Matt. 19:21*, 1539, thesis 63: WA 39.II:42.27: "One may not pay attention ⟨to⟩ a judge... ⟨who⟩ orders that this animal ⟨i.e., the *Beerwolf*⟩ be allowed to run away free or even be defended."

137. ⟨See above, n. 134.⟩

138. *Disputation on Matt. 19:21*, 1539, thesis 65: WA 39.II:42.31: "And if the judge... be killed by those who persecute this monster in such a tumult, ⟨he⟩ is not treated unjustly."

139. ⟨"Das Volk."⟩ Ibid., WA 39.II:59.30: "Because he ⟨i.e., the pope as grand tyrant⟩ is not *magistratus* ⟨see above, 421 nn. 126-127⟩, the people act...." ⟨Literally: "then it is a popular action."⟩ — This situation fits Berggrav's statement in "Staat und Kirche in lutherischer Sicht," in *Das lebendige Wort*, 79: "When a governmental authority becomes tyrannical through lawlessness and great arbitrariness, then exist demonic situations and, therefore, a governance which is not under God. Obedience to a devilish authority would be nothing other than sin.... In such circumstances exists the right to rebellion in one or the other form ⟨i.e., passive and active resistance⟩ in principle."

140. *Decretum Gratiani* c.11. D.I. de cons. ⟨Friedberg 1:1297⟩.

141. *Disputation on Matt. 19:21*, 1539: WA 39.II:58.6: "... each one has to fight by

means of strength and body.... Before I would let my soul go into hell, I would rather put up all that I have, and rebel." ⟨See also ibid., WA 39.II:49.25: "In order to kill the animal (i.e., the *Beerwolf*), it is necessary that all cities and villages, and all men join together, and still [the monster] might escape."⟩

142. WA.TR 4:No. 4342 (on p. 237.17). See also *Disputation on Matt. 19:21*, 1539: WA 39.II:80.9: "... whoever kills a highway robber, functions in the office of the prince's magistrate. ..." — For the position of the Christian congregation in the political world, see Gollwitzer, *Christliche Gemeinde*, 26, 28, 32.

143. ⟨"Office of governmental authority" has to be understood in the widest sense possible. The term can designate the prince, or the members of his government, or what we would call civil and judicial service.⟩

144. For the history of this problem in Luther's thought, see Karl Müller, "Luther und Melanchthon über das ius gladii 1521," in *Geschichtliche Studien Albert Hauck zum 70. Geburtstag dargebracht* (Leipzig, 1916), 235ff. For the problem, see instead of other authors, Wingren, *Luthers Lehre vom Beruf*, passim. — See also Tertullian, *Apologeticum* 38.3 ⟨Loeb text⟩: "... nothing is more foreign to us ⟨Christians⟩ than the State. One state we know, of which all are citizens — the universe."

145. ⟨See above, 381 n. 190.⟩

146. *Psalm 82 Explained*, 1530: WA 31.I:208.1ff. See also *Sermons on the First Epistle of St. Peter*, 1523 (first version): WA 12:330.7ff. ⟨*LW* 30:75f.⟩: "For although pious Christians do not need the sword and law — since they live in such a way that no one can complain about them, and since they wrong nobody but do good to all and gladly suffer everything done to them — yet the sword must be wielded for the sake of the non-Christians, to punish them for the harm they inflict on the others. Public peace must be preserved, and the pious must be protected. Here God has established another method of government ⟨literally: 'governance'⟩, which should use force to compel those who are unwilling of their own accord to abstain from doing wrong to refrain from doing harm. Therefore God has instituted government for the sake of the unbelievers. Consequently, Christians, too, may exercise the power of the sword. They have the obligation to serve their neighbors and to restrain the wicked with it, in order that the pious may remain in peace among them"; ibid., WA 12:333.15 ⟨*LW* 30:79⟩: "Therefore I do not want to be compelled to be subject to secular princes and lords; but I will be subject to them of my own accord, not because they command me but to render a service to my neighbor."

147. *Sermons on Matthew, Chapters 5-7*, 1530-32: WA 32:390.8.19, 391.23 ⟨*LW* 21:109, 110⟩: "A related question is this: May a Christian be a secular official and administer the office and work of a ruler or a judge? This would mean that the two persons or the two types of office are combined in one man. In addition to being a Christian, he would be a prince or a judge or a lord or a servant or a maid — all of which are termed 'secular' persons because they are part of the secular realm. To this we say: Yes; ... There is no getting around it, a Christian has to be a secular person of some sort. As regards his own person, according to his life as a Christian, he is in subjection to no one but Christ, without any obligation either to the emperor or to any other man. But at least outwardly, according to his body and property, he is related by subjection and obligation to the emperor, inasmuch as he occupies some office or station in life or has a house and home, a wife and children; for all these things pertain to the emperor.... Just learn the difference between the two persons that a Christian must carry simultaneously on earth, because he lives in

human society and has to make use of secular and imperial things, the same way that the heathen do. For until he has been transferred bodily from this life to another one, his flesh and blood is identical with theirs; and what he needs to provide for it does not come from the spiritual realm but from the land and soil, which belongs to the emperor"; ibid., WA 32:439.39: "... one has to differentiate between a ... world-person and a Christian-person ...." For these materials, see Törnvall, *Geistliches und weltliches Regiment bei Luther,* 166ff.; Ernst Wolf, *Peregrinatio,* 1:235ff. — In view of the distinction, mentioned in the text above, Oepke (*Das neue Gottesvolk,* 464) doubted "that Luther's two kingdoms doctrine may be considered to be ‹the final word›." ‹In whatever way one responds to this argument, it is certain that› in his sermon *On Two Kinds of Righteousness,* 1519, Luther differentiated between "public" and "private" person: WA 2:150.36 ‹*LW* 31:304.›; see also already *Sermons on the Ten Commandments,* 1518: WA 1:513.35 (sermon of Jan. 25, 1517). See also Luther to Philip Melanchthon: July 21, 1530: WA.B 5:493.46 ‹*LW* 49:385: "... the church is a twofold person *(persona duplex)* in one and the same man"›; Bornkamm, *Luthers Lehre von den zwei Reichen,* 22; *Matthew, Chapters 18-24 Explained in Sermons,* 1537-40: WA 47:247.18: "A prince may very well remain a prince and yet also be a Christian. . . . For ‹his› *Christentum* ‹see above, 365 n. 63› has a different origin than secular governance or the estate of marriage"; *Sermons on the First Epistle of St. Peter,* 1523: WA 12:330.19 ‹*LW* 30:76›: "Yet the injunction of the Lord not to resist evil remains in force, so that even if a Christian wields the sword, he does not use it for himself and does not avenge himself but uses it solely for others. Thus it is also a work of Christian love to protect and defend a whole community with the sword and not to let the people be abused." — For the interpretation of the formula 'Christ-person — world-person', see Steck, *Luther und die Schwärmer,* 38. We find a first trace of this differentiation in Luther's letter to George Mascov: May 17, 1517: WA.B 1:98.14.

148. Especially Troeltsch criticized Luther for ‹supposedly› having affirmed a "double morality" (*Die Soziallehren der christlichen Kirchen und Gruppen,* 486 n. 223, on p. 488). Even though Holl refuted this criticism (*Luther,* 282ff.), Troeltsch's critique is being repeated even today and far-reaching consequences are drawn from it. Niebuhr (*Nature and Destiny of Man,* 2:194ff.), using Luther's position in the Peasants' War, argued: "By transposing an 'inner' ethic into a private one, and making the 'outer' or 'earthly' ethic authoritative for government, Luther achieves a curiously perverse social morality. He places a perfectionist private ethic in juxtaposition to a realistic, not to say cynical, official ethic. He demands that the state maintain order without too scrupulous a regard for justice; yet he asks suffering and nonresistant love of the individual without allowing him to participate in the claims and counter-claims which constitute the stuff of social justice. The inevitable consequence of such an ethic is to encourage tyranny; for resistance to government is as important a principle of justice as maintenance of government. Luther's inordinate fear of anarchy, prompted by his pessimism, and his corresponding indifference to the injustice of tyranny has had a fateful consequence in the history of German civilization. . . . Even without this particular error, the Lutheran political ethic would have led to defeatism in the field of social politics. Its absolute distinction between the 'heavenly' or 'spiritual' kingdom and the 'earthly' one, destroys the tension between the final demands of God upon the conscience, and all the relative possibilities of realizing the good in history. . . . The weakness of the Lutheran position in the field of social ethics is accentuated to a further degree by its inability to define consistent criteria for the achieve-

ment of relative justice. Despite its conception of sanctification as an ecstatic love which transcends all law, and of its doctrine of justification which eases the conscience in its inability to realize the good perfectly, it is forced, nevertheless, to find some standards of relative good and evil. Since it rightly has less confidence than Catholicism in the untainted character of reason, it relegates the 'natural law', that is, the rational analysis of social obligations, to the background, as an inadequate guide. But it has only odds and ends of systems of order to put in the place of 'natural law'. These consist primarily of two conceptions. The one is the order and justice which any state may happen to establish. This order is accepted uncritically precisely because a principle of justice, by which the justice of a given state could be criticized, is lacking. The other is the idea of a *Schoepfungsordnung,* an 'order of creation', which is presumably the directive given by God in the very structure of the created world. The difficulty with this concept is that human freedom alters and transmutes the 'given' facts of creation so much that no human institutions can be judged purely by the criterion of fixed principles of 'creation'." — These materials prove the necessity to arrive at a clear picture of the substantive and the institutional secular natural law in Luther's thought. See also above, 273 n. 12.

Friedrich Naumann (*Briefe über Religion* [Berlin, 1916], epilogue) pointed out the "conflict" existing between "morality in the daily struggle of surviving" and "morality of mercy"; Wehrung, *Welt und Reich,* 228f., criticized this position. Heinz Zwicker (*Reich Gottes, Nachfolge und Neuschöpfung. Beiträge zur Christlichen Ethik* [Bern, 1948], 123) opposed Luther's differentiation between the duty of love and the duty of office; see Wehrung, *Welt und Reich,* 229ff. — For the "division between official person and private person, and for the distribution of specific tasks to each of the two persons," see Wendland, "Weltherrschaft Christi," in *Stählin Festschrift,* 32.

149. *First Lectures on the Psalms,* 1513-15: WA 4:156.4 ⟨*LW* 11:307⟩: ". . . neither does the world associate *(communicare)* with them ⟨i.e., 'all who want to lead a godly life'⟩, nor they with the world." — Vajta (*Theologie des Gottesdienstes bei Luther,* 201 n. 18) included also the pastor among the "world-persons" because "all offices belong to life on earth." This statement is correct, of course. Luther's argumentation regarding the "world-person" deals, however, only with the offices in the kingdom of the world (Vajta, ibid., 261 n. 99, 274, presented a different position) for only they belong to the secular governance; see above, n. 147. — For the position of the pastor in terms of ecclesiastical law, see above, 386 n. 27.

150. Törnvall (*Geistliches und weltliches Regiment bei Luther,* 169) presented a different position: "The participation of a Christian in the affairs of the world can be determined without the aid of the revelation in Christ." Törnvall overlooked that through the reception into Christ's kingdom a complete change in man's legal situation has occurred, and that, therefore, it has to be clarified why and in what sense a Christian nevertheless may still be a world-person. — Bornkamm (*Luthers Lehre von den zwei Reichen,* 28, and ibid., n. 69) emphasized that the formula ⟨'Christ-person — world-person'⟩ is not only "polemically powerful" but also "thoroughly constructive." The legal question raised in the text above ⟨i.e., how is it possible that a Christian can serve in the office of governmental authority without denying his Lord?⟩ cannot be answered with Bornkamm's argument that a Christian "as 'old man' . . . is subject to secular laws," and "as a Christian ⟨i.e., as 'new man'⟩ has to serve his neighbor with the means made available by the secular order."

The issue is that precisely as a *Christian* ‹i.e., as 'new man'› a Christian has obligations to the secular governance.

151. Otherwise the permitted use of man-made law would result in an idolatrous service to reason, which considers itself to be autonomous; *Second Lectures on Galatians*, 1531: WA 40.I:176.1: "‹To man› God has given all creatures ‹and therefore also man-made law› for use and benefit but not for worship and religion."

152. *Sermons on the First Epistle of St. Peter*, 1523: WA 12:332.21 ‹LW 30:78›: "Even though you — if you are Christians — are free in all external matters and should not be compelled by law to be subject to the secular government, since . . . no law is laid down for the just (1 Tim. 1:9), yet of your own accord you should be willing and unconstrained. It is not that you must obey the law out of necessity, but you must do so to please God and to serve your neighbor."

153. And this is the case even when a ruler is not a Christian; *Psalm 101 Explained*, 1534-35: WA 51:238.24: "Nevertheless ‹God› calls such a secular governance of the godless his order and creature"; sermon of Dec. 26, 1544: WA 49:643.12ff.

154. Important is the "lawful use of the law of Moses" ‹i.e., of the secular natural law›; *The Book of Deuteronomy with Notes*, 1525: WA 14:612.21 ‹LW 9:70›: ". . . the fulfilling of the Law is love from a good heart and from faith that is not feigned (1 Tim. 1:5), which uses law lawfully when it has no laws and has all laws — no laws, because none bind unless they serve faith and love; all, because all bind when they serve faith and love."

155. ‹Literally: "walk in love."› *On Secular Authority*, 1523: WA 11:272.3. See also *Summer Postilla*, 1526: WA 10.I.2:393.28, 394.1.

156. ‹I.e., as a means for showing love for his neighbor.› For the meaning of 'use', see Gustaf Törnvall, "Der Christ in den zwei Reichen," *EvTh* 10 (1950/51): 76.

157. *On Keeping Children in School*, 1530: WA 30.II:564.2: "Does one not serve God when one assists in maintaining God's order and secular governance?"; *Second Lectures on the Psalms*, 1518-21: WA 5:577.3: "To know . . . that ‹God› has called ‹me› to a certain work adds strength and makes ‹me› courageous for ‹I› know that whatever ‹I› do, I do according to God's will and command. Because one is content with one's superior strength ‹and› God's command, one has to be careful not to miss asking God for help, and do so humbly and with fear."

158. For the *divina vocatio* (divine call) of an earthly vocation, see *Second Lectures on Galatians*, 1531: WA 40.2:155.2 ‹the text of the lecture deals with the office of preaching, though Luther also touches the role of the housefather; in the edited version (*LW* 27:120f.) only the office of preaching is mentioned›; *On Secular Authority*, 1523: WA 11:258.5ff.: Christians in a secular office (including an office of governmental authority) "are God's servants and craftsmen"; *Psalm 101 Explained*, 1534-35: WA 51:240.17: in his secular office a Christian is "a humble subject and faithful servant" of God; Luther to Justus Jonas: beginning of Sept., 1529: WA.B 5:144.10: a "public person" ‹i.e., world-person› is superior to a monastic.

159. Sermon of Sept. 29, 1530: WA 47:857.35: God wants us to be his *Mitarbeiter* (co-worker) but not his co-creator; God alone is creator. See also Ernst Wolf, "Politia Christi. Das Problem der Sozialethik im Luthertum," *EvTh* 8 (1948/49): 59, 63, and Wingren, *Luthers Lehre vom Beruf*, 30ff., 86ff. See also above, 376 n. 155.

160. *Open Letter on the Harsh Book against the Peasants*, 1525: WA 18:390.17: "Those

who are in God's kingdom should . . . nevertheless not obstruct the law and actions of the secular kingdom but assist in promoting them."

161. *Lectures on Psalms 120–134*, 1532-33: WA 40.III:207.8. ⟨Therefore Luther criticized the monks (ibid., 207.14ff.), who (ibid., 208.1ff.) "want to lick the fat which is on top of the soup but do not want to eat the soup," (i.e.,) "they do not want to rule people or families" (i.e., they do not want to serve in the *politia* or the *oeconomia*).⟩ For this passage, and for the following, see Carl Stange, "Luthers Lehre vom gesellschaftlichen Leben," *ZSTh* 7 (1929): 57ff.; Gollwitzer, *Christliche Gemeinde*, 12; Ernst Wolf, *Peregrinatio*, 1:231.

162. ⟨For "natural man," see above, 358 n. 10.⟩ *On Secular Authority*, 1523: WA 11:258.1, 274.25.

163. *The Book of Deuteronomy with Notes*, 1525: WA 14:552.1.5.28: "Wisdom is most highly required ⟨for⟩ princes. . . . The kingdom of men ⟨rules⟩ over rational creatures; therefore it is ruled only by means of word⟨s⟩, which consist of wisdom and understanding. . . . ⟨*LW* 9:18:⟩ They are the wise men who understand affairs divine and human, especially those who know the statutes and laws and all that is necessary for the life of the people. In Hebrew those are called 'understanding' who are watchful and keep looking out with sharp judgment and vigilant mind, so that they may judge properly and sensibly about all matters and practice moderation."

164. Ibid., WA 14:552.34 ⟨*LW* 9:19⟩: "You see, therefore, that in divine Law no account is taken of the rich, powerful, noble, strong, and friendly, for handling public office, as is the custom of the world; but of the wise, understanding, and experienced, even if they are poor, lowly, weak, etc."

165. Ibid., WA 14:553.21 ⟨*LW* 9:19⟩: "The question has been properly raised whether a prince is better if he is good and imprudent or prudent yet also evil. Here Moses ⟨Deut. 1:13⟩ certainly demands both. Nevertheless, if one cannot have both, it is better for ⟨a prince⟩ to be prudent and not good than good and not prudent; for the good man would actually rule nothing but would be ruled only by others, and at that only by the worst people. Even if the prudent man harms good people, yet at the same time he governs the evil ones, which is the most necessary and suitable thing for the world, since the world is nothing else than a crowd of evil people."

166. Ibid., WA 14:550.23. See also Luther to George Spalatin: soon after Dec. 21, 1518: WA.B 1:284.6: the correct use of the 'form' of God ⟨i.e., God's power⟩ is the 'form' of the servant.

167. *The Book of Deuteronomy with Notes*, 1525: WA 14:552.10; ibid., WA 14:552.23 ⟨*LW* 9:18⟩: "Here you see that the magistrates should be chosen by the votes of the people, as reason also demands."

168. *The Bondage of the Will*, 1525: WA 18:651.7 ⟨*LW* 33:87⟩: ". . . from the beginning of the world there has always been more outstanding talent, greater learning, and more earnest application among the heathen than among Christians or the People of God. . ."; *Psalm 101 Explained*, 1534-35: WA 51.226.26 ⟨*LW* 13:179⟩: "The godless often receive much better and nobler gifts and skills from God in secular affairs, so that they are almost indispensable at home or in the government; in fact, the pious are not even pupils in comparison with them"; ibid., WA 51:242.7.11 ⟨*LW* 13:198⟩: ". . . to tell the truth, they ⟨i.e, the heathen⟩ are far more skillful in such matters ⟨i.e., of the secular government⟩ than the Christians. . . . Every day we find out how swift, tricky, clever, smart, and quick the children of the world are in contrast to us devout, stupid, good, simple wethers and sheep";

Sermons on Exodus, 1524-27: WA 16:354.6: "... reason ⟨is⟩ wiser in the secular people than in the saints.... ⟨This⟩ you see ⟨in⟩ the fine laws of the heathen, such as the Romans ⟨and⟩ Greeks."

169. *Lectures on Hebrews,* 1517-18: WA 57.III:137.5 ⟨to Heb. 3:1; *LW* 29:143⟩: "... all our doing *(operatio)* is a confession...." — See also the important materials in Barth, *Christengemeinde und Bürgergemeinde,* 20ff. However, Luther did not maintain Barth's idea that church and *politia* are related with each other as if they were an inner and an outer circle. For Luther the image of two concentric circles was valid only for the relationship of the membership in the *ecclesia abscondita* (hidden, spiritual church) with that in the *ecclesia manifesta* (manifest church); see Johannes Heckel, *Initia iuris,* 14, and Gollwitzer, *Christliche Gemeinde,* 25f.

170. *Second Lectures on Galatians,* 1531: WA 40.II:72.4: "Man is naturally disposed for the political and the social life."

171. Ibid., WA 40.II:76.4: "... harmony in the variety of many activities."

172. For examples of principles for governing practiced by a Christian prince, see above, 79, and 350 nn. 459-61, and 351 n. 462. Additional materials: (1) Limiting the number of laws to the minimum needed, while maintaining the secular natural law; *On Secular Authority,* 1523: WA 11:279.25.30; *Postilla for Lent,* 1525: WA 17.II:94.24: "One should issue, command, and obey all sorts of laws, not for their sake..., but only for the sake of practicing love, which is the true meaning of law... ⟨Rom. 13:8⟩." (2) Readiness to compromise; *Against the Robbing and Murderous Hordes of Peasants,* 1525: WA 18:359.35 ⟨*LW* 46:52⟩. (3) Mercy toward the defeated enemy: ibid., WA 18:361.16 ⟨*LW* 46:54⟩. — Troeltsch has to be corrected when he argued (*Die Soziallehren der christlichen Kirchen und Gruppen,* 538f.) that in matters of public law ⟨and criminal law⟩ Luther excluded the principle of equity.

173. *On Secular Authority,* 1523: WA 11:271.35 ⟨*LW* 45:118⟩: "He who would be ⟨literally: 'who wills to be'⟩ a Christian prince must certainly lay aside any intent to exercise lordship or to proceed with force. For cursed and condemned is every sort of life lived and sought for the benefit and good of self; cursed are all works not done in love. They are done in love, however, when they are directed wholeheartedly toward the benefit, honor, and salvation ⟨or: 'well-being'⟩ of others, and not toward the pleasure, benefit, honor, comfort, and salvation ⟨or: 'well-being'⟩ of self."

174. See ibid., WA 11:255.12 ⟨*LW* 45:95f.⟩.

175. *Whether Soldiers, Too, Can Be Saved,* 1526: WA 19:652.25: "... a superior person ⟨*Oberperson* in the sense of the person in the office of governmental authority⟩... should be a public ⟨or: 'common'⟩ person *(gemeine Person)* and not ⟨a person who⟩ lives only for himself."

176. *Second Lectures on Galatians,* 1531: WA 40.II:153.1: "... magistrate,... do your job and stay in your vocation...."

177. The model of the godly ruler is David. He, "filled with fear ⟨or: 'reverence'⟩ and wisdom of God, directs and executes all his tasks according to God's command and not according to his reason"; *Magnificat,* 1521: WA 7:601.30; ibid., WA 7:602.17: from the ruler "God will demand an account of his ⟨conduct in his⟩ estate and office..."; ibid., WA 7:603.5 ⟨*LW* 21:356ff.⟩; *Second Lectures on the Psalms,* 1518-21: WA 5:370.23: "He who... is faithful to God is also faithful to men. For without faith and God's grace it is impossible that a man does not seek his own (i.e., also be unfaithful toward men)." — For man's ac-

countability before God in the hour of death, see *Second Lectures on Galatians,* 1531: WA 40.II:154.7 ⟨and the edited version of these lectures, *LW* 27:120f.⟩.

178. For a ruler who is not responsible to the people on the basis of positive law it is necessary to fear God; *Magnificat,* 1521: WA 7:545.14: "... because they do not have to fear men, it is necessary that all overlords (*Uberherren;* see also above, 428 n. 175) fear God more than other people do, know him and his work well, and act diligently. ..."

179. *Lectures on Genesis,* 1535-45: WA 43:513.22, 514.5 ⟨*LW* 5:123, 124⟩: "... if you are in the government, beware of depending on your own wisdom; beware of yourself, and pray privately with folded hands: 'Heavenly Father, be Thou with me; help, guide, and direct me.' ... it is completely certain that you will never achieve anything without prayer. For governing is a divine power, and for this reason God calls all magistrates gods (cf. Ps. 82:6), not because of the creation ⟨i.e., the magistrates are not 'created' gods⟩ but because of the administration ⟨i.e., of their duties⟩ which belongs to God alone." ⟨Now follow some observations about what will happen when officials in church, state, and family do not act with such an awareness regarding the nature of their offices.⟩

180. *Matthew, Chapters 18-24 Explained in Sermons,* 1537-40: WA 47:452.8: "... a lord and prince should ... command ⟨his⟩ subjects ⟨to do only⟩ what is right and godly. For such estates should rule and teach the subjects in such a way that they are led to God ..."; ibid., WA 47:247.1.5: "The purpose of the estate of marriage and of secular governance is to increase the number of Christians and to ⟨help them⟩ remain Christians.... ⟨But⟩ such estates do not help people come into God's kingdom or to Christendom because they are secular estates and do not belong in the kingdom of heaven."

181. *Magnificat,* 1521: WA 7:595.34: "No one serves ... God unless he lets God be his God and lets God's work be active in him. ..."

182. See above, 426 n. 157.

183. *On Monastic Vows,* 1521: WA 8:609.38: "... a Christian can observe all the laws, rites, and customs of all people and accommodate himself to them, as long as they are not contrary to the divine commandments, and he does not put the trust of his conscience in them."

184. As Holl (*Luther,* 347) has correctly argued; see also Oepke, *Das neue Gottesvolk,* 457.

185. Or *respublica bene instituta;* see *The Book of Deuteronomy with Notes,* 1525: WA 14:710.1 ⟨*LW* 9:233⟩; e.g., in such a well-ordered commonwealth prostitution is outlawed⟩.

186. See Johannes Heckel, "Cura religionis, ius in sacra, ius circa sacra," in *Festschrift Ulrich Stutz zum siebzigsten Geburtstag dargebracht von Schülern, Freunden und Verehrern* (Stuttgart, 1938), 224ff.

187. See above, Appendix II.

188. *On Good Works,* 1520: WA 6:207.26 ⟨*LW* 44:27⟩: "... a Christian ... knows all things, can do all things, ventures everything that needs to be done, and does everything gladly and willingly, not that he may gather merits and good works, but because it is a pleasure for him to please God in doing these things. He simply serves God with no thought of reward, content that his service pleases God."

189. *To the Christian Nobility,* 1520: WA 6:408.10 ⟨*LW* 44:129⟩: the office of "those who exercise secular authority ... has a proper and useful place in the Christian community," because the officeholder shares with the believers the same Baptism, faith, and gospel. See also above, 122.

190. See above, 317 n. 123.

191. *On Secular Authority*, 1523: WA 11:255.1 ⟨LW 45:95⟩: "... if you see that there is a lack of hangmen, constables, judges, lords, or princes, and you find that you are qualified, you should offer your services and seek the position, that the essential governmental authority may not be despised and become enfeebled or perish. The world cannot and dare not dispense with it."

192. *Lectures on Hebrews*, 1517-18: WA 57.III:217.5. ⟨The context of the quotation deals with observing ceremonies; see *LW* 29:218f.⟩.

193. See Gollwitzer, *Christliche Gemeinde*, 14.

194. See Luther's negative view of secular rulers in *On Secular Authority*, 1523: WA 11:267.30, 268.11 ⟨LW 45:113⟩: "You must know that since the beginning of the world a wise prince is a mighty rare bird, and an upright prince even rarer. They are generally the biggest fools or the worst scoundrels on earth; therefore, one must constantly expect the worst from them and look for little good, especially in divine matters which concern the salvation of souls. They are God's executioners and hangmen; his divine wrath uses them to punish the wicked and to maintain outward peace. Our God is a great lord and ruler; this is why he must have such noble, highborn, and rich hangmen and constables.... If a prince should happen to be wise, upright, or a Christian, that is one of the great miracles, the most precious token of divine grace upon that land"; *Matthew, Chapters 18-24 Explained in Sermons*, 1537-40: WA 47:499.32; Luther to Nicholas Hausmann: Aug. 1, 1529: WA.B 5:128.6. This negative view makes necessary that a Christian use his office "in the fear of God"; *Magnificat*, 1521: WA 7:590.8 ⟨LW 21:344⟩. — See also Wehrung, *Welt und Reich*, 220.

195. *Psalm 101 Explained*, 1534: WA 51:254.9.21 ⟨LW 13:212f.⟩: "'No matter how minor the office, it is worth hanging for.' The offices of princes and officials are divine and right, but those who are in them and use them are usually of the devil. And if a prince is a rare dish in heaven, this is even more true of the officials and the court personnel. This is caused by the evil, depraved nature, which cannot stand success; that is, it cannot use honor, power, and authority in a divine way. No matter how insignificant the little office may be, they take a foot though they do not have an inch, and always want to be God themselves when they ought to be God's maid.... Now, if the maid herself wants to be God and to rule tyrannically with Lucifer..., thinking that everything is to be done for her own benefit, greed, rest, and pomp, then she may also expect what is written in the Magnificat (Luke 1:52): 'He pushes down the mighty from their seat, and exalts the humble.' Thus it has happened, and is still happening daily to all the empires, to high and low authorities, to princes as well as to officials"; *Sermons on Matthew, Chapters 5-7*, 1530-32: WA 32:512.4: "Though a prince wears a golden chain and a mink coat, if he is a godly man, then in this mink coat ⟨walks⟩ a man so mortified and miserable that we find no one similar to him in a monastery." — For the need of "the gift of counsel... to those who... have already been called and placed in some position" ⟨of governmental authority⟩ because they "are surrounded on all sides by snares, temptations, and dangers," see *First Lectures on the Psalms*, 1513-15: WA 4:326.34 ⟨LW 11:445⟩. — See further, *On the Councils and the Church*, 1539: WA 50:569.7: "... the devil searches especially ⟨for the big lords⟩, ⟨because⟩ through them he is able to accomplish the greatest damage"; *Matthew, Chapters 18-24 Explained in Sermons*, 1537-40: WA 47:563.40; Luther to Duke Frederick, elector of Saxony: March 28, 1522(?): WA.B 2:487.18: "A prince has to consider that injustice might be mixed into his

Notes to Page 117

governance; blessed is the prince in whose governance is the smallest amount of injustice!"; to George Spalatin: June 9, 1523: WA.B 3:83.5: "... it is the fate of all princes that almost by some sort of necessity they sin toward both parties by favoring ⟨literally: 'exalting'⟩ those who are unworthy and by oppressing those who deserve otherwise"; to Duke Charles III of Savoy: Sept. 7, 1523: WA.B 3:150.11.

196. *Lectures on Genesis,* 1535-45: WA 42:401.11: "To be a powerful man on earth is not evil by itself"; *First Lectures on the Psalms,* 1513-15: WA 3:295.13: "... all power is from God, and from God comes nothing other than what is good"; *Second Lectures on the Psalms,* 1518-21: WA 5:161.39: "... I do ⟨not⟩ condemn power, peace, life because without them one cannot live, and they are God's best creatures."

197. See Wingren, *Schöpfung und Gesetz,* 50, with reference to Luther's *Lectures on Psalm 2,* 1532: WA 40.II:203.6. ⟨The problem is not the office of authority and power, but their misuse by not using them spiritually.⟩ See also Luther to Nicholas Hausmann: Aug. 1, 1529: WA.B 5:128.6: "The court is the devil's chair and bed, even if a prince would be the best one."

198. *Second Lectures on Galatians,* 1531: WA 40.I:202.4: "Ceremonies, the law and its works are necessary in this world; yet there is always the danger that from these things the denial of Christ will come; from laws grows at once trust in works..."; *Matthew, Chapters 5-7 Explained in Sermons,* 1530-32: WA 32:524.13: "When God graces a person with outstanding, special gifts, there is a real danger that that person does become proud and not remain humble."

199. *Psalm 101 Explained,* 1534-35: WA 51:244.36; ibid., WA 51:245.5 ⟨*LW* 13:201⟩: "While the devil is also hostile and opposed to the secular government of the heathen, still he hates the government of the saints of God on earth much more fanatically"; Luther to John Frederick and John William, dukes of Saxony: Sept. 6, 1541: WA.B 9:510.18ff.; to Duke John Frederick, elector of Saxony: March 17, 1543: WA.B 10:279.20.

200. ⟨"Venison," i.e., something seldom available. See also above, 430 nn. 194-95.⟩

201. *The Book of Deuteronomy with Notes,* 1525: WA 14:551.18 ⟨*LW* 9:17f.⟩: "Yes, as Scripture has it (John 10:35), 'They ⟨i.e., the magistrates⟩ are called gods'; for they certainly ought to shine with godly virtues far beyond human measure, since they should successfully provide for that weak and diversified mass of the people subject to Satan in a hostile land"; for this passage, see Bornkamm, *Luther und das Alte Testament,* 55. — For the Christian in the office of judge, see *On Good Works,* 1521: WA 6:267.21 ⟨*LW* 44:102f.⟩.

202. For the high spirit with which a Christian serves in an office, see *Lectures on Genesis,* 1535-45: WA 43:210.3, 211.9 ⟨*LW* 4:103f., 105⟩: "... it is most certainly true that when anyone in his vocation is convinced... that God desires and has commanded in His Word what he is doing, he will experience such force and effectiveness of that divine command as he will not find in the oration of any orator, either of Demosthenes or of Cicero.... anyone can be certain about his calling from the Word of God, whether it is a calling in civi⟨c⟩ life or in the church."

203. *On Secular Authority,* 1523: WA 11:272.27: "... the estate of princes is a dangerous estate"; *Sermons on Exodus,* 1524-27: WA 16:360.4; *Sermons on Deuteronomy,* 1529: WA 28:525.10, 530.12. ⟨In the last two texts Luther dealt more with magistrates and ruling in general than with princes.⟩

204. See also Gerhard Ritter, *Die Dämonie der Macht* (6th ed. Munich, 1948), 114.

205. ⟨See below, Index of Subjects: *Law,* s.v. "law, of wrath."⟩

206. See Lau, *Luthers Lehre von den beiden Reichen,* 37, ⟨57f.⟩; id., "Bemerkungen zu Luthers Lehre von den beiden Reichen," *ELKZ* 6 (1952): 236; Gollwitzer, *Christliche Gemeinde,* 15.

207. *On Secular Authority,* 1523: WA 11:251.22 ⟨*LW* 45:91⟩: "If anyone attempted to rule the world by the gospel and to abolish all temporal law and sword on the plea that all are baptized and Christian, and that, according to the gospel, there shall be among them no law or sword — or need for either — pray tell me, friend, what would he be doing? He would be loosing the ropes and chains of the savage wild beasts and letting them bite and mangle everyone, meanwhile insisting that they were harmless, tame, and gentle creatures; but I would have the proof in my wounds. Just so would the wicked under the name of Christian abuse evangelical freedom, carry on their rascality, and insist that they were Christians subject neither to law nor sword, as some are already raving and ranting"; *Admonition to Peace,* 1525: WA 18:326.32 ⟨*LW* 46:39⟩; *Against the Robbing and Murdering Hordes of Peasants,* 1525: WA 18:358.35 ⟨*LW* 46:51⟩.

208. See Ernst Wolf's fitting comments in "Frage des Naturrechts bei Thomas und bei Luther," 15. See also Luther's sermon of March 25, 1540: WA 49:82.36: "Secular lordship has to command and rule with coercion, . . . and yet it should understand it as a service."

209. Therefore a Christian who serves in an office of governmental authority has to use the severity which is characteristic of the secular law; *Open Letter on the Harsh Book against the Peasants,* 1525: WA 18:390.4 ⟨*LW* 46:70⟩. But he may not forget equity derived from the secular natural law. Such a tempered severity is a "good wrath"; *Second Lectures on Galatians,* 1531: WA 40.I:310.5ff ⟨and the edited version of these lectures, *LW* 26:187⟩; Luther to the City Council of Danzig: May 5(7?), 1525: WA.B 3:484.5: ". . . the gospel is a spiritual law with which one cannot rule. . . . Therefore one has to differentiate clearly between the spiritual governance of the gospel and the external, secular governance, and absolutely not intermingle both."

210. ⟨See above, 108-14. When the incumbent of the office of governmental authority violates the institutional or the substantive secular natural law, when he is the grand tyrant, then the actions of this "wicked man" are not very similar to the actions of a godly man.⟩

211. *The Book of Deuteronomy with Notes,* 1525: WA 14:577.14.

212. For God's order functioning 'without God' though it is 'with God' ⟨i.e., is God's order nevertheless⟩, see ⟨esp.⟩ Lau, "*Äußerliche Ordnung,*" 59. See also Ernst Wolf, "Frage des Naturrechts bei Thomas und bei Luther," 11.

213. Luther to Wenceslas Link: Jan. 15, 1531: WA.B 6:17.9: ". . . a prince as prince is a political person; when he acts as such a person, he does not act as a Christian . . ."; *Sermons on Matthew, Chapter 5-7,* 1530-32: WA 32:440.9: "A prince can very well be a Christian, but as a Christian he does not have to rule; when he rules, he is not called a Christian but a prince. Certainly, the person is a Christian, but the office . . . has nothing to do with his being a Christian ⟨*Christentum;* see above, 365 n. 63⟩."

214. *Psalm 127 Explained,* 1524: WA 15:373.3. See also *Second Lectures on Galatians,* 1531: WA 40.I:43.9: "I have to learn ⟨for myself⟩ and to teach the people to ignore the law and act as if there were no law; conversely, while ⟨we are⟩ in this world, ⟨I have⟩ to press and drive the law ⟨upon them⟩ as if there were no grace."

215. ⟨To do what (I) can. For the Scholastics, see Heiko A. Oberman, "Facientibus

quod in se est Deus non denegat gratiam. Robert Holcot, O.P., and the Beginnings of Luther's Theology," *HThR* 55 (1962): 317ff.> *Second Lectures on Galatians,* 1531: WA 40.I:292.6: "When I am in the kingdom of reason ‹i.e., the kingdom of the world›, ... I do as much as I am able to do; there I am excused ‹for not being perfect›. In the *politia* and *oeconomia* belongs the saying 'one has to do as much ‹as one is able to do›' — but it is not so in the spiritual kingdom"; sermons of ca. 1514-20: WA 4:651.18: "If a person does what is in his power, he always sins"; *Disputation of Henry Schmedenstede,* 1542, thesis 32: WA 39.II:189.15.

216. A Christian has to ascribe the positive results of his actions in the kingdom of the world to God and not to his own ability; *Psalm 127 Explained,* 1524: WA 15:372.2: "Even though God does not intend to preserve anything unless man works with diligence and care, yet God does not wish that man thinks his diligence and care accomplish what alone God's goodness and grace accomplish."

217. ‹WA 6:404ff., or *LW* 44:123ff.›

218. ‹Or *corpus christianum* in the sense of Christian commonwealth, a commonwealth in which church and state are united.›

219. ‹See above, 97.›

220. ‹*Corpus christianum* or *respublica christiana*.›

221. See, e.g., Karl Riecker, *Die rechtliche Stellung der evangelischen Kirche Deutschlands* (Leipzig, 1893), 65ff.; see further, Emil Sehling, *Geschichte der protestantischen Kirchenverfassung* (2d ed. Leipzig, 1914), 6.

222. *Affirmative:* esp. Matthes, *Das Corpus Christianum bei Luther* (see above, 256 n. 35); Arnold Hirsch, "Luther et le Corpus Christianum," *RHMC* 4 (1957): 111. *Negative:* Oepke, *Das neue Gottesvolk,* 449ff., 453, 459: Luther always differentiated between the human society and the people of God, not in terms of space, but in terms of functioning (as an afterthought, however, Oepke saw human society and the people of God amazingly closely connected in concrete situations); Kohlmeyer, "Die Bedeutung der Kirche für Luther," *ZKG* 47 (1928): 508ff. Schlink (*Theologie der Bekenntnisschriften,* 317 n. 8) had doubts. For Lau (*Luthers Lehre von den beiden Reichen,* 62 n. 144) the question is open. — See also Harald Diem, *Luthers Lehre von den beiden Reichen,* 127ff.

223. ‹As defined in n. 218.› For the medieval basis of the term *corpus christianum,* see esp. Josef Bohatec, *Calvins Lehre von Staat und Kirche mit besonderer Berücksichtigung des Organismusgedankens* (Breslau, 1937), 581ff.; for additional literature, see Hans Liermann, "Studien zur Geschichte des corpus christianum in der Neuzeit," *ZSRG*.K 27 (1938): 486 n. 1.

224. *To the Christian Nobility,* 1520: WA 6:410.4 ‹*LW* 44:131›.

225. Ibid., WA 6:409.18, 413.28 ‹*LW* 44:130, 137›. For similar phrases, see *First Lectures on the Psalms,* 1513-15: WA 3:11.23, 295.29, 4:183.20; *Third Disputation against the Antinomians,* 1538: WA 39.I:491.7: "... godless and evil people are not a part of the body of the church..."; *The Blessed Sacrament of the Body of Christ and the Brotherhoods,* 1519: WA 2:743.11: "... Christ together with all saints is one spiritual body, just as the people of one city are a community and body. ..."

226. See Otto Gierke, *Das deutsche Genossenschaftsrecht,* 3 (Berlin, 1881), 517f.

227. *Decretum Gratiani* c.3. D.XI.; c.6. D.I. de cons. ‹Friedberg 1:23, 1295›.

228. Turrecremata, *Summa de ecclesia domini,* l.III. cap. 64.

229. Ibid., l.c., l.II. cap. 116. — During the first interrogation at the Diet of Worms,

the Imperial party reminded Luther to keep in mind "the unity of the holy, catholic, and apostolic church, ⟨and(?), or(?), i.e.(?)⟩ the public *(communis)* peace and quiet of the Christian commonwealth *(respublica christiana)*"; WA 7:827.28ff.

230. Compare *To the Christian Nobility*, 1520, with two of Luther's writings from later years, *Against Jack Sausage*, 1541, and *Against the Roman Papacy*, 1545. *Against Jack Sausage:* WA 51:479.25 ⟨LW 41:195⟩: "If then we have the same baptism as the original, ancient (and as the creed says, 'catholic,' that is, 'universal') Christian church, and are baptized in it, we belong to the same ancient universal church"; ibid., WA 51:483.20: "All of Christendom"; ibid., WA 51:487.18 ⟨LW 41:199⟩: "Thus we have proved that we are the true, ancient church, one body and one communion of saints with the holy, universal, Christian church"; ibid., WA 51:494.24 ⟨LW 41:203⟩: ". . . who has commanded you to make this sacrilegious innovation in the church, which is a spiritual kingdom, of giving it a bodily head, whom you call His All-Holiness, when there can be no other head than a spiritual one, that is, Christ?"; see also ibid., WA 51:479.33, 480.21.22.28.34, 534.20. — *Against the Roman Papacy:* WA 54:243.29: ". . . all of Christendom in this world has no head above itself . . . except the Savior, Jesus Christ, God's son; according to St. Paul, he is the head of his body, which is all of Christendom; Eph. 4⟨:15⟩." — See also Ernst Wolf, *Peregrinatio*, 1:159ff.

231. See the carefully collected list of the pertinent phrases in Walther Köhler, "Zu Luthers Schrift 'An den christlichen Adel deutscher Nation,'" *ZSRG*.K 14 (1925): 24ff.

232. *To the Christian Nobility*, 1520: WA 6:405.16 ⟨LW 44:124⟩, and many other places.

233. Ibid., WA 6:406.23 ⟨LW 44:126⟩. For Canon law materials, see, e.g., *Decretum Gratiani* c.1. D.XXIII ⟨Friedberg 1:77ff.⟩.

234. ⟨I.e., the institutional church on earth.⟩ See Johannes Heckel, *Initia iuris*, 39ff.

235. ⟨Freely: "a body of equals."⟩

236. *To the Christian Nobility*, 1520: WA 6:407.18: ". . . Baptism, gospel, and faith alone make us spiritual and Christian people. . . . therefore through Baptism we all are consecrated as priests, as St. Peter says in 1 Pet. 2⟨:9⟩ . . ."; *The Holy and Blessed Sacrament of Baptism*, 1519: WA 2:727.20: "Baptism is an external sign . . . , which separates us from all unbaptized people; by this sign we are recognized as a people of our duke, Christ, under whose flag (i.e., the holy cross) we constantly fight against sin."

237. *To the Christian Nobility*, 1520: WA 6:407.22: "Through Baptism all of us are consecrated to be priests . . ."; *German Exposition of the Lord's Prayer for Simple Laymen*, 1519: WA 2:88.9; *The Private Mass and the Consecration of Priests*, 1533: WA 38.229.20: priests are not made by the pope's bishops; through the Holy Spirit and Baptism we are "born priests," we have inherited our priesthood; ibid., WA 38:230.8: we are priests "by birth ⟨in the sense of rebirth through Baptism⟩ and inheritance".

238. *To the Christian Nobility*, 1520: WA 6:407.19 ⟨LW 44:127⟩: "The pope . . . ordains, consecrates, and prescribes garb different from that of the laity, but he can never make a man into a Christian or into a spiritual man by so doing. He might well make a man a hypocrite or a humbug and blockhead, but never a Christian or a spiritual man. As far as that goes, we are all consecrated priests through baptism."

239. Ibid., WA 6:407.13 ⟨LW 44:127⟩: ". . . all Christians are truly of the spiritual estate, and there is no difference among them except that of office." ⟨See also above, 260 n. 14.⟩

240. For a definition, see *Receiving Bread and Wine in the Sacrament*, 1522: WA

10.II:37.12: "... those who believe and love, i.e., who are true Christians...." See also Luther's notes on the sermons of Tauler, 1516: WA 9:104.3: "Spiritual ⟨people⟩ — true Christians."

241. In a slightly altered form this phrase can be found, e.g., in *Against Jack Sausage,* 1541: WA 51:511.25. ⟨See also above, 98.⟩

242. *Decretum Gratiani* c.1. D.XXIII ⟨Friedberg 1:77ff.⟩. Instead of other medieval authors, see Biel, *Expositio missae,* lect. 22.G: "In Canon law, the name church . . . is restricted to the clergy." For additional materials, see Johannes Heckel, *Initia iuris,* 12 n. 36. See also *The Papacy at Rome,* 1520, WA 6:296.19, and *Against Jack Sausage,* 1541: WA 51.530.31.

243. *To the Christian Nobility,* 1520: WA 6:411.27 ⟨LW 44:134⟩.

244. ⟨For this equation of 'reform of the church' with 'reform of the Christian estate' (or 'estate of Christians'), and vice versa,⟩ see Luther to Wenceslas Link: July 20, 1520: WA.B 2:146.14 ("Our little book against the pope about the need to reform the church is being published"), and Aug. 19, 1520: WA.B 2:168.13 (Luther mentioned the little book "about the improvement of the estate of the Christians"); to John Voigt: August 3, 1520: WA.B 2:162.13 (Luther mentioned "the German book against the pope about the improvement of the estate *[status]* of the church").

245. As early as in a sermon of Oct. 1515 Luther derived the mutual connection which Christians have in their vocational life on earth from the connection which they have in Christ's mystical body; WA 4:669.10.16: "We all are in one faith, ⟨and⟩ one is a member of the other. Just as in a ⟨biological⟩ body one limb serves the other, so it also happens in the mystical body, . . . ⟨otherwise⟩ the true church body could not exist." See also *On the Power of Excommunication,* 1518: WA 1: 639.2: "... the communion of the faithful is twofold: one is internal and spiritual, the other is external and corporeal"; *Explanations of the Ninety-five Theses,* 1518: WA 1: 607.40. — For 'Christian body' in the sense of Christ's body, see the parallelly constructed phrase "divine law and Christian law (in the sense of Christ's law)" in *On Trade and Usury,* 1524: WA 15:312.6.

246. *To the Christian Nobility,* 1520: WA 6:412.15.16f. ⟨LW 44:135⟩.

247. Sermon of Aug. 2, 1523: WA 12:649.15: ⟨If the canons of the All Saints Chapter in Wittenberg, who still practice old ecclesiastical customs, do not know that among these customs are hidden misuses, then they should,⟩ "if they were godly people and were serious about serving God, . . . come to their brothers, who understand these matters, humble themselves, and obey these brothers."

248. *To the Christian Nobility,* 1520: WA 6:412.23 ⟨LW 44:135⟩. For the background, see Johannes Heckel, *Initia iuris,* 124f.

249. For citizenship as legal title authorizing the presentation of reform proposals, see *To the Christian Nobilty,* 1520: WA 6:413.36ff. ⟨LW 44:137⟩.

250. These lip-Christians are not "of the church" ⟨though they are in the church because they have been baptized⟩; *The Babylonian Captivity of the Church,* 1520: WA 6:561.23 ⟨the passage deals with the papal clergy⟩.

251. This legal situation is not changed by the fact that, according to human judgment, these *baptized* lip-Christians are considered to be holy; see Johannes Heckel, *Initia iuris,* 41 n. 171.

252. *To the Christian Nobility,* 1520: WA 6:413.28.38 ⟨LW 44:137: "true member of the whole body"⟩.

253. Ibid., WA 6:415.10 ⟨LW 44:139, and ibid., n. 44⟩.

254. ⟨Literally: "previous interpretations, which in their variety sound helpless, of Luther's statements . . . ." See above, 118, where these interpretations are listed in the form of questions.⟩

255. ⟨Some examples:⟩ Richard Rothe, *Theologische Ethik*, 3.I (Wittenberg, 1848), 1011: "⟨In the Reformation,⟩ Christendom itself on principle has done away with the church." — Rieker, *Rechtliche Stellung der evangelischen Kirche Deutschlands*, 69: "The question whether Luther's view of the unity of all Christian life does not mean that the church disappears, . . . can be answered affirmatively. Church which is not organized in legal forms, i.e., an invisible church, as Luther teaches, is no longer church according to the . . . understanding which thus far has been connected with this word ⟨i.e., church⟩." For other, identical materials, see ibid., 70. — Erich Förster, *Die Entstehung der preußischen Landeskirche unter der Regierung König Friedrich Wilhelms des Dritten nach den Quellen erzählt*, 1 (Tübingen, 1905), 168: "In the homeland of the Lutheran Reformation, the temperament of the people . . . instinctively rejects 'the church'. For 'church' is something of ⟨Roman⟩ Catholic piety; . . . Lutheran . . . piety . . . can, of course, accept 'church', but that piety never feels at home in it without second thoughts . . . . The . . . homeland of Lutheran piety can be nothing other than the state, the organization of the people which, contrary to appearance, for faith is Christendom and thus, according to Luther's thinking, church. . . . Therefore . . . the form of the religious communal life, which is most faithful to the essence of Protestantism, is the state church. . . ." In later years Förster changed his position to the effect that the "*Volkskirche* ⟨i.e., people's church in the sense of the identity of society and church; one is being born into the church, not by Baptism but by birth, so that the church has been absorbed into the structured society, i.e., the state⟩ is the only form which is adequate to . . . the gospel proclamation"; see his "Fragen zu Luthers Kirchenbegriff aus der Gedankenwelt seines Alters," in *Kaftan Festgabe*, 94. *Volkskirche* is an unclear term which stands between 'universal church' and 'particular churches'. ⟨*Volkskirche* has to be considered one of the particular churches; therefore one has to assume that, as a manifestation of the universal church, this particular church, called *Volkskirche*, shares in the legal organization of the universal church, which according to Luther is appropriate for the universal church; see Johannes Heckel, "Recht und Gesetz," ZSRG.K 26 (1937): 361. Yet according to Förster, the *Volkskirche* does not have a legal organization. He ignored the legal organization of the universal church in its connection with the particular churches and argued (*Kaftan Festgabe*, 95) that *Volkskirche* is not "a special ecclesiastical community," i.e., not a legally organized particular church which is independent from the state. For Luther, see also above, 98.⟩ — Holl, *Der Westen*, 374: At the time of the War of Liberation against Napoleon "the oecomenical idea is totally missing in all interpretations of the church. When one thought of the visible evangelical church, one always focused on the individual territorial church, without remembering that that church also has a worldwide task." ⟨In spite of this affirmation,⟩ Holl did not find a way back to Luther's concept 'universal church'.

256. ⟨It was Holl (*Luther*, 342 n. 1) who argued that Luther "fought" the concept 'universal church'.⟩ In support, Holl quoted from Luther's *On Proposition XIII concerning the Power of the Pope*, 1519: WA 2:224.7ff. ⟨Luther quoted (ibid., 224.5) one of Eck's arguments: "'You [Luther] should have known that God created in the firmament of heaven two big lights, the brighter [literally: 'greater'] one to rule day, the duller [literally: 'smaller'] one to rule night; both are great, but one is greater. Therefore, to the firma-

ment of heaven, i.e., of the universal church, God fastened two great lights; i.e., he established two grandeurs *(dignitates)*, the papal authority and the royal authority. The one which rules the days, i.e., spiritual matters, is the greater one; the one which rules carnal matters is the smaller one. And it is known that as great as the difference is between sun and moon, so great is the difference between popes and kings.'" [From Luther's comments, ibid., 224.24:] "What is one to say? Does from this argument follow that Julius [Caesar], Augustus, and other heathen emperors have been in the church because they were the God-created duller lights of [heaven, i.e.,] the church? And what is even a bigger joke: Julius and Augustus were those duller lights before the firmament, i.e., the church, was made, even before Christ, the head and creator of this firmament [i.e., the universal church] had been born; [more,] for a long time the universal church has been without that brighter light [i.e., the pope], as it is even now in Greece and India; maybe the people there are still in darkness. . . ." Heckel's comments on Holl's argument:⟩ In this passage Luther opposed only the doctrine of the two lights in the universal church, but not the concept 'universal church' itself. As the following references document, throughout his life Luther used the concept 'universal church' *(ecclesia universalis, catholica kirch, gemeine christliche Kirche)* without having any second thoughts. These materials show that, when Holl argued that Luther "fought" against the concept 'universal church', he was at least correct at one point, namely, that often and esp. in later writings Luther replaced the phrase 'universal church' with other phrases. *Explanations of Luther's Theses Debated in Leipzig,* 1519: WA 2:405.14f.; *The Babylonian Captivity of the Church,* 1520: WA 6:505.27.28.31, 561.26; *Against the Bull of Antichrist* ⟨Latin text⟩, 1520: WA 6:606.28.31.36, 607.7.9.17.20, 609.4.13; ⟨German text:⟩ WA 6:615.5; *Confession concerning Christ's Supper,* 1528: WA 26:506.30f.35; *Avoiding the Doctrines of Men,* 1522: WA 10.II:89.34, 90.4; *Second Lectures on Galatians,* 1531: WA 40.I:203.6, 40.II:86.11; *First Lectures on the Psalms,* 1513-15: WA 3:344.3; ibid., WA 4:180.25; *Second Lectures on the Psalms,* 1518-21: WA 5:75.8, 451.33, 530.18; *Sermons on John, Chapter 16,* 1538: WA 46:11.22; sermon of Jan. 18, 1545: WA 49:683.10; *Against the Roman Papacy,* 1545: WA 54:243.29; *On the Councils and the Church,* 1539: WA 50:625.1, 626.15; brief by Luther and other theologians: prior to July 18, 1540: WA.B 9:181.14; Luther to Philip Melanchthon: Nov. 21, 1540: WA.B 9:272.20.

257. For a different view, see Scheel, *Evangelium, Kirche und Volk,* 17: "According to Luther, one can speak about the church only if one focuses on its invisibility."

258. See Johannes Heckel, *Initia iuris,* 15. See also *Lectures on Psalm 45,* 1532: WA 40.II:560.10: ". . . the face of the church *(facies ecclesiae)* is the face of a sinner, vexed, forsaken, dying, afflicted, and whatever else is of the devil."

259. ⟨Literally: "face of the church."⟩

260. *To the Christian Nobility,* 1520: WA 6:445.28 ⟨LW 44:182⟩. For this passage, see Walther Köhler, "Luthers Schrift 'An den christlichen Adel,'" *ZSRG*.K 14 (1925):27f. Köhler saw that the phrase presents "the sacred nucleus of the 'whole', true, and essential Christendom" as "soul in the body" of the church. But he did not see that and why Luther equated this "nucleus" with the universal church.

261. See above, 100.

262. For the description of the universal church as 'holy', see *To the Christian Nobility,* 1520: WA 6:412.16 ⟨LW 44:135⟩, and Johannes Heckel, *Initia iuris,* 26f.; *Third Disputation against the Antinomians,* 1538: WA 39.I:491.8: ". . . therefore the church is holy, . . . be-

cause of the trope synecdoche, i.e., because of that part which is holy ⟨i.e., those who have been baptized and in faith maintain this consecration to be spiritual people and fight sin; see above, 119⟩, not because of the number of all who are in the church . . . ."

263. See Johannes Heckel, *Initia iuris,* 60ff.

264. As esp. Holl, *Luther,* 345f. argued. See also Harald Diem, *Luthers Lehre von den beiden Reichen,* 128. — Rudolf Stadelmann connected *corpus christianum* with "universale Christengemeinde" (universal congregation of Christians), but he also connected it with "mystical body of Christ"; it does not become clear how these two suggestions agree; see *Das Zeitalter der Reformation,* in *Handbuch der deutschen Geschichte,* new ed. by Leo Just, 2.I, prepared by Eberhard Naujoks (Darmstadt, 1956), 61, 62.

265. Walther Köhler, "Luthers Schrift 'An den Christlichen Adel,'" *ZSRG*.K 14 (1925): 36. — The term 'Christendom' is unclear in Sohm, *Kirchenrecht,* 1:465, 492, 542, 558ff. ⟨italics by this ed.⟩. According to Sohm, *Christendom* is the *community of the true believers* and, therefore, the *invisible church.* Yet at the same time this community *can be externally recognized* through the true preaching of the Word and the administration of the sacraments, and, therefore, it is a *visible* community. But in both cases, *Christendom is a purely spiritual community.* Nevertheless, according to Sohm (ibid., 558), "in Luther's doctrine the medieval idea of the two swords ⟨the spiritual, ecclesiastical one and the secular one⟩, which are placed above Christendom, is still effective with unbroken strength; secular authority is called to rule Christendom, that same community which is spiritually ruled by the ecclesiastical authority." In this last passage *Christendom is the totality of those who are baptized,* ⟨a visible community⟩, as it is appropriate for the medieval understanding of the universal church in relationship with the two swords doctrine. ⟨See *DMA,* s.v. "Two Swords, doctrine of."⟩ The first understanding of Christendom ⟨that it is the community of the true believers and, therefore, invisible⟩ and the last one ⟨that it is the totality of those who are baptized and, therefore, a visible community to be ruled by the representatives of the two swords⟩ do not agree with each other.

266. For materials from Luther's later period, see above, 434 n. 230.

267. Kohlmeyer, "Die Bedeutung der Kirche für Luther," *ZKG* 47 (1928): 509 n. 2, had arrived at the same result.

268. ⟨See above, 30, 31, 86, 93, 97f., 119, 260 n. 14.⟩

269. *To the Christian Nobility,* 1520: WA 6:406.21 ⟨*LW* 44:126⟩.

270. Ibid., WA 6:407.9 ⟨*LW* 44:127⟩. For the exemption of the clergy from the jurisdiction of secular courts, see c.1 in VI⁰ ⟨*Liber sextus*⟩. III.2 ⟨Friedberg 2:1019⟩.

271. ⟨Freely: "A body of unequals."⟩

272. ⟨I.e., ecclesiastical.⟩

273. ⟨In Baptism.⟩

274. *To the Christian Nobility,* 1520: WA 6:408.26 ⟨*LW* 44:129⟩: "It follows from this argument that there is no true, basic difference between laymen and priests, princes and bishops, between religious and secular, except for the sake of office and work, but not for the sake of status. They all are of the spiritual estate. . . . But they do not have the same work to do." In *The Private Mass and the Consecration of Priests,* 1533, Luther pointed out that between a bishop and a pastor there is no difference in terms of the estate: "Bishop and pastor are one thing"; WA 38:237. 22.

275. ⟨See n. 276: "bodily and spiritual welfare of the community."⟩

276. *To the Christian Nobility,* 1520: WA 6:409.1 ⟨*LW* 44:130⟩: "Therefore, just as

those who are now called 'spiritual,' that is, priests, bishops, or popes, are neither different from other Christians nor superior to them, except that they are charged with the administration of the word of God and the sacraments, which is their work and office, so it is with the temporal authorities. They bear the sword and rod in their hand to punish the wicked and protect the good. A cobbler, a smith, a peasant — each has the work and office of his trade, and yet they are all alike consecrated priests and bishops. Further, everyone must benefit and serve every other by means of his own work or office so that in this way many kinds of work may be done for the bodily and spiritual welfare of the community, just as all the members of a body serve one another [I Cor. 12:14-26]." — This difficult passage is often used to prove that Luther affirmed "the idea of a unified, spiritual-secular commonwealth"; so esp. Friedrich Meinecke, "Luther über christliches Gemeinwesen und christlichen Staat," *HZ* 121 (1920): 11. But in so doing the meaning of Luther's argumentation is not caught. He compared offices of church and state, or vocations, in their relationship with man-made law on the one hand, and with divine law on the other hand. But from this does not follow that these offices or vocations belong to a "unified commonwealth." — Holl (*Luther*, 347; italics by Holl) also erred. According to him, "Luther ... sees an *all-encompassing order* in the world, which reaches its height in the preservation and growth of Christendom. The kingdom of God is the higher unit, which encompasses state and church as its means ⟨i.e., for accomplishing this preservation and growth⟩, and thus also connects them with each other. Therefore in the passage cited ⟨at the beginning of this note⟩ Luther can designate the thus accomplished *whole* as a body, a community." Holl ignored that the kingdom of God is a kingdom at the right and at the left of God, and that one may speak of the kingdom of God as one unit only if one also includes these two sides of God's kingdom. Further, in the passage quoted above Luther did not deal at all with the relationship of state and visible church with each other, and then with a community placed above them. He dealt with the vocational life of the Christians in the world, either in ecclesiastical or secular estates ⟨or offices⟩, and he described how the spiritual community, which exists among Christians in the world, is effective in the earthly life. — See also Ernst Kohlmeyer, *Staat und Kirche in der Deutschen Reformation* (Bonn, 1935), 9ff.

277. *To the Christian Nobility*, 1520: WA 6:410.4 ⟨*LW* 44:131⟩.

278. Ibid., WA 6:407.17f., 408.8 ⟨*LW* 44:127, 129⟩.

279. A different view is presented by Herbert Olsson, "Sichtbarkeit und Unsichtbarkeit der Kirche nach Luther," in *Ein Buch von der Kirche*, 359: "Since the Word ⟨of God⟩ is effective in these secular estates as law, they belong to the church (Christ's body). In other words, they are ecclesiastical estates, regardless whether or not they who do ⟨secular⟩ works have faith"; ibid., 359 n. 2: "Therefore in his book addressed to the nobility Luther can speak ... of the 'body of Christendom,' to which all secular estates belong."

280. *To the Christian Nobility*, 1520: WA 6:410.5 ⟨*LW* 44:131⟩.

281. ⟨Literally: "vocation" in the sense of occupation *(Beruf)*.⟩

282. *To the Christian Nobility*, 1520: WA 6:408.8 ⟨*LW* 44:129⟩: "... those who exercise secular authority ... , have the same faith ... as the rest of us, ... ⟨have⟩ a proper and useful place in the Christian community." See also above, 427 n. 162.

283. ⟨I.e., the legally fixed privilege of the clergy and religious to be exempt from secular jurisdiction (be tried in ecclesiastical courts only), from secular taxation, and from communal burdens. See also *BLD*, s.v. "Benefit of the Clergy."⟩

284. *To the Christian Nobility,* 1520: WA 6:409.7, as above, 438 n. 276.
285. Ibid., WA 6:409.18 ⟨*LW* 44:130⟩.
286. Ibid., WA 6:411.8 ⟨*LW* 44:133⟩.
287. For details, see Johannes Heckel, *Initia iuris,* 27.
288. According to Luther, the position of the Romanists "would reduce the Christian church to one man" ⟨i.e., the pope⟩; *To the Christian Nobility,* 1520: WA 6:412.18 ⟨*LW* 44:135⟩.
289. Ibid., WA 6:412.37 ⟨*LW* 44:136⟩: "Therefore, it is the duty of every Christian to espouse the cause of the faith, to understand and defend it, and to denounce every error."
290. Ibid., WA 6:413.1 ⟨*LW* 44:136⟩.
291. Ibid., WA 6:413.27 ⟨*LW* 44:137⟩: "Therefore, when necessity demands it, and the pope is an offense to Christendom, the first man who is able should, as a true member of the whole body, do what he can to bring about a truly free council ⟨i.e., a council which is not controlled by the pope⟩. No one can do this so well as the temporal authorities, especially since they are also fellow-Christians, fellow-priests, fellow-members of the spiritual estate, fellow-lords over all things. Whenever it is necessary or profitable they ought to exercise the office and work which they have received from God over everyone."
292. Walther Köhler, "Luthers Schrift 'An den christlichen Adel,'" *ZSRG*.K 14 (1925): 31f.: ". . . Christian society in which secular authority acts as the chief functionary." See also id., *Luther und das Luthertum in ihrer weltgeschichtlichen Auswirkung* (Leipzig, 1933), 96; Bohatec, *Calvins Lehre von Staat und Kirche,* 631.
293. According to Wehrung (*Welt und Reich,* 213), "das christliche Abendland" (the Christian West) was the "unchallenged" presupposition of Luther's thinking, "not to say the *corpus christianum;* astonishingly, the value of the concept *corpus christianum* in Luther's thinking is controversial since various ideas are connected with it" ⟨it should be clear, of course, that Luther understood *corpus christianum* differently than it was understood in the Roman Catholic Church⟩. Wehrung refers to Luther's *Psalm 82 Explained,* 1530; here (WA 31.I:208.12.25.36 ⟨*LW* 13:61f.⟩) Luther mentioned the "common articles of all Christendom, which are believed throughout the world," and which belong to the "law of the city." Wehrung ignored that Luther spoke here of a *respublica bene instituta* (a well-ordered commonwealth), and a *respublica* is never a 'Christian' body; see above, 116 and 429 n. 185.
294. According to Ludwig Richter, *Geschichte der evangelischen Kirchenverfassung* (Leipzig, 1851), 17ff., Luther changed his position on the relationship between secular authority and church "within a few years" ⟨i.e., after *To the Christian Nobility*⟩. For a critique, see Sohm, *Kirchenrecht,* 1:543 n. 2; Rieker, *Rechtliche Stellung der evangelischen Kirche Deutschlands,* 69 n. 1.
295. See above, 347 n. 435. ⟨See also above, 266 n. 8.⟩ *On the Councils and the Church,* 1539: WA 50:652.18 ⟨*LW* 41:177⟩; *Disputation on Matt. 19:21,* 1539: WA 39.II:44.8. See also Ernst Wolf, "Politia Christi," *EvTh* 8 (1948/49): 60ff.
296. ⟨"Orders" in the sense of occupations, or offices, or institutions, or estates, not commands; see, e.g., also 'monastic' order.⟩ *Confession concerning Christ's Supper,* 1528: WA 26:504.30, as above, 347 n. 435.
297. Ibid., WA 26:504.35, 505.7: "Before God these are nothing but holy works . . . because these three institutions or orders are contained in ⟨or: 'set up in,' or: 'based on'⟩ God's Word and commandment."

298. ⟨I.e., the medieval *corpus christianum* or *respublica christiana*.⟩ Hermann Diem (*Luthers Predigt in den zwei Reichen,* 29) presented a different view. His basis was Ernst Wolf, "Zur Sozialethik des Luthertums," in *Kirche, Bekenntnis und Sozialethos,* ed. by Forschungsabteilung des Oekumenischen Rates für praktisches Christentum (Geneva, 1934), 52ff. ⟨Heckel referred to p. 22 of an offprint with new pagination⟩; see also Ernst Wolf, *Peregrinatio,* 1:218f., 223, 231, and id., *Libertas christiana* (Munich, 1949), 30. Diem dealt with the problem whether today the author of a "political sermon" has to consider other presuppositions than Luther had to. ⟨This problem is valid, of course;⟩ but as a criterion for the difference one may not use the thesis that Luther presupposed the ⟨medieval⟩ *corpus christianum.* Hermann Diem, *Lutherische Volkskirche in West und Ost* (Munich, 1951), 39ff.: "Luther's preaching in the two kingdoms has to do with the *corpus christianum* in the sense of a ⟨unified,⟩ closed society of Christians; in this society the governmental authority and the subjects are open to be addressed by the office of preaching because both belong to the church. After this presupposition has been eliminated ⟨in the present⟩, the task of the preacher remains, of course, the same in principle ⟨i.e., to address governmental authority and subjects with the gospel⟩ . . . ." On p. 40, n. 1, Diem assumed that "even today Luther's central intention, i.e., to declericalize society and thus to avoid the splitting of a Christian's existence into two different realms, . . . still can be implemented with the help of Luther's concept of the two kingdoms." — See also Wehrung, *Welt und Reich,* 46.

299. *On the War Against the Turks,* 1529: WA 30.II:130.27: ". . . the emperor is not the head of Christendom nor the protector of the gospel or of the faith." See also below, 460 n. 21; the draft of a letter of the evangelical estates meeting at the 1529 Diet of Speyer in Johannes Kühn, *Die Geschichte des Speyrer Reichstages, 1529* (Leipzig, 1929), 152: not the emperor but Christ is "the head of his church, i.e., the head of Christendom." — Lau (*Luthers Lehre von den beiden Reichen,* 60f.) has a different position. His basis is the thesis that Luther still knew of "Christendom" as "the unity which transcended *politia, oeconomia,* and *ecclesia* . . ." ⟨i.e.,⟩ as a community. There is, of course, *one* passage which could be cited in support of such a thesis; it is in Luther's Jan. 25, 1521, letter to Duke Frederick, elector of Saxony. Here (WA.B 2:254.32ff. ⟨LW 48:196⟩) Luther spoke of Emperor Charles "as secular head of holy Christendom." This phrase was a fixed formula in bureaucratic writing and, probably, did not originate with Luther but with a draft by Spalatin. Luther adopted the phrase in an effort to exhort the emperor as a Christian in the office of governmental authority to act so that "my opponents, the papists, cease their storming and un-Christian actions against me." Luther's text expressed the same ideas about the Christian governmental authority as we find them in *To the Christian Nobility.* — In cap. II.2 and 3 of the Golden Bull of 1356 we find the phrase "temporal head ⟨of the Christian people⟩." ⟨For the Golden Bull, see *DMA,* s.v. "Golden Bull of 1356."⟩

300. Esp. the phrase "secular Christian authority" (*To the Christian Nobility,* 1520: WA 6:409.27.31 ⟨LW 44:131: "temporal Christian authority"⟩) may not be understood in this sense. — Sohm, *Kirchenrecht,* 1:558, presented a different position; ibid., 559: "⟨Secular governmental authority⟩ cannot be excluded from Christendom, over which the spiritual sword is placed, just as, conversely, ecclesiastical authority cannot be excluded from Christendom, over which the secular sword is placed."

301. Sohm, *Kirchenrecht,* 1:468.

302. Walther Köhler, "Luthers Schrift 'An den christlichen Adel,'" ZSRG.K 14 (1925): 31, 35.

303. Ibid., ZSRG.K 14 (1925): 36: "It is the spirit which builds for itself 'the body' ⟨of Christendom⟩, and the spirit has its vital force in the mystical body" ⟨of Christ, or in the spiritual church⟩.

304. ⟨I.e., Christians who have been baptized but have not preserved their baptismal consecration in faith; see above, 119.⟩

305. *On Good Works,* 1520: WA 6:207.1: ". . . all members live, work, and have their name from the head, and without the head no member can live, work, or have a name."

306. Walther Köhler, "Luthers Schrift 'An den christlichen Adel,'" ZSRG.K 14 (1925): 37.

307. ⟨"Foremost member of the church" in the sense of being distinguished and therefore being the primary functionary (above, 440 n. 292) of a territorial church.⟩

308. Walther Köhler, "Luthers Schrift 'An den christlichen Adel,'" ZSRG.K 14 (1925): 32 ⟨See also above, 440 n. 291. The *believing* prince (a "true member of the whole body") is the foremost member of the church; therefore, when necesssary, he may, can, should be the church's "chief functionary."⟩

309. Luther did not adopt Augustine's concept *ecclesia permixta* (mixed church). See Spörl, "Augustinus — Schöpfer einer Staatslehre?" *HJ* 74 (1955): 67. — For a position different from the one presented above in the text, see Matthes, *Luther und die Obrigkeit,* 47: "A wonderful . . . sociological unit . . . , the 'secular kingdom' having come to faith."

310. Förster, "Fragen zu Luthers Kirchenbegriff," in *Kaftan Festgabe,* 95f., makes a prince's attribute 'Christian' dependent on the "Christian education" of a prince, i.e., an external matter, and not "on the faith" of a prince, ⟨an internal matter⟩.

311. So also Walther Köhler, "Luthers Schrift 'An den christlichen Adel,'" ZSRG.K 14 (1925): 37: "The internal law ⟨of a Christian governmental authority's action⟩ has its roots always in the structure of the mystical body ⟨of Christ⟩"; ibid., 38: "The decisive factor is the belonging of a governmental authority to the mystical body as a member of equal legal rank." But for Köhler this was not the only mark ⟨necessary for establishing the 'Christian' quality of a governmental authority⟩.

312. *Second Lectures on Galatians,* 1531: WA 40.I:342.5.10; ibid., WA 40.I:348.1: "Spirit is whatever happens and is done in us through the spirit"; ⟨see also the edited version of these lectures, *LW* 26:212f., 216f.⟩.

313. In *Second Lectures on Galatians,* 1531: WA 40.II:87.4, Luther developed what it means for someone in a God-constituted office to "walk by ⟨or: 'in'⟩ the Spirit"; ⟨see also the edited version of these lectures, *LW* 27:69f.⟩.

314. ⟨I.e., the membership in the spiritual church.⟩

315. *The Book of Deuteronomy with Notes,* 1525: WA 14:616.21 ⟨*LW* 9:73⟩: ". . . man should remain in the service of God alone, learn to relate everything to Him, and to do, possess, use, and endure all in His name."

316. *Psalm 101 Explained,* 1534-35: WA 51:244.35: ". . . godly, Christian princes ⟨should⟩ at the same time serve God and rule the people."

317. *Psalm 127 Explained,* 1524: WA 15:372.9: ". . . God wills . . . that we fulfill the duties of our office . . . in free, true faith and not worry when things do not turn out right, or be self-confident when things turn out well. No one does this unless he has a believing heart."

318. *On Christian Freedom* ⟨Latin text⟩, 1520: WA 7:51.17: "Faith alone is the salutary and efficacious use of God's Word...."

319. *Second Lectures on the Palms,* 1518-21: WA 5:221.17, 234.7; *Defense Against the Charge of Inciting Rebellion,* 1533: WA 38:113.5; sermon of Nov. 24, 1532: WA 36:362.37, 363.10.17, 364.32, 365.8, 366.23.32, 367.36, 371.22, 371.37 ⟨capital letters as in the original print⟩: "Now follows the other part, ⟨namely,⟩ ABOUT THE GOOD CONSCIENCE. Love should come from a heart which has a joyful ⟨or maybe: 'courageous'⟩, certain conscience, both toward people and God.... Each Christian... should have the reputation that in his relationship with everyone he lives, practices, and demonstrates his love in such a way that no one may accuse him of something which would terrify his conscience or make him despondent; to the contrary, people, if they are honest, should have to say that he has conducted himself in such a way that his actions resulted in nothing other than improvement ⟨of things for⟩ whoever was willing to accept it. To be able to boast before God of ⟨such a reputation⟩ and contrary to what ⟨some⟩ people might say — that means to have a good conscience before God and the people. Of course, such a conscience accomplishes nothing in God's court, just as that purity of the heart manifested in external living or works of love ⟨accomplishes nothing in God's court⟩, because before God we always remain sinners. Nevertheless, we are to have such a heart that enables us ... to say: 'God commanded this..., therefore I do it with a pure heart and good conscience.... What I speak and do has been ordered by God and commanded to me.'... Before God we are still lacking many things and have much that is punishable, even if in the eyes of the people all things we do were perfect.... Now has to be added... FAITH. This is the true chief part and the highest commandment, which contains all the other commandments, ⟨namely,⟩ that we know that faith has to be added when love is not perfect, the heart not pure enough, and the conscience not at peace, because God still finds things to punish even when the world cannot punish anything.... FAITH ... ⟨dares⟩ to appear before God... and say: 'Dear Lord, before the world I am innocent and certain that the world cannot punish me.... Before you I have... to confess, however, that I am guilty of all things.... Therefore if the law is to be valid, I am unable to argue with you, but I shall at once appeal... from your throne of judgment to your throne of mercy. Before the world's court I accept that one deals with me according to the law, and I shall answer and do what I have to do. But before you I do not want to know of any law but crawl to the cross, where I can beg and take grace.'... For where the throne of mercy rules, there is nothing but forgiveness... of all sins.... Now look, if one preaches about faith in this way, then all would be right with man, and then all those other things would come, a pure heart and good conscience through true, perfect love. For who through faith is certain in his heart that he has a merciful God..., moves on and does all things joyfully ⟨or: 'courageously'⟩, and he also can live with people accordingly, love everyone and do good.... Before God he is certain for the sake of Christ the mediator that God does not wish to push him into hell but smiles at him friendly and opens heaven to him. This is the highest certainty, the top and basis of our Salvation. Then I proceed from this basis, ⟨giving⟩ my life to the neighbor and doing to him the best that I am able to do according to the duties of my office and estate; if I do not enough ⟨see also above, 118⟩, I go to him and ask for his forgiveness. Therefore I have a good conscience toward God and the people.... In this way, in his relationship with people, man is called perfect in all things because of love; but before God ⟨he is called perfect⟩ not because ⟨he fulfills⟩ the law, but because of Christ, whom he grasps in

faith at the throne of mercy, and who sets up for me his holiness and grants to me that I have in him what I need for Salvation." — See also Ernst Wolf, "Vom Problem des Gewissens," in *Peregrinatio*, 1:81ff., 111, and esp. Schott, *Fleisch und Geist nach Luthers Lehre*, 20ff., 36ff. — For the "twofold joy" <or: "courage"> of the believer toward God and man, see Althaus, "Liebe und Heilsgewißheit bei Luther," in *Lortz Festgabe*, 1:74ff.; for the various interpretations of 1 John 4:17a, see ibid., 70ff.

320. Sermon of Nov. 24, 1532: WA 36:361.24.

321. Ibid., WA 36:361.24ff.

322. <"Well-being" or "Salvation."> *On Secular Authority*, 1523: WA 11:272.5 <*LW* 45:118>.

323. *Second Lectures on Galatians*, 1531, and *Second Commentary on Galatians*, 1535: WA 40.I:427.5.11 <*LW*:26:272>: "The Law is not faith, <but> in a concrete ... situation they come together.... Therefore faith always justifies and makes alive; and yet it does not remain alone, that is, idle. Not that it does not remain alone on its own level and in its own function, for it always justifies alone. But it is incarnate and becomes man; that is, it neither is nor remains idle or without love."

324. Sermon of Oct. 25, 1522: WA 10.III:282.3.11.

325. Therefore one has to question Wünsch, *Ethik des Politischen*, 133: "One cannot deny that Luther connected other, more radical demands with a Christian person than with a Christian office." A "Christian office" as an institution in the kingdom of the world did not exist for Luther. <See also above, 432 n. 213.>

326. *On Secular Authority*, 1523: WA 11:264.11 <*LW* 45:108>: "... every man runs his own risk in believing as he does, and he must see to it himself that he believes rightly." — See also Gogarten, *Kirche in der Welt*, 163; Wehrung, *Welt und Reich*, 49: "The meaning of an office is ... always personalistic — in Luther's thinking all things are personalisticly understood —: the princely office is called 'common person', i.e., person for others, work of a prince is work for others." <See also above, 428 n. 175.>

327. *That These Words of Christ, "This is My Body," Still Stand Firm against the Fanatics*, 1527: WA 23:188.8: "... all <things> which our body does externally ..., when God's Word comes to them and they are done in faith, are things spiritually done ...." See also Vajta, *Theologie des Gottesdienstes bei Luther*, 163.

328. *Psalm 127 Explained*, 1524: WA 15:373.13.

329. *Second Lectures on Galatians*, 1531: WA 40.II:30.3: "In Christ all spiritual things happen."

330. See above, 13f.

331. <Or: "Word in which it is set" either in the sense of set up, or of being set in, the way a precious stone is set in gold.> *That These Words, "This is My Body," Still Stand Firm against the Fanatics*, 1527: WA 23:263.22.

332. *Second Lectures on the Psalms*, 1518-21: WA 5:217.3: "Only Christ's cross provides instruction in the Word of God, the purest theology."

333. Ibid., WA 5:132.7: "... <a man> does not know God's righteousness unless God has instructed him." See also *D. Martin Luther's Preface to Ecclesiastes*, 1532: WA 20:8.19; *On Psalms 23-25*, 1513-16: WA 31.I:464.19: "... outside of Christ <exists> no knowledge and wisdom ..."; *Lectures on Psalms 120-134*, 1532-33: WA 40.III:202.3.6: "Solomon ... is a political doctor, who deals with ... those things in which he is well versed and in which the Lord has set him up, i.e., ... the political and the domestic governance. He deals with

them as no philosopher or man on earth has done, i.e., in faith; he relates whatever is done either politically or domestically to the divine governance ⟨literally: 'administration'⟩. No other writer does this. All the others . . . (ibid., 203.12) are unable to teach in this way about the commonwealth and matters of law as the Holy Spirit does, who is in the son of David. . . ."

334. *Lectures on Psalms 120-134,* 1532-33: WA 40.III:204.31.

335. Ibid., WA 40.III:209.11; ibid., WA 40.III:253.11: "⟨Solomon⟩ taught the true reason *(causam)* and foundation *(principium),* the giver and ruler of the *politia* and *oeconomia,* i.e., God himself"; *Second Lectures on Galatians,* 1531: WA 40.I:410.11: "We teach moral philosophy" ⟨instead of the "purest theology"; see above⟩ "in order not to know anything about God"; ⟨see also the edited version of these lectures, *LW* 26:261f.⟩.

336. ⟨The efficient and final cause of the world.⟩

337. ⟨The natural order of the world, i.e., the order of the world prior to Christ's work.⟩

338. ⟨God's official and co-worker.⟩ *Lectures on Psalms 120-134,* 1532-33: WA 40.III:210.14: ". . . we are God's officials *(ministri)* and co-workers, the *causa instrumentalis* (instrumental cause) — God governs the world through us. . . ."

339. Ibid., WA 40.III:206.7: "Only the Holy Spirit teaches that we anchor . . . *oeconomia* in the bosom of the divine majesty and trust him. . . ."

340. *Lectures on Psalm 45,* 1532-33: WA 40.II:544.8: "In the whole world no one ⟨but Christians⟩ can set forth what the *politia* is. . . . Therefore the wisdom of the world does not know what it is"; *Second Lectures on the Psalms,* 1518-21: WA 5:405.34: "There is no other legitimate use of ⟨law⟩ except faith and love . . ."; *Sermons on Matthew, Chapters 5-7,* 1530-32: WA 32:415.22: ". . . the present and future . . . of the spiritual and the secular governance are maintained through prayer."

341. *Second Lectures on Galatians,* 1531: WA 40.I:106.6: "Grace brings the judgment about all things, affirms the magistrate, the *oeconomia,* and orders" ⟨see also the edited version of these lectures, *LW* 26:48: ". . . the doctrine of grace and salvation . . . brings with it every benefit, both spiritual and physical, namely, the forgiveness of sins, peace of heart, and eternal life. It also brings light and sound judgment about everything. It approves and supports civi⟨c⟩ government, the home, and every way of life that has been ordained and established by God"⟩.

342. See above, 79, and 351 n. 467.

343. Gustaf Wingren ("Kirche und Beruf," in *Ein Buch von der Kirche,* 432) was correct when he argued: "Church and vocation *(Beruf)* are two entities which may not be separated . . . . Without the church a vocation would not at all be a call ⟨in the sense of appointment to a vocation, or internal calling for a vocation⟩ but a form of the curse of the law."

344. ⟨See above, 358 n. 10.⟩

345. ⟨The legitimate spiritual and corporeal use of law.⟩

346. Wolf-Dieter Marsch, "Ist das Recht eine notwendige Funktion der Kirche?" *ZEvKR* 5 (1956): 143 n. 93, saw in this sentence a "dangerous" statement! "Even before one is able to formulate this ecclesiastical law, which is not open to the world, it is necessary to think about the ⟨*sic*⟩ concept 'law'. . . . In any case, it has to be affirmed that the church — as an entity of the *eschaton* having been realized — does not emancipate itself from the world. The language of law remains bound to the world." I did not deny this; see above, 100, and 398 n. 86. Marsch also was not correct when he argued on p. 153 that ecclesiasti-

cal law "remains bound to the language of jurisprudence, that is <!>, to the public law concerning ecclesiastical matters <Staatskirchenrecht>."

347. <Literally: "the Christian congregation.">

348. <From here to "quite different" Heckel's text is freely translated.>

349. See above, 116, and 429 n. 184; Ernst Wolf, "Frage des Naturrechts bei Thomas und bei Luther," 15. Erich Seeberg (*Grundzüge der Theologie Luthers*, 209) was more restrained when he argued: "In practical terms, a Christian state will never exist."

350. <In the sense of the medieval *respublica christiana*.>

Notes to *What Happened to Luther's Doctrine of Law?*

1. <See above, 118f.>

2. For Melanchthon, see Werner Elert, "Humanität und Kirche. Zum 450. Geburtstag Melanchthons," in Elert, *Zwischen Gnade und Ungnade*, 92ff., esp. 96.

3. Instead of other authors, see Clemens Bauer, "Die Naturrechtsvorstellungen des jüngeren Melanchthon," in *Festschrift für Gerhard Ritter zu seinem 60. Geburtstag*, ed. by Richard Nürnberger (Tübingen, 1950), 244ff. In the theological starting point Melanchthon's doctrine of law agreed with that of Luther, and it received from this agreement its internal unity. Almost all the individual statements about natural law, mentioned by Bauer, can be found also in Luther's writings. The degree to which Melanchthon might have influenced Luther, or whether both independently derived their positions from older sources, are problems with which we cannot deal at this point. In any case, Melanchthon's concept 'natural law' was by no means "an alien element in <his> new theology" (as Bauer argued, 255) — just as one may not argue this in Luther's case — but certainly fits into the frame of that new theology. — It is totally without foundation to think that Melanchthon returned "to the image of the natural law held by Thomas and during the High Middle Ages" (as Wieacker, *Privatrechtsgeschichte der Neuzeit*, 146, argued). Such a return would sharply contradict Melanchthon's doctrine of Original Sin. — Friedrich Heer (*Europäische Geistesgeschichte* [Stuttgart, 1953], 266) argued: On the basis of Aristotle and biblical theology, Melanchthon developed a new doctrine of natural law, which sometimes is as identical with that of Thomas as one egg is identical with another one; he based his argument (ibid., 685, note to p. 266) on Clemens Bauer, "Die Naturrechts-Lehre Melanchthons," *Hochland* 44 (1952): 313ff. — Arnold *(Naturrecht bei Luther)* found a striking agreement between Luther and the Thomistic doctrine of natural law. For the opposite view, see Ernst Wolf, "Frage des Naturrechts bei Thomas und bei Luther," *JGGPÖ* 67 (1951): 192ff.; together with Johannes Heckel, Wolf emphasized Luther's basis in Occamist thought and the "radical spiritualizing of the divine law."

4. See Werner Elert, "Zur Terminologie der Staatslehre Melanchthons und seiner Schüler," *ZSTh* 9 (1931): 529f. Melanchthon affirmed this concept until the beginning of 1535, i.e., until he developed his doctrine of the *custodia utriusque tabulae*. See also Johannes Heckel, "Cura religionis," in *Stutz Festschrift*, 229.

5. See Johannes Heckel, "Cura religionis," in *Stutz Festschrift*, 231. <See also above, Appendix II.>

6. See Elert, *Morphologie*, 2:306ff.

7. For a different view, see Ebeling, "Triplex usus legis," *ThLZ* 75 (1950): 243: "The

profound difference between Luther and Melanchthon could be made clear already when one considers <Luther's> concept 'law'. For Luther, 'law' is not a statutorily revealed norm, to which man responds in one way or the other, but 'law' is for Luther an existential category; and in this category the theological interpretation of what it is to be a human being is summarized. Therefore 'law' is not an idea, or a sum of statements, but the reality of fallen man. "Law, sin, death, these three are inseparable." (WA 39.I:354.24.)

8. For the new rationale for metaphysics developed at the beginning of the seventeenth century, see Bengt Hägglund, *Die Heilige Schrift und ihre Deutung in der Theologie Johann Gerhards* (Lund, 1951), 9ff.

9. *De schismate Donatistorum* <or: *Adversus* (or: *Contra*) *Parmenianum Donatistam*>, book III. chapt. 3; *CSEL* 26:74.3.13. <See also *NCE* (2d ed.), 10:611f.>

10. Typical of this line of thinking is esp. the title of Theodor Reinkingk's <1590-1664> book, *Tractatus de regimine saeculari et ecclesiastico*, 1619. (I use the seventh edition, Augsburg, 1717.) For his political views, see Erik Wolf, "Idee und Wirklichkeit des Reiches im deutschen Rechtsdenken des 16. und 17. Jahrhunderts," in *Reich und Recht in der deutschen Philosophie*, ed. by Karl Larenz (Stuttgart, 1943), 1:94ff. <See also Martin Heckel, *Staat und Kirche*, s.v. "Reinkingk, Theodor.">

11. See Reinkingk, *Tractatus*, l. c. 1. III Cl. I cap.1. No.17, p. 809: "The authority of Christian princes in *respublica christiana*."

12. See Ulrich Stutz, *Kurfürst Johann Sigismund von Brandenburg und das Reformationsrecht*. SPAW.PH 1922.II, 20ff., and Johannes Heckel, "Höchstes Regal," *ZSRG*.K 13 (1924): 521f.

13. <As defined above, 433 n. 218.>

14. See also Gollwitzer, *Christliche Gemeinde*, 16f.

15. For some of the problems which arise in this connection, see Karl G. Steck, "Luthers Autorität," in *Ecclesia semper reformanda. Theologische Aufsätze Ernst Wolf zum 50. Geburtstag* (Munich, 1952), 104ff.; Heinz-Dietrich Wendland, "Die Situation am Ende der Neuzeit," *Dok*. 13 (1957): 217.

Notes to Appendix I

1. <*Widerstandsrecht*, i.e., the *right* to resist in the sense of a privilege ('inalienable right'), but also in the sense of the *law(s)* in which the details of this right are fixed.>

2. <One has to keep in mind that Luther developed his ideas in the frame of specific situations created by intentions or actions of Emperor Charles V. If one considers that 'emperor' is identical with 'head of state' both in terms of political symbolism and reality, then Luther's ideas are important even without their historic frame.>

3. See Ludwig Cardauns, "Die Lehre vom Widerstandsrecht des Volkes gegen die rechtmäßige Obrigkeit im Luthertum und im Calvinismus des 16. Jahrhunderts" (phil. diss. Bonn, 1903); Hans von Schubert, *Bekenntnisbildung und Religionspolitik 1529/30 (1524-1530)* (Gotha, 1910); Karl Müller, *Luthers Äußerungen über das Recht des bewaffneten Widerstands gegen den Kaiser*. SBAW.PH 1915.VIII (this work is fundamentally important); Fritz Kern, "Luther und das Widerstandsrecht," *ZSRG*.K 6 (1916): 331ff.; Kurt Wolzendorff, *Staatsrecht und Naturrecht in der Lehre vom Widerstandsrecht des Volkes gegen rechtswidrige Ausübung der Staatsgewalt* (Breslau, 1916); Hans Fehr, "Das Widerstandsrecht," *MIÖG* 38

(1920): 20ff.; Josef Bohatec, *Calvin und das Recht* (Graz, 1934), 144ff., and id., *Calvins Lehre von Staat und Kirche*, 84ff.; Hermann, "Luthers Zirkulardisputation über Matth. 19,21," *LuJ* 23 (1941): 35ff.; Matthes, *Luther und die Obrigkeit*, 130ff.; Wilhelm A. Schulze, "Reformation und Widerstandsrecht," *EvTh* 8 (1948/49): 372ff.; Carl Heyland, *Das Widerstandsrecht des Volkes* (Tübingen, 1950), 36ff.; Loy, "Das Widerstandsrecht und seine Grenzen bei Luther und heute," in *Zur politischen Predigt*, 67ff.; Iwand and Ernst Wolf, "Gutachten zur Frage des Widerstandsrechts," see above, 418 n. 109; Berggrav, "Staat und Kirche in lutherischer Sicht," see above, 412 n. 61; Carl Hinrichs, *Luther und Müntzer. Ihre Auseinandersetzung über Obrigkeit und Widerstandsrecht* (Berlin, 1952), 153ff.; Peter Meinhold, "Revolution im Namen Christi," *Saeculum* 10 (1959): 398ff.; Karl-Heinz Becker, "Die Probleme des Widerstandsrechtes in ökumenischer Sicht," *NELKB* 10 (1955): 5ff.; id., "Lutherische Demokratie," *Deutsche Universitätszeitung* 8 (1953.No.24): 4ff.; id., "Widerstandsrecht und Staatsgewalt," *ELKZ* 9 (1955): 129f.; Watson, *The State as a Servant of God*, 71 (a critical position); Pfeiffer, *Totaler Staat — und Luther?* 29ff.; Kurt D. Schmidt, "Das Widerstandsrecht im Sinne der Kirchen," *Informationsblatt für die Gemeinden in den Niederdeutschen Lutherischen Landeskirchen* 8 (1959): 81ff.; Thielicke, *Theologische Ethik*, 2.II. *Ethik des Politischen:* Nos. 2196, 2479f., 2526ff., 2540; Steck, *Luther und die Schwärmer*, 53f.; Gollwitzer, *Christliche Gemeinde*, 45ff.; *Macht und Recht. Beiträge zur lutherischen Staatslehre der Gegenwart*, ed. by Hans Dombois and Erwin Wilkens (Berlin, 1956), esp. the articles by Friedrich K. Schumann ("Widerstandsrecht und Rechfertigung," 34ff.) and by Eberhard Klügel ("Prinzipielles Recht zum Aufruhr? Fragen der politischen Aktivität des Glaubens," 44ff.); Gunnar Hillerdal, "Luther och tysk evangelisk politik 1530. Till frågan om Luthers syn på rätten til motstånd mot kejsaren, *KHÅ* 55 (1955): 124ff.

4. This resulted in uncertainties which, in turn, caused serious consequences; see the justified critical remarks by the Roman Catholic scholar Max Pribilla, "An den Grenzen der Staatsgewalt," *StZ* 146 (1948): 423ff., and id., *Deutsche Schicksalsfragen* (Frankfurt/Main, 1950), 287ff., esp. 306ff.

5. See esp. Fehr, "Widerstandsrecht," *MIÖG* 38 (1920): 23. See also Holl, *Luther*, 269, 491; Hermann Weinkauff, *Über das Widerstandsrecht* (Karlsruhe, 1956), 8: "As is known, Luther... fought his way through to the limited approval of the right of resistance held by the estates, though his fundamental position made this extremely difficult for him."

6. Kern, "Luther und das Widerstandsrecht," *ZSRG*.K 6 (1916): 339, was correct on this point.

7. See the important collection of Luther materials on the task preachers have toward secular governmental authority in Lau, *Luthers Lehre von den beiden Reichen*, 76 n. 176. Lau described this task as a "vicarious" task, and he cited Luther's *To Pastors, That They Preach against Usury*, 1540: WA 51:352.12-253.17. (Here Luther argued that it is the task of the jurists to instruct the public about the natural-law commandment of equity; preachers have to do this only because the jurists do not do their job.) Yet it would be better not to use the word 'vicarious', for a preacher does not have the competency to exercise the governance in the kingdom of the world 'vicariously'. His instruction about the secular natural law has a totally different quality than that of the jurists. They present a binding interpretation of the *secular* law, preachers proclaim the meaning of the *spiritual* ⟨divine natural⟩ law; when they mention the secular natural law, they do it as a warning not to violate the law of wrath *(lex irae)* externally, i.e., it is a part of preaching repentance.

8. Kern ("Luther und das Widerstandsrecht," *ZSRG*.K 6 [1916]: 334 n. 3) differenti-

Notes to Page 134

ated between the religious-moral *duty* of resistance and the *right* of resistance; a theologian has the competency for deciding whether the duty of resistance has to be implemented, a jurist has the competency for deciding matters connected with the right of resistance. Contrary to Kern, the situation is as presented above in the text. It is esp. a mistake when from this limitation of a theologian's competency Kern derived (ibid., 334) a "separation of the university faculties" in matters of judging the legal problem; ⟨supposedly⟩ "theologians have to deal only with the duties of the conscience, but they have to let the law function independently in its realm." There does not exist a "Humanistic-Protestant theology of Luther," according to which "a theologian is removed from the area of the jurist." (Ibid., 335f.) — Holl (*Luther*, 491) rejected the idea that in matters of the resistance to governmental authority Luther was interested "in natural law ideas"; "the Reformation deliberately ignored natural law." But it is precisely Luther's doctrine of the right of resistance that demonstrates that Holl's position cannot be maintained; see above, 238 n. 36; Luther to Duke John, elector of Saxony: Dec. 24, 1529: WA.B 5:209.33 ⟨*LW* 49:257, and ibid, n. 26⟩: a war of prevention "is unjust and also against the natural law."

9. See Luther to Duke Frederick, elector of Saxony: March 5, 1522: WA.B 2:456.102 ⟨*LW* 48:392⟩: ". . . no one should overthrow or resist authority save him who ordained it; otherwise it is rebellion and an action against God"; ⟨see also ibid., 456.96, or *LW* 48:392, the first lines of the paragraph in which this citation can be found;⟩ to John Rühel: May 4(5?), 1525: WA.B 3:480.22 ⟨*LW* 49:109⟩.

10. ⟨I.e., if the emperor, a legitimate governmental authority, would order to make war against the evangelical estates of the Empire, he would issue a command which in terms of the secular natural law is illegitimate.⟩

11. *A Sermon against the Turk*, 1529: WA 30.II:197.8; *Warning of His Dear German People*, 1531: WA 30.III:291.20, 299.9 ⟨Luther differentiated between disobedience and resistance⟩.

12. *Warning of His Dear German People*, 1531: WA 30.III:282.22 ⟨*LW* 47:19⟩.

13. ⟨Given to the Imperial estates in his election proclamation.⟩

14. Luther and Melanchthon to Duke John, elector of Saxony: May 1(2?), 1528: WA.B 4:448.23: an Imperial mandate was issued by "our God-established legitimate governmental authority which we are obligated to obey" ⟨for this letter see also *LW* 49:No. 181⟩; to Duke John, elector of Saxony: March 6, 1530: WA.B 5:258.31 ⟨*LW* 49:276⟩. — A different situation develops when God charges a "miracle man" to remove a tyrannical governmental authority; Hillerdal, *Gehorsam gegen Gott und Menschen*, 117ff. Luther always warned people not to feel that they are to play such a role.

15. ⟨This is a reference to the aftermath of the protest, filed by the evangelical minority against the Roman Catholic majority at the 1529 Diet of Speyer.⟩ Following his doctrine of the duty of a Christian to protest the illegitimate commands of a governmental authority ⟨see above, 108f.⟩, Luther accused the secular governmental authority of the Empire of violating the secular natural law ⟨the basis of the positive Imperial law⟩ through its illegitimate proceedings against the evangelicals ⟨after the Diet of Speyer, and with the saber-rattling resolution of the 1530 Diet of Augsburg⟩; see *Warning of His Dear German People*, 1531: WA 30.III:284.9 ⟨*LW* 47:21⟩.

16. Luther to Duke John, elector of Saxony: March 6, 1530: WA 5:259.55 ⟨*LW* 49:277f.⟩.

17. ⟨Luther considered the princes to be the emperor's subjects, i.e., the princes and the emperor did not have equal rank in law; see also below, 453 n. 55.⟩

18. I.e., to justify self-defense, or the protection of legal associates or subjects. See Luther to Duke John, elector of Saxony: March 6, 1530: WA.B 5:259.44 ⟨LW 49:276f.⟩, and Dec. 24, 1529: WA.B 5:209.33, 210.43 ⟨LW 49:257f.⟩. — For 'vim vi repellere licet' as natural law in the decretals, see, e.g., c.3. X⟨Liber extra⟩. V.39 ⟨Friedberg 2:890⟩; above, 316 n. 112.

19. On the basis of Luther's letter to Duke John, elector of Saxony, dated Dec. 24, 1529 (WA.B 5:209.29, 210.39 ⟨LW 49:257f.⟩), Karl Müller (*Luthers Äußerungen über das Recht des bewaffneten Widerstands,* 29) concluded that the reformer granted the right of active resistance to the evangelical princes, *if* the emperor issued the ban against them because they did not obey his command to suppress the gospel, and then made war against them to execute the ban. — For the same argument, see Ekkehart Fabian, *Die Entstehung des Schmalkaldischen Bundes und seiner Verfassung 1529-1531/33* (Tübingen 1956), 49. For the way in which the Electoral Saxon chancellor Gregory Brück dealt with Luther in this matter, and for Melanchthon's criticism of Brück, see my remarks in ZSRG.K 43 (1957): 478ff., esp. 482 ⟨review of Ekkehart Fabian, *Dr. Gregor Brück 1557 bis 1957* (Tübingen, 1957)⟩. For the textual history of Luther's letter, see Reinhold Jauernig, "Die Konkurrenz der Jenaer mit der Wittenberger Ausgabe von Martin Luthers Werken," *LuJ* 26 (1959): 85f. — Yet in this letter Luther did not speak in such a positive way. He only discussed the question whether in terms of the secular natural law a *preventive* ⟨'first strike'⟩ *war* against the emperor was permissible, and he answered negatively; see also Otto Clemen in WA.B 5:249. Luther said nothing about the question whether in terms of the secular natural law a *war of defense* against the emperor was permissible. ⟨In order to demonstrate that Luther did not totally reject armed resistance⟩, Hermann ("Luthers Zirkulardisputation über Matth. 19,21," *LuJ* 23 [1941]: 48, and ibid., n. 1) referred to WA.B 5:209.34f. ⟨or *LW* 49:257: *if* there is no "actual violence or an unavoidable necessity" present, armed resistance is to be avoided; this passage is found in the letter mentioned at the beginning of this note⟩. But here Luther spoke only in general terms about the permissibleness of a war of defense when the problem is viewed in light of the secular natural law.

20. See Luther to Duke John, elector of Saxony: March 6, 1530: WA.B 5:258.13 ⟨LW 49:275⟩; to Lazarus Spengler(?): March 18, 1531: WA.B 6:56.9; *Disputation on Matt. 19:21,* 1539: WA 39.II:72.33.

21. Therefore one has to correct Fehr who argued ("Widerstandsrecht," *MIÖG* 38 [1920]: 23): "If you jurists can demonstrate the existence of the right of resistance on the basis of the positive law and the secular natural law, then the reformer does not oppose you with Holy Scripture."

22. ⟨Staatsrecht.⟩ In a Febr. 15, 1531, letter to Lazarus Spengler (WA.B 6:37.27.29 ⟨LW 50:12⟩), Luther emphasized that now he does not deal with secular natural law and divine law but with a "new law which goes beyond ⟨in the sense of being different⟩ natural law — [that is] . . . the law of state and the Imperial law . . . ."

23. See WA.B 5:662.1 ⟨LW 49:No. 235⟩.

24. See WA.B 5:662.18 ⟨LW 49:No. 235⟩; Luther to Wenceslas Link: Jan. 15, 1531: WA.B 6:16.14; to Lazarus Spengler: Feb. 15, 1531: WA.B 6:37.15 ⟨LW 50:11⟩.

25. ⟨See above, 134.⟩

26. *First Lectures on the Psalms,* 1513-15: WA 4:398.2, 414.24f.

27. Luther to Lazarus Spengler(?): March 18, 1531: WA.B 6:56.18.

28. *Disputation on Matt. 19:21*, 1539: WA 39.II:75.22.

29. From early on Luther had always maintained this position. See *First Lectures on the Psalms*, 1513-15: WA 3:519.31: "... the church is not established for ⟨the use of⟩ carnal arms and it does not trust in them, as the synagogue did in days of old"; ibid., WA 4:231.1: "... ⟨Christ⟩ does not rely on material arms"; ibid., WA 3:524.18, 4:42.33; Luther to George Spalatin: Nov. 4, 1520: WA.B 2:210.10: "If the gospel were something that could be spread or preserved through the mighty ones of this world, God would not have entrusted it to fishermen"; to Duke John, elector of Saxony: May 22, 1529: WA.B 5:77.47 ⟨*LW* 49:227⟩, and Nov. 18, 1529: WA.B 5:182.14 ⟨*LW* 49:248⟩: "We would rather wish to be ten times dead than to have on our consciences the thought that our gospel should have been the cause of such bloodshed and damage, done because of us"; WA.TR 3:No. 3830 (on p. 644.38f.).

30. ⟨Heckel used *Christentum;* see above, 365 n. 63.⟩

31. This is probably the way in which one has to understand the following sentence in Luther's Jan. 15, 1531, letter to Wenceslas Link: WA.B 6:17.9: "This I have ... conceded, that a prince as prince is a political person ⟨see also above, 428 n. 175, 432 n. 213⟩; when he acts as such a person, he does not act as a Christian, who is neither a prince, nor a male, nor any of the other persons in the world." For Luther's phrasing, see *On Psalms 23-25*, 1513-16: WA 31.I:473.4; *Sermons on Matthew, Chapters 5-7*, 1530-32: WA 32:440.2: "A Christian ⟨is⟩ neither male nor female, nor young, old, lord, servant, emperor, prince, peasant, citizen, nor anything that is in the world ...." ⟨See Gal. 3:28.⟩ For similar statements, see Luther to Nicholas von Amsdorf: ca. Feb. 3, 1542: WA.B 9:610.51; to Wenceslas Link: Jan. 15, 1531: WA.B 6:17.13: "Certainly ⟨no armed resistance to the emperor⟩ is permitted to a *Christian* ⟨italics by this ed.⟩ because he is a person who has died to the world"; in this letter Luther dealt with the argument of the jurists that a prince as Christian guardian of the church has the right of active resistance. Luther's statement seems to take care of the concerns voiced by Hermann, "Luthers Zirkulardisputation über Matth. 19,21," *LuJ* 23 (1941): 51.

32. Luther to Lazarus Spengler(?): March 18, 1531: WA.B 6:57.33, as above, 379 n. 175.

33. ⟨I.e., if the emperor would make war against the evangelical princes for the sake of their faith, is he then a legitimate governmental authority?⟩

34. ⟨See above, 57.⟩

35. For this dualism as illustrated with the relationship of the Two Tables with each other, see above, 410 n. 54. ⟨See also below, Index of Subjects: *Law*, s.v. "natural law, dualism in."⟩

36. Theses 8 and 9 of *Disputation on Matt. 19:21*, 1539: WA 39.II:39.16.18: "... it is certain that Christ had not come to do away with the law of the Second Table, but rather to confirm it. In fact, everywhere he confirmed the ⟨office of the⟩ magistrate and the laws of the *politia*...." ⟨For Luther, the Fourth Commandment connected the Second Table with the *politia;* see, e.g., *BC* 384.141ff.⟩

37. Theses 21 and 22 of *Disputation on Matt. 19:21*, 1539: WA 39.II:40.16.18: "Christ speaks ⟨Matt. 13:44-46, 19:21,29⟩ about abandoning and selling all things because of the First Table or the public confession of the faith ⟨literally: 'the confession and public cause of the faith'⟩. Because of the First Table ⟨literally: 'in the cause of the First Table'⟩ and the matter of retaining and acquiring that precious pearl of the kingdom of heaven, the field has to be sold, and all things have to be abandoned and given away."

38. The evil is inflicted not by the emperor. For a different view, see Hermann, "Luthers Zirkulardisputation über Matth. 19,21," *LuJ* 23 (1941): 68ff.

39. This should answer the question raised by Hermann, "Luthers Zirkulardisputation über Matth. 19,21," *LuJ* 23 (1941): 69. He asked: Why did Luther in theses 36-50 deal only with the passive disobedience of the princes, and then in theses 51ff. he spoke of the right of active resistance? In thesis 40 Luther rejected the right of active resistance for "private persons of whatever social position" (Hermann, 69f.); that thesis dealt with citizens in the sense of subjects but also with lower magistrates, which were subordinated to the territorial governmental authority.

40. For a first ‹cumbersome› step toward this new idea, see Luther's *Sermons on Matthew 5-7*, 1530-32: WA 32:391.35, 392.7.11.18, 393.5.

41. See above, 423 n. 142.

42. Thesis 32 of *Disputation on Matt. 19:21*, 1539: WA 39.II:41.1: "... as the magistrate, whose member you are, himself fights ‹the robber›, so he commands you to fight ‹the robber› on the basis of the Second Table, which you are bound to obey."

43. Ibid., theses 24 and 25: WA 39.II:40.23.25: "Outside of matters pertaining to the First Table ‹literally: 'the cause of the First Table'›, or the confession ‹of faith›, all things are to be acquired, preserved, defended, and administered, because we are bound to obey the Second Table; i.e., by divine and by natural law ‹we are bound› to take care of the body and this life, feed, protect, and keep them in good order."

44. Ibid., theses 31 and 35: WA 39.II:40.38, 41.8: "If... a robber or thief wishes to inflict violence upon you, or steal something from you, because you are a Christian he has to be resisted, if you wish to be a godly citizen of this world.... One need not worry if ‹the robber› pretends to act because of Christ, i.e., the First Table, because it is certain that he does not seek to kill you because of Christ but seeks to kill you because of your property."

45. Ibid., thesis 39: WA 39.II:41.17: "... the magistrate, ‹regardless of his position,› always and everywhere commands to preserve the peace among the subjects, whatever religion they might have."

46. Ibid., thesis 49: WA 39.II:41.38: "It is not up to us, in fact, it is prohibited to us, to destroy the God-instituted magistrate and political institutions *(politias)* ...."

47. *Matthew, Chapters 18-24 Explained in Sermons*, 1537-40: WA 47:347.24: "A Christian has to reach the point where he even gives up his life for the sake of the confession of Christ and of love ‹for the neighbor›, if need demands it. ‹Example:› I am living under a godless prince, and he expels me from the territory or persecutes me ‹literally: 'burns me'›, what am I to do in this situation? I should not only sell my goods, abandon wife, children, father and mother, but even risk my neck ‹for the sake of confessing Christ and loving the neighbor›. This is the right beginning of obeying God's command." See also Luther and Bugenhagen to the Einsiedel brothers (Dec. 28, 1527; WA.B 4:306.5), and to George Spalatin (Jan. 5, 1528: WA.B 4:340.3).

48. According to Luther, matters of faith, i.e., the First Table of the commandments, could be the only reason for a confrontation between a governmental authority and its *evangelical* subjects, because in matters of the Second Table they maintain the strictest obedience; thesis 45 of *Disputation on Matt. 19:21*, 1539: WA 39.II:41.30: "... the magistrate, who inflicts evil ‹upon his subjects› for the sake of the First Table (he cannot have another reason), is not to be resisted." The clause in parentheses is not to be understood ironically ‹in the sense that the emperor and his party could or would have another rea-

son, namely, to get their hands on the property of the evangelicals⟩, as Hermann, "Luthers Zirkulardisputation über Matth. 19,21," *LuJ* 23 (1941): 70, seems to suggest.

49. *Matthew, Chapters 18–24 Explained in Sermons*, 1537-40: WA 47:564.3 (sermon of Nov. 2, 1539?): ". . . the Apostles . . . were commanded to be silent and preach no more about Christ ⟨Acts 5:40⟩, though they had Christ's command to preach the gospel to all people. Which command were the Apostles to follow? Which one was just? St. Peter stood up and said: '. . . Dear secular lords, I am obligated to obey you provided that you do not oppose the overlord, i.e., that you do not oppose God, who prohibits me from doing what you command me to do. Therefore I intend to obey you in the realm covered by your authority, ⟨which⟩ is not to interfere with God's authority.'" — See also Matthes, *Luther und die Obrigkeit*, 43f.

50. Thesis 42 of *Disputation on Matt. 19:21*, 1539: WA 39.II:41.23: "If they ⟨i.e., the magistrates who proceed with force against the evangelicals because of their disobedience but pretend that their actions are considered to be the result of concern for religion⟩ do not wish to be better informed, then Christ's doctrine enters the situation: 'Go, sell, abandon, loose, throw away all things, even life itself.'" ⟨See also Matt. 19:21.⟩ — An alliance behind the back of such a governmental authority, or directed against it, is not permissible; Luther to Count Albrecht of Mansfeld: (beginning? of) 1525: WA.B 3:416.56.

51. *Admonition to Peace*, 1525: WA 18:323.25 ⟨*LW* 46:36⟩: ". . . let the ruler have his city; you follow the gospel. Thus you permit men to wrong you and drive you away; and yet, at the same time, you do not permit men to take the gospel from you or keep it from you." ⟨See also above, 412 n. 64.⟩

52. Thesis 45 of *Disputation on Matt. 19:21*, 1539: WA 39.II:41.30, as in above, 452 n. 48.

53. ⟨The jurists justified armed resistance of the believing Christian, who 'serves God with all his strength' ('extending the church and serving Christ with all his ability'), against his legitimate ruler, who persecutes his evangelical subject.⟩ *Disputation on Matt. 19:21*, 1539: WA 39.II:78.23: "⟨The jurists affirm that there is a right of resistance,⟩ because each individual, be he subject or prince, has to extend the church and serve Christ with all his ability; therefore they also have to resist the tyrant"; see also ibid., WA 39.II:79.24.

54. ⟨I.e., the right of spiritual legal equality of all Christians in Christ's kingdom. For "spiritual basic rights," see above, 31, 86, 97f., 247 n. 53, 285 n. 46.⟩

55. *Whether Soldiers, Too, Can Be Saved*, 1526: WA 19:652.25 ⟨*LW* 46:126⟩: "Overlords . . . are appointed to be persons who exist for the sake of the community ⟨literally: 'to be a public person'; see above, 428 n. 175, 432 n. 213⟩, and not for themselves alone. They are to have the support of their subjects and are to bear the sword. Compared to his overlord⟨,⟩ the emperor, a prince is not a prince, but an individual who owes obedience to the emperor, as do all others, each for himself. But when he is seen in relationship to his own subjects he is as many persons as he has people under him and attached to him. So the emperor, too, when compared with God, is not an emperor, but an individual person like all others; compared with his subjects, however, he is as many times emperor as he has people under him. The same thing can be said of all other rulers. When compared to their overlord, they are not rulers at all and are stripped of all authority. When compared with their subjects, they are adorned with all authority. Thus, in the end, all authority comes from God, whose alone it is"; Luther to Duke John, elector of Saxony: Dec. 24, 1529:

WA.B 5:210.58 ⟨LW 49:259⟩: "... the emperor, of course, is the lord and governmental superior of these sovereigns"; to Duke John, elector of Saxony: March 6, 1530: WA.B 5:258.13 ⟨LW 49:275⟩. See also Matthes, *Luther und die Obrigkeit,* 106ff. — Ernst Reibstein (*Johannes Althusius als Fortsetzer der Schule von Salamanca. Untersuchungen zur Ideengeschichte des Rechtsstaates und zur altprotestantischen Naturrechtslehre* [Karlsruhe, 1955]) totally misunderstood Luther's position on the contrast between "individual" ⟨or private, or *einzel*⟩ and "public" ⟨or *gemeine*⟩ person. He argued (63) that Luther "let the governmental authority step into ⟨in the sense of take over⟩ the laws of the *Gemeinde* (community)," because for him "to resist governmental authority" means "to oppose the *Gemeinde.*" But Luther did not speak about resisting the *Gemeinde* but the *gemeine Person* ⟨the public person, i.e., the prince⟩. This nullifies Reibstein's thesis about the close bond between the church and the power of the state which, supposedly, was the nucleus of the reformer's structure of the church-state relationship.

56. They were based on the statements made by Emperor Charles at the time of his election, July 3, 1519.

57. ⟨I.e., the Empire is the sum of the estates.⟩

58. See WA.TR 4:No. 4342 (Febr. 1539), on p. 236.14, and Karl Müller, *Luthers Äußerungen über das Recht des bewaffneten Widerstands,* 76 n. 1. ⟨See also below, nn. 60 and 66.⟩

59. *Disputation on Matt. 19:21,* 1539: WA 39.II:78.3: "An elector is not a private person, but the electors are the emperor's equals; seven electors are the parts *(partes)* which set up ⟨or: 'make up'; *constituere*⟩ the emperor. The emperor is the head, they are the members, etc. They are part of the Empire *(pars imperii),* and, therefore, they are also part of the emperor. I am ... a finger; ... if one finger wants to poke the eye, the other finger fights it. So ⟨it is⟩ also in the *forma* of the Empire." See also Luther to John Lüdike: Febr. 8, 1539: WA.B 8:367.49.

60. ⟨Or: *in parte sollicitudinis.* There seems to be no standard English version of this phrase; in German texts of the late medieval and early modern period, e.g., it is translated in many ways. For our interpretations, see *Mediae Latinitatis Lexicon minus* (2.ed. 2002), s.v. "pars, 4.11.12.14." — As part of the Empire, the electors, together with the emperor, are to govern the Empire, because emperor and electors share the responsibility of caring for the Empire in the best possible way.⟩ WA.TR 4:No. 4342 (Febr. 1539), on p. 237.3: "Because of this solicitude *(in hac parte sollicitudinis)* the electors must not be silent." ⟨I.e., the responsibility of caring for the Empire does not allow the electors to be silent, or not oppose the emperor. See also ibid., 239.36 (a German version of this text): "The electors, insofar as they are members of the Empire and of the emperor, are secular members and not Christians; therefore they are not to be silent in matters pertaining to the Empire and their office, but they ought to ... do what their duty demands."⟩ — For *in parte(m) sollicitudinis,* see also Marsilius of Padua, *Defensor Pacis,* ed. by Richard Scholz (Hannover, 1932), 446 n. 1, where other references can be found.

61. ⟨From now on, this new insight into the constitution of the Empire shaped Luther's position on resistance to the emperor, if he would make war against the evangelical estates.⟩

62. See Luther's *Smalcald Articles,* 1537: WA 50:213.11 ⟨BC 298.1⟩.

63. *Decretum Gratiani* c.11. C.II.q.6 ⟨Friedberg 1:469⟩.

64. ⟨In the following, down to "... the emperor's unilateral action ... ," it was neces-

sary to expand or paraphrase Heckel's text. We are grateful to Martin Heckel for helping us understand the text.⟩

65. ⟨For the most part they were ceremonial in nature.⟩

66. WA.TR 4:No. 4342 (Febr. 1539), on pp. 236.16, 237.19 ⟨for our text we have combined Heckel's quotations with additional materials from a German version of this table talk, ibid., 239.29ff., 240.23ff.⟩: "⟨The electors⟩ are members of the emperor; . . . each one is charged with the care for the Empire *(cura imperii)*, albeit not in the first place ⟨i.e., in the first place the emperor is charged with this care⟩. There ⟨in the first place, i.e., when it comes to the emperor⟩ these seven ⟨electors⟩ have the same authority as the emperor has. . . . Summary: In the German Empire the emperor is not a monarch and exclusive lord, as are the kings of France and England, who rule in their kingdoms all by themselves, but the electors and the emperor have one common authority and ⟨duty⟩ of administration. Therefore the emperor does not have the authority or right to issue laws . . . by himself, much less does he have the authority, competency, or right to draw the sword and make war against the subjects and members of the Empire . . . without . . . approval of the whole Empire." — For materials from late medieval Imperial law, see Ernst Heymann, review of Wolzendorff, *Staatsrecht und Naturrecht,* in *ZSRG*.G 37 (1916): 566.

67. ⟨See also above, 109.⟩

68. ⟨See also above, 59, 107f. 313 n. 98.⟩

69. *Disputation on Matt. 19:21,* 1539: WA 39.II:77.26 (B text): "The emperor, or ⟨his brother⟩ Ferdinand, is . . . seeking our possessions, yet ⟨does it⟩ under the pretext of the pope" ⟨i.e., the emperor pretends that it is religion (the pope's condemnation of the evangelicals), which authorizes him to make war against the evangelical princes, whom the pope has declared to be heretics⟩.

70. It was jesting, and yet it was also more than jesting, when as early as Aug. 15, 1521, Luther wrote to George Spalatin: WA.B 2:380.49 ⟨*LW* 48:294⟩: ". . . to be a ruler and not to a certain degree a robber is not at all — or hardly — possible. The greater the ruler, the bigger the robber." See also Luther to George Spalatin: Jan. 1, 1527: WA.B 4:151.54.

71. See above, 452 n. 44; Luther to John Ludicke: Feb. 8, 1539: WA.B 8:367.22; Luther and others to Duke John Frederick, elector of Saxony: July(?), 1539: WA.B 8:517.59.

72. ⟨See above, 452 nn. 43-44.⟩

73. *Disputation on Matt. 19:21,* 1539: WA 39.II:77.3: ". . . if the emperor as tyrant would persecute ⟨God's doctrine⟩ of his own will, not because of the pope's authority as the true motivation, is he then to be resisted? That evil has to be resisted. We must leave ⟨our⟩ doctrine and church to our descendants in good order." See further, above, Appendix II.

74. See Johannes Heckel, "Cura religionis," in *Stutz Festschrift,* 229ff.; Hans Lüthje, "Melanchthons Anschauung über das Recht des Widerstands gegen die Staatsgewalt," *ZKG* 47 (1928): 512ff.

75. See Melanchthon's brief, signed also by Luther, dated Dec. 20, 1543: WA.B 10:470.43, and Melanchthon's letter, signed also by Luther, dated May 14, 1544: WA.B 10.568.20.

76. ⟨Literally: "the papacy." See also above, 421 n. 121, 422 n. 139.⟩

77. Luther to John Ludicke: Feb. 8, 1539: WA.B 8:367.26.

78. ⟨See above, 112.⟩

79. See above, 421 n. 121. ⟨See also above, 421 n. 119.⟩

Notes to Appendix II

1. Sometimes Luther focused on a secular governmental authority as such, i.e., that authority of which the incumbent was not an evangelical believer, sometimes on a Christian evangelical governmental authority ⟨of which the incumbent was an evangelical believer⟩. Therefore we find contradictory statements regarding the *cura religionis*.

2. *Psalm 101 Explained*, 1534-35: WA 51:230.36 ⟨LW 13:184: "spiritual rule" of David⟩. In this passage Luther understood the spiritual governance of a prince as the guardianship *(custodia)* of the First Table of the Decalogue, implemented by a Christian prince; it supplements the work of the ministry of the Word in its spiritual governance; see ibid., WA 51:240.13, 241.16.35 ⟨LW 13:195, 197⟩; *The Book of Deuteronomy with Notes*, 1525: WA 14:614.3. — As is known, the phrase *custodia primae tabulae* (guardianship of the First Table) originated with Melanchthon; see Johannes Heckel, "Cura religionis," in *Stutz Festschrift*, 229ff.; in terms of substance there is not the slightest difference between Luther and Melanchthon in this matter. — Holl (*Luther,* 347 n. 3) pointed out that there is no documentation available for Luther having "assigned the duty of the guardianship of the First Table (maintaining true worship in a territory) to the prince *as prince* ⟨italics by this ed.⟩." Yet that documentation can be found in *Psalm 101 Explained*. See also below, 460 n. 22; Luther to Duke Henry of Saxony: July 25, 1539: WA.B 8:506.6.

3. *Psalm 101 Explained*, 1534-35: WA 51:216.12: "In the following three verses ⟨Ps. 101:2-4, David⟩ demonstrates how he has managed his house and ruled his kingdom according to the spiritual estate, that is, in the Word and service of God. The other four verses demonstrate how he has ruled in the secular estate."

4. See above, 126.

5. Holl's view of the situation was too narrow when he wrote (*Luther,* 347): "The content of their actions is proscribed to Christians not in ⟨the Christian faith⟩ but rather already in the divine natural order." "Divine natural order" was for Holl identical with the Second Table of the Decalogue.

6. *Magnificat,* 1521: WA 7:584.30; for this passage, see Maurer, *Freiheit eines Christenmenschen,* 99.

7. Kühn (*Toleranz und Offenbarung,* 104) was correct when he emphasized against Karl Müller, *Kirche, Gemeinde und Obrigkeit nach Luther* (Tübingen, 1910), 19, 21, that the actions of a secular governmental authority benefiting the church may not be described only in negative terms, only as a protection against something which is wrong. *Psalm 82 Explained,* 1530: WA 31.I:199.3.35: ⟨The first important virtue of a prince or lord is to⟩ "feed or protect" ⟨the pastor who promotes God's kingdom and creates a new world, an eternal beautiful paradise; see *LW* 13:52f.⟩; sermon of Feb. 22, 1540: WA 49:38:29: ⟨According to Isa. 49:23 and 60:16,⟩ "God wills that his Christians be preserved through godly kings, so that they can live on earth and have their food . . ."; of Feb. 29, 1540: WA 49:40.24; Luther to George Spalatin: Jan. 2, 1523: WA.B 3:2.18.

8. *Psalm 101 Explained,* 1534-35: WA 51:231.4 ⟨LW 13:184⟩: ⟨According to Ps. 101:4, David⟩ "leaves his court and visits the whole area of his kingdom, speaking especially of the false teachers and the idolatrous priests who were to be found now and then in the land." This passage augments Herman Diem's historical materials, presented in "Kirchenvisitation als Kirchenleitung," in *Ecclesia semper reformanda,* 45ff. — In *Second*

Lectures on the Psalms, 1518-21: WA 5:573.26, Luther dealt with prayer for the illumination of a prince in preparation for such a work.

9. *Psalm 101 Explained,* 1534-35: WA 51:234.18 ⟨LW 13:188⟩: "... ⟨David⟩ permitted all pious, faithful, and true teachers to move about in freedom and in peace, giving them shelter, protection, and provision. In addition he sought, demanded, called, ordained, and commanded everywhere that the Word of God be preached in its truth and purity and that God be properly worshiped." Primarily it is the responsibility of bishops to take care of these matters. When they neglect their duty, Christian governmental authorities have to act as 'emergency bishops' *(Notbischof); A Model for Consecrating a True Bishop,* 1542: WA 53:255.5, 256.3; for literature on this term, see WA 53:255 n. 2. See further, Luther to Count Henry of Schwarzburg: Dec. 12, 1522: WA.B 2:627.20: "... it is not against the law, in fact, it is the highest ⟨form of compliance with the⟩ law, to chase the wolf from the sheep pen and ignore whether this will harm his belly." Luther made similar statements as early as Apr. 28, 1522, in materials prepared for the City Council of Altenburg: WA.B 2: 507.7.

10. ⟨In dealing with heresy Luther made six points.⟩

(1) Heretics are people who "teach a righteousness which is different from God's righteousness"; *Second Lectures on the Psalms,* 1518-21: WA 5:352.32. In addition to this new definition, which is based on Luther's doctrine of law, we find older definitions, which are closer to Canon law; *Assertion of All Articles,* 1520: WA 7:123.22; *Defense and Explanation of All Articles,* 1521: WA 7:395.29 (for this passage, see also *Reply to Ambrosius Catharinus,* 1521: WA 7:711.13); *The Papacy at Rome,* 1520: WA 6:294.30: "Not to believe correctly makes heretics."

(2) It is the task of the church to find out whether heresy exists, and if it does, fight it. The only standard for the church's action is Holy Scripture, and the only means which the church has to fight heresy are spiritual means, i.e., the theological debate; *To the Christian Nobility,* 1520: WA 6:455.21 ⟨LW 44:196⟩: "We should overcome heretics with books, not with fire, as the ancient fathers did"; *Concerning Rebaptism,* 1528: WA 26:146.6: "One should oppose ... them with writings and God's Word, ⟨because⟩ one will accomplish little with fire"; *The Book of Deuteronomy with Notes,* 1525: WA 14:680.34 ⟨LW 9:183⟩. Excommunication is the church's strongest action against heretics; *Assertion of All Articles,* 1520: WA 7:139.26. — See also *Postilla for Lent,* 1525: WA 17. II:125.1.

(3) It is not permissible to force someone to believe; *The Book of Deuteronomy with Notes,* 1525: WA 14:680.29, 681.2 ⟨LW 9:183⟩; brief by Luther and Bugenhagen, dated Jan. 24, 1528: WA.B 4:358.40; above, 392 n. 50; *Decretum Gratiani* c.3-5. D.XLV ⟨Friedberg 1:160ff.⟩. — Permissible is, however, to insist that people attend the evangelical instruction in the basic tenets of the Christian faith, because in such an instruction people will also be taught the moral principles which are the foundation of the secular commonwealth; *The Small Catechism,* 1529: WA 30.I:349.17 ⟨BC 339.13⟩: "Although we cannot and should not compel anyone to believe, we should nevertheless insist that the people learn to know how to distinguish between right and wrong according to the standards of those among whom they live and make their living. For anyone who desires to reside in a city is bound to know and observe the laws under whose protection he lives, no matter whether he is a believer or, at heart, a scoundrel or knave"; Luther to Thomas Löscher: Aug. 26, 1529: WA.B 5:137. 13 ⟨LW 49:233f.⟩: "... since the Decalogue and the Catechism also teach matters pertaining to the political commonwealth and the management of household af-

fairs *(politia, oeconomia)*, and since such matters must often be dealt with in sermons, these people should be compelled to attend those sermons in which they can learn secular obedience and the [proper way] of managing a household — regardless of whether they believe the gospel or not — so that they are not a cause of offense to others...." — For the "common articles," believed by Christians throughout the world, as "law of the city," see *Psalm 82 Explained,* 1530: WA 31.I:208.11ff., 30ff. ⟨*LW* 13:61f.⟩. — See also Luther to Margrave George of Brandenburg-Ansbach: Sept. 14, 1531: WA.B 6:193.49.

(4) Secular authorities may not obstruct the church's theological debate on what might be heresy under the pretense that public order has to be maintained; *On Secular Authority,* 1523: WA 11:268.19 ⟨*LW* 45:114⟩: "... you say, 'The temporal power is not forcing men to believe; it is simply seeing to it externally that no one deceives the people by false doctrine; how could heretics otherwise be restrained?' Answer: This the bishops should do; it is a function entrusted to them and not to the princes. Heresy can never be restrained by force.... Here God's word must do the fighting.... Heresy is a spiritual matter..."; ibid., WA 11:269.10 ⟨*LW* 45:115⟩; *The Book of Deuteronomy with Notes,* 1525: WA 14: 720.14 ⟨*LW* 9:250f.⟩: "... the preachers and ministers of the works of the Law and ⟨those⟩ of the Gospel of grace ... constantly fight about works and righteousness.... the wise nation ⟨i.e., the children of the world⟩ ... wants to settle this strife by forbidding instruction and by imposing a uniform way of teaching, to impede the ministry of the Word.... its work and effort ⟨i.e., the work of the "wise nation"⟩ is to be utterly condemned, because this struggle is never settled except through God as Judge. Wrath and argument are indeed to be put away where the matter of love is at stake; but in the case of faith they neither can nor should be put away, because it is necessary that there be heresies (1 Cor. 11:19)." — Luther, therefore, would not at all have supported the principle 'cuius regio, eius religio' (the ruler determines the religion of his territory), just as Melanchthon did not support it; see Johannes Heckel, "Cura religionis," in *Stutz Festschrift,* 233ff., and id., "Melanchthon und das heutige deutsche Staatskirchenrecht," in *Kaufmann Festgabe,* 96. The reformers were of the opinion that it would be easy for the truth of their teachings to become evident if secular authorities stayed out of the theological debate.

(5) An evangelical prince has to impede the public spreading of a doctrine which in a theological examination based on Holy Scripture has been judged to be false. Luther changed his position on the way in which a secular governmental authority was to deal with the public teaching of heresies; see Heinrich Bornkamm, "Das Problem der Toleranz im 16. Jahrhundert," in id., *Das Jahrhundert der Reformation* (Göttingen, 1961), 262ff. Originally Luther argued that one should let "the spirits confront each other and fight it out.... One should let them preach ... whatever they are able to preach and against whomever they want to preach, for ... there must be sects, and God's Word has to do battle..."; *Letter to the Princes of Saxony concerning the Rebellious Spirit,* 1524: WA 15:219.1, 218.19. His experiences in the Peasants' War and with the preaching of the Anabaptists taught him that discordant preaching in a territory or city was identical with an attack on the peace in a secular commonwealth. Therefore he demanded that secular governmental authorities prohibited the public spreading of a doctrine which on the basis of a theologial examination had been judged to be contrary to Holy Scripture. See below, 459 n. 11, ⟨below, 483 n. 167⟩.

(6) Insofar as the public teaching of heresy is also a crime against the secular natural-law order of a commonwealth, secular governmental authority has the compe-

tency of punishment. See n. 11 below; Walther Köhler, *Reformation und Ketzerprozeß* (Tübingen, 1901); Holl, *Luther,* 367, 369ff., 485f.; Heinrich Hoffman, "Reformation und Gewissensfreiheit," *ARG* 37 (1940): 170ff.

11. *Psalm 82 Explained,* 1530: WA 31.I:208.11 ⟨*LW* 13:61⟩: "If some were to teach doctrines contradicting an article of faith clearly grounded in Scripture and believed throughout the world by all Christendom, such as the articles which we teach the children in the Creed ... such teachers should not be tolerated, but punished as ⟨public; *sic*⟩ blasphemers. For they are not mere heretics but open blasphemers; and rulers are in duty bound to punish ⟨public; *sic*⟩ blasphemers as they punish those who curse, swear, revile, abuse, defame, and slander, ⟨etc.⟩"; *A Secular Governmental Authority Has the Duty to Restrain the Anabaptists,* 1536: WA 50:11.30: "Just as secular governmental authority is in duty bound to fight and punish public blasphemy, ... so it is duty bound to fight and punish in its territory ... false doctrine taught publicly, ... and heresies"; ibid., WA 50:12.1: "Everyone is duty bound to prevent and fight blasphemy in accordance with his estate and office. On the basis of this commandment ⟨i.e., the Second Commandment⟩ princes and governmental authorities have the authority and command to abolish false worship of God, and in opposition to it organize the ⟨teaching of⟩ true doctrine and true services of God. This commandment ... teaches them to fight false doctrine taught in public and punish the stiff-necked ⟨heretics⟩. This is also supported in Lev. 24:16 ..."; ibid., WA 50:13.12: "This is true: both offices, the office of preaching and the office of secular governance, are different. Nevertheless, both are to serve the ⟨honor⟩ of God. Princes ought not only protect the property and life of the subjects, but their most noble office ⟨in the sense of task⟩ is the promotion of God's honor and the fight against blasphemy and idolatry." See also *Psalm 101 Explained,* 1534-35: WA 51:231.4, 234.16, 235.14 ⟨*LW* 13:184, 188, 189f.⟩; Luther to Duke John, elector of Saxony: Feb. 9, 1526: WA.B 4:28.23, 29.48; to George Spalatin: Nov. 11, 1525: WA.B 3:616.30; Luther's brief of Sept. 1530: WA.B 5:615.58.

12. ⟨See above, 31, 86, 97f., 247 n. 53, 285 n. 46.⟩

13. *To the Christian Nobility,* 1520: WA 6:446.14: "Every community, council, or governing authority not only has the authority to abolish and oppose what is contrary to God and injurious to men's bodies and souls, ⟨and do so⟩ without the knowledge and consent of the pope or bishop, but indeed is also bound at the risk of the Salvation of their souls to oppose ⟨these things⟩, even though popes and bishops, who ought to be the first to do so, do not consent"; *A Model for Consecrating a True Bishop,* 1542: WA 53:237.34, 239.24.

14. ⟨Literally: "the Christian congregation."⟩

15. *Luther's Sincere Admonition to All Christians to Guard against Insurrection,* 1522: WA 8:679.24: "... secular governmental authorities and the nobility should ... take action ⟨against the pope and his anti-Christian governance; see ibid., 678.4⟩ ... by virtue of the obligations incumbent upon such duly constituted authority; for what is done by duly constituted authority cannot be regarded as insurrection."

16. ⟨Literally: "of an ecclesiastical ordinance."⟩ This is the result of the discussion of the problem in *Psalm 101 Explained,* 1534-35: WA 51:239.31 ⟨*LW* 13:195⟩. See also the sermon of June 25, 1538: WA 46:450.2.

17. *Psalm 101 Explained,* 1534-35: WA 51:240.27 ⟨*LW* 13:196⟩.

18. In his doctrine of the godly magistrate as *praecipuum membrum ecclesiae,* Melanchthon expressed this same idea, though juristically he was more precise; see Johannes Heckel, "Cura religionis," in *Stutz Festschrift,* 247ff.

19. Sermon of Aug. 2, 1523: WA 12:649.18: ⟨The canons of the Collegiate Chapter of All Saints in Wittenberg, who oppose the gospel and refuse to initiate liturgical reforms⟩ "may . . . not excuse themselves with the argument that the Elector ⟨i.e., Frederick the Wise⟩ commands not to change anything and to maintain things as they always have been. What do we care about him? He may command only in secular matters. If he would go beyond secular matters, we would say: 'Gracious Lord, you take care of your governance, ⟨but we⟩ have to obey God rather than man.' Therefore the canons are not excused." — For Luther's polemic against "secular princes who rule spiritually," see *On Secular Authority*, 1523: WA 11:270.2 ⟨LW 45:116⟩. See further, Johannes Heckel, *Initia iuris*, 81ff. — Eugen Rosenstock-Huessy (*Die europäischen Revolutionen und der Charakter der Nationen* [Stuttgart, 1951], 223) argued that in Germany the Reformation changed the medieval office of bishop, which had become that of a "military prince of the Empire," in such a way that "now the military prince became a supervising spiritual prelate and civic person." If one evaluates this aperçu in light of a Protestant prince's understanding of his faith, then the term 'supervising spiritual prelate' is inaccurate.

20. ⟨Or *Kirchenvogtei*. In a narrow sense, *advocatio ecclesiae* designated the prince's or lord's rights as a patron of a church (e.g., his right to nominate a candidate for a benefice which for several reasons the prince controlled); in a wider sense, it designated the prince's or lord's rights in the church, which resulted from his duties to protect the church (being *custos ecclesiae*).⟩

21. *On Two Imperial Contradictory Commands concerning Luther*, 1524: WA 15:278.1: "Here you see how that poor, mortal bag of maggots, the emperor, whose life isn't safe for one moment, impertinently brags to be the true, supreme protector of the Christian faith"; *On the War against the Turks*, 1529: WA 30.II:130.27: ". . . the emperor is not the head of Christendom nor the protector of the gospel or of the faith. The church and the faith must have another protector than the emperor and the kings; in general, they are the worst enemies of Christendom and faith . . ."; *On Secular Authority*, 1523: WA 11:270.3 ⟨LW 45:116⟩; *First Lectures on the Psalms*, 1513-15: WA 3:150.31, 379.39, 380.5, 406.25, 442.10; ibid., WA 4:90.19, 231.1, 409.15, 414.24; *Second Lectures on the Psalms*, 1518-21: WA 5:257.2, 515.28, 525.30, 649.37; Holl, *Luther*, 349 n. 2.

22. *On the Councils and the Church*, 1539: WA 50:652.10.15: ". . . on earth are only two corporeal governances, city and house ⟨i.e., *politia* and *oeconomia*⟩. . . . Then comes the third ⟨governance⟩, God's own house and city, i.e., the church; from the house it has to have people, from the city it has to have protection. . . ."

23. *Decretum Gratiani* c.20. C.XXIII.q.5 ⟨Friedberg 1:936f.⟩.

24. Turrecremata, *Summa de ecclesia domini*, book 2. chapt. 78: "This method of maintaining and protecting the church . . . is suited . . . for the faithful *(fidelis)* secular princes."

25. It was Sohm's central error when he argued (*Kirchenrecht*, 1:559) that Luther and the Lutheran Reformation affirmed the medieval view of the position held by governmental authority within Christendom. Therefore Holl's critique (*Luther*, 349, 344) of Sohm was justified.

26. I.e., as the externally recognizable totality of those who are baptized and entitled to receive the sacraments, regardless whether or not they have faith. See Johannes Heckel, *Initia iuris*, 27.

27. *To the Christian Nobility*, 1520: WA 6:413.27 ⟨LW 44:137⟩: ". . . when necessity de-

mands it, and the pope is an offense to Christendom, the first man who is able should, as a true member of the whole body, do what he can to bring about a free council. No one can do this so well as the temporal authorities, especially since they are also fellow-Christians, fellow-priests, fellow-members of the spiritual estate, fellow-lords over all things." See also Holl, *Luther,* 333, 349.

28. ⟨The conduct of the ecclesiastical officials creates an emergency *within* the church (not society), and that emergency provides the legal basis for acting.⟩

29. See Luther's instruction for the City Council of Altenburg: Apr. 28, 1522: WA.B 2:507.11: ⟨The council of Altenburg is obligated to serve the Salvation of the souls living in Altenburg because it has two duties: the duty to implement the corporeal governance and the duty to implement brotherly Christian love;⟩ Luther to George Spalatin: May 5, 1522: WA.B 2:515.22: "... it is important for a prince as a Christian brother, and also for the sake of his office ⟨literally: 'and also in the name of prince'⟩ to oppose the wolf and be responsible ⟨or: 'concerned'; *sollicitum esse;* see above,137: *in partem sollicitudinis*⟩ for the Salvation of his people"; to Duke Frederick, elector of Saxony: May 8, 1522: WA.B 2:521.56: "Your Electoral Grace is unable to have a good conscience while protecting the rights ... of the ⟨papal clergy⟩ in this matter, i.e., their opposition to ⟨the appointment of⟩ preachers of the gospel. You yourself, as a Christian member ⟨of the church⟩, are obligated to assist ... in ⟨such an appointment⟩, and as a Christian prince you ought to oppose the wolves as much as possible." See also Holl, *Luther,* 354 n. 4.

30. *Kirchenrecht,* 1:549, 559, 566ff.

31. ⟨See above, 31f., 97f., 98f., 119f., 121f., 260 n. 14.⟩

32. *Luther,* 349; italics by Holl.

33. ⟨See also above, 84 n. 16.⟩

34. In the quotation ("When the church [in Holl's terminology this is the visible church] itself does its duty, then a Christian prince is in the church nothing other than another Christian") "Christian" designated for Holl the member of external Christendom. He documented this understanding (*Luther,* 349 n. 3) with Luther's Jan. 15, 1531, letter to Wenceslas Link: WA.B 6:17.9f. But here 'Christian' designated the member of the spiritual and not of the corporeal ⟨visible⟩ church; therefore this passage does not substantiate Holl's argumentation.

35. ⟨See also above, 125f.⟩

36. ⟨I.e., to be a Christian in name only.⟩

37. See above, n. 34.

38. ⟨If something is wrong in the church, then something is wrong in society; if something is wrong in society, the prince has the duty and right to act; therefore he has the right to act in ecclesiastical matters in order to eliminate whatever is wrong in society.⟩

Notes to Appendix III

1. Schönfeld, *Grundlegung der Rechtswissenschaft,* 296.

2. Ernst Wolf, "Der christliche Glaube und das Recht," *ZevKR* 4 (1955): 234.

3. In "Der Ansatz einer evangelischen Sozialethik bei Martin Luther," in *Die evangelische Kirche in der modernen Gesellschaft,* ed. by Theodor Heckel (Munich, 1956), 25ff., I surveyed the history of the interpretation of Luther's kingdom doctrine and listed

the most recent secondary literature. Törnvall, *Geistliches und weltliches Regiment bei Luther*, is the best presentation of Luther's doctrine of the governances; Lau, *Luthers Lehre von den beiden Reichen*, is the best presentation of Luther's kingdom doctrine.

4. ⟨Althaus, "Die beiden Regimente bei Luther," *ThLZ* 81 (1956): 129f.⟩

5. See Schlink, "Gerechtigkeit und Gnade," *KuD* 2 (1956): 279. ⟨See also above, 13f., 126.⟩

6. Althaus, "Die beiden Regimente bei Luther," *ThLZ* 81 (1956): 132. ⟨Our text is a free translation of Althaus's text.⟩

7. *First Lectures on the Psalms*, 1513-15: WA 3:368.22: "... Christ is the end and center of all things; all things look and point to him...." See also ibid., WA 3:375.32.

8. Ibid., WA 3:357.24, 4:247.33.

9. Ibid., WA 4:254.35, 397.1.

10. Ibid., WA 4:417.9.

11. Ibid., WA 3:261.27, 4:397.1; *Second Lectures on the Psalms*, 1518-21: WA 5:277.33.

12. In his careful study, Einar Billing, *Luthers lära om staten* (Uppsala, 1900), 165ff., has seen Luther's different usages of 'kingdom', but he was unable to explain their systematic structure; so were the Luther scholars who since Billing have dealt with this topic.

13. *First Lectures on the Psalms*, 1513-15: WA 3:254.27, 357.23, 449.32, 4:42.5; *Lectures on Romans*, 1515-16: WA 56:60.5, 118.17; *Psalm 110 Explained*, 1518: WA 1:703.31. For the understanding of kingdom as body, see also the important passages in *The Blessed Sacrament of the Body of Christ and the Brotherhoods*, 1519: WA 2:743.11.20: "... Christ together with all saints is a spiritual body, just as the people of a city are a community and body, and each citizen is a member of the other one and of the whole city. Thus all saints are members of Christ and of the church, which is God's spiritual, eternal city. Reception into this city is reception into the community of saints, incorporation in Christ's spiritual body, and becoming a member of that body.... Receiving this sacrament in bread and wine is nothing other than receiving a sure sign of this community and incorporation in Christ and all saints, just as a citizen is given a sign, document, or any kind of credential so that he may be certain that he is a citizen of the city and a member of that community."

14. *The Papacy at Rome*, 1520: WA 6:298.6; *On Good Works*, 1520: WA 6:207.1.

15. *First Lectures on the Psalms*, 1513-15: WA 3:335.31.

16. Ibid., WA 3:299.2.

17. Ibid., WA 3:11.22, 295.29; *The Leipzig Disputation*, 1519: WA 2:314.11.

18. *First Lectures on the Psalms*, 1513-15: WA 3:11.22, 532.21, 4:42.17, 405.14; *Lectures on Romans*, 1515-16: WA 56:175.2.8; above, 257 n. 40.

19. See above, 87f. ⟨See also above, 86f., 90f.⟩ This nullifies Gunnar Hillerdal's critique. In "Kirche und Politik," *LR* 5 (1955): 163, he argued that as a result of the "very schematic division of mankind into two groups, Christians and non-Christians," in *Lex charitatis*, "one no longer can clearly discern the position, which is fundamental for Luther's theology, that the believer always is simultaneously righteous and sinner." — On the basis of Luther's *On Secular Authority*, Kattenbusch ("Doppelschichtigkeit in Luthers Kirchenbegriff," *ThStKr* 100 [1928]: 325 n. 1) had already faulted Luther because of his "schematic division of mankind into two parts." — Hillerdal overlooked that in terms of the membership in a kingdom there is a difference between a Christian, in whom sin does not rule, and a non-Christian. The former is a member of Christ's kingdom, the lat-

ter is a member of the kingdom of the world. This has been already pointed out in *Lex charitatis,* above, 255 n. 24.

20. See above, 105f.

21. See above, 99f., 107ff.

22. *First Lectures on the Psalms,* 1513-15: WA 4:254.35: "... indeed ⟨Christ⟩ governs *(dominari)* all people, both the good and the evil ones...."

23. ⟨Or: "power."⟩

24. *First Lectures on the Psalms,* 1513-15: WA 3:250.18: "... ⟨he is⟩ king in the kingdom of the church and of the whole world"; *Second Lectures on the Psalms,* 1518-21: WA 5:282.11.

25. ⟨See below, Index of Subjects, s.v. "man, reborn, is afflicted with Original Sin."⟩

26. *German Exposition of the Lord's Prayer for Simple Laymen,* 1519: WA 2:96.19.24ff., 97.7.

27. ⟨I.e., Word of God spoken into us (as is the gospel), not spoken outside of us, around us, and thus directed toward us (as was the law of Moses).⟩ *First Lectures on the Psalms,* 1513-15: WA 4:9.28ff.

28. For the meaning of this phrase, see above, 54ff.

29. For the connection between this division of mankind into two kinds of people with Augustine's doctrine of the two cities, see above, 25f., and Johannes Heckel, "Ansatz einer evangelischen Sozialethik," in Theodor Heckel, *Die evangelische Kirche in der modernen Gesellchaft,* 37ff. For Augustine, see instead of other authors, Spörl, "Augustinus — Schöpfer einer Staatslehre? *HJ* 74 (1955): 66f. — For 'kingdom of God and kingdom of the world' in the thought of Augustine and of Luther, see Kinder, "Gottesreich und Weltreich bei Augustin und bei Luther," in *Elert Gedenkschrift,* 24ff. (where additional literature is cited).

30. *Second Lectures on the Psalms,* 1518-21: WA 5:523.25. See also above, 64 and 325 n. 193.

31. Criticizing *Lex charitatis,* Ragnar Bring ("Der Glaube und das Recht nach Luther," in *Elert Gedenkschrift,* 141, 152) pointed out that "in the final analysis the two kingdoms can be determined not by something that rests within man but only by the actions of God and of the devil; therefore the two kingdoms cannot be understood in terms of two groups of people." In *Lex charitatis* the division of mankind into two mystical bodies has indeed been derived from God's actions and Satan's counteractions *(influxus capitis in membra;* see also above, 148) because, upon being addressed by God's Word, mankind split into two parts. Nowhere in the book is it argued that that split was the result of something "which rests within man." It is esp. not true that in the book "natural law appears to be something which can be found in man as a predisposition," as Bring argued (150). To the contrary, in the book the divine natural law is emphatically described (above, 46) as "God's creative speaking into man, as a manifestation of God's power, which ceaselessly creates spiritual life in man,... as an 'active word.'" This also nullifies Hillerdal's critique ("Kirche und Politik," *LR* 5 [1955]: 162) that the author of *Lex charitatis* affirms "a more or less static dualism of the kingdom doctrine and of the doctrine of law and is unable to place in his system those statements of Luther in which the secular natural law and the divine natural law are connected with God's ceaselessly ongoing new Creation."

32. ⟨See above, 149.⟩

33. Sermon of June 5, 1534: WA 37:426.7.

34. ⟨Or: "worship."⟩

35. *On Secular Authority,* 1523: WA 11:251.1 ⟨*LW* 45:90⟩.

36. See also below, 465 n. 64.

37. ⟨See further, above, 86f., 89-92.⟩

38. ⟨See above, 148.⟩

39. Sermon of Oct. 25, 1522: WA 10.III:379.29: "Now the devil has assembled the biggest crowd under his governance. Therefore another governance has to exist, the secular sword; one has to have princes and magistrates, we need them."

40. "Die beiden Regimente bei Luther," *ThLZ* 81 (1956): 131.

41. See Kattenbusch, "Doppelschichtigkeit in Luthers Kirchenbegriff," *ThStKr* 100 (1928): 320ff.; Elert, *Morphologie,* 2:52; Ernst Wolf, *Peregrinatio,* 1:232ff.; Kinder, "Gottesreich und Weltreich bei Augustin und bei Luther," in *Elert Gedenkschrift,* 35f. — Luther presented the doctrine of the three basic estates ⟨or orders, or hierarchies⟩ of Christendom at the same time (1519/20) that he presented his doctrine of the two kingdoms, and he did not feel that both doctrines contradicted each other. Certainly, the doctrine of the hierarchies adds a new dimension to the doctrine of the governances, but in my opinion it dovetails with that doctrine in spite of Kinder's doubts.

42. ⟨See above, 149.⟩

43. See Johannes Heckel, "Luthers Lehre von den zwei Regimenten. Fragen und Antworten zu der Schrift von Gunnar Hillerdal," *ZEvKR* 4 (1955): 259.

44. *Psalm 110 Explained,* 1518: WA 1:701.27.

45. *First Lectures on the Psalms,* 1513-15: WA 3:252.6, 300.21.

46. Bring ("Der Glaube und das Recht nach Luther," in *Elert Gedenkschrift,* 152) presented a different position. On the basis of his starting point, he could have arrived at a position identical with that presented in *Lex charitatis* had he considered the understanding of kingdom as body *(regnum, corpus).*

47. See above, 150, the text for n. 35.

48. See above, 346 nn. 420-21.

49. Sermon of Jan. 16, 1529: WA 28:281.3.18: "The secular kingdom extends over rogues and hoodlums, the spiritual kingdom extends over Christians, and God's Son rules here." See also *Whether Soldiers, Too, Can Be Saved,* 1526: WA 19:640.4; above, 346 nn. 422-23.

50. *First Lectures on the Psalms,* 1513-15: WA 4:451.30.33.

51. ⟨I.e., at best, secular power can curtail evil, if necessary even destroy the evil ones, but it is unable to accomplish anything spiritually against evil. See also above, 28f.⟩

52. See above, 274 n. 14, 402 n. 4, 403 n. 7. ⟨This would be the "negative way"; for the "positive" way ("side"), see above, 154; below, 156.⟩

53. First version: WA 12:330.30 ⟨*LW* 30:76⟩.

54. WA.B 3:306.9.

55. WA 19:648.17. For this passage, see also Bengt Hägglund's review of Hillerdal, *Gehorsam gegen Gott und Menschen,* in *SvTK* 31 (1955): 289.

56. ⟨As Althaus did; see above, 164f.⟩

57. WA 11:245ff. ⟨*LW* 45:81ff.⟩. Typical of this lack of understanding is Jordan, *Luthers Staatsauffassung,* a book which otherwise is valuable for its wealth of material.

58. ⟨See above, 439 n. 283.⟩

59. ⟨In the sense of exemption from secular law.⟩

60. *To the Christian Nobility,* 1520: WA 6:407.14 ⟨LW 44:127⟩.

61. ⟨See also above, 119, 260 n. 14.⟩

62. ⟨See also above, 371 n. 116.⟩

63. ⟨See below, Index of Subjects, s.v. "man, reborn, is afflicted with Original Sin."⟩

64. Therefore Luther rejected the *privilegium fori* of the ⟨papal⟩ clergy and argued that one should let the office of the secular governmental authority "be freely active and unencumbered throughout the whole body of Christendom, no person excepted"; *To the Christian Nobility,* 1520: WA 6:409.18.

65. *On Christian Freedom* (Latin text), 1520: WA 7:67.29: ". . . in Rom. 13⟨:1⟩ and Titus 3⟨:1⟩ Paul commands Christians to be subject to the authorities and to be ready to do every good work, . . . so that by doing this they serve others and the authorities in the freedom of the Spirit and obey ⟨the command of the authorities⟩ freely and out of love." See also above, 107, 114ff.

66. ⟨Through the coercive power of the governmental authority.⟩

67. See above, 116f. See also *Sermons on Matthew, Chapters 5-7,* 1530-32: WA 32:511.27, 512.4: "If you are a prince, judge . . . and are to practice and prove your faith ⟨by⟩ implementing ⟨the duties of⟩ your office and estate faithfully and doing the right thing, then you certainly will acquire so much to do . . . that no Carthusian monk would have a more difficult life than you . . . . Though a prince wears a golden chain and a mink coat, if he is a godly man, then in this mink coat ⟨walks⟩ a man so mortified and miserable that we find no one similar to him in a monastery."

68. See above, 310 n. 67.

69. WA 6:408.8.10. For this passage and the following material, see *Psalm 110 Explained,* 1518: WA 1:697.29: "God's children do not run away from the company of evil people; in fact, they search out evil people in order to help them. God's children do not want to go to heaven alone, but they want to bring along the biggest sinners if they are able."

70. See above, 85ff., 98ff.

71. See above, 105.

72. ⟨See above, 28, 148.⟩

73. See above, 269 n. 19; *Commentary on Zechariah,* 1527: WA 23:514.19.

74. ⟨I.e., the pope.⟩

75. See above, 406 n. 32.

76. See above, 79, 99, 107ff., 133ff. See also Johannes Heckel, "Widerstand gegen die Obrigkeit? Pflicht und Recht zum Widerstand bei Luther," *Zeitwende. Die neue Furche* 25 (1954): 156ff. ⟨above, Appendix VII⟩, and id., "Stellungnahme der Kirche der Reformation — Die Lutheraner," in *Widerstandsrecht und Grenzen der Staatsgewalt. Bericht über die Tagung der Hochschule für Politische Wissenschaften, München, und der Evangelischen Akademie, Tutzing, 18.-20. Juni 1955, in der Akademie Tutzing,* ed. by Bernhard Pfister and Gerhard Hildmann (Berlin, 1956), 36.

77. ⟨See above, 148.⟩

78. *Second Lectures on the Psalms,* 1518-21: WA 5:649.24.29, 650.3ff. See also above, 406 n. 32.

79. ⟨See above, 31, 86, and esp. 97f., 247 n. 53, 285 n. 46.⟩

80. See above, n. 76.

81. Althaus, "Die beiden Regimente bei Luther," *ThLZ* 81 (1956): 134 n. 7, argued that

it is wrong to differentiate *types* of tyrants in Luther's thinking; "Luther did not differentiate between types but envisioned very real persons: princes, the Turk, the pope." Of course! But these real persons are also juristic types.

82. See above, 116.

83. See Lau, "Leges charitatis," *KuD* 2 (1956): 85f. In the present context, a critical discussion of this article has to be restricted to some remarks on Lau's dealing with the kingdom doctrine of *Lex charitatis*.

84. ⟨I.e., a law which in its essence is secular.⟩

85. ⟨The church is a *corpus mixtum*.⟩

86. See above, 463 n. 29.

87. ⟨In the sense of mixed ecclesiastical body.⟩ *City of God* 1.35: "In this world those two cities are totally intermixed and mixed together until such time that they will be separated through the final Judgment." See also Spörl, "Die 'Civitas Dei' im Geschichtsdenken Ottos von Freising," in *La Ciudad de Dios,* 2:580.

88. *Third Disputation Against the Antinomians,* 1538: WA 39.I:490.25, 496.3. Instead of citing many of the available titles on this subject, see Kohlmeyer, "Die Bedeutung der Kirche für Luther," *ZKG* 47 (1928): 497ff.

89. ⟨*Staatliches Körperschaftsrecht.*⟩

90. ⟨They belong to the mystical body of Christ not in reality, or according to their actions, but they have the potential of belonging.⟩ Instead of other authors ⟨and also for medieval materials⟩, see Holl, *Luther,* 294 n. 5.

91. *First Lectures on the Psalms,* 1513-15: WA 4:289.2.25. Occasionally Luther used the term 'dead member' in order to suggest that such a member did *not belong* to Christ's body; *Lectures on Romans,* 1515-16: WA 56:77.2.

92. *The Papacy at Rome,* 1520: WA 6:302.6. For this passage, see also Johannes Heckel, "Die zwo Kirchen," *ELKZ* 10 (1956), cited according to the enlarged reprint in the series Theologische Existenz heute, vol. 55 (Munich, 1957): 46f.

93. *Third Disputation Against the Antinomians,* 1538: WA 39.I:491.7.

94. ⟨What is the spiritual meaning of the corporeal church?⟩

95. *First Lectures on the Psalms,* 1513-15: WA 4:284.25.

96. See Johannes Heckel, "Die zwo Kirchen," 54f.

97. See above, 120f. — The concerns mentioned by Lau ("Leges charitatis," *KuD* 2 [1956]: 85) are the result of his not using these two criteria when he dealt with the universal church.

98. See Johannes Heckel, "Die zwo Kirchen," 46.

99. *The Bondage of the Will,* 1525: WA 18:652.23: "The church is hidden, the saints are unknown." For this concept, see Johannes Heckel, *Initia iuris,* 15ff.

100. *The Bondage of the Will,* 1525: WA 18:651.34 ⟨*LW* 33:88⟩: "I call them saints and regard them as such; I call them and believe them to be the Church of God; but I do so by the rule of love, not the rule of faith. For love, which always thinks well of everyone, and is not suspicious but believes and assumes the best about its neighbors, calls anyone who is baptized a saint.... But faith calls no one a saint unless he is declared so by a divine judgment...." See also Johannes Heckel, *Initia iuris,* 41 n. 171.

101. For the ungodly as "domestic enemies," see *Second Lectures on the Psalms,* 1518-21: WA 5:479.33. ⟨See also above, 257 n. 42.⟩

102. ⟨I.e., being inscribed in the church's roster.⟩

103. Second Lectures on the Psalms, 1518-21: WA 5:45.11.

104. ⟨I.e., membership in the church as a result of Baptism and being on the roster of the church.⟩

105. See above, 466 n. 100.

106. *The Bondage of the Will*, 1525: WA 18:650.27 ⟨*LW* 33:86⟩: ". . . the state of the Church of God throughout the whole course of the world from the beginning has always been such that some have been called the People and the saints of God who were not so, while others, a remnant in their midst, really were the People or the saints, but were never called so. . . ." See also Johannes Heckel, "Die zwo Kirchen," 54.

107. ⟨Heckel wrote "angefochtene Kirche." For *Anfechtung*, see above, 248 n. 55.⟩

108. ⟨Heckel wrote "Anfechtung des Satans."⟩

109. ⟨*Kirchenordnung*; see also above, 187, 221, and below, 504 n. 22.⟩

110. *First Commentary on Galatians*, 1519: WA 2:475.11, 617.1ff. See also above, 98, 389 n. 45.

111. This demanding love would be the legal title for the law of ecclesiastical discipline, for which Lau asked in "Leges charitatis," *KuD* 2 (1956): 87.

112. *First Commentary on Galatians*, 1519: WA 2:483.23.

113. Althaus, "Die beiden Regimente bei Luther," *ThLZ* 81 (1956): 133.

114. Ibid., 134.

115. ⟨E.g., ibid., 131, 133.⟩

116. Ibid., 135: "state . . . ; political world."

117. Ibid., 133 ⟨with reference to above, 34f.⟩: ". . . it is impossible to join Heckel ⟨in affirming⟩ that only 'the outer or corporeal people, i.e., the ungodly,' belong to God's kingdom at the left. Here . . . Luther's two meanings of 'kingdom of the world' are confused."

118. See above, 34ff., 105ff.

119. ⟨I.e., the difference in the status of the citizens in the two kingdoms.⟩

120. ⟨*Quaternio* stands for the number four (a quarto page, or a detachment of four soldiers, or the number four on a dice). A literal translation of *quaternio terminorum* would be: "a four of terms," a quadriga of terms. In syllogistics the phrase designates 'fallacy of four terms'. This is an inaccurate translation — *quaternio* as such has nothing to do with fallacy — which can be justified only on the basis of the use of the phrase. In a categorical syllogism there may be only three terms, and the middle term may be used only with one content. If the middle term is used with two contents or meanings, then one has four terms, or a *quaternio terminorum*, and the syllogism is not genuine, the conclusion is fallacious (hence 'fallacy [as a result] of four terms'). Example: Right is useful; only one of my hands is right; therefore only one of my hands is useful. (See *The Cambridge Dictionary of Philosophy*, ed. by Robert Audi [Cambridge, 1995], s.v. "syllogism.") In this case the fourth term is the result of a new content of 'right' (biological vs. pragmatic) connected with 'hands' (— or in light of Heckel's following statement: two different contents in the meaning of the *one word 'right'* are pulled together, creating a chaos in the understanding of this word; in the example that Heckel develops, the one word [for which in the argumentation different contents are pulled together] is 'citizenship'.) See also below, 468 n. 124.⟩

121. ⟨I.e., the chaos which is the result when "fundamentally different contents" in the meaning of one word are pulled together and thus confused.⟩

122. ⟨Since Heckel frequently cited Luther's *Second Lectures on the Psalms*, it is possible that he was thinking of Luther's comments on Ps. 1:2: WA 5:32.20-24 ⟨*LW* 14:294⟩: "See that you always separate most widely and distantly the Law *(lex)* of the Lord from the laws *(lex)* of any men, and watch with all diligence that the two, confused in one chaos — *in unum cahos utraeque confusae* — (as is done by the doctors of destruction), do not miserably destroy you. They either turn the Law of God into human tradition or human tradition into the Law of God." The "one word" would be "law"; the "chaos" would be what "the doctors of destruction" do with this one word; and the "two fundamentally different contents" pulled together so that the understanding of the one word 'law' presents a chaos would be "law of God" and "human tradition" or "laws of men". — Martin Brecht (Münster) contributed a passage from a set of theses by Luther (WA 6:29:19f.), which is an excellent commentary on Heckel's example: "If someone brings *terminos* ("terms"; in light of the context probably "conclusions") of logic and philosophy into theology, he necessarily creates a horrendous chaos of errors."⟩

123. ⟨In Heckel's example, this would be the difference between 'citizenship in Christ's kingdom' and 'citizenship in the kingdom of the world', a difference which is eliminated in the unqualified term 'citizenship' of statement (3).⟩

124. ⟨See also above, 467 n. 120. The argumentation is to show that one can after all obtain a positive statement (i.e., [4]) from a comparison of Althaus's kingdom in the absolute and in the not absolute sense. That statement is fallacious nevertheless. I.e. it is illogical to argue that a Christian is a citizen in both kingdoms (see the opening sentence of the next section) for the following reasons: The argumentation is not a genuine syllogism but a *quaternio terminorum*. The argumentation's three initial terms are: 'Christian', 'citizenship', 'organizational principle'. The second term, 'citizenship' (which in a genuine syllogism would be the middle term, would have to be used with one content, and could not appear in the conclusion), is used with two fundamentally different contents: citizenship as a spiritual relationship, citizenship as a relationship in terms of public law. This amounts to using two terms. What initially was the third term now is the fourth term; it is incorrectly used to establish what does not exist, i.e., the second term with one content. And then that non-existent second term is the result (4) of the argumentation; i.e., what was supposed to be the middle term appears in the conclusion.⟩

125. Althaus, "Die beiden Regimente bei Luther," *ThLZ* 81 (1956): 133.

126. See Gustaf Törnvall, "Regimentslärans socialteologiska huvuduppgift," *NKT* 25 (1956): 76.

127. Althaus, "Luther und die Bergpredigt," Luther 1956:7, and id., "Luthers Lehre von den beiden Reichen," *LuJ* 24 (1957): 46.

128. See n. 127.

129. Althaus, "Luthers Lehre von den beiden Reichen," *LuJ* 24 (1957): 42: "God rules the world in two ways," whereby Luther understood the secular governance to cover "all that serves the preservation and order of this temporal life" (ibid., 43).

130. ⟨Ibid., *LuJ* 24 (1957): 42.⟩

131. Ibid., *LuJ* 24 (1957): 43.

132. See above, 255 n. 19.

133. Althaus, "Luthers Lehre von den beiden Reichen," *LuJ* 24 (1957): 44.

134. ⟨*Disputation on Matt. 19:21:* WA 39.II:39ff.⟩

135. ⟨Ibid., WA 39.II:81.16f.⟩ See above, 382 n. 190 ⟨esp. the discussion of Arnold,

Naturrecht bei Luther⟩, and Althaus, "Die beiden Regimente bei Luther," *ThLZ* 81 (1956): 135f.

136. See above, 381 n. 190 ⟨first paragraph⟩.
137. ⟨Or carelessness?⟩
138. WA 27:417.24, 418.25.
139. WA 38:666.39, 667.11.
140. ⟨"Die beiden Regimente bei Luther," *ThLZ* 81 (1956): 131f.⟩
141. Ibid., *ThLZ* 81 (1956): 131.
142. See above, 72ff., together with 54ff.
143. See above, 77.
144. See the passage in *Commentary on Zechariah,* 1527: WA 23:514.1, used by Althaus, "Luther's Lehre von den beiden Reichen," *LuJ* 24 (1957): 43 n. 8.
145. See *On Secular Authority,* 1523: WA 11:266.24ff. ⟨*LW* 45:111⟩; *Sermons on John, Chapters 16–20,* 1528-29: WA 28:441.6; sermons of 1540: WA 49:137.10ff.; *Lectures on Psalms 120–34,* 1532-33: WA 40.III:222.5f., 223.1ff., 224.9.
146. ⟨In Gen. 1:28 the Vulgate reads "dominamini" and in Gen. 1:26 it reads "praesit." NRSV reads in both verses "have dominion over."⟩ This answers Lau's question ("Leges charitatis," *KuD* 2 [1956]: 78) whether for Luther *dominatio* did not exist already in the Original Status.
147. See above, 72.
148. Sermon of Nov. 11, 1530: WA 32:170.6: God gave man power *(potestas)* over all creatures, animals, fish, birds. To use this power one does not need the (or: a) special gift of the Holy Spirit because the unbelievers, the Turk, and those who persecute the gospel also have this power.
149. "Die beiden Regimente bei Luther," *ThLZ* 81 (1956): 131f.
150. See above, 149.
151. See above, 28.
152. See below, Index of Subjects, s.v., "devil, governance of."
153. Althaus, "Luthers Lehre von den beiden Reichen," *LuJ* 24 (1957): 55.
154. Althaus, "Die beiden Regimente bei Luther," *ThLZ* 81 (1956): 133f.
155. Ibid., 132.
156. ⟨Ibid., 133.⟩
157. Althaus, "Luthers Lehre von den beiden Reichen," *LuJ* 24 (1957): 55 n. 45.
158. See above, n. 155.
159. See above, 28f.
160. ⟨I.e., difference in the social status of people.⟩
161. *Lectures on Genesis,* 1535-45: WA 42:151.22; above, 338 n. 337.
162. Althaus, "Die beiden Regimente bei Luther," *ThLZ* 81 (1956): 133, and id., "Luthers Lehre von den beiden Reichen," *LuJ* 24 (1957): 42, 55 n. 45.
163. See above, 151ff.
164. *First Lectures on the Psalms,* 1513-15: WA 4:447.31.
165. Ibid., WA 3:103.24, and many other places.
166. Ibid., WA 3:490.6.23, and many other places.
167. Ibid., WA 4:38.18, 52.7.
168. Ibid., WA 3:251.22, 4:447.18.
169. Ibid., WA 3:406.11.

170. Ibid., WA 3:131.7, 480.32.
171. Ibid., WA 3:359.30.
172. ⟨Literally: "non-grace."⟩ Ibid., WA 3:359.30: "indignatio spiritualis."
173. *Psalm 110 Explained,* 1518: WA 1:690ff.
174. Ibid., WA 1:691.35ff.
175. Ibid., WA 1:692.9.
176. Ibid., WA 1:692.9f.
177. Ibid., WA 1:698.4.7.
178. Ibid., WA 1:698.15.33; *Second Lectures on the Psalms,* 1518-21: WA 5:38.20; for the opposite, the godly man, see ibid., 191.36.
179. *Psalm 110 Explained,* 1518: WA 1:692.6ff.
180. *First Lectures on the Psalms,* 1513-15: WA 3:346.9.
181. Althaus, "Die beiden Regimente bei Luther," *ThLZ* 81 (1956): 132f.
182. See above, 32.
183. ⟨Althaus, "Die beiden Regimente bei Luther," *ThLZ* 81 (1956): 133.⟩
184. See above, 255 n. 18, together with 246 nn. 47-48, 247 nn. 49-50.
185. See above, 27.
186. See above, 243 n. 11.
187. See above, 445 n. 341.
188. ⟨We had difficulties with the text of Section XXVI, and we appreciated the help Martin Heckel gave us for understanding the text and shaping our version and comments.⟩
189. Althaus, "Luthers Lehre von den beiden Reichen," *LuJ* 24 (1957): 54: ". . . the kingdom of the world (including the empirical church) . . . ."
190. ⟨See above, 152f., 468 nn. 129-30.⟩
191. ⟨That legal structure may not be organized according to the principles which determine the secular governance over the members of the kingdom of Satan. *The nucleus of the church is Christ's kingdom in his mystical body, which externally exists in the corporeal church;* and that kingdom stands only under the governance of Christ, it never stands under the governance of the secular governmental authority, which deals with non-Christians. Therefore the law of the corporeal church may not be structured according to the principles which structure the kingdom of the world, but it has to be structured according to principles which structure the kingdom of Christ, i.e., divine love and the spiritual basic rights of a Christian. Luther rejected the Canon law and the papal supremacy as a distortion of the legal structures of the two governances and kingdoms.⟩
192. ⟨Literally: "The kingdom of Christ in his mystical body."⟩
193. ⟨See the first paragraph of this section.⟩
194. ⟨In Section XXVII Heckel develops the test case mentioned in Section XXVI.⟩
195. ⟨So according to Althaus; see the first paragraph of Section XXVI.⟩
196. Althaus, "Luthers Lehre von den beiden Reichen," *LuJ* 24 (1957): 43.
197. *Instructions for the Visitors,* 1528: WA 26:197.26 ⟨*LW* 40:271; see also ibid., 273⟩.
198. ⟨I.e., do what a bishop is supposed to do.⟩
199. *Addition to Goat Emser's Book,* 1519: WA 2:678.4.
200. *Reply to Ambrosius Catharinus,* 1521: WA 7:721.30. ⟨See also above, 99.⟩
201. ⟨See above, 148, 163.⟩

202. Thielicke, *Theologische Ethik*, 1:No. 1783 <"Schlachtenlärm," i.e., literally: "noise of battle">.
203. <See above, 148.>

Notes to Appendix IV

1. See Ernst Wolf in *Für Kirche und Recht. Festschrift für Johannes Heckel zum 70. Geburtstag*, ed. by Siegfried Grundmann (Cologne, Graz, 1959), 287ff.; in *ZevKR* 1 (1951): 102ff., 4 (1955): 225ff., 6 (1957/58): 255ff.; in *Staatsverfassung und Kirchenordnung. Festgabe für Rudolf Smend zum 80. Geburtstag am 15. Januar 1962*, ed by Konrad Hesse et al. (Tübingen, 1962), 443ff.; and Ernst Wolf, *Peregrinatio*, 1 (2d ed. Munich, 1962).

2. *Etliche Gewissensfragen hinsichtlich der Lehre von Kirche, Kirchenamt und Kirchenregiment* (Stuttgart, 1862), 9ff. For Harleß, see Theodor Heckel, *Adolph von Harleß. Theologie und Kirchenpolitik eines lutherischen Bischofs in Bayern* (Munich, 1933), 189ff. For the history of the problem in the 19th century, see Holsten Fagerberg, *Bekenntnis, Kirche und Amt in der deutschen konfessionellen Theologie des 19. Jahrhunderts* (Uppsala, 1952), and the additions to this book in my review in *ZSRG*. K 42 (1956): 507ff. — For our topic, Kinder, *Der evangelische Glaube und die Kirche*, presented a carefully assembled collection of the secondary literature. See also the pertinent articles in *EKL* and *RGG* (3d ed., 1957-65). — Three jurists, working in the tradition of either the Lutheran or the Reformed or the Union Church, presented books which in many ways are fundamentally important for our topic: Siegfried Grundmann, *Der Lutherische Weltbund* (Cologne, 1957), reviewed by Hans Liermann in *ZSRG*.K 44 (1958): 510ff.; Erik Wolf, *Ordnung der Kirche* (Frankfurt/Main, 1961), reviewed by Karl Brinkel in *ZSRG*.K 48 (1962): 503ff.; Otto Friedrich, *Einführung in das evangelische Kirchenrecht* (Göttingen, 1961), reviewed by Siegfried Grundmann in *ZSRG*.K 48 (1962): 499ff. If in the following sketch it was possible or necessary to deal with these contributions to our topic, it was done in the text without special references. — After the present study was completed, Hans Dombois, *Das Recht der Gnade* (Witten, 1961) was published. On pages 955-994 the author critically reviews "Luther's doctrine of ecclesiastical law according to Johannes Heckel's presentation." In spite of the author's efforts, his critique accomplishes nothing since it lacks sufficient knowledge of the sources.

3. *Kirchenrecht*, 1 (Leipzig, 1892).
4. WA 50:250.1 <*BC* 315.XII>.
5. Emil Brunner, *Das Mißverständnis der Kirche*, 7.
6. Törnvall, *Geistliches und weltliches Regiment bei Luther*, 9.
7. See above, Heckel, *Lex charitatis*. The following study is the result of the preparation of a new edition of *Lex charitatis;* it was to replace the chapter "The Christian as a Member of the Church in the World" (above, 97).
8. Johannes Heckel, "Zwei-Reiche-Lehre," in *EKL* 3 (1959): 1936ff. (above, 204ff.). For a different position, see Paul Althaus in *EKL* 3 (1959): 1928ff. For the consequences which result from these two different positions, see the article by Siegfried Grundmann, "Kirche und Staat nach der Zwei-Reiche-Lehre Luthers"; this article is now being published in *Im Dienste des Rechtes in Kirche und Staat. Festschrift zum 70. Geburtstag von Franz Arnold*, ed. by Willibald M. Plöchl et al. (Vienna, 1963), 38ff.

9. See Ernst Wolf, "Sinn und Grenze der Anwendung der Zwei-Reiche-Lehre auf das Kirchenrecht," in *Smend Festgabe*, 451; Bornkamm, *Luthers Lehre von den zwei Reichen*, 29.

10. Luther to George Spalatin: Oct. 4, 1522: WA.B 2:605.8: "The kingdom of God is Christ's church. . . ."

11. See *The Small Catechism*, 1529: WA 30.I:296.27 ⟨*BC* 345.6⟩.

12. For documentation, see Wehrung, *Kirche nach evangelischem Verständnis*, 31.

13. *The Papacy at Rome*, 1520: WA 6:298.6.17.27. For this passage, see also Johannes Heckel, "Die zwo Kirchen," and id., *Im Irrgarten der Zwei-Reiche-Lehre*, above, 145ff. See further, *Against Jack Sausage*, 1541: WA 51:494.25: ". . . the church, . . . is a spiritual kingdom, . . . ⟨and⟩ cannot have another head than a spiritual one, which is Christ."

14. *The Papacy at Rome*, 1520: WA 6:297.39: ". . . ⟨here, in the church⟩ Christ in heaven is the head, and he alone rules"; *Against Jack Sausage*, 1541: WA 51:494.25, as in n. 13.

15. ⟨*Caput ministeriale.*⟩

16. During the Leipzig Disputation Luther was still willing to accept the jurisdictional primacy of the pope as an institution of man-made ecclesiastical law; *Explanations of Luther's Theses Debated in Leipzig*, 1519: WA 2:397.3, as above, 390 n. 49; see also Luther to the Franciscans in Jüterbog: May 15, 1519: WA.B 1:392.141: ". . . the pope is Christ's vicar only *humano iure*. . . ."

17. Luther to Margrave Albrecht of Brandenburg, grand master of the Teutonic Order: Dec. 1523: WA.B 3:210.31: ". . . if the church is not ruled by means of faith, love, and the other gifts of the Holy Spirit, it is neither ruled at all, nor is it the church, but it is Satan's synagogue. Christ alone rules the church ⟨through the gifts of the Holy Spirit⟩. . . ."

18. *Matthew, Chapters 18–24 Explained in Sermons*, 1537-40: WA 47:233.9: "In this way ⟨Christ⟩ wills his kingdom to be different from the kingdom of the world. In the world there has to be a difference among people so that some sit at the top and rule, but others let themselves be ruled"; ibid., WA 47:233.32: ". . . in his church the Lord Christ does not will any lordship at all to exist, but all that we do — I when I preach, you when you listen — is to be directed toward getting to know Christ"; ibid., WA 47:239.17: "Here superiority *(maioritas)* and prestige cease to exist. One has to pay attention to the Word and teaching of the Lord Christ and let oneself be ruled by them. The Word has to do it, aside from this, we are all equal."

19. *Addition to Goat Emser's Book*, 1519: WA 2:678.4: ". . . in the ⟨church⟩ is no superiority, because Christ has forbidden it . . ."; *Reply to Ambrosius Catharinus*, 1521: WA 7:721.30: "The gospel and the church do not know of any jurisdictions, which are nothing other than tyrannical inventions of people. ⟨The gospel⟩ knows only love and service, not power and tyranny."

20. ⟨In the sense of serving rather than the *professional* ministry.⟩ *Reply to Ambrosius Catharinus*, 1521: WA 7:773.37: ". . . jurisdiction in the church is nothing other than the service *(ministerium)* of love. . . ."

21. Luther to Margrave Albrecht of Brandenburg, grand master of the Teutonic Order: Dec. 1523; WA.B 3:210.34: ". . . Christ alone is the ruler *(rector)*, pastor, foundation, and teacher of the church . . ."; *On the Keys*, 1530: WA 30.II:487.12: ". . . God did not order any man to rule his church, but he reserved ruling the church for himself and retained it. . . ."

22. *Against Jack Sausage*, 1541: WA 51:535.18: "... in the church God cannot and will not tolerate anyone next to himself, one is to listen only to him and his Word ...."

23. *John, Chapters 3 and 4 Explained*, 1538-40: WA 47:192.5: "⟨Appointment to the preaching office⟩ comes through man ⟨but⟩ is not of man."

24. See Siegfried Grundmann, "Sacerdotium — Ministerium — Ecclesia Particularis," in *Johannes Heckel Festschrift*, 150ff.; Wilhelm Brunotte, *Das geistliche Amt bei Luther* (Berlin, 1959); Heinz Brunotte, "Sacerdotium und Ministerium als Grundbegriffe im lutherischen Kirchenrecht," in *Smend Festgabe*, 263ff.

25. Sermon of Jan. 17, 1535: WA 41:10.5: "Whoever ⟨is⟩ a Christian ... has been called into Christ's military service."

26. ⟨Ministry of the Word in the sense of service to the Word, not in the sense of ministry as a profession.⟩ *Concerning the Ministry*, 1523: WA 12:191.37: "... through Baptism we have been ⟨re⟩born and called to such ministry *(ministerium)*." In light of this passage Heinz Brunotte's argument ("Sacerdotium und Ministerium," in *Smend Festgabe*, 275) that "Luther ... never used 'ministerium' to designate the universal priesthood ⟨of believers⟩" has to be corrected.

27. *Concerning the Ministry*, 1523: WA 12:178.9: "A priest is not a ⟨professional⟩ minister; a priest is born ⟨i.e., through Baptism⟩, a ⟨professional⟩ minister is made ⟨i.e., through Ordination⟩"; ibid., WA 12:178.26: "A priest ... is born not ordained. ... He is born not of the flesh but through the spiritual birth, i.e., ⟨through⟩ water and the Spirit in the bath of regeneration."

28. See Luther's brief on the Private Mass: July 27, 1530: WA.B 5:504.8ff.

29. For the call procedure, see *Concerning the Ministry*, 1523: WA 12:191.19, 195.35 ⟨*LW* 40:37, 43f.⟩, ⟨and above, 192-96⟩.

30. See Karl Barth, *Die Ordnung der Gemeinde* (Munich, 1955), 11ff.

31. *Sermons on John, Chapters 14 and 15*, 1537: WA 45:521.32f.

32. Therefore a sacrament administered according to Holy Scripture retains for Luther the sacramental quality even if an unbelieving priest administers the sacrament; sermons of 1538: WA 46:170.31: "Even if he who baptizes, or he who is being baptized, does not believe, Baptism is true, and its power is present ⟨with the rite⟩, for we did not establish Baptism; it does not depend on us but on God's Word ..."; *The Babylonian Captivity of the Church*, 1520: WA 6:525.33; *Disputation of Henry Schmedenstede*, 1542: WA 39.II:198.20.

33. *Reply to Ambrosius Catharinus*, 1521: WA 7:742.34: "... 'church' signifies nothing other than the holy congregation of believers, who live and act by God's Spirit, ⟨and⟩ who are the body and fulness of Christ. ..."

34. Luther to Jhan von Schleinitz: June 18, 1523: WA.B 3:92.81: "... all of us have one Baptism, Lord's Supper, God, and Spirit, through which we all become spiritual brothers and sisters"; *Concerning the Ministry*, 1523: WA 12:189.10; sermon of Apr. 22, 1538: WA 46:337.26ff.

35. *The Papacy at Rome*, 1520: WA 6:296.8.

36. *The Large Catechism*, 1529: WA 30.I:189.6 ⟨*BC* 416.47⟩.

37. Ibid., WA 30.I:190.4 ⟨*BC* 417.51⟩.

38. *On the Keys*, 1530: WA 30.II:452.20, 484.4.

39. Sermon of Nov. 18, 1526: WA 20:559.7f.

40. For 'rule of faith' and 'rule of love', see *The Bondage of the Will*, 1525: WA 18:651.31ff. ⟨LW 33:88⟩, and above, 161 and 466 n. 100.

41. *The Papacy at Rome*, 1520: WA 6:293.35; *Reply to Ambrosius Catharinus*, 1521: WA 7:722.15.

42. *Disputation of John Macchabäus Scotus*, 1542: WA 39.II:182.10: "The members of the church are corporeally dispersed, ⟨yet⟩ they are united and assembled together in the Spirit, they are spiritually collected together in Christ."

43. Ibid., WA 39.II:176.5: "Succession ⟨in the church⟩ is tied to the gospel. If the bishop, who in this church comes after Bugenhagen, would teach the devil, I must not obey him because it says: 'Flee the false prophets ⟨Matt. 7:15⟩.' One has to pay attention to where the Word is, and then act accordingly.... Where the Word is, there is the church"; ibid., WA 39.II:177.2: "The gospel has to be the succession."

44. ⟨For "ministry," see above, 473 n. 26.⟩

45. *Disputation of John Macchabäus Scotus*, 1542: WA 39.II:181.13.

46. WA 18:652.23 ⟨LW 33:89⟩.

47. Luther to Margrave George of Brandenburg-Ansbach-Kulmbach: Nov. 16, 1531: WA.B 6:227.14: "⟨Christ⟩ conceals his Christendom in distress, factions, frailty, and weakness so that one is unable to find it through reason; one only can see it through faith, and one has to recognize it through the ⟨presence of the⟩ gospel, as we say in the Creed: 'I believe ⟨in⟩ one holy, Christian church.'"

48. *Answer to the Book of Goat Emser*, 1521: WA 7:683.11.

49. ⟨Literally: "face of the church."⟩

50. *Reply to Ambrosius Catharinus*, 1521: WA 7:710.1: "... just as that Petra ⟨i.e., the spiritual rock, Christ, as the foundation of the church⟩ is without sin, invisible, spiritual, and perceptible only through faith, so it is necessary that the church, too, is without sin, invisible, spiritual, and perceptible only through faith."

51. *Disputation of John Macchabäus Scotus*, 1542: WA 39.II:149.6: "... the catholic church ... is such a congregation ... which we cannot comprehend unless the Holy Spirit would reveal it because the church is in the flesh and appears visibly, it is in the world and appears in the world, yet nevertheless it is not the world, nor is it in the world, and no one sees it ..."; ibid., WA 39.II:161.14: "Through the confession ⟨of faith⟩ the church is recognized, according to ... ⟨Rom. 10:10⟩. It is necessary that the church is wrapped in flesh, but the church is not flesh, nor does it live according to the flesh; likewise, the church exists in the world, but it is not the world, nor does it live according to the world; it is in a person, and yet it is not a person ... ; therefore to the degree that the church is in the flesh, the world, a person, it is visible, i.e., through the confession."

52. For the following, see Johannes Heckel, "Die zwo Kirchen," 46, 52ff.

53. *Reply to Ambrosius Catharinus*, 1521: WA 7:709.20: "External church."

54. Other names: All of Christendom, universal Christendom, Christian people, ecclesiastical people, ecclesiastical body, *ecclesia universa*, catholic church, whole church, Christian world, ecclesiastical or Christian commonwealth (*respublica ecclesiastica* or *christiana*). See above, 98; Johannes Heckel, "Die zwo Kirchen," 51 n. 49; Oepke, *Das neue Gottesvolk*, 406ff.

55. Luther also called them collections ⟨or assemblies of Christians⟩, congregations, individual or particular churches. See above, 98.

56. *Assertion of All Articles*, 1520: WA 7:136.6; *Against the Roman Papacy*, 1545: WA 54:276.28: "... in Christ all churches are equal."

57. See Johannes Heckel, *Initia iuris*, 15 n. 52; see also Ernst Wolf's review of this title in *ZEvKR* 1 (1951): 102ff.

58. See Johannes Heckel, *Initia iuris*, 12 n. 36.

59. *Warning of His Dear German People*, 1531: WA 30.III:317.23.32, 318.18.

60. See Heinrich Bornkamm, "Die Kirche in der Confessio Augustana," in id., *Das Jahrhundert der Reformation*, 138f.

61. *Against Jack Sausage*, 1541: WA 51:545.23; *On the Councils and the Church*, 1539: WA 50:625.5.16.32. ⟨See also WA 30.III:348.21.⟩

62. *Disputation on Faith and Law*, 1535: WA 39.I:48.5 ⟨LW 34:113, thesis 61⟩.

63. *Lectures on Psalm 45*, 1532: WA 40.II:560.10.

64. Sermon of March 30, 1540: WA 49:109.31: "God is not without the church, the church is not without God"; ibid., WA 49:110.10: "The Word creates the church."

65. *The Private Mass and the Consecration of Priests*, 1533: WA 38:216.2.5: "In the Lord's Prayer the church confesses that it sins and errs, but that it is forgiven.... For before God the church will always be a humble sinner until Judgment Day, it is holy only in Christ its Savior through grace and forgiveness of sins." See also Johannes Heckel, *Initia iuris*, 40.

66. ⟨See above, 178f.⟩

67. *Against Jack Sausage*, 1541: WA 51:507.31.

68. *On the Councils and the Church*, 1539: WA 50:629.34; *Against Jack Sausage*, 1541: WA 51:515.30, 518.33.

69. ⟨Isa. 55:11.⟩

70. The phrase 'efficax et infallibile signum' has been adopted from Luther's *Disputation on Excommunication*, 1520: WA 7:236.19.

71. ⟨In contrast to the Apostolic Sucession of the office holder; see above, 179.⟩ *On the Councils and the Church*, 1539: WA 50:593.7: "There always have to be saints on earth, and when they die, other saints have to live, and this from the beginning of the world to its end; otherwise the article 'I believe ⟨in⟩ one, holy, Christian church, the communion of saints' would be wrong"; ibid., WA 50:593.11.

72. ⟨See also above, 161f.⟩

73. ⟨I.e., that the church has "the face of a sinner"; see above, 180.⟩

74. The division of mankind into two kinds ('families') of people, as developed in the basic meaning of the kingdom doctrine ⟨see above, 148f.; see also above, 64f., 91f., 149f., 357 n. 50⟩, nullifies the value of the argument that in the kingdom doctrine "the Lutheran principle 'simul iustus et peccator' is basically ignored"; see Heinz Brunotte in *Informationsblatt für die Gemeinden in den Niederdeutschen Lutherischen Landeskirchen* 7 (1958): 344. That this is not the case we can learn from Luther himself; *Disputation of Palladius and Tilemann*, 1537: WA 39.I:221.9: "Mercy rules only over the righteous and holy ones, God's wrath rules over those who are not righteous and the ungodly ones. As long as someone is not righteous and is an unbelieving sinner, and not penitent, he is not in ⟨God's⟩ mercy. But when he is converted and accepts faith in Christ, he is righteous and holy, even though sin still exists in his flesh. Mercy does not embrace the ungodly, but it embraces the righteous ones who desire to believe ⟨while⟩ they are sinners." See also *Sec-*

ond *Commentary on Galatians*, 1535: WA 40.I:528 ⟨*LW* 26:343ff.⟩, and Johannes Heckel, "Luthers Lehre von den zwei Regimenten," *ZevKR* 4 (1955): 258f.

75. *Matthew, Chapters 18–24 Explained in Sermons*, 1537-40: WA 47:263.40: "... these two kings and potentates, the Lord Christ and the devil ..., have two armies which confront each other ... in battle...."

76. ⟨Therefore the church on earth never exists without *Anfechtung* (see above, 248 n. 55).⟩ For the threefold *Anfechtung* of the church, see Luther to Wenceslas Link: Sept. 8, 1541: WA.B 9:510.8. Link had complained that people despise God's Word. Luther answered: "I have strengthened my heart this way: The church's first *tentatio (Anfechtung)*, which exists since the beginning of the world, always comes from the tyrants who shed our blood. When the tyrants are almost finished ⟨with us⟩, then follows the *tentatio* of the heretics, which does much more damage and strengthens the violence of the tyrants. Once the heretics are somewhat subdued, then follows the most damaging *tentatio* ..., namely, licentiousness and cupidity to live without law, without the Word, since we are saturated with, and tired of, the Word, which ⟨supposedly⟩ is no longer needed, since the enemies are defeated. Thus the worst enemies of man are the members of his own household ⟨see also above, 466 n. 101⟩. These are the three *tentationes* directed against the Father, the Son, and the Holy Spirit. I always thought that the pope and the tyrants do not pose any ⟨real⟩ danger ⟨for us⟩, or that we would not be overthrown by Müntzer, Karlstadt, and the Anabaptists. But ⟨now⟩ I suspect that our people will be the despisers and scoffers among us...."

77. ⟨Literally: "church of knights."⟩

78. Sermon of Sept. 22, 1538: WA 46:499.13; ibid., WA 46:500.16: "Therefore ⟨the church⟩ is called a fighting church, a church of knights, which is in a continuous battle against sin."

79. *Against Jack Sausage*, 1541: WA 51:516.32: "If we judge according to living, then holy church is not without sin, as it confesses in the Lord's Prayer: 'Forgive us our trespasses'"; ibid., WA 51:517.1: "But the teaching ⟨of the church⟩ must not be sin."

80. For the following, see Johannes Heckel, "Die zwo Kirchen," 57ff.

81. *Against Jack Sausage*, 1541: WA 51:477.25.

82. *Concerning the Ministry*, 1523: WA 12.188.29 ⟨*LW* 40:33⟩: "How much more ought we not then confidently judge the church of Rome in its insincerity and feigned authority *(simulatricem et simulatam Ecclesiam Romanam)*. We are not to be judged by this church...."

83. ⟨See below, Index of Subjects, s.v. "devil, mystical body of."⟩

84. *The Papacy at Rome*, 1520: WA 6:297.2.

85. ⟨I.e., spiritual and corporeal.⟩

86. *The Papacy at Rome*, 1520: WA 6:296.38: "zwo kirchen." For the history of this term, see Johannes Heckel, *Initia iuris*, 41 n. 170, and id., "Die zwo Kirchen," 58 n. 71.

87. Sermon of May 21, 1531: WA 34.I:432.9: "These are the two Christian churches which oppose each other: one which condemns and curses, the other which endures this."

88. *Against Jack Sausage*, 1541: WA 51:477.31: "... the Lord Christ himself ... differentiates between two churches, a true and a false one...."

89. Sermon of Oct. 5, 1544: WA 49:619.23: "... in Christ is one body, in Christ you have one head of the church."

90. See above, 159f.

91. ⟨See above, 160.⟩

92. See Bornkamm, "Die Kirche in der Confessio Augustana," in id., *Das Jahrhundert der Reformation,* 138f.

93. *First Lectures on the Psalms,* 1513-15: WA 4:289.2.25. Occasionally Luther used the phrase 'dead member' in order to show that such a member does not belong to Christ's body. See *Lectures on Romans,* 1515-16: WA 56:77.2; sermon of Feb. 7, 1546: WA 51:177.16 (dealing with the excommunication of a member who is "totally rotten and dead").

94. *Third Disputation against the Antinomians,* 1538: WA 39.I:491.7: therefore 'ecclesiastical body' ⟨or 'church body'⟩ and 'members of Christ' designate the same thing; Luther's brief of Sept. 1530: WA.B 5:615.70: "⟨The Jews⟩ do not belong to our ecclesiastical or civic body, but are prisoners"; Luther to Lazarus Spengler(?): March 18, 1531: WA.B 6:56.11: "If the jurists are right that a Christian not as a Christian but as a citizen or member of the political body may resist ⟨the emperor⟩, then so be it. We are talking about the members of Christ and the ecclesiastical body. We certainly know that a Christian as a citizen or member of the political body may use the sword and have a secular office, and we have often written about this. But our office does not permit us to advise a member of the political body ⟨to engage in⟩ such a resistance, nor do we know the jurists' law."

95. *The Papacy at Rome,* 1520: WA 6:302.6.

96. See the following paragraphs.

97. See above, 161f., 466 n. 100.

98. ⟨I.e., a *baptized believer* has *citizenship* in the spiritual and the corporeal church; the *illegal excommunication of a baptized and believing Christian;* the *legal status of a baptized unbeliever.*⟩

99. *The Papacy at Rome,* 1520: WA 6:297.17; Johannes Heckel, "Die zwo Kirchen," 59ff.

100. ⟨Because a *baptized and believing* Christian may not be excommunicated.⟩

101. ⟨I.e., he is removed from the roster and may not receive the sacraments.⟩

102. See *On the Power of Excommunication,* 1518: WA 1:638ff.

103. ⟨Or the spiritual church.⟩

104. ⟨I.e., Baptism.⟩ For the means of grace as marks of the church, see Prenter, *Spiritus creator,* 260f.

105. ⟨See above, 161f., 466 n. 100.⟩ For the church in the world as a *concordia fidei* and a *concordia caritatis,* see Luther's preface to Antonius Corvinus, *Quatenus expediat aeditam recens Erasmi de sarcienda Ecclesiae concordia Rationem sequi,* 1534: WA 38:276.16.

106. For the church as a community of love, see esp. *The Blessed Sacrament of the Body of Christ and the Brotherhoods,* 1519: WA 2:742ff. ⟨*LW* 35:49ff.⟩.

107. *Against Jack Sausage,* 1541: WA 51:505.27: ". . . we say that you are and remain in the church. . . . But you are no longer of the church or members of the church. . . ."

108. For the roots of this phrase in the patristic tradition, see Johannes Heckel, *Initia iuris,* 14 n. 45.

109. *Against Jack Sausage,* 1541: WA 51:521.33: "They are in the church but not of the church, ⟨or⟩ according to the number *(numero)* but not according to the quality *(merito)*. . . . Therefore one has the following difference: not all are Christians who pretend to be Christians. But when one arrives at the point that one disagrees in matters of doc-

trine, then a separation takes place, and one finds out who the true Christians are, namely, those who have God's Word, true and clear."

110. This phrase also originated in traditional church doctrine. See, e.g., the gloss ⟨see above, 246 n. 44⟩ to *Decretum Gratiani* c.70. D.I. de poen. ⟨Friedberg 1:1179⟩: "There is a difference between 'to be of the church,' which here ⟨i.e., in c.70⟩ is denied ⟨to⟩ the evil ones, and 'to be in the church,' which is granted ⟨to⟩ those who oppose" ⟨the church, i.e., the nominal Christians, the 'chaff' on the 'thrashing floor'⟩; *Second Lectures on the Psalms,* 1518-21: WA 5:430.34 ⟨to Ps. 15:1⟩: ". . . here the question is not posed regarding everyone who is in God's church, since on the thrashing floor much chaff is among the wheat, but only regarding those who truly are of the church. . . ."

111. *Disputation on Matt. 22:1-14,* 1537: WA 39.I:291.9: ". . . in the church are mixed together good and bad or evil people, whom we call hypocrites; even though they use the sacraments, they use ⟨only⟩ externally what the godly people use in truth."

112. *On the Councils and the Church,* 1539: WA 50:616.2: ". . . a council judges ⟨or: 'condemns'⟩ a heretic not in an arbitrary way, but according to the law of the kingdom, i.e., according to Holy Scripture, . . . which is the law of holy church. At the threat of eternal damnation, ⟨this⟩ law, kingdom, and judge are to be feared because this law is God's Word, this kingdom is God's church, this judge is the officer or servant of both."

113. See above, 472 n. 17.

114. Sermon of July 1, 1538: WA 46:466.8: "It is not church . . . unless it is ruled by the Holy Spirit. . . ."

115. See above, 82f., 92f., and Johannes Heckel, "Die zwo Kirchen," 62ff.

116. See Lau, *Luthers Lehre von den beiden Reichen.*

117. *How Christians Should Regard Moses,* 1527: WA 24:6.5. See also Merz, "Gesetz Gottes und Volksnomos," *LuJ* 16 (1934): 56ff.

118. *How Christians Should Regard Moses,* 1527: WA 24:5.28.

119. *On the Keys,* 1530: WA 30.II:498.18: ". . . the Keys are . . . an office ⟨in the sense of task⟩, authority, or command given by God to Christendom through Christ for the purpose of retaining or forgiving the sins of man"; ibid., WA 30.II:503.18: "The Key of binding is the authority or office to punish a sinner (who does not want to repent) with the public judgment of eternal death by separating him from Christendom. When such a judgment is pronounced, it is as if Christ himself has judged. If the sinner remains in his sin, he certainly is eternally condemned. The Key of loosening is the authority or office to absolve a sinner (who confesses ⟨his sin⟩ and turns ⟨from his sinful ways⟩) of his sin and to promise him eternal life. This, too, is as if Christ himself judges. And if a sinner believes and remains ⟨in the right way⟩, he certainly is eternally blessed. . . ."

120. ⟨Literally: "ecclesiastical ban," the small ban.⟩ For the relationship of the 'common absolution' ⟨i.e., the publicly pronounced, general absolution of the congregation in contrast to a privately pronounced absolution of an individual⟩ with excommunication, see Luther and others to the City Council of Nuremberg: Oct. 8, 1533: WA.B 6:529.62.64.69: ". . . the gospel itself is a common absolution. . . . Therefore we are unable to prohibit and condemn common absolution as something unchristian because it serves to remind the audience that each one should accept the gospel, and that the gospel is an absolution which also belongs to him. . . . Regarding the counterargument — one may not absolve the crowd ⟨because⟩ there are many in it who should be bound rather than absolved, and one should not absolve anyone who does not desire it, etc. — one has

to know the following: there is a difference between preaching and jurisdiction. Jurisdiction deals with publicly committed sins. There are also many more secret sins which one cannot bind or punish in any other way than through the . . . preaching office. Therefore the sermon binds all unbelievers, and, in contrast, at the same time it grants forgiveness to all believers, even to him who has been bound through jurisdiction; if through ⟨listening to⟩ the sermon he would come again to obedience and faith, he would be forgiven before God; but thereafter he also should reconcile himself again with the church since he also has offended it ⟨and not only God. The argument that repentance and faith are the conditions for such an absolution⟩ also applies to the common sermon ⟨as common absolution⟩. Each kind of absolution, the common one and the private one, is based on faith — without faith neither absolution loosens. Therefore the Key of loosening has not been used in a wrong way ⟨in common absolution⟩. For faith does not count on one's worth, it only accepts absolution and affirms it."

121. *Smalcald Articles,* 1537: WA 50:247.15 ⟨*BC* 314.IX⟩.

122. See Rudolf Hermann, "Die Probleme der Exkommunikation bei Luther und Thomas Erastus," in id., *Gesammelte Studien zur Theologie und der Reformation* (Göttingen, 1960), 446ff.; Ruth Götze, *Wie Luther Kirchenzucht übte* (Göttingen, 1959).

123. *On the Keys,* 1530: WA 30.II:501.20.

124. Ibid., WA 30.II:502.22.35: ". . . the congregation, who is to consider such a person to be excommunicated, has to know and be certain that he deserves to be excommunicated, and how he got into this situation. . . . The congregation has to join in being judge. . . ."

125. Ibid., WA 30.II:502.5: ". . . the specific sin has to be publicly committed by a known person ⟨of whom one is certain that he committed the sin, namely,⟩ when one brother sees the other one commit the sin. In addition, the sin has to be censured in a brotherly way first, and in a last step the sin has to be publicly confirmed before the congregation." ⟨The literal translation of the verb in the last clause, "confirmed," would be "convinced"; i.e., the congregation has to be publicly convinced that the sin had been committed and dealt with as outlined.⟩

126. *Exhortation to All Clergy Assembled at Augsburg,* 1530, WA 30.II:310.5: Luther listed robbery, adultery, fornication, murder, hatred, usury, drunkenness, heresy, blasphemy, "and similar things."

127. Luther to Leonard Beyer: 1533: WA.B 6:564.1: "Those who despise godliness and do not go to Holy Communion we usually first terrify by mentioning the authority and prestige of our most illustrious prince and threatening them with exile and punishment, as we do with blasphemers. Then, if they do not come to their senses, we order the pastors to inform, instruct, and reprimand them for a month or longer. Finally, if they are obstinate, they are to be excluded from the assembly of the church and avoided as heathen. In Scripture there is a clear passage on excommunication ⟨Matt. 18:17⟩."

128. ⟨In the following sentence this situation is described as "internal excommunication, executed by God."⟩

129. *Disputation on Excommunication,* 1520: WA 7:236.15: "Someone who is to be excommunicated because of the wickedness of his heart and public offenses is already excluded prior to being ⟨publicly⟩ excommunicated. Consequently, external excommunication is only a sign of the internal excommunication."

130. ⟨By which that "semblance of membership" in the corporeal church is revealed for what it is, and is nullified.⟩

131. ⟨As established in the internal excommunication, executed by God.⟩

132. *On the Keys*, 1530: WA 30.II:505.28: "... the Keys demand faith in our hearts. Without faith you are unable to use them beneficially."

133. Luther summarized the presented materials in a sermon on excommunication in *Matthew, Chapters 18–24 Explained in Sermons*, 1537-40: WA 47:281.20ff., 282.2.14, 284.17; for excommunication as the verbal establishment of a prior fact, see ibid., WA 47:285.12, 289.3; for the legal effect of excommunication according to divine positive law, see ibid., WA 47:285.30; for excommunication as a penalty aiming at improvement, see ibid., WA 47:286.31ff.

134. ⟨See above, 180f.⟩

135. *Disputation on Excommunication*, 1520: WA 7:236.19: "External excommunication is not an efficacious and infallible sign of the internal excommunication — often it is a most fallacious sign."

136. Canonists dealt with this in the topic 'The Erring Key'. Early on, Luther affirmed their position; later he sharply criticized it because 'Key' was to be understood as God's Word, which never errs. For Luther, it was rather the priest who erred, i.e., the human executor of the divine Word, a situation which was obscured in the phrase 'erring Key'; *On the Keys*, 1530: WA 30.II:475.20ff., and Johannes Heckel, *Initia iuris*, 104 n. 437.

137. *On the Keys*, 1530: WA 30.II:503.31: "⟨Preachers⟩ are executors, deliverers, and drovers of the gospel, which simply preaches these two things: Repentance ⟨i.e., the work of the law implemented in the Key of binding⟩ and forgiveness of sin ⟨i.e., the work of the gospel implemented in the Key of loosening⟩, Luke 24⟨:47⟩."

138. ⟨See above, 467 n. 109, below, 504 n. 22.⟩ For the following, see Bornkamm, "Bindung und Freiheit in der Ordnung der Kirche," in id., *Das Jahrhundert der Reformation*, 185ff.; Siegfried Grundmann, "Das Gesetz als kirchenrechtliches Problem," *ZEvKR* 8 (1962): 326ff.

139. *On the Councils and the Church*, 1539: WA 50:552.21: "... matters of ... the external, temporal governance of the churches...." ⟨*LW* 41:59: "... the temporal, external rule of the church."⟩

140. *The German Mass*, 1526: WA 19:73.14 ⟨*LW* 53:62⟩: "But such orders are needed for those who are still becoming Christians or need to be strengthened.... ⟨Such orders⟩ are essential especially for the ⟨simple folk⟩ and the young who must be trained and educated in the Scripture and God's Word daily..."; *On the Councils and the Church*, 1539: WA 50:649.18 ⟨*LW* 41:173⟩.

141. *On the Councils and the Church*, 1539: WA 50:614.8 ⟨*LW* 41:131⟩: "... a council has the power to institute some ceremonies, provided, ... that they are useful and profitable to the people and show fine, orderly discipline and conduct. Thus it is necessary, for example, to have certain days, and also places where one can assemble; also certain hours for preaching and for the public administration of the sacraments, for praying, singing, praising and thanking God, etc. — as St. Paul says, I Corinthians 14[:40], 'All things should be done decently and in order.' ... In summary, these must and cannot be dispensed with if the church is to survive."

142. Sermon of Feb. 27, 1523: WA 11:38.32: "... the externals of worshipping God are left to our judgment ⟨literally: 'will'⟩."

143. Luther to Margrave Albrecht of Brandenburg, grand master of the Teutonic Order: Dec. 1523: WA.B 3:212.106: "⟨The ceremonies of the pope⟩ are not . . . God's mysteries; therefore having observed them I do not live or shall be in God's church, nor shall I die or be outside of the church by having neglected them."

144. *Reply to Ambrosius Catharinus*, 1521: WA 7:720.2: ". . . without place and institution *(corpus)* there is no church, and yet institution and place are not the church, nor do they belong to the church"; ibid., WA 7:720.8: ". . . all things are indifferent and free"; ibid., WA 7:720.11: "For here rules the freedom of the Spirit which makes all things indifferent, nothing necessary, whatever be corporeal or earthly"; Luther to Margrave Albrecht of Brandenburg, duke of Prussia: Feb. 17, 1543: WA.B 10:266.19: ". . . we want to be humble servants of the faith (i.e., of God), and we have to be, but we want to be masters of the ceremonies and will not tolerate that they become equal to faith. . . ."

145. Luther to Margrave Albrecht of Brandenburg, grand master of the Teutonic Order: Dec. 1523: WA.B 3:212.108: "⟨The laws of the pope⟩ are free and indifferent, just like any other externals suitable to be used by the body."

146. ⟨See also above, 241 n. 65.⟩

147. *The Babylonian Captivity of the Church*, 1520: WA 6:536.20: "In support of their traditions ⟨the papal theologians⟩ with puffed cheeks blow up this word ⟨of Christ: 'Who listens to you, listens to me'; Luke 10:16⟩." — The first abuse of the Power of the Keys is the wrong interpretation of Matt. 16:19 and 18:18, dealing with the power to bind and loosen. The papal theologians "took from these verses the word 'binding' and twisted it to mean 'command' or 'prohibit', or making laws and commandments for Christendom. Therefore they give to the pope the authority to bind the souls and consciences of Christians with laws . . ."; *On the Keys*, 1530: WA 30.II:465.20. See also *Some Short Sermons of D. Martin Luther*, 1537: WA 45:460.27, and the exchange of letters between Melanchthon and Luther at the time of the 1530 Diet of Augsburg: July ⟨14,⟩ 20, and 21, 1530: WA.B 5:475ff., 490.11ff., 492.27, 493.38.44 ⟨LW 49:No. 225⟩.

148. *Ex necessitate legis*. Luther to Margrave Albrecht of Brandenburg, grand master of the Teutonic Order: Dec. 1523: WA.B 3:212.117: "It is very stupid and abominable if one wishes to rule the church with external works and laws; they pertain to eating, drinking, clothing, time, and place, things from which, however, one is not able to live or be saved because they are temporal matters . . ."; to Charles III, duke of Savoy: Sept. 7, 1523: WA.B 3:152.94: "Salvation rules in us not through the laws of man but alone through Christ's power"; ibid., WA.B 3:152.96: "Those who are not Christians are to be kept in check by other means than the traditions of man. Those people are to be avoided, and . . . one ought not to have any dealings with them. ⟨These other means are⟩ the secular sword (as they call it) and the magistrates; it is their task through the fear of the sword to prevent the evil ones from committing evil. . . . But a bishop will rule the Christians without the sword, only with God's Word, since it is certain that those who are not voluntarily good are not Christians. . . . What kind of insanity is it to harass those who voluntarily are good with laws which are applicable to the evil ones or those who do not want to be good? Certainly, as Christians do all things voluntarily, so they also subordinate themselves to the sword and the laws for the evil ones; they even use the sword, not for their good (since except for faith they need nothing other for righteousness and Salvation) but as an example for others, and for the ⟨maintenance⟩ of public peace and strengthening the law of the sword. Therefore they are free and ought to use whatever traditions and ceremonies in a free

way." — Even the use of Canon law could be endured were it used in this sense; Luther to Margrave Albrecht of Brandenburg, grand master of the Teutonic Order: Dec. 1523: WA.B 3:212.112.

149. *Ex necessitate fratris. The German Mass,* 1526: WA 19:72.23.27 ⟨LW 53:61⟩: "... we must make sure that freedom shall be and remain a servant of love and of our fellowman.... Seeing then that this external order, while it cannot affect the conscience before God, may yet serve the neighbor, we should seek to be of one mind in Christian love.... As far as possible we should observe the same rites and ceremonies, just as all Christians have the same baptism and the same sacrament [of the altar] and no one has received a special one of his own from God"; Luther to Anthony Lauterbach: Oct. 19, 1545: WA.B 11:200.16: "... in those temporal and indifferent matters ⟨i.e., the ceremonies⟩... we ⟨should⟩ serve... according to the need and weakness of the brothers...."

150. *First Commentary on Galatians,* 1519: WA 2:617.1.

151. I am grateful to my student Knut Nörr for calling my attention to *Panormitani* ⟨Nicholas of Tudeschi, 1386-1445⟩ *Proemium 'Gregorius Episcopus',* no. 16, in *Commentarius in Primum Librum Decretalium* (Lyons, 1534), 1:fol. 4v. Panormitanus refers to Johannes Andreae, *Questiones Mercuriales super regulis iuris. De reg. possessor.* (Lyons, 1510), fol. 72. — See also Ludwig Buisson, *Potestas und Caritas. Die päpstliche Gewalt im Spätmittelalter* (Cologne, 1958; 2d ed. enlarged, Cologne, 1982).

152. *Psalm 117 Explained,* 1530: WA 31.I:241.12: "... Christian existence is something higher and totally different from all secular and spiritual ⟨in the sense of ecclesiastical, i.e., Canon law⟩ rights, laws, external holiness, governance, whatever one calls these matters, be it among Jews or heathen."

153. ⟨See above, 237 n. 20.⟩

154. Luther to Philip Melanchthon: July 21, 1530: WA.B 5:493.63 ⟨LW 49:386f.⟩: "⟨We are unable,...⟩ either on the basis of the ecclesiastical or the secular law ⟨to grant to the bishops the power to impose anything on the church...⟩."

155. *On the Councils and the Church,* 1539: WA 50:649.34: "Such matters ⟨i.e., when and where to preach⟩ are totally external; they also are totally subordinated to the rule of reason (as the circumstances of time, place, and person demand)"; ibid., WA 50:553.18: "The Holy Spirit is to explain Christ and not deal with such matters ⟨i.e., legal matters pertaining to the conduct of the clergy⟩, which are subordinated to reason." For a similar statement, see *The Private Mass and the Consecration of Priests,* 1533: WA 38:187.1.

156. *The Papacy at Rome,* 1520: WA 6:291.8; *Second Lectures on Galatians,* 1531: WA 40.I:418.7.

157. *The Right and Power of a Christian Congregation,* 1523: WA 11:415.23.

158. ⟨For "Christ's royal rule," see above, 148f.⟩

159. ⟨See above, 31, 86, 97f., 247 n. 53, 285 n. 46.⟩

160. Luther to Christopher Jörger: Dec. 31, 1543(?): WA.B 10:485.26: "In such matters ⟨of conscience⟩ your king is not God's servant. Therefore even though in temporal matters every man owes obedience to your king, one may not obey him in spiritual matters (which pertain to eternal life). He is unable to give eternal life; ⟨also,⟩ he has no command, but God has clearly forbidden him to dare meddling in matters pertaining to spiritual eternal life and master them in his governance. Rather, he should be a student of, and subject to, God's Word, as are all creatures, etc."

161. *Defense against the Charge of Inciting Rebellion,* 1533: WA 38:110.21: "The author-

ity ⟨of the princes⟩ extends only to body and goods, or secular matters. But they . . . also investigate the secrets of the heart and conscience and want to rule there . . . ." See also n. 162.

162. *Sermons on the First Epistle of St. Peter*, 1523: WA 12:331.32. "Among a Christian people there should and may not be coercion; when one begins to bind consciences with external laws, faith and Christian life will soon perish"; Luther to Daniel Greiser: Oct. 22, 1543: WA.B 10:436.3: "I am unable to expect any good from the form of excommunication which ⟨now⟩ one takes for granted at your court. For if it will happen that the courts want to rule the churches according to the courts' desire, God will not bless it, and these most recent events will be worse than the former ones ⟨see Matt. 27:64b⟩ because what is done without faith is not good. What is done without a call ⟨see above, 193f., esp. 194⟩ is done without faith and will perish, no doubt. Either they themselves ⟨i.e., the princes and their officials⟩ might become pastors and preach, baptize, visit the sick, distribute the Lord's Supper, and do all the ecclesiastical things, or they should stop confusing the calls. They should take care of their courts and leave the churches to those who are called to the churches and are accountable ⟨for their ministry⟩ to God. One may not tolerate that other people do something and we are burdened with having to give an account for it. We want the offices of the church to be different from those of the court. . . . Satan continues to be Satan. ⟨When the pope ruled, Satan⟩ mixed the church into the *politia*, in our days he wants to mix the *politia* into the church. But with God's help we shall resist and do all in our strength to preserve the different calls." For the background of this letter, see *EKO* 1:287 (a law of Duke Maurice of Saxony, dated May 21, 1543), and WA.B 10:436 n. 1. ⟨See also above, 108.⟩

163. Luther to Margrave Albrecht of Brandenburg, grand master of the Teutonic Order: Dec. 1523: WA.B 3:212.122: ". . . external matters have to be ruled by parents and princes of the world; it is their task to rule bodies and corporeal matters, in which there is neither Salvation nor damnation but only the *pax politica* in the world."

164. If a secular governmental authority transgresses this God-given limit of its authority to command, a Christian congregation has to resist by emphatically confessing that it wishes to uphold its church ordinance. See, e.g., the brief by Luther and Melanchthon, dated Oct. 24 or 25, 1544: WA.B 10:671.28ff.

165. Luther to Cardinal Albrecht, archbishop of Mainz: 1530: WA 30.II:400.8; Bornkamm, "Das Problem der Toleranz," in id., *Das Jahrhundert der Reformation*, 268ff. (which has to be augmented according to the materials presented above). For the further development, see Martin Heckel, *Staat und Kirche* (also in *ZSRG*.K 42 [1956]:117ff., 43 [1957]: 202ff.), and id., "Autonomia and Pacis Compositio," *ZSRG*.K 45 (1959): 141ff. (also in id., *Gesammelte Schriften. Staat, Kirche, Recht, Geschichte*, 1 [Tübingen, 1989]).

166. Brief of Melanchton, Luther, and others concerning Martin Bucer's *Reformation:* Jan. 14, 1545: WA.B 11:17.58: ". . . we are unable to consider it profitable to . . . work toward ⟨the emperor⟩ undertaking a general reformation. It would be more profitable if ⟨the preaching of⟩ the gospel itself would continue as it has been until now, and if one could accomplish that external peace be granted to ⟨the evangelical⟩ estates."

167. Protection of civic peace includes also the care for the uniform preaching in a lordship; Luther to Duke John, elector of Saxony: Feb. 9, 1526: WA.B 4:28.23: ". . . it is the task of a secular ruler not to tolerate that obstinate preachers cause division and discord among his subjects; one has to worry that from this situation might finally come rebellion

and mob-actions. Rather, in one place ⟨in the sense of one territory or city and its surrounding area⟩ there should be uniform preaching. This was the reason that ⟨the authorities in⟩ Nuremberg silenced their monks and closed the monasteries." ⟨See also above, 458 n. 10 (5) and (6).⟩

168. Luther and others to Droste Simon: Nov. 8, 1539: WA.B 8:591.8: "... God has commanded all secular governmental authorities to spread, promote, and maintain ⟨or: 'preserve'⟩ his holy gospel and the true worship of God"; ibid., WA.B 8: 592.12: "... this is the true and highest worship of God, which a governmental authority is to do and can do...."

169. For a significant example, see Luther to George Spalatin: Nov. 11, 1521: WA.B 2:402.5 ⟨LW 48:326⟩: "... I will not put up with your statement that the Sovereign ⟨i.e., Elector Frederick of Saxony, Luther's territorial prince⟩ will not allow anything to be written against Mainz ⟨i.e., Cardinal Albrecht, archbishop of Mainz, with whom Luther had crossed swords regarding indulgences⟩, or anything that could disturb the public peace. I would rather lose you, the Sovereign himself, and the whole world [than be quiet].... Not so, Spalatin! Not so, Elector! For the sake of the sheep of Christ, we must resist that most atrocious wolf ⟨i.e., the cardinal⟩, with all our strength...."

170. ⟨See above, Appendix II.⟩

171. Luther to Duke John, elector of Saxony: Oct. 31, 1525: WA.B 3:595.36 ⟨LW 49:134ff.⟩: as secular governmental authority, the elector should see to it that the poor financial conditions of pastors and parishes in the territory are improved and that the local governmental institutions are "visited" ⟨in the sense of examined⟩; to Duke John, elector of Saxony: Nov. 30, 1525: WA.B 3:628.5 ⟨LW 49:138⟩: an electoral commission, consisting of lay people, should visit all parishes in the territory and organize a system for paying the salaries of pastors, "for ... it is Your Electoral Grace's duty to see to it" that pastors receive the reward of their labors (Matt. 10:10, Luke 10:7); Luther to Duke Henry of Saxony: July 25, 1539: WA.B 8:506.6: "God has especially commanded the ... rulers to organize and maintain the churches according to the needs of the churches."

172. ⟨Heckel wrote "organisatorische Nothilfe." Poor external or spiritual conditions have developed in the church(es) of a territory (or city). Thus an *emergency* has developed because the officials of the church, who are responsible for the church's well-being, do nothing to remedy the situation. Therefore the prince (or city council) has to provide *relief* by organizing the means for eliminating the *emergency*.⟩

173. *Psalm 101 Explained*, 1534: WA 51:216.12: "⟨David⟩ shows in these three verses ⟨Ps. 101:2-4⟩ how he managed and ruled his kingdom according to the spiritual estate, namely, with the Word and worship of God. The remaining four verses ⟨5-8⟩ show how he has ruled as a secular estate."

174. Ibid., WA 51:222.31: "... now secular kings ... interfere in the matters of the gospel ⟨and,⟩ following the example of the pope, prohibit what God has commanded, as, e.g., receiving both bread and wine in the Lord's Supper, Christian freedom, marriage ⟨i.e., of priests⟩"; ibid., WA 51:239.25: "In the name of the devil secular lords always want to teach and dominate Christ, how he is to govern his church and implement his spiritual governance"; ibid., WA 51:246.7: "... ⟨the secular governmental authorities⟩ command what is to be preached and believed."

175. ⟨See above, 466 n. 100.⟩

176. ⟨I.e., the baptized believers.⟩

177. *On the Councils and the Church*, 1539: WA 50:651.9: "... ceremonies ought to be

regulated so that in the end they do not become a burden . . ."; *Propositions against the School of Satan,* 1530: WA 30.II:421.1: "God's church has the authority to set up ceremonies pertaining to festivals, food, fasting, prayers, vigils, etc., but not for others, only for itself; the church has never acted differently nor will it. ⟨The actions of the church are governed by the following conditions:⟩ These ceremonies may not contradict the articles of faith or the commandment of works; the ceremonies exist as a possibility ⟨i.e., they are not final matters⟩, and the church controls them; they may neither bind nor disturb consciences; they are observed for a period of time and not perpetually; they can be changed according to the circumstances of time and situation; they can be abolished."

178. Luther to Nicholas Hausmann: March 21, 1534: WA.B 7:45.5: Luther advises against the publication of a church ordinance *(ordinatio ceremoniarum),* authored by Hausmann for the city of Dessau, ". . . for we are already sorry that our reformation ⟨i.e., Luther's *The German Mass*⟩ has been published because ⟨thus⟩ an example has been made for all the others also to publish ⟨their orders of worship⟩. And so the variety and multitude of ceremonies has grown *ad infinitum* so that in a short time we will outdo the . . . papists. Rather, I have advised that ⟨your⟩ manuscript be retained and the pastors simply be informed article by article what and how much they should do at this time — just as under the papacy the divine order ⟨of worship⟩ (as it is called) was handed down — so that they would gradually become established by use. . . . ⟨"They," i.e., "article by article" and the subjects treated in them⟩. Finally, ⟨I have done this⟩ so that matters with us or other neighbors may be preserved as uniform as possible ⟨and we⟩ do not open the mouth of papists and sects to bark and slander us for discord among us (as they brag). . . ."

179. Luther to Landgrave Philip of Hesse: Jan. 7, 1527: WA.B 4:157.12: Luther advises against the publication of a church ordinance for Hesse. "For until now I have not been so courageous, nor am I able to be, as to introduce among us such a multitude of laws ⟨written down⟩ with such powerful words. This would be an option: Follow the way Moses acted; he took the laws, of which the larger part was already used among the people by tradition, wrote them down, and put them in the proper order"; ibid., WA.B 4:158.20: the best way of proceeding would be if some pastors could agree on some matters, and then others would gradually follow so that "usage and custom ⟨would develop⟩"; ibid., WA.B 4:158.26: ". . . if laws are made too soon, before custom and usage exist, they seldom turn out to be good laws. People are not as ready ⟨for laws⟩ as those assume who sit by themselves and paint with words . . . how things ought to be. There is a big difference between prescribing laws and following laws"; ibid., WA.B 4:158.31: "But if some matters have become custom . . . , then it is easy to add the ⟨written⟩ order to them. Certainly, making laws is an important, dangerous, and far-reaching undertaking, and without God's Spirit nothing good will come of it. Therefore one has to act with fear and humility before God and observe this rule: concise and good, few and good, careful and steadfast."

180. Luther to Prince George of Anhalt: July 10, 1545: WA.B 11:132.7: "I admit that I have no positive attitude even to those ceremonies which are necessary, but I am hostile toward those which are not necessary. Once burned, twice careful: There is my experience with ceremonies in the papacy, and the example of the early church. ⟨According to ibid., n. 7, Luther suggested that under the papacy ceremonies had an inappropriate significance, in the early church they were insignificant.⟩ For it is easy for ceremonies to grow into laws; once they have become laws, they soon become traps for consciences, and finally pure doctrine is obscured and destroyed. This could especially be the case if the next

generation is cold and unlearned, and quarrels more about ceremonies that mortify the carnal mind. We see this now already while we are still alive and experience the rise of sects and discord, when everyone follows his own mind"; ibid., WA.B 11:133.17: "Since . . . certainly the end is at hand, it seems to me that, at least in this blessed age, it is not necessary to be much concerned about setting up ceremonies and making them uniform, worse, fixing them through a permanent law. But one thing has to be done, namely, that the Word is purely and abundantly taught, and that learned and qualified ministers are ordained; they, first of all, should care for being of one heart and soul in the Lord. Through this, it will, of course, be easy for ceremonies to become uniform or be tolerated. Without such a heart there will be no end . . . to discord regarding ceremonies, for the next generation will adopt the same authority which we ⟨would⟩ use now ⟨for setting up uniform ceremonies⟩. And so it will be flesh against flesh, the result of the corrupt nature. Therefore I am unable to advise that in each place throughout the land there should be uniformity in the ceremonies. But where obviously ungodly or absurd ceremonies have been abolished, one should tolerate differences in ceremonies; if somewhere some ceremonies have been abolished, they should not be restored; when they have been retained, they should not be abolished. ⟨Examples would be⟩ the altars which have been placed at the usual place, or the sacred or secular vestments of the preachers, and other similar things. For if one heart and one soul in the Lord is present, it will be easy for someone to endure ⟨the lack of uniformity which exists in these external matters⟩. But if the zeal for unity in heart and soul is not present, that external unity in ceremonies will accomplish little; further, that unity would not last long among the next generation because these are ⟨matters⟩ which depend on local customs and are subject to time, person, and accidental circumstances; God's kingdom does not consist in these things because by their very nature they are subject to change. Whatever will be, one has to be careful that it not be turned into necessary laws. To me the following seems to be desirable: A schoolmaster or housefather rules without laws; alone through supervision he corrects, according to God's law, what is wrong in school and household when he sees that good discipline is transgressed. Likewise, in the church all things ought to be governed through the present supervision ⟨i.e., the visitation of parishes⟩ rather than through laws which one ignores. For where the supervision by the housefather ceases to exist, there also ceases to exist discipline among the members of the household"; ibid., WA.B 11:133.44: "⟨The implementation of all authority in the church⟩ depends on qualified and (as Christ says) prudent and faithful persons ⟨Luke 12:42⟩. If we do not involve such persons in the government of the church, then without such qualified persons we try in vain to govern through laws. Why is it necessary to make all things uniform?"

181. See Luther's brief on a compromise in matters of churchly practices, proposed by Martin Bucer and George Witzel: Dec. 1539(?): WA.B 8:653.34. Luther dealt with the procedure for creating law in the church: "This is one of the positive features ⟨literally: 'grace'⟩ of our ⟨Augsburg⟩ Confession; it simply narrates what at one time has been going on in our churches ⟨in the sense of congregation, but also in the sense of congregations of a particular territory or city⟩, and what the situation is now; it is as if one hears a story and not a prescription or law. If ⟨the confession⟩ would have been put together before ⟨its content⟩ was practiced, who knows when and how much of it would have been practiced?" ⟨This is a reference to the *Augsburg Confession* (1530), in which some articles begin with the phrase "our churches teach with great unanimity," or a similar one; see, e.g., *BC*

27. This suggests that the text of the confession only formulates what was being taught, believed, and practiced in the congregations of the territories or cities of which the political authorities signed the confession. This indeed was the case. For the Margraviate of Brandenburg-Ansbach-Kulmbach (of which the prince, Margrave George, had signed the confession) we have a large number of 'confessions' written by the pastors of that territory; in most cases, these texts simply describe the situation in a particular congregation in terms of doctrine and practice. These statements were mailed to the government in Ansbach prior to the creation of the *Augsburg Confession*. We do not know whether they had any influence at all on the formulations of the *Augsburg Confession*, though it is doubtful.> Ibid., WA.B 8:653.45: most important are good preachers "who would diligently disseminate these main subjects <i.e., justification by faith and the celebration of the Lord's Supper by giving bread and wine to the communicants> among the people. Then the ceremonies would have to adjust themselves accordingly." Now follows a sentence to the effect that if a man stands straight, his suit also stands straight; meaning: if a man has the right faith than the externals will also be right.

182. Luther to the pastors of Lübeck: Jan. 12, 1530: WA.B 5:221.13 <LW 49:262f.>: "... we ... beg and urge you most earnestly not to deal with change[s] in the ritual, which [changes] are dangerous, but to deal with them later. You should deal first with the center of our teaching and fix in the people's minds what [they must know] about our justification; that is, that it is an extrinsic righteousness — indeed it is Christ's — given to us through faith which comes by grace to those who are first terrified by the law and who, struck by the consciousness of [their] sins, ardently seek redemption.... Adequate reform of ungodly rites will come of itself, however, as soon as the fundamental[s] of [our] teaching, having been successfully communicated, have taken root in devout hearts."

183. *Propositions against the School of Satan*, 1530: WA 30.II:421.19: "The church <in the sense of congregation but also congregations of an area> ... is the number or gathering of those who are baptized and believe, <and live> under one pastor, be he the pastor of a city, or of a province, or the whole world. That pastor or prelate <i.e., bishop> may not set up anything (because he is not the church) unless his church consents to it. The pastor of the church can admonish and persuade it to agree that for certain urgent reasons, and for a given time, the church impose upon itself fasting, festival days, prayers, or other ceremonies, and <then> change and abolish them if it wants to."

184. <I.e., the bishop of a diocese.>

185. *Matthew, Chapters 18-24 Explained in Sermons*, 1537-40: WA 47:292.26.36.

186. <Or of congregations in a particular geographic area.>

187. Luther to Duke Charles III of Savoy: Sept. 7, 1523: WA.B 3:151.66: <Man-made ecclesiastical law (traditions, decrees of the Fathers, statutes of the councils) does not have the quality of a law which before God is binding; obeying it is of no use before God for taking away sins, neglecting them does not make one guilty>; *The German Mass*, 1526: WA 19:72.4 <LW 53:61>: "... I would kindly and for God's sake request all those who see this order of service or desire to follow it: Do not make it a rigid law to bind or entangle anyone's conscience, but use it in Christian liberty as long, when, where, and how you find it practical and useful."

188. Luther to Anthony Lauterbach: Oct. 19, 1545: WA.B 11:200.11: "... we have to serve each other according to Paul's teaching, who was all things to all people.... But as soon as he realized that doing this was a matter of servitude and necessity, he did not

yield an inch to anyone"; ibid., WA.B 11:200.15: "Unity in the Spirit, which pertains to life eternal, is by far to be preferred to these temporal and indifferent matters ⟨i.e., ceremonies⟩, which end when this life ends. Because of the need or weakness of the brothers we only have to serve in them for a moment ⟨Gal. 2:5⟩, just as we have to serve parents, little children, the infirm or sick people."

189. *On the Councils and the Church*, 1539: WA 50:649.7 ⟨LW 41:173⟩: "Besides these external signs and holy possessions the church has other externals that do not sanctify it either in body or soul, nor were they instituted or commanded by God; but . . . they are outwardly necessary or useful, proper and good — for instance, certain holidays and certain hours, forenoon or afternoon, set aside for preaching or praying, or the use of a church building or house, altar, pulpit, baptismal font, candlesticks, candles, bells, priestly vestments, and the like"; ibid., WA 50:649.26 ⟨LW 41:173f.⟩: "And no one should (as no Christian does) ignore such order without cause, out of mere pride or just to create disorder, but one should join in observing such order for the sake of the multitude, or at least should not disrupt or hinder it, for that would be acting contrary to love and friendliness"; *To the Livonians*, 1525: WA 18:419.7 ⟨LW 53:47⟩: "For even though from the viewpoint of faith, the external orders are free and can without scruples be changed by anyone at any time, yet from the viewpoint of love, you are not free to use this liberty, but bound to consider the edification of the common people . . ."; ibid., WA 18:419.18 ⟨LW 53:48⟩: "Now when your people are confused and offended by your lack of uniform order, you cannot plead, 'Externals are free. Here in my own place I am going to do as I please.' But you are bound to consider the effect of your attitude on others. By faith be free in your conscience toward God, but by love be bound to serve your neighbor's edification . . ."; ibid., WA 18:419.32 ⟨LW 53:48⟩: "⟨A pastor must explain to the people that ceremonies, etc., are not binding laws, but that ceremonies are⟩ done for their own good so that the unity of Christian people may also find expression in externals which in themselves are irrelevant. Since the ceremonies or rites are not needed for the conscience or for salvation and yet are useful and necessary to govern the people externally, one must not enforce or have them accepted for any other reason except to maintain peace and unity between men. For between God and men, it is faith that procures peace and unity."

190. ⟨See above, 482 n. 159.⟩

191. *The Right and Power of a Christian Congregation*, 1523: WA 11:415.26: "⟨In the church the office of preaching⟩ is the highest office; all other offices hang on it and come after it."

192. ⟨See above, 192-96, Sections XIV through XVIII.⟩

193. *First Commentary on Galatians*, 1519: WA 2:483.23: "But you see that the other Apostolic work is to be concerned for the poor"; *Ordinance of a Common Chest*, 1523: WA 12:13.26: "⟨There is⟩ no higher service of God than Christian love, which assists and serves the needy. . . ."

194. Sermon of Dec. 2, 1537: WA 45:328.23: ". . . the kingdom of Christ cannot exist without schools and the preaching of the Word"; *On the Councils and the Church*, 1539: WA 50:628ff. ⟨LW 41:148ff.⟩.

195. *Ordinance of a Common Chest*, 1523: WA 12:11ff. ⟨LW 45:169ff.⟩.

196. *On the Councils and the Church*, 1539: WA 50:641.18: "The church cannot be without . . . bishops, pastors, preachers, priests, and conversely, they cannot be without the church; ⟨church and pastors⟩ have to be together."

197. *Concerning the Ministry,* 1523: WA 12:180.17: "The first office, ⟨that of priest,⟩ indeed the office of the Word, is common to all Christians...." See esp. Maurer, *Pfarrerrecht und Bekenntnis.*

198. *Concerning the Ministry,* 1523: WA 12:181.17: "... the ministry of the Word is the highest office in the church, indeed it is unique and held in common by all who are Christians...."

199. In order to emphasize the difference between the interpretation of the priesthood in Canon law and his own interpretation, Luther differentiated between 'a priest by birth', ⟨i.e., the rebirth through Baptism⟩, and 'a priest because of the office'; he called the latter "minister of the Word," i.e., public minister. See the sermon of June 9, 1535: WA 41:207.11ff. ⟨See 193 n. 204. below.⟩

200. *On the Councils and the Church,* 1539: WA 50:632.35, 633.1.10.

201. ⟨See above, 178.⟩

202. *The Right and Power of a Christian Congregation,* 1523: WA 11:411.31.

203. See above 178 and 473 n. 26.

204. Sermon of June 9, 1535: WA 41:205.10: "Each Christian is to be called a born priest, born not by father or mother but by Baptism and the gospel, without man's help, alone through divine work."

205. ⟨Or: "a common law of the individual Christian and at the same time of the congregation" in the sense of law by which the individual and the congregation live. See also above, 97f.⟩ *Concerning the Ministry,* 1523: WA 12:189.17 ⟨*LW* 40:34⟩: "It is of the common rights ⟨'right' (or: 'law'); Luther used the singular!⟩ of Christians that we have been speaking. For since we have proved all of these things to be the common property of all Christians, no one individual can arise by his own authority and arrogate to himself alone what belongs to all. Lay hold then of this right and exercise it, where there is no one else who has the same ⟨right⟩. But ⟨this⟩ community ⟨right (or: 'law')⟩ demand⟨s⟩ that one, or as many as the community chooses, shall be chosen or approved who, in the name of all with ⟨this right: *vice et nomine omnium, qui idem iuris habent*⟩, shall perform these functions publicly. Otherwise, there might be shameful confusion among the people of God, and a kind of Babylon in the church, where everything should be done in order, as the Apostle teaches [I Cor. 14:40]. For it is one thing to exercise a right publicly; another to use it in time of emergency. Publicly one may not exercise a right without consent of the whole body or of the church. In time of emergency each may use it as he deems best."

206. ⟨I.e., the side of the *individual* baptized believer's *right* to practice this priesthood as over against the *right of the Christian congregation.*⟩

207. ⟨I.e., a quality which cannot be destroyed.⟩ *The Babylonian Captivity of the Church,* 1520: WA 6:535.8: "Baptism never becomes invalid as long as you do not in desperation turn away from ⟨your⟩ Salvation. For a while you might stray from ⟨Baptism as a⟩ sign, but because of this, the sign itself does not become invalid. You are baptized sacramentally once, yet you have to be baptized always through faith, ⟨i.e.,⟩ you always have to die and live ⟨Rom. 6:3-14⟩."

208. Ibid., WA 6:564.16: "... the sacrament of Ordination can be nothing other than a fixed rite to elect a preacher in the church."

209. *Concerning the Ministry,* 1523: WA 12:190.24 ⟨*LW* 40:35f.⟩: "In this view of the ministry, the so-called 'indelible character' vanishes and the perpetuity of the office is shown to be fictitious. A minister may be deposed if he proves unfaithful. On the other

hand he is to be permitted in the ministry as long as he is competent and has the favor of the church as a whole, just as in civil matters any administrator is treated as an equal among his brethren. In fact a spiritual minister is more readily removable than any civil administrator, since if he is unfaithful he should be less tolerable than a civil officer. The latter can be harmful only in matters of this life, whereas the former can be destructive of eternal possessions."

210. Luther to George Spalatin: Dec. 18, 1519: WA.B 1:595.30: "... this kind of priesthood, in which we are, does not at all appear to be different from the laity except for the ministry through which the sacraments and the Word are administered."

211. Against the distinction of his opponents that the right of the Keys *(ius clavium)* belongs to the church, but the use belongs to the pope, Luther argued that "Christ gave the right and the use of the Keys to any Christian"; *Concerning the Ministry*, 1523: WA 12:184.3.

212. ⟨I.e., of clergy vs. laity.⟩ *The Babylonian Captivity of the Church*, 1520: WA 6:566.26: "Be certain ... that all of us ⟨Christians⟩ are priests in the same way. That is, we have the same authority ⟨in matters of⟩ the Word and sacrament. Yet not everyone is permitted to use this authority unless it is done with the consent of the congregation, or as the result of a call by someone who has a higher position. For no individual may appropriate for himself what belongs to all unless he is called ⟨to do so⟩. Therefore the sacrament of Ordination, if it is anything at all, is nothing other than a fixed rite of calling someone into the ecclesiastical ministry ..."; Luther to Margrave Albrecht of Brandenburg, grand master of the Teutonic Order: Dec. 1523: WA.B 3:210.42: "... in these churches there cannot be anyone who is unequal, or people who are superior in the church."

213. *Concerning the Ministry*, 1523: WA 12:183.30: "We all who are Christians hold this office of the Keys in common."

214. ⟨See above, 439 n. 283.⟩ *To the Christian Nobility*, 1520: WA 6:409.11 ⟨LW 44:130f.⟩. — The argument that in the Imperial law and the Canon law the immunity from sharing in the burdens of the community ⟨esp. taxes⟩ is granted to the clergy has no value since abuse nullifies privilege (see *Decretum Gratiani* c.63. C.XI. qu.3 ⟨Friedberg 1:660⟩). Luther to the City Council of Stettin: Jan. 11, 1523: WA.B 3:14.21 ⟨LW 49:27⟩: "It is against God, conscience, and love, as well as against reason and right, to tolerate such privileges any longer. Therefore [the clergy] is obligated to renounce their privileges so that hardship for the community be avoided. ... For it is un-Christian, even unnatural, to derive benefit and protection from the community and not also to share in the common burden and expense, to let other people work but to harvest the fruit of their labors."

215. *The Right and Power of a Christian Congregation*, 1523: WA 11:414.12: except in an emergency ⟨see ibid., lines 5ff.⟩, "no bishop may install someone ⟨as pastor⟩ without the election, will, and call of the congregation. The bishop ⟨only⟩ is to confirm the person whom the congregation has elected and called; if he does not, then the ⟨called⟩ person nevertheless is confirmed ⟨in his office⟩ through the call of the congregation ⟨itself⟩."

216. Where no congregation is available, the sacramental call suffices. This is applicable also in other emergency situations. As examples for the public implementation of the preaching office without an extra-sacramental call by a particular church, Luther mentioned the work of the deacons Stephen and Philip ⟨Acts 7, 8:5ff.⟩, of the Ethiopian court official ⟨Acts 8:38f.⟩, and of Apollos in Ephesus ⟨Acts 18:24ff.⟩; *The Right and Power*

of a Christian Congregation, 1523: WA 11:412.14ff. ⟨*LW* 39:310⟩; *Concerning the Ministry,* 1523: WA 12:191.38ff., 192.8ff. ⟨*LW* 40:37f.*.*⟩.

217. *Concerning the Ministry,* 1523: WA 12:191.6 ⟨*LW* 40:36⟩: "If the office of teaching be entrusted to anyone, then everything accomplished by the Word in the church is entrusted, that is, the office of baptizing, consecrating, binding, loosing, praying, and judging doctrine. Inasmuch as the office of preaching the gospel is the greatest of all and certainly is apostolic, it becomes the foundation for all other functions, which are built upon it, such as the offices of teachers, prophets, governing [the church], speaking ⟨in⟩ tongues, the gifts of healing and helping...."

218. ⟨*Officia sacerdotalia.*⟩

219. ⟨See above, 193.⟩

220. See the addition to Luther's letter to George Spalatin, dated May 16, 1519: WA.B 1:397.48: "Remember, you are to be a priest, or a common and public minister."

221. *The Right and Power of a Christian Congregation,* 1523: WA 11:412.32: "... instead of, and by the command of the others...." ⟨See also above, 489 n. 205.⟩

222. *The Babylonian Captivity of the Church,* 1520: WA 6:564.6: "If they ⟨i.e., Luther's opponents⟩ would be forced to admit that we all who are baptized are priests of the same standing, as we are indeed, and to them ⟨i.e., the priests according to the Canon law⟩ is entrusted only the service *(ministerium),* yet with our consent, then they would also know that they have no right of ruling *(ius imperii)* over us except to the degree that we voluntarily agree."

223. *Against Jack Sausage,* 1541: WA 51:521.30: "... the teaching must publicly ... shine to direct life accordingly."

224. Luther to Oswald Lasan(?): June(?), 1531: WA.B 6:143.12; to Barbara Lißkirchen: March 7, 1535: WA.B 7:167.4. In his letter to Wolfgang Brauer (Dec. 30, 1535: WA.B 7:338.5) Luther developed details: "⟨A housefather⟩ is not obligated ... to celebrate Holy Communion for himself and the members of his household. Also, it is unnecessary; he is not called and he does not have a command to ⟨celebrate Holy Communion in this way⟩. Even if the tyrannical servants of the church, who are obligated to serve Holy Communion to him and the members of his household, refuse to do this, he nevertheless can be saved in his faith through the Word. Further, it would create a great offense were one to celebrate the sacrament here and there in the homes; in the long run nothing good would come from it, but only dissension and sects would develop, as now people are difficult and the devil is out of his mind. In Acts ⟨2:46⟩ the first Christians did not celebrate the sacrament separately in their homes, but they gathered together to do it. And even had they ⟨celebrated Holy Communion in their homes⟩, one could now no longer accept such an example, just as it is not acceptable to have all goods in common, as they had at that time ⟨Acts 2:44⟩. Now the gospel and the sacraments are public matters. But it is right that a housefather teaches God's Word to his people, and thus it should be. For God has commanded us to teach and educate our children and the members of our household, and ⟨this teaching of⟩ the Word is commanded to everyone. But the sacrament is a public confession and is to have publicly called servants because to the sacrament is added that it be celebrated in his memory, as Christ says; i.e., St. Paul says, one is to proclaim or preach the Lord's death until he comes ⟨1 Cor. 11:26⟩. And at the same place St. Paul also says ⟨1 Cor. 11:20f.⟩ that one should come together, and he severely reprimands those who separately, each one for himself, want to celebrate the Lord's Supper. It is not prohibited,

however, but commanded to us that each ⟨housefather⟩ teach God's Word especially to the members of his household and also to himself — but no one can baptize himself, etc. For there is a difference between a public office in the church ⟨and the office⟩ a housefather has for the members of his household. Therefore ⟨both offices⟩ are not to be intermingled or separated. Since in this situation ⟨mentioned by the addressee of the letter⟩ there is no need or call, one should not do anything without God's definite command, based ⟨only⟩ on one's own devotion, for nothing good will come from it."

225. *Reply to Ambrosius Catharinus,* 1521: WA 7:722.3: ". . . only through the . . . public voice of the gospel ⟨does one know⟩ where the church is . . . ."

226. ⟨For the Lord's Supper as a public confession, see the letters cited above, 491 n. 224.⟩ — For the same reason Luther opposed the Communion of sick people in their home; Luther to Anthony Lauterbach: Nov. 26, 1539: WA.B 8:609.5: ". . . I would wish that private Communion simply be abolished everywhere; in the sermon people should be taught to commune three or four times in a year, and then, strengthened through the Word, they may fall asleep, regardless whatever the circumstances of their death might be."

227. ⟨I.e. literally, "corner-preachers." This term (in use since the middle of the 15th century) designated anyone who without proper credentials or proper procedures of appointment occupied the pastoral office in a congregation; i.e., the person 'sneaked' *(einschleichen)* into a congregation; WA 30.III:518.5. Rather than retaining the German term, it is sometimes translated with "clandestine preachers"; *LW* 40:383. This does not do full justice to *Winkelprediger*. The issue is not only that a *Winkelprediger* acts 'secretly' or 'clandestinely'; to the contrary, in his congregations he acts publicly, "infecting our people with ⟨his⟩ poison" (WA 30.III: 518.6). The congregation is also in a corner, i.e. outside of the mainstream of the church, in which a pastor is to occupy the office by way of the proper procedure of appointment; therefore the pastor "preaches in a corner" (WA 30.III:518.17), in addition to being a *Schleicher,* someone who has sneaked into the congregation without an official call (WA 30.III: 518.18). Hence the authorities have to act.⟩

228. *Psalm 101 Explained,* 1534: WA 51:258.9: ". . . God does not value the secular governance as much as his own, eternal governance of the church . . . ."

229. Luther to Philip Melanchthon: Jan. 13, 1522: WA.B 2:424.16 ⟨*LW* 48:366⟩: ". . . God has never sent anyone, not even the Son himself, unless he was called through men or attested by signs. In the old days the prophets had their authority from the Law and the prophetic order, as we now receive authority through men."

230. Luther to George von Harstall and to the Mayor and City Council of Creuzburg: Jan. 27, 1543: WA.B 10:255.18: ". . . the office of pastor, the office of preaching, and the gospel do not belong to us or anyone else, not even an angel, but only to God, our Lord . . ."; ibid., WA.B 10:257.87: "You are not the lords over the parishes and the office of preaching, you did not establish them but God's Son established them. Also, you did not add anything to them, and you have less rights over them than the devil has over the kingdom of heaven. . . ."

231. *Concerning the Ministry,* 1523: WA 12:172.10 ⟨*LW* 40:10⟩: Those "who have faith and know the truth, possess full freedom and means to drive away unworthy ministers and to call and appoint only such worthy and devout men as they choose."

232. See above, 474 n. 51, below, 493 n. 239.

233. ⟨Literally, "lord of the business."⟩

234. *On the Councils and the Church*, 1539: WA 50:633.12: "... the Holy Spirit excluded women, children, and unfit persons ..."; ibid., WA 50:633.20: "For such a difference is also present in nature and among God's creatures, ⟨namely,⟩ that women (much less children or fools) cannot and should not have a governance, as experience teaches and Moses says in Gen. 3⟨:16⟩: 'You shall be subject to the man.' The gospel, however, does not do away with such natural law but confirms it as God's order and creatures."

235. Luther and others to John Lang, Peter Geltner, and the other pastors in Erfurt: Sept. 30, 1533: WA.B 6:522.14: "... your call has been ... issued with the knowledge of the magistrate, the councilors, and the trustees; they ratified it and promised to respect it ..."; ibid., WA.B 6:522.22: "Your call ... has been issued publicly, without reservation, and not secretly."

236. Luther to Frederick Myconius: Oct. 20, 1535: WA.B 7:302.3: "We are sending back your John, who has been called and elected by your people. He also has been examined by us; in public, before our congregation, with prayer and praise of God, he has been ordained and confirmed as your fellow minister, according to the order of our prince. It was not easy to have Dr. Bugenhagen ⟨i.e., the city pastor⟩ do this; he still thinks that one should be ordained in one's own congregation by one's pastors. This will finally happen when this new way of doing things and the Ordination have been solidly grounded and have become a firmer custom."

237. Luther to John Sutel: March 1, 1531: WA.B 6:44.18: "... publicly before the altar, with prayer and the laying on of hands by the other ministers receive the testimony ⟨of your call⟩ and the authority to celebrate the Lord's Supper."

238. *Concerning the Ministry*, 1523: WA 12:173.2 ⟨*LW* 40:11⟩: "The public ministry of the Word, I hold, by which the mysteries of God are made known, ought to be established by holy ordination as the highest and greatest of the functions of the church, on which the whole power *(vis)* of the church depends. . . ."

239. Luther to Nicholas von Amsdorf: Febr. 3(?), 1542: WA.B 9:610.47: "The church must ⟨exist⟩ in the world, but it can ⟨exist⟩ only in a mask *(larva)*. . . ."

240. ⟨See above, 104, 187.⟩

241. *On the Councils and the Church*, 1539: WA 50:559.31: "⟨The Council of Nicaea⟩ primarily dealt with the article that Christ is true God. . . . In addition, the council fathers dealt with some accidental, corporeal, external, temporal matters; it is correct to consider them to be secular, in no way comparable with the articles of faith, and not to be considered eternal law"; ibid., WA 50:579.28: "... to depose bishops is not an article of faith but an external ... work, which reason can and should do, and for which one does not need the Holy Spirit in a special way (as is the case in the articles of faith)"; see also ibid., WA 50:560.5. — For the different meanings of 'secular', see Lau, "*Äußerliche Ordnung.*" ⟨See also above, 152f.⟩

242. ⟨See above, 104, 187.⟩

243. Luther to Margrave Albrecht of Brandenburg, grand master of the Teutonic Order: Dec. 1523: WA.B 3:211.95: "What is one to do with the commandments of the pope? Answer: They are to be placed outside of the church, just as certain other things"; to John Heß: Apr. 22, 1526: WA.B 4:61.2: "... until now one has fought about secular matters, which are outside of Scripture, such as the pope, purgatory, and other trifles; but now one has come to the real battle about matters within Scripture."

244. ⟨I.e., the corporeal church.⟩

245. *On the Councils and the Church,* 1539: WA 50:553.16: "... to order such external matters, God-given reason suffices so that the Holy Spirit is not needed; he is to explain Christ and not deal with such matters which are subject to reason." See also ibid., WA 50:580.13, 583.24, 606.3.

246. Sermon of June 1, 1539: WA 47:778.40: "Whoever wishes ... to teach man-made rules, may do so in the secular governance and the domestic governance; he should not bother God's church with his man-made rules."

247. *Commentary on 1 Corinthians, Chapter 7,* 1523: WA 12:106.5: "... external works and matters ⟨are not spiritual, but⟩ faith in the heart ... is spirit and makes all things of man spiritual, both the external and the internal things"; *On the Councils and the Church,* 1539: WA 50:649.34: "... such matters ⟨i.e., a church ordinance⟩ are totally external and reason is to rule them powerfully and totally (as the circumstances of time, place, and people demand). God, Christ, and the Holy Spirit are not concerend with ⟨such matters⟩. . . ."

248. *On the Councils and the Church,* 1539: WA 50:619.21: "... ⟨ceremonies⟩ only serve the external discipline and order; they may be changed at any moment, and they are not to be considered eternal laws ... , commanded in the church and written down with tyrannical threats. For they are totally external matters, corporeal, transitory, changeable"; see also ibid., WA 50:557.22, 627.37, 649.8.

249. Rudolf Smend ("Wissenschafts- und Gestaltsprobleme im evangelischen Kirchenrecht," *ZevKR* 6 [1957/58]: 231) has called such matters "half secular."

250. See above, 151ff.

251. See above, 153, 164f.

252. Luther and others to Leonard Beyer: July 24, 1536: WA.B 7:477.1: "... our gospel and teaching insist that one differentiate between the two governances, the secular and the spiritual, and definitely not intermingle one with the other if not a real emergency or the absence of ⟨qualified⟩ persons would force one to do this. If persons are present, who rule city hall and city, and also persons who take care of the pastoral office and the church, no one is to interfere in the office of the other or usurp it, ... as St. Peter teaches ⟨1 Pet. 4:15⟩ that we are not to be people who strive for the office that belongs to someone else. ⟨The text reads *allotrioepiskopoi* (composite of *allotrios* and *episkopos*), a word which we find in the New Testament only in 1 Pet. 4:15. An English translation of the text of 1 Pet. 4:15 in Luther's 1522 September Testament would read: "(someone) searching for (or: 'eager for') alien goods." In the Vulgate the passage reads: "alienorum appetitor," i.e., someone who has an appetite for what belongs to other people. An English translation of the text in the final version of the Bible (1545), which Luther supervised, would read: "(someone) who interferes in an alien office," i.e., an office which is not entrusted to him; a marginal note explains the text in the sense that Luther used it in the present letter. In light of *episkopos* (supervisor, bishop) it would seem that the text of the NRSV, "mischief maker," does not do justice to the Greek text. The text of the New English Bible, "infringing the rights of others," is more to the point. See also *TDNT* 2:620ff.⟩ From the beginning Christ has separated these two offices, and experience provides much evidence that there cannot be peace where the council or the city wants to rule the parish, or the pastor wants to rule the council and the city, as the example of the papacy teaches us very well."

253. See above, 35, 170f., and esp. Grundmann, *Der Lutherische Weltbund,* 36.

254. See above, 107ff., 156ff.

255. <E.g., for its building, a congregation has to comply with the building codes of the secular community. Or, a congregation, or the church at large, has to manage its finances according to the standards of public accounting and accountability. The situation becomes critical in connection with the assumed, or claimed, or granted, or not granted 'sanctuary' quality of houses of worship, or when members of the church themselves violate the law of the church as a publicly incorporated and therefore by public law recognized and secured corporation.>

256. For a Christian's right of resistance if a governmental authority violates the secular natural law, see above, 107ff.

257. <Literally: "the congregation.">

258. See above, 474 n. 51, 492 n. 239.

259. <See above, the second paragraph of Section XIX, though the issue is not phrased as a question. The issue is picked up as a question in the second paragraph of Section XX ("... what is the situation regarding...") and dealt with: May one consider the man-made ecclesiastical law outside the matters dealing with the Power of the Keys to be 'secular', and if so, in what sense? That law is not 'spiritual' but 'secular' (i.e., it is different from the medieval, supposedly 'spiritual' Canon law). 'Secular' does not mean, however, that the secular governmental authority has the competency for creating and implementing this non-spiritual, secular law — only the believers have that competency; Section XX, last paragraph, Section XXI, and the last paragraph of the present section.>

260. See Theodor Heckel, *Kirche, Wahrheit, Recht* (Munich, 1961), 118ff.; id., "Reform des Kirchenrechts und die Reformen der Kirche," in *Johannes Heckel Festschrift*, 256ff.

261. See above, 189f.

262. See above, 43ff.

263. See above, 54ff.

264. <See below, Index of Subjects: *Law*, s.v. "law, of wrath.">

265. See above, 196f., 494 n. 245.

266. Therefore Luther did not list the creation of a church ordinance among the priestly duties; see above, 491 n. 217.

267. <Than that dealing with the governances.>

268. See above, 148ff.

269. See Bornkamm, "Bindung und Freiheit in der Ordnung der Kirche," in id., *Das Jahrhundert der Reformation*, 195.

270. <See above, 161f., 466 n. 100.>

271. *On the Councils and the Church*, 1539: WA 50:625.5.16.32.

272. <Heckel used "angefochten," the verb derived from *Anfechtung*; see above, 248 n. 55.>

273. See Johannes Heckel, "Decretum Gratiani," *StGra* 3 (1955): 485ff.

274. *The Babylonian Captivity of the Church*, 1520: WA 6:536.15: "... today ecclesiastical goods <e.g., land and tenancies> are the same as spiritual goods...."

275. *On the Keys*, 1530: WA 30.II:488.3; brief by Luther, Melanchthon (the author of the text), and others: Jan. 18, 1540: WA.B 9:30.399: "Paul makes sufficiently clear that the papal governance in the church is the governance of Antichrist. Therefore one cannot consent to <the pope's> sovereignty over the churches, which he has appropriated to himself; he wishes to possess that sovereignty by divine law, to have authority over the

churches for making laws . . . . This contradicts many articles of the gospel's teaching, which we confess. Therefore one cannot consent that he has this authority. In addition, one also is not to consent to his pretense that he is lord over all kings, that he could set up and depose kings, and that he brags to have received such a commandment from Christ, as is often cited in Canon law and in the histories"; *Against the Roman Papacy*, 1545: WA 54:245.25: "⟨The Roman church⟩ separates itself from universal Christendom . . . and invents for itself a carnal, secular . . . governmental authority over all of Christendom."

276. *Reply to Ambrosius Catharinus*, 1521: WA 7:732.25: "How great is . . . the sea of the laws about dignitaries, prelacies, benefices, legal cases, courts, privileges, immunities, and ⟨similar⟩ things which have to do with the church not more than Belial has to do with Christ"; ibid., WA 7:733.3: ". . . laws, statutes, manners, usages, dispensations, irregularities, and countless abominations of this kind — one is nauseated to mention them — rule ⟨the pope's⟩ kingdom."

277. Luther and Karlstadt to Duke Frederick, elector of Saxony: Aug. 18, 1519: WA.B 1:471.200: ". . . the Roman church is not above the other churches, but all churches are equal."

278. Erich Ruppel's impressive collection of objections to the position presented in *Lex charitatis* ("Fragen des kirchlichen Disziplinarwesens im Lichte der Zwei-Reiche-Lehre," in *Smend Festgabe*, 349ff.) demonstrates the difficulties which praxis and scholarship still have today. See also Hans Liermann, "Die gegenwärtige Lage der Wissenschaft vom evangelischen Kirchenrecht," *ZevKR* 8 (1962): 290ff.

279. Luther to Caspar Zeuner: Feb. 9, 1543: WA.B 10:259.7: ". . . when we start to make all things alike, then these things will become everywhere articles of faith and chains ⟨for consciences⟩, as has happened under the papacy; but it will be a very good remedy against this evil ⟨i.e., the development of new articles of faith and chains for consciences⟩ if things are not alike. ⟨For the translation, see WA.B 10:260 n. 5: "Apparently the text is doubtful."⟩ ⟨Even⟩ under the papacy it did quite some good that one thought that one church does not have to be like the ⟨Roman church so that⟩ church without any qualms of conscience followed its own rites. For if likeness and consensus in the most important and central things, i.e., doctrine, are preserved, it will be easy to reach a consensus on the difference in the external ceremonies; this would be the same as when head and body are equally healthy so that the difference in the works done by different members ⟨of the body⟩ does not create discord in the body, but rather creates a beautiful harmony of different voices, as in music."

280. ⟨See above, 31, 86, 97f., 247 n. 53, 285n. 46.⟩

281. Luther to William Pravest: March 14, 1528: WA.B 4:411.7: "Certainly, I condemn only those ceremonies which are contrary to the gospel; all the others I preserve unchanged in our church"; ibid., WA.B 4:412.15: "In summary: I hate no one more than those who put away the free and harmless ceremonies, and make out of freedom necessity."

282. See above, n. 276.

283. Luther to Duke John Frederick of Saxony: March 18, 1522: WA.B 2:477.14: ". . . one should follow love and adjust oneself to the congregation ⟨in connection with the question whether the Lord's Supper is to be received with bread and wine⟩, . . . until it has learned the freedom" ⟨which those have who have progressed in the faith⟩; to George Spalatin: Jan. 14, 1523: WA.B 3:16.7; to Justus Jonas and the All Saints Chapter in Wittenberg: March 1, 1523: WA.B 3:35.23.

284. If a public rite is ungodly, tolerance is at the end; Luther to the members of the All Saints Chapter in Wittenberg: Aug. 19, 1523: WA.B 3:131.24: "... it is one thing to tolerate those who are weak in neutral matters, but in matters which are openly ungodly it is ungodly to be tolerant ..."; ibid., WA.B 3:132.69: "... an open, ⟨ungodly⟩ and public religious practice may not be tolerated because of the offense it gives to those who are ignorant and weak ...." — For Luther's battle with the enthusiasts, see instead of other authors, Steck, *Luther und die Schwärmer*.

285. ⟨See above, 197f.⟩

286. See Sohm, *Kirchenrecht*, 1:623ff.

287. Sermons of 1540: WA 49:227.31: "The emperor and the Imperial Chamber Court intrude ⟨into the situation⟩, and they want to decide who is a heretic on the basis of ⟨Roman⟩ law and Canon law."

288. Luther and others to Duke John Frederick, elector of Saxony: Oct. 23, 1539: WA.B 8:573.45 ⟨LW 50:200; criticism of Henry VIII's Reformation policies⟩: "... the devil begins to use a new ruse: since the papal power has to fall, the devil now urges the great kings to use religion as it is opportune for them, for their profit and advantage"; ibid., WA.B 8:574.89 ⟨LW 50:202⟩: "Among tyrants he ⟨i.e., Bishop Stephen Gardiner with the consent of Henry VIII⟩ is the greatest." — Luther was very much vexed by the attempts of mayors and city councils to establish the governance of the city council over the church. E.g., in Zwickau and Joachimsthal ⟨today: Jáchymov in the Czech Republic⟩ they called and dismissed pastoral assistants without the consent of the competent pastor; or, e.g., in Torgau, they arbitrarily summoned pastors to appear in city hall. See Luther to the Mayor and City Council of Zwickau: March 4, 1531: WA.B 6:46.5; to the pastor of Joachimsthal, Sebastian Steude: Aug. 24, 1541: WA.B 9:501.7; to the pastor of Torgau, Gabriel Zwilling: Sept. 30, 1535: WA.B 7:280.3.

289. See Johannes Heckel, *Initia iuris*, 42 n. 172.

290. ⟨See above, 31, 86, 97f., 247 n. 53, 285 n. 46.⟩

291. Brief by Luther and others, sent to Duke John Frederick, elector of Saxony: July 1, 1539: WA.B 8:472.98: "The Private Mass, the prohibition to give both bread and wine to the communicants, celibacy, monastic life, calling on saints, lack of knowledge of the faith ⟨or: 'not knowing the Creed'⟩, wrong ideas about penance, about satisfaction, indulgence, serving ⟨or: 'worshipping'⟩ God through works without God's Word, and many other manifest errors are contrary to the holy gospel which, from the beginning of the true church, God has revealed through his Son; therefore by God's command we are forced to censure such errors, cast them away, and change the practice...."

292. *Disputation of John Macchabäus Scotus*, 1542: WA 39.II:167.8: "The church has always existed, even if invisibly. But where remained the external marks ⟨of the church⟩? In the church of the papists true Scripture remained and has been preserved through God's miraculous plan. ⟨Also,⟩ preserved through a divine miracle, Baptism, the sacrament of the altar, and absolution remained ⟨there⟩...." — The Roman church remained for Luther a holy church in spite of the faults which he found in it; *Second Lectures on Galatians*, 1531: WA 40.I:68.9, as above, 393 n. 58. See also Aulén, "Einheit der Kirche," in *Ein Buch von der Kirche*, 472ff.

293. Luther to Count Albrecht of Mansfeld: May 3, 1521: WA.B 2:324.107: "... authority and obedience end where there is false doctrine."

294. *On the Councils and the Church*, 1539: WA 50:512.25, 514.8 ⟨LW 41:12, 13f.; in or-

der to demonstrate what a true secession from the church is, Luther argued that the pope and his followers are the ones who secede from the church, or "put themselves out of the church"⟩.

295. ⟨And probably the minority. For *pars sanior* and *pars major* and their relationship with each other, see Ferdinand Elsener, *Studien zur Rezeption des gelehrten Rechts,* ed. by Friedrich Ebel et al. (Sigmaringen, 1989), 17ff.⟩

296. *The Private Mass and the Consecration of Priests,* 1533: WA 38:251.27: "Until Judgment Day it is impossible that we or holy church corporeally separate or isolate ourselves from the abomination, the papacy or the Antichrist...."

297. *Against Jack Sausage,* 1541: WA 51:487.18: "Thus we have now proved that we are the true, old church, one body and congregation of saints with the whole, holy Christian church"; ibid., WA 51:479.26: "... catholic, i.e., the whole Christian church...."

298. See Ernst Wolf, *Peregrinatio,* 1:162.

299. Luther to Count John Henry of Schwarzburg: Dec. 12, 1522: WA.B 2:627.20: "... it is absolutely right to chase the wolf out of the sheep pen, never mind what this does to his belly"; *The Right and Power of a Christian Congregation,* 1523: WA 11:411.20: "... it is divine law and demanded by the Salvation of the souls to dismiss or avoid such bishops, abbots, monasteries and ⟨their⟩ governance" ⟨i.e., line 18: people of whom it is "manifest that they teach and rule contrary to God and his Word"⟩.

300. See Luther's brief on the election of an evangelical bishop for Naumburg: Jan. 19, 1542: WA.B 9:597.7: "... this is God's order and commandment, and obedience to it supersedes all other duties: One has to flee from idolatrous teachers, and the church has to depose them, as Paul clearly states: 'If anyone proclaims to you another gospel, let that one be accursed ⟨Gal. 1:9⟩.'... the old canons have the same meaning, and in this matter the custom of the early church was for the church itself to depose a heretical bishop; this was the case in Antioch, where Paul of Samosata was deposed" ⟨see *WDCH,* s.v. "Paul of Samosata"⟩; ibid., WA.B 9:598.43: "One might object: So be it, one should avoid false teachers and depose them, etc., but one may not withhold secular obedience and fiefs, etc., from bishops or members of collegiate chapters. Answer: It is certain that the property of a parish ... should and must be used for service, as the Gospel ⟨Luke 10:7⟩ says: 'The laborer deserves to be paid.' These properties were not given ⟨to the church⟩ for the pomp and idleness of the members of a collegiate chapter, but they were given to meet the needs connected with the maintenance of the ecclesiastical offices, as the codex commands in clear words: 'Who does not meet the duties of his office, is not to use his benefice, and is to be deposed.'" ⟨According to WA.B 12:328 n. 55, "codex" refers probably to *Decretum Gratiani,* Friedberg 1:316f.⟩

301. Luther to Duke John, elector of Saxony: July 20, 1525: WA.B 3:546.30: "Who does not want to preach the gospel should not feed himself from preaching the gospel"; *Exhortation to All Clergy Assembled at Augsburg,* 1530: WA 30.II:316.6: "⟨This is the rule:⟩ The benefice because of the office, not the benefice because of wickedness."

302. See above, 488 n. 193.

303. *To the Councilmen of All Cities in Germany That They Establish and Maintain Christian Schools,* 1524: WA 15:27ff.⟨LW 45:347ff.⟩.

304. Brief by Luther and others on the draft of a church ordinance for the Margraviate of Brandenburg-Ansbach-Kulmbach and the City of Nuremberg: Aug. 1, 1532: WA.B 6:340.36 ⟨LW 50:64f.⟩: "At present we have instituted no other ban than that

those who live in public sins and do not desist are not admitted to the sacrament of Christ's body and blood. This can be accomplished because no one among us receives the holy sacrament unless he has first been examined by the pastor or deacon. Further, we do not see how at this time another ban could be introduced, for many matters occur for which a preliminary investigation would be necessary. We are unable to see how at this time such a procedure of investigation could be instituted and organized, since secular government does not wish to be bothered with such an investigation. Therefore we are content to withhold the holy sacrament from those who live and remain in public sins, even though the world is now so crude and beastly as to be in no hurry at all for the sacrament and church, so that this exclusion from the Lord's Supper might not be considered to be a punishment. If someone excommunicates himself in this way, be content; when even secular authority is ready to permit the existence of public vices [what are we to do?] Nevertheless, in their sermons the preachers ought to censure such pagan ways and behavior by reciting the divine threats in all seriousness; at the same time they ought to admonish the authorities to check such pagan ways. If discipline would again be restored by instituting examination prior to communion, as certainly would be very useful and good, then one could more easily come to the point where one could institute a system of ecclesiastical discipline which would hold parents responsible for urging their children and members of their household to go to the sacrament and to church, [and] for preventing the young people from falling into such pagan contempt of the sacraments and of all divine matters. If the public ban is also instituted, then, of course, the secular authority has to enforce an order for ostracizing the person who has been banned, if the public ban is to do any good at all; at the present this might cause many wrongs, especially in the large cities and territories. But our type of ban, by which someone is excluded in private from the sacrament, has no impact on citizenship and business dealing. In spite of this action, a Christian may work and have other civic dealings with the person who is banned, as one would have dealings with a pagan, but in such a way that he makes clear to the one who is banned and to others that he does not approve of, nor is pleased with, the ungodly and censurable teachings and actions [which caused the ban]."

See also Luther to Tilemann Schnabel and the other pastors of Hesse assembled at Homberg: June 26, 1533: WA.B 6:497.5: "With great joy I have become acquainted with your zeal for Christ and Christian discipline. But in these turbulent times, which are not yet sufficiently suitable for accepting discipline, I would not dare to advise accepting such a sudden innovation. One has to let the peasants first be a bit on a rampage, and a wagon full of hay should move aside for a drunk. Things will work out by themselves for we will not be able to push them ahead through laws. It is an important matter, not by itself but because of the persons involved who have the power to stir up troubles for us; ⟨at this point,⟩ these troubles cannot be calmed down since we are ⟨only⟩ a root in dry ground ⟨Isa. 53:2⟩ and have not yet grown into branches and leaves. In the meantime I would advise to begin slowly and in small pieces, as we are doing here. First, we keep those who seem to deserve excommunication away from the sacrament of the Eucharist; this is the true excommunication, which is called the small ban. Then we do not permit such people to be god-parents at Baptisms. Under no circumstances may we claim to practice the excommunication which prohibits secular dealings ⟨i.e., the large ban⟩; first, because it is outside of our law and it ⟨could⟩ deal with those who ⟨may⟩ want to be true Christians; second, because in this age the ⟨large ban⟩ cannot even become a part of our ⟨competency⟩, and we would look ridiculous were we to try handling what is now beyond our abilities. You seem to hope that the prince himself might implement such a ban, but that is quite uncertain; ⟨and further,⟩ I do not want the political magistrate mixed ⟨into this task⟩; in all aspects he should be separated from it so that the differentiation between both magistrates is fixed truly and certainly."

305. For the connection of excommunication with love, see Luther to Wolfgang Capito: Jan. 17, 1522: WA.B 2:432.59 ⟨LW 48:376⟩: "There is, however, no grace, no love, no kindness for those who condemn or despise doctrine itself and the ministry of the Word, or persecute it cunningly — or rather, it is the highest kind of love to resist their fury and ungodliness with all strength and in every possible way."

306. Luther and Bugenhagen to Cyriakus Gericke: Jan. 14, 1542: WA.B 9:594.4: "This is the custom in our congregation: Once a person who in his life stubbornly despised to commune with us has died, we have no fellowship ⟨literally: 'commune'⟩ with him; i.e., we let him be buried by whoever will bury him and in whatever way, outside or inside the cemetery. But we ⟨i.e., the pastors⟩ shall not follow ⟨the casket⟩ with ⟨our⟩ pupils, and we shall not sing ⟨at his grave⟩; those who bury him may cry, according to the statement: 'Let the dead bury the dead' ⟨Luke 9:60⟩." See also WA.TR 2:No. 1735: let those who do not partake of the Lord's Supper and learn the *Catechism* die "like the swine"; they should not be buried in the *Kirchhof* ⟨i.e., the area around a church, which sometimes is used for burials⟩; WA.TR 4:No. 5174: when those who do not partake of the Lord's Supper die, they should be buried "in the knackery."

307. Luther to Gregory Brück, chancellor of Electoral Saxony: Apr. 25, 1524: WA.B 3:274.3.12. — For the use of properties of monasteries and religious institutions which have been dissolved, see Luther's brief of the beginning of 1531: WA.B 6:6.55; Luther and others to the councilors of the dukes of Pomerania: May 30, 1544: WA.B 10:589.97: ". . . it is not right that these properties which ⟨were given⟩ for . . . the use by the churches, as, ⟨e.g.,⟩ for the episcopal office, for a visitation, for courts, etc., are confiscated ⟨by secular authorities⟩ so that the needs of the church are ignored. In this matter they sin who act ⟨or⟩ who help with word or action for, as everyone knows, it is unjust to covet the goods of someone else and withhold them from the community or a private person"; Luther to the City Council of Kiel: July 7, 1544: WA.B 10:603.4: "It is true, we theologians have taught until now, and still do, that the properties of dissolved monasteries are to be invested for the use by churches and the poor . . ." for this is right and godly . . ."; to the City Council of Herford: Oct. 24, 1534: WA.B 7:113.10ff.; *Against Jack Sausage*, 1541: WA 51:525.25: "⟨The church has been endowed with properties for⟩ maintaining . . . churches and schools, i.e., God's holy Word, the office of preaching and other services in the church, theologians, pastors, preachers, and, in addition, also the poor, widows, orphans, and the sick"; ibid., WA 51:526.22: "⟨The pope's followers argue unjustly that⟩ the properties of the church belong to them, ⟨and, therefore, they⟩ demand that we restore ⟨these properties to them⟩". — For the duty of Christians to maintain preachers, see *Against the Roman Papacy*, 1545: WA 54:280.19.

308. Luther to Wenceslas Link: Feb. 7, 1525: WA.B 3:437.18: ". . . it would be excellent and proper if in a city one ⟨pastor⟩ were the bishop, and the others the pastors . . ."; to George Spalatin: Jan. 12, 1541: WA.B 9:306.7: ". . . here in Wittenberg one has begun to organize a consistory. Yet once completed, it will not affect the visitors ⟨of the congregations in the territory⟩. Rather, ⟨it will deal⟩ with marriage matters (with which we here

⟨i.e., the theologians of the university⟩ are no longer able or willing to deal), and it will force the peasants to abide by a certain order of discipline and pay an income to the pastors; perhaps by necessity this will also touch the nobility and magistrates here and there." — See also Peter Brunner, *Vom Amt des Bischofs* (Witten, 1955), 55ff., and id., *Nikolaus von Amsdorf als Bischof von Naumburg* (Gütersloh, 1961), 56ff., 95ff. — Luther and Melanchthon affirmed that a particular church by law should have the office of bishop or superintendent. Sermon of June 5, 1535: WA 41:186.13: "A priest is to be an intercessor, sacrificer, and teacher. It is the highest honor to be a priest, higher than the honor of being a king or prince. To be a bishop is not such a glorious matter as the common people think; he is ⟨only⟩ a watchman or shepherd, as one has called him in prior times. ⟨Then⟩ the large congregations had an overseer. He was to have a superior position among the other priests so that one comes to him and consults with him; this is the case here with our pastor ⟨i.e., John Bugenhagen⟩, who is a bishop." ⟨The text does not make clear who the "one" is who comes to the bishop; maybe it is the priest, mentioned at the beginning of the text. But one could also think of people who want to consult with the bishop about their pastor.⟩ — For the tasks of a bishop, see Luther, Melanchthon (the author of the letter), and others to the dukes of Pomerania: May 14, 1544: WA.B 10:568. 33: ". . . it is true and obvious that, as an overseer, a bishop has to spread the pure Christian doctrine of the gospel and himself teach it, . . . also, he has to visit the churches, ordain qualified persons, supervise the studies, preside over the marriage courts and other ecclesiastical courts, and implement Christian discipline, tasks for which the dioceses have been established ⟨or: 'endowed'⟩ in the first place. . . ."

309. Luther to Lazarus Spengler: Aug. 15, 1528: WA.B 4:534.8 ⟨*LW* 49:205f.⟩: "First of all, it is proper and prudent not to compel anyone to come to or abstain from the ⟨Lord's Supper⟩, or to appoint particular times and places for it, thus trapping the consciences. Since St. Paul teaches, however, [in] I Corinthians 14[:40, that] among Christians all things should be done in an orderly fashion, it seems good to me that the Provosts ⟨i.e., the chief pastors of the two city churches in Nuremberg⟩ and ministers should get together and decide on a common and free procedure for this matter. The honorable city council should then see to it that this procedure is used, and thus preserve unity and uniformity."

310. A church ordinance should not be imposed upon congregations, either by a council of the evangelical party or a command of a territorial lord. See Luther to Nicholas Hausmann: Nov. 17, 1524: WA.B 3:373.16 ⟨*LW* 49:90f.⟩: "I do not consider it sufficiently safe to call a council of our party for establishing unity in the ceremonies. It would set a bad example, however praiseworthy the zeal with which it might be attempted, as all the councils of the church prove from the beginning. Even the Council of the Apostles ⟨Acts 15:1ff.⟩ dealt almost more with works and traditions than with faith. In the later councils, in fact, there was never any discussion of faith, but only of opinions and questions. As a result, the word 'council' is almost as suspect and distasteful to me as the term 'free will'. If in these external matters one congregation does not voluntarily want to follow another, why should it be compelled to do so by decrees of councils, which are soon converted into laws and snares for souls? Of its own accord a congregation should, therefore, follow another one, or else be allowed to enjoy its own customs; only the unity of the Spirit should be preserved in faith and in the Word, however great may be the diversity and variety in respect to the flesh and the elements of the world." See also Luther's Jan. 7, 1527, letter to

Landgrave Philip of Hesse (WA.B 4:157, as above, 485 n. 179), in which Luther advised not to publish a church ordinance.

311. ⟨In the sense of congregations *and* also of all congregations in a particular territory with those in another territory.⟩

312. Luther had no delusions about the possibility of arriving at a universally accepted evangelical ecclesiastical law; Luther to Gregory Brück, chancellor of Electoral Saxony: Jan. 6, 1543: WA.B 10:237.27: "I have no hope that we might more and more become one in the use of uniform ceremonies in all churches, as it also was impossible under the papacy. Even if in our territory we do things in a certain way, others will not follow us and do not want us to be their masters, as we clearly see. Even the Apostles experienced this with the ceremonies of Moses; they had to leave it a matter of choice, how people wanted to eat, dress, ⟨or⟩ handle themselves. More about this matter once I have arrived at a decision."

313. Luther did not strive for uniformity in the order of worship used in all evangelical congregations, but he hoped that uniformity might be accomplished within a lordship; *The German Mass*, 1526: WA 19:73.3.6 ⟨*LW* 53:62⟩: ". . . I do not propose that all of Germany should uniformly follow our Wittenberg order. . . . But it would be well if the service in every principality would be held in the same manner and if the order observed in a given city would also be followed by the surrounding towns and villages; whether those in other principalities hold the same order or add to it ought to be a matter of free choice and not of constraint."

314. ⟨See above, 184; see also above, 85, below, Index of Subjects: *Law*, s.v. "law, of Christ, is the authentic interpretation of the divine meaning of the divine natural law."⟩

315. *The Right and Power of a Christian Congregation,* 1523: WA 11:409.21: ". . . ⟨Christ⟩ gives the right and power to judge doctrine to each individual and all Christians together. . . ."

Notes to Appendix V

1. ⟨See also above, 471 n. 8.⟩
2. ⟨For the following, see also above, 148f.⟩
3. ⟨Literally: "power of the prince."⟩
4. ⟨I.e., the position of power.⟩
5. ⟨Or families.⟩
6. ⟨I.e., the use of power.⟩
7. ⟨See above, 463 n. 27.⟩
8. ⟨The unrighteous to be made righteous.⟩
9. ⟨The unrighteous not to be made righteous.⟩
10. ⟨Heckel used "angefochten"; see above, 495 n. 272.⟩
11. ⟨In the sense of command *and* institution.⟩
12. ⟨I.e., the sum of those who are subject to power, the royal people of believers, or the Babylonian body of the devil; see above, (1.*b*) and *(c)*.⟩
13. ⟨See above, 53.⟩
14. ⟨I.e., the community of the baptized.⟩
15. ⟨See also above, 118-27.⟩

16. ⟨See below, Index of Subjects: *Law,* s.v. "law, of wrath."⟩

17. ⟨*Geistliches Bettelwerk;* see above, 60, 69.⟩

18. ⟨To feed (or shepherd) with the Word.⟩

19. ⟨See above, 98.⟩

20. ⟨See above, 247 n. 170, 335 n. 305.⟩

21. ⟨*Staatskirchenrecht*.⟩

22. ⟨See above, 31, 86, 97f., 247 n. 53, 285 n. 46.⟩

23. ⟨Of belonging together and of being in tension.⟩

24. ⟨See above, 161f., 466 n. 100.⟩

25. ⟨I.e., Baptism.⟩

26. ⟨E.g., receiving the Lord's Supper or being a god-parent.⟩

27. ⟨See above, 98.⟩

28. ⟨Be it that of the state (which creates and implements law in the church), or of someone in the church (who claims to have such an authority).⟩

29. ⟨E.g., because that command does not deal with a specific issue, or because it is not a legitimate command, or because for whatever reasons it is not enforced.⟩

30. ⟨If "governmental authority" designates someone in the church, and if his command is "at an end" (n. 29), then the Christian brotherly love (which is the basis for the Christian's obligation of obedience to man-made ecclesiastical law) demands that a Christian act in the realm of the church in order to enforce that obedience to Christian brotherly love at all cost; Luther's conduct in connection with the indulgence traffic could illustrate this situation. If "governmental authority" designates a secular authority, and if its command is "at an end," then Christian brotherly love demands that the Christian extend his action beyond the ecclesiastical commonwealth and be active in the secular commonwealth in order to enforce the obedience to the commandment of Christian brotherly love at all cost.⟩

31. ⟨See above, 502 n. 10.⟩

32. ⟨I.e., not only externally by way of the connection with the domestic governance.⟩

33. ⟨I.e., a believing Christian is at the same time a sinner and a righteous person. See above, 255 n. 24, below, Index of Subjects, s.v. "man, reborn, is afflicted with Original Sin."⟩

34. ⟨See also above, 107-9.⟩

35. ⟨See also above, 116-18.⟩

36. ⟨See above, 248 n. 55.⟩

37. ⟨See above, 399 n. 90.⟩

38. ⟨Or hierarchies; see also above, 266 n. 8.⟩

39. ⟨See *WDCH,* s.v. "Marsilius of Padua," and Johannes Heckel, "Marsilius von Padua und Martin Luther. Ein Vergleich ihrer Rechts- und Soziallehre," *ZSRG*.K 44 (1958): 268ff.⟩

40. Christoph E. Luthardt, *Die Ethik Luthers in ihren Grundzügen* (2d. ed., enlarged. Leipzig, 1875).

41. Törnvall, *Geistliches und weltliches Regiment bei Luther.*

42. ⟨See above, 13f., 126.⟩

Notes to Appendix VI

1. ⟨According to Martin Heckel, since the days of the founding of *ZSRG*.K by Ulrich Stutz an opportunity is available for authors to announce their works in that journal.⟩
2. *ZSRG*.K 26 (1937): 285ff.
3. ⟨WA 1:233ff., or *LW* 31:25ff.⟩
4. ⟨WA vols. 3 and 4, or *LW* vols. 10 and 11.⟩
5. ⟨See above, 358 n. 10.⟩
6. ⟨Or the lecturer on the Psalms.⟩
7. See, e.g., Karl Holl's article, which in its time was an excellent study, "Die Entstehung von Luthers Kirchenbegriff," in Holl, *Luther,* 288ff.
8. ⟨I.e., *Lex charitatis.*⟩
9. ⟨WA 4:81.13; see also *LW* 11:229.⟩
10. ⟨WA vols. 56 and 57.I, or *LW* vol. 25.⟩
11. ⟨"God's will is (or: 'as') law."⟩
12. ⟨I.e., Purgatory.⟩
13. ⟨I.e., the basis for the God-imposed punishments just mentioned.⟩
14. ⟨To cancel punishments set up in this divine law.⟩
15. ⟨I.e., the sinner under God's judgment.⟩
16. ⟨I.e., in connection with the controversy on indulgences; see Johannes Heckel, *Initia iuris,* 23.⟩
17. ⟨I.e., it was not only a spiritual concept, but it was also the basis of the *iurisdictio externa* of the church; hence the questions at the end of Section I.⟩
18. ⟨As they had been in the Middle Ages; see above, 217.⟩
19. ⟨*Kirchengewalt.*⟩
20. ⟨See above, 467 n. 121, 468 n. 122; in the present context, the 'one' word is 'ecclesiastical authority'.⟩
21. ⟨See above, the last two paragraphs of Section III.⟩
22. ⟨See above, 467 n. 109. In a wide sense, as Heckel used it here, *Kirchenordnung* designates the order of the church by divine (natural and positive), heteronomous law *and* the order of the church by man-made, autonomous law. In a narrow sense (and in general) it designates the man-made order of the church; see, e.g., above, 187, 202f. We use 'constitutional law of the church' for the order of the church by divine law, and 'man-made law of the church' for the order of the church by man-made law; see below, Index of Subjects: *Law,* s.v. "Lutheran ecclesiastical law as divine, heteronomous, constitutional law of the church" and *Law:* "Lutheran ecclesiastical law as man-made, autonomous law of the church."⟩
23. ⟨Or proclaim God's Word and administer the sacraments as they have been instituted in Holy Scripture.⟩
24. ⟨See also above, 187.⟩
25. ⟨See also above, 187.⟩
26. ⟨See above, 98.⟩
27. ⟨WA 1:525ff., or *LW* 31:83ff.⟩
28. ⟨I.e., the church's internal court before which the sacramental penance of the individual sinner takes place; for details, see Johannes Heckel, *Initia iuris,* 90ff.⟩
29. ⟨See Johannes Heckel, *Initia iuris,* 96: in the forgiveness of sins "all depends on

faith. . . . Through faith man grasps God's hand of mercy. Only in this way does man participate in the sacrament (of Penance). He himself, not the priest, is the minister of the sacrament . . ."; ibid., 97: in matters of receiving the forgiveness of sins, man is in a direct legal relationship with God, and, therefore, he does not need a priest (or "minister"); ibid., 100: the priest only pronounces God's judgment.>

Notes to Appendix VII

1. <See above, 504 n. 1.>
2. Johannes Heckel, *Initia iuris;* see above, Appendix VI.
3. <See above, 341 n. 368.>
4. <I.e., the Roman Catholic church.>
5. <See also above, 423 nn. 143-44.>
6. <See above, 349 n. 455.>
7. <See above, Appendix II.>

Titles of Cited Luther Texts

Numbers in the left-hand column correspond to the listing of each item in Aland's *Hilfsbuch zum Lutherstudium*. Numbers in the right-hand column show the volume and first page number in the Weimar edition (WA). (See above, xx and 235 n. 19.)

728	*A Marriage Booklet for Simple Pastors*, 1529	30.III:74
87	*A Model for Consecrating a True Bishop*, 1542	53:231
767	*A Secular Governmental Authority Has the Duty to Restrain the Anabaptists*, 1536	50:8
732	*A Sermon against the Turk*, 1529	30.II:160
187	*Addition to Goat Emser's Book*, 1519	2:658
67	*Admonition to Peace*, 1525	18:291
733	*Admonition to Prayer against the Turk*, 1541	51:585
169	*Against Eck's Judgment*, 1519	2:625
777	*Against Jack Sausage*, 1541	51:469
399	*Against Latomus*, 1521	8:43
112	*Against the Bull of Antichrist* (Latin text), 1520	6:597
113	*Against the Bull of Antichrist* (German text), 1520	6:614
588	*Against the Heavenly Prophets*, 1525	18:62
450	*Against the Perverters and Forgers of the Imperial Mandate*, 1523	12:62
64	*Against the Robbing and Murdering Hordes of Peasants*, 1525	18:357
550	*Against the Roman Papacy*, 1545	54:206
651	*Against the Sabbatarians*, 1538	50:312
547	*Against the Spiritual Estate of the Pope and the Bishops, Falsely So Called*, 1522	10.II:105
190	*Answer to the Book of Goat Emser*, 1521	7:621

506

Titles of Cited Luther Texts

140	*Answer to the Theological Faculty of the University of Louvain and of Cologne,* 1520	6:174
41	*Assertion of All Articles,* 1520	7:94
165	*Asterisci,* 1518	1:281
501	*Avoiding the Doctrines of Men,* 1522	10.II:72
768	*Concerning Rebaptism,* 1528	26:144
188	*Concerning the Answer of the Goat in Leipzig,* 1521	7:271
575	*Concerning the Ministry,* 1523	12:169
	Concerning the Sacrament of Baptism, 1528. Aland, *Hilfsbuch:* register of *Predigten,* No. 821	27:32
2	*Confesssion concerning Christ's Supper,* 1528	26:261
114	*Defense and Explanation of All Articles,* 1521	7:308
243	*Defense against the Charge of Inciting Rebellion,* 1533	38:96
27, 28, 29	*First, Second, Third Disputation against the Antinomians,* 1537, 1538	39.I:360, 419, 489
263	*Disputation against Scholastic Theology,* 1517	1:224
451	*Disputation of John Marbach,* 1543	39.II:206
58, 537	*Disputation of Jerome Nopp and Frederick Bachofen,* 1543	39.II:235
543	*Disputation of Palladius and Tilemann,* 1537	39.I:202
673	*Disputation of Henry Schmedenstede,* 1542	39.II:187
681	*Disputation of John Macchabäus Scotus,* 1542	39.II:146
123	*Disputation on Christ's Divinity and Humanity,* 1540	39.II:93
211	*Disputation on Excommunication,* 1520	7:236
759	*Disputation on Faith and Law,* 1535	39.I:44
355	*Disputation on Justification,* 1536	39.I:82
403	*Disputation on Law and Faith,* 1519	6:24
292	*Disputation on Man,* 1536	39.I:175
765	*Disputation on Matt. 19:21,* 1539	39.II:39
747	*Disputation on Matt. 22:1-14,* 1537	39.I:265
748	*Disputation on Revenge,* 1520	6:575
75	*Disputation on the Power and Will of Man without Grace,* 1516	1:145
49	*Exhortation to All Clergy Assembled at Augsburg,* 1530	30.II:268
418	*Explanations of Luther's Theses Debated in Leipzig,* 1519	2:391
638	*Explanations of the Ninety-five Theses,* 1518	1:525
742	*German Exposition of the Lord's Prayer for Simple Laymen,* 1519	2:80
276	*Heidelberg Disputation,* 1518	1:353

Titles of Cited Luther Texts

518, 520	*How Christians Should Regard Moses*, 1525, 1526, 1527	16:363, 24:2 (and ibid., XXI)
204	*Instruction about Saints*, 1522	10.II:164
301	*Instruction for the Confession of Sinners*, 1518	1:258
751	*Instructions for the Visitors*, 1528	26:195
771	*Letter of D. Martin Luther concerning His Book on the Private Mass*, 1534	38:262
98	*Letter to the Princes of Saxony concerning the Rebellious Spirit*, 1524	15:210
779	*Long Sermon on Usury*, 1520	6:36
201	*D. Martin Luther's Offer and Protest*, 1520	6:476
45	*Luther's Sincere Admonition to All Christians to Guard against Insurrection*, 1522	8:676
565	Notes on the *Sentences* of Peter Lombard, 1510-11	9:29
716	Notes on the sermons of Tauler, 1516(?)	9:97
227	*On Christian Freedom*, 1520 (German text)	7:20
413	*On Christian Freedom*, 1520 (Latin text)	7:42
142	*On Confession*, 1520	6:157
761	*On Good Works*, 1520	6:202
357	*On Justification*, 1530	30.II:657
675	*On Keeping Children in School*, 1530	30.II:517
181	*On Marriage Matters*, 1530	30.III:205
755	*On Monastic Vows*, 1521	8:573
544	*On Proposition XIII concerning the Power of the Pope*, 1519	2:183
540	*On Secular Authority*, 1523	11:245
780	*On Trade and Usury*, 1524	15:293
60	*On the Ban*, 1520	6:63
382	*On the Councils and the Church*, 1539	50:509
670	*On the Keys*, 1530	30.II:435
173	*On the New Bulls and Lies of Eck*, 1520	6:579
502	*On the New Testament, That Is, the Mass*, 1520	6:353
212	*On the Power of Excommunication*, 1518	1:638
731	*On the War against the Turks*, 1529	30.II:107
235	*On Two Imperial Contradictory Commands concerning Luther*, 1524	15:254
359	*On Two Kinds of Righteousness*, 1519	2:145
65	*Open Letter on the Harsh Book against the Peasants*, 1525	18:384
241	*Ordinance of a Common Chest*, 1523	12:11
179	*Persons Who are Forbidden to Marry*, 1522	10.II:265

Titles of Cited Luther Texts

10	*Postilla for Advent*, 1522	10.I.2:1
758	*Postilla for Christmas*, 1522	10.I.1:1
216	*Postilla for Lent*, 1525	17.II:5
272	*Postilla for the Home*, 1544	52:1
689	*Summer Postilla*, 1526	21:197
145	*Preface to Antonius Corvinus, Quatenus expediat aeditam recens Erasmi de sarcienda Ecclesiae concordia Rationem sequi*, 1534	38:276
414	*Preface to John Lichtenberger's Prophecies*, 1527	23:7
710	*Propositions against the School of Satan*, 1530	30.II:420
663	*Receiving Bread and Wine in the Sacrament*, 1522	10.II:11
122	*Reply to Ambrosius Catharinus*, 1521	7:705
508	*Reply to the Bishop of Meissen*, 1520	6:144
582	*Reply to the Dialogue of Silvester Prierias on the Power of the Pope*, 1518	1:647
683	Sermons of ca. 1514-21	4:590
	Sermons of 1514-17. Aland, *Hilfsbuch:* register of Predigten, Nos. 6-61	
177	*Sermon on the Estate of Marriage*, 1519	2:166
6	*Sermon on the Pope's Indulgence and Grace*, 1518	1:383
573	*Sermons on the Ten Commandments*, 1518	1:398
778	*Short Sermon on Usury*, 1519	6:3
672	*Smalcald Articles*, 1537	50:192
136	*Some Short Sermons of D. Martin Luther*, 1537	45:421
679	*That These Words of Christ, "This is My Body," Still Stand Firm against the Fanatics*, 1527	23:64
120	*The Babylonian Captivity of the Church*, 1520	6:497
655	*The Blessed Sacrament of the Body of Christ and the Brotherhoods*, 1519	2:742
38	*The Bondage of the Will*, 1525	18:600
178	*The Estate of Marriage*, 1522	10.II:275
156	*The German Mass*, 1526	19:72
714	*The Holy and Blessed Sacrament of Baptism*, 1519	2:727
364	*The Large Catechism*, 1529	30.I:125
151	*The Last Words of David*, 1543	54:28
168	*The Leipzig Disputation*, 1519	2:254
503	*The Misuse of the Mass*, 1521	8:482
510	*The Order of the Mass*, 1523	12:205
548	*The Papacy at Rome*, 1520	6:285
770	*The Private Mass and the Consecration of Priests*, 1533	38:195
406	*The Right and Power of a Christian Congregation*, 1523	11:408
658	*The Sacrament of the Body and Blood of Christ, against the Fanatics*, 1526	19:482

Titles of Cited Luther Texts

365	*The Small Catechism*, 1529	30.I:243
556	*Two Sermons on Christ's Passion*, 1518	1:336
721	*Ninety-five Theses*, 1517	1:233
139	*Sixteen Theses on Faith and Ceremonies*, 1520	6:379
756	*Theses on Monastic Vows*, 1521	8:323
160	*Theses on the Remarriage of Widowed Pastors*, 1528	26:517
781	*To Pastors, That They Preach against Usury*, 1540	51:331
7	*To the Christian Nobility*, 1520	6:404
676	*To the Councilmen of All Cities in Germany That They Establish and Maintain Christian Schools*, 1524	15:27
88	*To the Goat in Leipzig*, 1521	7:262
420	*To the Livonians*, 1525	18:417
158	*Warning of His Dear German People*, 1531	30.III:276
393	*Whether Soldiers, Too, Can Be Saved*, 1526	19:623

OLD TESTAMENT

517	*Lectures on Genesis*, 1535-45	42-44
518	*Sermons on Genesis*, 1523-24, 1527	14:97, 24:1
520	*Sermons on Exodus*, 1524-27	16:1
523	*The Book of Deuteronomy with Notes*, 1525	14:497
524	*Sermons on Deuteronomy*, 1529	28:509
593	*First Lectures on the Psalms*, 1513-15	3, 4:1
594	*Second Lectures on the Psalms*, 1518-21	5
116	*The Seven Penitential Psalms*, 1517	1:158
597	*The First 25 Psalms Explained at the Coburg*, 1530	31.I:263
598	*On Psalms 23–25*, 1513-16	31.I:464
599	*Lectures on Psalms 120–134*, 1532-33	40.III:9
600	*Lectures on Psalm 2*, 1532	40.II:193
606	*Lectures on Psalm 45*, 1532	40.II:472
607	*Lectures on Psalm 51*, 1532	40.II:315
611	*Psalm 82 Explained*, 1530	31.I:189
612	*Psalm 90 Explained*, 1534-35	40.III:484
614	*Psalm 101 Explained*, 1534-35	51:200
615	*Psalm 110 Explained*, 1518	1:690
616	*Psalm 110 Explained*, 1535	41:79
619	*Psalm 117 Explained*, 1530	31.I:223
141	*Psalm 118 Explained*, 1530	31.I:65
622	*Psalm 127 Explained*, 1524	15:360
172	*D. Martin Luther's Preface to Ecclesiastes*, 1532	20:7
306	*Lectures on Isaiah*, 1527-30	25:87
283	*On Gog according to Ezekiel, Chapters 38 and 39*, 1530	30.II:223
22	*Lectures on Amos*, 1524-25	13:124
347	*Lectures on Jonah*, 1525	13:225

Titles of Cited Luther Texts

348	*Commentary on Jonah*, 1526	19:185
265	*Lectures on Habakkuk*, 1525	13:396
266	*Commentary on Habakkuk*, 1526	19:345
653	*Lectures on Zechariah*, 1525-26	13:546
654	*Commentary on Zechariah*, 1527	23:485
449	*Lectures on Malachi*, 1526	13:676

New Testament

	The New Testament in German, 1522	WA.DB 6, 7
458	*Notes on Some Chapters of Matthew*, 1538	38:447
465	*Sermons on Matthew, Chapters 5–7*, 1530-32	32:299
477	*Matthew, Chapters 18–24 Explained in Sermons*, 1537-40	47:232
56	*The Gospel of the Ten Lepers Explained*, 1521 (Luke 17:11-19)	8:340
316	*Sermons on John, Chapters 1 and 2*, 1537-38	46:538
318	*John, Chapters 3 and 4 Explained in Sermons*, 1538-40	47:1
324	*Sermons on John, Chapters 6–8*, 1530-32	33
328	*Sermons on John, Chapters 14 and 15*, 1537	45:465
333, 334	*Sermons on John, Chapters 16–19*, 1528-29, 1538 (including *Sermons on John, Chapter 16* and *Sermons on John, Chapter 17*)	28:70, 46:1
	Sermon on John 18:10f. Aland, *Hilfsbuch*: register of *Predigten*, No. 990	28:245
646	*Lectures on Romans*, 1515-16	56, 57.I
83.45	*Preface to Romans* (in *The New Testament in German*), 1522	WA
386	*Commentary on 1 Corinthians, Chapter 7*, 1523	12:92
230	*First Lectures on Galatians*, 1516-17	57.II
228	*First Commentary on Galatians*, 1519	2:443
229	*Second Lectures on Galatians*, 1531	40.I, II
229	*Second Commentary on Galatians*, 1535	40.I, II
274	*Lectures on Hebrews*, 1517-18	57.III
563	*Sermons on the First Epistle of St. Peter*, 1523	12:259
343	*Lectures on 1 John*, 1527	20:599

Short Titles and Place of Full Citation

See above, xix.

Not listed are book reviews and the titles of works listed in 233n3.

Adam, "Bericht," *DtPfrBl* 53 (1953)	369n97
Aegidius Romanus, *De ecclesiastica potestate*	373n132
Aegidius Romanus, *De regimine principum*	323n168
Aland, *Hilfsbuch*	xx, 235n18
Althaus, "Die beiden Regimente bei Luther," *ThLZ* 81 (1956)	268n17
Althaus, *Christliche Wahrheit*	363n39
Althaus, *Communio sanctorum*	387n31
Althaus, *Gebot und Gesetz*	247n53
Althaus, "Liebe und Heilsgewißheit bei Luther," in *Lortz Festgabe*, 1	371n111
Althaus, "Luther über die Autorität der Kirche," in *Lilje Festschrift*	394n58
Althaus, "Luther und die Bergpredigt," *Luther* 1956	382n190
Althaus, "Luthers Lehre von den beiden Reichen," *LuJ* 24 (1957)	146
Althaus, *Luther und die politische Welt*	316n111
Althaus, *Paulus und Luther*	373n130
Althaus, *Theologie der Ordnungen*	337n330
Althaus, *Todesstrafe*	348n445
Althaus, "'... und hätten allen Glauben,'" in *Elert Gedenkschrift*	348n445
Althaus, *Wahrheit des Evangeliums*	254n14
Andreae, *Questiones*	482n151
Arnold Festschrift	471n8
Arnold, *Naturrecht bei Luther*	237n8
Aubin Festgabe	333n402
Aulén, "Einheit der Kirche," in *Ein Buch von der Kirche*	394n58
Bainton, *Here I Stand*	248n55

Short Titles and Place of Full Citation

Barth, *Christengemeinde und Bürgergemeinde*	403n6
Barth, *Eine Schweizer Stimme*	241n66
Barth, *Ordnung der Gemeinde*	473n30
Bauer, "Die Naturrechts-Lehre Melanchthons," *Hochland* 44 (1952)	446n3
Bauer, "Naturrechtsvorstellungen des jüngeren Melanchthons," in *Ritter Festschrift*	446n3
Becker, "Die Probleme des Widerstandsrechtes," *NELKB* 10 (1955)	448n3
Becker, "Lutherische Demokratie," *Deutsche Universitätszeitung* 8 (1953)	448n3
Becker, "Widerstandsrecht und Staatsgewalt," *ELKZ* 9 (1955)	448n3
Beintker, *Die Überwindung der Anfechtung bei Luther*	243n11
Bekennende Kirche	390n47
Berggrav, "Staat und Kirche in lutherischer Sicht," in *Das lebendige Wort*	412n61
Bertholet Festschrift	239n43
Hermann W. Beyer, "Der Christ und die Bergpredigt," *LuJ* 14 (1932)	310n69
Hermann W. Beyer, "Glaube und Recht im Denken Luthers," *LuJ* 17 (1935)	239n45
Hermann W. Beyer, *Luther und das Recht*	322n159
Wilhelm R. Beyer, *Rechtsphilosophische Besinnung*	239n46
Biedermann, *Goethes Gespräche*	311n75
Biel, *Collectorium*	284n44
Biel, *Expositio missae*	242n7
Billing, *Luthers lära om staten*	262n12
Binder Festgabe	345n418
Binder, *Luthers Staatsauffassung*	263n42
Blanke, *Der verborgene Gott bei Luther*	281n16
Bluhm, "The Significance of Luther's Earliest Sermons," *HThR* 37 (1944)	248n60
Bogler, *Harthmut von Cronberg*	318n133
Bohatec, *Calvins Lehre von Staat und Kirche*	433n223
Bohatec, *Calvin und das Recht*	448n3
Bornkamm, "Äußerer und innerer Mensch bei Luther," in *Krüger Festgabe*	252n1
Bornkamm, "Bindung und Freiheit in der Ordnung der Kirche," in id., *Das Jahrhundert der Reformation*	480n138
Bornkamm, "Iustitia dei," *ARG* 39 (1942)	242n6
Bornkamm, *Das Jahrhundert der Reformation*	458n10 (5)
Bornkamm, "Die Kirche in der Confessio Augustana," in id., *Das Jahrhundert der Reformation*	475n60
Bornkamm, *Luther und das Alte Testament*	250n78
Bornkamm, *Luthers Lehre von den zwei Reichen*	251n7
Bornkamm, "Das Problem der Toleranz," in id., *Das Jahrhundert der Reformation*	458n10 (5)
Bornkamm, *Wort Gottes bei Luther*	286n55

Short Titles and Place of Full Citation

Bring, *Dualismen hos Luther*	243n13
Bring, "Gesetz und Evangelium," *Aus der Arbeit der Luther-Agricola Gesellschaft in Finnland* 1 (Helsinki, 1943)	359n21
Bring, "Der Glaube und das Recht nach Luther," in *Elert Gedenkschrift*	463n31
Bring, "Lutherische Theologie," *Luthertum* 1 (1951)	256n25
Bring, *Luthers Anschauung von der Bibel*	287n62
Emil Brunner, *Das Gebot und die Ordnungen*	274n13
Emil Brunner, *Gerechtigkeit*	248n61
Emil Brunner, *Das Mißverständnis der Kirche*	287n63
Peter Brunner, *Nikolaus von Amsdorf*	501n308
Peter Brunner, *Amt des Bischofs*	501n308
Peter Brunner, "Der Christ in den zwei Reichen," *ELKZ* 3 (1949)	269n19
Heinz Brunotte, "Obrigkeit," in *Handwörterbuch zur Lutherbibel*	256n34
Heinz Brunotte, "Sacerdotium und Ministerium," in *Smend Festgabe*	473n24
Wilhelm Brunotte, *Das geistliche Amt bei Luther*	473n24
Brunstäd, *Theologie der Bekenntnisschriften*	368n86
Buisson, *Potestas und Caritas*	482n151
Calasso, *Gli ordinamenti giuridici*	406n32
Calasso, *I glossatori*	406n32
Calvin, *Institutes*	329n242
Cambridge Dictionary of Philosophy	467n120
Campenhausen, "Reformatorisches Selbstbewußtsein," *ARG* 37 (1940)	242n2
Campenhausen and Bornkamm, *Bindung und Freiheit in der Ordnung der Kirche*	396n70
Cardauns, "Lehre vom Widerstandsrecht"	447n3
La Ciudad de Dios	251n4
Coing, "Die Naturrechtsdebatte," *Der Juristenrundbrief der Evangelischen Akademie* 2 (1950)	273n10
Coing, *Die obersten Grundsätze des Rechts*	310n65
Cronberg, *Christliche Schrift und Vermahnung*	318n133
Dahm, *Deutsches Recht*	248n62
Das lebendige Wort	412n61
Dehn and Ernst Wolf, *Gottesrecht und Menschenrecht*	305n24
Dempf, *Sacrum imperium*	406n32
Dictionary of Ecclesiastical Latin	234n10
Harald Diem, *Luthers Lehre von den beiden Reichen*	240n56
Hermann Diem, "Kirchenvisitation als Kirchenleitung," in *Ecclesia semper reformanda*	456n8
Hermann Diem, *Lutherische Volkskirche*	441n298
Hermann Diem, *Luthers Predigt in den zwei Reichen*	251n3
Hermann Diem, *Theologie als kirchliche Wissenschaft*	237n13

Short Titles and Place of Full Citation

Digest (Watson ed.)	316n108
Dombois, *Recht der Gnade*	471n2
Dörries, "Menschengehorsam und Gottesgehorsam bei Luther," *ARG* 39 (1942)	408n41
Ebeling, "Anfänge von Luthers Hermeneutik," *ZThK* 48 (1951)	250n79
Ebeling, *Evangelische Evangelienauslegung*	277n28
Ebeling, "Luthers Auslegung des 44.(45.) Psalms," in *Lutherforschung heute*	277n27
Ebeling, "Triplex usus legis," *ThLZ* 75 (1950)	287n59
Ecclesia semper reformanda	447n15
Ehrhardt, "La notion du droit naturel chez Luther," in *Études de théologie et d'histoire*	238n31
Eichmann, *Kaiserkrönung*	238n23
Ein Buch von der Kirche	271n31
Einführung in die Rechtswissenschaft	236n8
Elert Gedenkschrift	251n7
Elert, *Das christliche Ethos*	340n365
Elert, *Der christliche Glaube*	363n39
Elert, "Humanität und Kirche," in id., *Zwischen Gnade und Ungnade*	446n2
Elert, *Morphologie*	254n11
Elert, "Terminologie der Staatslehre Melanchthons," *ZSTh* 9 (1931)	446n4
Elert, *Zwischen Gnade und Ungnade*	273n4
Ellul, *Die theologische Begründung des Rechts*	239n41
Ellwein, *Vom neuen Leben*	377n162
Elsener, *Rezeption*	498n295
Elze, "Verständnis der Passion," in *Rückert Festgabe*	264n51
Erler, *Kirchenrecht*	240n57
Fabian, *Entstehung des Schmalkaldischen Bundes*	450n19
Fagerberg, *Bekenntnis, Kirche und Amt*	471n3
Fehr, "Widerstandsrecht," *MIÖG* 38 (1920)	447n3
Festschrift des Deutschen Juristentages	378n172
Ficker, *Konfutation*	317n123
Forck, *Königsherrschaft Jesu Christi*	299n159
Förster, *Entstehung der Preußischen Landeskirche*	436n255
Förster, "Fragen zu Luthers Kirchenbegriff," in *Kaftan Festgabe*	436n255
Friedberg, *Recht der Eheschließung*	338n333
Friedrich, *Einführung in das evangelische Kirchenrecht*	471n2
Geppert, *Ist Lehrchaos protestantisches Schicksal?*	362n37
Geppert, "Gegenwärtige Diskussion des tertius usus legis," *ELKZ* 9 (1955)	368n86
Gerechte Ordnung	305n25

Short Titles and Place of Full Citation

Gerner, "Entwicklungstendenzen im attischen Recht," *ZSRG*.R 67 (1950)	243n12
Gierke Festgabe	238n24
Gierke, *Althusius*	352n482
Gierke, *Deutsches Genossenschaftsrecht*	433n226
Giese Festschrift	319n49
Gogarten, *Kirche in der Welt*	311n75
Gogarten, "Die Lehre von den zwei Reichen und das 'natürliche Gesetz'," *DTh* 2 (1935)	305n24
Gogarten, *Der Mensch zwischen Gott und Welt*	315n105
Gollwitzer, *Christliche Gemeinde*	238n39
Gottschick, *Luthers Theologie*	371n111
Götze, *Wie Luther Kirchenzucht übte*	479n122
Grewe, *Gnade und Recht*	327n211
Grobmann, "Naturrecht bei Luther und Calvin"	239n46
Grundmann, "Das Gesetz als kirchenrechtliches Problem," *ZEvKR* 8 (1962)	480n138
Grundmann, "Kirche und Staat," in *Arnold Festschrift*	471n8
Grundmann, *Der Lutherische Weltbund*	471n2
Grundmann, "Sacerdotium — Ministerium — Ecclesia Particularis," in *Johannes Heckel Festschrift*	473n24
Gyllenkrok, "Die Anfänge von Luthers Theologie"	325n195
Gyllenkrok, *Rechtfertigung und Heiligung*	265n61
Hägglund, *Die Heilige Schrift in der Theologie Johann Gerhards*	447n8
Hägglund, *Theologie und Philosophie bei Luther*	242n5
Handwörterbuch zur Lutherbibel	256n34
Harleß, *Etliche Gewissensfragen*	471n2
Adolf von Harnack, *Dogmengeschichte*	249n70
Theodosius Harnack, *Die Kirche*	390n49
Theodosius Harnack, *Luthers Theologie*	243n12
Hartmann, *Das Problem des geistigen Seins*	235n3
Hauck Festgabe	423n144
Johannes Heckel Festschrift	471n1
Johannes Heckel, "Ansatz einer evangelischen Sozialethik," in Theodor Heckel, *Die evangelische Kirche in der modernen Gesellschaft*	461n3
Johannes Heckel, "Cura religionis," in *Stutz Festschrift*	429n186
Johannes Heckel, "Decretum Gratiani," *StGra* 3 (1955)	249n69
Johannes Heckel, "Die zwo Kirchen"	466n92
Johannes Heckel, "Höchstes Regal," *ZSRG*.K 13 (1924)	447n12
Johannes Heckel, *Im Irrgarten der Zwei-Reiche-Lehre*	149
Johannes Heckel, *Initia iuris*	216 and 241n68
Johannes Heckel, *Lex charitatis*, 1953	223
Johannes Heckel, "Luthers Lehre von den zwei Regimenten," *ZEvKR* 4 (1955)	464n43

Short Titles and Place of Full Citation

Johannes Heckel, "Marsilius of Padua und Luther," *ZSRG*.K 44 (1958)	503n39
Johannes Heckel, "Melanchthon und das heutige deutsche Staatskirchenrecht," in *Kaufmann Festgabe*	236n4
Johannes Heckel, "Naturrecht und christliche Verantwortung," in *Zur politischen Predigt*	1
Johannes Heckel, "Recht und Gesetz," *ZSRG*.K 26 (1937)	250n81
Johannes Heckel, "Stellungnahme der Kirche der Reformation — Die Lutheraner," in *Widerstandsrecht und Grenzen der Staatsgewalt*	465n76
Johannes Heckel, "Widerstand gegen die Obrigkeit?" *Zeitwende. Die neue Furche* 25 (1954)	223 and 465n76
Johannes Heckel, "Zwei-Reiche-Lehre," in *EKL* 3	204
Martin Heckel, "Autonomia und Pacis Compositio," *ZSRG*.K 45 (1959)	483n165
Martin Heckel, *Staat und Kirche*	418n84 and 483n165
Theodor Heckel, *Adolph von Harleß*	471.2
Theodor Heckel, *Die evangelische Kirche in der modernen Gesellschaft*	461n3
Theodor Heckel, *Kirche, Wahrheit, Recht*	495n260
Theodor Heckel, "Liebe und Gerechtigkeit," in *Schreiner Festgabe*	309n59
Theodor Heckel, "Reform des Kirchenrechts und die Reformen der Kirche," in *Johannes Heckel Festschrift*	495n260
Theodor Heckel, "Regula aurea," in *Zur Politischen Predigt*	373n127
Heer, *Europäische Geistesgeschichte*	446n3
Hering, "Aequitas bei Gratian," *StGra* 2 (1954)	319n141
Hermann, "Exkommunikation bei Luther und Thomas Erastus," in id., *Gesammelte Studien*	479n122
Hermann, *Fragen um den Begriff der natürlichen Theologie*	253n5
Hermann, *Gesammelte Studien*	479n122
Hermann, *Klarheit der Heiligen Schrift*	257n38
Hermann, *Luthers Lehre von Sünde und Rechtfertigung*	241n62
Hermann, *Luthers These "Gerecht und Sünder zugleich"*	244n28
Hermann, "Luthers Zirkulardisputation über Matth. 19,21," *LuJ* 23 (1941)	409n44
Herntrich, "Luther und das Alte Testament," *LuJ* 20 (1938)	369n30
Heydte, *Geburtsstunde des souveränen Staates*	256n33
Heyland, *Widerstandsrecht des Volkes*	448n3
Hillerdal, *Gehorsam gegen Gott und Menschen*	299n161
Hillerdal, "Kirche und Politik," *LR* 5 (1955)	463n31
Hillerdal, "Luther och tysk evangelisk politik 1530," *KHÅ* 55 (1955)	448n3
Carl Hinrichs, *Luther und Müntzer*	448n3
Hermann Hinrichs, *Geschichte des Natur- und Völkerrechts*	239n44
Arnold Hirsch, "Luther et le Corpus Christianum," *RHMC* 4 (1957)	433n222
Emanuel Hirsch, "Initium theologiae Lutheri," in *Kaftan Festgabe*	370n99
Emanuel Hirsch, *Lutherstudien*, 1	252n17

Short Titles and Place of Full Citation

Emanuel Hirsch, *Reich Gottes Begriffe des neueren europäischen Denkens*	237n15
Hochstetter, "Viator mundi," *FS* 32 (1950)	313n97
Hof, "Luthers Lehre von Gesetz und Evangelium," *ELKZ* 3 (1949)	297n142
Hoffmann, "Reformation und Gewissensfreiheit," *ARG* 37 (1940)	459n10
Holl, *Der Westen*	248n57
Holl, *Luther*	238n36
Holstein, *Grundlagen*	237n13
Iwand, *Glaubensgerechtigkeit nach Luthers Lehre*	267n11
Iwand, *Rechtfertigungslehre und Christusglaube*	244n22
Iwand and Ernst Wolf, "Gutachten zur Frage des Widerstandsrechts," *Junge Kirche* 13 (1952)	418n109
Jacob, *Gewissensbegriff in der Theologie Luthers*	247n52
Jauernig, "Die Konkurrenz der Jenaer mit der Wittenberger Ausgabe von Luthers Werken," *LuJ* 26 (1959)	450n19
Jedin, *Konzil von Trient*, 1	360n46
Joachimsen, *Sozialethik des Luthertums*	310n62
Joest, *Gesetz und Freiheit*	368n86
Jordan, *Luthers Staatsauffassung*	263n42
Kaftan Festgabe	279n3
Kahl, *Lehrsystem des Kirchenrechts und der Kirchenpolitik*, 1	236n7
Kahl, "Rechtsinhalt des Konkordienbuches," in *Gierke Festgabe*	238n24
Kattenbusch, "Deus absconditus bei Luther," in *Kaftan Festgabe*	279n3
Kattenbusch, "Doppelschichtigkeit in Luthers Kirchenbegriff," *ThStKr* 100 (1928)	275n14
Kaufmann Festgabe	236n4
Kaufmann, "Anthropologische Grundlagen der Staatstheorien," in *Smend Festschrift*	252n19
Kern, *Gottesgnadentum*	416n89
Kern, "Luther und das Widerstandsrecht," *ZSRG*.K 6 (1916)	447n3
Kinder, *Der evangelische Glaube und die Kirche*	387n30
Kinder, "Gottes Gebote und Gottes Gnade," *Kirchlich-theologische Hefte* 7 (1949)	238n39
Kinder, "Gottesreich und Weltreich bei Augustin und bei Luther," in *Elert Gedenkschrift*	251n7
Kinder, "Politische Verantwortung des Christen," *ELKZ* 8 (1954)	382n190
Kinder, "Verborgenheit der Kirche nach Luther," in *Lortz Festgabe*	336n317
Kirche, Bekenntnis und Sozialethos	441n298
Kisch, "Die Aequitaslehre des Marsilius von Padua," in *Rennefahrt Festgabe*	319n142
Kisch, *Erasmus und die Jurisprudenz*	320n144
Kisch, "Summum ius summa iniuria," in *Simonius Festgabe*	319n142

Short Titles and Place of Full Citation

Joseph Klein, *Kanonistische und moraltheologische Normierung in der katholischen Theologie*	407n39
Kurt Klein, *Kirche und Staat*	382n190
Klügel, *Das Evangelium und die Ordnungen des öffentlichen Lebens*	382n190
Klügel, "Recht zum Aufruhr?" in *Macht und Recht*	448n3
Hans Köhler, "Das Problem der politischen Ethik," *ELKZ* 9 (1955)	382n190
Walther Köhler, *Luther und Luthertum in ihrer weltgeschichtlichen Auswirkung*	440n292
Walther Köhler, "Luthers Schrift 'An den christlichen Adel,'" *ZSRG*.K 14 (1925)	434n231
Walther Köhler, *Reformation und Ketzerproze*	459n10
Walther Köhler, "Sozialwissenschaftliche Bemerkungen zur Lutherforschung," *ZGStW* 85 (1928)	238n36
Koellreutter, *Deutsches Staatsrecht*	237n13
Köttgen, "Glaube und Recht," *LuJ* 17 (1935)	274n13
Kohlmeyer, "Die Bedeutung der Kirche für Luther," *ZKG* 47 (1928)	236n12
Kohlmeyer, "Die Geschichtsbetrachtung Luthers," *ARG* 37 (1940)	305n22
Kohlmeyer, *Staat und Kirche in der Deutschen Reformation*	348n274
Kohlmeyer, *Von Augsburg nach Wittenberg*	251n7
Krause, *Kaiserrecht und Rezeption*	318n133
Krüger Festgabe	252n1
Krumwiede, *Glaube und Geschichte in der Theologie Luthers*	315n105
Kühn, *Toleranz und Offenbarung*	242n3
Kühn, *Geschichte des Speyrer Reichstags 1529*	441n299
Künneth, "Selbstverständnis der lutherischen Kirche," *ELKZ* 2 (1948)	396n73
Künneth, *Widerstandsrecht als theologisch-ethisches Problem*	407n39
Kuttner, "Sur les origines du terme 'droit positif,'" *RHDF* 1936	298n154
de Lagarde, *Recherches sur l'esprit politique de la Réforme*	239n43
Lammers, *Luthers Anschauung vom Willen*	279n2
Lang, "Die Reformation und das Naturrecht," *BFChTh* 13.IV (1909)	239n47
Latreille and Siegfried, "Les forces religieuses et la vie politique, Le Catholicisme, Le Protestantisme," *Cahiers de la Fondation nationale des sciences politiques* 23 (Paris, 1951)	249n70
Lau, *"Äußerliche Ordnung"*	238n31
Lau, "Bemerkungen zu Luthers Lehre von den beiden Reichen," *ELKZ* 6 (1952)	240n58
Lau, "Leges charitatis," *KuD* 2 (1956)	234n5
Lau, *Luthers Lehre von den beiden Reichen*	239n45
Laun, *Die Menschenrechte*	388n36
Lenz, "Luthers und Calvins Verhältnis zum Staat," *ELKZ* 5 (1951)	346n419
Liermann, *Deutsches Evangelisches Kirchenrecht*	401n20
Liermann, "Gegenwärtige Lage der Wissenschaft vom evangelischen Kirchenrecht," *ZevKR* 8 (1962)	496n278
Liermann, "Geschichte des corpus christianum in der Neuzeit," *ZSRG*.K 27 (1938)	433n223

Short Titles and Place of Full Citation

Liermann, *Grundlagen des kirchlichen Verfassungsrechts*	319n49
Liermann, "Zur Geschichte des Naturrechts," in *Bertholet Festschrift*	239n43
Lilje Festschrift	394n58
Link, *Das Ringen Luthers*	242n74
Loewenich, *Luther und das Johanneische Evangelium*	371n109
Loewenich, *Luthers evangelische Botschaft*	254n10
Loewenich, *Luthers theologia crucis*	241n63
Lohmann, "Ein Gott — zwei Regimente," *Luther* 74 (2003)	234n4
Lommatzsch, *Luthers Lehre vom ethisch-religiösen Standpunkt aus*	235n2
Loofs, "Der articulus stantis et cadentis ecclesiae," *ThStKr* 90 (1917)	370n99
Lortz Festgabe	336n317
Loy, "Das Widerstandsrecht und seine Grenzen bei Luther und heute," in *Zur politischen Predigt*	409n50
Luthardt, *Ethik Luthers*	503n40
Lutherforschung heute	269n18
Lüthje, "Melanchthons Anschauung über das Recht des Widerstands," *ZKG* 47 (1928)	455n74
Macht und Recht	448n3
Marsch, "Ist das Recht eine notwendige Funktion der Kirche?" *ZEvKR* 5 (1956)	445n346
Marsilius of Padua, *Defensor Pacis*	454n60
Matthes, *Das Corpus Christianum bei Luther*	256n35
Matthes, *Luther und die Obrigkeit*	333n281
Maurer, *Freiheit eines Christenmenschen*	241n59
Maurer, "Kirche und Geschichte," in *Lutherforschung heute*	269n18
Maurer, "Luther und die Doppelehe Landgraf Philipps von Hessen," *Luther* 1953	343n400
Maurer, "Luther und die Schwärmer," *SThKAB* 6 (1952)	287n57
Maurer, *Pfarrerrecht und Bekenntnis*	390n49
Mayer, "Darf der Christ sein eigenes Recht suchen?" *Zeitwende* 12.II (1936)	404n12
Mayer, *Strafrecht*	404n12
Mayer, "Strafrechtstheorie bei Luther und Melanchthon," in *Binder Festgabe*	345n418
Mediae Latinatis Lexicon	454n60
Meinecke, "Luther über christliches Gemeinwesen und christlichen Staat," *HZ* 121 (1920)	438n274
Meinhold, *Genesisvorlesung Luthers*	245n37
Meinhold, *Luthers Sprachphilosophie*	259n6
Meinhold, "Revolution im Namen Christi," *Saeculum* 10 (1959)	448n3
Meiser Festschrift	239n42
Meisner, *Discursus*	419n116
Meissinger, *Der katholische Luther*	242n1
Merz, "Gesetz Gottes und Volksnomos," *LuJ* 16 (1934)	396n70
Messner, *Naturrecht*	273n12

Short Titles and Place of Full Citation

Mezger, "Gerechtigkeit und soziale Ordnung in evangelischer Sicht," in *Zur politischen Predigt*	316n115
Mitteis, "Zur rechtsgeschichtlichen Forschung in Italien," *ZSRG*.G 69 (1952)	406n32
Mochi Onory, *Fonti canostiche*	406n32
Richard A. Muller, *Dictionary*	278n29
Alfred D. Müller, *Grundriß der praktischen Theologie*	399n93
Georg Müller, *Luthers Stellung zum Recht*	241n72
Hans M. Müller, "Das christliche Liebesgebot und die lex naturae," *ZThK*.NF 9 (1928)	273n11
Hans M. Müller, *Erfahrung und Glaube bei Luther*	305n25
Karl Müller, *Kirche, Gemeinde und Obrigkeit nach Luther*	459n7
Karl Müller, "Luther und Melanchthon über das ius gladii," in *Hauck Festgabe*	423n144
Karl Müller, *Luthers Äußerungen über das Recht des bewaffneten Widerstands*	447n3
Münter, *Kirche und Amt II*	238n25
Naumann, *Briefe über Religion*	425n148
Niebuhr, *Nature and Destiny of Man*	248n62
Nürnberger, "Lex naturae," *ARG* 37 (1940)	298n148
Nygren, *Agape and Eros*, Part I (1941)	276n19
Nygren, *Agape and Eros*, Part II.2 (1939)	251n7
Nygren, "Luthers Lehre von den zwei Reichen," *ThLZ* 74 (1949)	251n3
Nygren, "Staat und Kirche," in *Ein Buch von der Kirche*	271n31
Obendiek, *Der Teufel bei Martin Luther*	257n38
Oberman, "Facientibus quod in se est," *HThR* 55 (1962)	432n215
Oehler, "Evangelisches Kirchenrecht," in *Giese Festschrift*	391n49
Oepke, *Das neue Gottesvolk*	238n36
Olsson, *Grundproblemet*, 1	252n2
Olsson, "Sichtbarkeit und Unsichtbarkeit der Kirche nach Luther," in *Ein Buch von der Kirche*	439n279
Ott, "Recht und Gesetz bei Biel," *ZSRG*.K 38 (1952)	283n33
Oxenford, *Conversations of Goethe*	311n75
Pauls, *Luthers Anschauung von Staat und Volk*	411n58
Pelikan, "Kirche nach Luthers Genesisvorlesung," in *Lutherforschung heute*	335n300
Pfeiffer, *Totaler Staat — und Luther?*	303n6
Pflanz, *Geschichte und Eschatologie bei Luther*	268n14
Pinomaa, "Heiligung bei Luther," *ThZ* 10 (1954)	244n24
Pinomaa, *Zorn Gottes in der Theologie Luthers*	242n8
Prenter, "Luthers Lehre von der Heiligung," in *Lutherforschung heute*	377n166
Prenter, *Spiritus creator*	242n5

Short Titles and Place of Full Citation

Preuß, *Luther der Christenmensch*	307n38
Preuß, *Luther der Prophet*	242n2
Pribilla, "An den Grenzen der Staatsgewalt," *StZ* 146 (1948)	448n4
Pribilla, *Deutsche Schicksalsfragen*	448n4
Puchta, *Einleitung in das Recht der Kirche*	236n6
Quervain, *Kirche, Volk, Staat, Ethik*, 2.I	393n43
Quiring, "Luther und die Mystik," *ZSTh* 13 (1936)	286n50
Radbruch, *Rechtsphilosophie*	327n211
Reibstein, *Johannes Althusius*	454n55
Reich und Recht	447n10
Reicke, "Kirchenrecht," in *Einführung in die Rechtswissenschaft*	236n8
Reinkingk, *Tractatus*	447n10
Rennefahrt Festgabe	319n142
Richter, *Geschichte der evangelischen Kirchenverfassung*	440n294
Rieker, *Rechtliche Sellung der evangelischen Kirche Deutschlands*	433n221
Ritschl, *Dogmengeschichte*	278n35
Ritter Festschrift	446n3
Ritter, *Dämonie der Macht*	431n204
Ritter, *Neugestaltung Europas*	359n26
Ritter, *Weltwirkung der Reformation*	316n111
Rockwell, *Doppelehe des Landgrafen*	343n400
Rommen, *Ewige Wiederkehr des Naturrechts*	273n9
Rosenstock-Huessy, *Die europäischen Revolutionen*	460n19
Rothe, *Theologische Ethik*	436n255
Rückert Festgabe	264n51
Rupp, *Righteousness of God*	236n1
Ruppel, "Fragen des kirchlichen Disziplinarwesens," in *Smend Festgabe*	496n278
Saint-Blancat, "L'Augustinisme de Luther en 1510"	276n23
Saint-Blancat, "Luther und Petrus Lombardus," *ZSTh* 22 (1953)	276n23
Saint-Blancat, "Recherches," *VC* 8 (1954)	276n23
Sauter, *Die rechtsphilosophischen Grundlagen des Naturrechts*	273n12
Scheel, *Evangelium, Kirche und Volk*	314n98
Scheel, *Martin Luther*	242n1
Schlink, "Gerechtigkeit und Gnade," *KuD* 2 (1956)	327n211
Schlink, *Theologie der Bekenntnisschriften*	236n5
Schlink, "Das theologische Problem des Naturrechts," in *Meiser Festschrift*	239n42
Schlink, *Theology of the Lutheran Confessions*	255n24
Schlink, "Weisheit und Torheit," *KuD* 1 (1955)	276n18
Irmgard Schmidt, "Das göttliche Recht und seine Bedeutung im Bauernkrieg"	286n46

522

Short Titles and Place of Full Citation

Kurt D. Schmidt, "Luthers Lehre vom heiligen Geist," in *Schöffel Festschrift*	262n33
Kurt D. Schmidt, "Widerstandsrecht der Kirchen," *Informationsblatt* 8 (1959)	448n3
Schmitt, *Lage der europäischen Rechtswissenschaft*	236n10
Schöffel Festschrift	262n33
Schönfeld, *Grundlegung der Rechtswissenschaft*	239n42
Schönfeld, *Über die Gerechtigkeit*	238n26
Schoenstedt, *Tyrannenmord*	416n84
Schott, *Fleisch und Geist nach Luthers Lehre*	252n20
Schott, "Anfänge evangelischen Kirchenrechts?" *ZEvKR* 2 (1953)	361n33
Schott, "Ist das Kirchenrecht eine Funktion des Kirchenbegriffs?" *ThLZ* 79 (1954)	237n21
Schott, "Kirchliche Gesetzgebungsgewalt im Urteil Luthers," *WZ (H)* 4 (1954)	249n66
Schreiner Festgabe	309n59
Schreiner, *Recht der Kirche*	398n85
Schrey, *Die Bedeutung der biblischen Botschaft für die Welt des Rechts*	272n3
Schrey, *Gerechtigkeit in biblischer Sicht*	235n1
Schrey, "Wiedergeburt des Naturrechts," *ThR.NF* 19 (1951)	254n6
Schubert, *Bekenntnisbildung und Religionspolitik*	447n3
Schulte, *Quellen und Literatur zum Canonischen Recht*	246n44
Schulze, "Reformation und Widerstandsrecht," *EvTh* 8 (1948/49)	448n3
Schumann, "Bemerkungen zur Lehre vom Gesetz," *ZSTh* 16 (1939)	237n19
Schumann, "Widerstandsrecht und Rechtfertigung," in *Macht und Recht*	448n3
Erich Seeberg, *Grundzüge der Theologie Luthers*	255n21
Erich Seeberg, *Luthers Theologie*, 1	295n122
Erich Seeberg, *Luthers Theologie*, 2	249n67
Reinhold Seeberg, *Dogmengeschichte*, 4.I	363n40
Reinhold Seeberg, "Luthers Anschauung vom Geschlechtsleben und Ehe," *LuJ* 7 (1925)	300n168
Sehling, *Geschichte der protestantischen Kirchenverfassung*	433n221
Siegfried, "Le Protestantisme"	249n70
Simonius Festgabe	319n142
Smend Festgabe	471n1
Smend Festschrift	252n19
Smend, "Wissenschafts- und Gestaltsprobleme im evangelischen Kirchenrecht," *ZEvKR* 6 (1957/58)	494n249
Soden, "Verfassungen der deutschen evangelischen Landeskirchen," *ThR.NF* 5 (1933)	236n11
Sohm, *Kirchenrecht*	236n3
Söhngen, *Einheit in der Theologie*	258n8
Sommerlath, "Kirche und Reich Gottes," *ZSTh* 16 (1939)	360n29
Speiser-Sarasin Festschrift	319n142
Spörl, "Augustinus — Schöpfer einer Staatslehre?" *HJ* 74 (1955)	251n4

Short Titles and Place of Full Citation

Spörl, "Die 'Civitas Dei' im Geschichtsdenken Ottos von Freising," in *La Ciudad de Dios*	251n4
Spranger, "Zur Frage der Erneuerung des Naturrechts," *Universitas* 3 (1948)	317n115
Stadelmann, *Das Zeitalter der Reformation*	438n264
Stadtmüller, *Das Naturrecht im Lichte der geschichtlichen Erfahrung*	273n12
Stahl, *Kirchenverfassung nach Lehre und Recht der Protestanten*	236n9
Stählin Festschrift	251n3
Stange, *Theologische Aufsätze*	276n23
Stange, *Bernhard von Clairvaux*	276n23
Stange, "'Evangelisches Erwachen' in der katholischen Theologie," *ZSTh* 22 (1953)	249n73
Stange, "Luther über Gregor von Rimini," in id., *Theologische Aufsätze*	276n23
Stange, *Luther und das Evangelium*	248n57
Stange, "Luthers Lehre vom gesellschaftlichen Leben," *ZSTh* 7 (1929)	427n161
Stange, "Die Schmalkaldischen Artikel Luthers," *ZSTh* 14 (1937)	308n51
Stange, *Studien zur Theologie Luthers*	296n23
Stange, *Der johanneische Typus*	250n73
Steck, "Die beiden Reiche," *Stimme der Gemeinde* 3 (1951)	251n3
Steck, "Luthers Autorität," in *Ecclesia semper reformanda*	447n15
Steck, *Luther und die Schwärmer*	284n40
Steinlein, "Luthers Abgrenzung des Gehorsams gegen die Obrigkeit," *JMLB* 3 (1948)	408n41
Stephan, *Discursus*	421n123
Stephan, *Luther in den Wandlungen seiner Kirche*	268n15
Steubing, *Naturrecht und natürliche Theologie im Protestantismus*	274n13
Storck, *Das allgemeine Priestertum bei Luther*	386n28
Stratenwerth, *Die Naturrechtslehre des Duns Scotus*	283n32
Stroux, "Summum ius summa iniuria," in *Speiser-Sarasin Festschrift*	319n142
Stupperich, "Die guten Werke in der Theologie Luthers," in *Schreiner Festgabe*	377n156
Stutz Festschrift	429n186
Stutz, *Johann Sigismund von Brandenburg und das Reformationsrecht*	447n12
Suss, "La loi éternelle," *Positions luthériennes* 10 (1962)	282n27
Tarvainen, "Conformitas Christi in Luthers Theologie," *ZSTh* 22 (1953)	375n146
Thielicke, *Kirche und Öffentlichkeit*	332n271
Thielicke, *Theologische Ethik*, 1	243n15
Thielicke, *Theologische Ethik*, 2.II. *Ethik des Politischen*	422n130
Thieme, "Die Ehescheidung Heinrichs VIII als europäischer Rechtsfall," in *Aubin Festgabe*	343n402
Thieme, "Die Rechtsstellung des Fremden in Deutschland," *Recueils de la Société Jean Bodin* 10 (1958)	381n190

Short Titles and Place of Full Citation

Törnvall, "Der Christ in den zwei Reichen," *EvTh* 10 (1950/51)	273n7
Törnvall, *Geistliches und weltliches Regiment bei Luther*	256n28
Törnvall, "Regementslärans socialteologiska huvuduppgift," *NKT* 25 (1956)	468n126
Torrance, "Die Eschatologie der Reformation," *EvTh* 14 (1954)	267n12
Troeltsch, "Christliches Naturrecht," in id., *Gesammelte Schriften*, 4	323n169
Troeltsch, "Die kulturgeschichtliche Methode in der Dogmengeschichte," in id., *Gesammelte Schriften*, 4	249n71
Troeltsch, *Die Soziallehren der christlichen Kirchen und Gruppen*	238n34
Turrecremata, *Summa de ecclesia domini*	285n45
Vajta, *Theologie des Gottesdienstes bei Luther*	304n18
Veit, "Die Geistesgeschichtliche Situation des Naturrechts," *Merkur* 1 (1947)	407n39
Vignaux, "Luther commentateur," *EPhM* 21 (1935)	250n76
Vignaux, "Sur Luther et Ockham," *FS* 32 (1950)	250n76
Vogel, *Gott in Christo*	362n37
Vogel's Cross Reference	235n19
Vogelsang, *Anfänge von Luthers Christologie*	242n9
Vogelsang, *Luthers Werke in Auswahl*, 5	248n60
Walter, *Theologie Luthers*	280n12
Walz, "Die biblische Botschaft von der Gerechtigkeit Gottes und unser Recht," in *Gerechte Ordnung*	305n25
Watson, "Luther und die Heiligung," in *Lutherforschung heute*	377n166
Watson, *The State as a Servant of God*	347n437
Watson, *Um Gottes Gottheit*	254n11
Hans E. Weber, "Von den Kirchenrechtstheorien im alten Luthertum," *EvTh* 6 (1946/47)	392n51
Hans E. Weber, *Reformation, Orthodoxie und Rationalismus*	319n137
Max Weber, *Gesammelte Aufsätze zur Religionssoziologie*, 1	238n33
Wehrhahn, "Grundlagenproblematik," *ThR.NF* 18 (1950), 19 (1951)	237n16
Wehrhahn, "Der Stand des Methodenproblems in der evangelischen Kirchenrechtslehre," *ZEvKR* 1 (1951)	237n21
Wehrung, *Kirche nach evangelischem Verständnis*	240n49
Wehrung, "Theologie, Kirche, Kirchenleitung," *ZSTh* 22 (1953)	371n115
Wehrung, *Welt und Reich*	251n2
Weinkauff, "Naturrecht in evangelischer Sicht," *Zeitwende* 23 (1951/52)	307n49
Weinkauff, *Widerstandsrecht*	448n5
Welzel, *Naturrecht und materiale Gerechtigkeit*	248n62
Welzel, *Vom irrenden Gewissen*	378n172
Welzel, "Gesetz und Gewissen," in *Festschrift des Deutschen Juristentages*	378n172
Wendland, "Kritische Bedeutung der neutestamentlichen Lehre von den beiden Reichen," *ThLZ* 79 (1954)	251n3

Short Titles and Place of Full Citation

Wendland, "Situation am Ende der Neuzeit," *Dok* 13 (1957)	447n15
Wendland, "Weltherrschaft Christi," in *Stählin Festschrift*	251n3
Wenger, "Zur christlichen Begründung des Naturrechts," *ZSRG*.R 69 (1952)	273n12
Weyenborg, "La charité dans la première théologie de Luther (1509-1515)," *RHE* 45 (1950)	248n60
Widerstandsrecht und Staatsgewalt	465n76
Wieacker, *Privatrechtsgeschichte der Neuzeit*	273n10
Wingren, "Geistliches und weltliches Regiment bei Luther," *ThZ* 3 (1947)	255n24
Wingren, "Kirche und Beruf," in *Ein Buch von der Kirche*	445n343
Wingren, *Luthers Lehre vom Beruf*	255n24
Wingren, *Die Predigt*	240n53
Wingren, *Schöpfung und Gesetz*	352n471
Wohlhaupter, "Aequitas canonica," *VGG*.R 56 (1931)	319n141
Erik Wolf, "Idee und Wirklichkeit des Reiches," in *Reich und Recht*	447n10
Erik Wolf, *Ordnung der Kirche*	471n2
Erik Wolf, *Große Rechtsdenker*	236n2
Erik Wolf, *Rechtsgedanke und biblische Weisung*	288n67
Erik Wolf, "Zur Rechtsgestalt der Kirche," in *Bekennende Kirche*	390n47
Ernst Wolf, "Der christliche Glaube und das Recht," *ZevKR* 4 (1955)	461n2
Ernst Wolf, "'Evangelisches' Eherecht," in *Smend Festschrift*	338n337
Ernst Wolf, *Libertas christiana*	441n298
Ernst Wolf, "'Natürliches Gesetz' und 'Gesetz Christi' bei Luther," *EvTh* 2 (1935)	294n117
Ernst Wolf, "Naturrecht und Gerechtigkeit," *EvTh* 7 (1947/8)	251n9
Ernst Wolf, "Frage des Naturrechts bei Thomas und bei Luther"	240n48 and 446n3
Ernst Wolf, *Peregrinatio*, 1	242n3 and 471n1
Ernst Wolf, "Politia Christi," *EvTh* 8 (1948/49)	426n159
Ernst Wolf, "Sinn und Grenze der Anwendung der Zwei-Reiche-Lehre auf das Kirchenrecht," in *Smend Festgabe*	472n9
Ernst Wolf, "Sozialethik des Luthertums," in *Kirche, Bekenntnis und Sozialethos*	441n298
Ernst Wolf, "Vom Problem des Gewissens," in id., *Peregrinatio*, 1	380n183
Wolzendorff, *Staatsrecht und Naturrecht*	447n3
Wünsch, *Ethik des Politischen*	238n30
Wünsch, *Gotteserfahrung und sittliche Tat bei Luther*	246n43
Wünsch, *Wirtschaftsethik*	315n150
Würtenberger, "Wege zum Naturrecht in Deutschland," *ARSP* 38 (1949)	240n50
Zahrnt, *Luther deutet Geschichte*	414n76
Zickendraht, *Der Streit zwischen Erasmus und Luther*	279n8
Zur politischen Predigt	1
Zwicker, *Reich Gottes*	425n148

Index of Bible Passages

→ = see also.

Genesis

1:2	257n43
1:26	167
1:28	52, 167, 314n98
2:16	299n159
3:16	493n234; → 169f., 338n337
4:15	345n413
9:6	344n411, 345n413, 348n445
10:8	416n85
10:9	420n120
22:11	314n101
28:12	278n34, 358n6
32:24	244n22

Exodus

8:2	339n349
11:2	250n78
12:35	250n78
12:36	340n362
17:11	415n79
20:5	329n233
21	348n445
34:14	329n233
40:20	356n36

Leviticus

24:16	459n11

Deuteronomy

1:13	427n165
4	283n36
4:2	294n111
5:6	300n162
9:10	294n117, 295n119
18:15	358n8
19:4	350n461
21:15	340n360
24:1	340n361, 341n366
28:13	331n263
32:35	380n186

1 Samuel

2:6	281n20
16:7	225

2 Samuel

22:27	264n58

1 Kings

16:31	312n84

Psalms

1:1	277n28, 291n94, 303n10, 306n31
1:2	17, 277n28, 371n115
2:2	418n108
5:1	275n14
5:8	295n125
6:1f.	328n231
7:10	292n101
8:6	269n18
10:16	257n42
13:3	246n45
15:1	478n110
18:26	64, 264n58, 327n220
20:1	350n459
23:3	273n6
25:8	324n182
26:5	70
27:13	36, 271n36
33:9	49

527

Index of Bible Passages

33:16	415n79	8:10	314n99	18:18	481n147
42:7	283n31	9:14	264n55	18:23	331n268
51:5	292n101	49:23	456n7	19:6	299n161
51:10	336n320	53:2	499n304	19:8	75, 341n366, 342n377
51:16	400n9	55:11	85, 208, 475n69		
68:18	269n18	60:16	456n7	19:21	451n37, 453n50
76:4	420n120			19:29	451n37
78:40	265n63	**Jeremiah**		21:12	410n53
82:1	351n467	6:14	333n283	23:8	386n19
82:2	346n427			23:10	386n19
82:6	429n179	**Ezekiel**		25	35, 170, 171
85:4	331n261	13:10	333n283	25:31	395n65
89:8	279n5			25:35	309n60
91:11	270n29	**Daniel**		27:64b	483n162
99:4	8	11:36	421n125		
101:2	456n3, 484n173			**Luke**	
101:4	292n101, 456n8	**Hosea**		1:52	430n195
101:5	484n173	1:2	250n78	6:31	50
110	34			9:60	500n306
110:1	171	**Amos**		10:7	484n171, 498n300
110:2	269n19, 393n58	6:1	264n55		
111:1	217			10:16	481n147
117:1	383n191	**The Wisdom of Solomon**		12:42	486n180
119:10	289n78			14:1	318n134
119:18	277n27	15:2	378n170	16:8	93
119:37	286n52			24:47	480n137
119:105	286n56	**Ecclesiasticus**			
119:137	265n59	10:13	306n37	**John**	
119:143	275n14			2:13	410n53
119:168	272n36	**Matthew**		3:3	268n14
127	338n342	5:13	412n61	3:5	379n177
142:5	36	5:20	284n41	3:6	268n14
143:2	18	5:38	356n41, 403n7	4:23	45
143:10	287n56	5:44	375n140	6:63	334n294, 399n91
145:17	265n59	7:12	50, 291n90, 303n6		
146:9	381n190			10:3b	371n107, 376n155
		7:15	474n43		
Proverbs		7:17	294n117	10:9	371n107, 376n155
8:15	405n23	10:10	484n171		
26:23	292n101	13:44	451n37	10:35	431n201
		16	399n91	12:31	268n14
Ecclesiastes		16:19	481n147	14:6	398n78
1:2	323n174	17:27	166, 403n6	14:26	337n324
		18:15	395n67	16:11	270n29
Isaiah		18:17	396n74, 479n127		
6:10	314n99				

Index of Bible Passages

Acts

2:44	491n224
2:46	491n224
5:29	414n77
5:40	453n49
7	490n216
8:5	490n216
8:38	490n216
15	501n310
18:24	490n216

Romans

1:16	357n54
1:17	17
1:19	253n3
2:14	304n20
2:15	295n119, 305n26
3:9	310n66
3:11	255n16
3:27	370n103
4:1	273n6
4:15	296n135
4:17	296n136
5:5	294n117, 295n119, 368n87
6:3	489n207
7:1	17
7:8	66
7:11	66
7:14	292n98
7:16	378n169
7:17	378n169
8:2	295n119
8:3	277n26
8:14	289n75
10:4	366n69
10:10	412n62, 474n51
11:8	265n63
12	221
12:19	375n140, 418n107
13:1	126, 221, 406n29, 407n40, 411n56, 465n65
13:3	345n416
13:4	348n445
13:9	303n6
13:10	89, 370n102
14:4	302n5

1 Corinthians

2:14	225
2:15	101, 104, 156, 203, 372n116, 397n74
3:17	394n58
4:20	287n63
6:1	375n140
7	339n348
7:9	75
7:31	404n15
10:17	361n32
11:7	344n408
11:19	458n10
11:20	491n224
11:26	491n224
12:14	439n276
13:12	269n18
14:40	480n141, 489n205, 501n309
15:24	269n18
15:48	30

2 Corinthians

3:5	287n58
3:18	374n133
4:4	268n14, 270n29
11:20	375n140

Galatians

1:6	349n447
1:9	498n300
2:5	488n188
2:6	385n16
3:10	243n13, 297n138
3:15	343n395
3:23	249n66, 267n12, 330n250
3:28	451n31
4:3	323n171
4:22	343n395
5:14	380n180
5:22	297n138

Ephesians

1:3	261n17
1:9	282n27
2:8	297n138
2:19	381n190, 399n91
2:20	393n56
4:13	366n70, 374n134
4:15	434n230
5:23	264n53
5:30	264n53
6:17	348n445

Philippians

2:6	408n42
3:20	261n17, 272n36, 318n129, 382n190

Colossians

1:25	346n421
3:3	293n104

1 Thessalonians

5:21	400n95
5:23	289n78

2 Thessalonians

2:4	394n58
2:8	113

1 Timothy

1:5	426n154
1:8	330n251
1:9	123, 330n251,

Index of Bible Passages

		Hebrews		1 Peter	
	366n69,	4:12	293n108	2:4	399n91
	381n190,	8:10	368n87	2:9	434n236
	387n32,	10:28	277n26	2:13	271n34
	388n35,	11:1	281n20	4:15	404n12,
	405n26,	13:1	374n138		494n252
	426n152	13:5	375n140		
2 Timothy				**1 John**	
1:7	212	**James**		4:10	291n88
		2:10	243n19	4:17a	444n319
Titus		4:7b	112	**Revelation**	
3:1	465n65	5:16	417n101	19:16	421n125

Index of Subjects

See above, 234n8 and 235n15.

→ preceded by comma = *see;* preceded by semicolon or blank indent = *see further*.

For cross-references which are *not preceded* by *"Law,"* see the entries following the line of stars on 541 below.

Different or expanded or coordinating phrasings of subject titles or of their subentries are separated by a slash (/); qualifications of subject titles or of their subentries are placed in parentheses. In the cross-references such additional materials are listed only when they are significant for the cross-reference.

Technical terms and phrases are listed in their English version when this was possible or seemed wise to do so.

For "Luther, Martin," only biographical materials are listed.

For listings of Luther's juristic or theological materials, see the subjects.

Law/*lex/ius/Gesetz/Recht*.
For actions (e.g., adultery), institutions (e.g., kingdom), and persons (e.g., prince) connected with law, see below, the entries following the line of stars.

administrative law, 401n1; → *Law:* Lutheran ecclesiastical law as man-made, autonomous law of the church, is law for the corporeal church, as administrative law

Bill of Rights, 247n53

Canon law/canonistic literature/ canonistic teachings, 8f., 14f., 20, 40, 45, 51, 65, 73-75, 98, 99, 101, 118, 119, 131f., 144, 155f., 159, 178, 184, 185, 187, 188, 191, 193, 196, 200-203, 218-22, 230, 237nn18,20, 241nn65,72, 246n44,

531

Index of Subjects

260n13, 287n60, 292n104, 399n91, 406n32, 435n242, 478n110, 480n136, 481n148, 482nn151-52, 489n199, 490n214, 491n222, 495n259, 496n276, 497n287; → *Law: Decretum Gratiani; Law: Liber Extra; Law: Liber Sextus;* bishop; papacy

ceremonial law, 284n43, 328n222; → *Law:* Lutheran ecclesiastical law as man-made, autonomous law of the church, is law for the corporeal church, as law for worship

Christian law, 90, 106, 118, 127, 286n54, 302n5, 362n39, 374n140, 380n187

civil/civic law, 344n411, 401n1; → positive law

common law of believing Christians, 98, 119, 142, 193, 489nn197-98,205, 490nn211,213, 502n315

criminal law, 65, 67f., 270n27, 350n461, 353n11; → equity

Decalogue/law of Moses, 20, 69f., 74, 81-83, 86f., 144, 185f., 243n15, 249n66, 253n6, 274n14, 277n26, 296n135, 323n175, 324n183, 331n263, 334n291, 368n83, 403n7, 485n179

    and divine natural law, 45, 57f., 81f., 353n2

    and secular natural law, 82, 250n85; → *Law:* substantive secular natural law, and Decalogue

    belongs to the whole world because it is inscribed in the minds of all people and therefore is universally binding, 82, 311nn70,72-73, 313n87, 353n2, 354n14, 369n91

    does not change sinful man's misinterpretation of the divine natural law (is carnally interpreted as righteousness of works)/does not lead to Salvation, 41f., 82-83, 354n20, 355n24, 356nn38-39,42-43,45, 357nn47,53-54

    is law of wrath, → *Law:* law, of wrath

    is promulgated by Moses (a sinner, the ruler of the Jewish nation, the interpreter of the secular natural law) as transpositive human law, 81-82, 313n87, 328n222, 354n22, 355nn24,27

    is *Sachsenspiegel* of the Jews, 81f., 311n72

    its spiritual meaning is discovered only by spiritual man, 69f., 82f., 86f.; → man, reborn, and law, understands the spiritual meaning of law and uses law spiritually

    points to Christ and grace, 333n284, 354n21, 355n24, 356nn35-36, 368n84, 387n35; → *Law:* law, use of, theological

    → *Law:* divine law, as commandment and institution

Decretum Gratiani, 144, 243n19, 244n21, 246n44, 257n40, 258n53, 260n13, 276n24, 287n60, 296n132, 298n152, 316n112, 318n134, 319n140, 326n210, 327n213, 338n339, 341n368, 343n398, 373n132, 387n29, 389n40, 394n60, 408n41, 411n55, 422n140, 433n227, 434n233, 435n242, 454n63, 478n110, 490n214, 498n300

Digest, 315n108, 416n92

disciplinary law, 67, 330n258; → church, discipline of

divine law, 5-9, 16-18, 20f., 39, 41f., 52f., 130f., 239n40, 242n75, 284n44, 286nn53-54, 316n112, 324n183, 328n222; → *Law:* law, terminology of

    as commandment and institution, 52f., 227, 284n43, 286n54, 291n90, 300n162, 407n33,

Index of Subjects

413n71, 440n297; → *Law:* divine law as positive law; *Law:* Lutheran ecclesiastical law, and divine law; *Law:* institutional secular natural law; *Law:* substantive secular natural law; church; *oeconomia; politia*
  as positive legal order, 39f., 63-66, 326n200
  First Table and Second Table, 57, 69f., 209f., 285n46, 309n61, 312nn79,82, 346n425, 408nn41-42, 410n54, 451nn36-37, 452nn42-44,48, 456n2
  Ten Commandments, 45, 57f., 69, 81-83, 109, 242n73, 243n15, 244n27, 283n30, 289n73, 298n151, 301n171, 306n35, 311nn70,73, 312n81, 313nn87,93, 314nn99,104, 332n274, 334n290, 353n4, 368n83, 370n107, 371n111, 380n182, 408n42, 413n69, 451n36, 459n11
  → *Law:* law, superior vs. inferior
divine law as natural law is law for man in the incorrupt, the corrupt, and the redeemed status, 16-22, 49, 54-56, 69, 87f., 98-101, 107, 115f., 208-11, 218f., 229, 248n60, 315n108, 322n157, 380n187, 396n74, 410n54; → *Law:* law, terminology of
  and Christ's kingdom, 41, 92f., 208f.
  and Golden Rule, 50f.
  and reason, 18, 41-44, 48, 307n40
  as statute, 44-47
  cannot be obeyed by natural (sinner) man, 17f., 66, 87, 218f., 243n20
  causes the sinner to despair or blaspheme, 16-19, 43f., 244n22, 247n54; → *Law:* law, of wrath; *Anfechtung*
  claims man totally, 17, 41, 46-50, 52f., 289nn76,79; → *Law:* divine law as natural law, goal of
  condemns natural (sinner) man to spiritual death, 17, 64f., 245n37; → *Law:* law, of wrath
  content of, 49-51
  features of, 43-48
  goal of, 46-48 (→ 250n74), 50, 54f., 219, 288nn70-71, 289nn73-76, 297n141; → *Law:* divine law as natural law, claims man totally
  is a given of man's incorrupt nature, inscribed in his heart, 18, 44-50, 54, 87, 208f., 243n20, 286n48, 291n87
  is again proclaimed by God (Decalogue), 45, 81
  is connected with/different from the secular natural law, 54f., 58f., 62f., 68f., 225f., 228
  is covered in darkness caused by sin, 20, 44, 54f., 81, 83
  is different from man-made law, 41f., 45, 49f., 66, 218f., 220, 295n121
  is experienced by natural (sinner) man as perverse law, 18; → 44, 64f.
  is identical with divine love, and therefore is law of love (*lex charitatis*), 41, 47, 50, 52, 88, 127, 221, 290n86, 291n87, 295nn119,124
  is implemented by God, 49f., 296n135
  is law-creating divine sovereign will, 20, 39, 41, 43-46, 54, 66, 92f., 208-10, 225f., 239n40, 279n8, 305n26
  is the order for the life of the spiritual man, 4f., 49-51, 219, 227f.; → *Law:* divine law as positive law, is spiritual law which organizes the spiritual communal life of spiritual man; *Law:* law, of the Christian estate

Index of Subjects

is spiritual, perfect law and generates spiritual life, 45-48, 52f., 289n74, 297n141; → 84f.
is standard for all legal matters, 43
is understood and obeyed only by the believing Christian (a member of Christ's kingdom), 92f., 106, 126f., 208f., 219, 225f., 228, 312n82; → man, reborn, and law, understands the spiritual meaning of law and uses law spiritually
promulgation of, 48-50
relationship with the divine positive law, 51-53, 363n42
sovereignty and universality of, 16f., 48, 64f., 282n27
→ *Law:* law, of Christ, is the authentic interpretation of the divine meaning of the divine natural law

divine law as positive law is law for man in the incorrupt, the corrupt, and the redeemed status, 18f., 21, 40, 51f., 70, 85f., 137f., 202, 210f., 219f., 301n173, 362n39, 396n74, 492n230; → *Law:* law, terminology of
and Decalogue, 45
as commandment and institution, → *Law:* Lutheran ecclesiastical law as divine, heteronomous, constitutional law of the church; church, as institution of the divine positive law; marriage as institution of the divine positive law; office of public ministry
as statute, 44f.
is designed to facilitate spiritual man's obedience to the divine natural law, 52f.
is identical with divine love, 52
is law of the hidden (spiritual) church, 85, 184, 285n46
is spiritual law which organizes the spiritual communal life of spiritual man, 51f., 227f.
→ *Law:* Lutheran ecclesiastical law, and divine law

divine spiritual basic rights of a Christian (brotherly love, equality, freedom), 31, 97f., 137, 200f., 210f., 227f., 247n53, 285n46; → *Law:* Lutheran ecclesiastical law, and divine law; *cura religionis* of the evangelical prince, essence of; estate, spiritual/Christian

ecclesiastical law, 6-9, 160

Lutheran ecclesiastical law, 6-10, 101, 176f., 216-22, 228f., 504n22
and divine law, 6f., 21, 85f., 98-101, 119, 127, 184f., 188, 193, 203, 219-21, 228f., 286n53, 318n131; → *Law:* Lutheran ecclesiastical law as divine, heteronomous, constitutional law of the church; *Law:* Lutheran ecclesiastical law as man-made, autonomous law of the church, implements the divine natural law in Christ's interpretation, divine positive law, and the three spiritual basic rights of a Christian
and kingdom of God or Christ, 7-9, 30-32, 177; → governance, spiritual; kingdom, of God; kingdom of Christ
development after Luther, 129-32, 214f., 231

Lutheran ecclesiastical law as divine, heteronomous, constitutional law of the church, 104, 121, 123, 177-79, 185-87, 362n39, 492n230; → *Law:* common law of believing Christians; *Law:* divine law as positive law, is spiritual law which organizes the spiritual communal life of spiritual man; *Law:* divine spiritual basic rights of a Christian; *Law:* Lutheran ecclesiastical law, and divine law; *Law:* Lutheran

Index of Subjects

ecclesiastical law, and kingdom of God or Christ; *Law:* law, of Christ; Baptism; church, as corporeal spiritual communion; church, as institution of the divine positive law; church, governance of, spiritual; estate, spiritual/Christian; governance, spiritual; Keys, Power of; Lord's Supper; office of public ministry; priesthood of believers

Lutheran ecclesiastical law as man-made, autonomous law of the church, 100f., 104, 127, 162, 184-203, 211f., 480nn139-40, 504n22

and order of the *politia,* 197f.

circumstances and time for the enacting of, 190, 203, 484n177, 485nn178-79, 486n181, 487n182, 496n279, 501n310

competency for the enacting and implementing of, 98, 189-91, 197-99, 222, 387n31, 392n50, 400nn94-95, 481n147, 482n154, 487n183, 501n310; → 172-74; *Law:* Lutheran ecclesiastical law as man-made, autonomous law of the church, establishes the duty and right of the believer to participate in the creation of ecclesiastical law, in the judgment concerning its legitimacy, and in the supervision of its implementation; *Law:* Lutheran ecclesiastical law as man-made, autonomous law of the church, is created in a public process of voluntary cooperation by the believers; estate, spiritual/Christian

eliminates the spiritual legal differentiation between priest and layman, and all jurisdictions, ranks, and subordinations in the church, 97f., 118-19, 121, 178, 193, 373n131, 383n2, 385nn11,13-14,16, 386nn20,28, 392n50, 393n57, 434nn236-37, 435n239, 438n274, 472nn18-21, 481n147; → church, God in Christ is the only governmental authority in; estate, spiritual/Christian; priesthood of believers

establishes faith and brotherly love as the constructive principles for man-made laws in the church (so that all law-actions in the church are actions of love, service, and voluntary subordination), 97f., 127, 161f., 184, 188, 211-14, 221, 229, 384nn4-5,8, 385n14, 389n45, 395n68, 472n17, 482n149, 487n188, 496n279, 501n310

establishes the duty and right of the believer to participate in the creation of ecclesiastical law, in the judgment concerning its legitimacy, and in the supervision of its implementation, 101, 119, 123, 142, 192-95, 203, 394nn59,62, 400nn94-95, 440n289, 492n231, 502n315

→ *Law:* Lutheran ecclesiastical law as man-made, autonomous law of the church, competency for the enacting and implementing of; *Law:* Lutheran ecclesiastical law as man-made, autonomous law of the church, has to be reformed or resisted in certain circumstances; call, extrasacramental; Keys, Power of; office of public ministry, disciplining incumbent of

form (literary) of, 190f., 485n179, 486n181

goal/purpose of, 100, 161f., 187, 198f., 201, 203, 211f., 221, 480nn140-41, 482n149, 488n189

has to be reformed or resisted in certain circumstances, 21, 98-

535

100, 101, 112, 119, 121-23, 141, 183, 200-202, 212f., 219f., 222, 394nn59,62, 398n78, 411n56, 440n291, 497nn284,291; → *cura religionis* of the evangelical prince; man, reborn, is spiritual man who judges all things

implements (and therefore is controlled by) the divine natural law in Christ's interpretation, divine positive law, and the three spiritual basic rights of a Christian, 98-101, 104, 127, 162, 184-88, 193, 202f., 212f., 219f., 229, 318n131, 383n2, 396n74; → *Law:* divine spiritual basic rights of a Christian; *Law:* Lutheran ecclesiastical law, and divine law; *Law:* law, of Christ, is the authentic interpretation of the divine meaning of the divine natural law

is created in a public process of voluntary cooperation by the believers, which is guided by rational considerations (expediency), with reason having been illuminated by faith, 31f., 98, 100f., 188-91, 199, 203, 221, 384n4, 395n68, 398nn80-81,86, 400nn94-95, 482n155, 487n187, 493nn241-45, 494n247, 501nn309-10, 502n313; → 371n116, 445n341

is law for the corporeal church (which exists in particular churches or congregations), 98, 100, 127, 161f., 488n189

as administrative law for the external matters of the church, 100, 197f., 398n80, 488n194 → church, *diaconia* of; church, governance of, external; church, supervision in; office of public ministry, economics of; visitation, of congregations

as disciplinary law, → church, discipline of

as law for offices, esp. the office of public ministry, 99f., 192, 194f.; → call, extrasacramental

as law for weddings, 103f.

as law for worship, 85f., 187, 190f., 203, 396n71, 480nn141-42, 481nn143-44, 488n189, 496nn281,283, 497n284, 501n309, 502nn312-13; → God, worship of

is not binding in the absolute sense, is not legally necessary but is needed for the sake of Christian brothers, 98-100, 103, 187f., 191, 202f., 211f., 221, 229, 480n140, 481n148, 482n149, 487nn187-88, 488n189

is not part of Christ's spiritual governance and therefore is not spiritual or perfect law, 98f., 187f., 196f., 199, 398n86; → governance, spiritual

secures/demands legal and spiritual equality of particular churches, 98f., 389n40, 392n56, 495n275, 496n277; → church, as corporeal spiritual communion

secures/demands the independence of the (spiritual and external) governance of the church from the governance of the *politia*, 143, 189f., 203, 346n425, 408n43, 409n51, 432n209, 460n19, 483nn162,164, 484n174, 494n252, 497n288; → authority, governmental, competency/tasks of; *cura religionis* of the evangelical prince, essence of

Roman Catholic ecclesiastical law, 237n13; → *Law:* Canon law; bishop; conciliarism; papacy

Index of Subjects

emergency law, 143f.; → *cura religionis* of the evangelical prince, endows the prince with the duty and right to reform the church when conditions exist which create an emergency

family law, 77, 201, 228

geistliches Recht, 241n65; → *Law:* Canon law; *Law:* spiritual law
Golden Bull (1356), 441n299
Golden Rule, 50f., 57, 59f., 62, 90, 241n71, 309nn60-61, 311n78, 315n108, 316n114, 319n143, 322n166, 330n259

heathen law/law for heathen, 57, 381n189, 383n191, 427n168; → *Law:* Roman law; heathen

Imperial law, 76f., 189f., 316n112, 321nn152,155, 332n274, 409n49, 490n214; → *Law:* public law; *Law:* Roman law
ius utrumque, 100f., 188, 237n20

Jewish national law, 74f., 81f., 185, 285n46, 312n83, 340n362, 353n11

Kirchenordnung, 504n22

law, 317n116
 and faith, 14, 85-88; → justification by faith
 and gospel (grace), 35, 85f., 101, 241n60, 262n35, 267n12, 270n27, 313n90, 329n250, 355n24, 356n35, 358n9, 367n82, 369n88, 480n137, 487n182; → *Law:* law, use of, theological
 and justification by faith, 13f., 85-88, 126f., 146f., 174f., 213-15, 223-25; → justification by faith
 and Mysticism, 45f., 49
 and need, 61, 76f., 318n134, 319n140
 and Reformation, 12-15, 248nn61,62, 273n12
 as empty law, 47, 368n85, 379n177, 405n26,
 as genus, 353n2
 as letter/sign vs. substance/spirit (*figura, res, signum*), 42, 45-46, 63f., 69, 284n43, 292n102, 294nn116-17, 323n176, 324n183, 333nn281-83, 354n21, 410n54, 411n58; → 302n3, 356n36; *Law:* substantive secular natural law, and righteousness; symbol/reality
 as *Rechtsgesetz*, → *Law:* divine law, as positive legal order
 as school for understanding divine righteousness, 68f.
 as stopgap (make-do order, "beggary," dead law, *Notordnung*, sick law), 28f., 60f., 68f., 208f., 225-27, 323n175, 326n208, 340n355; → 46, 288n67; *Law:* law, as letter/sign vs. substance/spirit
 books of, 62, 301n173, 309nn60,61, 317nn118,123, 318n130, 321n155
 concept/doctrine/method/organization of, 1f., 5, 10-14, 18-21, 39f., 41f., 48-50, 53-55, 57, 66, 88, 129f., 174f., 213f., 225-27, 228
 disobedience to, → *Law:* positive law, disobedience to makes one guilty before God
 dispensation from, → *Law:* substantive secular natural law, dispensation from
 form of, 60f., 319n139
 formalism in, 48, 288n67
 goal of, 275n16, 298n146
 "is always an honest man, but the judge is often a scoundrel," 411n58

537

is God's gift, 323nn174,177
is simultaneously sacred and secular, 10f.
medieval doctrine/understanding of, 9, 12, 14, 18-21, 40-46, 58, 73f., 227, 283n32, 284n44, 285n45, 53, 207, 277n27, 287n60
needs/has new grammar, rules, vocabulary, 296n136, 297nn138,141, 301n177, 322n161; → 365n60, 366n71, 370n101
normativism in, 46
of Christ, 13, 20f., 31, 42, 45, 87-89, 210f., 225f., 229, 249n66, 284n43, 291n89, 294n117, 295n119, 355n32, 358n9
  as institution, 85f., 301n172
  interprets the Golden Rule spiritually, 50f., 90; → 310n63; *Law:* Golden Rule
  is the authentic (spiritual) interpretation of the divine meaning of the divine natural law as *lex charitatis,* or law of faith and love, the norms of the Christian existence, 50f., 84, 87-89, 92f., 125f., 184, 208f., 225f., 293n109, 358n13, 370n107, 371n111, 374n140
  with the law of faith having priority over the law of love, 88f., 263n48, 370nn102,106, 371n111, 384n10, 404n16
  is love poured into hearts by the Holy Spirit, 294n117, 295n119, 368n87, 370n102
  is spiritual law for the believing sinner and is grasped and obeyed in faith and love, 87-92, 174f., 225f., 284n43, 294n117, 372nn119-20
  → justification by faith
of the Christian estate, 21, 86-93, 119f.; → *Law:* divine spiritual basic rights of a Christian; estate, spiritual/Christian
of the city/secular commonwealth, 6f., 21, 144, 333n281, 440n293
of faith, 88; → *Law:* law, of Christ, is the authentic interpretation of the divine meaning of the divine natural law
of hidden love, 35, 66f., 225f.; → *Law:* law, of wrath; God, acts in contrasts
of Moses, → *Law:* Decalogue
of nations, 303n8, 315n108, 344n411
of wrath/kingdom of wrath, 32-36, 64-66, 68, 78f., 83, 86, 90-93, 98, 111, 117, 199, 208-10, 213f., 225f., 265n63, 294n116, 296n135, 379n176, 448n7, 475n74; → God, acts in contrasts; governance, secular; kingdom of the world
office of, → *Law:* law, use of
ontology of, 41
Positivism in, 6-7, 58, 407n39
secularism of, 54f.
superior vs. inferior, 107, 312n82, 318n134, 338n340, 339n343, 342n377, 370n106, 410n54
terminology of, xviif., 45, 219, 247n53, 249n64, 283n31, 285nn45-46, 298n154, 302n1, 302nn5-6, 303n8, 308n50, 320n148, 362n39, 374n140, 489n205
two kinds of, 41, 273n6, 274n14, 297n141; → *Law:* natural law, dualism in
use/office/task/work of, 63f., 68-70, 126f., 270n27, 298n146, 326nn203,206-7, 329nn242,250-51, 366n69, 367n82, 368n86, 445n340
  civic/political, 66-68, 150, 154f., 329n243, 366n69, 367n82; →

538

Index of Subjects

governance, secular; kingdom of the world
theological/proper, 65-67, 86f., 298n146, 326nn202-3,207, 329nn240,243,250, 355nn25,27, 356n35, 366n69, 367n82, 368nn83-85, 448n7, 487n182; → repentance
third, 368n86
→ doing/using things spiritually or corporeally
Lebensordnung, 310n69
Liber Extra, 341n368, 417n96, 450n18
Liber Sextus, 313n88, 438n270

"might makes right," 67, 113
moral law, 284n43

natural law, 9-11, 14f., 18-21, 40, 57, 61-63, 239n47, 253n6, 254n12, 273nn9-12, 274n13, 275n16, 286n54, 298n154, 313n98, 315n108, and knowledge of God, → God, knowledge of
and sin, 251n19, 252n16, 273n12, 274n13; → *Law:* substantive secular natural law, is the product of natural, sinful man's divine dowry and the infralapsarian, rational, corporeal misinterpretation of the divine natural law
Christian, 92f., 311n74, 380n182
dualism in (divine natural law vs. secular natural law), 40, 62f., 92f., 135, 208f., 227, 315n108, 410n54; → families of man
in science, 285n46
medieval and patristic theories of, 9, 14f., 18f., 44f., 54f., 58, 63, 227, 248n61, 284n44, 313n98
modern Roman Catholic position on, 9
secular natural law, 54-63, 69f., 74f., 77, 81, 110, 114-18, 126-28, 144, 208f., 212-14, 228, 302nn5-6, 309n60, 310n63, 311n78, 313n98, 317n123, 387n35, 413n73, 428n172
institutional secular natural law, 70, 285n46
and church, 70f.
and governmental authority, 77-80, 127f., 213f.
and marriage, → marriage as institution of the secular natural law
substantive secular natural law, 60, 76, 286n47, 302nn1,5-6
and Decalogue (the model for the secular natural law), 57-59, 69f., 73f., 82, 92f., 208f., 225-27, 311nn72-73, 312n86, 313n87, 354n15, 380n182, 407n33, 410n54
and equity, 61f., 74, 79, 317nn118,123, 319n143, 320nn144,146, 351n464, 428n172, 432n209
and history, 56, 59f.
and reason, 57-60, 309nn58,60-61, 313n98, 315n108, 318n133, 319n137; → 315n105
and righteousness (divine spiritual, human external), 54, 55-58, 62f., 68f., 83, 208f., 225-27, 302n3, 310n69, 322nn160-62,164-165,168, 328n229, 331n263, 356n36; → *Law:* law, as stopgap
as *Notordnung*, → *Law:* law as stopgap
dispensation from, 59, 61, 314n104; → marriage as institution of the secular natural law, bigamy, monogamy, polygamy; marriage as institution of the secular natural law, indissolubility and divorce
goal/motto of, 56, 59, 110, 118, 309n60
is based on man's awareness of human solidarity and mutual responsibility ("body of man-

539

Index of Subjects

kind"), which includes the duty to share common burdens and dangers, 56f., 308n53

is connected with/different from/opposed to the divine natural law, 54-56, 58, 69f., 127f., 208f., 302n5; → *Law:* substantive secular natural law, is the product of natural, sinful man's divine dowry and the infralapsarian, rational, corporeal misinterpretation of the divine natural law

is law of universal love for man, 56, 61, 68f., 79, 93, 125f., 208f.

is located in the kingdom of the world/not connected with Christ's kingdom, 54, 57, 63, 199

is normatively expressed in the corporeally understood Golden Rule, 56-62, 208f., 225f., 309n61, 315n108, 319n143

is the product of natural, sinful man's divine dowry and the infralapsarian, rational, corporeal misinterpretation of the divine natural law, 54-56, 62, 83f., 208f., 225f., 254n12, 305nn23,26

is standard for the conduct of non-Christians, 93

is source/standard for the positive law and actions derived from/based on it, 59-63, 69f., 79, 101, 107-9, 114, 116, 198f., 208f., 213f., 309n60, 313n98, 318nn131,133-134, 387n35

limits the power of governmental authority, → authority, governmental, competency/tasks of; resistance in the *politia*, justification for affirming or rejecting different forms of resistance

Naturgesetz, 247n53, 284n44

Naturrecht, 302nn1,5

"necessity <need> has no <positive> law," 113; → *Law:* law, and need

"one may fight force with force," 110, 134, 316n112

Polizeiordnung, 402n1

positive law/earthly/human/man-made/secular, 45, 49f., 54f., 63f., 81f., 107, 197, 295n121, 298n154

and constitution of God's kingdom at the left, 68; → kingdom, of God, as kingdom of God at the right and the left

and equity, → *Law:* substantive secular natural law, and equity

and righteousness, → *Law:* substantive secular natural law, and righteousness

as letter, 63f.; → *Law:* law, as letter/sign vs. substance/spirit

disobedience to makes one guilty before God, 68, 107; → 79

endangers man's relationship with God, 62, 66, 328n222

guidelines for the creating and implementing of, 60f.; → *Law:* substantive secular natural law, and equity

is "beggary," → *Law:* substantive secular natural law, as stopgap

is derived from and controlled by the secular natural law, → *Law:* substantive secular natural law, is source/standard for the positive law and actions derived from/based on it

secures peace and stability in the secular commonwealth (fights the devil and the evil ones, protects the good ones, and therefore is necessary), which pave the way for the proclamation of the gospel, 60f., 67f., 78, 157, 318n129, 321n154, 328n222, 329n243, 330nn251,253, 347nn428,430,439, 351n464; → 269n19; *pax politica*

spiritual characteristics of (is

Index of Subjects

God's gift/divine, external order serving God's will for law/God's "mummary"), 64-70, 78, 93, 114-16, 323nn174,177, 324n178, 333n287, 334n293; → *Law:* positive law, and constitution of God's kingdom at the left; doing/using things spiritually or corporeally; man, reborn, and law, understands the spiritual meaning of law and uses law spiritually

"wilderness" of, 60f.; → 66

procedural law, 311n78

public law, 6f., 130f., 134f., 137f., 161, 181f., 209-11, 236n4, 320n148, 445n346

right, → *Law:* law, terminology of
divine/spiritual, → *Law:* divine spiritual basic rights of a Christian
human, 247n53, 388n36
of reforming the church, → *Law:* Lutheran ecclesiastical law, as man-made, autonomous law of the church, has to be reformed or resisted in certain circumstances
of resistance, → *Law: Widerstandsrecht*

Roman law, 62, 131f., 322n164, 328n222, 427n168, 497n287; → *Law:* Imperial law

Sachsenspiegel, 81f., 311n72

spiritual law/addressing man's spirit/dealing with spiritual, noncorporeal matters/of the Holy Spirit, 8, 14f., 31, 184, 188, 282n27, 289n79, 290n84, 292n102, 297n141, 300n162; → 241n65; *Law:* common law of believing Christians; *Law:* divine law; *Law:* divine law as natural law; *Law:* divine law as positive law; *Law:* divine spiritual basic rights of a Christian; *Law:* Lutheran ecclesiastical law as divine, heteronomous, constitutional law of the church; *Law:* law, of Christ; *Law:* law, of the Christian estate

Staatsrecht, → *Law:* public law

"supreme justice/law is often supreme foolishness/injustice," 314n99, 319n142, 351n462

Venerabilem, 417n96

Weistum, 312n85

Widerstandsrecht, 447n1; → resistance in the church as duty and right; resistance in the *politia*

* * * * * * *

absolution, → Keys, Power of
adultery, → marriage as institution of the secular natural law, indissolubility and divorce
Amt, 234n12; → office; vocation
Anabaptists, 144, 476n76
anarchy (mob action, rebellion, rebelling peasants), 20f., 62, 79, 107, 144, 159, 286n54, 302n5, 321n155, 329n250, 349n451, 351n468, 374n140, 380n187, 411n55, 413n69, 417n101, 449n9; → 118, 273n12
Anfechtung, 16-18, 71, 102f., 213f., 243n11, 244n22, 247n54, 248n55, 295n125, 333n283, 467nn107-8, 476n76, 495n272, 502n10; → *Law:* divine law as natural law, causes the sinner to despair or blaspheme; *Law:* law, of wrath
Antichrist, → papacy
antinomian/antinomians, 20f., 101
atheism, 252n2
authority, governmental, 35, 234n12, 266n5, 423n143

541

and church, 122; → *Law:* Lutheran ecclesiastical law as man-made, autonomous law of the church, secures/demands the independence of the (spiritual and external) governance of the church from the governance of the *politia;* authority, governmental, competency/tasks of; *cura religionis* of the evangelical prince; *pax politica*

begins with the Fall and emerges from marriage (domestic governance), 72f., 77-79, 167-70, 212f., 228, 344nn409-11, 345nn413-14; → *oeconomia*

Christian quality of the incumbent of, → prince, his person (can be) is Christian

compared with the office of preaching, 77-79, 346nn421-22,427, 347nn428,430, 350n456, 459n11

competency/tasks of, 28f., 35, 74, 77-79, 108-9, 118, 123, 125-28, 141, 143-44, 157-59, 166, 186, 189f., 201, 212-14, 258nn53-54, 264n57, 266n3, 346nn421-22,425, 347nn428,430, 348nn440-41, 350n460, 351n464, 404n14, 405n19, 408n43, 409n51, 423n146, 429n180, 430n194, 431n201, 438n276, 440n291, 452n45, 456n7, 459nn11,13, 460nn21-22, 461n29, 481n148, 482nn160-61, 483n162-64,167, 484nn168,171,174, 492n230, 497n288; → 154; *cura religionis* of the evangelical prince, essence of; *pax politica*

is directed toward the common good and the welfare of the subjects, 79, 117f.

is God's gift/institution/representative/tool/vicar (hangman, mask, servant), even when the incumbent is a heathen, 35, 78-79, 151f., 157, 264n57, 268n17, 269n23, 270nn28-29, 271n34, 323n174, 333n287, 346n421, 347nn435,438, 348nn440-41,444,446, 349nn449-50, 405n23, 408n43, 411n56, 414n74, 426nn153,157-58, 430nn194-95, 440n291, 445n338; → 344n409; God, governance of

is God's institution for checking the wicked people and protecting the good people, and therefore is needed in the world, 78, 107, 150, 154-57, 166, 188, 206f., 212f., 258n53, 264n57, 266n3, 269n19, 270n27, 274n14, 345nn413,416, 405n19, 423n146, 427n165, 430n191, 464n39, 481n148; → 93; kingdom of the world

is highly praised by Luther, 78f., 154, 346n427

is to be censured, 411n56, 412n61

is to be honored and obeyed, 78f., 108f., 269n23, 348n446, 411n55

misuse of the office of, 79f., 108-9, 117, 350n459, 351n468, 411nn55-56, 413n68, 414n74; → God, punishes evil governmental authorities; resistance in the *politia*

negative judgment about, 154, 346n422, 407n40, 430n195

spiritual governance of, 140; → *cura religionis* of the evangelical prince

symbol of, → sword, secular

→ *Law:* substantive secular natural law, is source and standard for the positive law and actions derived from/based on it; elector; emperor; magistrate; *politia;* prince

authority, parental (housefather),

Index of Subjects

102f., 292n104, 301n171, 344n409, 396n72, 400n3, 408n42, 426n158, 483n163, 491n224; → *oeconomia*

Babylonian body, → devil, mystical body of
ban (large), 138, 203, 401n20; → Keys, Power of
Baptism/being baptized/to baptize, 30, 85-87, 93, 119, 122, 161f., 178-84, 193, 203, 207-11, 217, 245n31, 257n41, 259n4, 261n27, 266n11, 280n15, 339n352, 360n31, 362n39, 363n41, 365nn63,68, 366n72, 387n35, 393n58, 434nn230,236-38, 435n251, 437n262, 438n273, 473nn27,32,34, 489nn199,206, 491nn222,224, 497n292
battle
  between God/Christ and the devil, and their kingdoms, 17, 34, 36, 86f., 111f., 148, 157, 159, 181f., 206f., 245n38, 255n24, 268n14, 269n19, 270n29, 476n75
  between God and man, 244nn22,28, 246n43, 302n4
  within a Christian, 51, 86f., 90-92, 148, 367nn79-80; → man, reborn, is afflicted with Original Sin
Beruf, 234n12; → vocation
bishop/episcopal office (evangelical, papal), 137f., 144, 191, 285n46, 346n419, 392n50, 394nn59,62, 395n68, 398n87, 417n97, 438nn274,276, 457n9, 459n13, 460n19, 470n198, 474n43, 481n148, 482n154, 493n241, 494n251, 497n288, 498nn299-300, 500n308; → *Law*: Lutheran ecclesiastical law as man-made, autonomous law of the church, is law for the corporeal church, as administrative law; church, supervision in; papacy
blasphemy, 141; → 144

body
  and kingdom, 36, 148-50, 462n13
  Babylonian, → devil, mystical body of
  Christian/churchly (*civitas ecclesiastica, corpus christianum, respublica christiana, respublica ecclesiastica,* Christian body, *das irdische Kirchenwesen,* ecclesiastical body), 1f., 97f., 118-22, 157f., 160-62, 205-7, 256n35, 310n67, 388n38, 389n44, 477n94; → church, as corporeal spiritual communion;
  church, as mixed body
  civic/political, 138, 213f., 310n67, 477n94
  mystical, → Christ, mystical body of; devil, mystical body of
  of mankind, → families of man
Book of Concord, 6, 8f., 214, 236n5, 299n158
  Apology, 101, 236n5
  Apostles' Creed/Children's Faith, 178f., 315n105, 332n274, 337n324, 392n56, 434n230, 459n11, 474n47, 475n71, 497n291
  Augsburg Confession, 101, 189, 236n5, 321n154, 486n181
  The Large Catechism, 69f., 300n164, 304n18, 332n274, 339n346, 340n361, 344n409, 360nn27,29, 364n45, 380n182, 400nn5,7, 473nn36-37; → 144, 500n306
  A Marriage Booklet for Simple Pastors, 337nn328-29,332, 400n4, 401n18
  Smalcald Articles, 176f., 340n353, 361n33, 364n45, 401n20, 479n121
  The Small Catechism, 144, 262n33, 472n11; → 500n306
Buspiegel, 87

caesarism, 271n35

543

Index of Subjects

call
  extrasacramental, 178, 193-96, 395n66, 473n29, 490n215, 492n227; office of public ministry; Ordination
  sacramental, 178, 193; → priesthood of believers, Baptism is consecration for
chaos of one word, 220, 468n122
celibacy, 73, 484n174
character
  indelebilis, 193, 489n209
  of man, 48f., 255n24, 289n78, 292n102, 306n32; → 334n294, 383n191
chest, common, 395n65; → church, property of; office of public ministry, economics of
children, 102f.
  Christian education of, 102f.
  of God, 31f., 402n4
  of the world, 31, 144, 312n82, 427n168
  of wrath, 259n1; → *Law:* law, of wrath
  → families of man
Christ
  abolishes the law of Moses, 84, 86, 365n68, 366n70
  and laws of the *politia,* 451n36
  as head and king, 30, 177, 259n55, 266n3, 434n230; → Christ, mystical body of; kingdom of Christ
  as legislator, 85-88, 357nn2-3, 358n8, 362n38, 369n89
  as physician, 377n163
  as teacher, 84, 358n8; → *Law:* law, of Christ
  divinity of, 204, 264n53, 493n241
  governance of, 149, 178; → *Law:* Lutheran ecclesiastical law as divine, heteronomous, constitutional law of the church; governance, spiritual; kingdom of Christ
  humanity of, 34, 148, 177, 205f., 264n53, 268n18, 278nn34-35, 358n6
  Incarnation of, 89
  kingdom of, → kingdom of Christ
  law of, → *Law:* law, of Christ
  mystical body of, 28, 30, 85f., 120f., 124, 150, 157, 161, 178f., 184, 205-7, 256n29, 257n37, 264n53, 361n32, 364n49, 384n6, 393n58, 433n225, 435n245, 442n303, 462n13; → church, as body of Christ
  suffering of, 89, 263n51
  tasks/office/work of, 84-86, 127, 368n85
Christentum/das christliche Wesen, 86, 365n63, 386n25; → 30
Christian
  estate of, → estate, spiritual/Christian
  is a baptized believer (true Christian), 30, 119, 120-23, 178f., 183f., 477n98, 487n183
    who has rights in the church, 119-23; → *Law:* divine spiritual basic rights of a Christian; *Law:* Lutheran ecclesiastical law as man-made, autonomous law of the church, implements the divine natural law in Christ's interpretation, divine positive law, and the three spiritual basic rights of a Christian
  is an only baptized person ("lip"-Christian, hypocrite, nominal), 30, 93, 104, 119, 124, 181-84, 222, 257nn41-42, 334n288, 435n251, 477n109, 478nn110-11
  is a foreigner in this world and its kingdom, → man, reborn, is a citizen *only* in Christ's kingdom
  is a "rare bird," 90, 302n5
  marriage of, → marriage as institution of the secular natural law; marriage of Christians

544

Index of Subjects

prayers of, 86f., 90f., 110-12, 270n29, 359n26, 367n78, 417n101, 429n179

vocation of, 360n31, 426n158; → man, reborn, the world-person; vocation

weak, 119, 397n75

→ man, reborn

Christian order of society, 123f.

Christian social organism, 124f.

church/ecclesiology, 123, 172-74, 177-82, 193, 204-14, 217f., 228f., 236n12, 237n13, 266n5, 299n159, 344n410, 360n28; → families of man

a "blind" word, 101, 180, 200, 400n96

acts through the office of public ministry, 193f.; → 85; office of public ministry

and state, 70f., 108-11, 130-32, 157f., 189f., 201, 209-11, 214, 436n255, 476n76; → *Law:* Lutheran ecclesiastical law as man-made, autonomous law of the church, and order of the *politia; Law:* Lutheran ecclesiastical law as man-made, autonomous law of the church, secures/demands the independence of the (spiritual and external) governance of the church from the governance of the *politia;* authority, governmental, competency/tasks of; authority, governmental, misuse of the office of; *cura religionis* of the evangelical prince; guardianship/guardian, of the church; Kirchenregiment, landesherrliches/städtisches

as body of Christ with Christ as head ('Christian body'), 30, 85, 148, 161, 177-84, 194f., 260n11, 264n53, 384n8, 433n225, 434n230, 462n13, 473n33, 474n42, 476n89, 477nn93-94; → body, Christian/churchly; Christ, mystical body of

as commonwealth, → body, Christian/churchly

as communion of saints/true believers, 20, 120f., 178f., 205f., 225f., 236n5, 360n29, 363n41, 389n41, 433n225, 462n13, 466n100, 498n297; → 119, 161, 217; Christian, is a baptized believer; church, as spiritual church

as corporeal spiritual (legally organized) communion/congregation/particular (manifest) church, with spiritual legal equality between all particular churches, 19, 85, 97-99, 101, 118-20, 178-81, 184, 192-96, 210f., 217-20, 359nn25,26, 360nn27,29, 384n5, 389n40, 392n56, 462n13, 474n55, 487n183

is a sign of the true (spiritual) church, 161f., 181, 210f.

is constituted in/has to function according to the heteronomous ecclesiastical law, 85f., 98-101, 127, 180f., 184f., 194f., 200-203, 209-12, 229, 351n467, 475n64; → *Law:* Lutheran ecclesiastical law as divine, heteronomous, constitutional law of the church

membership in, 161f., 178f., 180-84, 477nn107,109, 478n110

→ church, two forms of

as counterchurch (church of the devil, of hypocrites, false church), 70f., 181-83, 201f., 211-14, 351n467, 392n56, 472n17, 476n88

as institution of the divine positive law in the status of the incorrupt

545

and of the corrupt nature, 51f., 70f., 85f.
as kingdom, 178f., 187
as mixed body, 160f., 181f., 442n309, 478n111
as spiritual church, 14, 19f., 74f., 85f., 119-23, 177, 179, 183f., 187, 194-96, 210f., 222, 225f., 399n91
   is connected with/in tension with the universal church, and through it with the particular churches as corporeal, spiritual, legally organized communions, 71f., 101, 119f., 123, 161f., 179-82, 186, 195, 201f., 209-12; → church, as corporeal spiritual communion; church, two forms of
   is hidden/members known only to God, scattered throughout the world, 30, 70f., 161f., 178-80, 209-11, 217-22, 336nn311,317, 380n181, 428n169
   → church, is the place where the Holy Spirit works; church, marks of; church, two forms of; man, reborn, is a citizen *only* in Christ's kingdom
as universal church existing in legally constituted particular churches/manifest church, 19, 74f., 98, 105, 119-21, 127, 141f., 179f., 198f., 204, 207-11, 217, 222, 388nn38-39, 389n40, 398n78, 434n230, 436n255, 460n26; → church, as corporeal spiritual communion; church, two forms of
definitions of/titles for, 98, 120f., 127, 142, 176f., 360n28, 388n39, 389n41, 460n26, 473n33, 474nn51,54-55, 487n183
diaconia of, 99f., 488n193, 500n307
discipline of, 184, 467n111, 500n306; → Keys, Power of

God in Christ is the only governmental authority in, to the exclusion of any earthly ruling authority, 97f., 108, 177-79, 189, 261nn20,26, 262nn28,30, 392n50, 393n57, 409n45, 472nn13-14,20-21, 473n22, 483n165; → authority, governmental, competency/tasks of; authority, governmental, misuse of the office of; bishop; church, and state; *cura religionis* of the evangelical prince; papacy
governance of, 178-80, 191, 386n26
   external, 100f., 187f., 191, 220, 398n81, 480n139
   spiritual, 100, 191, 194-96, 199, 492n230
   → *Law:* Lutheran ecclesiastical law as man-made, autonomous law of the church, secures/demands the independence of the (spiritual and external) governance of the church from the governance of the *politia; cura religionis* of the evangelical prince, essence of
holiness of, 262n33, 360n29, 369n97, 389n41, 393n58, 437n262, 473n33, 474n50, 475n65, 498n297; → church, as spiritual church; church, is the place where the Holy Spirit works
is in *Anfechtung* and danger of becoming 'world,' 70f., 99, 158f., 161f., 200f., 203, 211-14, 222, 467nn107-8, 476n76; → 248n55
is oppressed/persecuted, 70f., 181f., 212f., 336n322, 476n76
is the place where the Holy Spirit works, 85, 119, 177-80, 184, 262n33, 360nn27,29, 399n91, 473nn33-34; → church, as spiritual church is "wrapped in

flesh," 195, 474n51, 493n239; →
church, two forms of invisible/
visible, 6f., 179, 474n51,
497n292; → church, two forms
of
law of, 184-96, 286n53; → *Law:* Lutheran ecclesiastical law; *Law:*
Roman Catholic ecclesiastical
law
magisterial office of, 75, 133, 179
marks of, 178-81, 192-93, 207,
210f., 363n41, 477n104,
492n225, 497n292
militant, 181f., 476n78
ordinance of, 161f., 187f., 504n22
"outside of the church there is no
empire," 158, 406n32
property of (buildings, endowments, gifts), 197f., 395n65,
495n255, 498nn300-301,
500nn307-8; → church, governance of, external; office of public ministry, economics of
roster of, 161f., 179, 184, 222,
477nn101,107,109, 478n110
separation from, 99, 201f.
supervision in, 100, 202f.; →
bishop; visitation, of congregations
two forms/aspects/"faces"/persons
of, 71f., 120-21, 179f., 209-11,
217, 423n147, 437n258, 474n51,
475n65
→ *Volkskirche*
censura, 185; → 203
commonwealth
Christian, → body, Christian/
churchly
Christian, medieval meaning of
*(respublica christiana, corpus
christianum)*, 118, 123f., 157f.,
204, 208-11, 388n38, 433nn222-
23,229, 438n264, 439n277
secular, 6f., 7of., 144
belongs to God, 32, 79, 126f.,
270n28

is well ordered, 116, 127f.
→ kingdom of the world; *politia*
communicatio idiomatum, 255n24
conciliarism, 137
concupiscence, 102, 244nn21,27,
245n34, 254nn10,13-14, 378n170;
→ sin, Original
Confession (of sins), 18f., 77, 86f.,
91f., 478n119
confession (of faith), 13, 189, 403n9,
410n54, 428n169, 451n37,
452nn43,47
confessional state, 214
confessional writings of the Lutheran
church, → *Book of Concord*
Confutatio (1530), 317n123, 387n33
consistory, 500n308
council of the church, 123, 384n10,
397n76, 422n135, 460n27,
478n112, 480n141, 487n187,
493n241, 501n310
court people, 150, 270n29, 430n195;
→ 427n165
Creation/creatures, 9, 17, 25-27, 33,
43, 47, 50, 56, 65, 68, 149, 167,
272n38, 298n147, 304nn17,21,
307n41, 311n73, 315n105,
323n174, 324n182, 326n209,
347n439, 354n18, 360n27, 367n82;
→ God, as Creator
credit/creditor, 310n63
cuius regio, eius religio, 144
cura religionis of the evangelical
prince, 35, 116, 123, 127f., 131f.,
140, 231
basis of, 141-44, 189f., 457n9,
484n172; → guardianship/guard-
ian of Both Tables of the commandments; prince, his office,
benefits the church; prince, his
person (can be) is Christian;
prince, is *praecipuum membrum
ecclesiae*
charges the prince with fighting
blasphemy, heresy, idolatry, and
with maintaining and protecting

Index of Subjects

the church, 140f., 144, 189f., 456nn3,7, 459nn11,13, 460n22, 461n29, 483n167, 484nn168,171
endows the prince with the duty and right to reform the church when conditions exist which create an emergency, 141-43, 190, 440n291, 457n9, 459nn11,13, 461n28, 484nn171-72
essence of, 124-26, 140-44, 189f., 440n291, 456n2, 457n9, 460n19, 461nn29,34, 484nn168,172-74
interpretation of, 141-44, 460n25
is to enable the church to organize itself legally on the basis of the three spiritual basic rights of a Christian, 143

damage, 313n88
deceit/deceiver, 260n7, 285n46, 313n88, 321n151
devil/Lucifer/Satan, 32, 35, 39, 58f., 63, 67, 85f., 90-93, 113, 117, 149, 161f., 171f., 185, 213f., 230, 248n55, 252n18, 255n24, 256n30, 257nn38,45, 258n48, 259n3, 266n3, 272n38, 295n125, 322n161, 330n253, 332n272, 336n323, 337n324, 346n425, 350n459, 353n1, 363n42, 369n96, 398n78, 408n43, 419n119, 421n123, 430n195, 431nn199,201, 472n17, 474n43, 483n162, 484n174, 491n224, 492n230, 497n288
church of, → church, as counterchurch
governance of, 28-32, 148, 150, 158f., 206f., 255n20, 270n29, 421n121, 464n39
mystical body of, 28, 124, 148-53, 157f., 161, 181, 205-7, 255n20, 257n40
→ battle, between God/Christ and the devil, and their kingdoms; families of man; kingdom of the world

diet, 134
of Augsburg (1530), 449n15
of Speyer (1529), 449n15
of Worms (1521), 406n32, 433n229
divorce, → marriage as an institution of the secular natural law, indissolubility and divorce of
doing/using things spiritually (i.e., in a God-pleasing way) or corporeally (carnally), 52, 63f., 102f., 167, 229, 266n11, 292nn102,104, 298n147, 333n283, 334n294 and 375n145, 431n199, 442nn312-13, 444nn327,329; → man, reborn, and law, understands the spiritual meaning of law and uses law spiritually

ecstasy, 295n125
elector, 136-38
emergency bishop, 457n9; → 143f., 484n172
emperor, 93, 105, 133-39, 141, 166, 262n30, 264n53, 266n3, 321n156, 365n68, 379n175, 408n42, 409n49, 411n56, 413n69, 422n133, 423n147, 441n299, 447n2, 449n10, 450n17, 451n33, 453n55, 477n94, 483n166
Empire, Holy Roman, 134-39, 158, 351n467, 406n32, 449n13, 450n17, 453n55, 454n59
"outside of the church there is no empire," 158, 406n32
→ commonwealth, Christian, medieval meaning of; state, medieval
endowment, → church, property of
engagement, 337n331, 339n352, 341n373, 342nn378,385, 401n17
Enlightenment, 54-58, 158, 273n12, 338n342
enthusiasts, 20f., 46, 81f., 114, 144, 159, 300n163, 497n284; → 476n76
equity, → Law: substantive secular natural law, and equity

548

Index of Subjects

error vincibilis and *invincibilis*, 92
eschatology, 39f., 92f., 113, 124f., 177, 206f., 267n12; → battle, between God/Christ and Satan, and their kingdoms
estate, 266n5, 347n435, 385n15, 398n78
   ecclesiastical (professional), 121, 155f., 193f., 260nn13-14, 325n197, 362n35, 373n131, 386nn27-28, 421n123; → office of public ministry; priest/priesthood, and layman; priest/priesthood, medieval understanding of
   secular/corporeal, 78, 103, 260n14, 386n18, 438n276, 456n3; → marriage as institution of the secular natural law, is a corporeal estate; office, secular
   spiritual/Christian, 31, 50, 65, 86f., 93, 97f., 118-23, 140, 151f., 155f., 201, 260n14, 298n149, 325n197, 360n31, 385nn13,16, 386nn25-26, 438nn274,276, 440n291, 456n3; → *Law:* law, of the Christian estate; Christian, is a baptized believer; marriage of Christians
ethics, 118, 273n12, 298n147, 305n30, 308n51, 384n8
excommunication, → Keys, Power of

faith, 9, 243n17, 254n14, 284n43, 292n104, 371n115, 372n117, 380n183, 443n318; → Christian, is a baptized believer; justification by faith, content of faith
   "faith formed by love," 217, 370n105
Fall, → man, fallen; sin, Original
families of man (bodies, groups, kinds of man), 28, 35, 41, 92f., 148-55, 164f., 171f., 206-9, 215, 227f., 255nn19,24, 264n59, 266n3, 274n14, 277n27, 335n304, 336n316, 357n50, 380n186, 462n19, 463nn29,31, 464n49, 475n74; → *Law:* natural law, dualism in; church, as counterchurch; governance, secular, governance, spiritual
fasting, 377n164, 395n64, 397n75
Fathers (of the church)/early church, 25, 28, 41, 113, 130f., 168-71, 204, 244n21, 276n24, 284n43, 291n88, 300n170, 306n37, 372n127, 377n166, 397n76, 423n144, 442n309, 463n29, 466n87, 477n108, 487n187, 498n300; → *Law:* natural law, medieval and patristic theories of; *Book of Concord,* Apostles' Creed
Fürstenspiegel, 79, 231

geistliches Strafgericht, 33f.
Gentiles, → heathen
God, 277n27
   acts in contrasts, 35, 66f., 92f., 225f., 243n12, 246n46, 281nn20,23, 282n24, 328nn231-32, 329nn234,237-38; → *Law:* law, of wrath; *Anfechtung*
   as Creator, 27f., 35, 44-50, 53-59, 65, 73f., 90-93, 115, 156, 164-67, 227, 252n12, 296n136, 307n40, 324nn182-83, 326n209, 347n439; → Creation; God, Word of
   as devil or man's creature, 27f., 54f., 171f., 254n12, 254n9, 255n18; → *Anfechtung;* God, hatred for; God, knowledge of
   as efficient and final cause of the world, 126
   being/attributes of, 18f., 32, 41, 43f., 47, 64f., 225f., 236n1, 240n59, 243n11, 246nn44-45, 247n49, 248n57, 252n3, 264nn56,59, 265n63, 273n6, 277n29, 278n30, 279nn5-8, 280nn9,11-12,15, 281n23, 282nn27-29, 284n43, 290n86,

293nn105,107, 301n179, 303nn10,13, 322n162, 329n234, 333n287, 354n18, 357n51, 364n53, 372nn117-18, 378n170, 418n108, 445n341; → God, acts in contrasts; God, will of

controls the secular natural law, 58f.

court/throne of judgment/throne of mercy of, 17f., 62, 91f., 112, 127, 242n77, 246n41, 330n259, 368n84

evaluates man according to man's heart and will, 46f., 91f., 225f., 261n25, 289n76, 297n141, 373n131, 375n149, 385n16, 386n17; → man, heart and will of

governance of, 21, 32-34, 78f., 114f., 126f., 148-53, 156, 164f., 206-10, 215, 228, 270n29, 271nn31,35, 293n105, 333n287, 346n419, 426n153; → *Law:* law, of wrath; authority, governmental, is God's representative; authority, governmental, is God's institution for checking the wicked people and protecting the good people; families of man; God, Word of; governance, secular; governance, spiritual; kingdom, of God; kingdom of Christ; kingdom of the world

grants power over life and death in case of murder, 344n411

has heroes/miracle workers, → heroes/miracle workers, of God

hatred for, 41, 54f., 70f., 83, 171f., 225f., 247n49, 264n59, 372n121

impact on man, 32, 44, 64f., 282n28
  → families of man; God, Word of; man, reborn, the Christ-person; man, reborn, the world-person

institutions/orders of, → *Law:* divine law as positive law, as commandment and institution; *Law:* law, of Christ, as institution; God, governance of; order/orders, divine/God-established; priesthood of believers

is manifested/preached/revealed/ "wrapped in," 43, 280n15, 282n29, 333n287; → 82f.; authority, governmental, is God's representative; God, Word of; sacraments

kingdoms of, → kingdom, of God

knowledge of, 27, 43, 252n3, 253n6, 277n27, 278n34, 280n15, 281n21, 303n13, 305n24, 312n80, 360n28, 372n117; → God, Word of; Holy Spirit

law of, 45, 247n53, 284n41, 285n46, 326n202
  → *Law:* divine law; *Law:* divine law as natural law; *Law:* divine law as positive law; *Law:* law, of wrath; *Law:* law, use of

love for, → love, for God

punishes evil governmental authorities, 79f., 110-12, 412n63, 418n107, 430n195; → anarchy; resistance in the *politia*; resistance of a Christian

will of, 27, 48f., 68, 82f., 218f., 252n3, 282n29, 289n75, 296n127; → *Law:* divine law as natural law, is law-creating divine sovereign will

Word of (creative, living, powerful, tool), 32, 36, 45-50, 82, 85f., 178, 206f., 209f., 266n11, 271n35, 284n42, 286n56, 287nn57,62, 288n65, 290n81, 293n108, 294n118, 295nn122,125, 296n136, 299n159, 334n294, 355n34, 359n21, 360n31, 364n56, 370n102, 417n105, 443n318, 463n27
  → *Law:* law, and gospel; *Law:*

550

Index of Subjects

law, use of; call, sacramental; God, impact on man; Holy Spirit; vocation

worship of, 52, 70f., 85, 271n35, 299n159, 300n167, 312n83; → *Law:* Lutheran ecclesiastical law as man-made, autonomous law of the church, is law for the corporeal church, as law for worship

wrath of, → *Law:* law, of wrath; God, acts in contrast

governance/governances (general; doctrine; secular and spiritual governance side-by-side), 1f., 33f., 123f., 148-51, 153, 164f., 172-74, 197-99, 205-7, 255n24, 262n32, 266n5, 270n29, 271n35, 274n14, 346nn419,421, 380n186, 432n209, 445n340, 460n22, 494nn246,252

domestic, → *oeconomia*

of angels, 270n29

of Christ, → Christ, governance of

of the church, → church, governance of

of the devil, → devil, governance of

of God, → God, governance of

governance, secular (corporeal, with sword), 28f., 35f., 77f., 152-56, 164f., 168, 172-74, 197f., 255n24, 258n54, 262n31, 274n14, 339n350, 348n440

and the Christian, → man, reborn, the world-person

begins with the Fall and emerges from the domestic governance, → authority, governmental, begins with the Fall and emerges from marriage

functions (should function) with the severity of the law (sword), balanced with equity and mercy, and not with the gospel (the world cannot be ruled with the gospel), 77, 79, 199, 212f., 258nn52-53, 259n55, 266n3, 270n27, 277n25, 326n211, 347n430, 350n461, 351nn462,464, 427n163, 432nn207-9; → authority, governmental, competency/tasks of; authority, governmental, is God's institution for checking the wicked people and protecting the good people; sword, secular

is beneficial to the office of public ministry, 140, 157, 212f., 269n19, 347n428; → *cura religionis* of the evangelical prince; *pax politica*

is God's order, 346n421; → God, governance of

is implemented by governmental authority, → authority, governmental, competency/tasks of

over non-Christians and scoundrels, 77-79, 150, 154f., 258nn52-53, 266n3, 270n27, 274n14, 347n439, 351n464, 423n146, 464n49; → 164f.

over people of unequal status, 28f., 258n49, 386n18

governance, spiritual, 30f., 150, 152f., 189, 206-9, 255n24, 262n32, 270n29, 385n14, 445n340

means of, 31, 149f., 178f., 261n27, 262nn33,35, 266n11, 274n14; → *Law:* law, use of, theological; church, as corporeal spiritual communion; church as spiritual church; God, Word of; justification by faith, basis of; Keys, Power of; office of public ministry, competency/tasks of; sacraments

over people of equal status, 31f., 97f., 178, 258n49, 385nn13-14, 472n18; *Law:* law, of the Christian estate; estate, spiritual/Christian

guardianship/guardian

Index of Subjects

of Both Tables of the commandments, 130, 138f., 456n2, 459n11
of the church, 134f., 203, 222, 451n31, 460nn20-21

habitus, 244n28, 366n72, 367n77
heathen/Gentiles, 30, 57, 71, 92f., 102, 104, 107, 116, 124f., 140, 230, 248n59, 252n3, 255n21, 257n42, 286n48, 295n119, 302n5, 304n20, 311n73, 312n80, 315n108, 318n130, 321nn152,155, 334n288, 337n324, 353n10, 354n12, 379n174, 380n187, 381n189, 383n191, 399n91, 410n54, 411n56, 414n76, 423n147, 427n168, 431n199, 479n127, 482n152
heretics/false teachers/false teachings, 70f., 110f., 141, 144, 270n29, 272n38, 336nn311,320,323, 337n324, 409n47, 459n11, 474n43, 476n76
heroes/miracle workers
of God, 59, 314n103, 315n108, 416n83, 449n14
of the devil, 316n111
hierarchies, 123f., 152f., 266n5, 347n436
holiness/holy, 292n104, 349n448, 360n29, 373n131, 393n58, 399n91; → doing/using things spiritually or corporeally
Holy Spirit, 46, 63f., 90f., 119f., 120, 124, 126f., 181f., 199, 207, 210f., 240n59, 246n44, 252n3, 257n43, 261nn21,23, 262n33, 266n11, 271n36, 283n34, 284n42, 286nn55-56, 287nn57,64, 289n74, 290n84, 292n104, 294n117, 295nn119,124, 297nn138,141, 304n17, 306n35, 334n294, 348n445, 360n31, 368n87, 387n35, 398n86, 403n11, 444n333, 469n148, 472n17, 482n155, 493nn234,241, 494nn245,247; → church, is the place where the Holy Spirit works; God, Word of
Humanism, 130f., 448n8

indulgences, → Penance, sacrament of

Jansenism, 273n12
Jews, 28, 57, 71f., 124f., 292n104, 334n288, 337n324, 356n43, 357n53, 383n191, 396n70, 399n91, 410n54, 451n29, 477n94; → *Law:* Jewish national law; *Sachsenspiegel*
judge and jurist, 5, 11f., 35, 39, 45, 61f., 134f., 137, 216, 227, 259n54, 275n16, 302nn180, 306n34, 309n60, 311n78, 315n108, 317n126, 320n146, 321n155, 322nn159,161, 341n373, 352n480, 401n17, 411n58, 422nn136,138, 431n201, 448nn7-8, 451n31, 465n67, 477n94
individuals (up to ca. 1700), 315n108, 416n84, 421n123, 447nn10-11; → *Law:* Canon law; Scholasticism
rules of, → *Law:* law, needs/has new grammar, rules, vocabulary
→ *Law:* substantive secular natural law, and equity
Judgment Day, 34f., 39f., 57, 148, 170-72, 206f., 268nn14,18, 305n26, 360n31, 394n60, 395n65, 475n65, 498n296
justice, 236n1
justification by faith, 127, 249n73, 270n27, 276n19, 281n21, 367n77, 487n182; → *Law:* law, and justification by faith
basis/means of (grace of God, Word of God, Baptism), → *Law:* law, and gospel; Baptism; church, is the place where the Holy Spirit works; God, being/attributes of; God, Word of; Holy Spirit

Index of Subjects

content of
  man's response to God's law-Word, → *Law:* law, use of, theological; man, reborn, is afflicted with Original Sin; repentance
  divine action of not imputing sin to man because of Christ's work, and imputing Christ's righteousness to man as man's foreign righteousness/"exchange" of man's sinfulness for Christ's righteousness/rebirth of the 'old' (sinful, natural) man as the 'new' man of the Christian estate, 84-90, 127, 256n29, 257n37, 259n4, 359n20, 364nn49-50, 365nn59,61,68, 366nn70,72, 368nn85,96, 371n116, 487n182; → estate, spiritual/Christian; man, reborn, has evangelical freedom
faith, 127, 273n6, 277n28, 281n20, 296n130, 365n61, 370nn105,107, 488n189, 489n207
  as God's gift, 372n117
  as incorporation in Christ, 85f., 244n22, 364n49, 369n96; → Christ, mystical body of
  is active in love and works, 88-90, 290nn83-84, 292n100, 297n138, 324n179, 330n259, 332nn274,276, 334n294, 370n107, 371nn111-12, 372n127, 374nn135,137, 375n143, 376nn151-52,154-56, 377nn157-59, 380n182, 444n323; → *Law:* law, of Christ, is the authentic interpretation of the divine meaning of the divine natural law; love, Christian; man, reborn, is afflicted with Original Sin
  partial/total, 90-92
  structure of, 127, 370nn102,107, 374n135, 376n155
  → righteousness

Keys, Power of, 104, 110f., 144, 161f., 178f., 183-87, 192, 196, 203, 211f., 220-22, 261n27, 280n15, 361n33 and 396n74, 362n39, 387n31, 393n58, 395n67, 401n20, 477nn93,98, 478nn119-20, 481n147, 483n162, 490nn211,213, 497n292, 500n305; → repentance
kingdom
  general (doctrine and terminology of, controversy about, development after Luther), 7, 14, 25, 28, 39-41, 125, 145-51, 160-77, 197, 204-7, 214f., 225-27, 256n25, 259n6, 262n32, 263n46, 271n35, 407n38, 464n49, 471n8; → 129-32, 231; families of man
  of faith, 178f.
  of God/heaven, 6f., 10f., 33f., 36, 45, 50, 72, 126, 203, 236n9, 256n34, 261n26, 262n33, 472n10, 492n230
    as kingdom of God at the right (→ kingdom of Christ) and the left (→ kingdom of the world) of God, 32-36, 154, 170f.
  of glory, 34f.
  of grace, → kingdom of Christ
  of reason, → kingdom of the world
  of wrath, → *Law:* law, of wrath; kingdom of the world
kingdom of Christ/grace/Spirit (essence, citizen, functioning, law, ruler/head), 7-9, 13, 20f., 25, 28-36, 41, 51, 86, 91-93, 117f., 123-27, 147-51, 154-56, 166f., 177, 182, 185f., 204-15, 225-30, 236n5, 245n38, 250n83, 253n6,

553

Index of Subjects

255nn20,24, 256nn27,29-30, 257n37, 259nn4-6, 261n21-24,27, 262n32, 264n53, 266n3, 268nn17-18, 269n19, 292n104, 295n125, 312n82, 360n31, 367n82, 378n170, 383n191, 384n4, 403n6, 426n160, 464n49, 470n191, 472n18, 488n194; → *Law:* law, of Christ, is the authentic interpretation of the divine meaning of the divine natural law; *Law:* law, of the Christian estate; battle, between God/Christ and the devil, and their kingdoms; church, as body of Christ; church, as spiritual church; estate, spiritual/Christian; governance, spiritual; justification by faith, content of, divine action, rebirth; man, reborn, is a citizen *only* in Christ's kingdom; man, reborn, is simultaneously a Christ-person and a world-person

kingdom of the world/reason/sword (essence, citizen, functioning, law, ruler/head), 10f., 20f., 25-36, 41, 45, 51, 57, 63-79, 86, 91-93, 105, 118, 153-55, 166-69, 189, 197, 205-10, 214f., 228-30, 245n38, 257nn39,47, 258n48-53, 259nn1,3-4,6, 260n7, 264nn52-53,57, 266n3, 270nn27-29, 274n14, 300n170, 312n82, 326n210, 327n218, 332n272, 365n65, 367n82, 398n83, 464n49, 472n18; → *Law:* substantive secular natural law, is located in the kingdom of the world; *Law:* law, law of wrath; battle, between God/Christ and the devil, and their kingdoms; authority, governmental; governance, secular; man, reborn, is simultaneously a Christ-person and a world-person; magistrate; prince; *politia*

Kirchenordnung, 504n22

Kirchenregiment, → church, governance of

landesherrliches/städtisches, 131f., 141, 143f., 189f., 399n90, 460n19; → guardianship/guardian, of the church

Kulturprotestantismus, 358n16

Lebensordnung, 310n69

lese majesty, 17

Lord's Supper, 85, 150, 203, 301n172, 362nn37-39, 363nn41-42, 393n58, 397n75, 462n13, 473n34, 479n127, 482n149, 484n174, 486n181, 491n224, 492n226, 493n237, 496n283, 497nn291-92, 500n306, 501n309

love, 276n24

Christian (as manifestation of faith and of obedience to the divine natural law in Christ's interpretation, for the brother, neighbor, enemy), 31, 69, 89f., 103, 107, 161f., 184, 198-200, 211-14, 221, 228f., 263n48, 275n16, 276n19, 359n26, 370n102, 372nn124-26, 373n130, 374n138, 384n6, 389n45, 390n47, 404n16, 405n26, 406nn29-30, 461n29; → justification by faith, content of, faith, is active in love and works

for God, 25, 46-50, 62, 69, 89, 290n83, 297n143

for self, 25, 28f., 62, 89, 332n274, 372n123; → man, fallen

structured, 372n127

universal, → substantive secular natural law, is law of universal love for man

wrathful, 35; → God, acts in contrasts

Luther, Martin, 16-21, 62, 76f., 81f., 120, 183f., 200f., 216-25, 240n56, 337n331, 339n352, 341n372, 346n427, 349nn453-54, 390n49 and 472n16, 396n74, 433n229, 497n288

Index of Subjects

magistrate, 108, 113, 166, 203, 266n3, 268n17, 269n23, 317n123, 330nn253,258, 334n294, 337n332, 349n447, 408n41, 421nn126-27, 423n142, 428n176, 429n179, 445n341, 451n36, 452nn42,45-46, 464n39, 481n148

"when the magistrate does not function, the common people *(plebs)* are the magistrate," 113

man, 289n78, 428n170

character of, → character, of man

conscience of, 18f., 54f., 90-93, 125-27, 203, 240n56, 242n77, 244n22, 252n2, 261n27, 263n45, 291n95, 294n111, 305n26, 317n122, 324n179, 337n332, 340n355, 341n373, 363n42, 365n68, 368n84, 375n150, 379nn175-76, 380n183, 384n10, 387nn32-33, 400n12, 404n12, 407n34, 409n49, 429n183, 482n149, 487n187, 496n279; → 118; *Anfechtung;* man, reborn, has evangelical freedom

heart and will of, 17-18, 20, 25f., 32, 41, 45-50, 63-65, 68, 86, 89-91, 127, 165f., 225f., 240n56, 241n71, 243n14, 244n22, 247n49, 252nn14,18-19, 255n18, 259n2, 261n25, 276n20-23, 280n10, 288n70, 289nn74-77,79, 290nn80,83-85, 291n91, 292nn97,101, 294nn117-18, 296nn128,130, 297n141, 298n150, 301n173, 303n9, 304nn14-15,19, 305n26, 307n48, 309n61, 322n165, 323n177, 324n180, 327n213, 365n58, 376n155, 380n187, 387n34

kinds of, → families of man

reason of, 9, 18, 20, 31f., 41f., 43, 47f., 56, 58f., 63, 89, 197, 246nn43-44,47, 252nn,3,6,16 258n50, 262n32, 263n51, 284n43, 303nn9-10,12, 306n35, 307nn39-40,48, 309n61, 331nn262,266, 384n4, 386n26, 398nn80-81, 404n15; → *Law:* divine law as natural law, and reason; *Law:* Lutheran ecclesiastical law as man-made, autonomous law of the church, is created in a public process of voluntary cooperation by the believers, which is guided by rational considerations; *Law:* substantive secular natural law, and reason

man, before the Fall, 43-53, 208f., 212f., 243n20, 278n35, 345n414; → *Law:* divine law as natural law; *Law:* divine law as positive law

man, fallen/old man, 1f., 9, 16-18, 20f., 25-28, 51, 54-57, 72, 87, 91f., 170, 197, 224-28, 243n20, 245nn31,34, 254n14, 273n10, 275n15, 278n35, 280n15, 288n72, 294n113, 299n161, 300n166, 303n9, 304nn17,20-21, 306n37, 333n284, 337n325, 345n413, 366n72, 367n77; → 273n12; doing/using things spiritually or corporeally; status, equal/unequal

conscience of, → man, conscience of

discovers the secular natural law, → *Law:* substantive secular natural law, is the product of natural, sinful man's divine dowry and the infralapsarian, rational, corporeal misinterpretation of the divine natural law

has the divine natural law inscribed in his heart (and therefore has a notion of what is right) but does not understand and use it correctly, 54f., 83f., 167, 208f., 225f., 303n12, 305nn23,26, 353n1, 357n47; → *Law:* divine law as natural law, is a given of man's incorupt nature, inscribed in his heart

555

hates law, 66, 327nn213-14,217
heart and will of, → man, heart and will of
is cursed/enslaved/under wrath, 32, 86, 259nn1-3; → *Law:* divine law as natural law, condemns natural (sinner) man to spiritual death; *Law:* law, of wrath
is enemy of the divine natural law, → God, hatred for
is sinner/carnal/corrupt/evil/external/natural/perverse/wicked, 27-29, 57, 66, 83f., 126f., 218f., 224f., 259n1, 280n15, 306n36, 307n41, 324n182, 358n10; → 273n12; character, of man; concupiscence
reason of, → man, reason of
man, reborn/new man/believing/justified/righteous/spiritual, 85f., 89-92, 97, 115, 127, 208f., 227-31, 260n14, 289n74, 296n127, 298n149, 359n21, 365nn61,63, 371n116, 374n135, 380n187, 384n8, 433n216; → character, of man; Christian; doing/using things spiritually or corporeally; estate, spiritual/Christian; justification by faith
and courts, 384n4, 404n15, 405n19, 413n69; → man, reborn, and experienced injury
and experienced injury/injustice, 90, 413n72
ought not avenge himself, 404n14, 418n106-8
will act against it in certain circumstances, 106, 110, 404n14
will suffer it, but protest and point out God's judgment, 404n12, 411n59
→ *Law:* Christian law; resistance in the *politia;* resistance of a Christian; self-defense
and law, 252n20, 258n51
understands the spiritual meaning of law and uses law spiritually, 63-70, 82f., 92f., 107, 116f.
upholds the priority of the First Table of the commandments over the Second Table, 410n54
→ *Law:* Christian law; *Law:* law, of Christ; *Law:* law, use of; *Law:* positive law, spiritual chracteristics of; man, reborn, has insight in the structure of the divine sovereignty
and war, 109
conscience of, → man, conscience of; man, reborn, has evangelical freedom
grows in faith and love, 89f.
exists in the tensions between the divine natural law and the secular natural law, and between the secular natural law and the positive law, 117f., 127f.
has evangelical (spiritual) freedom from the coercive force of law and its institutions (is "free lord"), 31f., 86, 90, 98, 105-7, 154-56, 165f., 212-14, 263nn46-47, 291nn93-94, 365n68, 366nn69-70, 368n85, 375n150, 380n187, 384n10, 387nn32-33,35, 402n4, 403n7, 405n21, 405n24, 405n26, 426n152; → man, conscience of; man, reborn, is a citizen *only* in Christ's kingdom
has insight into the structure of the divine sovereignty over God's kingdom at the left and at the right and supports the spiritual meaning of the *oeconomia* and of the *politia,* and of every way of living ordained by God, 78f., 107, 115-17, 126f., 188, 266n3, 270n29, 349n447, 445nn335,339-41; → man, reborn, and law; man, reborn, the world-person

heart and will of, → man, heart and will of

is afflicted with Original Sin as with a wound which in this life only begins to heal (in the process of repentance and Sanctification) so that he is simultaneously a righteous and a sinful person (*simul iustus et peccator*), 66f., 86-92, 127, 149, 151f., 155f., 212-14, 255n24, 281n20, 285n46, 292n98, 367nn73,75,77,79-80,82, 368nn83,86, 369n97, 373n130, 377n167, 378n170, 387n35, 434n236, 448n7, 475n74; → *Law:* law, use of, theological; battle, within a Christian; Confession; Keys, Power of; repentance

is the best qualified person for the service in secular offices, 115f.; → man, reborn, the world-person

is Christ for the neighbor and "servant of all," 97, 291n94, 375n143, 376n155

is a citizen only in Christ's kingdom (and lives according to Christ's law), is a foreigner in the kingdom of the world, is not a citizen of both kingdoms, 34, 93, 97, 114, 163-68, 206f., 230, 380nn181,186, 383n192, 387n35, 396n74, 403n6

is consecrated as priest, → priesthood of believers

is endowed with three spiritual basic rights, → *Law:* Lutheran ecclesiastical law as man-made, autonomous law of the church, implements the divine natural law in Christ's interpretation, divine positive law, and the three spiritual basic rights of a Christian

is God's co-worker/minister/tool/vicar/viceroy, 90, 114f., 126f., 228, 301n171, 426nn158-59; → authority, governmental, is God's representative; man, reborn, the world-person

is simultaneously a Christ-person and a world-person/has two offices/is a private and a public person, 114-16, 383n192, 423n147; → man, reborn, is a citizen *only* in Christ's kingdom; man, reborn, is God's coworker; man, reborn, the Christ-person; man, reborn, the world-person; office, difference between office and officeholder; prince, as a Christ-person and a public person

is spiritual man who judges all things (including the interpretation of Scripture and the legitimacy of law), is judged by no one, 101, 103, 120, 123, 155f., 203, 302n180, 371n116, 380n180, 396n74

lives in a corporeal spiritual communion, → church, as corporeal spiritual communion

lives with the cross, 364n56, 375n142, 403n9, 434n236; → *Law:* Christian law

marriage of, → marriage of Christians

reason of, → man, reason of

man, reborn, the Christ-person is a baptized believer on the basis of his justification by faith (→ Christian, is a baptized believer; justification by faith); is a citizen in Christ's kingdom and is endowed with the rights of the Christian estate and with evangelical freedom (→ *Law:* divine spiritual basic rights; *Law:* law, of the Christian estate; estate, spiritual/Christian; man, reborn, has evangelical freedom; man, reborn, is a citizen *only*

Index of Subjects

in Christ's kingdom); lives under Christ's governance according to Christ's law, though he is still afflicted with Original Sin (→ *Law: law, of Christ; governance, spiritual; man, reborn, is afflicted with Original Sin*); is a priest (→ *priesthood of believers*); lives in a corporeal spiritual communion (→ *church, as corporeal spiritual communion*); lives with the cross (→ *man, reborn, lives with the cross*) → *man, reborn, is simultaneously a Christ-person and a world-person*

man, reborn, the world-person is a Christ-person (→ *man, reborn, the Christ-person*); has in his secular vocation/office (442n317; → *vocation*) the divine call (298n146, 426nn157-58, 431n202), a God-given duty (21, 155f., 383n193), to be God's co-worker (→ *man, reborn, is God's co-worker*) for the maintenance and promotion (426n160) of the kingdom of the world (the secular natural law order, 126f., 228, 414n74) in its totality, ranging from procreation to the protection of the secular commonwealth against its law-breaking enemies and the upholding of the common good (→ *authority, governmental, competency/tasks of; authority, parental; governance, secular; marriage as institution of the secular natural law; oeconomia; order/orders, divine/God-established; politia*); responds to this call with faith-incarnate (90, 442n317, 444n323), voluntarily (387n32, 402n4, 405n26, 406n29, 423n146, 465n65, 481n148) obeying the secular law and governmental authority as God's order and representative for the kingdom of the world (→ *Law: positive law, spiritual characteristics of; authority, governmental, is God's representative*) — though as a citizen in Christ's kingdom he is exempt from their jurisdiction (213f., 228, 385n14, 402n4, 405nn24,26, 406nn28-29; → *man, reborn, has evangelical freedom*) — maintaining and promoting that law and authority (93, 107, 156f., 349n447, 383n192, 426n160, 429n189), and conscientiously serving (when necessary with force/sword; 117, 264n57, 277n25, 351n464) in secular offices (114-18, 156, 423n147, 430n191, 477n94), and does this for the benefit of the neighbor because for himself he does not need law/sword (274n14, 406n29, 423n146, 465n65, 481n148); thus he manifests his love for God and neighbor/obedience to the divine natural law in Christ's interpretation (107, 127, 156, 213f., 291n94, 402n4, 426n152; → *Law: law, of Christ; justification by faith, content of, faith, is active in love and works*); his obedience to secular governmental authority is restricted to external, corporeal matters (107, 405n24, 406n28, 408n42, 423n147, 482nn160-61) and limited by the secular natural law (107-9, 127f., 198f., 213f., 408n41, 413n72); → *Law: institutional secular natural law, and governmental authority; Law: substantive secular natural law, and Decalogue; Law: substantive secular natural law, is source/standard for the positive law and actions derived from/based on it; authority, governmental, competency/tasks of; resistance in the politia; resistance of a Christian*)

558

Index of Subjects

→ man, reborn, is simultaneously a Christ-person and a world-person
Manichaeism, 273n12
marriage as institution of the divine positive law in the status of the incorrupt nature, 51f.
marriage as institution of the secular natural law, 72-77, 339n344
  bigamy, monogamy, polygamy, 74-77
  changes in the nature of marriage as a result of sin, 71-73, 169f., 337nn326-27,330, 338n337
  God-created and in spite of sin maintained as a necessary and blessed natural order, 71-73, 102f., 337n326, 339n348
  impediments of, 73f., 103f., 339n352, 340n355
  indissolubility of and divorce, 73-76, 102-4, 298n154, 338n340, 339n344
  is a corporeal/public/worldly estate/thing and subjected to the secular legal order (kingdom of the world), 71-77, 227-30, 337nn327,332, 339n350, 342n385, 353n11
  is fountain of *oeconomia* and *politia* and their orders, 77, 103, 167f., 344n411, 345n413
  purpose of, 337n325, 338n339, 339n349, 429n180
  two classes of natural-law commandments for, 73f.
  → engagement
marriage of Christians, 73-76, 102-4, 227-30, 300n168, 344n410, 429n180
  and Roman Catholic marriage courts, 230
  → consistory
matrimonium consummatum/ legitimum/ratum, 229-30, 341n368, 342n377

miracles, 45f., 285n46, 286nn54-55
  → heroes/miracle workers
mob, rule of, → anarchy
murderer, 352n472

oath, 313n88
Obrigkeit, 234n12
oeconomia/domestic governance, 52, 72f., 77, 113, 115, 123f., 144, 266n5, 299nn160-61, 313n98, 330n258, 338n335, 344nn410-11, 345n414, 350n456, 417n97, 494n246; → authority, parental; marriage as institution of the secular natural law
office/estate, 234n12; → estate
  as God's order, → order/orders, divine/God-established
  difference between office and officeholder, 324n182, 348n445, 411n58, 430n195; → 118; man, reborn, is simultaneously a Christ-person and a world-person
  ecclesiastical, 192, 408n43; → bishop; office of public ministry; order/orders, ecclesiastical/monastic
  secular, 114-17, 122, 494n252; → vocation
office of public ministry (preaching office, pastor's office), 31, 77f., 99f., 141, 151-53, 187f., 192-93, 209f., 214, 260n14, 330n253, 346n421, 350nn456-57, 361n34, 362n39, 386n27, 398n78, 411n58, 425n149, 459n11, 488nn191,196, 492n230, 494n252; → priesthood of believers
  competency/tasks of, 31-34, 79, 85, 108, 144, 178f., 191, 194f., 203, 330n253, 341n373, 362n36, 412n61, 448n7, 480n137, 488n189, 493n237, 495n266, 500n308; → call; church, governance of; Keys, Power of

559

Index of Subjects

disciplining incumbent of, 194f., 201f., 394nn59,62, 457n9, 489n209, 492n231, 493n241, 498nn299-301
economics of, 140, 395n66, 484n171, 498n299, 500n308; → church, property of
employment in, → call, extrasacramental; Ordination
qualifications for, 195, 203, 361n34, 492n231, 493n234
one for all, all for one, 308n53, 490n214; → priest/priesthood, medieval understanding/position of
order/orders/ordinances/institutions/estates
divine/God-established, 123f., 150, 292n104, 300n163, 324n178, 334n293, 344n409, 347n435, 348nn444-45, 432n212, 440n297, 452n46
of Creation, preservation, Salvation, 35, 66f., 101, 299n161, 304n21, 337n330, 345n414, 347n439, 367n82
ecclesiastical/monastic, 121-24, 155f., 260n14, 298n149, 325n197, 339n347, 373n131, 398nn78,87, 400n6, 426n158, 427n161
→ bishop; priest/priesthood, medieval understanding of
secular, 126, 250n1, 349n447
→ estate; office
Ordination, 193-96, 325n197, 473n27, 489nn208-9, 493nn236,238, 500n308
Orthodoxy, Lutheran, 6f., 214, 369n98, 419n116

papacy/papal theologians/pope/Roman church, 101, 113, 118f., 123f., 127, 142, 157, 178f., 200, 203, 219, 249n66, 292n104, 326n208, 334n294, 342n377, 363n42, 365n68, 388n38, 389n44, 392n56, 393n58, 394n60, 395n68, 398n87, 399n91, 400n96, 406n32, 413n69, 416n85, 417n97, 419nn116,119, 421n123, 422nn128-29,133,139, 434nn237-38, 438n276, 440n291, 459nn13,15, 460n27, 472n16, 476nn76,82, 481nn145,147, 483n162, 490n211, 493n243, 494n252, 495n275, 496nn276-77,279, 497nn288,292,294, 498n296, 500n307, 502n312; → *Law:* Canon law; bishop; church, as corporeal spiritual communion
Paradise, → status, Original
parents, → authority, parental
pars sanior, 99, 201-3
pax politica (peace in the secular commonwealth), 35, 66f., 79, 117, 153, 189, 212f., 269n19, 270n28, 330n253, 333n281, 347n428, 351n464, 402n4, 483n167; → *Law:* secular natural law, secures peace and stability in the secular commonwealth; authority, governmental, competency/tasks of
peasants, rebelling, → anarchy
Pelagianism, 273n12
Penance, sacrament of, 21, 183, 217, 219, 222
people
judgment about, 258n53, 307n46, 367n82
"when the magistrate does not function, the common people *(plebs)* are the magistrate," 113
personalistic thinking, 27-29, 39, 48-50, 87f., 151-56, 205f., 219, 227, 255n24, 287n59, 288n68, 289n76, 444n326
pessimism, 118, 273n12
Pietism, 359n21, 369n96
poena latae sententiae, 65, 245n37, 361n33
politia, 71f., 75, 77, 79, 82, 103-28, 131f., 135, 141, 144, 157, 197f., 202, 204, 209f., 230f., 266n5,

560

269n23, 299n161, 300n170, 313n98, 338n335, 344n410, 345n414, 350n456, 388n38, 401n1, 432n215, 445nn335,340, 451n36, 452n46, 460n22, 483n162; → authority, governmental; governance, secular; kingdom of the world
potestas, 234n12
praecipuum membrum ecclesiae, → prince, is *praecipuum membrum ecclesiae*
prayer, → Christian, prayers of
priest/priesthood
  and layman, 385n16, 438nn274,276
  medieval understanding/position of, 98, 119-24, 155f., 193, 292n100, 373nn131-32, 386n28, 434n238, 438n270, 439n279, 484n174, 489n199, 490n214; → 308n53
priesthood of believers, 101, 193, 387n31, 473n27, 491n222
  and professional evangelical priesthood, 98, 193-96, 386n28, 489nn197-98, 489n205; → office of public ministry
  Baptism is consecration for, 178, 193, 434n236-38, 473nn26-27, 489n204, 491n222; → Baptism
  competency/limitations of/tasks of, 102f., 178-79, 193f., 387n31, 473n26, 489nn198,205, 490n212, 491n224
prince/king/ruler/ruling, 115, 130f., 259n55, 266n3, 270n29, 317n126, 318n130, 349n455, 416n88
  as a Christ-person and a public person (officeholder), 108, 122f., 423n147, 428n175, 432n213, 451n31, 453n55; → man, reborn, is simultaneously a Christ-person and a world-person; office, difference between office and officeholder; prince, Christian prince/non-Christian prince
  Christian prince/non-Christian prince, 116, 125f., 140, 143f., 334n293, 349n449, 409n44, 426n153
  competency/tasks of, → authority, governmental, competency/tasks of
  David is the model for the godly prince, 428n177, 456nn3,8, 457n9, 484n173
  evaluation of, 60f., 78f., 115f., 317n123, 318n130, 321n156, 335n308, 346n422, 350nn459-60, 407n40, 427nn163,165, 430n194, 431n197, 455n70
  has a divine call to serve in a secular office of God's kingdom at the left so that ruling belongs to God, to whom the prince is responsible, 78, 212f., 334n293, 428n177, 429nn178-79; → 426n158, 431n202; authority, governmental, is God's representative; man, reborn, the world-person
  his office
    benefits the church, 116, 122f., 140, 347n428, 350n457; → *cura religionis* of the evangelical prince; *pax politica*
    does not function according to the gospel but according to the proper use of secular power, 79, 199, 264n57, 277n25, 330n258, 351n464, 432nn207,209,213; → *Law:* substantive secular natural law, and equity
    is not Christian but secular (corporeal, not spiritual), 77f., 122f., 429n180, 432n213
    is a dangerous and difficult one, 117, 270n29, 350n459, 431n203
    misuse of, 79f., 108f., 117, 189, 346n425, 408nn42-43,

Index of Subjects

482n161, 483nn162,164,174; → authority, governmental, competency/tasks of; *cura religionis* of the evangelical prince, essence of; resistance in the *politia*

ranks second after the office of public ministry, 77f., 346nn420-22,427, 347n430

his person (can be) is Christian, and this is manifested in the way in which he organizes his private and his public life (use of the power of his office/practice and principles of ruling), 79, 116, 122, 125f., 423n147, 427nn163,165, 428nn172-73,176, 429nn179-80, 442n316, 465n67; → Christian, is a baptized believer; man, reborn, the Christperson; man, reborn, the worldperson; prince, David is the model for the godly prince

is *praecipuum membrum ecclesiae*, 143, 393n57, 440n292, 442n307, 459n18

is responsible for uniform preaching in his territory, 144, 483n167, 484n168

→ authority, governmental; governance, secular; kingdom of the world; magistrate

privilegium fori/immunitatis, → priest/priesthood, medieval understanding/position of

prostitution, 429n185

punishment, 28f., 33f., 66, 219, 244n26, 262n32, 270n27, 274n14, 277n25, 327n218, 356n35, 405n19

capital, 335n309, 344n411, 348n445, 464n51

→ *Law:* law, use of; *censura;* Keys, Power of; *poena latae sententiae;* sword, secular

quaternio terminorum, 163f.

Rationalism, 57, 273n12

reason, → *Law:* divine law as natural law, and reason; *Law:* Lutheran ecclesiastical law as man-made, autonomous law of the church, is created in a public process of voluntary cooperation of believers, which is guided by rational considerations; *Law:* substantive secular natural law, and reason; *Law:* substantive secular natural law, is the product of natural, sinful man's divine dowry and the infralapsarian, rational, corporeal misinterpretation of the divine natural law; God, knowledge of; kingdom of the world; man, reason of

rebellion, → anarchy

Rechtsgenosse, 296n133, 403n8

Redemption, 33f., 51, 66f., 101, 272n38, 330n252, 360n27; → Christ, tasks of; justification by faith, content of, divine action

Regiment, 1f.; → governance

repentance/evangelical penance, 66f., 151f., 186, 285n46, 367n82, 373n130, 448n7; → *Law:* law, use of, theological; Keys, Power of; man, reborn, is afflicted with Original Sin

res/signum, → symbol/reality

resistance in the battle between opposing spiritual forces, → battle, within a Christian

resistance in the church as duty and right, → *Law:* Lutheran ecclesiastical law as man-made, autonomous law of the church, establishes the duty and right of the believer to participate in the creation of ecclesiastical law, the judgment concerning its legitimacy, and the supervision of its implementation; *Law:* Lutheran ecclesiastical law as man-made, autonomous law of the

Index of Subjects

church, has to be reformed or resisted in certain circumstances; man, reborn, is spiritual man who judges all things

resistance in the *politia*/disobedience to secular governmental authority/reaction to injury or injustice/ *Widerstandsrecht*, 418n109, 447nn1-2

issues in, 133f.

may a Christian resist injury or injustice inflicted upon him by a fellow citizen? 106, 136

how is a Christian to act when his governmental authority commands him to commit an unjust action against God or neighbor, or when his governmental authority inflicts injury upon him (esp. in connection with his faith)? 79, 108-13, 134-37, 413n72, 451n31

may a Christian as a governmental authority (elector) use force against the emperor when the emperor makes war against him for religious reasons? 134-37

justification (legal and spiritual) for affirming or rejecting different forms of resistance, 61, 79f., 107-14, 127f., 134-39, 231f., 413n69, 477n94; → *Law:* substantive secular natural law, is source/standard for the positive law and actions derived from/based on it; authority, governmental, competency/tasks of; self-defense

resistance of a Christian — citizen or governmental authority (elector) — to an illegitimate command, or to injury inflicted upon him by a fellow citizen or his territorial prince, or a fellow governmental authority, or the emperor, form and content

corporeally active (with armed force against the law-breaking robber (whatever his social position is)/grand tyrant/emperor, 106, 113f., 127f., 136-39

corporeally passive but spiritually/verbally active (acknowledging/respecting the God-given power of a governmental authority to issue commands/suffering injury and enduring injustice/prayer/publicly protesting the illegitimate action or command/publicly warning of God's coming judgment over the illegitimate action or command and its actor), 106-12, 127f., 136f., 404n12, 412nn62,65, 413n72, 418n108; → God, punishes evil governmental authorities; man, reborn, and experiences injury/injustice

difference between disobedience/resistance and rebellion, 134-37; → 413n69; anarchy

emigration, 136f., 412n64

uncompromising, 109

resistance of a non-Christian to injury and injustice, and to governmental authority, 110, 134f.

respublica christiana, → commonwealth, Christian, medieval meaning of

righteousness, 16f., 20f., 53, 84, 245n39, 290n84, 293n107 (and 236n1), 294n113, 298n144, 304n20, 333n284, 396n72

civic/carnal/earthly/human/of law/of works, 41f., 56, 63, 69, 83, 246n46, 296n130, 304n20, 306n33, 310n69, 323nn170,175, 324n178, 328n229, 331n262, 332nn272,274,278, 333nn281,283,285, 379n177;→

563

Index of Subjects

Law: substantive secular natural law, and righteousness; *Law:* law, use of, civic
 of faith/spiritual, 54, 87f., 244n21, 258n51, 270n27, 273n6, 277n28, 284n43, 291n94, 292n100, 301n179, 322n168, 330n259, 367n77, 379n177, 487n182; → *Law:* law, use of, theological; justification by faith, content of
robber/robbery, 107, 113, 136, 452n44, 479n126; → man, reborn, and experiences injury/injustice; resistance of a Christian
rule/rules
 of faith/truth, 161f., 178f., 182, 184, 190, 200, 211f., 466n100
 of jurists, 287n60; → *Law:* law, needs/has new grammar, rules, vocabulary
 of love, 161f., 184, 190, 200, 211f., 465n72
 of man, → traditions of man
 of reason, 246n43; → reason

sacraments, 21, 33f., 85, 102, 130f., 161f., 178-81, 185, 194, 207, 210-13, 227, 362nn37,39, 363n42, 364nn44-45, 384n5, 410n54, 417n105, 438n276, 473n32, 477n104, 478n111, 480n141
 → *Law:* Lutheran ecclesiastical law as divine, heteronomous law of the church; Baptism; church, marks of; Lord's Supper
saints
 evangelical, 367n82, 475n71; → Baptism; church, as communion of saints; doing/using things spiritually or corporeally; secular/spiritual, meaning of the medieval church, 272n38, 285n46, 292n104, 397n75
Sanctification, 33f., 368n85; → man, reborn, is afflicted with Original Sin; repentance

Scholasticism (schools, theology, theologians), 13, 16-20, 25f., 39, 44-46, 58, 63, 73f., 118, 145, 160, 170f., 181f., 204, 214, 217-19, 224f., 242n77, 251n8, 256n32, 264n55, 272n38, 276n23, 277n29, 282n27, 283nn32-34, 284n44, 285n45, 288n68-70, 296n128, 298n144, 304nn20-21, 313nn95-97, 322n168, 340n362-64, 341n368, 365nn58,67, 372nn121,127, 373n132, 378nn171,173, 384n5, 388n38, 406n32, 433n228, 434n230, 435n242, 454n60, 460n24; → 277n28, 468n122
schools/teachers, 99f., 187, 202, 396n72, 480n140, 488n194
secular/spiritual, meaning of, 152-54, 196f., 227, 241n65, 288n71, 292n104, 334n294; → character, of man; doing/using things spiritually or corporeally; estate/spiritual/Christian
self-defense, 107, 109, 313n88, 414n79, 450nn18-19
signum/res, → symbol/reality
simul iustus et peccator, → man, reborn, is afflicted with Original Sin
sin, 17, 32, 353n2; → 1f., 118, 273n12
 Original, 17, 25f., 30, 65, 86f., 90-92, 251nn11,19, 307n41
 mortal/venial, 244n30, 247n54, 304n19
 → concupiscence; man, fallen; man, reborn, is afflicted with Original Sin; status, corrupt; tinder
"so many lands, so many customs," 337n332
sollicitudo, 137f., 454n60
state, 28, 77, 126f., 130f., 143f., 167, 308n55, 401n1
 Christian, 116, 127f., 159f., 214
 medieval, 28, 93, 107, 127, 158, 256n33, 270n26, 317n126, 318n133, 388n38, 406n32; →

564

commonwealth, Christian, medieval meaning of; Empire, Holy Roman
→ authority, governmental; kingdom of the world; *politia*
status
   Christian/of a Christian, 86-89, 151f.; → 16f., 298n149; estate, spiritual/Christian
   corrupt, 86, 245n34; → man, fallen
   equal/unequal, → *Law:* law, of the Christian estate; governance, secular, over people of unequal status; governance, spiritual, over people of equal status; man, before the Fall; man, fallen
   Original/Paradise, 9, 27, 47, 52, 65, 85-89, 170, 212f., 228, 243n20, 245n34, 298n144, 299nn159-60, 300n166-68, 345n414, 365n61, 377n159, 396n71; → *Law:* divine law as natural law; *Law:* divine law as positive law; Creation; man, before the Fall
Succession, Apostolic, 179, 475n71
sun, effect of, 64-67, 265n61, 331n262
sword, 345n415, 348n444
   secular, 29-34, 115, 117, 150, 166, 189, 264n53, 266n3, 277n25, 317n118, 347n428, 384n6, 423n146, 432n207, 438n276, 464n39, 481n148; → governance, secular; kingdom of the world; man, reborn, the worldperson; *politia*
   spiritual, 31; → governance, spiritual; Keys, Power of
symbol (shadow)/reality, 69, 161f., 210f., 302n3, 356n36, 360n31, 363n42; → *Law:* law, as letter/sign vs. substance/spirit; *Law:* substantive secular natural law, and righteousness; church, as corporeal spiritual communion
synecdoche, 119, 437n262

synteresis, 25f., 252n17, 304n20; → 224f.

theft, 353n11
theocracy, 31
theodicy, 43
theology of the cross, 13, 126, 206f.
tinder, 244n27, 245n34, 366n72; → concupiscence; sin
"to do what I can," 127, 432n215
"to each his own," → *Law:* substantive secular natural law, goal/motto of
tolerance, 189f.
traditions of man, 101, 277n28, 323n171, 396n72, 402n4, 468n122
Turks, 57, 112f., 334n288, 337n324, 419nn113,116, 421nn121,123,125, 469n148
two lights, doctrine of, 127
two swords, doctrine of, 438n265
tyranny/tyrant, 231, 317n118, 411n55, 455n73, 476n76; → 118, 273n12
   and church, 110-13
   as spiritual battle between God and the devil, 417n105; → battle, between God/Christ and the devil, and their kingdoms
   definition/terminology of, 110, 112, 416nn84-85
   grand tyrant, 112
      actions/examples of, 113f., 127f., 159
      is condemned by God, 113, 418n108; → God, punishes evil governmental authorities
   petty tyrant, 112, 419n117
   → resistance in the *politia*; resistance of a Christian

usury, 285n46

visitation
   of congregations, 140, 173, 203, 385n12, 484n171, 500nn307-8;

Index of Subjects

→ *cura religionis* of the evangelical prince; emergency bishop of institutions of local secular administration, 484n171

vocation/appointment (call) to an occupation/*Beruf*/charge with the duties of an occupation/inner calling to an occupation/occupation, 50, 79, 121, 332n274, 408n41, 426n158, 431n202, 438n276, 445n343; → 93, 360n31, 483n162; call

Volkskirche, 436n255, 441n298

voluntarism, 43-46; → God, will of; man, heart and will of

war
   horror of, 414n76
   just/unjust, 109, 414n79, 415n82
   religious, 134, 137-39, 414n79

Wesen, christliches, 386n25

Winkelprediger, 194, 492n227

world, 27f., 35, 256n30, 257nn38,45,47, 258n49, 259n3, 260n7, 330n253, 335n298, 427n165
   cannot be ruled with the gospel, 117, 277n25, 432n207
   → kingdom of the world; secular/spiritual, meaning of

worship, → God, worship of

www.ingramcontent.com/pod-product-compliance
Lightning Source LLC
Chambersburg PA
CBHW031538300426
44111CB00006BA/100